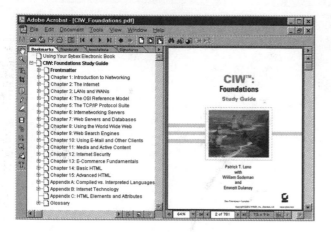

Search through the complete book in PDF!

- Access the entire *CIW: Foundations Study Guide*, complete with figures and tables, in electronic format.

- Search the *CIW: Foundations Study Guide* chapters to find information on any topic in seconds.

- Use Adobe Acrobat Reader (included on the CD-ROM) to view the electronic book.

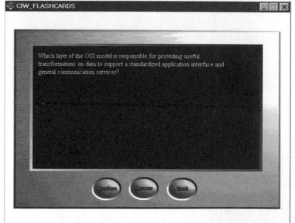

Use the Electronic Flashcards for PCs or Palm devices to jog your memory and prep last minute for the exam!

- Reinforce your understanding of key concepts with these hardcore flashcard-style questions.

Prepare for the Foundations exam on the go with your handheld device!

- Download the Flashcards to your Palm device and go on the road. Now you can study for the CIW Foundations exam anytime, anywhere.

SYBEX

CIW: Foundations Study Guide

Exam 1D0-410

OBJECTIVE GROUP	CHAPTER NUMBER
Internet Business Fundamentals	
Identify the infrastructure required to support Internet connections, including but not limited to: protocols, hardware and software components.	1, 2, 4
Identify Internet communications protocols and their roles in delivering basic Internet services, including but not limited to: SLIP, PPP, POP3, SMTP, HTTP, FTP, NNTP (news servers), Telnet, Gopher, and bandwidth technologies.	2, 4
Identify the purpose and function the Domain Name System (DNS).	2
Use Web browsers to access the World Wide Web and other computer resources.	8, 9
Use e-mail clients to send simple messages and files to other Internet users.	5, 10
Identify additional Internet services, including but not limited to: news, FTP, Gopher, Telnet, and network performance utilities such as ping and traceroute.	5, 10
Customize user features in Web browsers, including but not limited to: preferences, caching, and cookies.	8, 9
Identify security issues related to Web browsing and e-mail, including but not limited to: certificates, viruses, encryption and patches.	12
Use different types of Web search engines effectively.	9
Use the Web to obtain legal and international business information, including but not limited to: financial information, global work environment, and regulatory issues.	9
Identify various technologies for enhancing the user's Web experience, including but not limited to: programming languages, multimedia technologies, and plug-ins.	11
Define e-commerce, including technologies and concepts necessary to develop a secure storefront.	12
Identify issues in developing a corporate Web site, including but not limited to: project management, testing, and legal issues.	13

SYBEX

OBJECTIVE GROUP	CHAPTER NUMBER
HTML Fundamentals	
Format HTML files to maintain compatibility with older Web browsers.	14
Add images and graphical formatting to HTML files by manual coding in a text editor.	14, 15
Create a basic HTML form that accepts user input.	15
Test and analyze Web site performance.	15
Identify the purpose and function of Extensible Markup Language (XML).	15
Networking Fundamentals	
Identify networking and its role in the Internet, including but not limited to: TCP/IP, protocols, packets, and the OSI reference model.	1, 2, 3, 4
Identify the roles of networking hardware components, and configure common PC hardware for operation.	3, 4
Identify the relationships between IP addresses and domain names, including but not limited to: IP address classes, assignment of IP addresses within a subnet, and domain servers.	5
Identify the functions and components of Web servers, including but not limited to: various server types and related protocols, Internet connectivity, client-side and server-side scripting and applications, business needs and server selection criteria.	5, 6, 7
Identify common Internet security issues, including but not limited to: user-level and enterprise-level issues, access security, and security threats and attacks.	6, 12
Identify common performance issues affecting Internet servers and resources, including but not limited to: analysis and diagnosis, configuration, services and protocols.	6
Transmit text and binary files using popular Internet services, including but not limited to: the Web and e-mail.	10, 12

SYBEX

CIW:
Foundations
Study Guide

CIW™:
Foundations
Study Guide

Patrick T. Lane
with
William Sodeman
and
Emmett Dulaney

San Francisco • London

Associate Publisher: Neil Edde
Acquisitions and Developmental Editor: Heather O'Connor
Editor: Colleen Wheeler Strand
Production Editor: Molly Glover
Technical Editors: Kevin Lundy, Donald Fuller
Graphic Illustrator: Tony Jonick
Electronic Publishing Specialists: Interactive Composition Corporation
Proofreaders: Emily Hsuan, Dave Nash, Laurie O'Connell, Yariv Rabinovitch, Nancy Riddiough
Indexer: Ann Rogers
CD Coordinator: Dan Mummert
CD Technician: Kevin Ly
Book Designer: Bill Gibson
Cover Designer: Archer Design
Cover Photographer: Jeremy Woodhouse, PhotoDisc

SYBEX

To Our Valued Readers:

The Certified Internet Webmaster (CIW) program from ProsoftTraining™ has established itself as one of the leading Internet certifications in the IT industry. Sybex has partnered with ProsoftTraining to produce Study Guides—like the one you hold in your hand—for the Associate, Master Administrator, and Master Designer tracks. Each Sybex book is based on official courseware and is exclusively endorsed by ProsoftTraining.

Just as ProsoftTraining is committed to establishing measurable standards for certifying IT professionals working with Internet technologies, Sybex is committed to providing those professionals with the skills and knowledge needed to meet those standards. It has long been Sybex's desire to help bridge the knowledge and skills gap that currently confronts the IT industry.

The authors and editors have worked hard to ensure that this CIW Study Guide is comprehensive, in-depth, and pedagogically sound. We're confident that this book will meet and exceed the demanding standards of the certification marketplace and help you, the CIW certification candidate, succeed in your endeavors.

Good luck in pursuit of your CIW certification!

Neil Edde
Associate Publisher—Certification
Sybex, Inc.

Acknowledgments

This book is the product of a superb team. Sybex has devoted many resources to this first book in their new CIW Study Guide series. Heather O'Connor brought me into this project and helped me organize the Foundations material. Molly Glover kept the book on track as production editor. Colleen Strand edited the drafts, and provided many suggestions regarding the flow and structure. Emmett Dulaney contributed his expertise to revising some of the chapters, and Kevin Lundy did a great job as technical editor.

At ProsoftTraining, many individuals have contributed to the development and success of CIW Foundations. It would take another page to list all the subject-matter experts, writers, editors, instructors, and other participants who have contributed since 1998. Uday Om Pabrai, Gart Davis, John McNamara, and Max Miller made important contributions to Prosoft's early versions of Foundations. CIW would not exist without these individuals. Patrick Lane and James Stanger have done a great deal of the research and writing for the Foundations curriculum. It has been a pleasure to work with them, as well as with Jud Slusser, Jill McKenna, Susan Lane, and Chris Cambra in the Santa Ana office. In Austin, Rachel Zardiackas, Mike Hickey, and Bill Weronick deserve special recognition for their contributions to the CIW certification program.

Here at home, my family and friends gave me much encouragement during my marathon sessions at my Sony Vaio, while Kalin and Zosia Kitty kept me company. Lindsey Wegrzyn made sure that the little chicken, the tuna fish sandwich, and the fruit salad parade were always there when we needed them. Thank you Lindsey for making me a better person.

—Bill Sodeman

I would like to thank CIW and Sybex, in particular Heather O'Connor and Molly Glover, for the opportunity to work on this book. Thanks are also due to John Sleeva for keeping me on schedule and forever adding value to what I scribble.

—Emmett Dulaney

Patrick Lane would like to thank his wife, Susan, for her support and ability to make him see the lighter side of life during the time-consuming development of the CIW Foundations, CIW Internetworking Professional, and CIW Security Professional books. He would also like to thank Jud Slusser for his wisdom and long-view approach toward certification, and James Stanger for his technical expertise. He would also like to thank Heather O'Connor for the opportunity to author CIW books for Sybex.

Contents at a Glance

Contents

Table of Exercises

Introduction

The Prosoft CIW (Certified Internet Webmaster) certification affirms that you have the essential skills to create, run, and update a website. These skills are exactly what employers in today's economy are looking for, and you need to stay ahead of the competition in the current job market. CIW certification will prove to your current or future employer that you are serious about expanding your knowledge base. Obtaining CIW certification will also provide you with valuable skills, including basic networking, web page authoring, internetworking, maintaining security, and website design, and expose you to a variety of vendor products made for web design and implementation.

This book is meant to help you prepare for the Certified Internet Webmaster Foundations Exam 1D0-410. The Foundations exam is the prerequisite exam for the rest of the CIW certification levels and covers the basics of networking, the Internet, and web page authoring. Once you pass the CIW Foundations exam, you achieve CIW Associate status, and you can then move on to the many other learning opportunities in the CIW certification program.

The Certified Internet Webmaster Program

The CIW Internet skills certification program is aimed at professionals who design, develop, administer, secure, and support Internet- or intranet-related services. The CIW certification program offers industry-wide recognition of an individual's Internet and web knowledge and skills, and certification is frequently a factor in hiring and assignment decisions. It also provides tangible evidence of a person's competency as an Internet professional; holders of this certification can demonstrate to potential employers and clients that they have passed rigorous training and examination requirements that set them apart from non-certified competitors. All CIW certifications are endorsed by the International Webmasters Association (IWA) and the Association of Internet Professionals (AIP).

CIW Associate

The first step toward CIW certification is the CIW Foundations exam. A candidate for the CIW Associate certification and the Foundations exam has the basic hands-on skills and knowledge that an Internet professional is expected to understand and use. Foundations skills include basic knowledge of Internet technologies, network infrastructure, and web authoring using HTML.

The CIW Foundations program is designed for all professionals who use the Internet. The job expectations of a CIW Associate, a person who has completed the program and passed the Foundations exam, include:

- Understanding Internet, networking, and web page authoring basics

- Application of Foundations skills required for further specialization

There are a few prerequisites for becoming a CIW Associate. For instance, although you need not have Internet experience in order to start Foundations exam preparation, you should have an understanding of Microsoft Windows.

Table I.1 shows the CIW Foundations exam and the corresponding Sybex Study Guide that covers the CIW Associate certification.

TABLE I.1 The CIW Associate Exam and Corresponding Sybex Study Guide

Exam Name	Exam Number	Sybex Study Guide
Foundations	1D0-410	*CIW: Foundations Study Guide* (ISBN 0-7821-4081-5)

CIW accepts score reports from CIW Associate candidates who have passed the entry-level CompTIA i-Net+ exam (IKO-002) and will award Foundations certification to these individuals. For more information regarding the i-Net+ and other CompTIA exams, visit www.comptia.org/.

After passing the Foundations exam, students become CIW Associates and can choose from four Master CIW certification tracks, by choosing a path of interest and passing the required exams:

- Master CIW Designer

- Master CIW Administrator

- CIW Web Site Manager

- Master CIW Enterprise Developer

- CIW Security Analyst

Master CIW Designer

The Master Designer track is composed of two exams, each of which represents a specific aspect of the Internet job role:

- Site Designer
- E-Commerce Designer

Site Designer Exam   The CIW Site Designer applies human-factor principles to designing, implementing, and maintaining hypertext-based publishing sites. The Site Designer uses authoring and scripting languages, as well as digital media tools, plus provides content creation and website management.

E-Commerce Designer Exam   The CIW E-Commerce Designer is tested on e-commerce setup, human-factor principles regarding product selection and payment, and site security and administration.

Table I.2 shows the CIW Site Designer and E-Commerce Designer exams and the corresponding Sybex Study Guide for each of these steps toward the CIW Master Designer certification.

TABLE I.2   The Master Designer Exams and Corresponding Sybex Study Guides

Exam Names	Exam Numbers	Sybex Study Guide
Site Designer	1D0-420	*CIW: Master Designer Study Guide* (ISBN 0-7821-4082-3)
E-Commerce Designer	1D0-425	*CIW: Master Designer Study Guide* (ISBN 0-7821-4082-3)

Master CIW Administrator

The CIW Administrator is proficient in three areas of administration:

- Server
- Internetworking
- Security administration

After passing each test, you become a CIW Professional in that specific area.

Server Administrator Exam   The CIW Server Administrator manages and tunes corporate e-business infrastructure, including web, FTP, news, and mail servers for midsize to large businesses. Server administrators configure, manage, and deploy e-business solutions servers.

Internetworking Professional Exam   The Internetworking Professional defines network architecture, identifies infrastructure components, and monitors and analyzes network performance. The CIW Internetworking Professional is responsible for the design and management of enterprise TCP/IP networks.

Security Professional Exam   The CIW Security Professional implements policy, identifies security threats, and develops countermeasures using firewall systems and attack-recognition technologies. As a CIW Security Professional, you are responsible for managing the deployment of e-business transactions and payment security solutions.

The Exams in the Master Administrator track are listed in Table I.3.

TABLE I.3   The Master Administrator Exams and Corresponding Sybex Study Guides

Exam Names	Exam Numbers	Sybex Study Guide
Server Administrator	1D0-450	*CIW: Server Administrator Study Guide* (ISBN 0-7821-4085-8)
Internetworking Professional	1D0-460	*CIW: Internetworking Professional Study Guide* (ISBN 0-7821-4083-1)
Security Professional	1D0-470	*CIW: Security Professional Study Guide* (ISBN 0-7821-4084-X)

Other CIW Certifications

Prosoft also offers three additional certification series in website management, enterprise development, and security analysis.

Master CIW Web Site Manager   The Web Site Manager certification is composed of two Internet job role series exams (Site Designer 1D0-420

and Server Administrator 1D0-450) and two additional language exams (JavaScript 1D0-435 and Perl Fundamentals 1D0-437 from the CIW Web Languages series).

Master CIW Enterprise Developer   The Enterprise Developer certification is composed of three Internet job role series (Application Developer 1D0-430, Database Specialist 1D0-441, and Enterprise Specialist 1D0-442) and three additional language/theory series (Web Languages, Java Programming, and Object-Oriented Analysis).

CIW Security Analyst   The Security Analyst certification recognizes those who have already attained a networking certification and demonstrated (by passing the CIW Security Professional 1D0-470 exam) that they have the in-demand security skills to leverage their technical abilities against internal and external cyber threats.

For more information regarding all of Prosoft's certifications and exams, visit `www.ciwcertified.com`.

Special Features in This Book

What makes a Sybex Study Guide the book of choice for over 500,000 certification candidates across numerous technical fields? We take into account not only what you need to know to pass the exam, but what you need to know to apply what you've learned in the real world. Each book contains the following:

Objective information   Each chapter lists at the outset which CIW objective groups are going to be covered within.

Assessment Test   Directly following this Introduction is an Assessment Test that you can take to help you determine how much you already know about networking, the Internet, and web page authoring. Each question is tied to a topic discussed in the book. Using the results of the Assessment Test, you can figure out the areas where you need to focus your study. Of course, we do recommend you read the entire book.

Exam Essentials   To review what you've learned, you'll find a list of Exam Essentials at the end of each chapter. The Exam Essentials section briefly highlights the topics that need your particular attention as you prepare for the exam.

Key Terms and Glossary Throughout each chapter, you will be introduced to important terms and concepts that you will need to know for the exam. These terms appear in italic within the chapters, and a list of the Key Terms appears just after the Exam Essentials. At the end of the book, a detailed glossary gives definitions for these terms, as well as other general terms you should know.

Review Questions, complete with detailed explanations Each chapter is followed by a set of Review Questions that test what you learned in the chapter. The questions are written with the exam in mind, meaning that they are designed to have the same look and feel of what you'll see on the exam.

Hands-on exercises Throughout the book, you'll find exercises designed to give you the important hands-on experience that is critical for your exam preparation. The exercises support the topics of the chapter, and they walk you through the steps necessary to perform a particular function.

Interactive CD Every Sybex Study Guide comes with a CD complete with additional questions, flashcards for use with a palm device or PC, and a complete electronic version of this book. Details are in the following section.

What's on the CD?

Sybex's *CIW: Foundations Study Guide* companion CD includes quite an array of training resources and offer numerous test simulations, bonus exams, and flashcards to help you study for the exam. We have also included the complete contents of the study guide in electronic form. The CD's resources are described here:

The Sybex Ebook for the *CIW Foundations Study Guide* Many people like the convenience of being able to carry their whole study guide on a CD. They also like being able to search the text via computer to find specific information quickly and easily. For these reasons, the entire contents of this study guide are supplied on the CD, in PDF format. We've also included Adobe Acrobat Reader, which provides the interface for the PDF contents as well as search capabilities.

The Sybex CIW Edge Tests   The Edge Tests are a collection of multiple-choice questions that will help you prepare for your exam. There are three sets of questions:

- Two bonus exams designed to simulate the actual live exam

- All the Review Questions from the Study Guide, presented in an electronic test engine. You can review questions by chapter or by objective area, or you can take a random test.

- The Assessment Test

Sybex CIW Flashcards for PCs and Palm Devices   The "flashcard" style of question offers an effective way to quickly and efficiently test your understanding of the fundamental concepts covered in the exam. The Sybex CIW Flashcards set consists of 150 questions presented in a special engine developed specifically for this study guide series. We have also developed, in conjunction with Land-J Technologies, a version of the flashcard questions that you can take with you on your Palm OS PDA (including the Palm and Visor PDAs).

How to Use This Book

This book provides a solid foundation for the serious effort of preparing for the exam. To best benefit from this book, you may wish to use the following study method:

1. Take the Assessment Test to identify your weak areas.

2. Study each chapter carefully. Do your best to fully understand the information.

3. Study the Exam Essentials and Key Terms to make sure you are familiar with the areas you need to focus on.

4. Answer the review questions at the end of each chapter. If you prefer to answer the questions in a timed and graded format, install the Edge Tests from the book's CD and answer the chapter questions there instead of in the book.

5. Take note of the questions you did not understand, and study the corresponding sections of the book again.

6. Go back over the Exam Essentials and Key Terms.

7. Go through the study guide's other training resources, which are included on the book's CD. These include electronic flashcards, the electronic version of the chapter review questions (try taking them by objective), and the two bonus exams.

To learn all the material covered in this book, you will need to study regularly and with discipline. Try to set aside the same time every day to study, and select a comfortable and quiet place in which to do it. If you work hard, you will be surprised at how quickly you learn this material. Good luck!

Exam Registration

CIW certification exams are administered by Prometric, Inc. through Prometric Testing Centers and by Virtual University Enterprises (VUE) testing centers. You can reach Prometric at (800) 380-EXAM or VUE at (952) 995-8800, to schedule any CIW exam.

You may also register for your exams online at www.prometric.com or www.vue.com.

Exams cost $125 (U.S.) each and must be paid for in advance. Exams must be taken within one year of payment. Candidates can schedule exams up to six weeks in advance or as late as one working day prior to the date of the exam. To cancel or reschedule an exam, contact the center at least two working days prior to the scheduled exam date. Same-day registration is available in some locations, subject to space availability. Where same-day registration is available, registration must occur a minimum of two hours before test time.

When you schedule the exam, the testing center will provide you with instructions regarding appointment and cancellation procedures, ID requirements, and information about the testing center location. In addition, you will receive a registration and payment confirmation letter from Prometric or VUE.

Tips for Taking the CIW Foundations Exam

Here are some general tips for achieving success on your certification exam:

- Arrive early at the exam center so that you can relax and review your study materials. During this final review, you can look over tables and lists of exam-related information.

- Read the questions carefully. Don't be tempted to jump to an early conclusion. Make sure you know *exactly* what the question is asking.

- For questions you're not sure about, use a process of elimination to get rid of the obviously incorrect answers first. This improves your odds of selecting the correct answer when you need to make an educated guess.

- Mark questions that you aren't sure of and return to them later. Quite often something in a later question will act as a reminder or give you a clue to the correct answer of the earlier one.

Contacts and Resources

Here are some handy websites to keep in mind for future reference:

Prosoft Training and CIW Exam Information	www.CIWcertified.com
Prometric	www.prometric.com
VUE Testing Services	www.vue.com
Sybex Computer Books	www.sybex.com

Assessment Test

1. Mainframe computing is most limited by which one of the following issues?

    A. Terminal display size

    B. Terminal processing speed

    C. Latency

    D. Personal computer memory

2. Marcus is configuring his e-mail client. Which one of the following passwords must he supply to receive his e-mail messages?

    A. POP3 server password

    B. FTP password

    C. SMTP password

    D. Web password

3. In Microsoft Internet Explorer, you should enter the URL in what field?

    A. Location field

    B. Server field

    C. URL field

    D. Address field

4. What is the second stage of a project management cycle?

    A. Business requirements document

    B. Technology/architecture design

    C. Scope matrix documents

    D. Business process/functionality design

5. The Internet Corporation of Assigned Names and Numbers (ICANN) has reserved three blocks of IP address space for which of the following?

    A. Corporate networks

    B. Private networks

    C. Educational networks

    D. Non-profit networks

6. Which one of the following server software products provides support for IPX/SPX?

    A. Domino

    B. eDirectory

    C. IIS

    D. Apache

7. A full-text index is best used in which of the following situations?

    A. On an FTP search engine

    B. On a certificate server

    C. On an intranet website

    D. On a public web search engine

8. You have just download a Microsoft PowerPoint file and you do not have the PowerPoint program installed on your computer. What is the quickest and easiest way to view the file?

    A. Install the PowerPoint program

    B. View the file in your browser

    C. Install the PowerPoint viewer

    D. View the file in Adobe Acrobat Reader

9. Java is best described by which one of the following choices?

    A. An object-based programming language

    B. An object-oriented programming language

    C. An interpreted programming language

    D. A scripting language

10. Systems Network Architecture was developed for which one of the following purposes?

   A. Connecting personal computers in networks

   B. Connecting mainframes in networks

   C. Defining transmission media

   D. Presenting a framework for end-user application development

11. To upload a file with a command-line FTP client, you would:

   A. Log on to the FTP server and enter `put filename.ext`.

   B. Log on to the FTP server and enter `load filename.ext`.

   C. Log on to the FTP server and enter `upload filename.ext`.

   D. Log on to the FTP server and enter `get filename.ext`.

12. Which type of DNS record identifies the primary DNS server for a particular domain?

   A. Name server

   B. Start of authority

   C. Canonical name

   D. Address

13. Which of the following choices best describes an IP address?

   A. An address used to send e-mail to a specific user

   B. A server name, like `sybex.com`

   C. A 32-bit code used to identify specific computers

   D. A number that is burned into every network interface card

14. Which one of the following types of twisted-pair cable should be used for gigabit Ethernet networks?

   A. CAT3

   B. CAT5

   C. CAT7

   D. CAT1

15. Which attribute is used by the INPUT element to designate a text box, radio button, a submit or reset button, a password field, or a check box?

   A. TYPE

   B. NAME

   C. VALUE

   D. SIZE

16. The Media Access Control is associated with which layer of the OSI/RM?

   A. Physical

   B. Network

   C. Data Link

   D. Session

17. Which one of the following network devices can work with any networking protocol?

   A. Router

   B. Bridge

   C. Gateway

   D. Monitor

18. Active content can be created and programmed using what kind of file?

   A. HTML documents

   B. Token

   C. Objects

   D. Item

19. Hypertext Transfer Protocol (HTTP) works at which one of the following layers of the Internet architecture?

    A. Application layer

    B. Transport layer

    C. Internet layer

    D. Network Access layer

20. What type of HTML element will affect at least an entire paragraph?

    A. A block-level element

    B. A text-level element

    C. A paragraph-level element

    D. A content-level element

21. Which of the following characteristics are not associated with LDAP directory servers?

    A. Scalability

    B. Synchronization

    C. Complex directory structure

    D. Replication

22. In a database, a row and cell can be compared to which one of the following choices?

    A. table and record

    B. field and index

    C. record and field

    D. index and table

23. At what layer of the OSI/RM does a hub operate?

A. Session

B. Data link

C. Physical

D. Network

24. Which one of the following choices is not used as a protocol for sending an e-mail message?

A. FTP

B. POP

C. SMTP

D. IMAP

25. The World Wide Web is built upon which one of the following concepts?

A. Image viewing

B. Hypertext

C. E-mail

D. Server farms

26. System snooping is best defined as which one of the following?

A. The ability to link several databases together.

B. The action of mapping a server's database.

C. The ability to map the architecture of a computer system.

D. The action of entering a computer network and mapping the system's contents for malicious purposes.

27. In which network topology is a message repeated by each computer until the message reaches its destination?

   A. Ring

   B. Star

   C. Bus

   D. Server

28. Which of the following statements best describes ActiveX?

   A. ActiveX is a programming language.

   B. ActiveX is a set of technologies for creating active content.

   C. ActiveX is a feature of Netscape web browsers.

   D. ActiveX is a feature of the Linux operating system.

29. While creating a website, you include code in your HTML file that specifies a set of coordinates, creating a "hot spot" area on a particular image. What have you just created?

   A. A server-side image map

   B. A client-side image map

   C. An image transparency

   D. Animation

30. Which one of the following top-level domain codes was approved for use in the year 2000?

   A. .mil

   B. .biz

   C. .net

   D. .int

31. Which of the following default subnet masks corresponds to Class C?

   A. 255.255.255.255

   B. 255.255.255.0

   C. 255.255.0.0

   D. 255.0.0.0

32. John needs to connect his company's new T1 line to the existing LAN. What device does he need to make this connection?

   A. Hub

   B. Router

   C. Bridge

   D. Network interface card

33. Internetworking servers must have at least what level of permission from the operating system to bind ports?

   A. Guest

   B. User

   C. Administrator

   D. Superuser

34. Which one of the following choices is the best description of a packet?

   A. A protocol that enables information to be sent across a network.

   B. Another name for an e-mail message.

   C. A protocol that sends e-mail messages.

   D. A fixed piece of information sent across a network.

35. Anne opened her web browser, and noticed that a page she recently viewed was displayed. However, she was not connected to the Internet. What is the most likely reason she can see this page?

   A. The page was saved in her browser's cache.

   B. The page was saved as her home page.

   C. Her web browser displayed the page because of an internal error.

   D. The web server has overridden her browser settings.

36. The term Telnet should be applied to which of the following choices?

   A. A remote host connection

   B. A telephone connection

   C. A web browser

   D. An e-mail program

37. Cecelia designed a website for her company, Cecelia's Hard Disk Recovery Service. Which one of the following steps should Cecelia take to make sure that anyone using a web search engine can easily find her company when they search for hard disk recovery services?

A. She should wait for search engines to find and index her website.

B. She should select a memorable domain name to attract attention to her website.

C. She should submit her site's URL to several web search engines.

D. She should use the META tag to specify hard disk recovery services keywords for each page on her website.

38. IPv6 can accommodate how many different IP addresses?

A. 4 billion addresses

B. 40 billion addresses

C. 4 trillion addresses

D. An unlimited number of addresses

39. On a Windows network, what do you call the "computer name" of a Windows machine?

A. Domain name

B. NetBIOS name

C. Host name

D. WINS name

40. Which of the following is the best description of a routable protocol?

A. Only the TCP/IP suite is routable, because it follows the OSI/RM.

B. Routable protocols can choose from one of several paths to make a connection between two computers.

C. Routable protocols can send information without the need for error checking.

D. UNIX systems cannot use routable protocols.

41. Which language is used to simulate 3-dimensional spaces that have lifelike objects?

   A. 3DML

   B. HTML

   C. VRML

   D. XML

42. Which network topology uses a hub to connect computers?

   A. Bus

   B. Ring

   C. Star

   D. Peer-to-peer

43. Which attribute controls the length of a horizontal rule?

   A. SIZE

   B. ALIGN

   C. LENGTH

   D. WIDTH

44. Which of the following HTML table tags specifies cell contents?

   A. <TH>

   B. <TABLE>

   C. <TR>

   D. <TD>

45. In a three-tier client/server computing model, what task does the third tier perform?

   A. Requests data

   B. Retrieves data

   C. Formats data

   D. Displays data

40. Which one of the following types of internetworking servers is not a content server?

    A. HTTP

    B. FTP

    C. Directory

    D. Streaming media

47. Gerald is a network maintenance technician. He was told to work on a client's IEEE 802.5 network. What kind of network is this?

    A. Fast Ethernet

    B. Token ring

    C. 10Mbps Ethernet

    D. Novell NetWare 4

48. Which one of the following choices does not happen when a CGI program calls an out-of-process event?

    A. A separate process is launched.

    B. Another copy of the CGI program is loaded into the server's memory.

    C. The web server could slow down if many users are already using that CGI script.

    D. The process is launched as another thread within a single program.

49. Which one of the following is used to identify secure web forms in a web browser?

    A. A padlock icon

    B. Icons of keys placed next to the secure fields in the form

    C. Underlined text

    D. Flashing text

50. Hans wants to send Bronwen a copy of the e-mail he is mailing to his supervisor, David. John wants David to see that Bronwen is receiving a copy of the message for informational purposes. Which one of the following choices will work best?

A. Hans should include Bronwen along with David in the To field.

B. Hans should list David in the To field, and Bronwen in the Cc field.

C. Hans should list Bronwen in the To field, and David in the Cc field.

D. Hans should list Bronwen in the Bcc field, and David in the To field.

Answers to Assessment Test

1. C. Latency, the delay in sending data between two computers, is one factor that limits the mainframe computing model. Terminal display size is another issue, although it is not as crucial as latency. Terminals do not process data; that is done at the mainframe. Personal computer memory is not a consideration, as the mainframe model does not require PCs. For more information, see Chapter 1.

2. A. Marcus must have the POP3 server password to download messages to his client. He does not need FTP or web passwords. The SMTP password may be required to send mail messages, depending on his SMTP server's configuration. For more information, see Chapter 10.

3. D. It should be entered in the Address field. Netscape calls this the Location field. For more information, see Chapter 8.

4. B. The second stage of the project management cycle is the technology/architecture design stage; used to plan the project's design. For more information, see Chapter 13.

5. B. These blocks of IP addresses are used to identify workstations on LANs and WANs. Routers are programmed to filter out or block routing information about these addresses, so they cannot be used to identify hosts that are publicly accessible, such as web and e-mail servers. For more information, see Chapter 5.

6. B. eDirectory is a Novell product that can be integrated with NetWare. The other three products do not support NetWare. For more information, see Chapter 6.

7. C. Full-text search indexes are best used for indexing a small number of sites, because their storage requirements can be high. Certificate servers do not need full-text searching features. FTP sites can contain binary and text files, so full-text searching has limited value. For more information, see Chapter 9.

8. C. If you do not have the PowerPoint application, you should download and install the PowerPoint Viewer to display a PPT file. For more information, see Chapter 11.

9. B. Java is a powerful programming language that lets developers create their own objects. JavaScript and VBScript are examples of object-based scripting languages. JavaScript, VBScript, Perl, and PHP scripts are typically interpreted when they are executed. For more information, see Chapter 7.

10. B. IBM developed SNA to support its mainframe networking products. SNA defines appropriate networking protocols and topologies. For more information, see Chapter 4.

11. A. The put command is used to upload files to an FTP server. For more information, see Chapter 10.

12. B. The SOA record identifies the primary server for a domain. The name server record is used to identify all DNS servers for a domain. The canonical name record creates an alias for a host, such as a www alias for a web server. The address record maps a host name to an IP address. For more information, see Chapter 6.

13. C. An IP address is a 32-bit numeric address assigned to a specific computer. IP addresses are usually formatted as dotted quads, such as 127.0.0.1. E-mail addresses, such as user@yahoo.com, are used to send e-mail to a specific user. Server names are mapped to IP addresses using the domain name system (DNS). A unique Media Access Control (MAC) code is burned into each network interface card (NIC), and serves as a physical address for networking. For more on IP addresses, see Chapter 2.

14. C. Category 7 cable is the only type of twisted-pair cable that should be used on gigabit Ethernet networks. Category 3 cable can handle 10Mbps Ethernet. Category 5 can handle 100Mbps Ethernet. Category 1 is used for telephone connections only. For more information, see Chapter 3.

15. A. The TYPE attribute is used by the INPUT element to designate a text box, radio button, a submit or reset button, a password field, or a check box. For more information, see Chapter 15.

16. C. MAC addresses are associated with Layer 2, the data Link layer. For more information, see Chapter 4.

17. B.   Bridges can work with any network protocol. Routers handle one or more specific protocols. Gateways translate signals from one specific protocol to another. A monitor is the display screen used with a computer. For more information, see Chapter 3.

18. C.   Objects are used to create active content. HTML documents can be formatted to download objects and display them in a web browser. For more information, see Chapter 11.

19. A.   HTTP, along with FTP, SMTP, and other protocols used by client applications, works at the Application layer. The Transport layer accepts Application-layer data and manages the flow of data between two computers. The Internet layer addresses and routes packets. The Network Access layer is responsible for transmitting and receiving data on the transmission medium. For more information, see Chapter 5.

20. A.   A block-level element will affect an entire paragraph at the least. For more information, see Chapter 14.

21. C.   LDAP directory servers share these three characteristics with X.500 directory servers, as LDAP is based on X.500. LDAP has a simpler directory structure than X.500, however. For more information, see Chapter 6.

22. C.   In database and spreadsheet tables, a row can represent a record, while a cell represents a field. For more information, see Chapter 7.

23. C.   Hubs work at Layer 1, the Physical layer. Hubs server as a concentration point on the network, by connecting multiple computers to exchange unstructured bit transmissions. For more information, see Chapter 4.

24. A.   FTP is used for transferring large files. It is not used for transferring e-mail messages. POP is used for retrieving e-mail from a server to an e-mail client application. SMTP is used for sending an e-mail message. IMAP is used for retrieving e-mail from newer e-mail systems. For more information, see Chapter 2.

25. B.   Hypertext is the core concept of the World Wide Web. The images are an important part of the Web, but they are not mandatory. E-mail is a different service from the web. Server farms provide greater reliability for Internet services, and are sometimes used by websites. For more information, see Chapter 8.

26. D. System snooping is part of the discovery phase of the cracker process, in which the cracker attempts to identify potential targets within a network. For more information, see Chapter 12.

27. A. In a star network, the hub receives a signal and sends it to all computers. In a bus network, the messages are broadcast to all computers. A server is either a kind of network, or a computer that provides centralized functions on a network. For more information, see Chapter 1.

28. B. ActiveX is a Microsoft suite of technologies for creating active content. ActiveX objects can be created in several programming languages. Netscape and Linux do not support ActiveX objects; ActiveX is primarily used in Microsoft Windows and applications. For more information, see Chapter 11.

29. B. An example of a client-side image map is a "hot spot" area on a particular image. For more information, see Chapter 15.

30. B. ICANN approved seven new TLDs, including `.biz`, in 2000. The US military uses `.mil`; ISPs and other organizations use `.net`; and international organizations such as the European Union use `.int`. For more information, see Chapter 2.

31. B. The default subnet mask for a Class C address uses the first 3 bytes to identify the network. For more information, see Chapter 5.

32. B. John will need a router, which is commonly used as the interface between a LAN and a T1 line. A hub connects computers within a star network. A bridge connects two networks to each other. A NIC connects a computer to a LAN.

33. D. Internetworking servers require a user ID of 0, which is the superuser level. For more information, see Chapter 6.

34. D. Packets are best described as pieces of network data. The OSI/RM defines the packet-creation process. TCP/IP and IPX/SPX are examples of protocols that send information across networks. IMAP, SMTP and POP3 are examples of e-mail protocols. For more information, see Chapter 4

35. A. The web page was previously viewed and saved in the browser cache. Selecting the page as the home page increases the likelihood that it would also be saved in the cache. For more information, see Chapter 8.

36. **A.** Telnet is a terminal emulation program that allows users to control remote computers. For more information, see Chapter 10.

37. **D.** META tags can provide search engines with keywords and descriptions to include in their listings. Cecelia can wait for search engines to find her site, or submit her URL to search engines; but without META tags, the search engines may not list all possible keywords. Domain names are a good marketing tool, but have a limited life cycle. For more information, see Chapter 9.

38. **C.** IPv6 has a 128-bit address structure that can handle up to 4 trillion different addresses. IPv4 can handle up to 30 undecillion different addresses. For more information, see Chapter 2.

39. **B.** The NetBIOS name is the computer name of a Windows computer. The domain name should correspond to the company's DNS domain name. The host name is used as the computer name in DNS. The WINS name is used to map the NetBIOS name to an IP address. For more information, see Chapter 5.

40. **B.** Routable protocols can determine the optimal path between two networks by using routing tables. Error-checking functions are an important part of routable protocols. Error-checking helps the receiving computer determine if the packets have been damaged in transmission. UNIX systems use TCP/IP, a routable protocol, as their default networking operating system. For more information, see Chapter 4.

41. **C.** Virtual Reality Modeling Language is used to create simulated environments and animated objects. There is no such language as 3DML. HTML is the markup language used to create web documents. XML is used to create machine-readable data. For more information, see Chapter 11.

42. **C.** The star network uses a hub. The bus and ring topologies do not use a hub. Peer-to-peer is a type of network architecture. For more information, see Chapter 1.

43. **D.** The WIDTH attribute is used to control the length of a horizontal rule. For more information, see Chapter 14.

44. **D.** The <TD> HTML table tag specifies cell contents. For more information, see Chapter 15.

45. B.   In a three-tier client server model, the first tier is the client. The client is responsible for data formatting and display. The second tier requests the data. The third tier, the server, retrieves the data. For more information, see Chapter 1.

46. C.   Directory servers are database servers that provide contact information. For more information, see Chapter 6.

47. B.   Gerald will be working on a token ring networking standard. IEEE 802.3u defines Fast Ethernet. IEEE 802.3 defines 10Mbps Ethernet. Novell NetWare 4 uses IPX/SPX protocols, and is a proprietary network type. For more information, see Chapter 3.

48. D.   This describes an in-process model for handling CGI applications. This can be implmented with mod_perl on UNIX and Linux systems, and with DLLs on Windows servers. The other choices can all occur when a CGI program is launched as an out-of-process event. For more information, see Chapter 7.

49. A.   The padlock icon is commonly used to show that a secure web connection has been established between a browser and a web server. For more information, see Chapter 12.

50. B.   By listing David in the To field, the message is sent directly to him. By listing Bronwen in the Cc field she will receive a copy and David will also see her address on the Cc field of the message. David would not see Bronwen's address if she were listed in the Bcc field. If David saw his own address in the Cc field and Bronwen's address in the To field, David might believe the message was intended for Bronwen. For more information, see Chapter 10.

Chapter 1

Introduction to Networking

THE CIW EXAM OBJECTIVE GROUPS COVERED IN THIS CHAPTER:

- ✓ Identify networking and its role in the Internet.
- ✓ Identify the infrastructure required to support Internet connections.

The Internet has become a valuable part of our lives. It seems like any information you need is now available to you at the drop of a hat; if you just log on, you'll find what you're looking for in an instant. The Internet has made individuals, schools, towns, and businesses accessible from anywhere in the world, and its importance in our daily lives has reached new proportions.

As businesses and organizations continue to reach places farther and farther away through their websites, the need for knowledgeable professionals with specific skills to get those websites up and running, properly maintained, and flexible for innovation, has become vital.

The Certified Internet Webmaster (CIW) program tests individuals on the most important web functions and awards certifications based on knowledge and skill. The CIW Internet Foundations exam (1D0-410) is the initial exam for all CIW certifications, setting the pace for Internet professionals worldwide.

The CIW Internet Foundations exam covers the basic concepts of the Internet, from general networking to web authoring and e-business. We'll start our discussion with networking, since it lays the groundwork for how the Internet functions. If the Internet were an ocean, you would not have access to it without the rivers and lakes, or the *networks*, that flow to that ocean.

In this chapter, you will learn about networking basics, which include the history and evolution of networks, network categories, and network topologies.

Networking Evolution

Originally, computer networks were operated on a centralized, or *mainframe*, model. Early computers were very expensive to purchase, operate, and maintain. These computers had very little processing power and storage capability. Users concentrated their computer work on analyzing and storing important numerical data. There were few qualified professionals available to even configure and administer individual computers, much less entire networks. Early computers also suffered from reliability problems (that computer manufacturers later learned to resolve through improved hardware and software). All of these factors limited the existence of networks to large, well-funded institutions, such as universities and large companies.

By the late 1980s, however, the personal computer (PC) had gained wide popularity among business users. The personal computer was powerful, small, and relatively inexpensive. All sizes of businesses used the personal computer to automate routine tasks such as word processing and accounting. Also, new kinds of software such as spreadsheets and personal information managers became easier to use on a PC.

Many business networks eventually adopted the client/server model, which used a more modular approach than the mainframe scenario had provided. Personal computers could be used as client *workstations*, connected to mainframes. Personal computer manufacturers developed specialized servers to store files and run printing services. This allowed small to medium-sized businesses to create powerful networking solutions at a lower price than that of mainframe solutions.

The advent of the Internet led to another shift to web-based, increasingly decentralized computing. Changes in the telecommunications industry, along with many technological advances, made networking an affordable and necessary feature of doing business.

Mainframes

Mainframe computing, also called centralized computing, provided the first practical network solution. This centralized approach employed central servers, or mainframes, and remote terminals. Usually, these terminals were diskless, or "dumb" stations or terminals, that could only request information. Diskless terminals could not store or read data locally, but data storage was relatively expensive and providing local storage was cost prohibitive.

In these systems, most information processing occurs on the mainframe, not on the terminal. One example of a mainframe application is a Customer Information Control System (CICS) transaction program. CICS mainframe servers specialize in enabling transactions in a distributed environment, using the COBOL (Common Business Oriented Language) programming language. Sending properly formatted information from a mainframe to a client involves a great deal of processing by the mainframe. When a terminal sends an information request, this query is sent to the mainframe. The mainframe processes the query and obtains the desired information from a database or other source. After this processing is finished, the mainframe structures the information, which is then returned to the terminal. Figure 1.1 shows a mainframe model.

FIGURE 1.1 Mainframe model

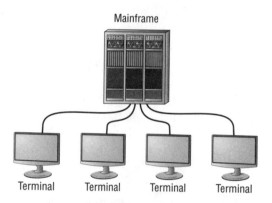

The mainframe computing model has two principal liabilities. The first is that the mainframe must handle all the processing work. The users are limited by the mainframe's computing capacity and storage space.

The second liability is that the data sent between the terminal and the mainframe occupy a relatively large amount of the network's *bandwidth*. Bandwidth refers to the amount of data a connection can carry within a given time. The mainframe wastes time waiting to communicate, when that time could be used for actual computations. This delay is called *latency*. In heavily used networks, these two liabilities can combine to create unacceptable network congestion.

Because of the massive investments in mainframes over the decades by universities, businesses, and other institutions, the mainframe model is still quite prevalent and will not disappear soon. However, with the advent of the Web and more sophisticated computing technologies, web-based interfaces and other bridging technologies will change or replace the traditional "dumb terminal" and mainframe environment.

Client/Server Model

The *client/server model*, also called *distributed computing*, reduces network congestion by dividing processing tasks between the client (the front end) and the server (the back end). The *client* is a system or application that requests a service from another computer (the server), while the *server* provides information or connections to other computers on the network. The back-end computer is generally more powerful than the front end and is responsible for storing and presenting information. A client/server example is illustrated in Figure 1.2.

FIGURE 1.2 The client/server model

Client   Server

The Client/Server Model Database

The information passed between client and server in this model is stored in an organized, tabular format in a *database*. To enable transactions between these databases and users, the client/server model must translate human-readable language into machine-readable code. Thus far, the most efficient way to accomplish this is by using SQL (pronounced as "sequel"), the programming language. SQL allows users to phrase queries on the front end that can be understood by the back end. Requesting data from a server in SQL involves the following process:

1. The user requests data.
2. The client machine translates the request into SQL.
3. The client sends the request to the server.
4. The server processes the request, which might involve communicating with a remote database or server.
5. The server delivers the response to the client.
6. The client delivers the response to the computer screen.

The key difference between this retrieval model and the one used by mainframes is that the client processes much of this request. In both models, the data is stored on a central computer—a mainframe or a server.

The client/server model contains two types of databases: single database servers and distributed databases. In a system with a single database, one computer would contain the data and would also have to answer any search or transaction requests.

A distributed database involves information storage across several machines, while still allowing searches and transactions to occur as if the information were stored centrally. The primary advantage of this approach is that it divides the task among several powerful computers and network connections. Such distribution tends to decrease the number of network bottlenecks. As you might expect, any bottleneck can lead to increased latency in a computer system.

Client/Server Advantages

In addition to sharing task processing, client/server benefits include a modular approach to computing. Because the client/server model allows you to add new system components, you may not be limited to one specific solution.

In the early years of networking, network administrators had to choose among several competing proprietary networking standards. Large computer companies such as IBM, Xerox, and DEC had each developed their own networking systems, and they were usually incompatible with one another. It was difficult and expensive to install DEC equipment on an IBM network, for example.

However, with the advent of open standards such as Transmission Control Protocol/Internet Protocol (TCP/IP) and Open Database Connectivity (ODBC), systems from different manufacturers could work together more efficiently. For example, today, Linux and Windows NT/2000 servers can use the TCP/IP protocols to work together, allowing businesses to scale solutions according to customer demand.

The client/server model is deemed *scalable* because it gives you the ability to adjust to new demands. This model also allows users more control over their own files, including where the files are stored, who may have access, and other important features.

Two-Tier and Three-Tier Computing

In *two-tier computing*, one computer is responsible only for formatting the information on the screen. The other computer is responsible for both the processing logic and the data storage. Traditional client/server relationships are similar to two-tier computing in that both computers are responsible for part of the processing task. Client/server relationships distribute the task more evenly between the two computers than the traditional systems do. This allows network administrators to choose and install computers that may be specialized for data storage, display, and other specific needs.

To reduce network congestion, developers have further divided the client/server process into three parts. The client is the first tier, a shared server or other network element is the second tier, and the server and database are the third tier. In three-tier computing, the client is responsible only for rendering the information into a suitable user interface. The second tier acts as an intermediary that processes the information before sending it to the server, which then queries the database. Logical functions, such as the parsing of queries and statements, occur at this tier. The third tier in the conceptual model is the database. Three-tier computing requires additional investment in hardware and software, but the cost and time savings realized by users may be worth the additional expense.

Migration to Client/Server Architecture

The combined use of high-performance workstations (terminals or personal computers connected to a network) and server systems support the same features found in mainframe operating systems, but at a much lower price. Furthermore, thousands of off-the-shelf applications are available for workstation operating systems.

Client/server architecture allows considerable flexibility in distributing resources on the network. With this flexibility comes additional complexity; you'll need to understand the types of client nodes that are appropriate for your organization. Identifying a suitable client/server configuration involves the analysis of the following:

- The types of applications that characterize your computing environment

- The users and their requirements

- The computing and network architecture

We will revisit these general issues throughout this book.

Networking Evolved: Web-Based Networking

Anyone who has used the World Wide Web is familiar with web-based networking, also called *collaborative computing*. Because of its association with the Internet, web-based networking is a unique networking type. Web-based networking can use both mainframe and client/server models. Using TCP/IP and other protocols and the Web, internetworks have allowed networks to become more distributed and decentralized.

Intranets at School and in the Workplace

Intranets bring web-based networking in-house, supplying a network for use by employees or members of a specific organization. If you attend a college or university, there is a good chance that you have access to some kind of intranet. Academic institutions have found that a well-designed intranet can increase employee and student satisfaction by providing constant access to grades, schedules, forms, and other important information. This can make regular processes such as class registration more efficient. An academic intranet can also reduce publishing and distribution costs, eliminating the need to print and maintain forms, newsletters, and other materials.

Corporations have seen some of the benefits of intranets as well. Intranets can help control employee use of the Internet by offering a single point for relevant news and information. An intranet can also be used as a gateway to existing information systems that are housed on mainframes. Consolidating corporate information resources in an intranet can increase employee productivity and help focus corporate operations.

Some corporations use their intranets to leverage employee knowledge by having departmental representatives create and update relevant content. The St. Paul Companies developed an intranet system with easy-to-use standards and authoring applications, based on Microsoft products such as Front Page, Internet Information Server (IIS), and Word. The IT department was responsible for maintaining the intranet, while content development was distributed among the departments. Only one to two days of training was required, and one or two representatives of each department or work unit were recruited to maintain the content.

In some cases, web-based computing represents a radical form of three-tier computing. Heavily distributed networks, such as extranets and virtual private networks (VPNs), also rely on the web browser to provide a consistent user interface with complex server mechanisms.

The benefit of utilizing web-based networking is that it combines the power of mainframe computing with the scalability of the client/server model. Furthermore, because web-based networking relies on the use of a familiar, ubiquitous, and often free web browser, information can be obtained without specialized software.

The goal of web-based networking is to provide an open, global solution that allows users to obtain information and conduct transactions. With the advent of e-commerce solutions, such as online shopping, secure transactions, and personal information management, web-based networking continues to develop as a powerful computing model.

Businesses use *extranets* to connect enterprise intranets to the global Internet. Extranets are designed to provide access to selected external users to expedite the exchange of products, services, and key business information.

Networking Categories

We can describe networks as groups of computers, designed to communicate in certain ways. Each computer must be programmed to transmit and receive data in ways the other computers in the network can understand. Obviously, it is much easier and less expensive to use standard sets of technologies to set up the various parts of a network. As we will see in this section, than are many kinds of networking technology standards.

All computer networks consist of the same three basic elements:

Protocols   communication rules on which all network elements must agree. You will learn about networking protocols in the next chapter.

Transmission media   a method for all networking elements to interconnect. You will learn about transmission media later in the book.

Network services   resources (such as printers) that need to be shared with all network users. You will learn about network services later in the book.

Two basic types of networks exist, each using variations of these three basic elements: peer-to-peer and server-based. A third network architecture—enterprise network—combines features of both peer-to-peer and server-based networks.

Peer-to-Peer Networks

When two or more computers are linked to each other without centralized controls, a *peer-to-peer network* is created. In a peer-to-peer network, each computer in the network has as much control as the next. In this situation, each computer functions as a *host*. (A host computer is either a client or a workstation that other computers use to gain information. Any host can share its resources with other systems on the network.)

A peer-to-peer network architecture does not require dedicated resources, such as file servers.

Typically, peer-to-peer networks tend to be less expensive and easier to work with than client/server networks. However, a peer-to-peer network is less secure, because file and account management can be distributed across the networked computers. Additionally, the larger a peer-to-peer network becomes, the slower it can get. Peer-to-peer networks usually support about 10 or fewer users, which is much less than a properly configured server-based network could do. Figure 1.3 shows a peer-to-peer network.

FIGURE 1.3 Peer-to-peer network model

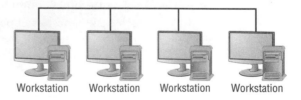

Examples of peer-to-peer PC networking products include the following:

- Artisoft LANtastic
- Novell NetWare Lite
- Microsoft Windows 95/98/Me

Server-Based Networks

A *server-based* network is a configuration of nodes, some of which are dedicated to providing resources to other hosts on the network. *Nodes* are processing locations on a network, such as a computer, printer, or other device. Each node has a unique network address. Dedicated nodes that make their resources available to other computers are called *servers*. These resources can include printers, applications, and documents. Figure 1.4 shows a server-based network.

FIGURE 1.4   Server-based network model

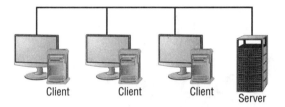

Server-based networks offer security because a central database can keep track of which resources each user can access. The server administrator can set up the network to allow each user access only to the specific files and directories they need to use. It is also much easier to backup and store duplicate copies of files stored on a server-based network, as network files are located in a central place.

However, dedicated servers can be expensive. Each server may require larger hard drives and more RAM than a typical client workstation requires. Servers are usually located in their own room, which should be locked to restrict physical access to these computers. An IT department that has its own servers may also require a full-time network administrator to configure, supervise, backup, and maintain their servers properly.

Examples of server nodes include such things as print servers, files servers, mail servers, and web servers. Client nodes can access these resources over the network. Examples of network operating systems that are suitable for installation on server nodes in a client/server network include:

- AppleTalk Network for Macintosh
- Linux
- Microsoft Windows NT/2000/XP
- Novell NetWare
- UNIX

Enterprise Networks

Enterprise networks provide connectivity among all nodes in an organization, regardless of their geographical location, and run the organization's mission-critical applications. Enterprise networks can include elements of both peer-to-peer and server-based networks.

An enterprise network may consist of several different networking protocols. *Protocols* are the rules that control network communications. An enterprise network can also combine network architectures.

Systems on enterprise networks are capable of translating packets of one architecture into another (acting as *gateways*). Additionally, an enterprise network can support multiple architectures (multiprotocol systems). (Gateways and multiprotocol systems will be discussed later, in Chapter 2.)

Network Topologies

Topologies are basic configurations that information systems professionals use to physically connect computer networks. Several popular topologies used to connect computer networks include the *bus*, *star*, *ring*, and *hybrid designs*.

Bus Topology

Bus topology networks require that all computers, or nodes, tap into the same cable. When a computer sends data on a bus network, that data is broadcast to all nodes on the network. The term *bus* describes the electrical bus or cable that connects all the computers in the network. Network data must be transmitted to each computer along the cable. Only the destination computer reads the sent message; the rest of the computers ignore the data. A bus topology is shown in Figure 1.5.

Small offices often use bus networks because they are easy and inexpensive to install. No dedicated server is needed, so bus networks are often less complex than other network types.

Bus networks usually need terminators, small electrical devices that absorb signals, at each end of the network to ensure that network traffic does not echo back through the network. Otherwise, the network can become congested with old traffic very quickly, much like a microphone getting feedback from being placed near a speaker. Since terminators are easy to find in computer-retail stores, it is easy to avoid this feedback effect on the bus network.

FIGURE 1.5   Bus topology with terminators

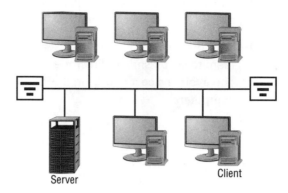

Using bus topologies has its advantages and disadvantages, as you can see in Table 1.1.

TABLE 1.1   Advantages and Disadvantages of Bus Topologies

Advantages	Disadvantages
Bus networks are relatively simple, inexpensive, easy to operate, and reliable.	Isolating problems is difficult; if a cable breaks, the entire network will be affected.
Bus networks use cable efficiently.	The network is likely to slow during peak traffic periods, because more data must pass by each computer.

 Real World Scenario

Installing a Bus Network in a Small Office

You are responsible for the personal computers in a small, three-person office. The computers run Windows Me. You and your colleagues have been passing files back and forth on floppy disks, but you are starting to get more and more large files that can't be shared this way.

One of your co-workers suggests purchasing a Zip drive for each of the three computers. A Zip drive is similar to a floppy drive, but uses special high-capacity disks that are slightly larger than floppy disks. This would allow your team to pass bigger files to one another. Depending on the model, a Zip drive can store 100 or 250MB on a Zip disk.

Your other co-worker suggests setting up a network. This would allow your team to set up shared directories on one or more of the three computers, and avoid the cost of buying the Zip drives for the current or any new computers.

In the real world, the easiest way to set up a network in this case is to use the peer-to-peer networking features in Windows Me. Because it is difficult to run cable in your particular office, you decide to install a bus network, as it requires the least amount of cabling. This reduces the cost of the network to just the setup time and the cable.

Star Topology

If a bus network grows too big, a *star* network will often be used as the replacement topology. Star topology networks connect network nodes through a central concentrating device, usually a hub. (We will discuss hubs in detail in Chapter 2.) Star networks, like the one shown in Figure 1.6, require more cabling than bus networks, because each computer must have its own network cable that connects to the hub.

FIGURE 1.6 Star topology

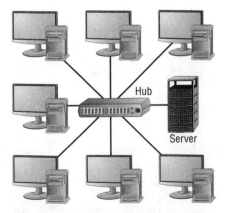

Because each computer's network connection terminates in the hub, the star topology arrangement greatly reduces the risk of an entire network failure. For example, if a cable breaks or a node fails, only that cable segment or node will be affected. The rest of the network will continue to function.

A common weak point of a star network is the hub itself, because if this central connection point fails, the entire star network will go down. Hubs are usually located in a hidden area, because the only time a hub is usually handled is when installing or disconnecting a new cable segment. This hidden placement can ensure that the hub will not be disturbed and reduce the likelihood of jeopardizing the stability of the network.

There are advantages and disadvantages to using star topologies, as listed in Table 1.2.

TABLE 1.2   Advantages and Disadvantages of Star Topologies

Advantages	Disadvantages
The network is usually not affected if one computer fails.	If the hub (or centralized connection point) malfunctions, the entire network can fail.
Network expansion and reconfiguration are relatively simple.	Star networks require more cable than bus networks.
Network management and monitoring can be centralized.	

 Real World Scenario

Converting a Bus Network to a Star Network

In the previous example of a bus network, adding an additional user to the network would require adding an additional segment of cable somewhere on the network. Bus networks can accommodate occasional additions like this.

Suppose, however, you knew you would be adding three computers to the bus network over the next six months. As you plan the installations, you are unsure where these computers will go. Each time you add a computer, you will have to insert a segment of cable somewhere in the network to maintain the bus. This makes the task of adding additional cable segments to the bus network increasingly difficult.

> It may be more practical to purchase a hub and rewire the bus network with a star topology. In a star network, you simply connect a new cable between the hub and each new computer. If you convert the network to a star configuration, you will no longer need the two terminators, so they should be removed from the network, also.

Ring Topology

Ring topologies do not have a central connection point. Instead, a cable connects one node to another, until a "ring" is formed, connecting each computer. When a node sends a message, each computer in the ring processes the message. If a computer is not the destination node, it will pass the message to the next node, until the message arrives at its destination. As each node retransmits or repeats the data, it also amplifies the signal. This allows ring networks to span a greater distance than star or bus networks.

If none of the nodes on the network accepts the message, it will make a loop around the entire ring and return to the sender.

An example of the ring topology is shown in Figure 1.7.

FIGURE 1.7 Ring topology

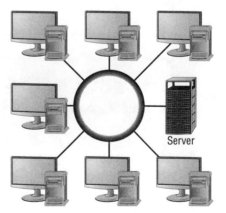

Server

Ring networks can connect through a central device called a Multistation Access Unit (MAU). The MAU can keep a ring network running, even if a mode isn't working. We'll go into more detail about MAUs in Chapter 2.

Table 1.3 discusses the advantages and disadvantages of ring topologies.

TABLE 1.3   Advantages and Disadvantages of Ring Topologies

Advantages	Disadvantages
All computers have equal access to data.	Network expansion or reconfiguration will affect network operation.
During peak usage periods, the performance is equal for all users.	Isolating problems is difficult on a ring topology network.
Ring networks perform well with heavy network traffic.	If one node fails, the entire network can fail.
Ring networks can span longer distances than other types of networks.	

Hybrid Networks

Larger networks usually combine elements of the bus, star, and ring topologies. This combination is called a *hybrid* topology. Hybrids allow the expansion of several existing networks by connecting them within an overall topology.

For instance, in a typical star ring network, two or more ring networks are connected into a star network, using a MAU as a centralized hub. Each ring network continues to serve its existing users, but by connecting them through a hub, users on one ring network can access resources on a different ring network.

In a star bus network, two or more star topologies are connected using a bus "trunk." In this situation, the bus trunk serves as the network's *backbone*. The backbone is the highest level in the computer network hierarchy, to which smaller networks typically connect. The backbone makes the connection between the star networks.

The star bus network shown in Figure 1.8 demonstrates that each star network contains two nodes and is connected by linear bus trunks. This topology is excellent for larger companies, because the backbone can implement media that support high data transmissions. However, the hybrid topology is not without its foibles. Table 1.4 discusses the advantages and disadvantages of hybrid topologies.

FIGURE 1.8 Star Bus Network

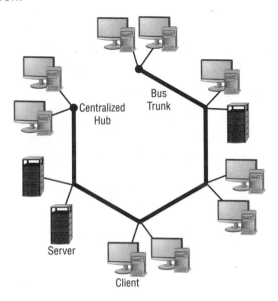

TABLE 1.4 Advantages and Disadvantages of Hybrid Topologies

Advantages	Disadvantages
Network expansion can be accomplished by choosing an appropriate network topology for the requirements.	Hybrid networks are more difficult to design, optimize and maintain than the star, bus, or ring topologies.
Server administrators can allow user access to the network through one or more methods.	

Mesh Topology

Mesh topologies connect devices with multiple paths so that redundancies exist, ensuring that a connection can always be made, even if one is lost. All devices are cross-connected so the best path can be chosen at any given moment in the event of a connection failure. Figure 1.9 shows a mesh topology based on the star bus hybrid topology.

FIGURE 1.9   Mesh topology

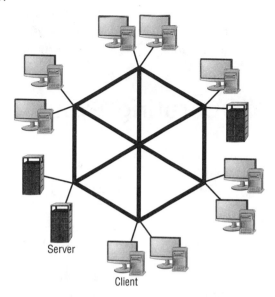

Server

Client

Table 1.5 lists the advantages and disadvantages of mesh topologies.

TABLE 1.5   Advantages and Disadvantages of Mesh topologies

Advantages	Disadvantages
If one connection is terminated, another can be chosen to deliver the data to the destination.	Additional hardware and cable can make mesh topologies more expensive and difficult to install and maintain.

Physical versus Logical Topologies

Star, bus, ring, hybrid networks, and mesh are all examples of *physical topologies* in that they refer to the way in which the various devices are connected to the network. But there is also something called *logical topologies*, a term which refers to a generated signal's actual path over a network. Bus and ring can also be classified as both logical and physical topologies.

For instance, a bus logical network generates a signal to all devices on the network and a ring logical network generates a signal that travels in one direction along a determined path. To put it more simply, physical topology connotes the actual connection to the network—the physical connection of cables and machines. Logical, however, refers to the type of signal running through the physical connection. This distinction between physical and logical topologies is very important for you to understand.

Network Operating Systems

A *network operating system (NOS)* is the program that allows users and administrators to manage and access resources on a computer network. A NOS helps integrate network computers by facilitating orderly, reliable communication throughout the entire network. Important functions of the operating system include managing multiple users on a network, providing access to file and print servers, and implementing network security.

A NOS enables clients to access remote drives (those drives not on the user's machine) as if they were on the client's own machine. A NOS can also allow servers to process requests from clients, and determine whether an individual client has permission to use a particular network resource.

Similar to a client/server relationship, part of the NOS must be run on the client workstation, while another part of the NOS must run on one or more servers. Some network operating systems can also be used to set up a peer-to-peer network. In this case, each node would serve as both the client and the server.

This section will discuss four of the most popular network operating systems:

- Novell NetWare

- Microsoft Windows NT/2000/XP

- UNIX

- Linux

The following sections explain important aspects of the four major NOSs and their vendors.

Novell NetWare

Novell Corporation was founded in 1983, and helped popularize the local area network (LAN) market. *Novell NetWare* is the most widely installed family of network operating systems. NetWare uses standalone servers that provide such LAN services as file storage, network printing, and directories. The most recent version is called NetWare 6.

Before version 5, NetWare was a proprietary NOS that communicated using the Internetwork Packet Exchange (IPX) protocol, the Sequenced Packet Exchange (SPX) protocol, and the NetWare Core Protocol (NCP). These protocols were necessary for all Novell network computers to communicate.

You will learn more about networking protocols later in the next chapter.

With version 5, NetWare started supporting TCP/IP as its networking protocol and Java as its primary application language. Because TCP/IP is the standard protocol of the Internet and Java is a programming language that operates across platforms (e.g., on Windows, UNIX, and so forth), server administrators could use NetWare 5 to easily integrate existing NetWare installations with Internet services such as web servers. In NetWare 6, Novell added remote file, printing, and directory services for Internet users.

Microsoft Windows NT, Windows 2000, and Windows XP

Originally, Novell NetWare overshadowed earlier Microsoft network operating systems in terms of features and market share, then Microsoft released the Windows NT network operating system in 1993. Eventually, the tables turned, and Windows NT became widely implemented in the corporate world because it supported a variety of networking schemes, including Novell NetWare and TCP/IP. The NT family included features that helped business users easily integrate and network Windows workstations, so businesses began adopting Windows 3.1 and Windows 95 computers as workstations. Back in the early days of implementation, the available versions of the Microsoft NOS were Windows NT Workstation, meant for use on client computers, and Windows NT Server, meant (as its name indicates) for the server.

In 1999, Microsoft introduced the Windows 2000 family of operating systems. Windows 2000 was the first Microsoft operating system specifically designed to use TCP/IP as its primary networking protocol, while still supporting other networking protocols. Three versions of Windows 2000 were released: Windows 2000 Server, Windows 2000 Advanced Server, and Windows 2000 Professional. Windows 2000 Server and Advanced Server provided businesses with a server operating system for applications and e-commerce. Windows 2000 Professional was designed for network clients, especially business users and advanced home users. Windows 2000 supported more types and brands of computer hardware and software than Windows NT did, including additional support for portable computers, advanced power management, and (Universal Serial Bus) USB connections.

Windows NT 4.0 and Windows 2000 both use TCP/IP as the default network protocol, and have a user interface similar to Windows 95/98/Me.

Then, in October 2001, Microsoft introduced the Windows XP desktop operating system. Windows XP is based on the Windows 2000 operating system, and is designed for high reliability and ease of use.

Like Windows NT and Windows 2000, Windows XP also uses TCP/IP as its default network protocol suite. However, Windows XP looks and behaves differently from earlier Windows operating systems; Microsoft introduced a streamlined, adaptive user interface that can customize itself based on the individual user's actions and patterns. Windows XP also incorporates advanced web technology into the operating system, providing easier user access to Internet services.

Microsoft XP is available in two versions:

- Microsoft XP Home Edition, which includes features such as digital imaging, audio file recording, an Internet firewall, broadband and dial-up connection management, and enhanced game compatibility. Home Edition is recommended for home use, hence the ingenious name.

- Microsoft XP Professional Edition, which adds corporate networking and Internet security features to the Home Edition features. XP Professional is recommended for business users and advanced home users.

UNIX

Computer scientists at AT&T developed the initial version of the *UNIX* operating system in 1969. UNIX (pronounced YOO-nicks) is used as a network operating system for the majority of non-PC networks. During the early development of the Internet, UNIX became the established choice of server administrators. Today, UNIX in its many forms remains the dominant Internet network operating system.

You should think of UNIX as a family of similar operating systems. At its core, UNIX offers a command-line interface that requires users to type in very specific commands. This facet of UNIX is often a difficult obstacle for beginning users. Although UNIX is a robust client/server operating system, the command-line interface sometimes resembles a mainframe computing model, where the user is explicitly requesting specific services from a remote server.

Because there are more than 600 UNIX commands, *graphical user interfaces (GUIs)* were developed to simplify UNIX operations. These GUIs include X-Windows, enhanced with the Open Look or Motif GUI. A GUI is a user-friendly environment that replaces the command line with a desktop. The user points and clicks on graphical pictures or icons and uses a handheld device called a mouse. (The developers of Microsoft Windows used these GUIs as a starting point for their work, which was originally developed to simplify command-based DOS operations.)

Many hardware vendors offer some variant of UNIX as a primary or secondary operating system. Popular UNIX versions include Sun Solaris, Digital UNIX, Berkeley Systems Distribution (BSD), Hewlett Packard HP-UX, Tarantella UNIXWare, and IBM AIX. Many IBM mainframes can run UNIX. The most recent Apple Macintosh operating system, OS X, is built on a version of UNIX, called Mach, developed at MIT.

Linux

While it is possible to run UNIX on a personal computer, relatively few users besides server administrators and advanced experts were interested in doing so. In 1991, a Finnish graduate student named Linus Torvalds decided to create his own version of UNIX for the personal computer, using portions of the UNIX operating system registered under the GNU licensing scheme; the GNU public license allowed developers to change the actual source code of UNIX and add new features, as long as the developers shared their innovations with any other interested people.

Torvalds decided to build his UNIX operating system completely within the GNU framework. He also posted requests for programming help on the Internet, and made the source code of his project available for anyone to download, use, and modify. This kind of software development model is called *open source computing*. Much of the early development of the Internet was done on an open source model. Over time, the Linux project grew, and Linus became the lead developer and coordinator for the operating system, which he called *Linux* (pronounced LIH-nucks).

Thousands of Individuals and hundreds of companies have assisted in the development of Linux. Some companies have developed retail Linux distributions, which often include additional applications, utilities, and features not provided in the freely available versions, called *distributions*. Popular Linux distributions include Red Hat, Mandrake, Caldera, and Debian.

Microsoft's competitors have also assisted in the development of Linux, partly as a response to the growing popularity of Microsoft operating systems and software. IBM, for instance, offers versions of Linux for use as a network operating system for some of its mainframe computers.

Linux is sometimes used as a desktop operating system on personal computers. Some users even choose to run Linux instead of Microsoft Windows. Some people and organizations prefer Linux because of its low cost, and its ability to run applications at high speed. The Brazilian and Chinese governments have selected Linux over Microsoft Windows as their preferred network operating system.

Depending upon the distribution, installing a Linux operating system can range from very easy to very difficult. You can also purchase a personal computer with a Linux distribution already installed and optimized for your needs.

Many Linux application programs are written by groups of programmers who are also Linux users and who follow open source guidelines. However, there are relatively few commercial software companies that have released Linux-compatible software, when compared to the large commercial market for Microsoft Windows software. Still, you can purchase software that allows Windows or Macintosh software to run on a Linux operating system. Microsoft Internet Explorer and Netscape web browsers are even available in versions compatible with some Linux distributions.

Linux is primarily used as a network operating system, and has become a popular way to host Internet services. Apache server, which runs on Linux, is the most widely used Internet server, based on the number of websites hosted.

Linux in the Workplace and Home

Many companies use Linux to help provide specific industrial solutions. The GNU public license allows anyone to create their own version of Linux, with the specific features they need. Developers can reduce the size of Linux by paring unneeded features, to the point that a Linux operating system can be burned onto a microchip and included in many kinds of computing products.

Several companies have developed inventory management systems and point-of-sale terminals using Linux operating systems.

Linux operating systems are often used in cable television set top boxes. Linux has also been used in the TiVo television recorder. In both of these devices, the cable or telephone line connection that is required for operation can also be used to send updates to the operating system.

Interoperability

All four NOSs can communicate across a network with one another. This feature, called *interoperability*, makes it easier for corporations with different clients and servers to create a network where the computers use different operating systems. Figure 1.10 shows a possible network that comprises a variety of NOSs, each of which can communicate with the others.

FIGURE 1.10 NOS interoperability

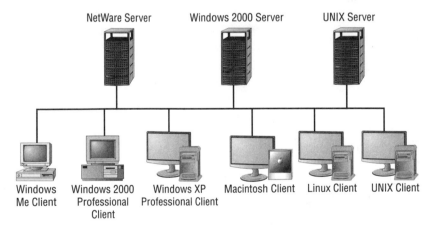

NetWare Server   Windows 2000 Server   UNIX Server

Windows Me Client   Windows 2000 Professional Client   Windows XP Professional Client   Macintosh Client   Linux Client   UNIX Client

Summary

In this chapter, you learned about the development of computer networks. Mainframe computing required one computer to handle all the users on a network. Client/server computing is the networking model on which the

Internet and the World Wide Web were developed. Web-based computing builds upon the mainframe and client/server models, and adds the ability to distribute network services across the Internet.

We also discussed how networks need protocols, media, and services to function. We reviewed three network models. Peer-to-peer networks allow two or more computers, or nodes, to communicate and share files with each other. Server-based computing adds a dedicated computer for file storage and other services. Enterprise computing combines aspects of peer-to-peer and server-based computing.

We also examined various network topologies, including the bus, star, ring, mesh, and hybrid designs. Each topology performs certain tasks better than others. The bus is easy to set up, but supports a small number of computers. Star networks require additional cable and hardware, but allow easier troubleshooting. Ring networks can span greater distances than bus and star networks, but require special hardware to increase network reliability. Mesh networks can transmit signals quickly and reliably, but require multiple cable hookups. Hybrid topologies allow network designers to use two or more different topologies to gain needed features.

For many computers, a NOS is required to access the Internet. We looked at popular NOSs from Microsoft and Novell, and also discussed UNIX and Linux. We discussed interoperability, and the role of TCP/IP as a common networking protocol.

In the next chapter, we will see how network elements fit into the Internet.

Exam Essentials

Understand networking and its importance in today's data communications marketplace.   Networking connects one or more computers to other computers in different locations. Utilizing networks, organizations cut costs by connecting quickly, sharing information, and benefiting from the use of cheaper, personal computers, thus breaking away from use of mainframes.

Be able to identify and describe the function of servers, workstations, and hosts.   Servers store and control access to information. Users can use a workstation to request and work on data. A workstation can also be called a host. Computers on networks can also be called nodes.

Be able to identify and describe the three kinds of network architectures.   A peer-to-peer network connects two or more computers without a server. Peer-to-peer networks are less secure and support fewer users than a server-based network, which has at least one server running a network operating system (NOS). Enterprise networks combine peer-to-peer and server-based networks, and may include gateways and multi-protocol systems.

Know the three basic elements of networks.   Protocols are communication rules for computers. Transmission media provide a method of connection. Network services are resources like printers and servers that are shared among network users.

Be able to identify and describe the five types of network topologies.   Bus networks connect two or more computers along a sequence of cable. Star networks use a central hub to connect computers. Ring networks pass network data around a ring of computers. Mesh networks interconnect computers to ensure reliability. Hybrid networks can combine elements of these topologies.

Understand the differences between logical and physical topologies.   A logical topology is the signal's actual path within a network. A physical topology is the actual physical connections of the network, such as hub, star, ring, or hybrid.

Know the major network operating systems.   Novell NetWare, Microsoft Windows NT/2000/XP, UNIX, and Linux are the most popular network operating systems. All these systems use TCP/IP for network communications. Each of these systems can also be configured to host a web server, mail server, and other kinds of Internet servers.

Key Terms

Before you take the exam, be certain you are familiar with the following terms:

backbone	client
bandwidth	client/server model
bus	database

Enterprise networks

extranets

graphical user interfaces (GUIs)

host

hybrid

interoperability

Intranets

latency

Linux

logical topologies

mainframe

mesh

network operating system (NOS)

network

nodes

Novell NetWare

open source computing

peer-to-peer network

protocol

ring

server

server-based

star

two-tier computing

UNIX

workstations

Review Questions

1. Which exam is required to receive any CIW certification?

    A. CIW Site Designer (1D0-420)

    B. CIW Foundations (1D0-410)

    C. CIW Server Administrator (1D0-450)

    D. CIW E-Commerce Designer (1D0-425)

2. In the early history of computing, before the personal computer, which model of networking was most commonly used?

    A. Microsoft Windows

    B. Enterprise

    C. Mainframe

    D. Web-based

3. Which term is defined as the communication delay caused by sending delays between two computers?

    A. Latency

    B. Mainframe

    C. Terminal

    D. Bus

4. In a two-tier client/server computing model, which of the following tasks does the client perform?

    A. Searches for data

    B. Formats and sends data

    C. Provides centralized data storage

    D. Requests and displays data

5. Amanda is designing part of a network using a three-tier client/server computing model. She is responsible for the second tier of the network. What task does the second tier perform?

A. Requests data

B. Retrieves data

C. Formats data

D. Displays data

6. The software application usually running on the end user's computer host can be called which one of the following?

A. Server

B. Client

C. Network

D. Mainframe

7. What type of network can connect customers and vendors to the internal networks of a business?

A. Intranet

B. Extranet

C. Internet

D. Internetwork

8. In web-based networks, the web browser provides what function?

A. Server

B. Client

C. Data storage

D. Protocols

9. Which one of the following choices best describes a peer-to-peer network?

   A. This network can connect as few as two computers.

   B. A hub is required.

   C. This network can connect up to 20 computers.

   D. A network operating system is required.

10. John is evaluating the following operating systems for installing on a server in a server-based network. Which choice is the least suitable?

    A. Microsoft Windows 2000

    B. Linux

    C. Microsoft Windows 95

    D. Novell NetWare 6

11. Which of the following choices apply to ring and bus networks?

    A. Cabling is easier on these networks than on star networks.

    B. If one node fails, the entire network can fail.

    C. These networks handle heavy traffic well.

    D. Network management is centralized.

12. Brad is installing a star network. Which one of the following pieces of hardware will he need to install?

    A. Server

    B. Terminator

    C. Multistation access unit

    D. Hub

13. Which type of network topology can use a Multistation Access Unit (MAU)?

    A. Peer-to-peer

    B. Bus

    C. Ring

    D. Star

14. Which network topology can span the greatest distance without the use of additional networking hardware?

    A. Hybrid

    B. Bus

    C. Mesh

    D. Ring

15. What is the name of the feature that allows all network operating systems to work with each other?

    A. Transparency

    B. Interoperability

    C. Scalability

    D. Latency

16. Which one of the following types of networks does not require dedicated servers?

    A. Enterprise

    B. Server-based

    C. Peer-to-peer

    D. NetWare

17. A network operating system most closely resembles which of the following network models?

   A. Mainframe

   B. Client/server

   C. Star

   D. Enterprise

18. Which of the following is the best description of the backbone of a computer network?

   A. The backbone is the level at which smaller networks are typically connected.

   B. The backbone connects computers on a peer-to-peer network.

   C. The backbone is the device that connects computers in a star network.

   D. The backbone is the device that connects computers in a ring network.

19. Which of the following network operating systems is used most often on Internet servers?

   A. UNIX

   B. Novell NetWare

   C. Microsoft Windows NT

   D. Microsoft Windows 2000

20. The Linux operating system is derived from which earlier operating system?

   A. Microsoft Windows

   B. Novell NetWare

   C. Mainframe operating systems

   D. UNIX

Answers to Review Questions

1. B. The CIW Foundations exam is required to receive any CIW certification. The code number at VUE and Prometric is 1D0-410. The CIW Site Designer (1D0-420) and CIW E-Commerce Designer (1D0-425) exams count towards the CIW Professional certification, and you must pass both to receive the Master CIW Designer certification. The CIW Server Administrator (1D0-450) exam also counts towards the CIW Professional certification, and is required for the Master CIW Administrator and Master CIW Web Site Manager certifications.

2. C. Mainframe computers were the first networking model to be used. Microsoft Windows was designed for the IBM personal computer. With the advent of personal computers, the other two models became possible.

3. A. Latency is the term that correctly describes the time one computer waits for another computer to receive a message. A mainframe is a type of computer. A terminal is used to communicate with a mainframe. A bus connects computers on a network, and is a type of network topology.

4. D. The client must send to the server a request for data. The server searches for the data in its storage areas and sends it. In a mainframe model, the server would also format the data for display.

5. A. In a three-tier client server model, the first tier is the client. The client is responsible for data formatting and display. The second tier requests the data. The third tier, the server, retrieves the data.

6. B. The term "client" can refer to the computer that is accessing a server or the software application on that computer. The server provides data that is requested by the end user, through a client application. Data is sent through the network. A mainframe provides data access and controls terminals.

7. B. An extranet is used to allow secure access by external parties into an internal business network. Intranets provide access for employees. An Internet and internetwork refer to large combinations of networks.

8. B. The web browser is sometimes called the universal client, because it is an application for viewing many different kinds of data. The server can provide network services, such as files and printing. Data storage is not performed within a web browser. Protocols are used to format data for transmission on a network.

9. A. A peer-to-peer network connects two or more computers, allowing each computer to act as a host. A star network topology requires a hub—a peer-to-peer network does not need a hub. Peer-to-peer networks are not recommended for connecting 10 or more computers. You do not need a network operating system to set up a peer-to-peer network.

10. C. John should not use Microsoft Windows 95. Windows 95 can be used as a network client, but does not have the recommended features for a network server. Microsoft Windows 2000, Novell NetWare 6, and Linux are suitable network server operating systems.

11. B. The only choice that applies to ring and bus networks is B. A token ring network without a MAU and a bus network can fail if a single node is not operating. Cabling a ring network can be more difficult than a star network if a central MAU is not used. Bus networks handle heavy traffic poorly, while ring networks do well. Bus networks lack a server, so network management is actually decentralized.

12. D. Brad will need to use a hub as a concentration point to tie all the computers in his star network together. A server is not required in a star topology. A terminator must be used at each end of a bus network. MAUs are use on ring networks.

13. C. The MAU is used in a ring network to help keep the network running if a node fails. Bus networks use a single cable to connect all computers. Peer-to-peer networks do not use a MAU and are not a network topology type. Star networks use a hub to connect all computers.

14. D. The ring topology can span the greatest distance without extra hardware, because each node amplifies the signal that is sent to the next computer. Without a specific design, we cannot say that a hybrid topology would work best. Bus networks work best at short distances. Mesh networks use a great deal of cable to interconnect nodes, which can limit signal distance.

15. B.   Interoperability refers to a general set of features and services that help define a network operating system. Transparency is an attribute of an image file. Scalability refers to the operating system's ability to handle larger amounts of data. Latency is the delay time between two computers.

16. C.   Server-based networks must have at least one server. Enterprise networks combine peer-to-peer and server-based networks, so there must be a server. In a peer-to-peer network, no servers are required. A Novell NetWare network uses a server for network file storage.

17. B.   Networking operating systems work on a client/server model. In the mainframe model, users access a mainframe computer by using a terminal. Star is a network topology—network operating systems tend to support multiple topologies. Peer-to-peer is a type of network. Network operating systems support enterprise networks.

18. A.   A backbone is the highest level in the computer network hierarchy. It typically connects two or more smaller networks to each other. Cables or another transmission medium connect peer-to-peer computers. Hubs connect computers on a star network. A MAU can be used to connect computers on a ring network.

19. A.   Of these choices, UNIX is installed on the most Internet servers.

20. D.   Linux is one of many variants of the UNIX operating system. Microsoft Windows and Novell NetWare were developed separately from Linux. There are many kinds of mainframe operating systems; IBM offers a version of Linux for mainframes.

Chapter

2

The Internet

THE CIW EXAM OBJECTIVE GROUPS COVERED IN THIS CHAPTER:

✓ Identify Networking and its role in the Internet, including but not limited to: TCP/IP protocols and packets.

✓ Identify the infrastructure required to support Internet connections, including but not limited to: protocols and hardware and software components.

✓ Identify Internet communications protocols and their roles in delivering basic Internet services, including but not limited to: SLIP, PPP, POP3, SMTP, HTTP, FTP, NNTP (news servers), Telnet, Gopher, and bandwidth technologies.

✓ Identify the purpose and function of the Domain Name System (DNS).

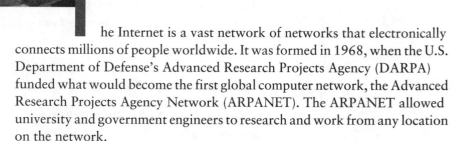

he Internet is a vast network of networks that electronically connects millions of people worldwide. It was formed in 1968, when the U.S. Department of Defense's Advanced Research Projects Agency (DARPA) funded what would become the first global computer network, the Advanced Research Projects Agency Network (ARPANET). The ARPANET allowed university and government engineers to research and work from any location on the network.

ARPANET's design for the Internet featured multiple hosts and multiple connections among those hosts (see Figure 2.1), which greatly reduced the chances of total network failure. There was (and is) no central hub for the ARPANET; a hub would have created a point of vulnerability, so control was distributed throughout the network. This decentralization resulted in a robust and reliable network design that would continue to function even if some of the hosts were unavailable or offline.

FIGURE 2.1 Multiple connections among hosts

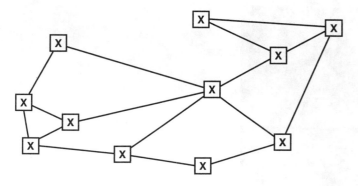

In the late 1980s, the Department of Defense decommissioned the ARPANET, and all the sites switched over to the National Science Foundation (NSF) network, called NSFnet. By 1986, the NSF had increased the number of supercomputers to five and added access to more networks, expanding the range of sites for businesses, universities, and government and military installations. The NSFnet—plus thousands of other organizations, including perhaps your school or business—compose what has become the largest network of networks: the Internet.

The hardware and communications links required to connect to the Internet were funded by a combination of private and government money, and, as years have passed, more private companies have joined the Internet. Despite continued predictions by some users that increasing business involvement would severely disable the Internet, growth has continued at an astounding rate. Business people everywhere see that connecting to the Internet via the Web is a good value, and they are willing to fund its phenomenal growth by paying for better, faster access.

Your understanding of how this vast global network works is vital to your success in the CIW Foundations program. This chapter builds the foundation for your understanding of the Internet, the various ways in which you can retrieve and contribute information, and the naming and addressing conventions you must understand in order to use the Web or any other aspect of the Internet.

How the Internet Works

Specific functions and devices allow you to access the Internet. First, Internet communication is made possible by the Transmission Control Protocol/Internet Protocol (TCP/IP) software on your computer, as we discussed in Chapter 1.

TCP/IP ensures that your information is transferred quickly and reliably. It divides your data into *packets*, or units of data, and sends each packet separately across the Internet. If a packet is lost, all your data is not resent; TCP/IP resends only the missing packet.

The World Wide Web vs. the Internet

It's likely that you are one of the millions of users who access the Internet every day. Surely you've noticed that material on the Internet presents information through multimedia formats: graphics, sound, animation, and video. It employs several tools to provide a visual layout: hypertext links, browser software, and code structure. This presentation of material on the Internet is an example of the World Wide Web.

The Web is not a network itself, like the Internet. The Web is a service that is offered on the Internet's networks. Thousands of computers called web servers offer content that you can access by using a program called a web browser. These programs can be used on many different computer networks, including the Internet and your company's computer network.

The Web resembles an electronic library, and therefore each location or website is like a book. Each book has a contents page that directs you to the other pages in the book, as well as to all the other books in the electronic library. These "books" are created using the *Hypertext Markup Language (HTML)*. These materials, along with interactive objects such as Java, JavaScript, and VBScript can add extensive functionality to web pages.

Next, the software on your computer sends information to the computer with which you are connected, which then passes it on to other computers until it reaches the intended destination. Your software does not have a map of the entire Internet, and does not know the route your transmission will take. Numerous possible routes exist between your workstation and any other; in essence, all paths through the Internet lead to your destination. A network device called a *router* determines the path to get you to the site you want. Routers help maintain network connections by recognizing damaged or slow connections, and then sending data through other routes.

The destination computer at the other end of your connection collects the TCP/IP packets and reassembles them into the data you see on your computer screen.

If one of the connections, or routes, between two computers is not working, there is no need for all the computers on the Internet to be informed. Instead, the nearby routers simply stop using that route until the connection is repaired.

IP Addresses

Every computer that is connected to the Internet has its own Internet Protocol (IP) address. The *IP address* helps the network deliver a packet to a specific computer.

As you can imagine, the original creators of the Internet recognized the need for a flexible addressing system powerful enough to accommodate the enormous number of current and future users. They decided that every device on the Internet would be given an *Internet Protocol (IP)* address, just like every house and business is given a street address. Instead of a street address format, such as 123 Main Street, a 32-bit address format is used, such as the following, where each one of the four sections of an IP address contains an 8-bit number:

204.115.34.10

Computers can use a binary format to represent all numbers. The basic unit of this format is the *bit*, which can represent the number zero or one. Numbers larger than 1 are written by stringing bits together, using base two arithmetic.

Binary, or *base two*, arithmetic values the number columns in powers of two, rather than powers of ten like the system we use in everyday life. Therefore, the number three in binary numbers would be written as 11, or "one-one." The first 1 has a value of two (whereas it would have a value of 10 in our conventional system). The second has a value of 1. You can convert the binary number into base ten by adding the 2 and the 1, which equals 3.

Larger numbers are represented in binary by adding more digits. Each digit represents two to an additional power. If we read out the previous example from left to right, the maximum value of the first digit is 2^1 or the number 2. The second digit represents 2^0 or the number 1.

An 8-digit binary number can represent any whole number between 0 and 255. This kind of number is also called an eight-bit number. Each section of an IP address contains eight bits, and can represent a number between 0 and 255. The number 255 (in base ten), or 11111111 (in base two), is broken down for you here:

Binary digits	1	1	1	1	1	1	1	1
Powers of two	2^7	2^6	2^5	2^4	2^3	2^2	2^1	2^0
Base ten value	128	64	32	16	8	4	2	1

The total value of a binary number can be determined by adding the values for every binary digit that is a 1. Here, we take a look at the binary number 10111010, which is the decimal number 186, or $128 + 32 + 16 + 8 + 2$.

Binary digits	1	0	1	1	1	0	1	0
Powers of two	2^7	2^6	2^5	2^4	2^3	2^2	2^1	2^0
Base ten value	128	64	32	16	8	4	2	1
Result	128	0	32	16	8	0	2	0

If we add up all the values in the Result row, we arrive at 186. Thus, this 3-digit section of the IP address represents 8 bits of information.

The IP address format is also referred to as a *dotted quad*, because the series of numbers is divided into four numbers, separated by a period, or "dot." As we will explain in Chapter 5, some number values are reserved in IP addresses. There are roughly $256 \times 256 \times 256 \times 256$ different IP addresses possible—approximately 4 billion.

Internet Protocol, Version 6 (IPv6)

As more commercial enterprises join the Internet, IP address demand continues to increase and it is possible that the current supply of IP addresses will be depleted. A new protocol called Internet Protocol, version 6 (IPv6) has been designed to solve this problem.

IPv6 supports approximately 340 undecillion IP addresses by using 128-bit IP addresses. The address format uses *hexadecimal numbers* instead of decimals. The word hexadecimal means "sixteen digits." In a hexadecimal number, each column represents a power of 16, starting with 16^0, or 1. (Computers must use a single character to represent a hexadecimal digit, so the letters A through F are used to represent the digits 10 through 15). Here is an example of a hexadecimal number:

`2EA7:4F00:000E:00D0:A267:97FF:FE6B:FE34`

To pronounce a hexadecimal number, you should say each of the single digits as if they were a single letter or number. You might also say the word "hex" or "hexadecimal" at the end of the number, as a further indication that this is not a base ten number. For example, the hexadecimal number 19 could be said as "one nine hex." You would not say this number as "nineteen," as 19 hexadecimal is actually 25 in our conventional base ten system. $(1 \times 16^1 + 9 \times 16^0 = 25)$

When writing hexadecimal numbers, some people add a capital "H" to the end of a number, if it is not clear from the context that the number is hexadecimal. We might present a number as 19H, which means it is the number 19 in hexadecimal. For IPv6 addresses, we do not need to add this notation, as we assume that all IPv6 numeric addresses are hexadecimal.

There are 8 segments, or *octets*, in an IPv6 address, with each octet carrying 4 hexadecimal digits. The entire numeric address is 128 bits, or 4 times a 32-bit IP address. Each octet contains 16 bits of information. The colon is used to separate each octet, rather than the period found in IPv4 addresses. Each octet holds a 4-digit hexadecimal number that converts to between 0 and 65535 in conventional numbers.

Let's look at the first set of digits in our example IPv6 address, 2EA7, and how it is translated into its decimal equivalent, 11943, or 8192 + 3584 + 160 + 7. We convert each hexadecimal digit to its base ten equivalent. Each succeeding digit of the hexadecimal number represents a number that is an increasing power of 16. We multiply the base ten by the appropriate power of 16 to obtain the decimal result for each digit.

Hexadecimal digits	2	E	A	7
Base ten equivalent	2	14	10	7
Powers of 16	$16^3 = 4096$	$16^2 = 256$	$16^1 = 16$	$16^0 = 1$
Result	8192	3584	160	7

IPv6 can help solve the address shortages of IPv4 and IPv6 is more efficient and requires less administrative overhead than IPv4. A server administrator would not need to set up private IP addresses for a network, a process we will explore in Chapter 5.

IPv6 will likely be implemented between 2005 and 2015, depending on how fast current addresses are depleted. Some Internet Service Providers

(ISPs) in Japan are already allocating IPv6 addresses to Internet clients in anticipation of IPv4 address depletion. Fortunately, IPv6 coexists with IPv4, and the two will function together on the Internet for many generations.

Client/Server Model on the Internet

Recall in Chapter 1 how we discussed the concept of networks and the client/server model. Most Internet programs use this client/server model. In this environment, client programs run on many desktops at once and interact with a server program that runs on a single central computer. This model allows a distributed computing system in which computing tasks are divided between the server and the client. Client programs conserve *bandwidth*—the amount of information, or traffic, that can be carried on a network at one time, by processing information locally before sending it out to the network.

When the client/server model is used on a network, such as the Internet, three elements are required:

Client   the software application usually running on the end user's computer host.

Server   the software application usually running on the information provider's computer host.

Network   the hardware that allows communication between the client and server.

The client software is the interface that allows the user to communicate and request information from the server. On the Internet, the client software is often a browser, such as Microsoft Internet Explorer or Netscape Navigator, or an e-mail program, such as Microsoft Outlook Express or Netscape Messenger.

As you can see in Figure 2.2, the client/server relationship is composed of a series of requests for information and the retrieval of that information. Once a server receives a client's request through the network, the server processes the request and attempts to locate the information. For instance, if a client requests a stock quote, the server will query its database for the quote. The quote will be sent to the client and displayed on its computer.

FIGURE 2.2 Client/server model

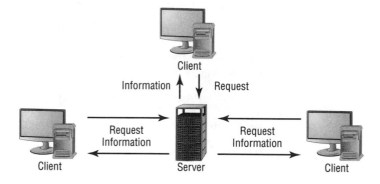

The client and server are able to communicate because they follow the same rules, or protocols, set up by the client/server model. Therefore, a client can access information from any server if both client and server understand the protocol already established.

🌐 **Real World Scenario**

Client/Server Model in Action

E-mail is a useful example of a technology that uses the client/server model. Once you install an e-mail client program on your computer, you can compose messages offline until you are ready to access the Internet connection and send your message. When the message is finished, and you press the Send button, the e-mail client computer can then connect to the Internet, send the message to an e-mail server, and close the connection. The server does not have to perform complex error checking, because the client formatted the message in the appropriate protocol. The recipient can then connect with his or her e-mail server to retrieve the message.

Connecting to the Internet

As we have learned, a client computer is necessary to connect to a network. The client cannot connect to a network without assistance. The following six elements are required to support a client in connecting to the Internet, or any other network:

Computer   PC, WebTV, mobile phone, or handheld device

Operating System   Windows 95/98/Me, Windows NT/2000/XP, Linux, UNIX, Mac OS

TCP/IP   Protocol stack used to communicate with the Internet.

Client Software   Web browser, e-mail, or news client program.

Internet Connection   Dial-up or direct connection to an Internet Service Provider (ISP)

Internet Addresses   Web addresses (www.CIWcertified.com), e-mail addresses (student1@class.com), or server addresses (mail.yahoo.com).

At first glance, this may seem like an intimidating list, but the operating system, TCP/IP, and the client software are included when you purchase one of the devices listed in the computer category. The computer cannot run without an operating system. The operating system contains the computer's basic set of instructions for receiving, presenting, and saving any kind of information the user requests. If the computer features Internet connectivity, then it must have some kind of TCP/IP software to connect to the Internet. Plus, most computers come with some sort of browser software so you can get up and running on the Internet almost immediately.

To initiate your connection to the Internet, you need an *ISP* or *Internet service provider*. An ISP is a company or organization that maintains a gateway to the Internet and rents access to customers on a per-use or subscription basis, much like the telephone company provides you with telephone service at your home or on your cell phone. ISPs are sometimes called *Internet Access Providers, or IAPs.*

ISP Trivia

Most ISPs do not provide extensive content or a protected environment; they usually provide a connection to the Internet, e-mail service, and a customizable home page. Many ISPs do provide Usenet service. ISPs like AOL and EarthLink, provide search engines, news, shopping services, and other types of proprietary content.

In North America, you typically purchase Internet access at a flat monthly rate. In Europe and other areas, the local telephone company may apply a per-minute fee to the call as a part of their standard billing practices. The cost for basic-service ISPs is dropping considerably. Some ISPs offer Internet connectivity for free, such as NetZero (www.netzero.com) in the United States and Freeserve (www.freeserve.com) in the United Kingdom.

There are thousands of ISPs worldwide that offer online services. A comprehensive list of ISPs is maintained at www.thelist.com.

While your ISP provides your connection to the Internet, you still need a device to connected your PC to the network. There are various methods and devices that can connect a user's computer to the Internet. There are modems, which provide access to the Internet on a case-by-case basis, and there are direct connections, which, while they utilize modems, are a very different breed of connection. We'll discuss both methods of Internet connection in the following sections.

Modems

One of the most popular devices individuals use to connect from their PCs to the Internet, is a modem. A *modem* is a device that adapts a computer to a phone line or cable TV network and connects the user to an ISP and ultimately to the Internet. The term "modem" is a combination of two words—MODulate and DEModulate. A modem performs these functions. It converts or modulates a digital signal to an analog form. It also receives analog signals and demodulates them to a digital signal.

An *analog* modem enables a computer to communicate with other computers over telephone lines, by translating digital data into audio/analog signals on the sending computer and back into digital form on the receiving computer. Many personal computers are sold with built-in analog modems.

Cable, DSL and ISDN modems are used on all-digital networks. These networks require the use of a digital modem, because no signal translation to analog is required to access a connection. As we will explain later in this chapter, digital modems use a different method to connect to a computer.

Dial-up Connections

Utilizing your modem, you can connect your PC to an ISP through a dial-up connection. Dial-up connections use an analog modem to access the Internet on a per-use basis. The user gains Internet access when his or her computer contacts an ISP and the ISP transfers the user to the Internet. When finished, the user disconnects from the ISP and hangs up the telephone line.

When you use a phone line and analog modem to connect to the Internet, you are most likely using a dial-up connection. Most dial-up connections use either *Serial Line Internet Protocol (SLIP)* or *Point-to-Point Protocol (PPP)* connections. Typically, the modem will dial the ISP and connect using PPP, which is an improved version of SLIP. If an ISP offers you a choice of a SLIP or a PPP connection, choose PPP.

SLIP is an older protocol that has been widely replaced by PPP for the following reasons:

- SLIP only supports IP, whereas PPP has implementations that support other networking protocols in addition to IP.

- SLIP does not support authentication. *Authentication* is the process of identifying a user who is logging on to a system. It usually requires a user name and a password.

A few older ISPs provide a service called a *shell account*, which is essentially the command-line interface of a UNIX server at the ISP. Shell accounts require users to enter commands to access and navigate the Internet. Today, most users use the point-and-click method through a browser's *graphical user interface (GUI)*.

Another type of connection, WebTV, uses dial-up connections to access the Internet. Even though a WebTV box sits on your TV and uses your TV as the monitor, it typically uses an analog modem and a phone line to connect to the Internet.

Integrated Services Digital Network (ISDN) is a type of dial-up connection that is often used in small offices. ISDN requires digital phone lines. Therefore, you must contact your local phone company and request it to install ISDN lines in your home or business.

An ISDN modem is attached to a computer. ISDN modems do not perform digital to analog modulation, because an ISDN line is a digital medium. However, the word modem is commonly used to describe this device. The ISDN line consists of several channels, which are used for transmitting the data. You can use one channel for normal telephone voice calls and the other for data connections.

The speed with which you can access the Internet is determined primarily by the speed capability of your analog modem. Table 2.1 displays common modem speeds for dial-up connections.

Connectivity speeds are measured in bits per second. A thousand bits per second is declared as "kilobits per second (Kbps)." A million bits per second is declared as "megabits per second (Mbps)." A billion bits per second is declared as "gigabits per second (Gbps)."

TABLE 2.1 Common Speeds for Dial-up Connections

Speed	Description
128Kbps	Two ISDN channels can be combined to increase the connection speed. Speeds of 128 Kbps are achieved by combining two 64Kbps channels using a special version of PPP, called Multilink PPP.
56Kbps	Fastest dial-up speed available using a single analog modem.
53Kbps	Fastest dial-up speed available using a single analog modem in the USA, because of Federal Communications Commission regulations.
33.6Kbps	Standard dial-up modem speed in the late 1990s.
28.8Kbps	Standard dial-up modem speed in the mid-1990s.
14.4Kbps	Moderately slow dial-up modem speed; may not support streaming audio and video.

Direct Connection

Unlike the connection a dial-up modem provides to the Internet, direct connections do not require activation each time you use them; they provide continuous access to the Internet. The direct connection is convenient and fast, because permanent network connections are generally capable of handling high bandwidth. If your company's network is connected to the Internet, or you have a cable or DSL modem installed on your computer, then your computer probably has a direct connection.

A direct, or continuous, connection can be obtained many ways. This section will discuss several direct connections used for Internet access including the following:

- Local area network (LAN)
- Cable modem
- Digital Subscriber Line (DSL)
- Wireless
- Hybrid

Local Area Networks (LANs)

A local area network (LAN) is group of computers connected within a confined geographic area so that their users can share files and services. Commonly found in offices and departments, LANs can be used to access the Internet through a router. The LAN router is connected to another router at the ISP by a high-speed communications line.

Each computer on the LAN needs a *network interface card* (NIC) to connect to the network. A NIC is a hardware device installed in a computer that serves as the interface between a computer and a network.

We will discuss LANs and NICs in detail in Chapter 3.

LANs are connected to the Internet using high-speed direct connections. High-speed connections are dedicated telecommunications lines that can also connect ISPs to other ISPs. These direct connections are identified by various names according to their speed, such as T1, T3, E1, and E3. We will review the various types of high-speed direct connections in Chapter 3.

Cable Modem

Just as you can with a LAN configuration, you can also create a direct connection to the Internet by using a cable modem (provided that your cable TV company has prepared your location for the technology). Cable modems access the Internet through cable TV lines.

To use this service, you must purchase or lease a cable modem, which connects your computer to the cable TV line. You may also require a network interface card (NIC) to attach your computer to the cable modem. When using a cable modem, an additional cable connects a computer's NIC to the modem.

Because a cable modem connection provides persistent or continuous access to the Internet, it is possible for other Internet users to access any computer you connect to the cable modem. Cable modem users should always take some additional security measures to protect their computers and data. We will discuss these security options, including personal firewalls and virus protection, later in Chapter 12.

Also, many cable modems must share the cable network with other users in their neighborhoods. The speed of the cable modem depends on how many users are online at a given time.

Digital Subscriber Line (DSL)

Another direct-connection method is *Digital Subscriber Line (DSL)*, which uses telephone lines and a DSL modem to provide high-speed access.

Speeds less than 512Kbps are common on both cable and DSL modems. Only ISPs are capable of achieving the maximum rates. Just as the speed of the cable modem depends on how many users are online at a given time, the speed of a DSL modem depends on the distance between the DSL modem and the phone company's main distribution frame.

If your local phone company supports DSL, its employees may have to visit your location and a local telephone company switching station for one or more installation visits, depending on the type of DSL offered. You will also need a DSL modem, which is usually provided by the DSL provider. You will also need a NIC to attach your computer to the DSL modem.

DSL may eventually replace ISDN, and DSL competes directly with cable modems.

Wireless Connections

Handheld devices and mobile phones can use a wireless connection to maintain a direct link to the Internet.

Mobile phones can provide the easiest wireless connections, as the phone itself becomes an Internet terminal. The mobile telephone company acts as an ISP. Mobile phone connections typically have low bandwidth, and are limited to text transmissions. The limited telephone keypad can make sending all but the shortest messages a slow, difficult process.

The new 3G, or third generation, technologies allow faster download speeds, letting users read longer e-mail messages and access multimedia content. This service was made available in Japan in late 2001. Deployment in North America and Europe will happen over the next few years, as telephone companies upgrade their infrastructure.

On a handheld device, a wireless modem is required. Wireless modems can use the cellular telephone network or a different radio frequency to transmit data. On some Palm devices in the USA, a wireless modem is built in to the hardware. For Pocket PCs and other Palm devices, various kinds of modems that attach to these devices are available. Some wireless modems can also be used with desktop and laptop computers. The user must also purchase service from a wireless ISP to gain Internet access.

Hybrid Connections

For some users, a hybrid connection may be more practical than wireless connections. Such a connection uses a direct connection to download data, and a dial-up connection to upload. The direct connection may be a cable modem, or a wireless connection like a microwave or satellite antenna.

Since hybrid cable modems are usually deployed in areas with limited bandwidth, users with a hybrid connection may experience some service problems. Latency is a particular issue, especially when uploading large e-mail messages and files. A hybrid cable connection may not even operate if the cable or telephone lines are not working. Wireless download connections require a clear line-of-sight between the user's antenna and the signal source. In relatively flat areas, a microwave antenna that provides connectivity for the local area may be mounted on top of a tall silo or other structure. Local weather, atmospheric conditions, and other factors may interfere with a direct wireless signal.

The Need for Speed

Compared to dial-up methods, the connection speeds associated with various types of direct connections are usually much faster. The speeds associated with some common types of direct connections are outlined in Table 2.2.

TABLE 2.2   Common Types of Direct Connections

Type	Speed
T3	44.736Mbps. Commonly used by North American ISPs to connect LANs and ISPs to the Internet infrastructure. Extremely fast and also one of the most costly types of access.
E3	34.368Mbps. European equivalent of T3.
T1	1.544Mbps. Commonly used by North American corporate LANs to connect to ISPs.
E1	2.048Mbps. European equivalent of T1.
Cable modem	512Kbps to 52Mbps.
DSL	512Kbps to 10Mbps.

Network Access Points

You have already learned that the Internet is a series of interconnected networks. Each ISP operates a network designed to accommodate large numbers of users so that they can each access the Internet. ISPs connect their networks to high-speed networks to give their users access to other Internet sites and servers. A Network Access Point (NAP) is a junction between one high-speed network and another. There are five NAPs in the United States, located in New York, Washington, D.C, Chicago, San Francisco, and Miami.

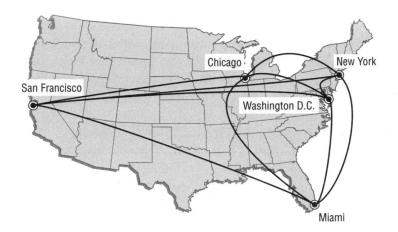

High-speed networks are called Internet *backbones*, because they provide essential connectivity for the rest of the Internet. Backbones carry the majority of network traffic using a high-speed transmission path. Backbones can cover long or short distances, and smaller networks typically connect to them. ISPs use NAPs for connectivity.

The backbone network connected by a NAP is a very high-speed Backbone Network Service (vBNS). These NAPs run in excess of 1Gbps, and are designed to reduce the network congestion caused by increasing Internet usage in the home, school, and workplace.

On the Internet, a *segment* is part of the backbone. A segment is any piece or part of a larger network; for instance, a segment connects San Francisco to Chicago in the NAP system. On a smaller scale, a segment can be the connection between your company's network and its NAP.

Besides the NAPs, there are secondary and tertiary public networks that provide Internet connectivity to ISPs, businesses, governments and other large customers. In North America and Europe, a number of companies and very large ISPs operate their own networks of private NAPs, often involving their own private fiber-optic networks. While a private NAP is very expensive to develop and maintain, these companies can provide themselves and clients with faster, less congested Internet connections.

As with traditional NAPs, ISPs and companies must purchase bandwidth from the NAP operator.

Internet Protocols

As we learned in Chapter 1, networking protocols are the rules that describe how clients and servers communicate across a network. The protocols used currently were developed many years ago, and are similar in concept to the rules of diplomatic interaction that dictate who speaks first, who bows to whom, and so forth. In the following sections you will examine these protocols, which include Hypertext Transfer Protocol (HTTP), File Transfer Protocol (FTP), the various electronic mail (e-mail) protocols, Telnet, news, and Gopher.

Hypertext Transfer Protocol (HTTP)

During the 1960s, the term hypertext was first used to describe a large database of many different kinds of files. An essential concept of hypertext is that files contain references to other files, so they are "linked" to one another, thus creating the protocols, or rules, to link the files.

Hypertext Transfer Protocol (HTTP) is a protocol used to transfer web pages from a web server to a web client. HTTP is the set of rules required to exchange files, such as text, images, video, and multimedia content, across the World Wide Web. HTTP is optimized to send several different files simultaneously, as the client web browser requests them. Not coincidentally, web servers are sometimes called HTTP servers.

File Transfer Protocol (FTP)

File Transfer Protocol (FTP) was originally developed to allow researchers access to programs and large data files on other computers. Recall the example we presented earlier in Chapter 1, with three coworkers in the same office who wanted to share their data. FTP was developed as a solution to allow Internet users in different locations access to the same files.

Businesses have discovered many uses for FTP servers as efficient information access, and distribution points. For instance, when you download software programs and documents from websites, you are usually transferred to FTP sites for the actual download. This process takes place transparently (e.g., the user is unaware of which protocol is downloading the program). FTP is also used to publish web pages to a web server. You simply upload your web page files to an FTP server. Once uploaded, web browsers using HTTP can access your web pages. We will cover this use of FTP in Chapters 14 and 15.

The early users of FTP protected most of their file access with simple user IDs and passwords, but many set aside small parts of FTP sites for anonymous, or general, access. To obtain access to files through an anonymous FTP server, you use the general user ID "anonymous" and provide your e-mail address as the password. Anonymous FTP site access is so popular that many FTP clients connect you automatically. FTP servers are scattered throughout the Internet, and are generally accessible to anyone.

E-Mail: SMTP, POP3, and IMAP4 Protocols

Although you likely use e-mail every day, you probably don't realize the essential rules that go along with sending and receiving mail. When you use e-mail, you do use protocols for sending and receiving messages. You send e-mail to others with an outgoing mail server using the *Simple Mail Transfer Protocol (SMTP)*. You receive e-mail from an incoming mail server using the *Post Office Protocol (POP)* or the *Internet Message Access Protocol (IMAP)*.

The Internet standard protocol for transferring e-mail messages is called Simple Mail Transfer Protocol (SMTP). SMTP Specifies how two mail systems interact, as well as the format of control messages they exchange to transfer mail.

POP is a protocol that is used to transfer e-mail from a user mailbox on a server to a client program. The user can read the messages on the client program. The latest version of this protocol is POP3.

Depending upon your ISP, you might use separate mail servers for outgoing and incoming e-mail, or a single server for both tasks. Although you can send e-mail to any user on the Internet, you will need an account and password to access your mailbox and see the messages.

In the last few years, many server administrators have required an account and password to send e-mail messages. The original Internet developers thought that e-mail would be a minor tool, and were amazed that it became the primary source of Internet traffic from the beginning.

Another protocol called *Internet Message Access Protocol (IMAP)* provides the same services as POP, but is more powerful. IMAP allows sharing of mailboxes and multiple mail server access. The latest version is IMAP4.

Telnet

A lesser-known protocol these days is the *Telnet* protocol, which is used with shell (text-only) accounts. It allows a user at one site to connect with a remote system at another site as if the user's terminal were connected directly. The remote system is typically a network server running Linux, UNIX, or Windows NT/2000.

In the past, universities and researchers used Telnet to access the Internet and read e-mail. Before graphical web browsers became popular, Telnet was the face of the Internet. Telnet is still widely used by administrators to remotely manage computers such as servers, firewalls, and routers.

Network News Transfer Protocol (NNTP)

Usenet (User Network) was developed in 1979 as an alternative to the Internet. As the Internet became increasingly popular, it absorbed Usenet, which is now often referred to as "newsgroups." The *Network News Transfer Protocol (NNTP)* was developed in 1985 and allows sites on the Internet to exchange Usenet news articles, which are organized into topics (for example, "Programming in C++" or "International trade issues"). Other newsgroups discuss topics far less relevant to business. *Newsgroups* allow many users a central area to share information. Usenet (User Network) is a very popular venue for newsgroups because it provides public access to several newsgroups and group mailing lists.

To use newsgroups, you must have access to a news server, which authorizes you to read and post news. Typically, your ISP or organization will have a paid subscription to portions of the Usenet. You can use a news client, such as Outlook Express or Netscape Messenger, to access a newsgroup.

You can also use a web-based newsreader service, such as groups.google.com, to search, read, and post newsgroup messages within a web browser. This is a popular method for users whose ISPs or organizations do not subscribe to Usenet.

Gopher

Developed at the University of Minnesota, *Gopher* is similar in concept and practice to today's Web: users follow text links from site to site in search of information. Gopher was one of the first tools developed to unite the Internet so that users could access the entire Internet rather than just one site. Gopher allows you to browse for text information without having to know exactly where the information is located.

The Web quickly became more popular than Gopher, as web content was easier to read and navigate. Web content also includes multiple images, while Gopher could display only one image at a time. As you might expect, most Gopher servers have been replaced with HTTP (web) servers.

Domain Name System (DNS)

When you access a website, you must enter the address of the web server in your browser. As previously mentioned, one way to identify the server is to provide the IP address. However, most users—professional and casual—prefer to use domain names because word-based names are much easier to remember.

The *Domain Name System (DNS)* translates easily recognizable names into IP addresses. For example, the CIW program has a web server at www.CIWcertified.com, which can be reached at 63.72.51.85.

www.CIWcertified.com = 63.72.51.85

Both the domain name and the dotted quad refer to the same web server, but the domain name is much easier to remember. Without DNS, end users would be forced to enter IP addresses every time access was needed to any part of the Internet.

DNS is an important Internet protocol. We will discuss DNS in more detail than the other protocols, because understanding its function facilitates the use of the other Internet protocols.

One way to remember a domain name is to understand its structure, which can reveal a great deal about the site. Businesses choose their domain names very carefully, so other businesses and users will be able to recall them for future reference.

Each domain name is unique. Once a name within a domain category (such as a specific name in the .com category) is assigned by a domain name registrar, no other organization or individual may use that name within that category. For example, there is only one company authorized to use the domain name CIWcertified.com.

A domain name consists of letters and numbers separated by dots and includes two or more words, called labels, as shown in Figure 2.3. The last label in a domain name is usually a two-letter or three-letter code, called a top-level domain, which will be discussed shortly. The other labels are limited to 63 characters each.

FIGURE 2.3 Typical domain name

WWW.CIWCERTIFIED.COM

Server (Host) Name | Registered Company Domain Name | Domain Category (Top-Level Domain)

Domain Name Syntax

A domain name signifies general divisions then specific companies, then departments within the company and even individual computers (such as a web server or an e-mail server). For example, the domain name www.CIWcertified.com is made up of the following components:

www   the name of the web server at the company, also called the website host.

CIWcertified   the name registered by the company that manages the CIW program. The name was chosen because it accurately represents the purpose of the website.

com   the designation that indicates this a commercial Internet site.

Domain names are not case sensitive. They are usually shown in lowercase characters. The CIW program capitalizes the CIW in its domain name as a marketing tool, to make these letters stand out from the domain name. Many other websites use the same technique. Be assured that you can enter either www.CIWcertified.com or www.ciwcertified.com in a web browser and arrive at the same website.

Some companies further subdivide their domain names into departments or individual workstations. For example, if a company wants to divide the domain companyname.com by department, it might choose to use research.companyname.com and sales.companyname.com. Or it might use tokyo.companyname.com and newyork.companyname.com, dividing by geography. For example, www.research.microsoft.com can be broken down in the following way:

www   the web server for this entity

research   the subdomain assigned to the research division of this company

microsoft   the registered domain name for the Microsoft Corporation

com   the designation that this is a commercial site

Some sites name each computer on the LAN and give each a unique domain name, such as sales1.companyname.com, sales2.companyname.com, and so forth.

There are some server names that are general standards, such as www for a web server, and mail for an e-mail server. However, there is no hard set of rules regarding server names. Common sense sometimes, but not always, prevails in the naming of publicly accessible servers.

A *fully qualified domain name (FQDN)* is the complete domain name of an Internet computer such as www.CIWcertified.com. The FQDN provides enough information to convert the domain name to a specific IP address. For instance, www.CIWcertified.com is an FQDN. The FQDN must include the server (host) name, the registered domain name, and the top-level domain.

Top-Level Domains

The right-side component of a domain name categorizes domains into groups by geography (country, state) or common topic (company, educational institution). These categories are called *top-level domains (TLDs)*. You are probably familiar with the .com top-level domain, which is often incorporated into company names to signify an Internet-related business.

The original top-level domains categorize domains by common topic, they are listed in Table 2.3.

Two-letter country codes categorize domains by country or region. The official list of these codes is located at www.iana.org/cctld/cctld-whois.htm; some examples are shown in Table 2.4.

TABLE 2.3   Original Top-Level Domain Codes

TLD	Description
.com	Commercial or company sites
.edu	U.S. educational institutions, typically universities and colleges
.gov	U.S. government departments and agencies
.mil	U.S. military
.org	Organizations; usually clubs, associations, and nonprofits
.net	Network sites, including commercial ISPs
.int	International organizations, including the European Union (eu.int)

TABLE 2.4   Examples of Country Codes

Country Code	Country
.au	Australla
.ca	Canada
.ch	Switzerland (Confédération Helvétique)
.de	Germany (Deutschland)
.fr	France
.id	Indonesia
.il	Israel
.mx	Mexico
.us	United States of America
.uk	United Kingdom

You do not need to memorize the two-letter country codes for the CIW Foundations exam. For your own benefit, you should become familiar with the country codes that are important to you or your business.

Domain names that end with country codes may feature categories or further geographical divisions before the company or organization name. For example, commercial sites in Australia all have domain names that end with .com.au, and university sites use .edu.au at the ends of their names.

Other countries use other abbreviations: In the United Kingdom, names ending with .ac.uk are universities (.ac stands for academic), and names ending in .co.uk are companies. In Canada, many names feature province abbreviations such as .on.ca or .mb.ca (for Ontario and Manitoba, respectively). Reading from right to left, you will eventually reach the organization name.

Additional domain categories were selected in the year 2000. They are categorized by topic, and listed in Table 2.5.

TABLE 2.5 Additional Top-Level Domains

TLD	Description
.aero	Airlines
.biz	Businesses
.coop	Cooperatives
.info	Content and research-related sites
.museum	Museums
.name	Personal Web addresses for individuals
.pro	Professional organizations

The .biz domain went live in late 2001.

EXERCISE 2.1

Reading Domain Names

See what information you can discern from the following domain names based on our discussion in this chapter.

1. microsoft.com

2. ukonline.co.uk

3. www.rutgers.edu

4. gopher.helsinki.fi

5. marketing.argonaut.com

6. mail.neulevel.biz

7. sports.yahoo.ca

The Business of Domain Names

In early 1993, the *Internet Network Information Center (InterNIC)* was established in the United States to run that country's domain name system. Out of that original collaborative effort grew the InterNIC Directory and Database server, which accommodated the InterNIC domain name registration service.

The InterNIC was a cooperative activity between the U.S. government and a company called Network Solutions. For years, Network Solutions was the only company allowed to register domain names in the .com, .net, and .org top-level domains, which were the three original top-level domains.

Today, the *Internet Corporation for Assigned Names and Numbers (ICANN)* is the organization responsible for defining and managing the domain name registration process. In 1998, as part of a Memorandum of Understanding issued by the U.S. Department of Commerce, ICANN inherited the responsibilities originally performed by the InterNIC. ICANN manages the DNS, including IP address space allocation, Internet protocol parameter assignment, and root domain name server management.

To register a domain name, your ISP (on your behalf and at your request), your employer (which acts as its own service provider), or you (if you are hosting your own website) must make a formal request to a domain name registrar. In the United States, the Internet Corporation for Assigned Names and Numbers (ICANN) verifies which companies can serve as domain name registrars.

Domain name registrars activate domain names on request, using a first-come, first-served basis. If your domain name of choice is available, you will receive notice via standard and electronic mail that your application has been accepted and your domain name has been added to the registrar's database.

In 1999, shared domain name registration was introduced in the U.S. Prior to this time, Network Solutions held a monopoly on registering .com, .net, and .org domain names. Network Solutions also maintained its own database of these domain names. Shared registration allows multiple companies to act as registrars for these three TLDs. Each registrar has access to the DNS registration database, and can add new domain names for their customers. Users may also transfer their domain name from one registrar to another. This has led to lower domain name fees, and increased competition among the U.S. registrars for customers.

ICANN is responsible for accrediting the domain name registrars, and it chose Network Solutions (www.netsol.com) as one of the original five registrars in the shared system. There are now many more ICANN accredited registrars. A list of these registrars is available at www.icann.org/registrars/accredited-list.html.

Some of these registrars can register domain names for country codes outside the United States. Some countries have outsourced domain name registration, especially as demand for domain names and DNS services outstrips a domestic registrar's ability to process requests.

The domain name registrars provide the following services:

- Domain name registration

- Registration service forms for domain name transfers, modifications, and so forth

- Resource links for payment options and policies

- Search capabilities for registered domain names, host IP addresses, and last name/first name queries using WHOIS, a utility used to query databases to determine registered hosts. Table 2.6 lists URLs for several WHOIS services.

TABLE 2.6   WHOIS Services for Selected Countries

Country	WHOIS URL
Canada	www.cira.ca
United States	www.opensrs.org/whois
United Kingdom	www.nic.uk

When you are searching the WHOIS services for a domain name, do not type "www" in front of the domain name. Recall that "www" is a host name, not a domain name.

Virtual Domain

A *virtual domain* is a hosting service that provides your company with a private web address, regardless of where the website is actually hosted. For example, if you register the domain name yourcompany.com, users can enter www.yourcompany.com to access your site, even if your website is actually hosted by a third-party ISP whose domain name is webserver.com. Users enter only your name, not the name of the third party. ISPs usually host several virtual domains on a single server to increase their sales revenues and subscription base.

If you hosted your website with a third-party ISP using a non-virtual domain, you would not need to register your company's domain name. Instead, users might access your site at www.webserver.com/yourcompany.

A virtual domain allows your web address to be shorter, more direct, and possibly easier to remember. It also gives your company the prestige of its own web address for marketing and sales, even though a third party is hosting your website.

Summary

Chapter 2 covered a lot of information about the Internet. We discussed the history and development of the Internet from an experimental network connecting a few universities to a global internetwork touching almost every aspect of our lives.

Computers need a connection to the Internet. We looked at the most popular kinds of dial-up and connections, including ISDN, and direct connections, including LANs, DSL, cable modems, and wireless devices. We discussed several kinds of Internet connection hardware: routers are used to send network signals to other networks; modems and network interface cards (NICs) are used to give individual computers access to the Internet.

Various rules, or protocols, are used to communicate over an Internet connection, including HTTP (World Wide Web), NNTP (newsgroups), Telnet, SMTP (outgoing e-mail messages), POP (incoming e-mail messages), and Gopher.

We also noted that all Internet servers have a 32-bit numeric IP address. They also often have a domain name. We discussed how domain names are assigned, and what the various parts of a domain's name mean, including the TLD and country codes. We reviewed the roles that the InterNIC and ICANN have played in domain name system management. We reviewed the services provided by domain name registrars, including the WHOIS service. We also discussed virtual domains, which allow several domain names to point to different areas of a single web server.

Exam Essentials

Be able to trace the evolution of the Internet.   The Internet was created in the late 1960s as an educational and governmental experiment, and has evolved into an essential communications and business tool.

Understand Transmission Control Protocol/Internet Protocol (TCP/IP) and state how the Internet uses it.   TCP/IP organizes and controls the flow of data on the Internet, by dividing information into small packets that are easily sent, distributed, and reassembled. TCP/IP is vital to internetworking because it provides the basic communications protocol for transmitting and receiving Internet data.

Understand how the client/server model functions on the Internet.
Internet users request data, such as web pages and e-mail messages from servers by using clients. Clients usually run on a personal computer, but sometimes another kind of device like a mobile telephone can be used.

Know the elements required to connect an Internet client to the Internet. Six elements are required. The user needs a computer. In this book, we use a PC, but there are alternatives including WebTV, mobile phones, and handheld devices. The computer must have an operating system (Windows, Linux, etc.) with TCP/IP installed, and client software to access the Web and e-mail. The computer must have an Internet connection, usually dial-up or direct. Finally, the proper Internet addresses must be used.

Be able to identify and describe the function of Network Access Points (NAPs). NAPs connect networks to other networks. They form the primary backbone of the Internet. There are five NAPs in the United States: San Francisco, Chicago, Washington, D.C., New York, and Miami.

Be able to identify and describe major Internet protocols. Hypertext Transfer Protocol (HTTP) is used to transfer web pages. E-mail messages are sent using Simple Mail Transfer Protocol (SMTP) and retrieved with Post Office Protocol 3 (POP3). File Transfer Protocol (FTP) is used to transfer files. Network News Transfer Protocol (NNTP) is used to post and retrieve newsgroup messages. Telnet is used to emulate a text-only terminal. Gopher is used to retrieve text-based information.

Understand domain names and virtual domains. Domain names are used as a substitute for the numeric IP addresses of servers. Domain names have a suffix that indicates the server's organization type or home country. Domain name registrars assign domain names, and match them to IP addresses provided by the user or an ISP. A virtual domain is a domain name that is mapped to an IP address on another server.

Understand the functions of ICANN. The Internet Corporation for Assigned Names and Numbers accredits the domain name registrars and sets rules and standards for domain name assignment.

Key Terms

Before you take the exam, be certain you are familiar with the following terms:

analog

authentication

backbone

bandwidth

Digital Subscriber Line (DSL)

Domain Name System (DNS)

dotted quad

File Transfer Protocol (FTP)

fully qualified domain name (FQDN)

Gopher

graphical user interface (GUI)

hexadecimal numbers

Hypertext Markup Language (HTML)

Hypertext Transfer Protocol (HTTP)

Internet Access Provider (IAP)

Internet Corporation for Assigned Names and Numbers (ICANN)

Internet Message Access Protocol (IMAP)

Internet Network Information Center (InterNIC)

Internet Protocol (IP)

Internet service provider (ISP)

IP address

modem

network interface card

Network News Transfer Protocol (NNTP)

newsgroups

packets

Point-to-Point Protocol (PPP)

Post Office Protocol (POP)

router

segment

Serial Line Internet Protocol (SLIP)

shell account

Simple Mail Transfer Protocol (SMTP)

Telnet

top-level domains (TLDs)

Usenet (User Network)

virtual domain

Review Questions

1. Which organization helped fund the early development of the Internet?

    A. NASA

    B. U.S. Department of Defense

    C. IBM

    D. Microsoft Corporation

2. Which one of the following choices best describes the function of a router?

    A. A router connects a computer to a network.

    B. A router helps send network signals on a good connection.

    C. A router connects a computer to the Internet by telephone.

    D. A router connects LANs to other LANs.

3. Hypertext Markup Language (HTML) is used in what kind of Internet service?

    A. Gopher

    B. The World Wide Web

    C. Printing

    D. Telnet

4. Which one of the following numbers should never appear in an IP address?

    A. 0

    B. 100

    C. 178

    D. 256

5. In what form does TCP/IP send information?

   A. Dotted quads

   B. Hexadecimals

   C. Bytes

   D. Packets

6. How many IP addresses are currently possible?

   A. 1 million

   B. 4 billion

   C. 400 million

   D. 4 trillion

7. IPv6 addresses support how many bits?

   A. 32

   B. 64

   C. 128

   D. 256

8. Which one of the following items is not required to support an Internet client?

   A. An Internet connection

   B. An operating system

   C. HTTP

   D. Internet addresses

9. Which one of the following services does an ISP usually not perform for customers?

   A. Provides connections to the Internet

   B. Assigns an IPv6 address

   C. Provides e-mail accounts

   D. Provides a POP server

10. Which one of the following connections uses a regular telephone line?

    A. DSL

    B. Cable modem

    C. Wireless

    D. LAN

11. Which one of the following terms best describes a group of computers connected within an office, so that users can share files and services?

    A. Peer-to-peer network

    B. Internet

    C. Local area network

    D. Intranet

12. Which of the following is the best definition of a network access point?

    A. A connection point between two computers

    B. A connection point between two local area networks

    C. A connection point between two office networks

    D. A connection point between two very high-speed networks

13. Which of the following describes a large database containing image and text files linked to each other by references?

    A. A client/server system

    B. Gopher

    C. FTP

    D. Hypertext

14. What is another name for an HTTP server?

    A. File server

    B. Gopher server

    C. Mail server

    D. Web server

15. Which of the following services is best suited for transferring large files from one Internet computer to another?

    A. HTTP

    B. FTP

    C. NNTP

    D. Gopher

16. John wants to read his e-mail messages on his personal computer. To set up his e-mail client, he needs to know which one of the following?

    A. POP3 server name

    B. SMTP server name

    C. NNTP server name

    D. E-mail address

17. What Internet service maps and easily remembered identifier to an IP address?

    A. Client/server model

    B. TCP/IP

    C. Domain Name System

    D. The network architecture

18. Emily has seen the website URL `internal.market.infospace.com`. Which part of this URL indicates the name of company that owns this site?

    A. `internal`

    B. `market`

    C. `infospace`

    D. `com`

19. The group into which a domain is categorized, by a common topic or a geographic location, is called what?

A. Host

B. Top-level domain

C. IP address

D. Server

20. ICANN is the organization that defines which one of the following?

A. TCP/IP

B. Network topologies

C. Domain name registration

D. Web browser design

Answers to Review Questions

1. **B.** The U.S. Department of Defense provided some of the original contracts and funding for the early development of the Internet. NASA, IBM, and Microsoft made later financial and technical contributions.

2. **D.** Routers are devices that connect LANs to other LANs, as well as WANs. Networks can use routers to switch signals away from poor connections, but cannot guarantee that a connection is always good. A NIC is used to connect a computer to a network. An analog modem connects a computer to the Internet by telephone.

3. **B.** HTML is used for writing web documents. Gopher uses a different text-based format. Printing is a general service provided by computers. Telnet is used for running a text-based session on another computer.

4. **D.** IPv4 uses the number 0 through 255 in addresses. 256 would be a higher number than what could be represented by 8 binary digits.

5. **D.** Packets are the small sections of data that TCP/IP helps transmit and decode. Hexadecimal is a type of numeric data. Dotted quads are the format of numeric IP addresses. Bytes are a measurement of computer file size.

6. **B.** IPv4 supports 4 billion addresses, or $256 \times 256 \times 256 \times 256$.

7. **C.** IPv6 supports 128-bit addresses. IPv4 supports only a 32-bit address.

8. **C.** HTTP is a protocol required only for web connectivity. The other three items are required for Internet access.

9. **B.** IPv6 has not been widely implemented on the Internet, and very few ISPs currently provide this service. An Internet Service Provider provides Internet connection services and e-mail access.

10. **A.** DSL connections run through normal telephone lines. Cable modems connect to cable television lines. Wireless connections are made by wireless modems or mobile phones. LAN connections can be made through any direct connection method.

11. C.   This description applies to a LAN. Peer-to-peer networks are not powerful enough to connect a large group of users in an office environment. The Internet describes the large global network, while an intranet is a special part of the Internet that is designed solely for use by internal employees.

12. D.   A network access point is a high-speed junction on the Internet backbone, used for connecting ISPs to each other. In most cases, a NAP would not be used to make local connections between small networks.

13. D.   This describes a hypertext system, such as the World Wide Web. The Web is a type of client/server system. Gopher is a collection of text-based files. FTP is an Internet service designed to share large files.

14. D.   There are many different kinds of file and mail servers. Gopher servers use the Gopher protocol. HTTP servers support the World Wide Web, and are often called web servers.

15. B.   Although HTTP is used for transferring files on the World Wide Web, FTP is a better choice, as it is often faster than HTTP. NNTP is used for newsgroup messages. There are few Gopher servers currently available, as many Gopher operators have replaced their Gopher servers with web servers.

16. A.   John needs to know the name of the POP3 server that is storing and sorting his e-mail. The SMTP server name is needed to send new e-mail messages. NNTP is used for newsgroups, not e-mail. John does not need to know his e-mail address to read his own e-mail.

17. C.   The Domain Name System provides a universal directory of domain names, which provide an alternative to memorizing numeric IP addresses. The client/server model describes the model upon which the Internet is built. TCP/IP is the protocol that controls communication over the Internet. Network architecture describes how computers are connected.

18. C.   `Infospace` is the domain name registered by that company. `Internal` or `Market` may be the name of the web server at that company. The TLD, `.com` indicates that this is a commercial site.

19. B.   The top-level domains (TLDs) provide an organizational structure for all domain names, by indicating the kind of organization that registered the domain name or the country in which the domain name was registered. A host is a computer that accesses the Internet. An IP address is the address assigned to each computer that is using the Internet. A server is a machine that stores Internet data.

20. C.   The Internet Corporation for Assigned Named and Numbers defines the processes for domain name registration and approves the domain name registrars. TCP/IP is a communications protocol that is defined and maintained by several groups. Network topologies are general designs for connecting computers. No one group controls the design of web browsers; they are rather the products of individual producers.

Chapter

3

LANs and WANs

THE CIW EXAM OBJECTIVE GROUPS COVERED IN THIS CHAPTER:

✓ Identify Networking and its role in the Internet, including but not limited to: TCP/IP protocols, packets, and the OSI reference model.

✓ Identify the roles of networking hardware components, and configure common PC hardware for operation.

Now that you understand the history of networks and networking protocols, it's time to move on to the integral pieces that make up those networks. In this chapter we will discuss the standards and hardware used in creating local area networks (LANs) and wide area networks (WANs).

A local area network, or LAN, is a group of computers connected within a confined geographic area, such as a building, floor, or room. LANs allow users to share files and services, and are commonly used for interoffice communication. A LAN can extend over several yards or several miles, but generally represents one locale, such as a corporate office in Chicago, for example.

A wide area network (WAN) is a group of computers connected over an expansive geographic area, such as a state or country, that allows users to share files and services. The Internet is sometimes described as a network of WANs.

LANs and WANs are the basic building blocks of the Internet. Remember that the Internet is a collection of networks. This chapter provides the basic knowledge you need for understanding how these networks are connected.

We will first discuss LANs, focusing on Ethernet, the LAN technology used in many networks today. There are several other types of LAN technologies that offer better speed and operation, including fast Ethernet and gigabit Ethernet. We will also look at token ring networks, another popular system for LANs.

We will then review various types of WANs, including frame relay, ATM, and FDDI. WANs form the backbone of the Internet, spanning countries and continents so that different networks can exchange information at high speeds.

Our next discussion will cover various devices that help connect computers and networks to each other such as routers, bridges, and hubs. These devices help place and direct signals along the network.

We will also discuss various transmission media such as cables, fiber optic lines, and wireless devices that transmit the signals between computers and networks. These various media provide a means for getting network signals from a client to its destination.

We will next explore various kinds of transmission types, including synchronous, asynchronous, baseband and broadband. These methods control how data is actually transmitted and exchanged along the media. We will end the chapter by reviewing the T-Carrier and E-Carrier systems that describe network capacity and speed.

IEEE LAN Standards

A *local area network*, or *LAN*, is a computer network that spans a small area, typically an office or several adjoining rooms. Businesses have adopted the LAN model because it is highly adaptable, and provides significant cost savings. With a LAN, users can share expensive network resources such as high-speed printers, color printers, high-capacity disk drives, and high-speed Internet connections. A LAN is usually run by a company's IT department. The IT department can use the LAN to help maintain the connected computers. Examples of maintenance include backing up and restoring files, installing updated software, and computer virus protection. Security issues can also be addresses, because a LAN often provides centralized control over what and how each computer is used. Figure 3.1 shows an example of a LAN.

A distinguishing factor among LAN technologies is the access methods they use. Access methods refer to the way data is placed on the physical wire for transmission. The *Institute of Electrical and Electronics Engineers (IEEE)* is an organization of scientists and engineers, accredited by the American National Standards Institute, that creates standards for computers and communications. The IEEE 802 Standards Committee is the leading official standards organization for LAN technologies.

FIGURE 3.1 LAN example

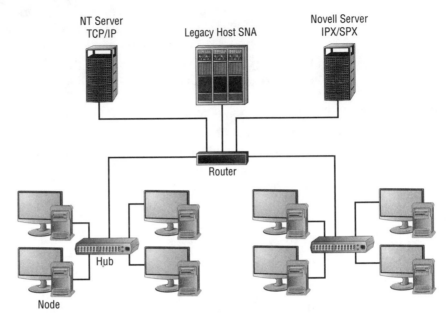

In this section, we'll cover the following IEEE 802 network standards:

- IEEE 802.2
- Ethernet/IEEE 802.3
- IEEE 802.3u—fast Ethernet
- IEEE 802.3z and 802.3ab—gigabit Ethernet
- IEEE 802.5—token ring

 The term "IEEE 802.3" is usually pronounced "eye triple e eight oh two dot three."

 You can consult the IEEE website at www.ieee.org for more information on the standard-setting process.

The IEEE 802.2 Standard

All standards in the IEEE 802 series use the 802.2 standard for determining how any computer on a LAN gets access to a network. The 802.2 standard also defines how network data is encoded and decoded into digital bits of information. This part of networking—the determination of how data is transferred across a physical connection—is also called the Data-Link layer. (We will discuss the Data-Link layer in more detail in Chapter 4.)

IEEE 802.2 defines two sublayers at which a computer can connect to a network: Logical Link Control (LLC) and Media Access Control (MAC). Each layer performs different services.

Logical Link Control (LLC)

The LLC sublayer provides connection-oriented and connectionless services at the Data-link layer, which manages network transmissions. LLC also provides flow control, and assists in checking the data for transmission errors. LLC is used in various proprietary networking protocols, such as Microsoft's NetBIOS and Novell's IPX/SPX.

Media Access Control (MAC)

Media Access Control (MAC) provides two essential networking services:

Access to the LAN Media   The MAC is responsible for placing the data on the network.

Provision of the MAC Address   This is also called a physical address, hardware address, or Ethernet address.

The MAC Address

The *MAC address* is a unique address number that is burned or permanently saved on each NIC. Each MAC address is assigned and burned by the NIC manufacturer, and can be used to identify a specific computer on a network.

MAC addresses are called physical addresses, as opposed to logical addresses. Physical addresses are used only to send data between two devices on a single network link. Physical addresses are similar to a building's street name and number.

Logical addresses are used to send data over internetworks to a remote destination. An example of a logical address is an IP address. You can compare a logical address to a set of arbitrary coordinates, like a hotel room number. The room number represents the MAC address, while the hotel's name is a logical address. If you wanted to call a guest at the hotel, you could tell the operator the guest's name. The operator would then dial the room number and connect the call. In networking terms, the telephone call has been routed first to the hotel, and then forwarded to the proper logical address.

MAC addresses use 12 hexadecimal digits to form a 48-bit address (6 bytes). Each half of the address is used for a different purpose, as shown in Figure 3.2.

FIGURE 3.2 MAC address components

$$00 - 80 - 5F - EA - C6 - 10$$

Vendor Code   Interface Serial Number

The vendor code is identified in the first 24 bits (3 bytes). The vendor code in Figure 3.2 is the one for Compaq. Other vendor codes include Sun (08-00-20) and Cisco (00-00-0c).

The interface serial number is identified in the last 24 bits. Determined by the vendor, the serial number is always unique to that vendor. In theory, no two MAC addresses are identical.

Microsoft is using MAC addresses as a unique identifier for computers. When you register Microsoft Windows XP, the operating system uses the MAC address of the computer's NIC to help identify the specific computer on which the operating system is installed. This information is sent back to Microsoft during the registration process, and can prevent users from installing the same copy of Windows XP on two or more computers.

Ethernet and IEEE 802.3

Ethernet is a term that describes a set of hardware technologies and networking protocols for LANs. In late 1972, Robert Metcalfe and his colleagues at Xerox PARC (Palo Alto Research Center) developed the first experimental Ethernet system to connect network workstations. Ethernet is one of the most successful LAN technologies ever developed, and is a predecessor to the IEEE 802.3 standard.

Ethernet does not technically use the 802.2 standard. The Ethernet standard is described in the IEEE 802.3 specifications. Ethernet is compatible with IEEE 802.2, and shares several important elements with the standard, such as the MAC sublayer.

All networks that use Ethernet/IEEE 802.3 use *CSMA/CD* or *Carrier Sense Multiple Access/Collision Detection*, the LAN access method used by Ethernet. CSMA/CD checks for network access availability with a specific signal, because Ethernet allows only one computer at a time to send a signal on a network. When two computers send signals simultaneously, a *collision* can take place between the two signals. This collision prevents other computers on the network from receiving signals properly. CSMA/CD allows each computer on the network to detect these collisions. After detecting a collision, each computer waits a random delay time and then attempts to retransmit their message. If the device detects a collision again, it waits twice as long to try to retransmit the message. Eventually, each computer gets an opportunity to transmit its message without collision.

This collision detection process can create heavy traffic on a network. Therefore, it is important to divide larger Ethernet networks into segments, by using a bridge or another hardware component.

Ethernet and IEEE 802.3 systems can operate at network speeds of 10Mbps.

IEEE 802.3u: Fast Ethernet

Fast Ethernet is a faster version of IEEE 802.3. It was originally developed by vendors such as 3Com, Cabletron, SynOptics, Digital, Grand Junction Networks, and Intel. The IEEE 802.3 committee is responsible for fast Ethernet. The major objective of the fast Ethernet standard is to promote the use of Ethernet at 100Mbps using the same access method, CSMA/CD.

Fast Ethernet supports the 100baseTX and 100baseT4 wiring standards, which require Category 5 UTP wiring to support 100Mbps. It can also use 100baseFX, which is fiber optic cabling. Vendors support fast Ethernet cards that use data rates of both 10Mbps and 100Mbps. (We'll discuss different specific types of transmission media later in the chapter.)

Many network administrators are upgrading their 10baseT networks to 100baseTX or 100baseT4. In many cases, replacing 10baseT NICs with 100baseTX or 100baseT4 NICs, and upgrading hubs to support both 10baseT and 100baseTX or 100baseT4 can accomplish this upgrade. This process is usually less expensive than upgrading to a 100baseFX, 16Mbps token ring, 100VG-AnyLAN, or FDDI network.

Table 3.1 displays the key differences between Ethernet and fast Ethernet.

TABLE 3.1 Ethernet vs. Fast Ethernet

Description	Ethernet	Fast Ethernet
Speed	10Mbps	100Mbps
IEEE standard	IEEE 802.3	IEEE 802.3u
Access method	CSMA/CD	CSMA/CD
Physical topology	Bus/Star	Star
Cable support	Coax/twisted-pair/fiber	Twisted-pair/fiber
UTP link distance (maximum)	100 meters	100 meters

IEEE 802.3z and 802.3ab: Gigabit Ethernet

Gigabit Ethernet is the fastest 802.3 LAN technology and is used primarily for network backbones. The gigabit Ethernet standard transfers data at 1,000Mbps using the access method CSMA/CD.

The two types of gigabit Ethernet are IEEE 802.3z and 802.3ab. The 802.3z standard is specified for specialty copper cable and fiber optic cable. The 802.3ab standard specifies gigabit Ethernet over Category 5 UTP cable.

Gigabit Ethernet supports the 1000baseT wiring standard, which uses Category 5 UTP wiring to support 1,000 Mbps. It can also use 1000baseCX, 1000baseSX and 1000baseLX, which use fiber optic cabling.

IEEE 802.5: Token Ring

The ring network topology we discussed in Chapter 2 forms the basis for token ring networking. The *token ring* network is specified in the IEEE 802.5 definition. IBM initially developed token ring for its mainframe environment, and the IEEE 802.5 standard complies with the corporation's original development: A data frame, or token, is passed from one node to the next around the network ring.

Whereas Ethernet uses the CSMA/CD access method, token ring networks use the *token passing* access method. Instead of sending broadcasts, as Ethernet does, a token ring network passes a token in one direction around the network. Each node processes the token to determine the destination. The node accepts the packet or places it back on the network ring. One or more tokens can circle the ring. With token passing, collisions do not occur; it is similar to a one-way street without cross traffic.

The IEEE standard does not specify a wiring standard, but some companies, like IBM, offer token ring networks that use twisted-pair wire. Token ring networks appear to use the star topology, but actually use a hub-like device called a *Multistation Access Unit (MAU)* to form a ring.

The MAU creates the ring using internal connections, as shown in Figure 3.3.

FIGURE 3.3   Token ring network with MAU

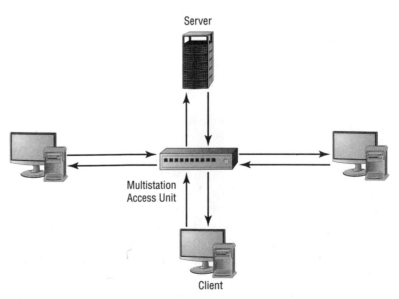

Server

Multistation
Access Unit

Client

The failure of one node in a ring topology can cause the network to fail, whereas MAUs can identify and bypass faulty nodes and network segments so the network can continue to function.

Data rates of 4 or 16Mbps are possible with token ring networks.

WAN Standards

*W*ide *area networks (WANs)* connect LANs to each other within a geographic region. With the continued growth of the Internet and with telecommunication companies investing in bandwidth to better serve businesses and consumers, WANs continue to expand the reach of networks across the country and across the world. WAN technologies and standards established by the IEEE, help network administrators build and run networks effectively and efficiently. Figure 3.4 shows a basic WAN.

FIGURE 3.4 WAN example

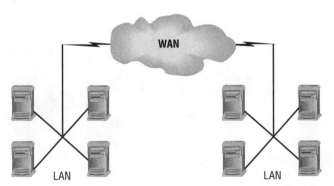

In recent years, wide area network technology has progressed quickly. WAN standards and technologies include FDDI, X.25, fast packet switching, frame relay, and ATM, which are discussed in this section. Each of these WAN standards has advantages that make them suitable for specific situations. You should already be familiar with PPP, SLIP and ISDN, which are also WAN methods we discussed in Chapter 2.

Fiber Distributed Data Interface (FDDI)

Fiber Distributed Data Interface (FDDI) is a high-speed LAN standard that is often used in WANs because of its high reliability. Like the IEEE 802.5 token ring standard, FDDI is token-based. The FDDI standard specifies the MAC sublayer of the Data-Link layer, as well as the Physical layers for a 100Mbps counter-rotating, token ring and fiber optic LAN. FDDI uses IEEE 802.5 as its LAN standard. An FDDI network is shown in Figure 3.5.

FIGURE 3.5   A Fiber Distributed Data Interface network

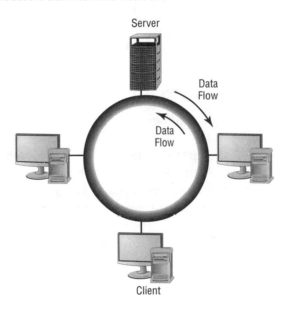

FDDI uses two counter-rotating rings to provide redundancy and allow the network to function if one ring fails. FDDI functions well over distances of up to 200 kilometers (with a single ring) with as many as 1,000 stations connected. In a dual-ring topology, each ring is limited to 100 kilometers. Because it is often used to cover a city or a specific geographic area, an FDDI network can be classified as a *municipal area network (MAN)*. FDDI supports both synchronous and asynchronous traffic, which we will discuss later in the chapter.

X.25

X.25 is a WAN standard developed from the ARPANET 1822 protocol, which was the original ARPANET packet-switching scheme. X.25 became an International Telecommunications Union (ITU) standard in 1976. It is currently used for automated teller machine transactions, credit card verifications, and many other point-of-sale transactions.

X.25 operates at 56Kbps or slower. Newer packet-switching technologies can outperform X.25, but it is still used worldwide. X.25 ensures error-free data delivery by checking errors at many points along the data's path. At the time X.25 was developed, error checking was an essential feature to include in this standard. Telecommunications lines did not support error-checking, and such features had not been included in networking protocols.

Fast Packet Switching

Fast packet switching refers to two different types of transmissions through mesh-type switching networks.

With fast packet switching, in tasks such as error correction, the network does not perform packet sequencing and acknowledgments. Eliminating error correction at the lower, physical layers of communications greatly improves performance. Any error checking is the responsibility of end systems. Because the network has less overhead associated with processing packets, it can move information quickly.

Frame relay and asynchronous transfer mode (ATM) are examples of fast packet switching technologies.

Frame Relay

Frame relay, as shown in Figure 3.6, is a fast packet switching technology that uses fiber optic and digital cabling. Frame relay is a streamlined version of X.25, and is designed for use on ISDN telephone lines. It uses variable-length packets and allows high-speed connections using shared network facilities. Frame relay does not extensively support error checking and acknowledgments, because frame relay is usually run on WAN connections. The various WAN protocols, including TCP/IP, already offer error-checking services.

FIGURE 3.6   Frame-relay packet switching

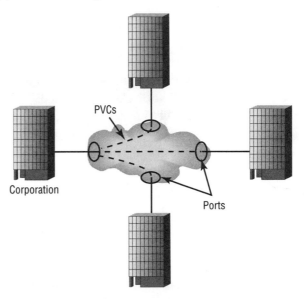

If your company wants to join a frame relay network, your local telephone company must connect your office to a frame relay "port," or Point
of Presence (POP). The POP must be a frame relay service provider. A frame
relay port is created for your company, giving it access to the frame relay
network.

Frame relay networks use Permanent Virtual Circuits (PVCs). These
logical, dedicated, end-to-end connections are used for data transfer. Once a
PVC is established, it exists until the transaction, transmission, or service is
terminated. In using PVCs, frame relay shares the physical network with
other frame relay networks.

Frame relay uses "bandwidth on demand," meaning that frame relay
customers can choose the amount of bandwidth they need. Each frame relay
port has its own port speed, usually at a transmission rate ranging from
64Kbps to 1.544Mbps (T1).

Asynchronous Transfer Mode (ATM)

Asynchronous transfer mode (ATM) is a fast packet–switching technology
that uses fixed-sized cells (instead of frame relay's variable-length packets)

and PVCs to support data as well as real-time video and voice. Both LANs and WANs can use ATM, but ATM is most commonly used as an Internet backbone.

ATM is referred to as a cell relay technology because it organizes data into 53-byte fixed-length cells. These cells are transmitted and segmented depending on the type of data sent. For example, bandwidth is allocated depending on the application class being used.

Because ATM uses fixed-length cells, it is faster than frame relay. Switching devices need not locate the beginning and end of each cell: these cells are all the same size. Although ATM typically operates at speeds ranging from 155Mbps to 622Mbps, it has a potential throughput rate of 1.2Gbps (gigabits per second).

Be careful when using the abbreviation ATM! In networking, ATM stands for Asynchronous Transfer Mode. X.25 allows error-correcting communications with automated teller machines, which some people call ATMs. Automated teller machines should not be confused with frame relay and asynchronous transfer mode!

Computer networks usually require a great deal of equipment to function properly. LANs and WANs typically include network interface cards, repeaters, hubs, bridges, routers, brouters, and switches so that they can make connections among the computers and to other networks. These devices place network signals on the transmission media and help direct the signals to their final destination.

Gateways connect different kinds of LANs to each other, by translating networking protocols. A *Channel Service Unit/Data (or Digital) Service Unit (CSU/DSU)* connects the LAN to external, high-speed networks. Patch panels are used to arrange the physical computer and network connections in an orderly way. Think of these devices as the everyday tools of a network administrator. A competent network administrator must be able to use *all* of these components together to build LANs, connect them to WANS, and provide fast, efficient network connections.

FIGURE 3.7 Networking devices

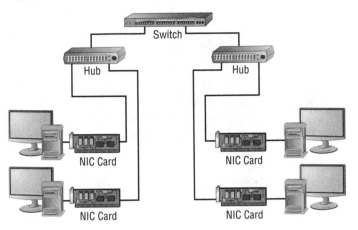

Network Interface Card (NIC)

Each node in a network contains a *network interface card (NIC)*, often called a *network adapter card*. The NIC is the interface between the computer and the network, as shown in Figure 3.8.

FIGURE 3.8 Network Interface Card (NIC)

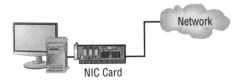

The NIC communicates with the computer and the operating system through a NIC device driver. A networking cable connects the NIC to the actual network. A NIC generally resides in a personal computer motherboard expansion slot, although more portable and desktop computers now include a built-in NIC as standard equipment.

Most NICs contain a *transceiver* (short for transmitter-receiver), a network device that transmits and receives analog or digital signals. Within a LAN, the transceiver places data onto the network wire, and detects and receives data traveling across the wire.

Real World Scenario

Looking at NICs

If you have access to a networked computer or if you have a cable modem or DSL connection, you should be able to locate the RJ-45 cable and the NIC. Desktop computers commonly have the NIC installed so that the RJ-45 connection port is on the back of the computer. NICs usually have two or more LEDs that light up to indicate network activity. These lights will help you find the NIC.

Some desktop and portable computer manufacturers have built a NIC directly into the computer, so that the RJ-45 port is located with the other computer ports, including the printer, serial, and USB ports.

If your portable computer does not have an RJ-45 port, you may have a PCMCIA NIC that is inserted on one side of your computer. Sometimes this PCMCIA card has an RJ-45 jack built in, but some PCMCIA cards use a device called a *dongle*. A dongle resembles a small cable with an RJ-45 port at one end, and a special connector that hooks into a small jack on the PCMICA card.

USB-equipped computers can use an external NIC that plugs into a USB port. The USB NIC has an RJ-45 port that hooks into the network, and usually has network activity lights on the front. USB NIC adapters are easy to install, because you do not need to open the computer. USB NICs tend to be slower than the other NICs described above, because early versions of USB supported a 3Mbps transfer speed. Because most USB NICs are used by home users, this is not a significant problem. Recall that most cable modems and DSL connections operate in the range of 512Kbps. As new versions of USB become available, USB NICs should be able to handle the 10Mbps network speeds commonly found on business LANs.

Repeaters

A *repeater*, shown in Figure 3.9, is a device that amplifies the electronic signal traveling on a cable segment. It ensures that electronic signals do not degrade. A repeater can connect computers that are farther apart than the defined network standards.

FIGURE 3.9   Repeater

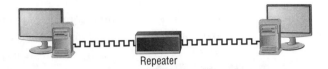

Repeater

Repeaters transmit binary code, the most basic form of digital information. When a cable segment approaches its maximum length, the data signal weakens and eventually breaks down because of attenuation. A repeater can strengthen this signal by retransmitting it.

Hubs

A *hub* connects computers in a star-configured network so they can exchange information. As you can see in Figure 3.10, the hub has several network cable ports, each of which connects to a single node or computer in the network. By interconnecting the nodes, a hub serves as the concentration point for a network. Most hubs are called active hubs because they can regenerate and amplify electronic signals, just as like a repeater.

FIGURE 3.10   Hub connecting workstations

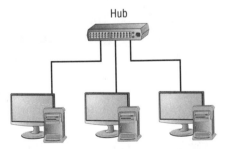

Hub

Hubs can be connected to other hubs, or "daisy-chained," to provide more ports for a larger network. You can also connect hubs to switches or routers to increase the number of network nodes.

Just as a power strip allows us to plug multiple electrical appliances into a single electrical outlet, a hub turns one network connection into multiple connections. Active hubs require their own power supply to amplify the signals. A hub usually includes an uplink port, which us used to connect to other hubs.

Bridges

Bridges are devices that filter frames to determine whether a specific frame belongs on a local segment or another LAN segment. A bridge uses hardware addresses to determine which segment will receive the frame, by recognizing hardware addresses (also known as media access control, or MAC, addresses) between networks.

Bridges can reduce network traffic by dividing one network into two segments. They can also connect network segments with the same or different data-link protocols, enabling them to communicate. For example, a bridge can connect an Ethernet network to a token ring network, or can connect two token ring networks to each other. Figure 3.11 illustrates two network segments connected by a bridge.

FIGURE 3.11 Bridge connecting network segments

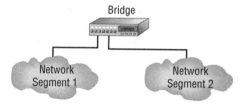

Suppose one computer sends information to another in an Ethernet network, for example. The bridge determines whether the destination computer resides on the same network segment by verifying the hardware address. If the destination machine resides outside that segment, the bridge passes the message to another segment. Through this screening process, network traffic is reduced and more bandwidth is made available to the network.

Bridges are independent of networking protocols. This independence enables bridges to forward frames from many different protocols.

Routers

Routers are conceptually similar to bridges in that they help connect networks to each other. Instead of using hardware addresses, as bridges do, routers use network protocols, such as IP and IPX. They forward, or route, data from one network to another, instead of only to network segments. Routers identify the destination machine's network address, then determine the most efficient route for transmitting data to it.

Take a look at the router connecting two networks illustrated in Figure 3.12. Suppose a machine on Network 2 sends data to another machine on Network 2. In the situation illustrated here, the router would not pass the data to Network 1, thus conserving network bandwidth.

FIGURE 3.12   Router connecting networks

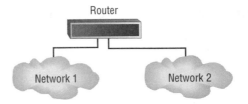

Routers are protocol dependent; they rely on the address system defined by the protocol used (IPX, IP and so forth). Different types of routers work with different protocols. For example, IP routers operate with the inherent IP 32-bit address structure. To use the IPX addressing protocol, a router that supports IPX is required.

Brouters

A *brouter* is a device that functions as both a router and a bridge. A brouter understands how to route specific types of packets, such as TCP/IP packets. Any other packets it receives are simply forwarded to other network(s) connected to the device, just as a bridge would do. Unlike a router, a brouter is protocol-*in*dependent. Brouters can route traffic from different kinds of LANs to a variety of external networks without specific rules. Network administrators can use brouters to connect two network segments that use different protocols, and then route outgoing network traffic to a WAN.

Gateways

A *gateway*, or protocol converter, is a more complicated network device than the ones we've discussed so far. A gateway must convert signals from one protocol stack to another. Routers can only forward a specific kind of protocol stack and brouters can forward any kind of protocol, but gateways, on the other hand, have the added responsibility of changing the signals to suit the protocol of the receiving system. While this is complicated for the gateway, it creates greater flexibility on the network. For example, a gateway may connect an AppleTalk network to nodes on a DECnet network, or a TCP/IP network to an IPX/SPX network, as shown in Figure 3.13.

FIGURE 3.13 Gateway

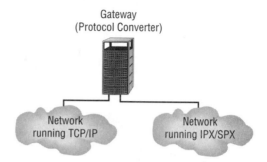

You will learn about a specific gateway type, the default gateway, in Chapter 4.

Switches

On a network, a *switch* directs the flow of information from one node to another. Switches operate faster than traditional network devices, such as hubs, bridges, and routers, and are increasingly replacing those devices. A switch can give each sender/receiver pair the line's entire bandwidth, instead of sharing the bandwidth with all other network nodes.

Switches offer the following benefits for Ethernet and token ring networks:

Simple installation For many bridges and hubs, installing a switch requires you to unplug connections from existing devices and plug the connections into the switch ports.

Higher speeds Switches have high-speed connections that allow full bandwidth between any two users or segments. This feature eliminates the switch as a potential network bottleneck.

More server bandwidth Servers can connect directly to switches. This capability allows network users to utilize the network's full bandwidth when accessing server resources.

Figure 3.14 illustrates a routing switch that connects two networks.

FIGURE 3.14   Switch connecting networks

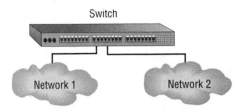

Network 1   Network 2

 Real World Scenario

Options for Handling Increased Network Traffic on a LAN

Patti is a network administrator for a medium-sized company that has added two new departments in the last six months. She has noticed that network traffic has increased, which has reduced the overall performance of her LAN. Her coworkers have noticed this slowdown in performance, as it takes them longer to retrieve files from the network servers.

Patti has three options for handling increased LAN traffic:

Use a bridge.   This method reduces the number of users on a network by separating it into two network segments.

Use a LAN switch.   LAN switches are available for Ethernet, fast Ethernet, token ring and FDDI, which we will discuss in this chapter.

Increase the network bandwidth.   One way to increase bandwidth is to move to a higher-speed standard such as FDDI. This approach requires Patti to change adapters, rewire the building, and possibly change system software. Upgrading to FDDI is expensive. Upgrading from Ethernet to fast Ethernet is more economical.

Channel Service Unit/Data (or Digital) Service Unit (CSU/DSU)

A *CSU/DSU* is a device that terminates physical connections, and it is required when using dedicated circuits, such as T1 lines. This device functions as a very high-powered and expensive modem. The digital data stream of the LAN is translated by the CSU/DSU into signals that are suitable for line transmission. As you can see in Figure 3.15, a dedicated T1 line enters a building through an RJ-45 connector to the CSU/DSU, which transmits the signal through the router and on to the network.

FIGURE 3.15 CSU/DSU

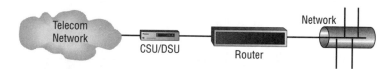

The CSU/DSU also performs some error-reporting and loopback functions that are necessary for troubleshooting and maintaining the LAN/WAN connection. The CSU/DSU is the primary connection between the LAN and a high-speed network WAN and is used to find glitches in the network. The error-reporting functions within the CSU/DSU can help a network professional determine if a connection problem is related to the LAN, or if something is wrong with the WAN connection. The loopback functions provide a way to test the CSU/DSU unit itself, to determine if it is functioning properly.

Patch Panels

A *patch panel* is a group of sockets (usually consisting of pin locations and ports) mounted on a rack. It is a central point where cables from different rooms or departments can be connected to one another, ultimately forming a LAN. It can then be used to connect a network to the Internet or other WAN.

One side of the patch panel contains rows of pin locations. A punch tool is used to "punch down" the wires to make a connection. These connections often originate from wall jacks throughout a building. For example, in an accounting department in a large cubicle-filled room, each accountant's computer may be connected to a hub. The hub is then connected to a wall jack, which is connected to the patch panel.

The other side of the patch panel contains a row of female ports, which are used to connect to other network devices, such as routers and switches. As you can see in Figure 3.16, the patch panel may be connected to a router, which is then connected to the Internet. Be aware that the patch panel is part of the physical network, not the logical network. The patch panel provides physical connections for cables and network devices.

FIGURE 3.16 Patch panel

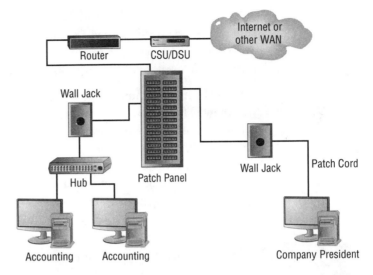

Patch cords are used in ports to cross-connect networked computers that are wired to the patch panel. Patch cords also connect network devices to a wall jack.

Patch panels are usually placed in a central point, such as a closet or your company's server room. They may have numerous ports and pin locations, depending on your company's size.

Transmission Media

To set up a network and support its computers and devices, you must have a transmission medium through which information can pass. This is where cables or even wireless methods enter the picture. The following section explains the most common cable types: twisted-pair, coaxial, and fiber optic. In this section, we will also cover wireless media.

Twisted-Pair cable

Twisted-pair cable is perhaps the most widely used cabling system in LANs. Two copper wires twist around each other to form the twisted-pair cable.

Twisted-pair cable is available in two basic types: *shielded twisted-pair (STP)* and *unshielded twisted-pair (UTP)*.

STP   Twisted-pair copper wire that is protected from external electromagnetic interference by a metal sheath wrapped around the wires. STP is harder to install and maintain than UTP.

UTP   The most common type of twisted-pair wiring. UTP is less expensive than STP, but less secure. Because UTP has less shielding than STP cable, it is possible to use electronic equipment to monitor the cable's radio frequency emissions or signals. These signals can be run through an analyzer or computer to display or save their contents. UTP cable is also prone to electromagnetic interference from other cables, electrical wiring, and atmospheric conditions.

Depending on the category, several insulated wire strands can reside in the cable.

STP and UTP are available with two varieties of wire: stranded and solid. *Stranded cable* is the most common type; flexible and easy to handle around corners and objects. Solid cable can span longer distances without as much attenuation (weakening of the signal) as stranded wire, but is less flexible. Solid cable will break in two if it is bent several times.

The TIA/EIA 568 Commercial Building Wiring standard specifies five twisted-pair standards. Two additional levels, Category 6 and Category 7, are also used commercially, but are not standardized. Table 3.2 outlines these categories.

TABLE 3.2   Twisted-Pair Categories

Category	Description
1	Used for voice, not data (UTP only).
2	Contains four twisted-pairs and has data transmission capacity of up to 4Mbps. Used for some token ring networks (UTP only).
3	Contains four twisted-pairs and has a data transmission capacity of up to 10Mbps. Used for Ethernet.

TABLE 3.2   Twisted-Pair Categories *(continued)*

Category	Description
4	Contains four twisted-pairs and has a data transmission capacity of up to 16Mbps. Used for some token ring networks.
5	Contains four twisted-pairs and has a data transmission capacity of up to 100Mbps. Used for Ethernet and fast Ethernet. Allows Ethernet to be easily upgraded to fast Ethernet.
6	Contains four twisted-pairs and has a data transmission capacity of up to 155Mbps. Used for fast Ethernet.
7	Contains four twisted-pairs and has a data transmission capacity of up to 1000Mbps. Used for gigabit Ethernet.

An ordinary home telephone cable is a good example of a category 1 cable. To see category 5 cables, just go to any computer store and look in the networking section.

Register Jack-45 (RJ-45) Connectors

RJ-45 connectors are commonly used on certain types of Ethernet and token ring networks, which you will learn about later in this chapter. The connector holds up to eight wires, and is used with twisted-pair wire. To attach an RJ-45 connector to a cable, the connector must be crimped using a tool called a crimper.

To crimp an RJ-45 connector, place the connector on the cable with the wires correctly positioned (the wire position depends on the network standard used). Place the connector in the crimper with the cable, and squeeze the crimper handles firmly.

The crimper pushes two plugs from the RJ-45 connector into the cable. One plug pushes into the cable jacket to attach the connector and cable. The other plug pushes eight pins through the cable jacket and into the respective wires. (See graphic.)

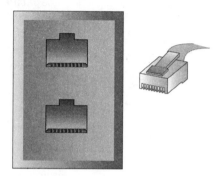

An ordinary home telephone cable in North America uses a four-wire RJ-11 connector. An RJ-45 connector is slightly larger than the RJ-11 standard telephone connector, and holds eight wires. Pre-assembled networking cables, available in any computer store, usually have an RJ-45 connector at each end.

Note: Be careful not to mix up the RJ-11 and RJ-45 connectors when hooking up computer and telephone equipment! You can force an RJ-11 connector into an RJ-45 jack, because RJ-11 connectors are smaller than RJ-45s. The electrical current from the telephone line may be high enough to damage or destroy the device on the RJ-45 jack and any connected devices.

Coaxial Cable

Coaxial cable, also called coax (pronounced "co-axe"), is a high-capacity cable used for video and communication networks. Coax provides higher bandwidth than twisted-pair cable.

Coaxial cable has two wires: a signal wire at the center, which is either stranded or solid, surrounded by a metallic shield that serves as a ground. The shield is either braided or solid and is wrapped in plastic. If a cable is meant to travel through a plenum, the space between building floors, it is coated in a fire-safe material such as Teflon.

Several types of coaxial cable exist for different purposes. For instance, there are special kinds of coaxial cable designed specifically for baseband, broadband, and television networks.

Thick Coaxial Cable (Thicknet)

Thick coaxial cable, or *thicknet*, is considered the Ethernet standard. It is often referred to as "yellow" cable, although the cable itself is available in a variety of colors.

Thicknet refers to one of several methods for connecting computers in a network environment. It is used for 10base5 Ethernet networks. 10base5 Ethernet is a network standard that runs at 10Mbps, uses baseband transmission and thick coaxial cable (such as 1/2 inch diameter), and has a maximum segment length of 500 meters. However, a network device, such as the repeater discussed earlier, can extend the network signal. Thicknet works well in environments where magnetic radiation may interfere with cable; it is commonly used in hospitals for computed tomography (CT) and magnetic resonance imaging (MRI) scanners.

Thin Coaxial Cable (Thinnet)

Thin coaxial cable, or *thinnet*, is an Ethernet standard for smaller networks. Unlike thicknet cable, thinnet is highly flexible and works well in small areas, such as office cubicles.

Thinnet is used for 10base2 Ethernet networks. 10base2 Ethernet is a network standard that runs at 10Mbps, uses baseband transmission and thin coaxial cable (such as 1/4 inch diameter), and has a maximum segment length of 185 meters.

BNC Connector

The British Naval Connector, or Bayonet Neill-Concelman (BNC) connector, is commonly used to connect coaxial cable to NICs, hubs, and other network devices. The *BNC connector* is crimped to the cable using a bayonet mount. The bayonet mount technique connects the two wires (signal and ground) in the coaxial cable to the connector. The connector is then inserted into another connector and turned, which pins the signal pin and ground into the BNC's locking groove. A BNC connector is shown in Figure 3.17.

FIGURE 3.17 BNC connector

Fiber Optic Cable

Fiber optic cable can accommodate data transmissions much faster than coaxial or twisted-pair cable. Fiber optic lines can transmit data in the gigabits-per-second range. Fiber optic cable sends data as pulses of light over threads of glass or plastic. Laser transmitters send the modulated light pulses through the cable and optical receivers receive them on the other end. The transmissions can travel for miles without signal degradation. No electrical signals are carried over the fiber optic line, so the lines are free of electromagnetic interference and are extremely difficult to tap.

Fiber optic cables consist of two small glass or plastic strands; one sends data, and one receives data. These strands are called the *core*. Glass or plastic cladding surrounds each core. Each core and cladding element is wrapped with a plastic reinforced with Kevlar fibers.

Two major types of fiber optic cable exist: single-mode and multimode.

Single-mode *Single-mode fiber optic cable* uses a specific light wavelength for transmission. The cable's core diameter is 8 to 10 microns. It is often used for inter-city telephone trunks and video applications.

Multimode *Multimode fiber optic cable* uses a large number of frequencies (or modes) for transmission. The cable's core is larger than that of single-mode. Multimode fiber is the type usually specified for LANs and WANs.

Fiber optic cable is expensive to produce and install and requires a professional to install the lines, as well as connect the network devices. As fiber optic becomes more widely used, it will require less expertise because technological advances are simplifying the installation and connection processes.

Many cable television and telephone companies are using fiber optic lines to provide high-bandwidth services, including cable modem and Internet. Typically, fiber optic lines are run through the local community and residential areas. Traditional cables, similar to coax and thicknet, are used to bring the signal from a connection box to each home. Coaxial cable is used within the building. Installation and maintenance of copper cables is less complicated and expensive than for fiber optic lines.

Wireless Media

As you have probably noticed, wireless network communications are becoming increasingly popular. While the word "wireless" implies that no cables are necessary in a wireless network, wireless networking is usually implemented in a hybrid environment, in which wireless components communicate with a network that uses cables. For example, a laptop computer may use wireless capabilities to communicate with a corporate LAN that uses cables.

The only difference between a wireless LAN and a cabled LAN is the medium itself, although the wireless LAN also requires a wireless NIC and transceiver for each wireless computer. You'll remember from earlier in this chapter, that the NIC (or network interface card) is the device in a computer that serves as the interface between a computer and a network. A transceiver is also required for the wireless LAN. The transceiver acts as an access point, sending and receiving signals to and from the network.

Transmission Types

Once a network is in place, and the proper devices and wires for connecting computers to LANs and WANs have been chosen, the data must be transmitted across the transmission media. There must be a stable, reliable method for getting information on and off the media; otherwise the network cannot function at a physical level.

How data flows through the network, the media, and its devices, is very important, because speed, accuracy, and efficiency are all affected by the manner in which data proceeds. In this section, we will discuss several data transmission concepts, including asynchronous and synchronous transmission modes, data transmission flow, and baseband and broadband.

Synchronous versus Asynchronous Transmission

To transmit data successfully, we need to understand how the data is structured. The use or absence of timing is one basic method of providing this structure.

Synchronous Transmission   With *synchronous* transmission, data is exchanged in character streams called message-framed data. In synchronous transmissions, the access device, such as a NIC, and a network device, such as a router, share a time clock and a transmission rate, and a start-and-stop sequence is associated with each transmission. The clock, transmission rate, and sequence act to synchronize the transmissions from the access device to the network device. The access and network devices need to be synchronized so that the entire message is received in the order it was transmitted.

T1 lines, which you will learn more about in just a few moments, use synchronous transmissions.

Asynchronous Transmission   *Asynchronous* is the opposite of synchronous transmission and is characterized by the absence of a clock in the transmission media. The access device is not synchronized with the network device; instead, data is transmitted as individual characters. Each character is synchronized by information contained in the start (header) and stop (trailer) bits.

Dial-up modems are an example of a device that uses asynchronous transmissions.

Data Transmission Flow

Once we have agreed on whether or not to use a timing sequence, we must then decide whether the sender and receiver can communicate at the same time. You may have experienced this situation before in a conversation. If both parties talk and neither party listens, the information may be lost.

Network communications can operate successfully in this manner, depending upon how well the connected devices can talk and listen to each other. The LAN and WAN standards must know when to communicate. The NIC must be configured to place data on the media at those times when another computer can receive the transmission. The three methods of circuit operation are as follows.

Simplex   Data travels in only one direction, similar to a public address (PA) system. Networks do not use simplex transmission methods, because the point of a network is to allow two computers to communicate with each other.

Half duplex   Data travels in two directions, but in only one direction at a time, similar to a walkie-talkie. Ethernet uses half-duplex transmissions. This is faster than simplex, but each side of the conversation must take turns talking and listening.

Full duplex   Data travels in two directions simultaneously, similar to a telephone conversation. Full-duplex Ethernet, an extension of Ethernet, supports full-duplex transmissions in a switched environment. Both sides of the conversation can talk and listen at the same time, if their networking hardware supports it.

Baseband and Broadband Transmissions

In networking, *bandwidth* is the measure of transmission capacity for a given medium. This rate is quantified as the number of bits that can be transmitted per second. A transmission medium's bandwidth can be divided into channels, where each channel is a portion of the total capacity available to transmit data. The two methods used to allocate bandwidth to channels are baseband and broadband.

Baseband

The *baseband* method of transmission uses the entire media bandwidth for a single channel. Baseband uses a transmission technology called *time division multiplexing (TDM)*. TDM sends multiple signals over one transmission path by interweaving the signals. For instance, three signals (X, Y, and Z) can be sent as XXYYZZXXYYZZ. The recipient device separates this single stream into its original three signals. StatTDM (Statistical TDM) gives priority to more urgent signals.

Although it is most commonly used for digital signaling, baseband can also conduct analog signals. However, most LANs, such as Ethernet and token ring networks, use digital baseband signaling.

Broadband

You've likely heard the term *broadband* frequently used these days to describe cable television, cable modem service, wireless systems, and DSL service. While these are the most common uses of broadband, there is a specific reason why it is convenient to use broadband for things such as cable TV and wireless, because the broadband method of transmission divides the media bandwidth into multiple channels, and each channel carries a separate signal. This method enables a single transmission medium to carry several conversations simultaneously and without interference.

Broadband uses a transmission technology called *frequency division multiplexing (FDM)*. Like TDM, FDM also transmits multiple signals over a single transmission path, however, FDM transmits each signal within a unique frequency range, or carrier.

The term broadband is also commonly used to describe any high-speed data transmission that provides services at T1 rates (1.544 Mbps) and higher. The capabilities of broadband technology vary greatly depending on the situation, and actual transmission rates can fail to reach T1 rates or may far exceed them. Generally, however, broadband implies higher transmission speeds than those that have been widely available in the past.

Broadband is used exclusively for analog signals; it cannot be applied to digital signals because digital signals can interfere with one another. In order to circumvent issues of analog and digital signals, broadband transmissions require a modem that converts digital signals to analog signals and vice versa.

T-Carrier System

The T-carrier system is a North American digital transmission format that provides dedicated and private line services for digital voice and data transmission at rates up to 45Mbps. T-carrier services are usually used to connect a LAN to a WAN, such as a company network to the Internet or a frame relay network. Currently, there are three types of T-Carrier services: T1, T2, and T3. Each service provides various bandwidth and speed to its customers.

T1

T1 is a common digital leased-line service that provides bandwidth of 1.544Mbps. Each T1 line supports 24 channels at 64Kbps. Each of the 24 channels in a T1 circuit can carry voice or data transmission.

Fractional T1, also called FT1, allows customers to lease the 64Kbps channels individually instead of the full T1 line.

To connect a T1 line to your LAN, you need the following systems.

CSU   The first point of contact for the T1 wires; it diagnoses and prepares the signals on the line for the LAN.

DSU   Connects to the CSU and converts LAN signals to T1 signaling formats.

The CSU/DSU combines both these units.

Multiplexor   Provides a mechanism to load multiple voice and data channels into the digital line. A multiplexor is used when a line is shared by two or more communications channels.

Router   Provides the interface between the LAN and the T1 line.

T2

T2 is an internal carrier specification that is equivalent to four T1 lines. T2 lines provide a bandwidth of 6.3Mbps. T2 is not offered to the public.

T3

T3 is equivalent to 28 T1 circuits and provides a total bandwidth of 44.736Mbps. Fractional T3 allows customers to lease channels, such as 3Mbps or 64Kbps channels, instead of the full T3 line.

The digital signal (DS) classification used in North America, Japan, South Korea and other countries provides a standardization for digital signal levels, and is synonymous with the T-carrier system. Table 3.3 shows the T-carrier system data transfer rates.

TABLE 3.3   T-Carrier System Used in North America, Japan, and South Korea

T-Carrier	Data Transfer Rate
T1	1.544Mbps
T2	6.312Mbps
T3	44.736Mbps
T4	274.176Mbps

E-Carrier System

The E-carrier system is a European digital transmission format that is analogous to the North American T-carrier system. Each transmission speed is a multiple of the E1 format, which operates at 2.048Mbps. Table 3.4 lists the five E-carrier speeds.

TABLE 3.4   E-Carrier System Used in Europe

E-Carrier	Data Transfer Rate
E1	2.048Mbps
E2	8.448Mbps
E3	34.368Mbps
E4	139.264Mbps
E5	565.148Mbps

Summary

In this chapter, you acquired a basic understanding of LANs and WANs. The hardware and transmission types we have discussed form the physical basis of computer networks. You discovered the communication devices involved, including network interface cards, repeaters, hubs, bridges, routers, switches, and CSU/DSUs. These communications devices physically connect computers and networks together.

Transmission media types were introduced, such as twisted-pair, coaxial and fiber optic cable, and wireless media. The cables and transmission media form an important part of the network infrastructure. Without transmission media, we could not build networks.

We also studied transmission types and learned about network standards, such as IEEE LAN standards, FDDI and WAN technologies. Networking standards describe how computers and networks actually communicate with each other over the transmission media and through the networking devices. We also reviewed the T-carrier and E-carrier digital transmission formats.

In the following chapters, we will use this information as we discuss how the Internet actually works. The OSI Reference Model, the Internet Architecture, and TCP/IP build upon the connections we have discussed in this chapter, and provide intelligence and reliability to the Internet.

Exam Essentials

Understand the basics of a local area network (LAN) and a wide area network (WAN).   A LAN connects computers in a small geographic area, such as an office. A WAN connects computers and networks over a larger area.

Be able to identify Carrier Sense Multiple Access/Collision Detection (CSMA/CD).   All Ethernet methods use CSMA/CD to control LAN access, which allows only one computer at a time to transmit a signal on the network.

Be able to identify the Institute of Electrical and Electronics Engineers (IEEE) 802.2 LAN standard, Ethernet, and CSMA/CD.   IEEE 802.2 defines the Logical Link Control (LLC) and MAC connection standards.

Be able to identify the Institute of Electrical and Electronics Engineers (IEEE) 802.3 LAN standard and Ethernet. IEEE 802.3 uses a MAC address along with Ethernet, in which only one LAN station at a time may broadcast a signal on the network, with an effective speed of 10Mbps, on star or bus networks using coax, twisted-pair, or fiber. IEEE 802u, also called fast Ethernet, operates at 100Mbps on star networks using twisted-pair or fiber. Both versions of Ethernet have a link distance of 100 meters. IEEE 803.3z and 802.3ab (gigabit Ethernet) allow transmissions speeds of 1000Mbps, and are used on network backbones.

Know the differences between logical and physical addresses. A logical address, such as an IP address, is used to send data between two networks. A physical address, such as a Media Access Control (MAC) address, is used to send data between two computers in the same physical link, such as a network or network segment.

Know the Token Ring networking standard. IEEE 802.5 defines the token ring network, in which a token identifies the destination of the signal. Token ring networks operate a 4 or 16Mbps. A MAU is used to tie the computers into a ring topology.

Know the FDDI networking standard and MANs. Fiber Distributed Data Interface (FDDI) uses two rings running opposite directions, tokens, and MAC addresses in a 100Mbps fiber optic network. When these networks are deployed over a specific area, they are called municipal area networks (MANs).

Understand WAN standards, including X.25, frame relay, and Asynchronous Transfer Mode (ATM). X.25 is a packet-level error-correcting protocol used for credit card and automated teller machine transactions at speeds of 56Kbps and less. Frame relay is a fast packet-switching technology that can connect dedicated lines at speeds between 64Kbps and 1.544Mbps. Asynchronous Transfer Mode transmits data at speeds up to 1.2Gbps using 53-byte cells.

Understand how the various LAN/WAN devices work together, including NICs, repeaters, hubs, bridges, routers, brouters, switches, gateways, CSU/DSU, and patch panels. Every computer in the network must have a network interface card (NIC) to provide a connection. Repeaters regenerate a network signal to help cover long distances. Hubs help connect several computers within a LAN. Bridges connect network segments by using hardware addresses. Routers connect networks to each other using IP addresses. Brouters can connect network segments and networks by using hardware addresses. Switches connect network nodes at a higher speed than hubs, bridges, and routers. Gateways translate protocols. The CSU/DSU terminates the physical connection of a dedicated circuit, such as a T1. A patch panel helps connect computers and networks at a specific location.

Understand the differences among common transmission media used in networking, such as twisted-pair, coaxial, fiber optic cable, and wireless media. Twisted-pair cable is frequently used in office LAN installations. It is available in seven categories. Network cables use RJ-45 eight-pin connectors. Coaxial cable is used for high-bandwidth installations in a building. The BNC connector is often used with coax. Of the two types of coaxial cable, thinnet is more flexible than thicknet, but thinnet has a shorter usable distance and is less resistant to interference. Fiber optic lines are used for very-high-bandwidth connections. Wireless media are usually implemented as part of a hybrid network, with wireless media connecting a workstation to the cabled network.

Know transmission types, including asynchronous and synchronous, simplex, half-duplex, full-duplex, baseband and broadband. Network lines use synchronous transmission, with a clock providing the same beat for the origin and destination. Dialup modems use asynchronous transmission, which has no clock, but requires the same speed for transmission and reception. In a half-duplex transmission, the data can travel in one direction at a time. In a full-duplex transmission, data travels in both directions simultaneously. Baseband uses the entire bandwidth to send one signal. Broadband dedicates a channel or portion of the bandwidth to each signal.

Know the function and types of T-carrier and E-carrier systems. The T-carrier system is the digital transmission format used in the United States, South Korea and Japan. The E-carrier system is used in Europe. Each system defines a set of speeds.

Key Terms

Before you take the exam, be certain you are familiar with the following terms:

asynchronous	gateway
Asynchronous transfer mode (ATM)	hub
bandwidth	Institute of Electrical and Electronics Engineers (IEEE)
baseband	local area network (LAN)
BNC connector	MAC address
bridge	Media Access Control (MAC)
broadband	multimode fiber optic cable
brouter	Multistation Access Unit (MAU)
Carrier Sense Multiple Access/ Collision Detection (CSMA/CD)	municipal area network (MAN)
Channel Service Unit/Data (or Digital) Service Unit (CSU/DSU)	network adapter card
coaxial cable	network interface card (NIC)
collision	patch cord
core	patch panel
dongle	repeater
Ethernet	router
fast packet switching	shielded twisted-pair (STP)
Fiber Distributed Data Interface (FDDI)	single-mode fiber optic cable
fiber optic cable	stranded cable
frame relay	switch
frequency division multiplexing (FDM)	synchronous

T1	token ring
T3	transceiver
thicknet	twisted-pair
thinnet	unshielded twisted-pair (UTP)
time division multiplexing (TDM)	wide area network (WAN)
token passing	X.25

Review Questions

1. Which one of the following choices best describes a group of computers connected within a confined geographic area so that their users can share files and services?

   A. Ring network

   B. Intranet

   C. Local Area Network (LAN)

   D. Extranet

2. Which of the following choices is most appropriate for networking an office with 10 computers in 3 adjoining rooms?

   A. MAN

   B. Local area network

   C. Wide area network

   D. Modem connections

3. The Internet is best described as which one of the following?

   A. A wide area network

   B. A local area network

   C. An e-mail network

   D. A commercial network

4. A NIC does not require which one of the following items to connect a computer to the Internet?

   A. Media

   B. Transceiver

   C. Device driver

   D. Cable modem

5. John has a computer on his local area network that is 300 meters away from the server. Which one of the following hardware devices would help him connect these two computers?

   A. Bridge

   B. Router

   C. Switch

   D. Repeater

6. A hub is most commonly associated with which of the following network topologies?

   A. Ring

   B. Star

   C. Peer-to-peer

   D. Hybrid

7. Rachel needs to connect two token ring networks to each other. The networks are in the same floor of her office buildings. Which hardware device is best suited to this task?

   A. Switch

   B. Router

   C. Bridge

   D. Hub

8. Which one of the following devices translates a signal from one networking protocol to the other?

   A. Switch

   B. Hub

   C. Gateway

   D. Router

9. How many twisted-pairs of wire are in a category 5 cable?

    A. Two

    B. Three

    C. Four

    D. Five

10. A British Naval Connector is usually seen on which of the following cable types?

    A. Category 1 cable

    B. Coaxial cable

    C. Category 5 cable

    D. Fiber optic lines

11. A normal Ethernet installation can always use which one of the following transmission flows?

    A. Full-duplex

    B. Half-duplex

    C. Simplex

    D. Bus

12. A token ring network uses which one of the following transmission methods?

    A. Baseband

    B. Full-duplex

    C. Simplex

    D. Broadband

13. Which of the following best describes a Media Access Control address?

   A. A number assigned to a computer by a server.

   B. A number permanently assigned to a NIC.

   C. A number assigned to a network by an ISP.

   D. A number assigned to a user by a server.

14. In the IEEE 802.3 specifications, how does a computer send a signal on the LAN?

   A. The computer asks the server when it can send the signal.

   B. The computer waits for an idle period to send a signal to all the other computers.

   C. The computer waits for an idle period to send a signal to a specific computer.

   D. The computer passes its signal to the next computer.

15. A Fiber Distributed Data Interface uses which of the following?

   A. One ring with very fast cable

   B. One ring with fiber optic lines

   C. Two rings running in opposite directions

   D. Two rings running in the same direction

16. Which one of the following choices best describes frame relay service?

   A. Provides fixed cell service at speeds of 1.544Mbps or greater.

   B. Provides dedicated connections at speeds of 1.544Mbps or less.

   C. Provides fixed cell service at speeds of 1.544Mbps or less.

   D. Provides dedicated connections at speeds of 1.544 Mbps or greater.

17. A T3 carrier can handle all but which of the following data transfer speeds?

    A. 64Kbps

    B. 800Kbps

    C. 1.5Mbps

    D. 50Mbps

18. Which of the following data speeds represents the maximum through-put of a T1 line?

    A. 512Kbps

    B. 1.544Mbps

    C. 44.736Mbps

    D. 56Kbps

19. The E-carrier system defines data transfer speeds based on the following multiple?

    A. 64Kbps

    B. 1.544Mbps

    C. 2.048Mbps

    D. 56Kbps

20. Which item is required to connect a cable modem to a personal computer?

    A. Phone cable

    B. Network interface card

    C. Router

    D. Hub

Answers to Review Questions

1. **C.** This is the basic description of a LAN. Intranets and extranets are types of internetworks, and both can be implemented for users in a wide geographic area. A ring network is one kind of topology used for implementing LANs.

2. **B.** A LAN is usually used for networking this many computers. A municipal area network would be difficult to set up with this many computers and rooms. A WAN is more appropriate for a network spanning several distant buildings. Modems would be relatively slow compared to a LAN.

3. **A.** The Internet is best compared to a WAN. It is much larger than a LAN, supports more services than e-mail, and is built on a combination of public and commercial networks.

4. **D.** The first three choices are required. Media of some sort, such as a cable or a wireless connection, must be used to connect the NIC to a network. A transceiver is often built into the NIC. A digital or analog modem is not always necessary for Internet connectivity.

5. **D.** John will want to use a repeater, which amplifies a network signal so that it can be sent down an additional length of cable, beyond the point where a signal would start to degrade. A bridge might help connect these two network segments, except for the distance involved. A router connects networks. A switch is meant to connect network nodes at high speeds, and would be an expensive solution to connect a single workstation to a network.

6. **B.** Explanation: Hubs are used in star networks to connect computers. Ring networks use a multistation access unit (MAU). Peer-to-peer networks connect one computer directly to the next computer. A hybrid network may use a hub if necessary.

7. **C.** Rachel should use a bridge to connect these two networks to each other. A switch is used for high-speed networks. A router connects networks using their software addresses, which is not appropriate for a token ring network. A hub is used to connect computers in a single network.

8. C. A gateway performs this task. The other devices provide connections. A switch connects two high-speed networks. A hub connects computers within a network. A router sends signals from one network to another.

9. C. There are four twisted-pairs in categories 2 through 7.

10. B. BNCs are used with coaxial cable. Category 1 cables are used for voice, and often have an RJ-11 connector. Category 5 cables use an RJ-45 connector. Fiber optic lines use an optical connection.

11. B. Ethernet can always use half-duplex. Full-duplex Ethernet is designed to also accept full-duplex transmissions. Simplex is not used in Ethernet. Bus is a network topology.

12. A. Token ring networks use baseband transmission. High-speed networks use broadband. Full-duplex and simplex are types of data transmission flows.

13. B. A MAC address is burned into a NIC card. It is a physical address for that particular piece of hardware. The other addresses are logical addresses that can be changed and reassigned.

14. B. In IEEE 802.3 networks, one computer at a time broadcasts its signal to the other computers on the network. The first choice describes an Apple Local Talk network. The third choice describes a token ring network. The last choice describes a bus network.

15. C. FDDI uses two counter-rotating rings to provide redundancy. One line can take over the network if the second line fails.

16. B. Frame relay provides a dedicated line at speeds between 64Kbps and 1.544Mbps. Frame relay does not use fixed cell lengths. These are used in asynchronous transfer mode.

17. D. The maximum data transfer rate for a T3 carrier is 44.736Mbps.

18. B. T1 lines have a maximum throughput of 1.544Mbps. 44.736Mbps is the maximum throughput of a T3 line.

19. C. Explanation: The E-carrier system uses 2.048Mbps as its multiple. This speed identifies an E1 carrier.

20. B. A NIC is necessary to connect a cable modem to a computer. Phone cables are used to connect computers to telephone lines. Routers and hubs are kinds of networking hardware.

Chapter

4

The OSI Reference Model

THE CIW EXAM OBJECTIVE GROUPS COVERED IN THIS CHAPTER:

- ✓ Identify the infrastructure required to support Internet connections, including but not limited to: protocols and hardware and software components.

- ✓ Identify Internet communications protocols and their roles in delivering basic Internet services.

- ✓ Identify Networking and its role in the Internet, including but not limited to: TCP/IP protocols, packets, and the OSI reference model.

- ✓ Identify the roles of networking hardware components, and configure common PC hardware for operation.

In this chapter, you'll learn about the Open Systems Interconnection Reference Model (OSI/RM, or OSI model), a very essential set of rules that provides the basis of internetworking. We will also discuss the protocols used to send information across networks covering the various aspects of protocols, such as connection state and routability. Using the network devices we presented in the last chapter, we will demonstrate how packets are created and sent across the Internet.

OSI Reference Model

The *OSI Reference Model (OSI/RM)* is a seven-layer model used to break down the many tasks involved in moving data from one host to another. OSI/RM was defined by the International Organization for Standardization (ISO) in 1983 (see www.iso.ch), based on proposals from several networking companies. The OSI/RM has three practical functions:

- The model gives developers necessary, universal concepts so they can develop and refine networking protocols.

- The model explains the framework used to connect heterogeneous systems. In other words, it allows clients and servers to communicate even if they are using different applications and operating systems; all they need is a common protocol, such as TCP/IP or IPX/SPX.

- The model describes the process of packet creation. You will learn more about packet creation shortly.

Networks can be built using the OSI/RM, just as a building is constructed from a blueprint. For instance, Novell NetWare, Microsoft Windows, and UNIX are based on the OSI/RM. This common framework allows these network operating systems to interoperate. The seven layers of the OSI/RM are described in Table 4.1.

TABLE 4.1 The Layers of the OSI/RM

Layer	Layer Number	Description
Application	7	This layer is the interface to the end user in an OSI environment. The Application layer supports file transfer, network management, and other services.
Presentation	6	This layer is responsible for providing useful transformations on data to support a standardized application interface and general communications services. For example, it converts text from American Standard Code for Information Interchange (ASCII) format to Extended Binary Coded Decimal Interchange Code (EBCDIC).
Session	5	This layer establishes, manages, and terminates connections or sessions between cooperating applications. It also adds traffic flow information. In many networking systems, this layer is barely or not at all implemented.
Transport	4	This layer provides reliable, transparent transport between the source and destination hosts. It also supports end-to-end error recovery and flow control.
Network	3	This layer organizes data into datagrams or packets. It forwards and routes datagrams to their destinations.

TABLE 4.1 The Layers of the OSI/RM *(continued)*

Layer	Layer Number	Description
Data Link	2	This layer provides reliable data transfer across the physical link. Frames are transmitted with the necessary synchronization, error control, and flow control. In short, it prepares the information so it can be placed on the transmission medium, such as a copper wire. In the IEEE 802.2 series of LAN standards, the Data Link layer is divided into two sublayers: the Logical Link Control (LLC) layer and the Media Access Control (MAC) layer. The LLC is responsible for error and flow control, and the MAC layer is responsible for placing data on the transmission media. This layer is also called the Data Link Control (DLC).
Physical	1	This layer manages the transmission of unstructured bit streams over a physical link. It is responsible for the mechanical, electrical, and procedural characteristics to establish, maintain, and deactivate the physical link.

You may have noticed that we have presented the OSI/RM layers in reverse numerical order. This is the usual way that the layers are described and presented.

You can use a mnemonic to help remember the seven OSI/RM layers. An example is "*All people seem to need data processing.*" The first letter of each word corresponds to the first letter of each OSI/RM layer.

Various combinations of software, protocols, and hardware are used throughout TCP/IP to transform and transmit network data. As Figure 4.1

demonstrates, the OSI/RM describes interaction between the individual layers as well as between hosts on a network. The left column contains the seven OSI/RM layers as they exist on a client computer. When the client sends data, it is creating a packet. We will discuss what a packet is in the next section.

The data is generated by a software application, operating at Layer 7, the Application layer. The software program could be a web browser, an e-mail client, or another program that is sending data through the Internet. As we move down this left column, each layer transforms and packages the data in a different way. As we move down the layer model, the computer is assembling a packet that can be sent across the network. When we reach Layer 1, the Physical layer, the packet has been converted to a signal that can be sent across the network media.

The right column contains the same seven layers as they exist on a server. The server receives the packet from the media. The server unwraps the packet layer-by-layer, moving up the layer model, until the server application receives the data sent by the client.

We will discuss the role of each OSI/RM layer in detail throughout this chapter, with a special focus on the TCP/IP protocol suite.

FIGURE 4.1   OSI model layers

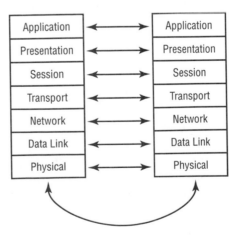

Packets

A *packet* is a fixed piece of information sent across a network. Whenever you send information across any network, you begin the packet-creation process. This packet creation process includes the journey through the OSI/RM layers we described in the previous section.

A packet consists of three elements:

Header   This is the first part of the packet, and it contains OSI/RM layer information used in decoding the packet.

Data   This section can include the client's request to a server, or a server's response to a client.

Trailer   This is the last part of the packet, and can contain Cyclical Redundancy Check (CRC) data used to correct any transmission errors that are found when the packet is received. (We'll go over CRC in detail in the next section.)

Many networking professionals use the terms "packet," "datagram," and "frame" interchangeably. Although this usage is accurate most of the time, "packet" is a generic term for any piece of information passed through a network. A *datagram* is a packet at the Network layer of the OSI/RM. A *frame* is a packet at the Data Link layer, used to traverse an Ethernet network. Even though the concepts are slightly different, these terms are usually used synonymously.

As you can see in Figure 4.2, a packet can have several headers. The header contains several different pieces of information, such as addressing information and an alert signal to the incoming computer. There is always one section of data, and there is usually only one trailer.

As we mentioned in the previous section, the packet-creation process begins with Layer 7, the Application layer of the OSI/RM, and continues through Layer 1, the Physical layer. For example, when you send an e-mail message or transfer a file from one computer to another, this message or file undergoes a transformation from a complete file into smaller pieces of information called packets. Beginning with the Application layer of the OSI/RM, the file continues to be divided until the initial discrete message becomes divided into smaller, more manageable pieces of information sent at the Physical layer.

FIGURE 4.2 Packet structure

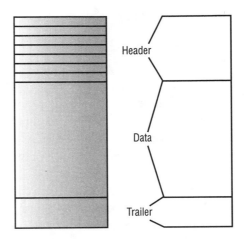

Figure 4.3 demonstrates how each layer adds its own information, called a *header*, to the packet. This information enables each layer to communicate with the others and also allows the receiving computer to process the message.

FIGURE 4.3 Headers added at each level of the OSI/RM

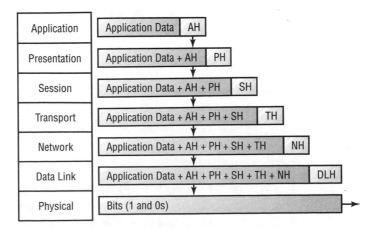

You have already seen how a sending host creates a packet. When a receiving host processes a packet, it reverses the packet-creation process and removes each header, beginning with Layer 1 and ending with Layer 7. All that is left at the end of this process is the original, unaltered data, which the host can then process.

CRC

A Cyclical Redundancy Check (CRC) is a mathematical calculation that allows the receiving computer to verify whether the data in the packet is valid and correct. When a sending host transmits a packet, it calculates a CRC, then adds this information to the trailer. When the receiving host reads the packet, it runs its own CRC, then compares it with the CRC stored in the trailer.

If the two CRCs match, then the computer assumes that the packet is not damaged and processes the packet. If the CRCs do not match, the receiving host discards the entire packet. Depending upon the networking protocol, the receiving computer may request a new, replacement packet from the sender.

Computer Speed, Memory, and Networking Performance

By now you may have realized that networking puts a lot of demands on a personal computer. The speed of a network connection does limit how fast your networked computer will retrieve information from the Internet. But there are other bottlenecks within your computer that can slow down the performance of Internet applications.

The speed of the CPU, or central processing unit, of the computer is an important factor in how quickly a computer can handle network traffic. Sending a simple e-mail message can require the computer to perform hundreds of CRC checks. Downloading a large file may require millions of CRC checks.

Computers need fast components to process network traffic quickly. Personal computers use CPUs such as Intel's Pentium series to help web browsing and e-mail client applications process CRCs and OSI/RM information as quickly as possible. The CPU has other tasks it must also perform while networking, including updating the display, retrieving and saving files, and running other applications.

Another common bottleneck is the amount of RAM installed in the computer. Windows and Linux operating systems can perform faster when they have additional RAM. Microsoft recommends a minimum of 128MB RAM for Windows XP. However, doubling the RAM to 256MB can significantly speed up network operations. This is because the CPU must also manage the amount of available RAM on the computer. When more RAM is installed, the CPU will spend less time managing memory, and devote more processor power to network connections.

Networking Protocols and the OSI Model

In this section, we'll take a look at the specific qualities of some networking protocols, some of which we've studied in earlier chapters, from the framework of the OSI model.

Protocol Categories

Before we discuss specific protocols, we should review some broader categories of networking protocols. First, protocols may be considered either connection-oriented (stateful) or connectionless (stateless). Additionally, we can consider whether a given protocol is routable or nonroutable. We'll discover more about what these categories mean in the following sections.

Connection-Oriented and Connectionless Protocols

Some network protocols, known as *connection-oriented protocols*, require that a host establish a connection, or session (also referred to as a state), before they transfer information. Because of this requirement, connection-oriented protocols are often called *stateful protocols*. A connection-oriented protocol must first gain a system's attention, prepare it to receive information, then send the information.

Receiving a phone call is an example of a connection-oriented activity. A call requires you to establish a continuous session before you can communicate. You can also immediately acknowledge that you received the information a caller has given you during the call. Your acknowledgment is part of that session.

Other network protocols do not require a previously established session. *Connectionless* or *stateless protocols* rely on a "best-effort" technology that sends the information to the network, hoping that the data will reach the intended system. Many connectionless protocols send information by short messages called datagrams.

If you were to send a message through your postal service, you would be involved in a connectionless activity, because you would not have initiated a continuous connection to transmit the message. You are simply mailing a letter, hoping that it will arrive. Rather than being able to send an immediate acknowledgment that the package was received, the recipient would have to send another message indicating that your transmission arrived. Although it might be tempting to regard a connection-oriented protocol as more important or reliable, for a network, connection-oriented protocols require more system overhead, and are not always appropriate for certain networking tasks.

Both the stateful and stateless protocols have a useful function in a network. For instance, on a network TCP acts as a stateful protocol because the connection is established as the communication begins, and as each segment of the communication is received, an acknowledgement is sent to the sender within a certain period of time. When sent data is damaged on the way, TCP sends no confirmation of receipt and original data is resent. On the other hand, IP is an example of a stateless protocol because no connection is established as communication begins. Since there is no data header in a stateless protocol and there is no acknowledgement of the transmission, information sent through a stateless protocol can often be transmitted faster than with stateful.

Routable and Nonroutable Protocols

Some protocols can travel through LANs and WANs and beyond because they can pass through a router. Recall from Chapter 3 that a router forwards packets from one network to another. The *routable* protocols, including TCP/IP and UDP/IP, are essential tools for creating the Internet. *Non-routable* protocols use predefined, or static, routes that cannot be changed. These protocols are used within networks and network segments. Some protocols are nonroutable because they do not use the functions of the OSI/RM Network layer. Nonroutable protocols include NetBEUI, NetBIOS, Systems Network Architecture (SNA), Local Area Transport (LAT) and the Data Link Control (DLC) protocol.

It is possible to use a nonroutable protocol when sending a message between two networks by adding a bridge. This would help connect two network segments that each use different protocols.

It is also possible to package, or encapsulate, the nonroutable protocol within a routable protocol, such as TCP/IP. Encapsulation, also called *tunneling*, is often used on extranets and intranets, when users need to access network data from a remote location. We will discuss tunneling in a later chapter.

Networking Protocols

Several networking protocols and architectures exist, all based on the OSI/RM. You were introduced to networking protocols such as TCP/IP and IPX/SPX in earlier chapters. This section will explain several important networking protocol properties, including:

- TCP/IP
- IPX/SPX
- NetBEUI and NetBIOS
- Data Link Control (DLC)
- Systems Network Architecture (SNA)

The TCP/IP Protocol Suite

As we learned in an earlier chapter, TCP/IP is a suite or collection of networking protocols that were developed for the Internet. We are using TCP/IP as an example to explain the OSI/RM because TCP/IP is a primary focus of the CIW Foundations certification. The OSI/RM can be readily applied to other protocols like Novell's IPX/SPX and IBM's SNA, and these are topics you will find covered in books for those protocols.

The TCP/IP protocol suite includes Transmission Control Protocol, Internet Protocol, User Datagram Protocol (UDP), Address Resolution Protocol (ARP), and many others that will be discussed later in this study guide. Each of these protocols has a specific function.

TCP

TCP ensures reliable communication and uses ports to deliver packets. It also fragments and reassembles messages, using a sequencing function to ensure that packets are reassembled in the correct order. TCP works at Layer 4, the Transport layer of the OSI/RM.

TCP packets also include CRC checksums in the data trailer. If the receiving computer finds an invalid CRC in a packet, the computer requests a new copy of the packet from the sending computer. This kind of error-checking is essential for protocols like HTTP and FTP, where it is crucial that the recipient get every piece of a file.

IP

IP is a connectionless protocol responsible for providing the numeric IP addresses of each computer. IP also is responsible for forwarding packets to their destination, an action called *routing*. IP works at Layer 3, the Network layer of the OSI/RM and IP relies upon TCP to make and maintain a network connection. This reliance that IP has on TCP is an example of how one protocol in the OSI/RM depends on another for certain services.

UDP

User Datagram Protocol (UDP) is a connectionless protocol that, like TCP, runs on top of IP networks and also works at Layer 4, the Transport layer of the OSI/RM. UDP is a fast, direct way to send and receive datagrams over an IP network and was originally designed for broadcasting short messages over a network. UDP packets include a CRC checksum in the data trailer. If the receiving computer finds an invalid CRC in a packet, the packet is simply discarded.

UDP can be used for communicating large messages across the network but only when the recipient does not need to receive every packet of that message. This kind of fast, sometimes unreliable delivery works well for certain applications like streaming audio where Internet users use a streaming audio application like Real Player or Windows Media Player to listen to music and radio. The data must be sent at a speed the client can handle easily, or the client will not receive a significant number of the packets. Sending UDP audio data too quickly can lead to audible skips in a song, for example.

UDP and TCP do have their differences. Unlike TCP, UDP provides very few error recovery services. UDP creates much less network overhead than TCP, because the client and server do not send acknowledgement messages to each other. Table 4.2 compares the advantages and disadvantages of TCP and UDP.

TABLE 4.2   TCP vs. UDP

Protocol	Uses	Advantages	Disadvantages
TCP	Sending files across the Internet	Provides error checking. Receiving computer can request copies of damaged packets.	Transmission of large files can be long, because the packets contain CRC data on their trailers.
UDP	Short broadcast messages on a LAN Sending streaming media files across the Internet	Very fast.	Does not provide error checking. Parts of the transmission may be lost.

ARP

Address Resolution Protocol (ARP) is a protocol used to convert a numeric IP address into a physical address, such as a MAC address. We will see in Chapter 5 that computers on the same LAN may all use the same network IP address, but for now, you can think of each computer on a LAN as having the same public telephone exchange. It is essential that these computers have a unique physical address, the MAC, to receive incoming TCP/IP data. To extend our telephone analogy, the MAC could be compared to the extension number of each individual telephone in an office. The ARP can be used to assign the MAC to what had been a numeric IP address.

Here's how it's done: A host can obtain a physical address by broadcasting an ARP request onto the TCP/IP network. The host on the network that has the IP address in the request then replies with its physical hardware address. A computer will usually save this information in a small file called an ARP cache for use throughout the session.

When a LAN computer sends IP packets onto an Ethernet network, it will include its MAC address in the Layer 3 (Network) packet header. Thus, the computer's unique address on the LAN is linked to its IP address. When a router on an Ethernet network places incoming IP packets on the LAN, each computer's NIC will perform its standard job of examining the MAC address of each packet. The receiving computer will take from the transmission medium only those packets containing the computer's MAC address.

IPX/SPX

Novell developed IPX/SPX, a LAN and WAN protocol suite, for its once dominant NetWare networking operating system. Internetwork Packet Exchange (IPX) is a connectionless protocol that resides at Layer 3, the Network layer of the OSI/RM. IPX is responsible for network addressing and packet routing. Sequenced Packet Exchange (SPX) is a connection-oriented Layer-4 transport protocol that uses services provided by IPX. SPX ensures that IPX packets arrive intact at their destination. Because SPX resides at the Transport layer, it ensures reliable data delivery and manages sessions.

IPX/SPX has certain performance advantages over TCP/IP. IPX/SPX is usually easier than TCP/IP to set up on an individual workstation. Some computer games that feature multiplayer capability support IPX/SPX for this reason. As we will see in later chapters, setting up TCP/IP correctly requires knowledge of numeric IP addresses and several networking protocols. IPX/SPX uses network, node, and socket numbers to send network traffic directly to a specific computer. If all you want to do is connect two computers in a LAN, IPX/SPX can do the job faster and easier than TCP/IP.

There are thousands of IPX/SPX WANs using private networks or virtual private networks (VPNs) to share network servers and files over long distances. Companies that have large Novell NetWare networks run most of these WANs, to connect their own offices and facilities.

The major disadvantage of IPX/SPX is that it is not a vendor-neutral protocol. It was developed by Novell and is used mostly with Novell NetWare networks. Before the Internet became popular, Microsoft included its own version of IPX/SPX, called NWLink, in its Windows operating systems.

Ultimately, TCP/IP has eclipsed IPX/SPX as the standard enterprise protocol, because it is an *open standard*. An open standard is based on specifications that are available to anyone. Open standards are usually administered by standards organizations, such as the International Organization for Standardization (ISO) and the European Computer Manufacturers Association (ECMA).

Web browsing requires TCP/IP to run. Plus, Microsoft Windows NT, 2000, and XP use TCP/IP as their default network protocol. As a result, the majority of business LANs that use personal computers and Windows now run TCP/IP.

Novell adopted TCP/IP as its default protocol in Novell NetWare 5. NetWare still supports IPX/SPX. Consequently, Novell Netware versions 5 and 6 are usually used within companies that have used earlier versions of NetWare as their corporate NOS.

NetBEUI and NetBIOS

NetBEUI (pronounced "net-boo-ee") is an acronym for Network Basic Input/Output System (NetBIOS) Extended User Interface. NetBEUI is a transport protocol first developed by IBM, but implemented by Microsoft as the standard networking protocol in some early versions of Windows NT. NetBEUI is a fast, efficient protocol for networks that are directly cabled together. NetBEUI is usually used within LANs; it cannot be easily used on a WAN, because it is a nonroutable protocol. Consequently, you cannot improve NetBEUI performance by adding routers and gateways to a network.

NetBIOS stands for Network Basic Input/Output System. It was originally designed for use with NetBEUI, but because NetBEUI is declining in popularity, NetBIOS is mainly used as a programming interface for applications. Microsoft Windows computers can use NetBIOS names to identify one another and communicate on a LAN. Windows NT 4, Windows 2000, and Windows XP use TCP/IP for these same functions, as there is less network overhead in using a single protocol to perform all these functions. Routable protocols such as TCP/IP and IPX/SPX can use NetBIOS to work with the physical addresses of computers.

NetBIOS resides at Layer 5, the Session layer of the OSI/RM.

Data Link Control

IBM originally developed Data Link Control (DLC) to enable client machines to work with mainframes. DLC is now used by Hewlett-Packard, which adopted DLC as a means to connect laser printers to LANs.

Some network protocols, such as Ethernet and token ring use the DLC addresses exclusively. Other protocols, such as TCP/IP, use a logical address at the Network layer to identify nodes. Ultimately, however, all network addresses must be translated to DLC addresses. In TCP/IP networks, this translation is performed with the Address Resolution Protocol (ARP). For networks that conform to the IEEE 802 standards, including Ethernet, the DLC address is usually called the Media Access Control (MAC) address.

Systems Network Architecture (SNA)

IBM introduced SNA in 1974 as a mainframe network architecture. Because it is an architecture, it includes a network topology and a series of protocols. The SNA model is quite similar to the OSI/RM. In fact, SNA inspired the creation of the OSI/RM. Even though SNA is an older architecture, it is still widely used within mainframe networks.

Mapping the OSI/RM

Now that you've learned about the various protocols involved with TCP/IP, IPX/SPX, NetBEUI, NetBIOS, and DLC we are ready to present a map of where the various network protocols and devices fit in the OSI/RM. This map is shown in Table 4.3.

TABLE 4.3 Mapping Protocols and Devices to the OSI/RM

Layer name	Number	Protocols	Devices	
Application	7	FTP HTTP NFS POP3 SMTP Telnet		
Presentation	6	ASCII EBCDIC Unicode Data compression Encryption		
Session	5	NetBIOS		
Transport	4	TCP NetBEUI SPX UDP	Layer-4 switches	
Network	3	IP IPX	Router	(Brouter) (Router switch)
Data Link	2	Ethernet LLC MAC	Bridge NIC LAN Switch	(Brouter) (Router switch)

TABLE 4.3   Mapping Protocols and Devices to the OSI/RM *(continued)*

Layer name	Number	Protocols	Devices
Physical	1	Binary	CSU/DSU Hub Switching hub Media Patch panel Repeater

Notice that we have placed the brouter at Layers 2 and 3 in this diagram. A brouter combines the functions of a router and a bridge. A router works at Layer 3, reading packet headers and using routing tables to determine where to send packets. Routers are protocol dependent. For a TCP/IP network, you must use a router that can support TCP/IP. A bridge works at Layer 2 to connect network segments and is protocol-independent. A brouter, therefore, is protocol dependent because of its router functions.

There are four kinds of switches listed in this diagram. A *switching hub* works at Layer 1; it is a faster version of a traditional hub. The *LAN switch* works at Layer 2, the Data Link layer, to filter and forward packets to network segments based upon their MAC addresses.

Another kind of switch, the *router switch*, works as a regular switch does, but also has many features of a router. Like a router, a routing switch can read packet headers and use routing tables to determine where to send packets. But the routing switch can also work with network segments, as a normal switch does. A routing switch is a network device that serves two functions, just as a brouter does. Routing switches are sometimes called Layer-3 switches.

Finally, there is the *Layer-4 switch*. This switch looks at the port information contained in the TCP or UDP header. By looking at this information, a Layer-4 switch can block packets based upon the application that sent them. The switch may let HTTP packets through by checking for the HTTP port number, 80. But the switch may block packets from applications that consume large amounts of bandwidth, such as streaming media.

Notice in Layer 6 that we have listed several protocols that we have not yet discussed. EBCDIC, ASCII, and Unicode are protocols for communicating and displaying text. EBCDIC was developed for use on mainframe computers, when paper punch cards were used for data storage. EBCDIC lists only the capital letters of the English alphabet, along with numbers and a few punctuation symbols.

ASCII replaced EBCDIC as a standard text protocol in the 1970s, because ASCII was designed to handle lower-case letters. ASCII uses a 7-bit numbering system. Each of the 128 ASCII characters is assigned a number from 0 to 127. ASCII became a worldwide standard, especially as IBM and other computer manufacturers developed methods to store additional sets of non-English characters. On Windows systems, for example, the language settings of the operating system help control what kind of keyboard layout and characters are used.

Unicode was developed to consolidate the various methods for mapping characters into a single system. The Unicode protocol system uses a 16-bit numbering method, which is sometimes known as double-byte. This numbering allows 65,000 characters to be mapped at once. This can easily accommodate most of the language alphabets, including Greek, Chinese, and Japanese.

You may also have noticed that Layer 5, the Session layer, has no network devices listed and only one protocol. The Session layer assumes that a reliable network connection has already been made. Many network specifications, including TCP/IP, contain few or no session specifications for the Session layer. These decisions are left to the client applications at Layer 7.

Finally, at Layer 1, the Physical layer, computers communicate in a binary format of ones and zeros. In each protocol, a letter or number is mapped to a specific binary code number.

Choosing and Combining Protocols

Despite its prevalence, TCP/IP is not the only protocol you need to learn and use. You should know about other protocols as well and know in which circumstances it will be helpful to use specific protocols. For example, small peer-to-peer networks do not require TCP/IP or IPX/SPX. A simple protocol such as NetBEUI would be the most appropriate for these networks, mainly because it is fast, has low overhead, and is easy to configure and maintain. On the other hand, a large LAN or a WAN would require a more capable protocol, such as TCP/IP.

In some cases, you might even need to use combined protocols on a network. Networks commonly use two routable protocols, such as TCP/IP and IPX/SPX, although this combination could cause problems with system overhead in large sites experiencing heavy traffic. Such a combination provides system redundancy and can speed connectivity by allowing clients and servers to use faster nonroutable protocols within a LAN.

Sometimes routable and nonroutable protocols should be combined, even in a routed network. A nonroutable protocol such as NetBEUI can be quite useful in a LAN because it can deliver traffic to local computers without the overhead associated with TCP/IP. If a user sends a message to an employee in the same LAN, NetBEUI will handle the entire transaction, as long as the client and server both have NetBEUI bound correctly. However, if someone sends a message to a recipient on another LAN, an activity that involves a router, the system will automatically use a routable protocol such as TCP/IP.

Binding a Protocol

Whenever you use a networking protocol such as TCP/IP, you must attach, or *bind*, it to your NIC within your operating system. By binding the networking protocol, you allow the computer to use the protocol in network communications. You can compare binding a protocol to giving yourself access to a spoken language like English. As long as anyone else you want to work with can understand English, you can communicate with them and exchange information.

WARNING Binding multiple protocols to a computer can increase the time required to maintain and troubleshoot both the computer and the LAN on which it is attached. In addition, the more protocols you use on a computer, the more system overhead you create for your computer and the network. Generally, you want to bind only those networking protocols that you know you will use on a regular basis.

In UNIX systems, you perform protocol binding by reconfiguring the kernel because the UNIX kernel incorporates all drivers and protocols. Whenever you want to change a driver or protocol, you must incorporate it directly into the kernel. In Windows NT/2000/XP, however, you bind a protocol to the NIC by accessing the Network dialog box, shown in Figure 4.4.

FIGURE 4.4 Windows XP Network dialog box

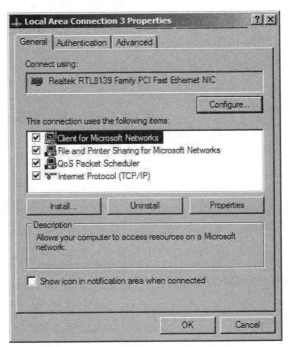

Protocols and Binding Order

If you are using multiple protocols, the binding order determines which protocol the system will use to send information first. If the first protocol is unavailable, the system will use the second protocol to deliver the packets.

 Windows NT, Windows 2000, and Windows XP each allow users to choose the binding order of network protocols. Windows 95/98/Me does not allow users to choose binding order. It automatically orders the protocols according to its own hierarchy.

EXERCISE 4.1

Binding Network Protocols to a NIC

In this exercise, you will view the network protocols installed on your Windows computer to understand how a protocol is bound to a NIC.

1. From the Desktop, right-click the My Network Places icon, as shown below. If the icon is not on your desktop, open the Windows Explorer, right click on the My Network Places entry in the left-hand pane, and select Properties.

My Network
Places

2. Select Properties. The Network window will appear, as shown below.

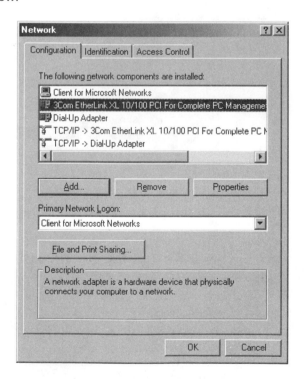

EXERCISE 4.1 *(continued)*

3. From the Network dialog box, in the The Following Network Components Are Installed field, there are two components that allow your computer to access the network. The first is the Network Interface Card (NIC), which connects your computer to the network. In the previous graphic, the NIC is highlighted. This computer has a 3COM Etherlink XL 10/100 PCI network interface card installed.

4. The second component (in this field) that allows your computer to access the network is the networking protocol. Here, your networking protocol is TCP/IP, and it must be bound to the NIC. In the graphic below, TCP/IP is highlighted. The TCP/IP protocol is bound to the 3COM Etherlink XL 10/100 PCI network interface card.

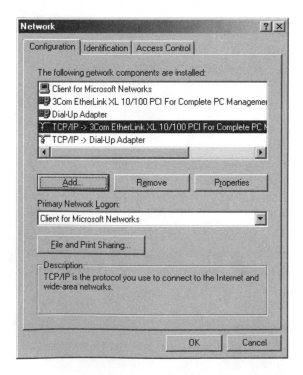

(Note: TCP/IP is the default networking protocol for Microsoft Windows Millennium Edition, Windows 2000/XP, NetWare versions 5 and higher, Linux, and UNIX. It is automatically installed during the operating system installation.)

5. You will configure your computer's TCP/IP properties later in this book. Select Cancel to return to your desktop.

This exercise was designed to explain the concept of binding a networking protocol to a NIC. A protocol can be bound to a NIC, even though the NIC is not connected to a network.

Summary

Each layer of the OSI model—from the Application Layer to the Physical Layer—provides the absolute necessities for a network to operate. Various stateful and stateless protocols, including TCP/IP, IPX/SPX, NetBEUI, NetBIOS, AppleTalk, DLC, and SNA, are based on and work within the OSI reference model. They also provide the rules of network functionality. Such protocols are defined as routable or nonroutable depending upon which functions of the OSI model they utilize. Finally, protocols can be combined or bound for use in networks to establish maximum functionality.

Exam Essentials

Understand the purpose of the Open Systems Interconnection reference model (OSI/RM). The OSI/RM is a networking model by the International Organization for Standardization. It is a framework for network protocol development. The OSI/RM also provides a model for connecting different networking systems.

Know the seven layers of the OSI/RM. Layer 7 is the Application layer, and supports the user's operations with and access to network data. Layer 6, the Presentation layer, supports the encoding and decoding of characters to a digital format. Layer 5, the Session layer, is not implemented in many networking systems, including TCP/IP. It is meant to manage connections and sessions among applications. Layer 4, the Transport layer, manages the movement of data between hosts. Layer 3, the Network layer, controls the direction of data to the hosts. Layer 2, the Data Link layer, is where network data is moved on and off the transmission medium. Layer 1, the Physical layer, is the electrical or electromagnetic transmission of the data.

Understand the packet-creation process. A packet is a fixed piece of information sent across a network. Packets have three parts. A header contains OSI/RM layer information used by the receiving computer for decoding the packet. The data portion contains the client's request or the server's response. The trailer can contain CRC information that is used by the receiving computer to detect transmission errors. The client computer creates packets starting at Level 7, the Application layer. Each additional layer is added as the data is broken up into smaller packets. The receiving computer reads the packet information in the reverse order that it was created, as the signal is received and reassembled.

Know how a Cyclical Redundancy Check (CRC) is used in TCP/IP packets. A CRC is a mathematical calculation that verifies the contents of a packet. The CRC is determined by the sending computer and attached to the trailer portion of the packet. The receiving computer calculates a CRC for each received packet, and then compares the two CRCs. If the CRCs do not match, the networking protocols on the receiving computer determine an appropriate remedy.

Understand the difference between a stateful and stateless protocol. Stateful protocols are also known as connection-oriented protocols. For example, protocols such as TCP require a constant connection between two computers. Stateless protocols are sometimes called connectionless protocols. For example, IP transmits network address information between computers, and uses a best-effort, low overhead approach to send that information.

Understand the difference between routable and nonroutable networking protocols. Routable protocols can be directed through LANs and WANs. Routable protocols such as IP and UDP are the backbone of Internet communication. Nonroutable protocols are used for networking services performed within a single LAN or network segment. These services include obtaining hardware addresses and exchanging network file information.

Know the differences in network protocols that reside at the network and transport layers of the OSI/RM. TCP and SPX are stateful protocols that work at Layer 4, the Transport layer, to provide stable network connections. IP and IPX are stateless protocols that work at Layer 3, the Network layer, to obtain network address and route packets to their proper destinations. IP uses logical addressing for packet routing and relies on ARP to map the physical addresses. IPX uses physical addressing for packet routing.

Know the functions of various TCP/IP protocols at the Application layer of the OSI/RM.   Protocols including HTTP, FTP, POP3, SMTP, and Telnet are used by client applications to request and display network data in a user-readable format.

Understand the functions of networking hardware at the various layers of the OSI/RM.   Routers work at Layer 3, the Network layer, and direct packets to external networks. Bridges and NICs work at Layer 2, the Data Link layer. Bridges connect two networks. NICs send and receive network data from the transmission medium. A variety of devices that handle raw network signals work at Layer 1, the Physical layer, including the CSU/DSU, hubs, patch panels, and repeaters. All transmission media also work at the Physical layer.

Key Terms

Before you take the exam, be certain you are familiar with the following terms:

Address Resolution Protocol (ARP)	open standard
bind	Open Systems Interconnection Reference Model (OSI/RM)
connectionless protocols	packet
connection-oriented protocols	routable
datagram	router switch
frame	routing
header	stateful protocols
LAN switch	stateless protocols
Layer-4 switch	switching hub
nonroutable	User Datagram Protocol (UDP)

Review Questions

1. Which of the OSI/RM layers is responsible for preparing data so it can be sent over a cable?

   A. Transport

   B. Data Link

   C. Physical

   D. Presentation

2. Layer 3 of the OSI/RM provides services that most closely match which one of the following choices?

   A. Transmits bits on a wire

   B. Provides an end user interface to network data

   C. Organizes data into packets

   D. Converts data into a readable text format

3. Which one of the following statements best describes the OSI/RM?

   A. The model describes how to design network topologies.

   B. The model describes key concepts used in networking protocols.

   C. The model contains standards for network operating systems.

   D. The model explains how to configure a web server.

4. What does the acronym OSI/RM mean?

   A. Open Systems Interconnection Reference Model

   B. Operating System Internet Reference Model

   C. Open System Internet Reference Model

   D. Operating System Interconnection Reference Model

5. Which one of the following choices is not part of the packet structure?

   A. Trailer

   B. Data

   C. Certificate

   D. Header

6. TCP is an example of what kind of protocol?

   A. Routable and stateless

   B. Nonroutable and stateless

   C. Routable and stateful

   D. Nonroutable and stateless

7. Which one of the following choices is the best description of a nonroutable protocol?

   A. Nonroutable protocols cannot be used on a TCP/IP network.

   B. Nonroutable protocols use static routes to send information from one network node to another.

   C. Nonroutable protocols can be used across several LANs without a bridge.

   D. Nonroutable protocols can find an optimal path for a network transmission.

8. Which one of the following choices is an appropriate use for the User Datagram Protocol?

   A. Transmitting FTP files

   B. Sending e-mail messages

   C. Web browsing

   D. Streaming audio

9. Which of the following statements about TCP/IP and the OSI/RM is the most correct?

    A. IP works at the Network layer, while TCP works at the Transport layer.

    B. IP works at the Data Link layer, while TCP works at the Presentation layer.

    C. IP works at the Transport layer, while TCP works at the Session layer.

    D. IP works at the Application layer, while TCP works at the Data Link layer.

10. User Datagram Protocol was originally developed to provide which one of the following services?

    A. Error-free file transfer

    B. Rapid delivery of short network messages

    C. E-mail

    D. Videoconferencing

11. Which one of the following protocols maps numeric IP addresses to physical IP addresses on a LAN?

    A. DNS

    B. ARP

    C. TCP

    D. IP

12. According to the OSI/RM, the function of Novell's SPX networking protocol is best compared to which of the following network protocols?

    A. IP

    B. SNA

    C. TCP

    D. Ethernet

13. NetBIOS belongs to which layer of the OSI/RM?

   A. Network

   B. Transport

   C. Data Link

   D. Session

14. Aimee is trying to trace the path of a packet from her computer through her LAN and to the Internet. Which one of the following choices describes a sequence of hardware devices that could be used on her LAN?

   A. Hub, media, patch panel

   B. Patch panel, media, repeater, NIC

   C. NIC, media, router, CSU/DSU

   D. CSU/DSU, hub, media, router

15. How many characters can the Unicode standard handle?

   A. 128

   B. 256

   C. 65,000

   D. 1 million

16. Which of the following statements about EBCDIC is not correct?

   A. EBCDIC maps uppercase characters to a numbering system.

   B. EBCDIC is mapped to the Layer 6 of the OSI/RM.

   C. EBCDIC maps lowercase characters to a numbering system.

   D. EBCDIC is mapped to the Presentation layer of the OSI/RM.

17. On Ethernet networks, what is the DLC address usually called?

    A. IP address

    B. MAC address

    C. DNS entry

    D. E-mail address

18. Which one of the following choices best describes the role of the TCP/IP header in the packet-creation process?

    A. At each layer of the OSI/RM, information is added to the packet trailer.

    B. At each layer of the OSI/RM, a separate packet header is added.

    C. At each layer of the OSI/RM, error-checking information is added to the packet header.

    D. At each layer of the OSI/RM, the network interface card adds diagnostic information.

19. Which layer of the OSI/RM corresponds most closely to an e-mail client?

    A. Network

    B. Application

    C. Session

    D. Data Link

20. Which one of the following choices describes the OSI/RM layer(s) at which a brouter operates?

    A. Layers 5 and 6

    B. Layers 2 and 3

    C. Layers 3 and 4

    D. Layers 1 and 2

Answers to Review Questions

1. **B.** Layer 2, the Data Link layer, prepares data to be placed on a transmission medium such as a cable. Layer 4, the Transport layer, supports end-to-end transmission of packets. Layer 1, the Physical layer, represents the optical or electrical signals on the network media. Layer 6, the Presentation layer, transforms data to a human-readable format such as ASCII or Unicode.

2. **C.** The Network layer, Layer 3, organizes data into packets. Layer 1, the Physical layer, is responsible for transmitting unstructured bit streams on a wire. Layer 7, the Application layer, provides an end user interface to network data. Layer 6, the Presentation layer, is responsible for text transformations.

3. **B.** The OSI/RM describes universal concepts that developers need for creating networking protocols. The OSI/RM also describes how to connect heterogeneous systems, and describes the packet-creation process. The OSI/RM does not deal with network topology design or server design.

4. **A.** The remaining three choices do not exist.

5. **C.** There is no certificate portion to a packet. The header contains OSI/RM layer information used for packet decoding. Data is kept in its own section. The trailer contains error-checking information, including CRCs.

6. **C.** TCP is both routable across WANs, and connection-oriented. SPX is also an example of such a protocol.

7. **B.** Nonroutable protocols use predefined, static routes to connect two computers. You can use nonroutable protocols in a TCP/IP network, but you must encapsulate or tunnel the nonroutable protocol first. Nonroutable protocols need a bridge to span network segments. By definition, nonroutable protocols do not use search for a best path.

8. **D.** UDP does not provide error-correction services. If one or more packets arrive in a damaged state, the computer will simply discard them. For the other three choices, it is important that all packets be received in an undamaged state. Otherwise, the receiving computer cannot assemble the completed files properly.

9. A. IP works at Layer 3, the Network layer, and provides IP address and packet routing services to TCP. TCP is responsible for maintaining the network connection.

10. B. The original purpose of UDP was fast delivery of very short messages. UDP simply discards bad packets, so it is not an error-free delivery method. This makes it inappropriate for e-mail, where all packets in an e-mail message must go through. UDP is well suited for videoconferencing, because occasionally lost packets may not be noticed by the receiving user.

11. B. Address Resolution Protocol performs this function by mapping an IP address to the Media Access Control address of a NIC. ARP is used within a network segment. The Domain Name System maps alphanumeric domain names to numeric IP addresses, and is essentially a WAN function. TCP provides a stable connection between Internet computers. IP provides numeric IP addresses, which are logical addresses. IP must be used with ARP to obtain a physical address.

12. C. SPX is a routable, Layer-4 transport protocol. It is most similar to TCP, which is also a routable transport protocol. IP is a Layer-3 Network protocol. Systems Network Architecture is a mainframe networking system that has similarities to the OSI/RM. An Ethernet network can use the SPX protocol, as well as many other networking protocols.

13. D. NetBIOS is a programming interface that is commonly used in LAN applications. NetBIOS works at the Session layer to identify computers on a LAN. NetBIOS works with NetBEUI and is a protocol used on Microsoft Windows networks. TCP/IP and IPX/SPX networks can also use NetBIOS services.

14. C. This choice correctly traces the path of the packet from the NIC onto a cable, across a router, and to a CSU/DSU. The sequencing in the other choices does not follow the OSI/RM and is incorrect.

15. C. Unicode is a 16-bit, double-byte standard for mapping international text characters. ASCII can handle between 128 and 256 characters, depending upon the version used.

16. C. EBCDIC is an older, Layer 6 standard that maps uppercase characters, numbers, and a few symbols to a numbering scheme.

17. B.   The Data Link Control address is called the Media Access Control address in the IEEE 802.2 networking standards.

18. B.   The packet-creation process allows each layer to add its own information, such as IP address, MAC address, and so forth, to a new piece of the packet header. These headers are read and stripped from the packet at each layer of the receiving computer.

19. B.   E-mail client applications work at the Application layer, Layer 7 of the OSI/RM.

20. B.   A brouter is a combination of a router and a bridge. Thus, it works at the Data Link and Network layers of the OSI/RM, Layers 2 and 3. The bridge function connects two or more network segments at Layer 2. The router function works at Layer 3.

Chapter

5

The TCP/IP Protocol Suite

THE CIW EXAM OBJECTIVE GROUPS COVERED IN THIS CHAPTER:

- ✓ Identify the relationships between IP addresses and domain names, including but not limited to: IP address classes, assignment of IP addresses within a subnet, and domain servers.

- ✓ Identify the functions and components of Web servers, including but not limited to: various server types and related protocols, Internet connectivity, client-side and server-side scripting and applications, business needs and server selection criteria.

- ✓ Identify additional Internet services, including but not limited to: news, FTP, Gopher, Telnet, and network performance utilities such as ping and traceroute.

In the previous chapters, we have discussed computer networking in a general sense. Networks consist of three elements. The first are the *network services*, which are the shared resources on the network, such as servers and printers. The second elements are the *transmission media*, such as cables and wireless, that carry the network signal to each computer with the assistance of networking hardware like NICs, routers and hubs. The third are the *networking protocols* that provide the rules and standards for network communications.

We have already discussed a few important Internet protocols, such as TCP/IP, HTTP, and others. Starting with this chapter, we will focus on the TCP/IP protocol suite, and how it supports the Internet applications we will study later in this book.

Since its implementation in 1983 by the major networks that made up the Internet, TCP/IP has far exceeded the expectations of its designers. Today, TCP/IP is the most widely used networking protocol suite in the world and is the *de facto* language of communication on the Internet.

The networking protocols themselves are often defined in Request for Comments documents, which will be our first topic of discussion. We will also discuss how TCP/IP protocols are developed and approved for use on the Internet.

We will then introduce and discuss the Internet architecture, a framework that builds upon the OSI/RM (we discussed in the last chapter) to help us categorize and map the common protocols used on the Internet. We will also cover IP addressing in detail, including the various address classes and how they are assigned. The chapter will conclude with a discussion of diagnostic tools used to troubleshoot TCP/IP networks, including command-line utilities and network analyzers.

Requests for Comments (RFCs)

*R*equests for Comments (RFCs) are published documents of interest to the Internet community. They include detailed information about standardized Internet protocols, such as IP and TCP, as well as those in various stages of development. They also include informational documents regarding protocol standards, assigned numbers (also called port numbers), host requirements (such as Data Link, Network, Transport and Application OSI layers), and router requirements.

RFCs are written by the individuals or organizations that are presenting the proposed topics. In the early days of the Internet, many RFCs were written by researchers, university employees, and government contractors involved in the development of the ARPANET. In recent years, more RFCs have been developed by committees.

Authors file RFCs with the *Internet Engineering Task Force (IETF)*, an organization of network designers, operators, vendors, and researchers concerned with the evolution of the Internet architecture and the smooth operation of the Internet. IETF membership is open to any interested individual. You can examine their website at www.ietf.org.

RFCs are identified by their number, which is assigned by the IETF's RFC editor, as each RFC is received. RFCs with the highest numbers were created most recently. You should make sure you are viewing the most recent RFC number when researching a particular topic. Two recommended RFC reference sites are located at www.rfc-editor.org/rfc.html and www.ietf.org/rfc.html. If an RFC has been updated, the index listing in the RFC editor query results will state the replacement RFC number.

You can read a detailed description of the IETF and associated organizations in RFC 3160, located at www.ietf.org/rfc/rfc3160.txt.

Protocol States

Before a protocol becomes a standard, it passes through several maturity level states: *experimental*, *proposed*, *draft*, and *standard*. If a protocol becomes obsolete, it is classified as *historic*. To progress through the steps, the protocol must be recommended by the Internet Engineering Steering

Group (IESG) of the IETF. There are four major levels of maturity for protocols:

Experimental   These are protocols that should only be used in laboratory situations. They are not intended for operation on systems other than those participating in the experiment. An important reason for this is that experimental protocols may interfere with draft and standard protocols that are in use on the Internet.

Proposed   These are protocols that may be considered for future standardization. The IETF encourages testing and research by several different groups of researchers, to help identify and resolve potential issues.

Draft   These protocols are being seriously considered by the IESG as potential Internet standards. Wide-scale testing is encouraged. Several parties analyze test results. Changes are often made at the draft stage; the protocol must then return to the proposed stage.

Internet standards   These are protocols determined by the IESG to be official standard protocols on the Internet. Standard protocols are of two types: those that apply to the entire Internet, and those that apply only to certain networks. Standard protocols are also called *full standards*.

Authors who submit an RFC at one of these last three levels are essentially relinquishing control of their protocol to the IETF and the appropriate working groups. *Working groups* are committees of technical experts who discuss and refine proposed, draft, and full standards. Working groups do most of their discussion on mailing lists, which we will discuss in the next chapter. Any interested individual may join and contribute to a working group.

A proposed protocol may be completely revised by a working group by the time it becomes an Internet protocol.

There are two additional protocol states that are designated in special situations; added to the above list, these protocol states describe the six different kinds of RFCs:

Historic   These are protocols that have been replaced by more recent ones or that never received enough interest to develop. Historic protocols are highly unlikely to become Internet standards.

Informational   These are protocols developed outside of the IETF/IESG, including protocols developed by vendors or by other standardization organizations. These protocols are posted for the benefit of the Internet community.

Internet Architecture

We now turn our attention to the *Internet architecture*. Similar to other networking models, the Internet architecture divides protocols into layers. Each layer of the Internet architecture is responsible for specific communication tasks. The Internet architecture consists of four layers. Each of the four Internet architecture layers coincides with one or two layers in the Open Systems Interconnection reference model (OSI/RM) that we discussed in Chapter 4.

The Internet architecture provides a reference to the internal workings of the Internet and TCPI/IP networks. As noted, the Internet architecture often combines the functions of two OSI/RM layers, usually when networking hardware or protocols can provide the appropriate support. This Internet architecture also provides guidance on connecting TCP/IP networks to other kinds of computer networks. Thus, our focus now shifts to how the Internet can be connected to other computer networks, and vice versa.

Figure 5.1 illustrates the Internet architecture, and Table 5.1 displays the OSI/RM and the Internet architecture equivalents.

TABLE 5.1 Internet Architecture Layers and the Corresponding OSI Reference Model Layers

Internet Architecture Layer	OSI/RM Layer
Application	7: Application 6: Presentation
Transport	5: Session 4: Transport
Internet	3: Network
Network Access	2: Data Link 1: Physical

In the next sections, we will present each of these four layers and discuss how each layer of the Internet architecture is related to the corresponding parts of the OSI/RM.

Application Layer

The *Application layer* of the Internet architecture corresponds to the Application and Presentation layers, Layers 7 and 6 of the OSI reference model. The Application layer incorporates the functionality of the Internet client, including the application programs and operating system, which presents data that the user has requested.

The Application layer of the Internet architecture is also called the *Process layer*.

The following protocols are used at the Application layer of the Internet architecture. Some of these protocols were introduced in Chapter 2; we are discussing these protocols again in this chapter so that you understand their relation to the OSI/RM. We'll also discover some new protocols in this section.

Hypertext Transfer Protocol (HTTP)   HTTP is used to transport HTML documents (web pages) across the Internet. HTTP 1.0 establishes a new protocol connection for each page requested, which creates unnecessary Internet traffic. HTTP 1.1 uses persistent connections, which allow multiple downloads with one connection. Both the client and the server must support HTTP 1.1 to benefit. Chapter 9 has an extensive discussion on how to use web browsers. HTTP is defined in RFCs 1945 and 2616.

File Transfer Protocol (FTP)   FTP is a system for transferring files between computers on a TCP/IP network. In Chapter 10, we will show you how to use command-line and graphical FTP clients. FTP is specified in RFC 959.

Telnet   Telnet is a terminal emulation protocol that allows a user at one site to log on and run programs from a remote system. We will demonstrate this in Chapter 10. Telnet is specified in RFC 855.

Network News Transfer Protocol (NNTP)   NNTP allows sites on the Internet to exchange Usenet news articles, which are organized into topic areas such as "Programming in C++" or "international trade issues." To use newsgroups, you must have access to an NNTP server with which you are authorized to read and post news. NNTP is specified in RFC 977.

Gopher   Gopher is a menu-based program used to find resources on the Internet. It is very similar in concept and practice to today's Web. Users follow links from site to site in search of information. It was one of the first tools developed to pull the Internet together so users could access the entire Internet rather than just one site. Web servers have largely replaced Gopher servers. Gopher is specified in RFC 1436.

Simple Mail Transfer Protocol (SMTP)   SMTP is the Internet standard protocol for transferring e-mail messages from one computer to another. It specifies how two mail systems interact. SMTP is often used with Post Office Protocol version 3 (POP3), which is a standard Internet mail service that uses the SMTP messaging protocol. POP3 stores incoming e-mail until users authenticate and download it. POP3 is defined in RFC 1939 and STD 53. SMTP is specified in RFC 821. POP3 is not considered part of the TCP/IP suite, but is integral to e-mail usage.

Domain Name System (DNS)   DNS is a mechanism used on the Internet to translate host computer names into Internet (IP) addresses. It is one of the most universal methods of centralized name resolution. For example, when a user requests the Fully Qualified Domain Name (FQDN), www.companyname.com, DNS servers translate the name into the IP address 201.198.25.108. DNS is defined in RFCs 1034 and 1035.

Trivial File Transfer Protocol (TFTP)   *TFTP* is used for initializing diskless systems. It works with the BOOTstrap (BOOTP) protocol. TFTP uses UDP, whereas FTP uses TCP. Because TFTP is simple and small, it can be embedded in read-only memory (ROM), which is ideal for diskless workstations or routers seeking configurations upon initialization. TFTP is specified in RFC 1350.

Simple Network Management Protocol (SNMP)   *SNMP* is used for managing TCP/IP networks. It is a standardized management scheme that vendors can support. Thus, an SNMP manager can centrally manage all SNMP-compliant network devices. SNMP also offers low resource requirements, portability, and wide acceptance. SNMP is specified in RFC 1157.

BOOTstrap Protocol (BOOTP) *BOOTP* is an alternative to RARP, an Internet layer protocol we will discuss shortly. BOOTP provides a method for diskless workstations and X terminals to determine their IP addresses. A single BOOTP message specifies many items needed at startup, including the diskless machine's IP address, the address of a gateway (router), and the address of a particular server (such as a DNS server). BOOTP is specified in RFC 951.

Dynamic Host Configuration Protocol (DHCP) *DHCP* is based on BOOTP. It is designed to assign Internet addresses to nodes on a TCP/IP network during initialization. It can also assign the address of a gateway (router) and the address of a particular server. Like BOOTP, it saves administrators a great deal of time because client systems do not require manual TCP/IP configuration. DHCP is defined in RFC 2131.

Transport Layer

The *Transport layer* of the Internet architecture corresponds to the Session and Transport layers, the fifth and fourth layers of the OSI model. In the previous chapter, we noted that the Session layer is not implemented in many networking models. Indeed, in the TCP/IP suite, the Application layer initiates sessions and connections.

The Transport layer of the Internet architecture is also known as the *host-to-host layer*, the *end-to-end layer*, or the *source-to-destination layer*.

The Transport layer accepts Application-layer data and requests, and provides the flow of information between two hosts using two different transport protocols that we discussed in the previous chapter:

Transmission Control Protocol (TCP) TCP provides session management between the source and destination systems. It ensures that data is delivered, that it is in sequence, and that no duplicate data is sent. Two machines must contact each other through a TCP connection before transferring data (i.e., a session must be established). TCP is defined in RFC 793.

User Datagram Protocol (UDP) UDP provides a simple datagram form of communication. One UDP packet is created for each output operation by an application, and a session is not necessary. UDP does not provide congestion control, use acknowledgments, retransmit lost datagrams, or guarantee reliability. UDP is defined in RFC 768.

The Transport layer also divides the data received from the Application layer into smaller pieces, called packets. Each packet is passed to the next layer of the Internet architecture, the Internet layer.

Internet Layer

The *Internet layer* of the Internet architecture corresponds to the Network layer, Layer 3 of the OSI/RM. A data packet received from the Transport layer is encapsulated in an IP packet, and given an IP header and trailer.

The Internet layer is also responsible for addressing and routing packets on TCP/IP networks. Based on the destination host information in the IP header, the Internet layer uses a routing algorithm to determine whether to deliver the packet locally or send it to a default gateway.

The following protocols are used at the Internet layer of the Internet architecture.

Internet Protocol (IP)   IP is the basic data-transfer method used throughout the Internet. It is responsible for IP addressing, and performs the routing function, which selects a path to send data to the destination IP address. IP is defined in RFC 791.

Address Resolution Protocol (ARP)   ARP translates Internet addresses to physical addresses. For instance, it uses your IP address to discover your computer's Ethernet address. ARP is specified in RFC 826.

Internet Control Message Protocol (ICMP)   *ICMP* is the troubleshooting protocol of TCP/IP. It allows Internet hosts and gateways to report errors through ICMP messages that are sent to network users. If a problem occurs on a TCP/IP network, an ICMP message will probably be generated. ICMP is specified in RFC 792.

Internet Group Management Protocol (IGMP)   *IGMP* is used for multicasting, in which one source sends a message to a group of subscribers who belong to a multicast group. A multicast group can receive the same data, such as the same e-mail message on a mailing list or a videoconference. For multicast delivery to be successful, members must identify themselves; this is usually handled by client applications. IGMP is defined in RFC 1112.

Reverse Address Resolution Protocol (RARP)   *RARP* performs the reverse function of ARP. It uses a node's hardware address to request an IP address. RARP is generally used for diskless workstations and X terminals. RARP is defined in RFC 903.

Figure 5.1 illustrates the relationships of all the Internet protocols within the Internet architecture.

FIGURE 5.1   Internet protocols and Internet architecture

HTTP	FTP	Telnet	NNTP	Gopher
SMTP	SNMP	DNS	BOOTP	DHCP
Application Layer				
TCP		UDP		
Transport Layer				
ICMP	IP	IGMP		
ARP		RARP		
Internet Layer				
Media				
Network Access Layer				

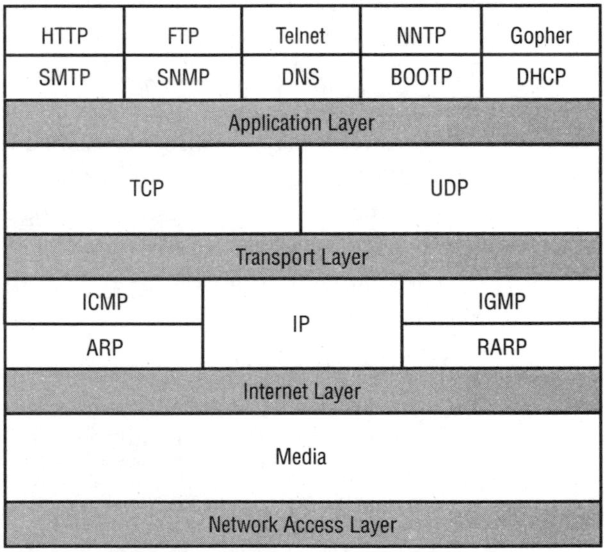

Network Access Layer

The *Network Access layer* of the Internet architecture corresponds to the Physical and Data Link layers, the first and second layers, of the OSI reference model. The Network Access layer accepts the higher-layer packets and transmits them over the attached network, handling all the hardware details of placing the information on the network media.

This layer usually consists of the following three elements:

- The operating system's device driver

- The corresponding network interface card (NIC)

- The physical connections

The contents of the Network Access layer can vary considerably, depending on which technologies are responsible for placing data on the network media and pulling data off the media. For instance, a dial-up connection would use modems and telephone lines to connect a computer to the Internet. A direct connection might use a cable modem and cable television lines. A LAN connection may involve a NIC and twisted-pair cable.

Examples of network access layer technologies include:

Local area networks (LANs)   Ethernet, token ring, and FDDI.

Wide area networks (WANs)   Frame relay, serial lines (T1, E1, and others), and ATM.

Demultiplexing

In the previous chapter, we mentioned that when the receiving computer receives a packet, it strips off the headers and trailers at each OSI/RM layer. *Demultiplexing* is the technical term for this process.

Figure 5.2 illustrates the demultiplexing process. Notice that this diagram resembles a flow chart. Each packet encapsulates a certain type of data generated by an application on the client. The data itself is contained within a protocol that supports the actual transmission of that data using IP and the Ethernet. The receiving computer moves through the flow chart from bottom to top to decode and check the data before it is processed by the proper application.

FIGURE 5.2   Demultiplexing of protocols

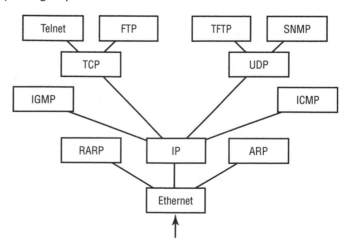

Routing

Now that we have discussed the Internet architecture and the IP packet creation process, we will cover how packets are sent over the Internet. *Routing* is an extremely important function of IP. It is the process of choosing a network path over which to send packets. The device that performs this task is called a *router*, which forwards packets from one physical network to another. Your knowledge of IP will enable you to see the correlation between IP and routing.

The Internet layer, or OSI/RM Network layer (Layer 3), performs the routing function. A packet, or datagram, carries sufficient information for routing from the originating host to the destination host using the IP address. Packets may traverse several networks before reaching their destination host.

Packets are routed transparently, but not necessarily reliably, to the destination host. The term "transparent," when applied to routing, means that after the routing hardware and software are installed, changes are undetectable by users because the routing process is largely automated along the network. The complexity of routing is not visible to the user. The Transport or Application layer is responsible for reliability, which ensures that the data arrives in a readable state at the receiving end.

The routing process is not totally reliable, however. Because routing is performed on the network, several nodes receive and pass along the packet on its journey. It is possible that one of these nodes may misdirect the packet.

Recall that the Transport layer is responsible for managing the network connection. If TCP is being used, TCP will request a replacement packet if the original packet contains errors or is not received. If UDP is the transport protocol, it will not request a replacement packet, and the application will continue processing without that packet's data.

Routing can be divided into two general classifications: direct and indirect. The type of routing that is performed depends on the proximity of the two nodes to each other.

Direct routing   If two computers on the same physical network need to communicate, the packets do not require a router. The computers are considered to be on the same local network. In an IEEE 802.3/Ethernet TCP/IP network, the sending entity encapsulates the packet in an Ethernet frame, binds the destination Internet address to an Ethernet address, and transmits the resulting frame directly to its destination. This process is referred to as *direct routing*. The Address Resolution Protocol (ARP) is an example of a direct routing protocol.

The destination system is on the same physical network if the network portions of the source and destination addresses are the same. We will discuss how to determine the network portions of IP addresses later in this chapter.

Indirect routing   If two computers that are not on the same physical network need to communicate, they must send the IP packet to a router for delivery. Whenever a router is involved in communication, the activity is considered *indirect routing*. As you might guess, indirect routing is essential for communications across the Internet.

The Routing Process

Routing involves the following two key elements.

- The host must know which router to use for a given destination; the router is determined by the default gateway. The *default gateway* is the IP address of the router on your local network; this router will route the packet to the destination network.

- The router must know where to send the packet; the destination is determined by the router's routing information table.

A *routing information table* is a database maintained by a router. The table contains the location of all networks in relation to the router's location. When a packet arrives at the router, the router examines the packet's destination network, then checks its own routing information table. It determines the next router to which to send the packet, and forwards the packet to that router. This part of the journey is considered a *hop*.

In some cases, the destination network is attached to the router, in which case the packet has reached its destination network. Figure 5.3 illustrates a simplified routing table so you can understand the basic process.

FIGURE 5.3 A simple routing information table

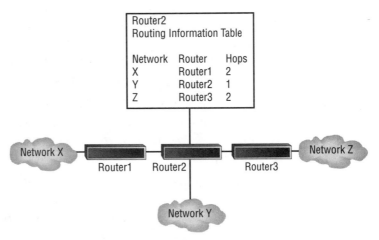

Static vs. Dynamic Routing

There are two methods routers can use for storing routing information tables: static and dynamic. *Static routers* contain routing information tables that must be built and updated manually. If a certain route does not exist in the static routing table, the router will be unable to communicate with that network. Static routers are often used within network segments, in situations where the network nodes are permanently installed and always operating—for example, a server room.

A *dynamic router* communicates with other dynamic routers to calculate routes automatically using routing protocols such as RIP (Routing Information Protocol) and OSPF (Open Shortest Path First), which we'll discuss shortly. Dynamic routers can exchange information about routes of known networks. When a route changes, the routers automatically update themselves by recalculating routes.

The convenience of dynamic routing comes at a price. Static routers are usually less expensive than dynamic routers. This is the main reason why some network administrators continue to use static routers. Once a network administrator learns how to program a routing information table, she can manually add any needed updates. If the network size becomes too large for the administrator to manage, dynamic routers should be considered to help reduce the maintenance time required.

Routing Protocols

At the beginning of the routing section, routing was defined as the process of selecting a path on which data will travel across networks. Routing also includes *routing protocols*, which determine how routers share information and how they report routing table changes to each other. Routing protocols enable networks to dynamically change without the need to enter static routing table entries for each adjustment.

There are the two basic types of routing protocols: exterior and interior.

Exterior routing protocols This approach is used for routing packets outside an organization's network. External Gateway Protocol (EGP) and Border Gateway Protocol (BGP) are examples of such protocols. These protocols can tell ISPs which routes you know your network can use to send external packets. We will not cover exterior routing protocols in this book, because such a discussion would also cover the actual installation and configuration of routers on a high-speed network. These topics require a deep knowledge of TCP/IP and network configuration.

Exterior Routing Protocols are part of the knowledge base tested in the Server Administration and Internetworking CIW exams.

Interior routing protocols This approach is used for routing packets within an organization's network. Examples of interior routing protocols are RIP and OSPF.

Routing Information Protocol (RIP)

The *Routing Information Protocol (RIP)* is commonly implemented on small to medium-sized LANs. RIP maintains only the best route to a destination. Old route information is replaced by new route information, causing network topology changes that are reflected in routing update messages. Routing update messages cause routers to exchange their tables and propagate the changes.

Two versions of RIP are currently used: RIPv1 (RFC 1058) and RIPv2 (RFC 2453). Because RIP requires routers to exchange their entire tables, RIP is somewhat inefficient and slow. Another disadvantage of RIP is that routes are selected on the basis of the closest path (fewest hops) between the source system and the destination system. No emphasis is placed on factors such as available bandwidth, multiple connections, or security. As the Internet continues to grow, RIP is gradually being replaced by a newer protocol, Open Shortest Path First.

Open Shortest Path First (OSPF)

The *Open Shortest Path First (OSPF)* routing protocol is an interior gateway routing protocol that overcomes many of RIP's shortcomings. OSPFv2 (RFC 2328) has recently become an Internet standard protocol. OSPF contains several practical features that help making routing faster and more reliable:

Routing table updates   Updates take place when necessary, rather than at regular intervals. This irregular frequency reduces traffic on the network and saves bandwidth.

Various types of service routing   OSPF makes it possible to install multiple routes to a given destination. Each route can be defined on the basis of a service, such as high bit rate and/or security.

Load balancing   If multiple routes exist to a given destination and all routes cost the same, OSPF distributes traffic evenly over all routes.

Network areas   OSPF provides the ability to partition a network into areas, allowing growth and organization. Each area's internal topology is hidden from other areas.

Authenticated exchanges   All exchanges between routers using the OSPF protocol are authenticated through the use of various authentication schemes. This arrangement is important because only trusted systems should propagate routing information.

Defined route support   OSPF allows the definition of host-specific or network-specific routes.

OSPF requires powerful routers with fast CPUs to make the required computations. While upgrading routers to OSPF from RIP can be expensive, the payoff in operating a faster network can be worth the investment.

Port Numbers

Once an IP packet has arrived at the destination host using the IP address, the packet is passed to the Transport layer of the Internet architecture. The Transport layer determines which service the packet is using by examining the packet's destination *port number*.

TCP and UDP protocol headers contain both source and destination port numbers. These port numbers are addresses by which Internet processes can be identified. Port numbers are an essential part of Internet computing, as several communication processes may be running simultaneously at any particular moment in an Internet session. For example, a client may be looking up a domain name while sending an e-mail message.

Each service or application, such as the Web and e-mail, use specific port numbers (see Table 5.2).

TABLE 5.2   Port Assignments for Popular Internet Protocols

Port Number	Assigned Protocols
21	FTP
25	SMTP
53	DNS
69	TFTP
70	Gopher
80	HTTP
110	POP3
213	IPX
143	IMAP4

To view many of the services and the ports associated with them, examine www.iana.org/assignments/port-numbers.

The port numbers themselves are grouped into two categories: reserved and registered port numbers. Table 5.3 lists the standard port assignments. These *well-known port numbers*, also called *reserved port numbers*, range from 1 to 1023 and are controlled by the Internet Corporation for Assigned Names and Numbers (ICANN). Well-known port numbers are used by TCP and UDP to identify well-known services that a host can provide.

The ICANN does not control *registered port numbers*. These port numbers range from 1024 to 65535 and are considered non-privileged. Therefore, any process can use them.

TABLE 5.3 Port Assignments in Internet Domain

Port Number Range	Description
1 to 1023	Well-known (reserved) port numbers
1024 to 65535	Registered port numbers

Ephemeral (short-lived or transitional) port numbers are unique port numbers typically assigned to client processes. The server process determines the ephemeral port number from the TCP or UDP header, and thereby knows the process with which to communicate at the remote system.

Internet Addressing

As we learned earlier, to ensure that each user on the Internet has a unique IP address, a central authority called the Internet Corporation for Assigned Names and Numbers (ICANN) issues all Internet addresses. The previous controlling organization, the IANA, was funded and overseen by the U.S. government. The ICANN is a private, non-governmental organization that performs the same tasks, such as Internet address space allocation.

To learn more about the ICANN, visit www.icann.org.

Most Internet addresses contain the *network* portion and the *host* portion. The network portion precedes the host portion:

```
network portion, host portion
```

Internet addresses are specified by four fields, separated by periods, which we discussed in Chapter 2:

`field1.field2.field3.field4`

Each field represents one byte of data. Each field has a value ranging from 0 to 255, as demonstrated by the following Internet address:

`208.157.25.111`

In this example, the network portion is 208.157.24, and the host portion is 111. To help distinguish the network portion from the host portion, Internet addresses are divided into classes, which are described in the next section.

Internet Address Classes

Without a classification system, the 3,720,314,628 possible Internet addresses would have no structure. To provide structure, IP addresses are categorized into classes. Classes can be determined by looking at the first byte of an Internet address.

Internet addresses are divided into five classes: A, B, C, D, and E. The IP address range for each class is shown in Table 5.4. The characteristics of each class are detailed in this section.

TABLE 5.4   IP Address Classes

Address class	IP address range
Class A	0.0.0.0 to 127.255.255.255
Class B	128.0.0.0 to 191.255.255.255
Class C	192.0.0.0 to 223.255.255.255
Class D	224.0.0.0 to 239.255.255.255
Class E	240.0.0.0 to 247.255.255.255

Class A

Class A addresses typically use the first byte for the network portion and the last three bytes for the host portion. Class A addresses range from 0.0.0.0 to 127.255.255.255.

The first byte can range from 1 to 126 (0 is a special case source address and 127 is a reserved loopback address, as you will discover later in this chapter). They provide the potential for 126 networks with 16,777,214 hosts each.

The following is an example of a Class A address (the first byte is the network address):

121.1.1.32

Class B

Class B addresses typically use the first two bytes for the network portion and the last two bytes for the host portion. Class B addresses range from 128.0.0.0 to 191.255.255.255.

The first byte can range from 128 to 191. Class B addresses provide the potential for 16,384 networks with up to 65,534 hosts each.

The following is an example of a Class B address (the first two bytes are the network address):

168.100.1.32

Class C

Class C addresses typically use the first three bytes for the network portion and the last byte for the host portion. Class C addresses range from 192.0.0.0 to 223.255.255.255.

The first byte can range from 192 to 223. Class C addresses provide the potential for 2,097,152 networks with up to 254 hosts each.

The following is an example of a Class C address (the first three bytes are the network address):

205.96.225.32

Class D

Class D addresses support multicasting. With multicasting, a packet is targeted to a group that is identified by a network address only. No host portion exists in the address. The first byte can range from 224 to 239. The following is an example of a Class D address (all four bytes are the network address):

230.5.125.62

Class E

Class E addresses are reserved for future use. The first byte can range from 240 to 247.

IP Addressing Rules

Internet addresses must follow several guidelines to function properly. Although you have learned about the ranges of class A, B, and C addresses, not all addresses within these ranges can be used. This section describes the exceptions.

Loopback Address

The *loopback* address 127 cannot be used as an Internet address. This address allows a client and server on the same host to communicate with each other. The loopback address is used for testing and troubleshooting a computer's Internet connection. For example, if your computer hosts a web server and you enter **http://127.0.0.1** in your web browser's address field (as a client), you will access your website. The loopback address can also be used to test local TCP/IP functionality by using the ping utility.

For UNIX and Windows NT/2000 systems, the loopback address is listed in the *hosts* file, and is typically the IP address 127.0.0.1 with the assigned name *localhost*.

Broadcast Address

Broadcast addresses send messages to all network hosts, and are used only as destination addresses. The network and/or host IP address portions cannot be the broadcast address 255, which is also represented as a number of all binary ones. There are four types of broadcast addresses:

Limited broadcast   (255.255.255.255) Used for configuring hosts when they start up. For example, a computer without an IP address can broadcast this address to obtain an IP address (i.e., from a DHCP or BOOTP server).

Net-directed broadcast   (netid.255.255.255) Used to broadcast to all hosts in a network. For example, if the network portion of your IP address is 192.35.200 and the host portion is 12, your computer can broadcast messages to all network hosts by using the destination address 192.35.200.255.

Subnet-directed broadcast   If a network is divided into several subnets, a broadcast can be limited to the hosts within a subnet. You will learn about subnets later in this chapter.

All-subnets-directed broadcast   If a network is divided into several subnets, a broadcast can be sent to all hosts within all network subnets. This type of broadcast has become obsolete; multicasting using Class D addresses is the preferred method.

Network and Special-Case Source Addresses

The network and/or host IP address portions can contain zeros, but they cannot be entirely zeros. For instance, the Class C address 198.168.3.0 is a network addresses, and cannot be assigned to a node.

The special-case source IP address of a computer is all zeros (0.0.0.0) when it initializes and requests an IP address (e.g., from a DHCP or BOOTP server). Although the computer broadcasts the request for the IP address, its source address is initially 0.0.0.0, until it is assigned a network IP address. The special-case source address can also specify a host on the network during initialization. For instance, the network portion of a Class C address can be all zeros, and the host portion can be 11, which is 0.0.0.11. These addresses cannot be used as valid IP addresses for a node.

Reserved IP Addressing

As we mentioned earlier, IPv4 supports about 4 billion addresses. A typical LAN has access to only a small range of IP addresses, because ISPs usually allocate IP addresses to LANs in small ranges or blocks. A web server that is open to the public, for example, will need a dedicated or static IP address that is linked to a domain name. But users at individual workstations usually do not need a static IP address, especially if they are only using Internet services.

Fortunately, there is a way to create internal IP addresses within a network to expand the number of network computers that can connect to the Internet. This method is called reserved IP addressing.

The ICANN has reserved the following three blocks of the IP address space for private networks, as defined in RFC 1918:

- 10.0.0.0 through 10.255.255.255.

- 172.16.0.0 through 172.31.255.255.

- 192.168.0.0 through 192.168.255.255.

Most Internet users who use dial-up access or use the Internet at an office computer are assigned one of the private IP addresses by their network.

These private network addresses have no global meaning. Therefore, Internet routers are expected to reject (filter out) routing information about them. The rejection will not be treated as a routing protocol error. The benefits of using private network addresses include:

- Conservation of globally unique IP addresses when global uniqueness is not required.

- More flexibility in enterprise design because of large address space.

- Prevention of IP-address clashes when an enterprise gains Internet connectivity without receiving addresses from the ICANN.

If your company merges with another and all hosts use private network addresses, you will probably have to combine several private Internets into one. Addresses within the combined private Internet may not be unique, and you will have to renumber hosts to accommodate identical IP addresses.

Subnet Masks

A *subnet mask*, also called a *net mask*, is a 32-bit number (similar to an IP address) with a one-to-one correspondence between each of the 32 bits in the Internet address.

Subnet masks serve two main purposes:

- Distinguish the network and host portions of an IP address.

- Specify whether a destination address is local or remote.

First, the subnet mask distinguishes network and host portions of an IP address. Because the system does not know which bits in the host field should be interpreted as the subnetwork part of the Internet address, it refers to the subnet mask. The subnet mask tells the system which bits of the Internet address should be interpreted as the network, subnetwork, and host addresses.

The simplest type of subnet mask is the default subnet mask. By default, each 8-bit field is turned on (255—all binary ones) or off (0—all binary zeros), depending on the address class (A, B or C).

The following list identifies the default subnet masks for Class A, B, and C addresses:

Class	Default Subnet Mask
A	255.0.0.0
B	255.255.0.0
C	255.255.255.0

Class D and E addresses do not have hosts, and therefore do not require subnet masks.

Subnet masks also specify whether a destination address is local or remote. Note that the subnet mask is used to "mask" the network address, so only the host address remains. In routing, this masking is extremely important. It allows a computer to determine whether a destination address is intended for a computer on the same (local) network, or a different (remote) one.

If the destination address is on the same network, the information can be transmitted locally. If the destination address is on a different network, the information must be sent to a router, which can locate the remote network.

Normal TCP/IP Desktop Configurations

The following list contains the normal configuration parameters for a workstation on a TCP/IP network. A network host must have at least an IP address and a subnet mask to communicate on a network. WAN communication requires at least an IP address, a subnet mask, and a default gateway.

Basic Configurations

The following items are used by client computers that connect to the Internet on a dialup, direct, hybrid, or wireless connection.

IP address   The 32-bit IP address that is unique to your workstation on the network. If you enter the IP address manually, it is considered a static IP address.

Subnet mask   The 32-bit number used to distinguish the network and host portions of your IP address; also used to calculate whether a destination address is local or remote.

Default gateway   If your computer calculates that a destination address is remote, your computer will send the packet to the default gateway, which is a local computer's IP address (usually a router). The router will send the packet to the remote network.

DHCP client   If you are a DHCP client, your TCP/IP configurations will automatically be sent to your computer when you initialize your system, which is the easiest way to configure clients on a network. Obtaining an IP address from a DHCP server is the alternative to entering a static IP address.

Name Resolution Configurations

You can also configure your computer to use name resolution systems, including DNS, WINS, or both.

Host name   If you use DNS, you must specify the name of your computer, which is the host name. Your computer will be identified by this name (e.g., *student11*) on the network.

Domain name   If you use DNS, you need to specify the domain name (e.g., yourcompany.com) to which your computer belongs.

DNS server   If you use DNS, you need to identify the DNS servers that will provide you with the DNS service.

NetBIOS name   On a Windows network, this name is the "computer name" of a Windows machine. Microsoft Windows uses NetBIOS names for computer identification on a network.

WINS server   The Windows Internet Naming Service (WINS) is a Microsoft name resolution protocol that maps NetBIOS names (instead of host names) to IP addresses. If your network uses WINS, you must identify the WINS servers that will provide you with WINS. WINS uses the NetBIOS name of your computer.

Dynamic Host Configuration Protocol (DHCP)

DHCP is a protocol that assigns IP addresses automatically on a TCP/IP network. Because DHCP automatically assigns IP addresses, it has become a central part of large enterprise LANs and WANs. DHCP can save a great deal of time because IT personnel are not required to manually configure each computer on the network.

DHCP assigns more than just an IP address, subnet mask, and default gateway. It can also assign DNS server information, WINS server information, and almost any other TCP/IP configurations needed by network clients.

With DHCP, a client system receives its TCP/IP configurations automatically at startup. DHCP assigns these configurations on a lease basis. The lease contains all of the TCP/IP configurations for a system. For instance, the leased IP address your computer receives may expire after 24 hours. After the address expires, it can be leased to another computer on the network or renewed by the same computer. If the client system is removed from one network and connected to another, it will automatically relinquish its old lease and be assigned a new one when it's connected to the new network.

In Windows 95/98/Me, you can release and renew your DHCP TCP/IP configurations by selecting the Start menu, choosing Run, and then entering **winipcfg** in the Open field. The IP configuration window will appear, as shown in Figure 5.4.

FIGURE 5.4   Releasing and renewing DHCP leases

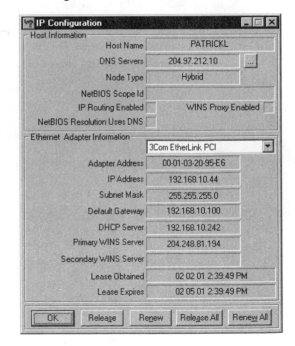

To release the current DHCP configuration, click the Release button. To renew your DHCP configurations, click the Renew button. Your lease will either be renewed, or you will receive a new lease that contains a different IP address.

The DHCP server has a pool of IP addresses that it can assign to network computers. The DHCP server then distributes those addresses to the network computers. The range of addresses could be private IP addresses, or addresses assigned to the company from an ISP.

Diagnostic Tools for Internet Troubleshooting

Now that you are familiar with IP addresses, you can learn how certain diagnostic tools use IP addresses to discover information within a TCP/IP network. This section will introduce tools that are used on a regular basis by system administrators to troubleshoot TCP/IP networks:

- ping
- tracert
- netstat
- ipconfig
- winipcfg
- arp
- network analyzers

The *ping* Command

The *ping* utility (Packet Internet Groper) tests connectivity between source and destination systems, by sending a small number of packets using ICMP. The ping command can then obtain and display the status and round trip time necessary for each packet. The ping command is a helpful diagnostic tool. Users can ping another computer to determine if their Internet connection is functioning or if the other computer is available.

The command syntax of ping is as follows:

`ping ip_address`

In this format, `ip_address` identifies the remote system. Options will vary depending on the operating system.

Using Windows, open the command prompt and enter the following:

`ping 192.168.3.13`

This command yields the following result:

```
Pinging 192.168.3.13 with 32 bytes of data:
Reply from 192.168.3.13: bytes=32 time<10ms TTL=64
Reply from 192.168.3.13: bytes=32 time<10ms TTL=64
Reply from 192.168.3.13: bytes=32 time<10ms TTL=64
Reply from 192.168.3.13: bytes=32 time<10ms TTL=64
```

Because a reply was received, a connection exists between your computer and the computer at IP address 192.168.3.13. To stop `ping` replies at any time, simultaneously press the Ctrl and C keys. The `ping` command is not always reliable because some Internet computers are configured to ignore ICMP packets. For example, Microsoft has disabled ICMP on several of its public Internet servers, such as `microsoft.com` and `www.microsoft.com`. This is because users often selected these domain names as ping targets.

Also, ping cannot deliver a step-by-step description of a packet's progress. (We will discuss the `tracert` command shortly, which can provide such information.)

EXERCISE 5.1

Testing Connectivity Using the *ping* Command

In this exercise, you will use the `ping` command to test connectivity between your computer and other computers on the network.

1. From the Desktop, Select Start ➢ Programs ➢ Accessories ➢ MS-DOS Prompt.

2. Test your own TCP/IP configurations by pinging the loopback address by entering the following at the MS-DOS prompt:

   `ping 127.0.0.1`

3. You should receive a successful reply, like this:

```
MS-DOS Prompt                                                    _ □ ×

Auto        ▼   [ ] 🗐 🗐  🔲  🗐🗐  A

C:\WINDOWS>ping 127.0.0.1

Pinging 127.0.0.1 with 32 bytes of data:

Reply from 127.0.0.1: bytes=32 time<10ms TTL=128
Reply from 127.0.0.1: bytes=32 time<10ms TTL=128
Reply from 127.0.0.1: bytes=32 time<10ms TTL=128
Reply from 127.0.0.1: bytes=32 time<10ms TTL=128

Ping statistics for 127.0.0.1:
    Packets: Sent = 4, Received = 4, Lost = 0 (0% loss),
Approximate round trip times in milli-seconds:
    Minimum = 0ms, Maximum =  0ms, Average =  0ms

C:\WINDOWS>
```

4. Test connectivity with another computer by pinging that computer's IP address. For instance, if the IP address is 192.168.3.7, enter:

ping 192.168.3.7

5. You should receive a successful reply.

Important: If your computer is configured with a different subnet mask than the other computers on the network, you will be unable to ping or communicate with them. However, the loopback ping will succeed, because it is testing only your local system.

6. Close the MS-DOS prompt.

The *tracert* Command

The trace route utility can determine the path between the source and destination systems. This command also provides information on round-trip propagation time between each router and the source system.

The command syntax for Windows is as follows:

`tracert ip_address`

In this example, `ip_address` identifies the remote system.

UNIX and Linux systems use the `traceroute` command, which provides similar information to `tracert`.

Sometimes network problems located far from your local network can compromise your network's performance. For example, if a company router or gateway fails, your Internet access may be interrupted. This disruption may cause name service failure, loss of e-mail service, or complaints from users who cannot use the Web. The trace route program can locate such failures.

The following is an example of output returned by `tracert` on a personal computer running Windows 2000:

```
Tracing route to www.ciwcertified.com [63.72.51.85] over a
maximum of 30 hops:
1   <10 ms <10 ms   10 ms  192.168.123.254
2   220 ms  191 ms  130 ms  24.27.4.1
3   101 ms   60 ms   40 ms  66.68.0.33
4    90 ms   60 ms   90 ms  66.68.1.253
5   100 ms   90 ms  100 ms  66.68.1.234
6   120 ms   70 ms  121 ms  6207507pos5-0-0.austin.rr.com
    ↳[24.93.33.29]
7   270 ms  100 ms   70 ms  500.POS3-2.GW3.DFW9.ALTER.NET
    ↳[157.130.139.233]
8   130 ms   80 ms  110 ms  143.at-6-0-0.XR1.DFW9.ALTER.NET
    ↳[152.63.98.170]
9   171 ms  100 ms   60 ms  0.so-2-1-0.XL1.DFW9.ALTER.NET
    ↳[152.63.101.249]
10  171 ms   70 ms  140 ms  0.so-0-0-0.TL1.DFW9.ALTER.NET
    ↳[152.63.0.193]
11  180 ms   11 ms   80 ms  0.so-3-0-0.TL1.LAX9.ALTER.NET
    ↳[152.63.0.53]
12   60 ms   90 ms   90 ms  0.so-2-0-0.XL1.LAX2.ALTER.NET
    ↳[152.63.115.225]
13  711 ms  150 ms   90 ms  POS4-0.XR1.LAX2.ALTER.NET
    ↳[152.63.115.218]
14  120 ms   71 ms  110 ms  195.ATM7-0.GW3.LAX2.ALTER.NET
    ↳[152.63.53.49]
```

```
15 270 ms  121 ms  120 ms  63.72.51.98
16 210 ms  100 ms  100 ms  63.72.51.97
17 200 ms  110 ms  111 ms  63.72.51.85
Trace complete.
```

The output from `tracert` shows the sequence of machines that the packets cross on the route from the local machine to the specified machine. In this case, the packets are traveling from the Austin RoadRunner cable modem network, through several hosts on UUNET's AlterNet nationwide high-speed network, to the web server `www.CIWcertified.com`. In this example, the path from the client to the web server involves 17 hops.

The tracert program tries each stage of the path three times and reports the average round-trip time for each stage.

The *netstat* Command

The *netstat* command displays the contents of various network-related data structures, such as the state of *sockets*. A socket is the end point of a connection (either side), which usually includes the TCP or UDP port used and the IP address. The `netstat` command displays information about packets processed by your system on the network. The command syntax is as follows:

```
netstat    options
```

Options will vary depending on the operating system. To learn about options for commands, open the command prompt and enter the following:

```
netstat -? or netstat /?
```

By itself, the `netstat` command displays only established active connections on the system. This command results in the following response:

```
Active Connections
Proto  Local Address         Foreign Address       State
TCP    workstation12:1037    192.168.3.13:1040     ESTABLISHED
TCP    workstation12:1041    192.168.3.13:1050     ESTABLISHED
TCP    workstation12:1046    192.168.3.13:1040     ESTABLISHED
TCP    workstation12:1050    192.168.3.13:1050     ESTABLISHED
TCP    workstation12:1599    207.199.11.24:ftp     ESTABLISHED
```

In the response, four TCP connections have been established between workstation12 and a server with IP address 192.168.3.13. Another TCP connection has been established with an FTP server at 207.199.11.25. These TCP connections use the registered TCP port numbers 1037, 1040, 1041,

1046, 1050 and 1599. The FTP connection uses the reserved TCP port number for FTP, which is 21.

The *ipconfig* Command—Windows NT/2000/XP

The Windows NT/2000/XP `ipconfig` command is used to display the Windows NT/2000/XP IP configuration. You have already used the `ipconfig` command to determine your physical address in a previous chapter. By default, this command displays only the IP address, subnet mask, and default gateway.

The command syntax is as follows:

```
ipconfig     options
```

To view all the IP-related configuration information, use the /all option. This option displays additional information, such as the hardware address. Following is an example of using the `ipconfig` command with the /all option:

```
ipconfig /all
```

This command yields the following results:

```
Windows IP Configuration:
Host Name                     workstation12
DNS Servers
Node Type                     Broadcast
NetBIOS Scope ID
IP Routing Enabled            No
WINS Proxy Enabled            No
NetBIOS Resolution Uses DNS   No
Ethernet adapter RTL80291:
Description                   Novell 2000 Adapter
Physical Address              00-00-1C-3A-62-BD
DHCP Enabled                  No
IP Address                    192.168.3.13
Subnet Mask                   255.255.255.0
Default Gateway               192.168.3.1
```

The `ipconfig` command also renews and releases IP addresses from a DHCP server. If no adapter name is specified, all IP leases will be released.

For example:

```
ipconfig /release adapter
ipconfig /renew adapter
```

The *winipcfg* Command—Windows 95/98/Me

The Windows 95/98/Me *winipcfg* command is used to determine your network card's IP configuration and Ethernet address. Select the Start button and choose Run. The run command line will appear. Enter the following command:

```
winipcfg
```

You can also enter winipcfg at the MS-DOS prompt. You will access your computer's IP configuration and hardware address in the next exercise.

EXERCISE 5.2

Identifying IP Configuration and Hardware Address Information

In this exercise, you will locate your computer's IP address configuration and hardware address.

1. Select the Start menu and choose Run.

2. Enter the following command:
```
winipcfg
```

3. The Windows IP configuration and Ethernet Adapter Information will appear. From the drop-down menu, select your computer's NIC, such as 3COM Etherlink PCI. Your screen should resemble this, depending on your IP configuration and NIC.

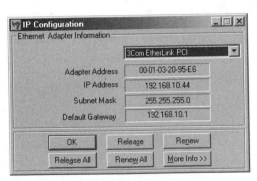

4. Select OK to close the IP configuration window.

The *arp* Command

To understand the arp command, you should review the Address Resolution Protocol (ARP) discussed earlier in this book. ARP resolves software addresses to hardware addresses.

Assume that the following two hosts exist on a TCP/IP Ethernet network: node1 and node2. Node1 knows the IP address of node2. However, node1 cannot send data to node2 unless node1 knows the Ethernet (hardware) address of node2. ARP resolves IP addresses to Ethernet addresses.

The arp command displays ARP information. It will show the physical (MAC) address of computers with which you have recently communicated. The command for viewing the ARP cache is as follows:

```
arp -a
```

This command yields the following result:

```
Interface: 192.168.3.13
Internet Address        Physical Address        Type
192.168.3.11            00-60-83-7c-24-a2       Dynamic
192.168.3.15            00-60-97-24-db-df       Dynamic
192.168.5.12            00-aa-00-38-e7-c3       Dynamic
```

To delete an entry from the ARP cache, use the following syntax:

```
arp -d IP address
```

In this example, IP address identifies the entry you want to delete.

Network Analyzers

Network analyzers allow network administrators to analyze data traversing a network. The data is "captured" by the network analyzer as it is transmitted across the network. Once captured, the data can be closely studied. For example, you can view the Ethernet header, which indicates the physical (MAC) addresses of both the source and the destination nodes.

Network analyzers can help an administrator troubleshoot and manage a network. Most network analyzers support several network protocols, such as TCP/IP and IPX/SPX. If you are viewing the packets on your network and notice a computer sending error messages, you can identify the computer and determine the problem. Popular network analyzers are the Network Associates Sniffer Basic (previously NetXRay) and Sniffer Pro products.

A network analyzer provides the following services:

Monitoring network traffic to identify network trends This practice helps establish a network baseline. For example, you may notice that network traffic is heaviest in the morning when all users start their machines.

Identifying network problems and sending alert messages Problems (such as traffic exceeding a given parameter) can be predefined by the network administrator.

Identifying specific problems Problems might include error messages generated by a network device, which can then be repaired.

Testing network connections, devices, and cables Network analyzers can send test packets over the network. The packets can be traced to discover faulty components or cables.

Figure 5.5 shows the results of a `ping` command packet capture using Network Associates Sniffer Basic.

FIGURE 5.5 Sniffer Basic (NetXRay) packet capture

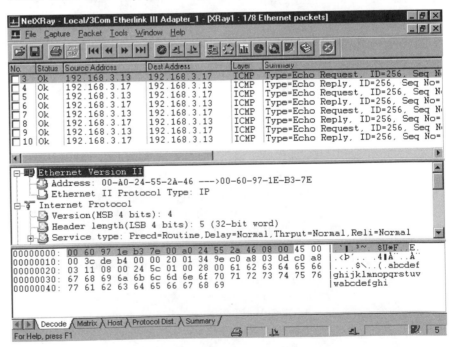

LAN and cable modem users should consult with their network administrator or ISP before installing and using any TCP/IP network analyzer application. Because LAN and cable modem users are sharing a network segment with other users, the network analyzer will be able to see packets from these users. In many cases, this may be a violation of the authorized use policies for your network.

Summary

In this chapter, we discussed the TCP/IP protocol suite, which provides the communications rules for Internet services. Requests for Comments (RFCs) are documents that define protocol specifications. They are submitted to and published by the Internet Engineering Task Force (IETF). RFCs are issued in one of six states: experimental, proposed, draft, standard, historical, and informational.

The Internet Architecture is a four-layer model that builds upon the seven-layer OS reference model. The four layers are Application (OSI/RM Layers 6 and 7, Presentation and Application), Transport (Layers 4 and 5, Transport and Session), Internet (Layer 3, Network), and Network Access (Layers 1 and 2, Physical and Data Link).

The Application layer includes several protocols we have already discussed in previous chapters, including HTTP, FTP, Telnet, NNTP, Gopher, SMTP and DNS. Other application protocols include Trivial File Transfer Protocol (TFTP), Simple Network Management Protocol (SNMP), BOOTstrap Protocol (BOOTP), and Dynamic Host Configuration Protocol (DHCP).

The Transport layer includes TCP and UDP.

The Internet layer includes IP, Address Resolution Protocol (ARP), Internet Control Message Protocol (ICMP), Internet Group Management Protocol (IGMP), and Reverse Address Resolution Protocol (RARP).

The Network Access layer includes the hardware and media required to send and receive network signals, including NICs, routers, and cables.

Demultiplexing is the process computers use to decode a network signal, by stripping away protocol headers until the actual transmitted data is revealed.

Routing is the process of directing packets to their proper destination. When two computers are on the same network, direct routing is used.

Otherwise, indirect routing is required, and routers try to send packets on a good connection. The computer must know which router to use, based on its gateway setting. The router must know where to send the packet. The router determines this by using a routing information table. Static routers have a manually programmed table, while dynamic routers can send and receive table updates with other routers. Routing protocols include Router Information Protocol (RIP) and Open Shortest Path First (OSPF).

Each Internet protocol or service has its own port number. This information is stored in the TCP or UDP header, and can be used by routers and other network hardware to help direct packets. The well-known port numbers (1 to 1023) are assigned and maintained by ICANN. Other registered port numbers (1024 to 65535) may be used as needed by applications.

Internet addresses have a network portion and a host portion. These are IPv4 addresses that are broken into four parts or dotted quads, with each part containing 1 byte of information. There are five classes of addresses, from A to E. Classes A, B and C are used to assign addresses to computers. Class D is reserved for multicasting. Class E is reserved for future use.

Some numerical addresses are reserved for specific uses. Addresses that begin with 127 are called loopback addresses, and are used to test computers. The number 255 is used for network broadcast messages. The address 0.0.0.0 is used by computers when they start up and request a real IP address. There are also three ranges of reserved addresses, which can be used to assign IP addresses within LANs.

Subnet masks look like IP addresses, but are meant to help distinguish between the network and host portions of an IP address. Subnet masks are assigned based upon the network's class identification.

At a minimum, Internet clients must be configured with an IP address, subnet mask, and gateway. Most clients also need a DHCP client so they can be assigned an IP address from the network's allocated range of addresses. Additional configuration may be needed for some networks, including DNS, NetBIOS, and WINS names.

Finally, we discussed several commands and utilities that are used in troubleshooting Internet connections. The `ping` command can test to see if a remote server is responding. The `tracert` command shows the number of hops or intermediate connections needed to reach a destination. The `netstat` command shows the status of sockets. The `ipconfig` and `winipcfg` commands are used in various versions of Microsoft Windows to display network configuration information. The `arp` command resolves IP addresses to physical addresses, such as MAC addresses. Network analyzers can intercept and read packets sent between two computers on a network.

Exam Essentials

Understand the purpose of Requests for Comments (RFC). RFC documents include detailed information about Internet standard protocols, assigned port numbers, host and server requirements. RFCs also describe the development of Internet protocols in the following stages: experimental, proposed, draft, standard. Obsolete protocols are classified as historic, and non-Internet protocols are described as informational.

Know the Internet architecture model and various Internet protocols. The Internet architecture model is a four-layer presentation of the TCPI/IP protocol suite. This model remaps the OSI reference model to reflect the Internet infrastructure. It includes the Application layer (the Application and Presentation layers of the OSI/RM), the Transport layer (the Session and Transport OSI/RM layers), the Internet layer (the OSI/RM Network layer), and the Network Access layer (the Data Link and Physical layers of the OSI/RM).

Understand demultiplexing. Demultiplexing is the process used by a receiving computer to read and strip off the headers and trailers of an incoming IP packet. This process takes the data received by the NIC, checks it, and renders it so that client applications may use the data.

Understand the routing process, including direct versus indirect routing, and static versus dynamic routing. Routing is the process of choosing a network path over which to send packets. Routing occurs in the Internet layer, (or the OSI/RM Network layer). The host must know which router to use for a given destination (determined by the gateway), and the router must know where to send the packet (determined by the routing information table). Direct routing occurs when two computers exist on the same physical network. Indirect routing occurs when packets are sent between two different networks. Static routing uses manually programmed routing information tables. Dynamic routing allows routers to exchange table information about known networks.

Be able to compare and contrast Routing Information Protocol (RIP) with Open Shortest Path First (OSPF). RIP allows routers to exchange entire routing information tables and uses the routers with the fewest hops. OSPF allows networks to be defined as areas. It also takes into account bandwidth and load balancing, and allows automated, partial table updates.

Understand port numbers and their functions, including well-known and registered port numbers.   TCP and UDP headers include port numbers, used to identify the Internet process for each packet. Well-known port numbers (1 to 1023) are assigned by ICANN, and include e-mail, the Web, FTP, and Telnet. Registered port numbers (1024 to 65535) are not assigned by ICANN, and can be used by any Internet process.

Understand IP addressing and address classes.   ICANN assigns ranges of numeric IP addresses, which contain a network and a host portion. There are five classes of IP addresses. Class A (0.0.0.0 to 127.255.255.255) uses the first byte to identify the network. Class B (128.0.0.0 to 191.255.255.255) uses the first two bytes for the network. Class C (192.0.0.0 to 223.255.255.255) uses the first three bytes for the network. Class D (224.0.0.0 to 239.255.255.255) is used for multicasting. Class E (240.0.0.0 to 247.255.255.255) are reserved for future use. Class D and E addresses specify network address information only; these addresses do not have hosts.

Understand loopback, broadcast, and special-case IP addresses.   The loopback address (127.0.0.1 to 127.255.255.255) is reserved to test and troubleshoot Internet connections. 127.0.0.1 is usually set up as the loopback address for testing an individual Linux, UNIX, or Windows computer with a TCP/IP stack. Broadcast addresses are used to send messages to all network hosts and are used only as destination addresses. These addresses have the number 255 in the network or host portion of the IP address. The special-case address 0.0.0.0 is used by a computer when it is requesting an IP address, usually at startup or when it is connected to the network. This address must be replaced by a valid IP address before the computer can be used as an Internet node.

Know the use of private addresses.   ICANN has designated several ranges of private IP addresses that can be used within networks. These ranges are 10.0.0.0 to 10.255.255.255, 172.16.0.0 to 172.31.255.255, and 192.168.0.0 to 192.168.255.255. Private addresses are used within networks for computers that will not be used as hosts or servers, including workstations on dial-up and local area networks. This helps conserve the IP address space and allows organizations to use their public IP address range efficiently.

Be able to identify default subnet masks and explain their function.
Subnet masks distinguish the network and host portions of a numeric IP address, and specify whether an address is local or remote. The default

subnet masks are 255.0.0.0 (Class A), 255.255.0.0 (Class B), and 255.255.255.0 (Class C). Subnet masks are used with Class A, B, and C addresses only, as Class D and E addresses do not have hosts.

Know the TCP/IP properties needed to configure a typical workstation. A basic configuration includes a numeric IP address, a subnet mask, and a default gateway. A static IP address or a DHCP client is also needed. You must also configure the workstation to use a name resolution system, such as DNS, WINS or NetBIOS.

Understand what Dynamic Host configuration Protocol (DHCP) does. DHCP assigns IP addresses automatically on a DHCP network. It is used on LANs, WANs, and by ISPs to dynamically configure subnet masks, and DNS information when the computer starts.

Know various diagnostic tools for troubleshooting TCP/IP networks. The `ping` command tests Internet connectivity between two computers. The `tracert` command shows information about the network route between two computers, including response time and hop information. The `netstat` command displays information about active Internet connections, including socket information. Windows 2000/NT/XP supports the `ipconfig` command, while Windows 95/98/ME supports the `winipcfg` command. Both versions show IP configuration information. The `arp` command displays the MAC addresses of other computers. Network analyzer software such as Sniffer is used to read IP packets on a local network or network segment.

Key Terms

Before you take the exam, be certain you are familiar with the following terms:

Application layer	draft
BOOTP	Dynamic Host Configuration Protocol (DHCP)
broadcast addresses	dynamic router
default gateway	end-to-end layer
demultiplexing	ephemeral port numbers
direct routing	experimental

full standards

historic

hop

host-to-host layer

indirect routing

Internet architecture

Internet Control Message
Protocol (ICMP)

Internet Engineering Task
Force (IETF)

Internet layer

loopback

net mask

netstat

Network Access layer

network analyzers

Open Shortest Path First
(OSPF)

ping

port number

Process layer

proposed

registered port numbers

Requests for Comments (RFCs)

reserved port numbers

Reverse Address Resolution
Protocol (RARP)

router

routing

Routing Information Protocol (RIP)

routing information table

routing protocols

Simple Network Management
Protocol (SNMP)

sockets

source-to-destination layer

standard

static routers

subnet mask

Trivial File Transfer Protocol
(TFTP)

Transport layer

well-known port numbers

winipcfg

working groups

Lab Exercises

1. Fill in the table below, indicating the class of each IP address and whether it is valid or not. If it is not valid, explain why.

	IP address	Class	Valid? yes or no	If not valid, why?
1	192.23.111.8			
2	10.1.1.256			
3	148.108.62.95			
4	127.0.0.1			
5	245.255.123.49			
6	100.54.100.90			
7	162.34.0.0			
8	127.65.18.191			
9	1.1.1.1			
10	208.152.84.255			
11	225.37.257.34			
12	255.255.255.255			

2. Determine the default subnet mask for the IP address 17.223.13.222.

3. Determine the default subnet mask for the IP address 195.10.99.2.

4. Determine the default subnet mask for the IP address 211.35.126.10.

5. Determine the default subnet mask for the IP address 152.5.202.69.

6. Determine the default subnet mask for the IP address 128.156.88.1.

Answers to Lab Exercises

1. Your table should look something like this:

	IP Address	Class	Valid?	If not valid, why?
1	192.23.111.8	C	Yes	
2	10.1.1.256	A	No	The fourth octet (256) is higher than 255.
3	148.108.62.95	B	Yes	
4	127.0.0.1	A	No	This is usually reserved in the hosts file as the loopback address for client computers.
5	245.255.123.49	E	No	Class E is reserved for future use.
6	100.54.100.90	A	Yes	
7	162.34.0.0	B	No	The host portion cannot be all zeros; this represents a network address.
8	127.65.18.191	A	No	This address is in the loopback address range; its first octet is 127.
9	1.1.1.1	A	Yes	
10	208.152.84.255	C	No	The last octet is 255, which indicates this Net-directed broadcast.
11	225.37.257.34	D	No	Third octet is higher than 255.
12	255.255.255.255	N/A	No	This is a broadcast address.

2. 255.0.0.0

3. 255.255.255.0

4. 255.255.255.0

5. 255.255.0.0

6. 255.255.0.0

Review Questions

1. Which one of the following states does an Internet protocol not have to reach before it becomes a standard?

   A. Informational

   B. Draft

   C. Proposed

   D. Experimental

2. The Internet layer of the Internet architecture model performs which one of the following tasks?

   A. Transmits datagrams over the attached network.

   B. Addresses and routes packets on TCP/IP.

   C. Accepts Application-layer data and provides the flow of information between hosts.

   D. Interacts with the Transport-layer protocols to present data.

3. At which layer of the Internet architecture is the network interface card?

   A. Application layer

   B. Transport layer

   C. Internet layer

   D. Network access layer

4. Which one of the following protocols is used by the `ping` command to obtain and report network status information?

   A. IGMP

   B. ICMP

   C. IP

   D. TCP

5. Address Resolution Protocol (ARP) is used at which one of the following Internet architecture layers?

   A. Network Access layer

   B. Application layer

   C. Transport layer

   D. Internet layer

6. Which one of the following protocols is used for multicasting?

   A. Reverse Address Resolution Protocol

   B. Internet Group Management Protocol

   C. Address Resolution Protocol

   D. Internet Message Access Protocol

7. Which routing protocol is sensitive to such criteria as available bandwidth and security?

   A. Open Shortest Path First (OSPF)

   B. Routing Information Protocol (RIP)

   C. File Transfer Protocol (FTP)

   D. Transmission Control Protocol (TCP)

8. Lindsey has connected two computers on the same physical network. What kind of routing is performed when these computers communicate?

   A. Static

   B. Indirect

   C. Direct

   D. Dynamic

9. Which one of the following statements is the best description of well-known port numbers?

   A. Port numbers ranging from 1 to 1023 assigned by ICANN to well-known Internet services.

   B. Port numbers ranging from 1024 to 65535 that any Internet process may use.

   C. Reserved IP address numbers that are used for broadcast messages within a network.

   D. Reserved IP address numbers that are used by a workstation at startup for obtaining a valid IP address.

10. Which reserved port number is used by FTP to transfer files?

    A. Port 21

    B. Port 80

    C. Port 25

    D. Port 53

11. Bob sees the IP address 65.80.0.19 in an e-mail message. Which one of the following statements can John assume is true about this address?

    A. It is a network address because there is a 0 in the address.

    B. It is a Class A address.

    C. It is the IP address of a web server, because it uses the number 80.

    D. It is a private address.

12. Beatrice sees the IP address 172.24.127.50 is assigned to her workstation. Which one of the following statements is true about her workstation?

    A. Her workstation has a Class C public IP address.

    B. Her workstation has a Class B public IP address.

    C. Her workstation is using a private IP address.

    D. Her workstation is set up to receive a multicast of a videoconference.

13. Which of the following Internet address classes is reserved for experimental or future use?

A. Class A

B. Class B

C. Class D

D. Class E

14. Which of the following default subnet masks corresponds to Class A?

A. 255.255.255.255

B. 255.255.255.0

C. 255.255.0.0

D. 255.0.0.0

15. A computer on the LAN has just started up and is using the IP address 0.0.0.0. Which one of the following protocols must this computer use before it can use SMTP to send an e-mail message to another machine on the Internet?

A. Telnet

B. DHCP

C. TFTP

D. DNS

16. After configuring a valid IP address and subnet mask on your computer, Hal successfully pings other computers on his local network. However, Hal is unable to ping computers outside his network. What TCP/IP configuration is required to communicate outside his local network?

A. WINS server

B. Default gateway

C. DNS server

D. NetBIOS name

17. Roberta is trying to determine how many hops exist between her Windows Me workstation and a Web server at another company. Which one of the following utilities should she use?

    A. `ipconfig`

    B. `tracert`

    C. `winipcfg`

    D. `ping`

18. Todd is trying to troubleshoot his Windows 2000 computer. He believes there is a problem with the IP configuration. Which utility should he use to view this information?

    A. `winipcfg`

    B. `netstat`

    C. `ipconfig`

    D. `ping`

19. Which of the following diagnostic tools displays information about the path between two computers on the Internet?

    A. `tracert`

    B. `ipconfig`

    C. `ping`

    D. `netstat`

20. Caitlin wants to determine the physical address of another computer on her LAN. She just used her FTP client to retrieve a file from that computer. Which one of the following commands should she use?

    A. `netstat`

    B. `arp`

    C. `tracert`

    D. `ping`

Answers to Review Questions

1. **A.** The informational state is normally used for protocols that were developed outside of the IETF procedures, but are listed for the benefit of the Internet community. Standard protocols must pass through the experimental, proposed, and draft stages before they become standards.

2. **B.** The Internet layer corresponds with the Network layer (Layer 3) of the OSI reference model. At this layer, IP is used to address and route packets. The Network Access layer accepts the higher-layer packets and transmits data over the network. The Transport layer accepts Application-layer data and manages the flow of data between two computers, using TCP in this example. The Application layer presents data to the user through client applications, and also contains client requests.

3. **D.** The NIC works at the Network Access layer. It sends and receives network signals across the transmission medium. It lies at Layer 2 (the Data Link layer) of the OSI reference model. The Application layer presents data to the user through client applications and also contains client requests. The Transport layer accepts Application-layer data and manages the flow of data between two computers. The Internet layer addresses and routes packets.

4. **B.** Internet Control Message Protocol provides troubleshooting information for Internet packets, including response time and time to live. Internet Group Management Protocol is used to manage multicasts of the same data to several computers on the same network. IP is used to address and route packets. TCP is used to maintain a connection between two computers.

5. **D.** ARP is used to translate IP addresses to physical addresses, such as MAC addresses. It operates at the Internet layer of the Internet architecture.

6. **B.** IGMP is used by a host to tell its router that the host will accept multicast messages. RARP uses a computer's hardware or MAC address to request an IP address. ARP translates IP addresses into physical or MAC addresses. IMAP is an alternative mail protocol that allows users to store and manage e-mail messages remotely.

7. **A.** OSPF is designed to consider bandwidth, authentication, load balancing, and other factors. It is an improvement over RIP. FTP is used for transferring large files across the Internet. TCP is used to set up a connection between two computers.

8. **C.** This is an example of direct routing. If the computers were on two different networks, indirect routing would be performed. Static and dynamic routing refer to the methods used for updating routing information tables.

9. **A.** Well-known or reserved port numbers identify Internet communication processes, including the Web, e-mail, FTP, and Telnet. Port numbers do not correspond with IP addresses.

10. **A.** All of the choices are from the well-known or reserved port numbers. FTP uses port 21. HTTP uses port 80. SMTP uses port 25. DNS uses port 53.

11. **B.** The only statement Bob can choose is B, that this is a Class A address within the range 0.0.0.0 to 127.255.255.255. Network addresses are not necessarily limited by the numeric IP address. We cannot tell from the IP address what the machine with this address is doing. The address is not within any of the three private address ranges.

12. **C.** The IP address is within one of the three reserved IP address ranges, 172.16.0.0 to 172.31.255.255. The address is also a Class B address, but it is not publicly accessible because routers are programmed to filter out packets sent from external networks directed to this address. Class D addresses (224.0.0.0 to 239.255.255.255) are used for multicasting.

13. **D.** Class E is reserved for future use. Classes A, B, and C are in use. Class D is reserved for multicasting.

14. **D.** The default subnet mask for Class A addresses uses the first byte to identify the network.

15. **B.** The computer must obtain a valid IP address from a DHCP server, because it is using the special case 0.0.0.0 address. E-mail, Telnet, TFTP, and DNS cannot be used until DHCP completes the address assignment.

16. B. John must have a default gateway address configured to send packets outside the local network. He also must have a DNS server address in his computer's IP configuration. Both of these items may be manually configured or setup automatically with DHCP. However, the DNS server is not the problem here, as John is pinging a numeric IP address. No DNS lookup is required. The WINS server and NetBIOS name are needed to communicate with local computers using Windows, but are not necessary for external Internet communication.

17. B. The `tracert` command will give Roberta the number of hops between the two computers. To view her computer's IP configuration, she would use `winipcfg`. On a Windows NT/2000/XP computer, she would use `ipconfig`. The `ping` command would tell her if the other computer is responding to ICMP packets, but would not tell her how many hops lie between the two computers.

18. C. The `ipconfig` command is supported in Windows NT/2000/XP. The `winipcfg` command provides the same information in Windows 95/98/Me. `Netstat` reports information about active connections. The `ping` command reports troubleshooting information about packets sent to another computer.

19. A. `Tracert` reports path information between two computers. `Ping` confirms connectivity. `Netstat` reports the active connections on a computer. `Ipconfig` is the Windows NT/2000/XP command for reporting IP-related configuration information.

20. B. The `arp` command will retrieve and display the physical or MAC address of the other computer. `Netstat` reports the active connections on a computer. `Tracert` reports path information between two computers, but does not report the physical address; it reports the IP or logical address. `Ping` reports the status of packets sent to another computer, as well as that computer's IP address.

Chapter

6

Internetworking Servers

THE CIW EXAM OBJECTIVE GROUPS COVERED IN THIS CHAPTER:

✓ Identify the functions and components of web servers, including but not limited to: various server types and related protocols, Internet connectivity, client-side and server-side scripting and applications, business needs, and server selection criteria.

✓ Identify common Internet security issues, including but not limited to: user-level and enterprise-level issues, access security, and security threats and attacks.

✓ Identify common performance issues affecting Internet servers and resources, including but not limited to: analysis and diagnosis, configuration, services, and protocols.

Now that we have discussed networking and its parts and protocols, we turn our attention to why these networks and the Internet itself exist. Traditional networks are designed to use LANs and WANs to store files in central sites and databases and then present the information contained therein to users at remote workstations. These files and databases that network users share are called *network services*.

Before TCP/IP, LANs and WANs were limited by the kinds of networking technology that were available. Today on the Internet, network services have become more distributed, or decentralized. Companies, organizations, and even individuals store, retrieve, and share information on a global scale.

This distribution and management of network services across the Internet is called *internetworking*. In this chapter, you will learn how internetworking services actually work. These services are installed on computers, called *servers*, and can provide data and services to fill a variety of needs.

We will first discuss how server software runs on a network operating system. Microsoft Windows implements server software as services that are controlled within the operating system. For Linux and UNIX network servers, the *inetd* daemon controls the server processes.

We'll then review the functions that servers provide to the Internet. There are several servers that support the *content* that we will study in depth in the second part of this book. These servers include HTTP, mail, mailing list, streaming media, FTP, and news.

We will also examine servers that support or enhance the *performance* of the Internet, by providing services that make the user's experience faster and more convenient. These servers provide the DNS, proxy, and caching services that work behind the scenes of Internet sessions.

We will also look at four *database* server types that are used for building high-performance websites. These are the certificate, directory, catalog, and transaction servers.

We will conclude the chapter with a brief review of popular server software suites for the Windows, Linux, and UNIX network operating systems. These suites can offer integrated solutions that allow the network administrator to easily configure and implement more than one of the internetworking server types listed here.

Server Implementation

Internetworking servers are usually hosted on powerful network computers. These computers are designed to handle requests for files and data very quickly. There may be additional hardware in these computers that provide speed and performance enhancements, such as multiple CPUs and NICs, and additional RAM. These computers often look different from a typical desktop computer, because special cases are used to house the computers. These cases are designed for mounting in a type of shelf called a *rack*, which allows many computers to be installed in a small amount of floor space.

These powerful computers are called servers, because they host and run the internetworking server software, which can be part of the operating system or separate programs. Throughout this book, we will use the term *server* to refer to both the internetworking server software and the computers that run this software.

An internetworking server runs as a *process* on a computer. A process is a task that is started by a computer program. The computer must have adequate permission to create a process that is bound to a well-known or reserved port number. The user ID of the process must be 0, or a user account with unlimited access privileges. This applies to Windows, Linux, and UNIX operating systems.

UNIX and Linux Server Implementation

UNIX and Linux use a special program called a *daemon* (pronounced like demon) called inetd to start other Internet servers. The inetd daemon has superuser access privileges, which gives inetd permission to bind ports to any processes it starts.

Inetd is called a daemon because it waits and listens in the background until summoned by another process. Because of its ability to launch, or "spawn," other services and servers, the Internet daemon is often referred to as a super-server.

The `inetd` service runs when the UNIX or Linux system starts up. By configuring the `inetd.conf` file, shown in Figure 6.1, you can use `inetd` to listen on specified well-known TCP and UDP ports (0 to 1023). When the `inetd` daemon receives a request for a recognized port, it will launch other services to support the request.

FIGURE 6.1   Sample `inetd.conf` file

```
page% more /etc/inetd.conf
#
# @(#)inetd.conf        5.2 (LINUX) 3/4/99
# This is the inetd.conf file created for the page server
#
#echo     stream   tcp      nowait   /etc/miscd         echod
#echo     dgram    udp      wait     /etc/miscd         echod
.
.
.
ftp       stream   tcp      nowait   /usr/local/etc/ftpd      ftpd -a -1
telnet    stream   tcp      nowait   /etc/telnetd       telnetd
smtp      dgram    udp      wait     /etc/smtpd         smtpd
.
.
.
```

You can use `inetd` to launch any UNIX or Linux service. These services typically include the following servers:

smtpd   the SMTP daemon

ftpd   the File Transport Protocol (FTP) daemon, used for FTP sessions

telnetd   the Telnet daemon

Additional servers include `smbd` and `nmbd`, which are the SAMBA service daemons that allow a UNIX system to participate in a Microsoft NetBIOS network. Some web administrators use `inetd` to start their web servers in response to client requests.

Because it launches other servers and services, `inetd` can present a security problem if it is not configured properly. It has superuser, or "root," permission, which can be purposefully misdirected to cause problems on the server. Also, `inetd` spawns a new process each time you use it. Therefore, use it carefully because it can deplete system resources on the server.

Microsoft Windows Server Implementation

Microsoft Windows uses *services* to run internetworking processes. Services are similar to daemons, as they wait in the background to be activated. Windows services must be set up by a user with administrator access privileges, which gives the services permission to bind to well-known port numbers. Windows operating systems offer a graphical control panel to help administrators configure each service, as opposed to the command-line interface used in UNIX and Linux.

HTTP   Included in Microsoft Internet Information Services (IIS), which is installed by default with the Windows NT and 2000 Server operating system. An HTTP server can also be installed as a software application provided by a third-party application, such as Apache.

FTP   Included in Microsoft Internet Information Services (IIS), which is installed by default with the Windows NT and 2000 Server operating system. An FTP server can also be installed as a software application provided by a third-party application.

SMTP   This service can be run by Microsoft Exchange Server, or a third-party software application such as Novell GroupWise or Lotus Notes.

Content Servers

We begin our discussion of specific types of internetworking servers by looking at services that support the common tasks Internet, LAN, and WAN users perform every day, such as web surfing, e-mail, FTP, viewing audio/video, and reading newsgroups. All of these servers function as *pull servers*, transmitting files when a user requests specific kinds of Internet content through a client application.

Web Servers

Web or HTTP servers send documents for viewing on a web browser. A typical web page may include an HTML file and several image files. The web browser is a client application that requests documents from web servers, based on the URL that the user enters. The documents the web server sends may be from a disk archive, or they may be created dynamically when the client requests them.

The site is organized around a web server process, which runs as a daemon process on UNIX machines and as a service on Windows NT/2000/XP machines. The web server process binds to TCP port 80, and listens for incoming requests from clients such as web browsers. These requests are formed in the simple language called *Hypertext Markup Language (HTML)*.

The server has access to a set of documents that it may return to a client in response to an appropriate request. These documents are located in a mass storage device, such as a hard drive, in a specific location that the server can read. These documents can be in a wide range of formats. For example, the server probably has access to a large collection of HTML documents as well as the associated image files in a range of formats. In addition, the server may be able to supply many other multimedia documents, such as sound files and video clips.

Web Gateways

Not all client requests are for particular static documents that exist as files on the web server. Some requests pass data to the server and specify a program for the server to execute on its host machine. This program might be a simple instruction, such as inserting a graphic onto the page. It also might be a more complex program that accesses a database. The server passes the client's data to the program, then returns the program's output to the client. This mechanism is called a *gateway*. Some servers use executable programs and scripts to perform this task. Others pass data to subroutines contained in an object library dynamically linked to the server. This method provides the same functionality as executing co-processes through a gateway, but with better performance.

Later in this book, you will learn more about CGI scripts and Server Application Programming Interfaces (SAPIs), such as Microsoft Internet Server Application Programming Interface (ISAPI). These scripts and dynamic libraries extend the HTTP server's capabilities by allowing it to create active content and communicate with databases and other servers.

HTTP Servers and MIME

An HTTP server can download any file type to a browser. However, the web browser must be preconfigured to accept each file type. The *Multipurpose Internet Mail Extensions (MIME)* system allows HTTP and e-mail attachments to identify the files they must use. A version of MIME that encrypts MIME data, called *Secure MIME (S/MIME)*, is used for secure transmissions.

The different MIME types are classified under broad headings (text, image, application, audio and video), then subclassified by exact type. For example, an HTML document has MIME type "text/html," whereas a plain text document has type "text/plain."

Whenever data is passed between a web server and a browser, the data is labeled with its MIME type. The recipient uses the MIME type to render the information. For example, when a web server sends an HTML document to a browser, it labels the document with its MIME type (text/html) so the browser can display the document properly. When a web server sends an Adobe Acrobat file (application/x-pdf) to a browser, the browser will open the correct plug-in (Adobe Acrobat Reader) to view the file.

When a web browser requests a server resource, the server deduces the resource's MIME type from the extension part of the document name. For example, the server understands a request for the URL `http://www.CIWcertified.com/default.asp` refers to a document of type text/html and labels the document with that type when it returns the document to the browser. The MIME type is included in the HTTP header, which is contained in a TCP/IP packet.

The correspondence between file name extensions and MIME types may be preprogrammed into the web server, or may be configured by the server administrator. In most cases, the preprogrammed MIME types are used, to maintain a standard set of MIME types that are supported by popular web browsers and operating systems.

Although most servers allow you to define any name for the initial document, many servers use `index.html` as the file name. Some servers use `index.htm`. Other common initial document names are listed in Table 6.1. Keep in mind that web server administrators can choose any initial document name they want. They can also choose to configure one or both of the file extensions `.htm` and `.html` to represent web documents on their web server.

When you want to create a page that will automatically render in a client's web browser, you should determine the name and extension that your server is configured to report. You can usually do this by checking the server's preferences or settings or by asking the system administrator. If you have a virtual domain on a web server, you should consult the web service provider's setup information.

TABLE 6.1 Common Initial Website Document Names

Name	Comment
index.htm or index.html	The most common initial document name; used as a default on Apache and other web servers.
default.htm or default.html	Used on Microsoft web servers.
default.asp	Used on Microsoft web servers.
home.htm or home.html	
main.htm or main.html	

HTTP Servers and the Operating System

HTTP servers work closely with the computer's operating system, because a web server is a high-performance file-sharing system. The performance of an HTTP server therefore depends on how well it works with a particular network operating system.

For instance, Microsoft Internet Information Services (IIS) is an integrated part of the Windows NT and Windows 2000 server operating systems. Other servers, such as Apache or iPlanet Enterprise Server, are available software versions that will work with a variety of operating systems. Apache is open source software, and its development process is similar to that of the Linux operating system. Because the source code is readily available, developers have translated or ported Apache to a variety of operating systems. iPlanet has its origins in Netscape's web server software, which was available for several different operating systems.

Most web servers can restrict files, folders, and directories by establishing *permissions*. Permissions include the ability to read a file (read permission), create or delete a file (write permission), execute programs (execute permission), or deny access (no access). Operating systems can also establish permissions.

For example, the Linux operating system can restrict access to a certain file or directory. Apache web server (or any other server) can restrict access to a specific resource. Operating system permissions generally take precedence over those granted by an HTTP server. The operating system and HTTP server permissions should be combined to ensure that a folder is secure.

However, permissions can also become confused. CGI scripts and programs require execute permissions. Therefore, the folder or directory in which a script resides must also have execute permission. Naturally, you must determine whether both the web server and the operating system allow execute permission. If the operating system itself forbids all executables in that folder, the Administrator must change this setting, even though the Webmaster has already given execute permission.

Access Control

An important part of setting up and managing a web server is access control, which is similar to permissions. Most websites offer access to the general public; users do not need special permission to access such server resources. This type of access is often called *anonymous access*. However, some sites want to restrict access to some or all of their server resources. An *access control list* defines the permissions for a resource by specifying which users and groups have access to the resource.

For example, the website may offer certain documents only to registered or paying users. Alternatively, the site may offer access to personal information, which must be supplied only to the owner of that information. The traditional method of restricting access to server resources is based on a database of permitted users, who must supply a password to access particular server information. The database of permitted users may be either:

- Users with accounts on the host operating system. IIS, for example, uses the system account database on the host computer as its database of permitted users.

- A special database managed by the server itself. The second method separates people with permission to access web server information from those with more global permissions on the host system. Because thousands of users may be allowed to access information, the second method is much better for restricting access.

 WARNING

Web servers that limit access to resources need a method for users to identify themselves. Usually some form of password is required. Password-based access to the server is vulnerable to password sniffing, unless the server uses a method for exchanging encrypted passwords.

Access Control and the Server Account

The access control restrictions discussed previously are enforced in two stages.

1. The web server process checks to see whether certain actions are allowed based on its configuration information.

2. The operating system enforces restrictions on actions the web server process can perform.

The operating system restrictions are based on the fact that the web server process is owned by a user account on the host machine and is subject to limitations imposed on that account. For example, if the web server process is owned by an account called "http" and the http user does not have read permission in a certain directory, the server cannot access that directory regardless of the server's internal configuration. In general, the restrictions imposed by the operating system are more reliable than those imposed by the web server alone.

To take advantage of the security mechanisms provided by the operating system, the web server process must be owned by an account with the fewest permissions needed for it to perform its task. In particular, the server should not be owned by a super-user or administrator account, because a web server process with these permissions is unconstrained by the operating system. For example, people use e-mail every day to communicate. Using an e-mail account requires a user name and password coupled with authentication. Remember that the web server may demand permissions that the operating system may deny, especially when using CGI scripts.

Aliases and Virtual Directories

As part of their configuration options, most web servers allow flexible mapping of URL path names to file names. This kind of mapping has various names, including virtual directories and aliases. Some of the advantages of flexible mapping of URL path names to file names include the following examples.

- The more flexible the mapping from URL path names to file names, the more freedom the administrator has to arrange files on the disk.

- If a set of documents may be reasonably accessed under several URL path names, all these URL path names can be mapped to the same file names.

For example, suppose you want a server to be able to supply a collection of documents called `doc1.html`, `doc2.html`, and so forth, located in the directory `/home/exams/docs`. The server root directory is `/usr/local/etc/httpd`, but you want browsers to access the `file doc1.html` under the URL `http://www.CIWcertified.com/exams/doc1.html`. To allow this access, you must configure the server to map the URL path `/exams/doc1.html` to the actual file path `/home/exams/docs`, instead of to `/usr/local/etc/httpd/docs/exams/doc1.html`.

Logging

Web servers (and a majority of other server types) generate a log of the requests they handle. In addition to helping monitor correct server operation, these logs eventually contain information about who uses the server resources, which resources are most popular, and how users initially find the site. The following three types of information are usually collected in web server logs.

Access data   Each time a client issues an HTTP command to the server, the command is logged.

Referrer data   Part of the information transmitted by a browser to a server is the URL at which the browser is pointing when it makes the request. This information may be logged to indicate how users enter the site.

Error data   Server errors (including improperly formatted HTTP requests, dropped TCP connections, and access violations) are logged to help monitor server operations.

Mail Servers

As we discussed in an earlier chapter, there are two ways to store and access Internet e-mail messages. We can use IMAP/SMTP, which handles both retrieving and sending e-mail messages, or we can use POP3/SMTP. SMTP sends Internet messages, while POP3 retrieves mail that the mail server has received. An Internet *mail server* uses one or both of these methods. The first is by the simple and more accepted POP3 protocol. Mail servers can store messages. The mail client uses POP3 to retrieve these messages from the server. For example, if you were to successfully send an e-mail message, the message would be stored in the appropriate mail server until the recipient downloaded it from the server. The POP3 server responds to a request, asks for a password, then transmits the messages to the client. SMTP is responsible solely for sending e-mail messages. In UNIX and Linux, the sendmail daemon is activated in response to a command, and sends the requested message.

IMAP handles messages in a more sophisticated manner because it allows a user to browse and manage files remotely, whereas a POP3 server forces a user to download files before reading, deleting, or otherwise managing them. IMAP servers can require more administration and disk drive space than SMTP/POP3 servers, because IMAP users will tend to leave more of their own mail messages for storage in their inboxes and folders.

In some corporate environments, your computer may be configured to support an e-mail system that supports both Internet and a different, internal e-mail message format. There are many large corporations that used internal e-mail systems before Internet e-mail became popular. As corporations added Internet access to their LANs and WANs, they often maintained the internal e-mail systems for certain employees, departments, and business functions. If you are using Microsoft Windows, your e-mail client application will use SMTP to send Internet e-mail to external sites. You may use a corporate e-mail system that supports a server application such as Microsoft Exchange Server, Lotus Notes, Novell GroupWise, or another product.

MIME

The MIME types that we discussed with HTTP servers are also used to transmit files with e-mail. For instance, your e-mail client application uses MIME to attach a GIF image or a Microsoft Word document to an e-mail message. MIME identifies a file type, encodes the file, and decodes it at the receiving end so it will display properly. MIME performs these steps by adding a header to each file. The MIME header contains the encoding method and the type of data contained within.

Whenever data is passed between an e-mail sender and recipient, the data is labeled with its MIME type by the client application. The recipient's client uses the MIME type to render the information. For example, when an e-mail client sends a QuickTime video to a recipient, it labels the file with its MIME type (video/quicktime) so the recipient can execute the file properly. A web server uses the same procedure to transmit files to browser clients.

Mail servers do not set MIME types in messages, but they can be configured to remove certain MIME attachments. This is often done to prevent mail servers from sending messages that are infected with viruses. This strategy can also be used to delete or quarantine any infected messages that are received by the mail server. We will discuss this further in Chapter 12.

MIME types may not define unusual documents or graphic formats. In this case, you must manually associate a file with the appropriate program. For example, you may receive a DOC file type attachment that you cannot open. There are several reasons why you cannot open this DOC file. You may not have a program needed to run or read it, such as Microsoft Word, or a MIME type may not have been defined. In either case, you can save the file to your desktop, right-click the file, and select the Open With option. Choose the proper application to run the file, and the file will execute. If you do not have the proper application, you need to install the application on your computer to run the file.

Mailing List Servers

A mailing list server is a standard SMTP server that can automatically forward an e-mail message to every member on a distribution list. Some mailing list servers, such as L-Soft LISTSERV, are designed expressly for this purpose. Other SMTP servers, such as Microsoft Exchange Server, can be configured to act as mailing list servers by adding third-party software or programming. A mailing list server allows people to work together even though their e-mail accounts reside on different e-mail servers across the Internet. Basically, a mailing list server allows you to imitate a newsgroup. The main difference is that any e-mail message you send does not remain persistent on a central server for a given time. Mailing lists have become popular because many users consider e-mail messages easier to manage than newsgroup postings. We will discuss how to find mailing lists in Chapter 9, and how to use mailing lists in Chapter 10.

The interface that allows you to configure a mailing list server is often called a *Mailing List Manager (MLM)*. Using an MLM, you can customize the behavior of the mailing list server. For example, you can configure a moderated list, which means that a designated individual will screen all submissions before they are sent to everyone on the list.

Table 6.2 lists several popular e-mail list server products, and the companies that offer them.

TABLE 6.2 Popular Mailing List Servers

List Server	URL
Cren Corporation ListProc	www.cren.net
L-Soft LISTSERV	www.l-soft.com
Microsoft Exchange Server	www.microsoft.com
SparkList	www.sparklist.com

Streaming Media Servers

A media server offers *streaming media* over a computer network. Streaming media is designed to emulate traditional broadcast media such as radio and television, but can provide on-demand access of a wide variety of programming to audiences of any size, especially a single user. Popular uses for streaming media include audio and video data, such as songs, talk shows, radio broadcasts, and other information. Popular vendors of streaming media products include RealNetworks, Microsoft, and Apple.

Streaming media servers use UDP to achieve the effect of a real-time broadcast. Remember that UDP is a connectionless protocol that does not guarantee reliable packet transmission. Unlike other content servers, the client does not have to receive the entire media file to present the data to the user. In fact, the client usually discards the streaming media data as it is being presented to the user.

A streaming media client is designed to show audio or video while it receives the data stream. The client uses buffers to store the media data in the client computer's memory. A *buffer* is a cache of memory used by a computer to store frequently used data. Buffers create the illusion of faster access times and can help reduce skips and pauses in media playback.

Client applications usually include self-configuration features that let the client test the computer and connection, and then determine the maximum supported download speed and audio/video quality. The client also considers the amount of time that the client will have to spend downloading the data. Few users want to download a streaming video file that takes more time to transmit than it does to view.

The streaming media server sends the UDP data at the specific speed requested by the client. Because of the way streaming media is implemented, the server cannot make adjustments if the client is unable to support that download speed. If the download speed is too fast for the client to handle, or if the download speed is too fast for the Internet connection to support, too much of the UDP data will be discarded, leading to skips and pauses in the media presentation.

On a dial-up connection, streaming audio generally has the sound quality of a radio broadcast. Faster connections can support audio that approaches CD quality. Streaming video is shown in a small window, perhaps 150 by 100 pixels, and the number of frames shown per second may be half what a normal television broadcast would show. The video will be small and jerky. On a faster connection, the client can view the video in a larger window. A computer user can improve the streaming media client's performance by installing more RAM, using a faster processor, and using a higher-bandwidth Internet connection.

Because streaming media clients can discard data once it is shown, streaming media has become a popular way to provide access to copyrighted audio and video materials. For example, radio stations usually pay a royalty fee to the owner of each song that is broadcast. This royalty fee is much lower than the retail price that an individual would pay for a recording of the song. Streaming media providers also pay broadcast royalties to audio and video owners, and the owners are assured that individual users cannot easily make a copy of the streaming media they have received. We will further discuss copyright issues in Chapter 10.

Streaming media servers are well suited for intranets. Businesses and other organizations can use streaming media and corporate networks to distribute audio and video material, including employee meetings, training films, and marketing materials. There are also a variety of software and hardware products available that support real-time audio- and video-conferencing over the Internet.

FTP Servers

Even though FTP is one of the oldest protocols, it remains the workhorse of all the servers discussed in this lesson. FTP is different from SMTP because FTP allows you to transfer files between servers in real time, and those files can be much larger than those transferred over SMTP.

In most situations, if you have a file that is 2MB or larger, you should transfer it via FTP; sending such a large file through an e-mail server slows that server and the network. Also, if the e-mail server has difficulty transferring a large file, it will no longer forward that message. Many ISPs and businesses restrict their file attachment size supported by their e-mail servers, so that users cannot send or receive file attachments that are over a certain size, such as 3 or 5MB.

With FTP, on the other hand, if a problem occurs with the file, you need only request the file again. Some FTP clients can do this automatically. Thus, little administrative intervention is needed. Finally, sending files via FTP is faster than with e-mail and HTTP.

Logging and Access Control with FTP

An FTP server logs all traffic, which is usually anonymous. The server administrator can consult the FTP server logs to determine the amount of traffic the site has handled.

Although it is possible to password-protect an FTP site, many administrators choose to allow anonymous access. To strengthen security, they verify that no sensitive information resides on the FTP server. One reason that FTP servers generally use anonymous logons is that the protocol requires passwords to be sent unencrypted. This allows hackers to obtain FTP passwords by monitoring a workstation with a network analyzer program.

News Servers

A news server uses the Network News Transfer Protocol (NNTP). Like an e-mail server, it has a written text output that users can access at their convenience. However, like a conference call, it has multiuser input. Like the low-tech standard office bulletin board, it allows users to post information in an easily accessible location. Using a news server, you can secure specific newsgroups, or you can leave them open to the public. One of the most important uses for a newsgroup is to provide a forum for groups to communicate while developing projects.

A network news service consists of objects, both physical and virtual. A service can usually be configured to accept file attachments, which can allow members to exchange files as part of a public conversation. These files will remain persistent for a specified period, creating a message-based forum. The news server thus allows a company to document a project and enhance collaboration.

The newsgroup's name is also its network address, written in hierarchy index form. For example, `rec.sport.football.college` is a newsgroup for U.S. college football, whereas `rec.sport.soccer` is for soccer. Both hierarchies begin with `rec` (recreation) and `sport` before subdividing into different types of sports.

To read a newsgroup, the user opens a news reader software program, such as Netscape Communicator. When the user gives commands, the reader complies by accessing a news client. The client in turn locates the news server containing the newsgroup and requests access. The server/client relationship is like the file server linking the client computers on a typical office network.

When one newsgroup server communicates with another to gain access to the central newsgroup files, the action is called a *newsfeed*.

Classic Internet newsgroups are generated and maintained by contributors. Some of these classic newsgroups were formed in the 1980s and early 1990s, before Internet use became widespread. Generally, whoever maintains a classic newsgroup charges no access fees and has no formal means of enforcing standards for articles. Contributors often identify themselves only by an e-mail address.

Newsgroup Policies and Security

The news server helps organize resources with the emphasis on distributing and locating information rather than owning or controlling it. *Usenet* is a public collection of newsgroups originally developed in the university community, with rules and procedures based on academic freedom and peer review. For example, users can call for a vote on banning offensive material, but they lack the means to enforce a ban.

Many ISPs regulate the types of newsgroups that are offered to their subscribers. Because ISPs must subscribe to a newsfeed to offer newsgroups, an ISP can easily opt out of certain newsgroups in the feed, and thus restrict user access. For example, some ISPs do not offer certain newsgroups in the alt hierarchy, such as `alt.warez.*`. The `alt.warez` newsgroups frequently list FTP servers and other resources that post illegal copies of commercial software.

Public newsgroups have no restrictions on which users can access the newsgroup. Private newsgroups are restricted to specific users. Secure newsgroups encrypt articles in transmission between users and servers. Usenet newsgroups are always nonsecure, reflecting the academic culture of open dissemination.

Sometimes the newsgroup is controlled or supervised by one or more users. *Moderated newsgroups* carry only articles approved by a moderator, who has the authority to remove or allow any posting that is sent to the group. Unmoderated newsgroups operate without restrictions on content. While this allows users to communicate more quickly than they can on a moderated group, it does allow users to post off-topic items. The first appearance of *spam*, or off-topic commercial postings, appeared on several unmoderated newsgroups in 1993.

Many administrators use news servers to create secure newsgroups. You can do this by enabling user-specific password protection, or through a Secure Sockets Layer (SSL) session. Although both of these solutions are secure, an SSL session provides even greater security. To enable an SSL session, you need to obtain a certificate that enables encryption. You can obtain a certificate from a company such as VeriSign, or configure and use a certificate server.

Intranet and extranet newsgroups can help a company develop and track projects. Often, these groups are password-protected at the server level, so that only specified users can gain access.

Performance Servers

We will now discuss the second type of internetworking server, which we'll call performance servers. These servers enhance the user experience by making Internet access easier, safer, or faster. Performance servers work behind the scenes to improve or manage the user's Internet experience.

The most common kind of performance server is the DNS server, which is implemented across the entire Internet. Two other kinds of performance servers, called proxy and caching servers, are often used on large corporate networks to help control Internet access and performance. Caching servers are also used on public networks to increase the performance of streaming media servers.

DNS Servers

The function of the Domain Name System (DNS) is to translate host computer names into IP addresses. Without DNS, users would be forced to enter numeric IP addresses every time they needed access to any part of the Internet. As we learned in Chapter 2, the Internet Corporation for Assigned Names and Numbers (ICANN) is responsible for DNS management.

For example, the CIW Certification Program has a web server that can be accessed using the Fully Qualified Domain Name (FQDN) of `www.CIWcertified.com`. The same web server can also be reached by entering the IP address 63.72.51.85. Both the name and the IP address refer to the same web server, but the former is much easier to remember.

DNS servers, also called name servers, contain the server application that supports name-to-address translation. Typically, the system on which the name server resides is called the name server system.

DNS is a decentralized system that is also its own network. It does not depend on one source for updates, and one server does not store all the data. Instead, DNS is a distributed database that exists on name servers scattered across the Internet.

The Hosts File

Until DNS was implemented, a single file called the hosts table was managed and updated by the Stanford Research Institute's Network Information Center (SRI-NIC). Whenever network administrators needed the latest hosts table for their name servers, they downloaded it from the SRI-NIC FTP server. As the Internet grew, this file became very large and difficult to manage, and no longer provided an effective way to distribute name-to-address data.

Many computer systems still use the hosts file system to enhance DNS performance. The hosts file on your computer is similar to the hosts table used earlier for the Internet. The *hosts file* is a simple text file that is referenced locally by applications and commands for name-to-address resolution. The format for entries is as follows:

```
Internet-address    official-host-name    aliases
```

For the hosts file to provide local diagnostics, the loopback address (127.0.0.1) must be included. After the loopback address is entered, you can add any IP address and corresponding host name that you require. The number sign [#] is used to add comments to the file. This technique can increase system performance, because the operating system does not have to query a DNS server for addresses included in the hosts file. The user can also use the nickname at the end of the line to refer to that server. With the hosts file shown in Listing 6.1, a user can enter "ciw" in the address line of their web browser to access the `www.CIWcertified.com` website.

Listing 6.1: A sample HOSTS file for Microsoft Windows

```
# This file contains the mappings of IP addresses to host
# names.
# Each entry should be kept on an individual line.
# The IP address should be placed in the first column
# followed by the corresponding host name.
# The IP address and the host name should be separated by
# at least one space.
#
# Additionally, comments (such as these) may be inserted
# on individual lines or following the machine name denoted
# by a '#' symbol.
#
# For example:
#
# 102.54.94.97    rhino.acme.com     # source server
# 38.25.63.10     x.acme.com         # x client host

# List the loopback address.
127.0.0.1         localhost

# User-defined entries
192.168.3.15      workstation12              lindsey
63.72.81.85       www.CIWcertified.com    ciw
```

In Windows NT/2000/XP, the hosts file can be opened with the Notepad text-editing application that is included with the operating system. The hosts file is located at:

```
%systemroot%\system32\drivers\etc
```

The location of the %systemroot% directory varies on each system, and depends upon how the operating system was first installed. The default location for this directory is usually c:\winnt\ or c:\windows.

On Linux and UNIX systems, the hosts file can be edited with a text-editing application such as vi. The hosts file is located at:

```
/etc
```

You will need root access privileges to modify this file, so you should contact your system administrator if you need assistance.

DNS Hierarchy

DNS is a network system that runs as a distributed database. It consists of three levels—root-level, top-level and second-level domains—and is often referred to as the domain name space. Figure 6.2 shows the domain name space.

FIGURE 6.2   Domain name space

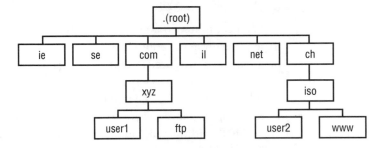

The root-level domain is the top of the hierarchy. The root-level domain contains entries for each top-level domain. The root-level domain is updated daily and replicated on root domain servers across the Internet. It is expressed by a period (.). This period is usually removed from the end of domain names. For example, www.CIWcertified.com instead of www.CIWcertified.com., which includes the final period.

The top-level domain is one level below the root-level domain. The top-level domain consists of categories found at the end of domain names, such as .com or .uk. Each top-level domain has a master server that contains entries for all registered second-level domains.

The second-level domain is one level below the top-level domain. Second-level domains include the businesses and institutions that register their domain names with the top-level domains, through their respective registrars. Second-level domains include registered names such as CIWcertified.com.

Second-level domains can also be categories of top-level domains. For example, the United States domain (.us) is categorized into a second-level domain for each state, such as Texas, which uses tx.us.

Companies and academic institutions in the United Kingdom and Australia are also categorized, as shown below:

- co.uk

- ac.uk

- com.au

- edu.au

Finally, second-level domains can also be divided into subdomains. This is usually done by the organization that has registered the domain name. Some sample subdomains may be:

- `office.microsoft.com`

- `bbc.co.uk`

- `au.sports.yahoo.com`

Each computer in a network needs a host name to access the Internet, depending upon the configuration requirements of your ISP or network. The host name is configured in that computer's DNS settings. A computer named "computer12" in the sales department of the CIW Certification program could be identified by the name `computer12.sales.CIWcertified.com`.

Remember that many corporate LANs use the private IP address ranges and DHCP. Although a computer may have the name `computer12.sales .CIWcertified.com`, it cannot run internetworking services that are available outside the LAN. This is because the routers will filter outgoing packets with private IP addresses. Therefore, no one outside the LAN should be able to access that workstation by its name, unless the server administrator has configured Network Address Translation (NAT) or provided another solution.

DNS Components

The Domain Name Service consists of these two key network components:

Name server   This is a server that supports name-to-address translation and runs the DNS service. The name server may also have a *cache* or archive of DNS entries it has previously received from the name resolver.

Name resolver   This is software that uses the services of one or more name servers to resolve an unknown request. For example, if a host requests `www.CIWcertified.com`, and the DNS server does not have the name information, it will use name resolver software to ask another name server on the DNS hierarchy. DNS clients and servers use name resolver software.

On UNIX and Linux systems, the resolver is actually a group of routines that reside in the C library `/usr/lib/libc.a`. This name resolver is actually run on the client computer. On Windows systems, the TCP/IP properties have a DNS tab that must be configured with the IP addresses of the DNS servers. The name resolver is running on another server. This configuration is sometimes done using DHCP.

DNS Server Types

DNS follows the standard client/server model: the client makes a request, and the server attempts to fulfill that request. DNS servers can fill several different roles, depending on the organization's needs. No matter what role the server takes, the client must specify the name server's domain name or IP address. The following server types are included in the DNS model:

Root server   Root servers can identify all top-level domains on the Internet. If a client requests information about a host in another domain, any server (except the slave server) can communicate that request to the root server.

Primary server   A primary server is the authority for a domain and maintains the DNS databases for its domain. It is the first DNS server in a domain. Companies and ISPs that implement their own DNS and participate on the Internet require a primary server.

Secondary server   A secondary server receives its authority and database from the primary server. Secondary servers provide fault tolerance, load distribution, and easier remote name resolution for the primary DNS server.

Windows NT/2000 Server contains a DNS service that can be installed as a service. Once installed, the NT Server computer can also function as a DNS server. The service is a fully functional DNS server and can be easily implemented for an intranet. It can also serve as a primary DNS server that can be registered with a top-level domain registrar. Many corporate LANs and ISPs operate their own DNS servers, to reduce the number of hops in looking up a domain name.

The name daemon, also called named (pronounced name-DEE), allows a UNIX or Linux computer to function as a DNS server. The most common implementation of UNIX DNS is the Berkeley Internet Name Domain (BIND).

Microsoft DNS is based on the BIND implementation, but does not adhere strictly to it. UNIX BIND servers are the most widely used DNS servers on the Internet.

DNS Records

Every domain consists of DNS records. A DNS record is an entry in a DNS database that provides additional routing and resolution information. Many different types of records can be configured, but only a few are needed for full address resolution and routing. Table 6.3 lists the most common DNS records.

TABLE 6.3 Common DNS Records

DNS Record	Function
Name Server (NS)	Identifies DNS servers for the DNS domain.
Start of Authority (SOA)	Identifies the DNS server that is the best source of information for the DNS domain. Because several backup DNS servers may exist, this record identifies the primary server for the specified DNS domain.
Address (A)	The most commonly used record; associates a host to an IP address. For example, you can establish an association between an IP address and a web server by creating an address record.
Canonical Name (CNAME)	Creates an alias for a specified host. For example, the name of a WWW server is server1.CIWcertfied.com. A CNAME record creates a "WWW" alias to the "server1.company.com" host, so it can also be accessed at www.CIWcertfiied.com.
Mail Exchanger (MX)	Identifies a server used to process and deliver e-mail messages for the domain.

These records are the most widely used. Many other types of records are used with DNS for different functions, but you do not need to know these unless you are involved in DNS server maintenance.

Real World Scenario

Sending an E-Mail Message

You work at the XYZ company, which uses the domain name xyz.com. As shown in Step A in the figure here, you send an e-mail message to an e-mail account at Yahoo!, which has the domain name yahoo.com. Your message has now gone to your company's SMTP server for processing.

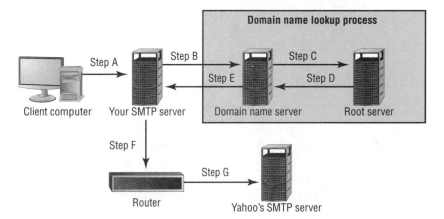

Before your SMTP server relays the e-mail message, it needs to match the domain name to its IP address. In Step B, the SMTP server sends a DNS request to a configured domain name server.

The name server first queries itself for the requested entry. Let's assume that the name server was just started, and its cache is empty. Because the entry does not exist in its cache, the name server forwards the request to the name resolver, which will then forward the request to one of the Internet's root servers in Step C.

In Step D, the root server will send your name server the reference information for the requested domain's (yahoo.com) primary and secondary name servers.

Your name server will query the yahoo.com name server for the request record. The request will be fulfilled, with the yahoo.com name server sending the requested IP address back to your name resolver and name server. This is shown in Step E.

Your name server will provide your SMTP server with the IP address, and save the information to its cache for later use.

In Step F, the SMTP server has reformatted the message, and forwarded the packets to the LAN's router. In Step G, the router forwards the packets to continue their journey across the Internet, to the yahoo.com SMTP server.

After this initial domain name lookup has been completed, the remaining TCP/IP packets will use the IP address for yahoo.com in the IP header. Each packet will follow Steps A, F, and G to find their destination at the Yahoo SMTP server.

Proxy Servers

A proxy server is an intermediary between a network host and other hosts outside the network. Its main functions are to provide enhanced security, manage TCP/IP addresses, and speed access to the Internet by providing caching server functions for frequently used documents.

In a network setting, a proxy server serves as the default gateway for IP communications. This process effectively hides the actual IP address from the client application. Proxy servers can provide the following additional services.

Caching of web documents If corporate users access information on a web server from the Internet, that information is cached to the local proxy server. This caching allows anyone in the corporate intranet to access the same information from the local system instead of repeatedly downloading the files from the Internet. This feature reduces the amount of network traffic produced on the Internet, which leads to improved performance for the corporate intranet and the Internet.

Corporate firewall access A proxy server can provide safe passage for corporate users to the Internet through a firewall, allowing protected use of HTTP and FTP. You will learn more about firewalls later in this book.

Filtering client transactions A proxy can control access to remote web servers and their resources by filtering client transactions. Filtering is accomplished by limiting or denying access to specific URLs or URL wildcard patterns, specific host IP addresses, domain names, host or computer names, web contents, and specific users. For example, you can deny access by anyone in a company to www.nonsense.com by specifying that URL in a proxy server's configuration. You can also deny access *from* a particular computer within a company, using the computer's name or IP address to limit access. In addition, you can deny access to an individual by specifying that person's user name.

Transaction logging   Generally, a proxy server supports transaction logging. Network administrators can track client activity and customize which data to record. Some of the data that can be logged includes accessed URLs, dates and times, and the byte counts of all data that has been transferred. Information on routing and success of a transaction can also be logged and used to evaluate network performance.

Securing the host   A proxy server can secure or block the host from users accessing the site from the Internet and help web servers handle a high volume of requests, if one proxy server is dedicated to this role and another is used to control outgoing access. In essence, the blocking proxy can act as a server outside your company's firewall, and your web server and its content can reside safely inside the firewall.

Enhanced administration   Management features are vital in daily proxy server implementation. Advanced logging and reporting, monitoring, automatic proxy configuring, remote management, SNMP, proxy scripting, and the server plug-in API are included to allow simplified management.

If your network uses a proxy server, you must ensure that all the clients are properly configured. For example, to browse the Web, you must enter the correct address of that proxy server into your browser. Otherwise, the proxy server will not receive any requests you make.

You must configure every application to work with your proxy server, including web browsers, Telnet applications, and FTP programs. Otherwise, not all applications will be able to access outside networks. Browsers from both Netscape and Microsoft provide proxy server configuration, and you can obtain third-party programs that will allow almost any Internet application to work properly with a proxy server.

Caching Servers

A *caching server* is a dedicated server, or a service within a server, that speeds data access by storing data retrieved by users (such as web pages), then presenting it directly to users who later request the same data. Web caching is a common service provided by proxy servers. Caching services are also sold as "cache-in-a-box" products.

There are several companies that operate large banks of caching servers. Content providers often use these to cache content such as websites and streaming media, rather than installing additional servers. By outsourcing the cache, content providers can concentrate on their core business. The cache server operators are responsible for providing enough servers and bandwidth to handle the streaming media traffic.

Companies and ISPs also use cache servers to reduce network traffic by storing web files that are frequently accessed but seldom changed. Cache servers, by themselves or as part of proxy servers, reduce the latency between the user and the web data. The cache server can check the file's date or the Expires field of the HTTP header to determine if a file can be cached. Expires headers are supported by practically every web client. Web caching is very effective for certain types of files that do not change often, including image files that are used as website menus.

For example, CNN uses Akamai to cache popular streaming media content at locations around the United States. When someone on the CNN website requests a video of a breaking news story, that request may be forwarded from CNN's streaming media server to an Akamai server farm, which will actually send the streaming media to the user. This transaction is transparent to the user, but is designed to decrease latency and provide a better streaming media presentation.

Database Servers

We now turn to the third type of internetworking server. Database servers are specialized applications that can store and retrieve information quickly, usually using SQL or another database language as a programming interface. Database servers are often connected to web servers through gateways.

Database servers are typically hosted on computers that have large, fast disk drives. The database servers we will discuss are certificate, directory, catalog, and transaction servers.

Certificate Servers

Transmitting information over the Internet can be risky. Information you send is passed from one computer to the next until it reaches its destination.

During the transmission, other users can intercept your information using network analyzer programs. It is possible that these eavesdropping users can change the contents of your message.

Certificate servers validate, or certify, keys. *Keys* are strings of text generated from a complex series of encryption algorithms that allow you to secure communications for a company or group of users.

Many web servers, such as IIS, can create and use keys that can be applied to other servers, such as news servers, mail servers, or web servers. Keys allow users to communicate in a secure manner.

A certificate provides digital proof of your real identity to the recipient of your message. Because e-mail and newsgroup servers use unencrypted protocols by default, any unencrypted messages are sent in plain text, and can be used for identity theft. Digital certificates help minimize this security risk by authenticating users before they transmit information. You will learn more about certificates later in this book.

Directory Servers

A *directory server* is a dedicated server that identifies all resources on a network. It then makes these resources available to authenticated users. For example, these server types allow a company to provide a directory of names, network services, e-mail addresses, department heads, company contacts, and address information to all users.

The most efficient solution does not include storage of current company or individual contact list databases. Most employees do not take the time to update their own contact lists. This outdated information can affect accuracy and performance. An effective way to improve access to such information is to use only one database and one access protocol.

For example, a directory server allows users to remotely access such information quickly from a central location, because it allows them to query the database without affecting network performance. An administrator need only configure employee e-mail programs to query the database.

Some companies give their employees access to electronic address books that are linked to a centralized list of e-mail addresses and contact information. The IT department updates the address book so the latest version is always available. Thus, company employees can automatically access it using their e-mail programs.

Directory Service Uses

A directory service enables a company to reuse the information in its directory, keep management costs from increasing, and avoid re-entry of user information for every application that requires such information. A directory service can also help administrators manage applications or users, and can help users locate other users or e-mail addresses.

In addition, a directory server can help with the following procedures:

- Locating and managing all company accounts with the same directory.

- Allowing users, both inside and outside the network, to use the service. For example, an office in one city can store the directory information about all its members on one server. Users outside that office can also access the information, if they have permission or a valid password.

- Maintaining a single database of e-mail contacts.

Directory Services

A specification and a protocol serve as the basis for most directory services: X.500 and the Lightweight Directory Access Protocol (LDAP).

X.500 is a specification used to manage user and resource directories. It is based on a hierarchical system that can classify entries by country, state, city, and street, for example. The X.500 specification was designed to offer a global directory. It has had limited success on its own because it is complex and difficult to implement, but it has been the basis for many other directory services.

X.500 directories offer the following characteristics:

Scalability   X.500 directories can be offered as global databases, but can also be divided into smaller databases for efficient management.

Synchronization   X.500 directories can synchronize with other directories to ensure all data is current.

Replication   X.500 directories can replicate with other X.500 directories, thereby making all database copies identical (for reducing retrieval time) and creating backup copies.

Lightweight Directory Access Protocol (LDAP) was developed from X.500 at the University of Michigan. It is easier to implement than X.500

because it is based on TCP/IP, which allows communication on both intranets and the Internet. LDAP uses a simplified X.500 directory structure and a simplified directory access method. The LDAP directory structure is hierarchical, similar to an X.500 directory.

Whereas the X.500 directory access method is also called the Directory Access Protocol (DAP), LDAP is considered "lightweight" because it uses a simpler hierarchical structure.

When Netscape adopted LDAP as its standard directory method in 1997, many other software companies such as Microsoft and Novell followed suit by adding LDAP support to their products.

Catalog Servers

A *catalog server* provides a single point of access that allows users to centrally search for information across a distributed network. In other words, it indexes databases, files, and information across a large network and allows keyword, Boolean, and other searches. If you need to provide a comprehensive searching service for your intranet, extranet, or even the Internet, a catalog server is the standard solution.

A catalog server keeps an index, or catalog, of all the documents for which it is responsible. The catalog server prevents users from having to browse an enormous number of documents.

Catalog servers can automate the indexing process with the use of programs that use algorithms and search parameters to find and index files, folders, and other materials. These programs are called *robots* or *spiders*. Most catalog servers have robots that are preconfigured to search for the most common file name extensions, such as `.html`, `.mpeg`, `.pdf`, `.txt`, and others.

You can customize search results to present full documents or summaries. Most catalog servers can also conduct secure sessions to ensure that search queries remain confidential.

Transaction Servers

When a financial transaction takes place, such as ordering office supplies over the Internet with a company credit card, a *transaction server* can guarantee that all required databases are updated. It verifies that all parts of a transaction have taken place successfully. In some cases, this task is complicated. For example, the online merchant's database must reflect the transaction, as well as the credit card company's, and in some cases, the manufacturer's database.

Transaction servers are intended as client/server replacements for older systems, such as Customer Information Control System (CICS) mainframe servers. Transaction servers are web-based and can provide both a stand-alone solution and a bridging tool to mainframe servers. Some transaction servers, such as Microsoft Transaction Server, are designed to interface with web-specific databases through the use of Active Server Pages (ASP).

A transaction server also comes preconfigured to connect to databases, thereby enabling spontaneous information transfer. If a financial transaction is unsuccessful because one of the databases has failed, it will take preprogrammed actions, such as canceling the transaction. Transaction servers are specifically built to support a three-tier client/server solution and allow high-volume transactions with minimum network overhead.

Mirrored Servers

Although a mirrored server is not an internetworking server itself, it can provide data redundancy to protect data on any type of server. *Mirroring* causes two sets of writes to occur for each write that takes place. A mirror set is established between two physical hard drives or partitions. The mirrored set can exist on one computer or two separate computers, as shown in Figure 6.3. The mirrored set of drives are usually local to each other, although it is possible to set up mirrors in remote locations on a LAN or WAN.

FIGURE 6.3 Mirrored server

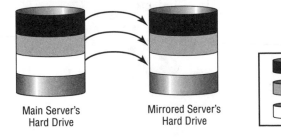

Main Server's Hard Drive

Mirrored Server's Hard Drive

File 1

File 2

File 3

Data is written to the primary, or original, drive when a write request is issued. Data is then copied to the mirrored drive, providing a mirror image of the primary drive. If one of the hard drives fails, all data is protected from loss.

Most network operating systems allow any portion of a drive to be mirrored, including the operating system files, which protect the entire system.

There is another meaning for the term "mirror" in internetworking. Mirrored servers can also provide supplemental access to data, by providing an additional server that contains the same information as a primary server. Some web and FTP sites have mirror sites, which are updated frequently to present the same information as the original sites. Mirror sites are usually used to reduce the load on a primary site, or to provide users in a specific geographic region a faster connection to data.

Choosing the Ideal Server

As a networking professional, you will have to make and justify decisions. Part of this decision-making process is learning what a company truly requires and then making the appropriate choices. You have already learned about types of servers used on the Web.

Popular Server Products

The following are descriptions of some industry-standard internetworking server software for UNIX, Linux, and Microsoft Windows operating systems. These products include stand-alone web servers as well as larger suites with additional internetworking servers such as mail and directory services. This list is not comprehensive and does not constitute an endorsement of any product. This discussion provides an overview of the popular internetworking servers and their basic capabilities.

Apache Web Server

Apache web server is a tested, well-accepted solution. As of this writing, more than half of all websites deliver their information with this server software. Originally designed to support UNIX, Apache now supports Windows NT and 2000 as well. All versions are available free of charge.

Apache server includes no formal support system, such as a customer support desk. A not-for-profit, membership-based group called the Apache Software Foundation (www.apache.org) is responsible for product development. The Apache web server is another example of the open-source movement. However, you can obtain configuration and support information from many sources by entering the keyword "Apache" in your favorite web search engine.

A downloadable version is available at the Apache HTTP Server Project site (www.apache.org/httpd.html). Apache is also included in some distributions of Linux. The Apache web server is not packaged with additional Internet services. You must obtain other server programs for news, FTP, and so forth.

Microsoft Internet Information Services

Microsoft's Internet Information Services (IIS) is now in its fifth version, and is closely integrated with the Windows NT and Windows 2000 Server operating systems. The IIS in NT is installed on more server computers than any other HTTP server software. IIS includes HTTP, FTP, NNTP, SMTP, Certificate, Active Server Pages (ASP), Index (catalog), and Transaction services. IIS has become popular because it provides many internetworking server solutions, along with native support for Windows LAN and WAN networks.

Another strength of IIS is that it allows you to use a remote server to store and retrieve files. The remote server need not be a web server itself. Using a remote server allows you to distribute processing load across several computers.

Because IIS is a Microsoft product, you can obtain worldwide, fee-based support from Microsoft. You can also administer it from a GUI-based interface or through HTML forms. Additionally, you can issue commands from a DOS session.

Personal Web Server (PWS) is a Microsoft web server product that is intended for website development and testing. Several versions of Personal Web Server are available from Microsoft as a free download. PWS is often used for the development and testing of server-side applications. Personal Web Server should not be used in place of IIS, because it lacks the features to support a production web server.

Lotus Domino

The Lotus Domino series includes all of the most-used types of Internet servers, including certificate, HTTP, SMTP, and FTP. One of the strengths of the Domino server series is its ability to serve Lotus Notes applications over intranets and the Internet. Additionally, the Domino series is adept at connecting with databases and supports Java servlets as a preferred database connection method.

An additional consideration is that Domino supports several operating systems, including AS/400, S/390, Linux, Windows NT/2000, Solaris, AIX, and HP-UX. For more information, consult the Lotus Domino home page at www.lotus.com/home.nsf/welcome/domino.

Novell NetWare

Novell offers its own suite of internetworking severs, integrated with its NetWare operating system. Novell has concentrated on directory servers for corporate LANs, building upon NetWare's strengths in user account management. The Novell eDirectory suite runs on a variety of networking operating systems, including NetWare, Solaris, Windows 2000/NT, Linux, UNIX, and AIX. Novell also offers certificate servers and the GroupWise e-mail system, which support Internet protocols and eDirectory services. Novell's website is located at www.novell.com.

iPlanet

Two of the more established server vendors, Netscape and Sun Microsystems, formed an alliance called iPlanet in 1999. This alliance provides services similar to those of its competitors. Because these companies have helped define the Web, their servers are among the most tested, and they provide fee-based support. Additionally, their products support many platforms, including OS/2, Windows NT/2000, Solaris, AIX, and HP-UX.

The iPlanet product line includes servers with server-side JavaScript interpreters, which allow you to use JavaScript to connect to databases and implement other server-side scripting applications. For more information, consult the iPlanet site at www.iplanet.com.

Summary

In this chapter, we have examined how internetworking servers are used to provide Internet services. The term "servers" can mean the software that provides internetworking services or the high-powered computers that run this software. Internetworking servers are run as services or processes on networking operating systems.

We have discussed three types of internetworking servers. Content servers provide the data that users can manipulate and read, in web browsers, FTP clients, e-mail programs, and media viewers. Performance servers help enhance the user's experience by providing faster, easier, or more secure Internet service. Proxy servers are used on corporate LANs to restrict access to external Internet sites. Caching servers can reduce latency by providing access to cached content, including streaming media.

Database servers provide web servers and other internetworking services with quick access to large quantities of information. Certificate servers help validate user identities. Corporate users can look up employee information using directory servers. Catalog servers provide indexes of network information. Transaction servers process financial transactions quickly.

We finished the chapter by reviewing internetworking software from several sources, including the Apache Project, Microsoft, Lotus, Novell, and iPlanet.

Exam Essentials

Know how internetworking servers are implemented, including the terms "service" and "daemon."   Internetworking servers are software products that provide Internet services. These servers are run as services on network computers. On UNIX and Linux computers, supervisory programs called daemons control them. The powerful computers that run these programs are also called servers. They typically have large hard drives, multiple processors, and extra RAM.

Know the three types of internetworking servers.   Content servers send files and data that can be manipulated and viewed by a user in a client application. These include web, FTP, mail, streaming media, and news servers. Performance servers work behind the scenes to improve or manage the user's experience. These include DNS, proxy, and caching servers. Database servers provide fast lookup of specific information that is used by content servers. These include certificate, transaction, catalog, and directory servers.

Understand the functions of web servers.   Web or HTTP servers send files that are requested by web browsers, using the HTTP protocol. The files can be text files, image files, or multimedia files.

Know the access and security features of a web server, including permissions, access control, aliases, virtual directories, and logging.   The operating system on a web server restricts access to files, folders, and directories by establishing permissions. These permissions help ensure that users cannot view or change important files on the server. Access control features are used by the web server process to make further restrictions on which specific users can view content, by setting up user accounts. When a user requests a web page, the web servers processes access rules first, and then the operating system enforces permissions. The server administrator can set up aliases or virtual directories that connect directories or folders to specific URLs. The web server can record or log the requests it receives, including HTTP commands, referrer information, and error data.

Be able to identify and describe the functions and features of other content servers, including mail, mailing list, streaming media, FTP, and news servers.   Mail servers send and store e-mail messages using the SMTP, POP3, and IMAP protocols. Mailing list servers use SMTP to send messages to lists or groups of users. Streaming media servers use UDP to send audio and video streams to users in a simulated real-time transmission. FTP servers help users send and retrieve large files. News servers give users access to newsgroups on specific topics.

Understand MIME and explain how MIME types are used by HTTP and mail servers.   The Multipurpose Internet Mail Extensions (MIME) system provides a method for web and mail servers to identify the many different kinds that can be transmitted to a client's system. MIME types are enclosed in application headers and are used by the client to identify an application program that can open and use the data.

Be able to identify and describe the functions and features of DNS. Domain name servers map domain names to IP addresses. The DNS service uses a name server, which supports the name-to-address translation, and a name resolver, which requests mappings for unknown names from root, primary, and secondary servers. DNS records are stored in databases, and use a hierarchy that helps identify the country, company, and department of a domain name.

Be able to identify and describe the functions and features of proxy and caching servers.   Proxy servers help hide the actual IP address of a host from other nodes on a network. They are used on LANs and WANs to restrict access to Internet sites and may provide firewall protection from external users. Proxies can also cache frequently used websites to reduce network traffic and can record logs of Internet activity. Caching servers are used to place website and streaming media content on convenient network locations, thus transparently providing more efficient access for the user.

Be able to identify and describe the functions and features of the database servers, including certificate, directory, catalog, and transaction servers. Certificate servers store and issue encrypted strings, or keys, that can be used to secure transactions and sessions. Directory servers contain a database of employees or individuals on a network and use the LDAP protocols to transmit this information to clients. Catalog servers provide searchable indexes of content. Transaction servers support the processing of financial transactions.

Know how mirroring is used by internetworking servers.   Mirroring is used in two ways. A network operating system can use mirroring features to simultaneously save data to another hard drive. Server administrators can also set up mirror servers in remote locations on a LAN or WAN. These mirror servers can host content from a primary server, such as a web or FTP server.

Be able to describe and identify popular internetworking server software. Apache is an open source web server that is available for Windows, UNIX, and Linux systems. Microsoft Internet Information Services (IIS) is a suite of internetworking servers for Microsoft operating systems. Lotus Domino and iPlanet provide content servers for several different operating systems. Novell NetWare provides directory and content services on Novell LANs and WANs.

Key Terms

Before you take the exam, be certain you are familiar with the following terms:

access control list	mirroring
buffer	Multipurpose Internet Mail Extensions (MIME)
cache	newsfeed
caching server	permissions
catalog server	process
certificate servers	pull servers
daemon	robots
directory server	Secure MIME (S/MIME)
gateway	server
hosts file	services
Hypertext Markup Language (HTML)	spiders
`inetd`	streaming media
keys	transaction server
Lightweight Directory Access Protocol (LDAP)	Usenet
mail server	X.500

Review Questions

1. A server computer is most likely to have which one of the following features?

   A. A fast modem

   B. Microsoft Windows

   C. Large quantities of RAM

   D. A large monitor

2. UNIX and Linux computers use a special program to start internet-working servers. Which of the following choices best describes the name of this program?

   A. webd

   B. netd

   C. super-server

   D. spawner

3. Microsoft Windows implements internetworking servers as which one of the following choices?

   A. Daemons

   B. Services

   C. Resources

   D. Systems

4. HTTP servers use which one of the following methods to let web browsers know which kinds of files they are sending?

   A. File extensions such as `.html`

   B. MIME

   C. Certificates

   D. Permissions

5. Hibba is configuring her department's Linux web server to run CGI scripts. Which one of the following must she change on the server in order to run the CGI scripts properly?

  A. httpd

  B. Services

  C. Permissions

  D. Access rights

6. Which one of the following networking protocols is usually associated with a mail server?

  A. NNTP

  B. UDP

  C. IMAP

  D. FTP

7. Which one of the following statements explains how mailing lists are different from newsgroups?

  A. Users need to subscribe to mailing lists in order to post messages. They do not need to subscribe to newsgroups.

  B. All mailing list messages are kept on the mailing list server for search and retrieval. News servers perform the same service for newsgroup messages.

  C. Mailing lists can be made private, while newsgroups are always open to the public.

  D. Mailing list messages are received as e-mail messages, while newsgroups use a different kind of message viewed through a different type of client software.

8. Streaming media servers use which one of the following kinds of technology to send video files to clients for viewing?

  A. Buffers

  B. User Datagram Protocol

  C. File Transfer Protocol

  D. Transmission Control Protocol

9. Tristan wants to send a 30MB customer database file to his colleague Ericka, who works in another country. Which one of the following statements best explains the method he should use?

   A. Tristan should put the file on the company's website and send Ericka the URL.

   B. Tristan should send the file as an e-mail attachment.

   C. Tristan should store the file on an FTP server, and send the URL to Ericka in a newsgroup message.

   D. Tristan should store the file on an FTP server, and send the URL to Ericka in an e-mail message.

10. Paige has been told to allow her company's employees to access public newsgroups on agriculture. Which one of the following choices should Paige implement?

    A. Paige should subscribe the company to a newsfeed and select the appropriate newsgroups to download.

    B. Paige should send an e-mail to all employees telling them how to access newsgroups through the Web.

    C. Paige should subscribe to several agriculture newsgroups and distribute appropriate messages as e-mails.

    D. Paige should install a public news server and start several newsgroups on agriculture.

11. Name servers perform which one of the following functions?

    A. They look up e-mail addresses based on a person's name.

    B. They translate domain names into IP addresses.

    C. They look up unknown domain names.

    D. They provide the index file name for a web server.

12. How does a computer know what its proper IP loopback address is?

   A. The loopback address is set by a DHCP server.

   B. The loopback address is listed in the computer's hosts file.

   C. The loopback address is set by the computer's NIC.

   D. The loopback address is set by the local server.

13. Which one of the following types of domain name servers contains information about all top-level domains?

   A. Primary server

   B. Root server

   C. Secondary server

   D. Name resolver

14. Everett is the network manager for a local company. In the last year, the company has grown from 50 to 250 employees. Several users have told him that the download time for web pages has increased significantly. Which one of the following choices is the best solution for Everett to decrease download times for web pages?

   A. Install a mirrored web server.

   B. Install a proxy server.

   C. Install a caching server.

   D. Install a gateway server.

15. Which one of the following services does a proxy server usually not provide?

   A. Transaction logging

   B. Caching of frequently accessed web documents

   C. Transaction filtering

   D. File and print services

16. Which of the following statements best describes a certificate?

    A. The part of a packet that identifies the IP address of the sender

    B. A credit card receipt sent by a website

    C. An encrypted text string that verifies the identity of an individual or company over the Internet

    D. A security mechanism used by websites that requires a user name and password to log onto the site

17. John has been asked to create an electronic employee list for his company. The HR department will update the list weekly. The HR department wants a solution that will work easily with the company's e-mail system. The company has 500 employees. Which one of the following solutions should he implement?

    A. John should create a spreadsheet that will be put on the intranet.

    B. John should install a directory server that uses LDAP.

    C. John should create a web page and post it on the company web site.

    D. John should create a text file that will be placed on the internal FTP site.

18. The marketing department has asked Molly to add an index of the company's website. This index should let users do keyword searches of the website. The index should be updated daily, as the marketing department regularly changes the web pages to support new promotions and products. Which one of the following solutions is best suited to this situation?

    A. Molly should post a list of keywords that are frequently mentioned on the site.

    B. Molly should add a link to a web search engine.

    C. Molly should install a catalog server.

    D. Molly should install a cache server.

19. Transaction servers are specifically designed to support which one of the following computing models?

A. Two-tier computing

B. Three-tier computing

C. Client/server systems

D. Mainframe systems

20. Which one of the following web servers is an open source product that runs on Windows operating systems?

A. Apache

B. Microsoft IIS

C. iPlanet

D. Lotus Domino

Answers to Review Questions

1. C.   Additional RAM can help speed up a server computer's operations, by letting the operating system keep more data in memory and reducing the amount of hard disk activity. Servers can use several different operating systems, including Windows, UNIX, Linux, and NetWare. Servers are usually connected to the Internet through NICs and high-speed lines. Servers do not require a large monitor. In fact, servers are often installed with shared monitors that are used by several computers.

2. C.   Inetd is also known as a super-server, because it can start internetworking serves in response to requests from other processes. There is no such program as webd or netd. Inetd can be described as a program that spawns other processes, but it is not known as a spawner.

3. B.   Microsoft calls internetworking servers "services." Services are another name for daemon, the term used by UNIX and Linux. Both services and daemons consume system resources when they are running.

4. B.   Multipurpose Internet Mail Extensions (MIME) are used to label files with an identifier. The web client uses that identifier to open an appropriate viewer for the data, if that viewer is installed on the client system. MIME labels are sometimes based on file extensions, but the web client relies on the MIME code in the packet header rather than the file name. Certificates are used to validate a user's identity. Permissions are used by the operating system to control access to files, folders, and directories.

5. C.   Hibba must change the operating system permissions to allow CGI scripts to execute. She would not need to change httpd to do this. Internetworking servers are started by daemons on Linux systems. They are controlled as services on Windows servers. The access rights are used to control user access to web server data.

6. C.   IMAP is the only one of the four protocols shown that is used by mail servers. NNTP is used by news servers. UDP is a transmission protocol commonly used by streaming media servers. FTP is used by FTP servers.

7. D.   Mailing lists and newsgroups use different message formats. Users must subscribe to mailing lists and newsgroups to post their messages. Mailing list servers may not store messages for later retrieval. Mailing lists and newsgroups can be made private, and restricted to certain users.

8. B.   Streaming media servers use UDP to send files, because UDP allows faster transmission than TCP. UDP does not get every packet to the client, but streaming media is designed to allow losses in transmission. The streaming media client uses buffers to store the media data before playback. FTP is not used for streaming media because it does not support real-time transmission and playback.

9. D.   Tristan should use FTP, and send Ericka an e-mail telling her where to find it. The file is 30MB, which may be too large to send as an e-mail attachment. The file is a customer database, so he should not put the file on the public web server or post the file's location on a newsgroup.

10. A.   The best course of action is to get a newsfeed and select only the agriculture newsgroups for download. Paige must also install an internal news server to store these messages for her fellow employees, but she does not need to start any new newsgroups. She should not tell employees how to access newsgroups on the Web, because some employees may subscribe to non-agriculture newsgroups.

11. B.   Name servers perform a URL to IP address lookup that most client applications require. Directory servers can be used to look up personal information. The name resolver is the DNS component that finds information on unknown domain names. The index file name for a web server is a configuration setting made by the server administrator.

12. B.   The loopback address (usually 127.0.0.1) is usually listed in the computer's hosts file. The loopback address must be set at that computer, because it is used to test IP connectivity. Without a connection, it would be impossible to send a loopback address to a computer. DHCP is used to provide a valid IP address to the computer, but it does not provide a loopback address. The NIC does not know what IP address it will be using—it must be told by the operating system or set manually.

13. **B.**   The root servers store and distribute top-level domain information for the Internet. Primary servers are used on ISPs and LANs to provide a local domain name service. Secondary servers are backups to the primary servers. The name resolver looks up unknown domain names from primary and root servers.

14. **B.**   The proxy server will cache frequently accessed web pages, and can also restrict access to external websites. This would be the best solution. A mirrored web server would not work, because the employees are probably accessing many different external web sites. Operating a caching server might require Everett to select and configure which sites are cached; a proxy server would manage this automatically. Gateway servers are used to connect web servers to other network services.

15. **D.**   Proxy servers provide transaction logging and filtering, web caching, Internet access through firewalls, and web server security. Proxy servers do not provide file and print services.

16. **C.**   A certificate contains a key that is issued or validated by a certificate server. The key is used to verify identity. The IP address is located in the IP header portion of a packet. Credit card receipts issued by websites usually do not include certificates. Websites can use accounts and passwords to control user access. Certificates can also be used, but are not required in default configurations.

17. **B.**   A directory server that supports LDAP will allow employees to look up information in their e-mail programs, along with other applications. A spreadsheet placed on the intranet is a good temporary solution, but will be harder to keep updated. If John were required to make the list publicly accessible, placing it on the website would work. Creating the list as a text file is not a good choice, as it will be difficult for employees to look up names in the file.

18. **C.**   A catalog server will provide an updated, searchable index of the website's contents. Posting a list of keywords will not be helpful for users. An external search engine may provide some search capabilities, but the links may not be updated often. A cache server helps store frequently accessed information in additional servers.

19. **B.**   Transaction servers support the three-tier client/server model.

20. **A.**   The Apache Group coordinates the open source development of the Apache web server. Apache is available in a Windows version, but is usually run on Linux systems. The other three products are sold on the traditional corporate model.

Chapter

7

Web Servers
and Databases

**THE CIW EXAM OBJECTIVE GROUPS COVERED
IN THIS CHAPTER:**

✓ Identify the functions and components of web servers,
  including but not limited to: various server types and related
  protocols, Internet connectivity, client-side and server-side
  scripting and applications, business needs, and server
  selection criteria.

The common perception is that the Web consists solely of HTML pages that contain attractive graphics and a few eye-opening pieces of animated, active content. However, the Web provides an effective tool for presenting and collecting data, as well. That is the focus of this chapter.

Today's websites are as transaction-based as they are graphics-based, meaning that beyond providing attractive visuals, they allow users to buy, sell, and exchange information. This level of functionality requires database gateways that work with web servers. To make your website ready for e-commerce, you must learn how to extend the functionality of a web server so it can enable transactions, access databases, and provide a sophisticated web presence.

We will begin our discussion with databases, and how they can be combined with web servers to provide data-driven websites. We will cover various kinds of database systems, including relational and object-oriented databases.

We will present several systems that provide this functionality. The web browser can use technologies such as client-side scripting and HTML forms to collect and present data. On the web server, the Common Gateway Interface (CGI) is a popular method for linking web servers and databases. Faster technologies, such as Server Application Programming Interfaces (SAPIs) and server-side scripting languages, and Java have become popular alternatives to CGI. We close the chapter with a brief discussion of database connectivity methods.

Databases

Let's start with the basic concept of a database. A *database* is a file or series of files used to organize information. It stores information in a consistent format, so that users can search the files for specific information. A sample database is illustrated in Table 7.1.

TABLE 7.1   Example of a Database Table

Record number	First_name	Last_name	Telephone	Email
1	Aimee	Mann	617-555-3492	aimeemann@yahoo.com
2	Roberto	Clemente	412-555-2648	slugger@pitt.com
3	Guy	Patterson	814-555-7587	guypa@msn.com
4	Barry	Allen	816-555-4567	barry@flash.net

A database is composed of several important components, the *field*, *record*, *table*, and *index*:

Field   This is a space allocated for the storage of a particular item of information. Fields are usually the smallest unit of information in a database. A field has several attributes, such as the type of data (such as text, numeric, object) and length or size (number of characters, significant digits, or object size). A field may also be calculated or determined by other fields. Each field in a specific database has its own unique name by which it is identified. In a spreadsheet, an individual field is represented as a cell.

Record   This constitutes a single, complete set of information composed of fields. A record can represent an individual customer, account, or other unit as appropriate to the business processes that the database supports. Records are sometimes assigned numbers to aid in identification. In a spreadsheet, a record is represented as a row. In relational databases, records are also called *tuples*.

Table   This is a file or unit in which records are stored. Database tables are often represented as having rows of records, and columns made up of individual fields.

Index   This is a list of unique identifiers or *keys* that identify each record. In a relational database table, unique keys are used to help maintain the integrity of the data table. The index is also used by a database management system to provide faster searches of the data table.

Transactions

In discussing databases, we often use the term *transaction* in two different senses. A financial transaction may represent a purchase in a store, a withdrawal from a checking account, or another event that involves an exchange of value. Databases are well suited for tracking and recording these events.

Over time, database professionals adopted the financial term transaction to represent an important database concept. In the IT sense, a transaction represents an event that changes or alters one or more records. When a user changes a record's contents and commits those changes to the database, we can say that a database transaction has occurred. IT professionals and database developers focus on maintaining the reliability and integrity of a database before, during, and after a database transaction.

Databases are essential for e-commerce transaction processing. The term *transaction processing* means the process of updating master files or databases immediately when a financial transaction takes place. Another commonly used name for this kind of transaction processing is *Online Transaction Processing (OLTP)*.

The Client/Server Model

The client/server model that we discussed in Chapter 2 has evolved into the primary model for deploying databases on networks. When you use a database, three major elements of the client/server model are involved:

User interface   The user interface determines how the client computer will render received information on the screen. A graphical operating system such as Windows or Linux provides a basic level of support for presenting the graphical user interface (GUI). Programmers write the rules and develop the screens that the application uses to present the data in its final form.

Process logic   This term refers to the way you access the physical database. This includes SQL and other languages. Process logic is sometimes called *business rules* or *business logic*, because these rules should be modeled after the actual business practices that the database supports.

Data storage   This layer is the database itself, which is hosted on one or more database servers.

The mainframe model for database access, also called the one-tier model, makes one computer responsible for all processes. The second model, called the two-tier model, separates the elements, making one computer responsible for both the process logic and the data storage; the other computer is responsible only for formatting the information on the screen. A diagram of this relationship is shown in Figure 7.1.

FIGURE 7.1 Two-tier architecture

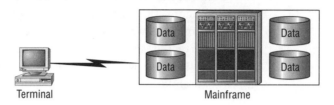

The three-tier architecture spreads the three elements across three different systems, as shown in Figure 7.2.

FIGURE 7.2 Three-tier architecture

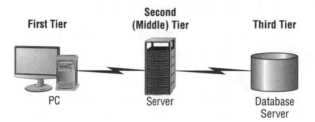

N-tier architecture distributes the middle-tier across several systems, as shown in Figure 7.3. N-tier solutions are also used when implementing an RDBMS or ODBMS solution, which we'll learn more about later in this chapter.

FIGURE 7.3 N-tier architecture

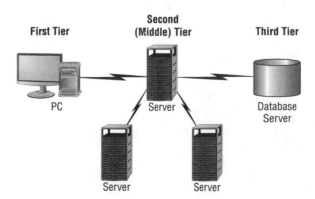

Real World Scenario

MapQuest.com and the N-Tier Architecture

R.R. Donnelley & Sons, a large publisher of road maps, operates MapQuest.com. This website offers interactive graphical maps, travel directions, and other services. A user can type an address or location name into a web form on the MapQuest.com home page, and see a graphical map that shows that location. MapQuest handles millions of requests per day using an N-tier architecture.

MapQuest's web server directs the inquiry to a set of database servers that contain physical address information. If the address is found, MapQuest can present a customized HTML page with images, text, and advertisements that relate to the requested address. To generate this content, MapQuest has several database server farms. These groups of linked servers are highly specialized.

A group of map servers locates and renders a custom graphical map of a requested address.

Another group of advertising servers locates images, text, and other content that ties the requested address to one or more of MapQuest's advertisers. The user can check one or more items they would like included on the map, such as restaurants, stores, and other businesses. These businesses are also referred to the address servers and map servers, so that they may be placed on the graphical map.

Other server farms help present the information in specific formats for Palm computers, telephones, and other portable devices.

A *thin client solution* uses a web browser to access a database via a web server. It is also an example of a three-tier solution: The process logic occurs on a server, the database resides on another, and our client application, the web browser formats the received information.

A thin-client solution could also be an example of an n-tier solution, because many different systems might be used in the middle tier. For example, an e-commerce site may use a certificate server, a transaction server, and a catalog server to present and process a secure order form. We will discuss e-commerce in more detail in Chapter 13.

Database Reliability

Two benefits of an n-tier solution include load balancing and fault tolerance. These are important attributes for a database system. Suppose a user is using their web browser to change a record in the database. The database system should be reliable and robust, so that a database record is not corrupted by physical or network problems.

Load balancing is the process of distributing processing and communications activity evenly across a computer network so that no single device is overwhelmed. Load balancing is especially important for networks where it's difficult to predict the number of requests that will be issued to a server.

Busy websites typically employ two or more web servers in a load-balancing scheme. The servers cooperate in handling incoming requests, so that a single server does not approach its processing capacity. These servers may contain entire sets or portions of duplicate data. This web server may be co-located with the first web server, or it may be located in another department or geographic region. To handle greater loads, you can simply add more servers. A set of load-balanced servers is also called a *server farm*. Server administrators use load balancing to provide a flexible, proactive approach for managing web server capacity.

Fault tolerance is the ability of a system to respond gracefully to an unexpected hardware or software failure. There are many levels of fault tolerance, the lowest being the ability to continue operation in the event of a power failure. At a network level, a fault-tolerant system may monitor network connectivity and traffic, and help reroute connections if one server in the system is unreachable.

Database software usually includes additional features for maintaining reliability. For example, SQL is based around individual database transactions. A programmer can use SQL features to lock a database record that a user is changing. This record lock prevents other users from changing that record until the database finalizes or commits the transaction. If the database detects a record error, another SQL command can rollback a record to its previous state. Many database systems use SQL features to provide an additional software level of database reliability.

Real World Scenario

MapQuest.com and Load Balancing

MapQuest operates a number of server farms in locations around the world. Load balancing is important for a site such as MapQuest. The website handles millions of requests daily, and is designed to provide complex, custom web pages quickly.

There are several sets of server farms located in North America, and containing mapping information for the United States, Canada, and Mexico. The MapQuest web servers use a load-balancing scheme that allocates queries to specific server farms, so that no set of servers becomes overloaded. MapQuest uses internal networks and communications lines to ferry requests between the server farms.

MapQuest also offers mapping services for other countries. MapQuest places some server farms in specific geographic locations, to reduce latency and increase site capacity. The MapQuest servers in Europe are focused on providing European mapping data, while servers in Asia focus on Asian countries. This enables the local server farms to handle mapping requests for what are probably local users.

Database Systems

Now that we have discussed what a database is, we can go over the various types of database management systems. Database systems provide the architecture and methods for working with data. There are three types of database models: *relational*, *non-relational*, and *object-oriented*.

Relational In this model, data is stored in a series of related tables. You can create small tables, called lookup tables, which are a list of entries that can be used in a particular field. For example, the State/Province field in a customer's address can be linked to a short table that lists the U.S. states and Canadian provinces, along with their two-letter abbreviations. The two-letter code would be entered in the customer's State field, rather than the complete name of the state or province. Using lookup tables helps enforce *referential integrity*, or the consistent entry of data across related tables. You can also create tables that contain the details for a particular record, such as an order. The details would be related or linked to the order by a unique order number. Relational databases have predefined types of data that must be used, such as numbers and strings of text.

Non-relational In this type of database, all data is kept in a single table. This type of database is also called a *flat file database*. This model is convenient for small quantities of data. However, it is easy to create erroneous or duplicate data, because you cannot easily use lookup tables to help enforce referential integrity. For example, a user can use the wrong code or spelling for an entry in the State field.

Object-oriented In this model, users and developers can easily define their own types of data, called *objects*. Objects may also be defined on other, more basic objects. This model works well with object-oriented programming languages, which let developers use complex data types.

Regardless of the type of database you are using, you need software that will allow you to store, access, or manipulate the data in an organized, secure way. Database management systems are designed to provide the process logic that enables a client to manipulate a database.

The software that performs this task for a non-relational database is called a *database management system (DBMS)*. If you plan to work with relational databases, you must use a *relational database management system (RDBMS)*. Similarly, whenever you work with an object-oriented database, you must use an *object database management system (ODBMS)*. Database management systems can be distributed, and therefore include solutions that reside on both the client and server. As you will learn, some database management systems are more distributed than others.

In addition to ease of access, each management system is designed to ensure orderly access to the information. Another goal is to ensure that the data maintains its integrity. For example, imagine what would happen if more than one person at a time were allowed to update the same database file. A management system also maintains integrity by making sure that programmers do not enter duplicate information into the system. Security is also an important feature of a DBMS, RDBMS, or ODBMS. For example, database files can be password protected or encrypted.

A DBMS allows you to work with two database types:

Hierarchical One record contains physical links to another. Only one user can access such a database record at a time. Older mainframes use this type of database.

Network Similar to a hierarchical database, but allows many users to access the record.

An RDBMS works only with relational databases. Rather than using static links between information, a relational database uses tables that are indexed or tagged so users can access the information by issuing different queries. These queries do not reorganize the table itself. They only allow the information found within the tables to be presented differently. Microsoft Access, shown in Figure 7.4, is an example of an RDBMS application, because it allows you to create, manipulate, and program a relational database.

FIGURE 7.4 RDBMS application

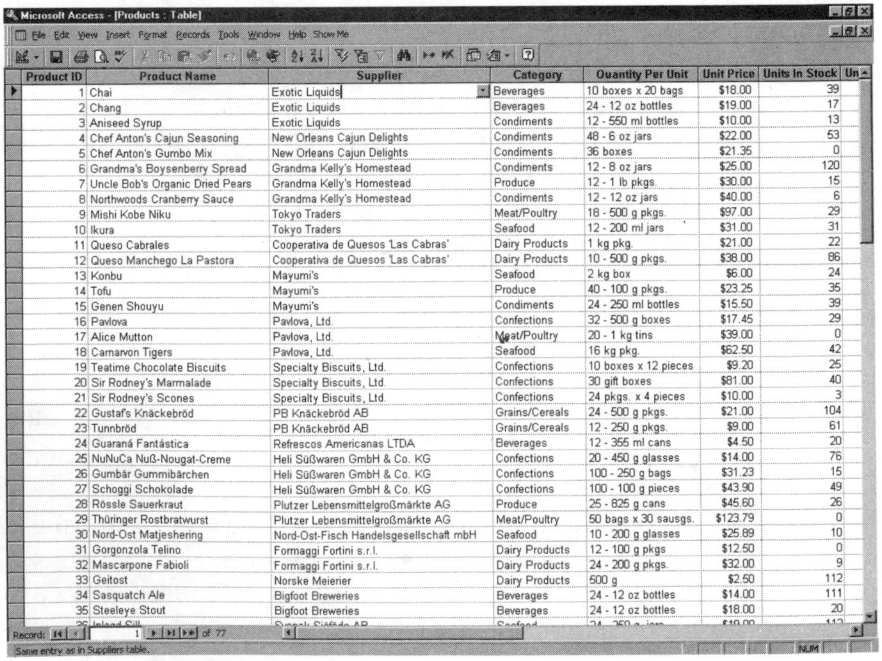

Product ID	Product Name	Supplier	Category	Quantity Per Unit	Unit Price	Units In Stock
1	Chai	Exotic Liquids	Beverages	10 boxes x 20 bags	$18.00	39
2	Chang	Exotic Liquids	Beverages	24 - 12 oz bottles	$19.00	17
3	Aniseed Syrup	Exotic Liquids	Condiments	12 - 550 ml bottles	$10.00	13
4	Chef Anton's Cajun Seasoning	New Orleans Cajun Delights	Condiments	48 - 6 oz jars	$22.00	53
5	Chef Anton's Gumbo Mix	New Orleans Cajun Delights	Condiments	36 boxes	$21.35	0
6	Grandma's Boysenberry Spread	Grandma Kelly's Homestead	Condiments	12 - 8 oz jars	$25.00	120
7	Uncle Bob's Organic Dried Pears	Grandma Kelly's Homestead	Produce	12 - 1 lb pkgs.	$30.00	15
8	Northwoods Cranberry Sauce	Grandma Kelly's Homestead	Condiments	12 - 12 oz jars	$40.00	6
9	Mishi Kobe Niku	Tokyo Traders	Meat/Poultry	18 - 500 g pkgs.	$97.00	29
10	Ikura	Tokyo Traders	Seafood	12 - 200 ml jars	$31.00	31
11	Queso Cabrales	Cooperativa de Quesos 'Las Cabras'	Dairy Products	1 kg pkg.	$21.00	22
12	Queso Manchego La Pastora	Cooperativa de Quesos 'Las Cabras'	Dairy Products	10 - 500 g pkgs.	$38.00	86
13	Konbu	Mayumi's	Seafood	2 kg box	$6.00	24
14	Tofu	Mayumi's	Produce	40 - 100 g pkgs.	$23.25	35
15	Genen Shouyu	Mayumi's	Condiments	24 - 250 ml bottles	$15.50	39
16	Pavlova	Pavlova, Ltd.	Confections	32 - 500 g boxes	$17.45	29
17	Alice Mutton	Pavlova, Ltd.	Meat/Poultry	20 - 1 kg tins	$39.00	0
18	Carnarvon Tigers	Pavlova, Ltd.	Seafood	16 kg pkg.	$62.50	42
19	Teatime Chocolate Biscuits	Specialty Biscuits, Ltd.	Confections	10 boxes x 12 pieces	$9.20	25
20	Sir Rodney's Marmalade	Specialty Biscuits, Ltd.	Confections	30 gift boxes	$81.00	40
21	Sir Rodney's Scones	Specialty Biscuits, Ltd.	Confections	24 pkgs. x 4 pieces	$10.00	3
22	Gustaf's Knäckebröd	PB Knäckebröd AB	Grains/Cereals	24 - 500 g pkgs.	$21.00	104
23	Tunnbröd	PB Knäckebröd AB	Grains/Cereals	12 - 250 g pkgs.	$9.00	61
24	Guaraná Fantástica	Refrescos Americanas LTDA	Beverages	12 - 355 ml cans	$4.50	20
25	NuNuCa Nuß-Nougat-Creme	Heli Süßwaren GmbH & Co. KG	Confections	20 - 450 g glasses	$14.00	76
26	Gumbär Gummibärchen	Heli Süßwaren GmbH & Co. KG	Confections	100 - 250 g bags	$31.23	15
27	Schoggi Schokolade	Heli Süßwaren GmbH & Co. KG	Confections	100 - 100 g pieces	$43.90	49
28	Rössle Sauerkraut	Plutzer Lebensmittelgroßmärkte AG	Produce	25 - 825 g cans	$45.60	26
29	Thüringer Rostbratwurst	Plutzer Lebensmittelgroßmärkte AG	Meat/Poultry	50 bags x 30 sausgs.	$123.79	0
30	Nord-Ost Matjeshering	Nord-Ost-Fisch Handelsgesellschaft mbH	Seafood	10 - 200 g glasses	$25.89	10
31	Gorgonzola Telino	Formaggi Fortini s.r.l.	Dairy Products	12 - 100 g pkgs	$12.50	0
32	Mascarpone Fabioli	Formaggi Fortini s.r.l.	Dairy Products	24 - 200 g pkgs.	$32.00	9
33	Geitost	Norske Meierier	Dairy Products	500 g	$2.50	112
34	Sasquatch Ale	Bigfoot Breweries	Beverages	24 - 12 oz bottles	$14.00	111
35	Steeleye Stout	Bigfoot Breweries	Beverages	24 - 12 oz bottles	$18.00	20

Table 7.2 lists various enterprise RDBMS providers and their products. An enterprise RDBMS is designed for high-volume transaction processing environments, using dedicated database servers to store and retrieve information.

TABLE 7.2 Enterprise Relational Database Management Systems

Developer	Product	URL
Borland	Interbase	www.borland.com
IBM	DB2	www.ibm.com
iPlanet	IPlanet Application Server	www.iPlanet.com
Microsoft	SQL Server 2000	www.microsoft.com
Oracle	Oracle 9i	www.oracle.com

Object-oriented database management systems (ODBMS) attempt to mimic real-world data relationships. The most popular form of ODBMS uses Java as a programming language, which will discuss later in this chapter.

Introduction to Database Gateways for Web Servers

Not all web client requests are for static documents, such as simple HTML files. Some HTML requests require the web server to pass data from itself to another server, application, or database. Furthermore, such requests must also include instructions that tell the web server to activate a specific program for the server to execute on its host machine. This process invokes programs that combine the web server and a database into an effective unit. An HTTP gateway is the script such as a Perl script or a mini-application, like a Java servlet or dynamic link library that allows a web server to pass a client's data to a program or database and then returns the program's output to the client.

At one time, whenever an administrator wanted to create an image map, a server-side script had to be used. Furthermore, a server-side script was needed to detect a browser (and customize a user's experience according to that browser) or to include programs such as hit counters, clocks, and other active content. Server-side scripts can also determine whether a user has entered the correct data type in a field. For example, you would not want a user to enter numbers in a State/Province field, which normally expects two-letter abbreviations. This function is called *data validation*. To perform server-side data validation, the user must send or submit the data to the server.

However, client-side scripting now allows web browsers to handle many of these tasks. In client-side scripting, the instructions for active content, such as Java, JavaScript, and ActiveX, are all embedded in simple HTML files. Data validation can also be performed on the client-side before the data is sent to the web server. This method reduces the load on the server, freeing it to process more clients. Also, certain techniques like animation must be handled on the client-side, as the client's operating system must provide the necessary graphic support.

With server-side scripting, you can create a *server-side include* that will create custom web pages based upon a user's request. A server-side include is a piece of code written into an HTML page that activates programs and interpreters on the server. An include is designed to create active web pages and reduce server overhead.

Client-Side Scripting

In the struggle to access databases and still ensure effective processing and bandwidth use, web programmers have developed both client-side and server-side solutions. As mentioned before, a client-side solution using JavaScript, Java, or ActiveX can help you create an impressive web page. When a user visits a website that has any active content, client-side scripts and programs perform operations *after* they are downloaded, thereby distributing the work between the client and the server. This distribution ultimately speeds up the website because the server is not bogged down with calculations for every client. The web server can use this additional CPU time that was lost to perform calculations to be used for fulfilling client requests.

In many cases, distributing the work to clients is fastest and easiest; each client can decide which data should be displayed. With the advent of advanced HTML technologies, one might think that server-side scripting is outdated. However, server-side scripting is still useful and necessary for certain applications.

Transactions and Download Time

Overuse of client-side scripting can result in long downloads. Even though a client-side script might reduce the server's processing load, download time for large files full of JavaScript, ActiveX, and Java applets may cause users to avoid those web pages and sites.

There are additional client-side drawbacks. For example, a dynamic web page might be built from data that is managed by another application. The client would need special drivers to access that data, meaning every visitor to the website would have to download extra driver files.

Another important part of optimizing Internet performance is to minimize the number of network transactions. Downloading one large file is faster than creating many smaller connections, because every TCP/IP connection has an overhead cost.

In addition to these performance issues, security risks are inherent in allowing every client to have access to data sources. The data source often cannot manage its own security. Giving different clients variable degrees of access to data makes the issue even more difficult to resolve from the client side. If the client has any kind of third-party contact, security is virtually impossible for the server to manage. The use of back-end data sources allows pages to be far more dynamic than they are when only client-side scripting is employed.

Combining Client-Side and Server-Side Scripting

The optimal web page combines server-side and client-side scripting, creating a load balanced client/server system where tasks are assigned to the most appropriate layer. Here as some general guidelines:

- Access to any data that resides on the client, such as the time or type of browser, should be implemented with client-side scripting.

- Access to any data that resides anywhere except the client should be implemented with server-side scripting.

- Minor changes to HTML layout and properties should be managed on the client side.

If you plan to customize an HTML page based on a user request, deliver alternative media such as plug-ins and other files, or access databases, you should perform these tasks on the server side.

HTML Forms and Form Processing

Currently, most web-based transactions occur through HTML forms. HTML files are plain text files that have been marked up with special language elements called *tags*, which are embedded in the text. Tags are pieces of text, enclosed in angle brackets and invisible in the final display, that provide instructions to programs designed to interpret HTML. For example, you may want to change the color of some text on your web page. You would apply this formatting by embedding opening and closing tags around the text that you want colored. We will discuss HTML in detail in Chapters 14 and 15.

When a content designer creates an HTML form, she uses the <FORM> tag to associate that form with a server resource. This server resource is a program or a subroutine dynamically linked into the server process. It receives the field information from the HTML form and processes it.

Every HTML form includes a submit button; when the user clicks it, the browser program packages the user data from the form fields and sends it to the server, along with the URL of the server resources that must handle the data. Two attributes are associated with the <FORM> tag: METHOD and ACTION.

The METHOD attribute sets the method by which the browser sends the form data to the server for processing. The two possible methods are:

GET   Form data is appended to the URL string that points to the location where the form is submitted. This method puts the data in an environment variable called query_string, and indicates how much data it is sending in another environment variable called content_length. You can read data sent using the GET method by reading the query_string variable for a number of bytes equal to the value of the content_length variable.

POST   Form data is sent separately from the actual call to the script. The POST method sends the data within the HTTP header and can take advantage of encryption methods.

POST is the preferred method and is the safer option for transferring large blocks of data or when data security is an issue. The GET method passes the form data in the URL where it can be easily accessed by network analyzers and viewed in the address box of a web browser.

The ACTION attribute specifies the database gateway, in this case a CGI script, and a web server path used to process the form. The form's contents will be uploaded to a CGI script and then sent via e-mail to the specified address.

An example of the <FORM> tag using the ACTION attribute follows:

```
<FORM METHOD=POST ACTION="http://www.uunet.net/cgi-bin/form/
person@company.com">
```

Now that you have reviewed how an HTML form sends information to a server, we are ready to discuss the various methods for creating a gateway between the client, the server and the database. Several alternatives to Common Gateway Interface (CGI) scripts have appeared over the years. Some of these solutions are proprietary, such as Microsoft Internet Server Application Program Interface (ISAPI), whereas others use open standards, such as Java servlets. Each solution, including CGI, uses an *application program interface (API)*. An API is a well-documented method that allows programmers to make requests of an operating system or application. The API describes what tasks can be performed by a software application, and defines how the programmer must request and structure these tasks.

With CGI and its various alternatives, some servers can pass data to subroutines contained within an object library that is dynamically linked to the server. This method provides the same functionality as executing co-processes through a gateway, but with better performance. We will discuss the essentials of such gateways, and why some are more popular than others. It will help you understand the concepts of client-side and server-side scripting, and how they help facilitate such gateways.

Common Gateway Interface (CGI)

The Common Gateway Interface (CGI) represents the most simple and universal database gateway on web servers. The CGI was included in early web server software and was one of the original defined standards for the Web. Thus, CGI is available for many web server software applications.

In CGI, the web server responds to an HTML form by running or executing a co-process. This co-process is another program that manipulates the data. The co-process returns the output from the process to the CGI interface, and the web server then sends the results to the client. This entire sequence is responsible for constructing a correctly formatted HTTP reply that can be rendered correctly in a web browser.

As shown in Figure 7.5, a CGI script allows you to create applications that enable transactions between a web server and a database.

FIGURE 7.5   The traffic flow when using a CGI program

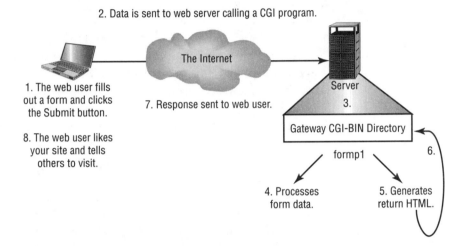

2. Data is sent to web server calling a CGI program.

The Internet

1. The web user fills out a form and clicks the Submit button.

7. Response sent to web user.

8. The web user likes your site and tells others to visit.

Server
3.

Gateway CGI-BIN Directory

formp1

6.

4. Processes form data.

5. Generates return HTML.

Many websites rely on CGI as their database gateway. Most programs executed by servers are written in the script language Perl, but any language can be used. The programs executed through CGI are usually called scripts. CGI scripts are located in a directory called CGI-BIN. As we discussed in the previous chapter, this directory must have execute permissions because the scripts, as well as the programs, must have access to the processor. A common problem is that the operating system denies such permissions, whereas the web server grants them by default. The web server will attempt to run the CGI script, but the operating system will not allow execution.

CGI Benefits

The chief benefit of CGI is that it is a time-tested technology that stands at the core of the Web. CGI scripts written in languages such as Perl, Python, C++, and Tcl/Tk are popular solutions used on thousands of websites. Many developers and server administrators can support this technology. Because it is time-tested, many developers know how to implement it quickly and effectively.

Another significant benefit is that most CGI solutions are not platform-specific. Because most scripts are written in Perl, you can copy a script that works well to another machine; many CGI programs are written in *interpreted languages* rather than *compiled languages*. An interpreted language, such as JavaScript or VBScript, need not be compiled. These programming languages require specific software to run, called *interpreters*. Interpreters run scripts by executing one line after another when the script is executed. The script is a text file, so the developer can easily modify the script as needed.

Applications written in Java, C, and C++ must be compiled, or translated into a machine-readable executable form, before they can be run on a computer. Compiled languages can create larger, faster programs than interpreted languages, but they tend to be more complex and difficult than interpreted languages.

CGI Drawbacks

One of the drawbacks of CGI is that it creates *out-of-process* events, meaning that each script runs as a separate process on your server. An out-of-process event occurs when an executable program launches a separate process each time it is loaded or referenced. If one person accesses your CGI script to process a form that orders a book, for example, it is as if that person has launched one instance of that CGI program. If another user accesses the same CGI script, a separate instance of that same program loads into the computer's memory. Each subsequent query will load yet another instance of that program into memory.

If you are hosting a site with light to medium traffic, such activity might not present a problem. However, if your site experiences heavy traffic, and if thousands of users call too many instances of your CGI script simultaneously, your processor utilization could rise to near 100 percent. When this overload occurs, your server will be unable to sustain more sessions, and your site may be unavailable to potential customers.

A CGI program that is written in Perl can be brought *in process* by making `perl.exe` part of the web server program. With an in-process model, an executable program provides a threading model that allows it to handle requests from multiple users. This eliminates the need to launch a separate process each time it is accessed. Under UNIX and Linux, the `mod_perl` extension to the Apache web server accomplishes this task. Under Windows, Perl interpreters implemented as dynamic link libraries (DLLs) extend the web server to solve this problem.

Another drawback with CGI programs is that unless they are very well written, they probably will not account for unexpected user entries and choices. If a script does not account for all possibilities, it will not deliver the user's information correctly, resulting in lost information.

Because CGI can call events out of process, CGI can also invite security problems. Hackers often attempt to get a script to operate in unexpected ways. There are several sample Perl CGI scripts that are installed with Linux, for example. These scripts were designed for demonstration purposes only, and the developers did not include adequate security measures in their programming. The server administrator should delete or disable these scripts on a public web server. Hackers can scan Linux web servers to detect whether these scripts are running. Because CGI scripts require permissions to execute instructions, a hacker can assimilate CGI-based permissions and instructions to gain root and administrative access to the web server's Linux operating system.

Even legitimate users can create problems by making unexpected or naive choices. There are CGI web form submission scripts available that crash or fail when the user types a punctuation mark in a data field. At best, these CGI scripts are a nuisance for users. At worst, these scripts can tax a web server's capacity if many users crash the script at once.

Finally, a CGI script cannot tell the difference between one session and another; it is stateless. Therefore, a script must start a new process every time it is accessed, even if the same user accesses it. This additional work requires more processor time. If the script could recognize where and when a session ended, it could provide ways to continue the transaction at the point at which it was stopped. Newer stateful technologies such as ISAPI and Java servlets allow sessions to continue, which help ease the processor load, conserve bandwidth, and speed transactions. Nevertheless, CGI is a well-tested and viable solution that remains quite popular.

 Real World Scenario

How MapQuest Uses CGI

MapQuest launched its consumer-oriented website in February 1996. At the time, the only available database gateway was CGI. Over the years, MapQuest has enhanced its CGI capabilities to handle its growing website.

MapQuest uses a suite of in-process programs to handle CGI requests, as an out-of-process model would quickly use up the available memory on an ordinary web server. This software is installed on a series of dedicated web server farms. These server farms take the data requests from web clients, and use CGI and Perl to convert them into SQL data queries that are sent to the address, mapping, and advertiser server farms for additional processing. Each CGI server can handle thousands of user requests simultaneously.

MapQuest sells its services to other websites. MapQuest can host the server farms, or a company can buy the software and host the data on its own servers. This kind of enterprise, N-tier architecture solution is an excellent example of how CGI is used in e-commerce.

Server Application Programming Interfaces (SAPIs)

To solve these problems presented by CGI, server developers have designed gateways using dynamically loaded object libraries. Rather than being executables, as CGI programs are, ISAPI applications are generally implemented as *dynamic link library (DLL)* files. The web server generates the reply document by calling a dynamically loaded subroutine and returning the subroutine's output to the client. A DLL is a program that can be shared and executed by several applications at once. Once loaded, these dynamic link library files can handle every request without being reloaded into the system's memory.

Using dynamically loaded libraries eliminates the substantial overhead involved in starting a new process on the host, thus providing better performance. As you will see, although these solutions improve processing speed and security, they also present new challenges.

Server application programming interfaces (SAPIs) present viable solutions to CGI, by supporting libraries and reducing the number of concurrent threads on a server. There are two popular web server SAPIs: Microsoft's ISAPI, and Netscape's NSAPI. Each gateway method uses proprietary technology, meaning that the program code and functions are tied to a specific vendor. By using a SAPI, you tend to limit yourself to one company's solution, rather than relying on an open standard.

The *Internet Server Application Programming Interface (ISAPI)* is a proprietary web server extension that allows the server to execute other programs and scripts without the expensive processing associated with CGI. It is supported only on Microsoft web servers, such as IIS, and some third-party proprietary gateways.

ISAPI applications run as threads or sub-processes of the web server process. The main benefit of this technique is that you can support more user requests without taxing the server's processor and input/output system. Another benefit of ISAPI is that you can use it to track client state across requests. ISAPI supports both client-side and server-side scripting with VBScript or JScript.

The Netscape Server Application Programming Interface (NSAPI) is a web server extension that allows the web server to execute other programs and scripts without the server-intensive process associated with CGI.

The main difference between the NSAPI and ISAPI is that NSAPI supports different languages, and runs in a slightly different environment than ISAPI. Therefore, even though the two operate on the same principle that allows them to use multiple server threads, significant differences still exist.

NSAPI was supported mostly on Netscape web servers and proprietary gateway products. NSAPI is now considered a legacy API, as iPlanet has ceased development of NSAPI enhancements in favor of other technologies. NSAPI uses JavaScript as its preferred server-side programming language, but it does support C++ and VBScript. ISAPI favors Microsoft VBScript, although both languages are supported to a certain extent in both SAPIs.

Because they are dynamic link libraries, ISAPI and NSAPI files have the .dll extension and are stored in folders specific to either the operating system or the web server.

Server-Side Scripting Technologies

Additional popular scripting products used to connect to databases and other programs are Microsoft Active Server Pages (ASP), Netscape Server-Side JavaScript (SSJS), and Macromedia ColdFusion. These scripting technologies provide effective alternatives to CGI, but they are also proprietary. JavaServer Pages (JSP) and Personal Home Page (PHP), which are similar in function to ASP and SSJS, are not proprietary. This section will cover the following server-side scripting solutions:

- Server-Side JavaScript (SSJS)
- Active Server Pages (ASP)
- Personal Home Page (PHP)
- JavaServer Pages (JSP)
- Java Servlets
- Cold Fusion

Server-Side JavaScript (SSJS)

Netscape originally developed the iPlanet server-scripting technology, *Server-Side JavaScript (SSJS)* in 1997, as a part of its Enterprise Server and LiveWire offerings. SSJS is similar to Microsoft ASP (which we'll cover in the next section) in that it relies on objects and is interpreted by the server. However, because SSJS supports JavaScript, the object names are different from those used in Active Server Pages, which we will discuss shortly. Another consideration is that because JavaScript is more universal than VBScript, you can find more people able to code the necessary scripts. You must use iPlanet web Server software, because it is the only product that contains the server-side interpreter used by JavaScript to connect to databases.

Despite the fact that objects are named differently, porting from one system to the other is relatively easy for many who understand scripting languages. The real advantage of SSJS over Active Server Pages is that it can run Windows, UNIX, Linux, Macintosh, and Novell NetWare. This, and the fact that SSJS implies the use of JavaScript instead of JScript or VBScript, is the essential difference between ASP and SSJS.

You can also embed Server-Side JavaScript into HTML pages, as well as in stand-alone files, as long as you use the .js extension. Special HTML tags allow commands to be executed on the server before the resulting value is returned to the client.

Active Server Pages (ASP)

Active Server Pages (ASP) is a Microsoft server-side scripting technology. It is superior to standard CGI in many ways. ASP technology is well integrated with Microsoft server products. They also give reasonably reliable perfor mance. You can use Active Server Pages to create server-side includes, as well as to connect to a database. Other uses include creating hit counters and clocks.

An ASP file is an HTML page with special commands embedded in it. These commands are executed on the server, and the resulting value is sent to the client. Because the ASP commands operate behind the scenes, the client does not see them.

ASP commands use a set of built-in server-side objects designed to simplify database connectivity. ASP files replace the .html file name extension with .asp. Other than this and the objects to which you refer, the HTML page remains the same. When the server receives a request for a file with this extension, it automatically checks the document for embedded commands. A standard HTML document with the .asp extension is simply an Active Server Pages file with no commands.

IIS, ASP, and ISAPI are designed to work together as a complete solution. Before using Active Server Pages, you must install a web server that supports ASP. Microsoft Internet Information Services (IIS) is the most common ASP web server, and is included with Windows NT/2000 Server. For testing and development purposes, Microsoft Personal Web Server can be used on individual workstations.

ASP can operate on other web servers by installing Sun's Chili!Soft ASP software. Chili!Soft provides ASP functionality on multiple operating systems, including Windows NT/2000, UNIX, Linux, AIX, HP-UX, Sun Cobalt, and Macintosh. Chili!Soft also supports several different web servers, including IIS, Apache, and iPlanet. For more information about this software, visit www.chilisoft.com.

You can use any of several interpreted scripting languages with Active Server Pages, including VBScript, Jscript, JavaScript, and Perl. However, ASP is optimized to work with VBScript and ActiveX/COM components. Only Microsoft web browsers support VBScript and ActiveX technologies on the client side, but any web browsers can access ASP applications, because the ASP commands execute on the server side.

Another way to access databases and other applications on the server side is to use Microsoft *ActiveX Data Objects (ADO)*. Active Server Pages works with ADO to provide data-access capabilities to a website.

ADO is a part of the Component Object Model (COM), the Microsoft model for creating applications that can work together across a network even though they were created using different computer languages. ADO uses the Microsoft proprietary Object Linking and Embedding Database (OLE DB) model to actually access the database or other information. In addition to its server-side capabilities, one of the ways ADO enables database access is through the use of client-side ActiveX controls, which can obtain database information and embed it within an HTML page. For more information, consult www.microsoft.com/data/ado.

Personal Home Page (PHP)

Personal Home Page (PHP) is another server-side scripting language you can embed in HTML pages to make them dynamic. Similar to other server-side scripting languages, PHP enables web pages to automatically obtain a user's browser version, as well as handle forms. It also works well when connecting the web server to databases.

PHP is currently in its fourth version, which is called PHP4. Because PHP is an interpreted language, you will need to download and install the PHP interpreter on your web server. PHP interpreters for Apache and IIS are available, supporting Windows, Linux, and UNIX operating systems. You can download the PHP interpreter of your choice, along with programming information, from www.php.net/.

This technology has become a popular alternative to Microsoft's ASP. PHP is available free of charge, and provides another example of the open source software movement. The goal of this movement is to allow users to download and customize applications and server programs for free. In exchange, users are asked to diligently report bugs and improvement suggestions to the creators.

HTML

Some database products offer the choice to save the actual database as an HTML file. This feature allows you to directly publish the database tables to a web server. These database files are generally used for viewing or displaying data. HTML was designed to format and display text, so it provides no support for editing or changing data. For any applications that require changing a record, another solution such as CGI, ASP, or an enterprise data server should be considered.

The industry standard is to implement an HTML gateway as an add-on to the database product, because its ability to support scripting and other application logic is fairly limited. HTML gateways tend to use a proprietary engine or an ISAPI-based engine to convert data to HTML. In the case of static HTML, the database application parses the database tables and inserts HTML table elements between the database table cell contents to provide a static HTML table.

Some applications, such as Microsoft Access 2000/XP, offer some options as to how the database will function. For example, you could publish the database as HTML, or Dynamic HTML with ASP files. Dynamic HTML provides support for larger database files, by providing data search and sort functions in the Microsoft Internet Explorer web browser. We will discuss Dynamic HTML, which uses client-side scripting to extend regular HTML, in Chapter 15.

Dynamic HTML generally requires a product such as IBM Net.Data. Such programs generally implement an HTML conversion engine as a shared library to avoid the performance overhead usually associated with CGI.

Java and Java Servlets

Servlets are small Java services that complement the web server. A Java servlet is far more powerful than any scripting language because Java is compiled. Java is not a scripting language. It is a full-fledged object-oriented programming language that can be used to create major applications, as well as Java servlets. Because Java is a cross-platform language, Java servlet technology is a compelling solution for many organizations.

A Java program, such as a Java servlet, can operate in many platforms because of the *Java Virtual Machine (JVM)*. A JVM is a small, efficient operating system that resides on top of other operating systems. The JVM creates a computing environment that runs Java applications, and also protects the computer's data. This environment is sometimes referred to as the *sandbox*.

To clarify, suppose a parent places a child in a sandbox and tells her not to leave. The parent gives her a few toys with which to play. With Java, the computer acts as the parent. The JVM is the sandbox. The tools are the computer resources the JVM may use. The child is the Java application.

Inside the sandbox, the JVMs have limited access to the computer's resources. A Java program can do only certain tasks that can be run in a secure manner without crashing the computer. Even with these restrictions, a JVM can run powerful Java games and office software.

Instead of being compiled to a specific processor, a Java program is compiled to run on a JVM. As long as a system is running a compatible JVM, the servlet or application will run. Windows and Macintosh operating systems, as well as Netscape Navigator and Microsoft Internet Explorer, all include JVMs.

Once a web server loads a Java servlet into memory, the servlet is persistent. It stays loaded until the server is restarted or the servlet is ended. This approach is similar to the in-process CGI model we discussed earlier, but servlets tend to be less expensive to develop and implement.

Java also enables programmers to use the *Common Object Request Broker Architecture (CORBA)*, an architecture designed to allow programs written in different languages to work together, regardless of which operating system they use. CORBA was developed by an industry consortium known as the Object Management Group (`www.omg.org`). There are several implementations of CORBA, the most widely used being IBM's SOM and DSOM architectures. CORBA has also been embraced by iPlanet as part of its Integration Server platform.

Java servlets and many scripting languages have the same basic architecture: They both use objects and are platform-independent. Servlets, however, have some special abilities that scripts do not. One example is a capability called *servlet chaining*. Servlets are created as modular pieces of code, and can be linked together, as if in a chain. The first servlet receives a request, processes it, then sends output. When servlets are chained, each one's output goes to another servlet, rather than back to the client. After processing, the information is sent either back to the client or to another servlet. Such practice allows you to distribute processing over a network.

Another advantage is that servlets are created using Java. Java's advantage over any other scripting language is complexity. Although Java is not as difficult to program as C or C++, it is fairly powerful, because you can create objects whose life cycles are unconnected to the server. In other words, Java, unlike JavaScript, can easily maintain the state or information of a client/server transaction, thereby allowing complex Internet sessions. Whereas JavaScript relies on cookies, Java has an innate ability to prolong web-based networking sessions.

Servlets can also forward requests to other machines as part of their ability to work with other servers. Thus, when a servlet receives a request, it could determine that a system is being used beyond its capacity. The servlet could then respond to this problem by sending the request to a different system on the network.

Because Java is less platform-specific than SAPIs, servlets have become popular for implementing web gateways. In this way, they are like Perl CGI scripts. Unlike CGI, however, Java servlets run in threads and not separate processes, and therefore are more efficient than CGI scripts.

JavaServer Pages (JSP)

The JavaServer Pages technology represents Java's entry into the realm of server-side scripting. Instead of using a Perl, SSJS, or ASP interpreter, JSP uses a specialized *Java servlet*. A Java servlet is a dedicated Java program that resides on a server, which extends a server's functionality. The servlet used by JSP is called the JSP engine. It will run on Windows NT/2000, Novell NetWare, UNIX, and Linux platforms. JSP is not proprietary, as are ASP and SSJS, which require specific Microsoft and Netscape software, respectively.

Figure 7.6 shows how a JSP file downloaded by a user communicates with the JSP engine, which resides on a web server. All server-side scripting technologies work similar to the JSP model. JavaServer Pages use a `.jsp` filename extension.

FIGURE 7.6 Using JavaServer Pages technology

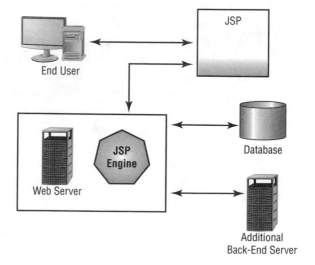

JSP Advantages

JSP technology is similar to ASP and SSJS in that it allows sophisticated database connectivity. However, JSP can provide even more sophisticated data handling. For example, JSP excels at processing the information contained in an HTML document separately from the way it is presented on the page.

JavaServer Pages technology is similar to Perl and PHP3 in that it is vendor neutral and free of charge. However, the chief difference between JSP and Perl and PHP3 is that JSP is more *extensible* and allows you to process information in a more sophisticated manner. An extensible system can be customized and expanded.

For more information, refer to the Sun JSP web page at `java.sun.com/products/jsp/index.html`. This site provides JSP server software and suggestions on getting started with JSP.

ColdFusion

ColdFusion is a web database gateway marketed by Macromedia. It was originally developed in 1996 by Allaire to provide web developers with a more robust database gateway than CGI. The advantage of ColdFusion is that it was originally designed to facilitate server-end database access. Although ASP technology provides extra components to allow database access, these components are somewhat limited and were added as a secondary consideration. ColdFusion does not use the Server Object Model to a great degree, but it is written with its own proprietary language: ColdFusion Markup Language (CFML).

The main advantage of ColdFusion is its simplicity. One of the motivations for developing ColdFusion was to create an application development environment that could be used by non-programmers. Most of the scripting languages we have presented in this chapter are derived from programming languages. ColdFusion uses the syntax of HTML tags. The special tags, which all start with the letters CF, are parsed and executed by the ColdFusion data server before the web page is returned to the client. ColdFusion files are called templates and use the extension `.cfm`.

ColdFusion has a scripting engine that can run in process on IIS and Apache web servers, on Linux, UNIX, Windows, and Solaris operating systems. Because ColdFusion is added to the server as a plug-in, it uses the server's API. ColdFusion is also sophisticated enough to determine which SAPI to use. If a service is added to ColdFusion running on a Netscape server, it will use NSAPI. If IIS is running, the service will use ISAPI.

You should be aware that because ColdFusion is a proprietary solution, it might have drawbacks, especially if you plan to change to a web server that it does not support. For example, if you must rely on a SAPI, but ColdFusion does not support it, you will have to use ColdFusion with CGI. However, CGI is not recommended because this environment is not very stable for use with ColdFusion.

Database Connectivity

So far, you have learned about various gateway methods. However, you have not learned how they can communicate with the actual database. Rather than attempting to access the file directly, gateway programs and scripts access the system's registry. The *registry* is a special database of configurations and settings maintained by the operating system.

At one time, programmers used several different means to access the registry because no universal standard existed. Currently, however, two standards allow users to program the operating system registry to recognize a database for use with CGI, JSP, PHP, ASP, SSJS, Java servlets, and other gateway applications. These are the Open Database Connectivity (ODBC) and Java Database Connectivity (JDBC) standards.

Open Database Connectivity (ODBC)

ODBC is a Microsoft technology that allows programmers to refer to databases. It is based on the X-Open standard call-level interface, and is one of the industry standard APIs for using SQL to access relational databases. Many web-based solutions use ODBC to program the registry so they can connect web pages to databases.

In ODBC, the client application communicates with the ODBC driver manager, which finds the requested ODBC data source and its associated database-specific ODBC driver. Then the ODBC driver communicates directly with the data source to enact the SQL command. You can then use a gateway, such as a CGI script, IDC file, or Net.Data macro, to access the database. For the database to operate with ODBC, it must be ODBC-compliant. Most commercial database products, such as Access, Excel, and DB2, comply with this near-universal standard.

In Windows NT/2000 Server, to use an ODBC-compliant database in a web-based environment, you must register it as a system data source with the driver manager if you want the database to be available to the system.

Registering a Database with ODBC

To use the database with a web server, you must first register it with the operating system so that it understands where to go when it processes a request from your gateway script or application. You register the database by creating a Data Source Name (DSN) that allows your operating system to interface with the scripts or dynamic link libraries referred to by the HTML form.

The standard Office 97/2000/XP installations provide all the drivers necessary for ODBC. One of the problems programmers face, however, is that they must connect databases that require older drivers. If you require older ODBC drivers, contact Microsoft at www.microsoft.com/data.

Java Database Connectivity (JDBC)

Developed by the Sun Microsystems subsidiary JavaSoft, JDBC allows a server to work with any SQL-compliant database, rather than forcing a DBMS to comply with a standard created by one company. JDBC is designed to use an operating system's registry to make databases available to Java through the Java API. JDBC allows Java to process SQL statements within Java programs, allowing a programmer to configure a database as a Java object. Therefore, a Java program can manipulate the database as if it were part of the program's structure. This ability to manipulate the database greatly simplifies the connection method. It also provides more possibilities for manipulating information within the database.

Because many programmers have deemed ODBC too proprietary and complex, they are using Java for its simplicity. Both ODBC and JDBC require drivers to operate; however, with Java, this driver can be used in various operating systems.

The key to this effort is the desire to create an effective open solution, rather than an effective proprietary one. JDBC uses four different types of drivers. Type 1 drivers use bridging technologies to access the database. Type 2 drivers use native API drivers (Java code calls C/C++ code provided by the vendor). Type 3 drivers give clients a generic network API that is translated to database-specific access at the server level. Finally, a Type 4 driver communicates directly with the database engine.

Summary

In this chapter, we have discussed what databases are and how they are integrated with web servers. We first discussed the various components of a database, including the field, record, table, and index. The term transaction is used in two senses. A transaction can be a financial exchange, which can be recorded in a database. Or the term can be used to refer to a database transaction, which occurs when a user requests or changes data from a database server. The database is an important part of the client/server model, and we discussed how databases are used in two-tier, three-tier, and N-tier architectures. We also presented two concepts of database reliability, load balancing and fault tolerance.

We next discussed database gateways that are used with web servers. Programmers use client- and server-side scripting techniques to handle tasks at different layers of the web client/server model. Web servers can collect data from users by presenting an HTML form on the web browser. When the user sends that data to the server, a GET or POST method determines how the data is transmitted. The HTML form also includes the action that the server should execute when receiving the data.

Common Gateway Interface (CGI) is the original web gateway solution. Using CGI, the web server can call out-of-process applications to handle database activities. The out-of-process model can consume large amounts of memory. An in process CGI model can be used that consolidates users' queries into a single process. Common CGI scripting languages include Perl and C++.

Server application programming interfaces (SAPIs) offered by Microsoft (ISAPI) and Netscape (NSAPI) use dynamic link libraries as a database gateway replacement for CGI. Various server-side scripting technologies are also available. These include Server-Side JavaScript (SSJS), Active Server Pages (ASP), and Personal Home Page (PHP).

Exam Essentials

Understand databases and their components. A database is a file that contains data in fields and records. These fields and records are contained in a table. The table may be indexed on one or more fields, as long as these fields can uniquely identify each record.

Understand the client/server model and how it is used with databases.
The client/server model includes a user interface to data, process logic, and
data storage. Two-tier, three-tier, and N-tier models allow developers and
server administrators to configure their client/server systems for optimal
performance, by isolating or integrating database operations.

Understand database reliability. For a database to be reliable, it should
incorporate load balancing and fault tolerance. Load balancing is the process of distributing tasks over two or more servers; many types of servers,
including database and web servers, use this technique to better handle
network traffic. Fault tolerance is the ability of a system to respond gracefully to an unexpected hardware or software failure. Database software
has additional features to maintain reliability, including transaction
processing features in SQL.

**Be able to list the different types of databases and database management
systems, including DBMS, RDBMS, and ODBMS.** A database management system (DBMS) uses a non-relational or flat-file model, where all
data is contained in a single file. A relational database management system (RDBMS) uses a relational model, where multiple data tables are
linked together through the use of common fields. An object-oriented
database management system (ODBMS) uses an object-oriented model,
which allows developers to define their own data types.

Be able to differentiate between client-side and server-side scripting.
Client-side scripting is used to control or program events that appear in
the web browser, including animations and data validation. Server-side
scripting is used by web servers to create custom web pages, based upon
the user's requests. A server-side include is used to tell the web server
where server-side code should be executed. Client-side and server-side
scripting can be combined to assign tasks to an appropriate layer of the
client/server model, and to attempt load balancing.

Know how HTML forms are processed, including actions and methods.
HTML forms are used by the web browser to collect data from a user.
When the user presses the Submit button on the form, the form's contents
are sent to the web server for processing, the data can be included in the
HTTP header with the POST method. The data can also be appended to
the URL string, using the GET method. The GET method is less secure,
because the form contents are always transmitted as plain text. The
POST method can use encryption to protect the form's contents during

transmission. Each form is assigned an action, which is the address of the appropriate database gateway for processing the form.

Understand the Common Gateway Interface (CGI), and describe how CGI programs process data. The CGI connects the web server software to external programs and scripts, and can be used as a database gateway. CGI executes these external programs as a co-process on the web server, creating an out-of-process event. Each out-of-process event handles one user's request. A busy web server that uses CGI can generate many out-of-process events, which can slow down the web server's performance. An in-process version of CGI programs can be used, which consolidates all the requests into a single thread of computer activity.

Know how server application programming interfaces work. SAPIs are sets of dynamic link libraries that web servers use to add functionality. Microsoft's Internet Server Application Programming Interface (ISAPI) is the leading SAPI, and works with IIS. Netscape's NSAPI is still in use, although it has become a legacy product.

Understand server-side scripting technologies, including Server-Side JavaScript, Active Server Pages, and Personal Home Page. Server-Side JavaScript (SSJS) was developed by Netscape to provide a database access language for its web servers. Microsoft Active Server Pages (ASP) has emerged as a leading rival to CGI. ASP can use a number of scripting languages, and can be implemented on IIS, Apache, and other web servers. Personal Home Page (PHP) is an open source solution that works on IIS and Apache. PHP uses its own scripting language.

Know HTML database gateway solutions. You can save HTML versions of database files and publish them to web servers. Access and other database clients can perform these conversions. There are also HTML gateway packages that use ISAPI and NSAPI to convert data to HTML.

Be able to describe the Java programming language. Java is a cross-platform, object-oriented programming language that is used for developing Internet-enabled applications. A piece of software called a Java Virtual Machine (JVM) is used to run Java applications on a computer. A well-written Java application can be run on any computer that has a JVM.

Know the functions of Java servlets and how they differ from scripting languages. Java servlets are small Java services or applications that can be used with a web server. Servlets may be chained together, passing requests and output to other servlets to process a task.

Be able to describe other database gateway technologies, including JavaServer Pages and ColdFusion.   JavaServer Pages is a database scripting language that uses a Java servlet to extend a web server's abilities. JSP is more extensible than Perl, PHP, and ASP because developers can use the Java programming language to create sophisticated applications. Macromedia ColdFusion uses HTML-like tags and SAPIs to provide a web database gateway.

Be able to differentiate between Open Database Connectivity (ODBC) and Java Database Connectivity (JDBC).   ODBC is a Microsoft technology that is used for referencing databases. A client can communicate with a database by using an ODBC driver manager. The driver manager is responsible for requesting data. JDBC is a standard for working with SQL-compliant databases, using four different types of drivers for database communication.

Key Terms

Before you take the exam, be certain you are familiar with the following terms:

Active Server Pages (ASP)	dynamic link library (DLL)
ActiveX Data Objects (ADO)	Enterprise JavaBeans (EJB)
application program interface (API)	extensible
business logic	fault tolerance
business rules	field
Common Object Request Broker Architecture (CORBA)	flat file database
compiled languages	in process
data validation	index
database	Internet Server Application Programming Interface (ISAPI)
database management system (DBMS)	interpreted languages

interpreters	referential integrity
Java servlet	relational
Java Virtual Machine (JVM)	relational database management system (RDBMS)
keys	sandbox
load balancing	server application programming interfaces (SAPIs)
non-relational	server farm
object database management system (ODBMS)	server-side include
Object Query Language (OQL)	Server-Side JavaScript (SSJS)
object-oriented	servlet chaining
object-oriented database management systems (ODBMS)	table
objects	thin client solution
Online Transaction Processing (OLTP)	transaction
out-of-process	transaction processing
record	tuples

Review Questions

1. Which one of the following database components can speed up a search process?

   A. Field

   B. Record

   C. Table

   D. Index

2. Jose administers two web servers at his company. The two computers have identical hardware. He has noticed that one web server is very busy at certain times of the day, while the other server is rarely used. Which of the following solutions will allow him to use both web servers to solve his capacity issues?

   A. Online Transaction Processing

   B. Load balancing

   C. Fault tolerance

   D. Common Gateway Interface

3. Gabrielle is trying to load a database file into an application. The database is a text file, with each line arranged as a record. Gabrielle knows this was the only file used in this database application. Each line contains a complete set of information. What kind of database best describes this file?

   A. Relational

   B. Non-relational

   C. Object-oriented

   D. ODBC

4. Which one of the following database systems attempt to replicate the real-world relationships in data?

   A. Database management system

   B. Relational database management system

   C. Java servlets

   D. Object-oriented database management system

5. Which one of the following is the best description of an API?

   A. An API is a set of methods used by programmers to make requests of an operating system.

   B. An API is a type of web page that includes data.

   C. An API is a programming language used for creating web applications.

   D. An API is an Internet protocol used for installing programs.

6. Which one of the following scripting tasks is best handled on the web server, rather than the web browser?

   A. Accessing data that is on another server.

   B. Minor changes to an HTML file's layout.

   C. Accessing information on the type of web browser the user has installed.

   D. Displaying an animation on the user's computer.

7. Neschan wants to have the web browser check data fields on an HTML form. Which one of the following solutions can perform this task without increasing the download time for this page?

   A. Java

   B. JavaScript

   C. ActiveX

   D. Perl

8. Raymond is looking at the HTML code for an order form on a website. He notices that the <FORM> tag is using the POST method. Which one of the following choices best explains why the POST method is included in this web page?

   A. The POST method is required for using Perl scripts.

   B. The POST method sends data from the web client in the URL.

   C. The POST method sends data from the web client in the HTTP header.

   D. The POST method will send the data after the user has completed the form.

9. Which of the following describes a service that uses a server-side script and an HTTP server to pass a client's data to a program or database and then return the program's output to the client.

   A. Common Gateway Interface

   B. Gateway service

   C. Default gateway

   D. HTTP Gateway Interface

10. Which one of the following choices is an interpreted language?

   A. VBScript

   B. Java

   C. C++

   D. C

11. Which server-side scripting solution is most often used with Windows web servers?

   A. Active Server Pages

   B. Perl

   C. Server-Side JavaScript

   D. Personal Home Page

12. Mario is writing a server-side script for use with Personal Home Page. What scripting language should he use to obtain the best results?

    A. Perl

    B. VBScript

    C. PHP

    D. JavaScript

13. Viola needs to post a price list on a web page. This price list has 52 items, and is saved as a Microsoft Access database. The prices are changed once a month. Which one of the following solutions will let Viola post this page in the least amount of time?

    A. Using CGI to link the web server to the price list by using Perl

    B. Saving the database as an HTML page

    C. Setting up an ODBMS

    D. Posting the database file to the company's web page

14. Which of the following does a Java Virtual Machine always do?

    A. The JVM connects clients to database servers.

    B. The JVM provides an environment for running Java applications.

    C. The JVM runs JavaScript applications.

    D. The JVM runs web browsers.

15. Which one of the following database access solutions is the most extensible?

    A. Personal Home Pages

    B. Active Server Pages

    C. Server-Side JavaScript

    D. JavaServer Pages

16. ISAPI files are usually implemented as which one of the following choices?

    A. Dynamic Link Libraries

    B. A Common Gateway Interface

    C. A Java servlet

    D. A server-side script

17. What function does process logic perform in the client/server model?

    A. These are rules for presenting data on the screen.

    B. These are rules for database access, based on how the database will actually be used.

    C. These are rules for storing data in a file.

    D. These are rules for accessing data through a web server.

18. Which one of the following choices is the proper term for describing how Java servlets can be connected together to process data?

    A. Linking

    B. Tagging

    C. Chaining

    D. Extending

19. Which one of the following technologies makes databases available through the Java API?

    A. ODBC

    B. JDBC

    C. ColdFusion

    D. Java servlets

20. A method of programming the Windows operating system registry to recognize a database, based on the X-Open standard call-level interface, is called:

A. Open Database Connectivity

B. Active Server Pages

C. Java Database Connectivity

D. ColdFusion

Answers to Review Questions

1. D.   Database systems can use an index to speed up searches through a table. Fields contain individual pieces of data, and a record is a single instance of data, described by different fields.

2. B.   Jose should combine these two web servers using a load balancing solution. This allows one web server to send traffic to the other, when the first server is overwhelmed by traffic. OLTP is another name for financial transaction processing. Fault tolerance is the ability to respond gracefully to hardware and software failures. CGI is used as a database gateway on web servers.

3. B.   This text file meets the criteria of a non-relational or flat file database. If the file had several linked tables, it might be a relational database. Object-oriented databases are usually used to store complex data, and are accessed by Java or C++ applications. ODBC is a type of database connectivity solution that can use non-relational and relational databases.

4. D.   An ODBMS attempts to do this. An RDBMS uses relational logic to link data among several tables. Java servlets can be used managing data relationships. A DBMS uses a non-relational database.

5. A.   An application programming interface (API) is a set of well-documented methods that can also be used for making requests of applications.

6. A.   Anytime a web application accesses data on a database server, server-side scripting can be used. Changes that involve the web browser display, including layout changes and animation, should be performed on the client-side. Animations are generally controlled on the client side, also.

7. B.   JavaScript can be used on the client-side to perform data validation. Java and ActiveX could also be used, but would require sending applications and objects to the web browser. Perl is used as a server-side scripting solution.

8. C. The POST method lets the web client use encryption to secure the data. Perl scripts can use data obtained from both the POST and GET methods. The GET method sends form data in the URL, which can allow other users to see this data easily. Both the GET and POST methods send the data after the user has submitted the form.

9. A. The proper name for this method is Common Gateway interface, or CGI. It is supported in most web server software.

10. A. VBScript is interpreted line-by-line as it is executed. Applications written in the languages must be compiled before they can be executed.

11. A. ASP is the default Microsoft solution for server-side scripting on IIS. Perl and PHP are used more often on Linux and UNIX systems. Server-Side JavaScript is used on Netscape and iPlanet servers, which have a lower market share than Microsoft IIS.

12. C. Mario must use PHP, as that is the only language supported on Personal Home Page.

13. B. Saving the list as an HTML page is the fastest option, and is supported within Access. The other solutions require programming or administrative skills. She could post the Access file, but users would need the Access application to open the file.

14. B. The JVM is designed to provide a secure place for Java programs to be executed on a computer. JDBC is a database connectivity solution used on web servers. JVMs cannot run JavaScript. You can run a Java web browser in a JVM, but this approach is not widely used.

15. D. JSP is the most extensible, because programmers can use Java to handle complex data processing.

16. A. ISAPI files extend the functionality of Microsoft IIS. These are implemented as DLLs, a common method used for Windows programming.

17. B. Process logic is also called business rules or business logic. These are rules that should be modeled on the actual business practices supported by the database. The user interface controls presentation of the data to the user. Data storage handles how the data is saved to one or more servers. CGI, APIs, and other solutions provide rules for accessing data through web servers.

18. C.   Servlet chaining is the term that describes how Java servlets can be linked together to process data.

19. B.   JDBC uses the operating system and four different types of database drivers to let programmers access databases. ODBC is a Microsoft solution that uses the Windows operating system. ColdFusion can use a variety of APIs to access databases. Java Servlets can use JDBC to access databases.

20. A.   ODBC is the Microsoft technology that performs these functions. ASP is a Microsoft scripting technology used for developing data-driven web pages. JDBC is the Java solution for database connectivity. Cold Fusion is another scripting solution for database connectivity. It can use ODBC to connect to databases.

Chapter 8

Using the World Wide Web

THE CIW EXAM OBJECTIVE GROUPS COVERED IN THIS CHAPTER:

✓ Use Web browsers to access the World Wide Web and other computer resources.

✓ Customize user features in web browsers, including but not limited to: preferences, caching, and cookies.

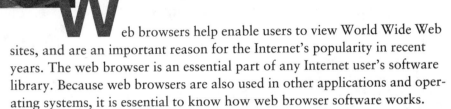

Web browsers help enable users to view World Wide Web sites, and are an important reason for the Internet's popularity in recent years. The web browser is an essential part of any Internet user's software library. Because web browsers are also used in other applications and operating systems, it is essential to know how web browser software works.

In this chapter, we will discuss how you can use two popular web browsers, Microsoft Internet Explorer and Netscape Navigator, to access, view, and navigate web pages. You will access Internet resources and learn how to configure your web browser using browser preferences. You will learn to customize your browser using the available preference options. You will determine the default fonts, your home page, the history folder, bookmarks and favorites. We will also discuss how browser preferences allow businesses and users to customize browsers to company or personal standards.

We will close the chapter with a brief discussion of wireless web access, which allows users to view websites on mobile devices such as telephones.

Evolution of the World Wide Web

As we discussed in Chapters 2 and 6, the World Wide Web is a hypertext information and communication system that has become extremely popular on the Internet. Hypertext connects web content. Each hypertext page is written using Hypertext Markup Language (HTML). Hypertext *links*, or *anchors*, connect one hypertext page to another. Any work on the Web can be a potential anchor destination of any hypertext page.

These anchors are displayed in a graphical web browser as highlighted or underlined text or images, so that users can easily identify them. These links can connect a hypertext page to other information on the Internet, such as additional Web and FTP servers. Links can also connect to multimedia resources, including video clips, graphics, sound, and active content. Figure 8.1 shows the basic organization of hypertext.

FIGURE 8.1 Hypertext organization

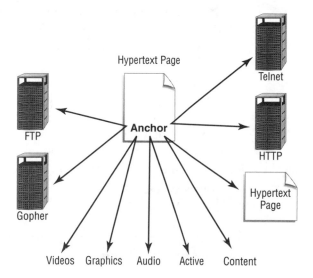

Like many other programming and computer languages, HTML is a published standard that can be downloaded and read by any interested individual. Companies can also take the HTML standard and add it to their products, so that they can read or write HTML documents. The *World Wide Web Consortium (W3C)* is the organization that controls the HTML standard. The W3C headed by the Laboratory for Computer Science at the Massachusetts Institute of Technology (MIT), promotes standards and encourages interoperability among Web products. The W3C is an international industry consortium founded in 1994 to develop common standards for the World Wide Web. It is funded by industry members, and works with the global community to produce specifications and reference software.

Even though the web has experienced rapid growth, it contains the same basic components it did when it was first created. The web is not a network itself, like the Internet, but a set of software programs that run on the Internet and other TCP/IP networks, which enable data communications that operate using the client/server model. Web programs can be used on many different computer networks, or on no network at all.

Web Browser Software

A *web browser* is a client application that can request and display HTML documents from an HTTP server. The first web browsers, which were developed and released in the early 1990s, displayed text only. As the HTTP standard developed, image support was added. Graphical web browsers can also request and display image files that are included with web documents. Modern graphical web browsers can often act as clients for other Internet applications, including FTP, news, and e-mail.

Many different Web browsers are available today. Several are free or relatively inexpensive. The most popular browsers are Microsoft Internet Explorer and Netscape Navigator, both of which have gone through several versions since they were first released in 1995. Together, these two browsers dominate the market.

Beyond the Big Guys

There are a few other browsers that you might encounter from time to time. These include the following:

America Online client application includes a built-in web browser. For Windows versions, AOL uses Microsoft Internet Explorer.

Mosaic was the first graphical web browser application released to the general public, and first appeared in 1993. Many of the programmers involved with Mosaic joined Netscape in the mid-nineties. Microsoft also licensed the Mosaic program code for their initial versions of Internet Explorer. Today, Mosaic is often used as a built-in web browser for cable television boxes and mobile devices.

Opera is a graphical web browser developed in Norway. Opera includes some functionality seen in Netscape and Microsoft products, including JavaScript and Java support. Opera is also available for several PC operating systems. One distinctive feature in Opera is extensive support for users with disabilities. Many of Opera's commands and functions are mapped to the keyboard, which can make web navigation much easier. Like Mosaic, Opera is also used as an embedded web browser in various devices. You can download the Opera browser for personal computers at www.opera.com.

Many businesses prefer one browser to another. By supporting only one brand of web browser, IT departments can focus on maintaining and supporting that browser. As we will discuss in this chapter, Microsoft and Netscape web browsers have their own special features. In business environments, IT departments tend to choose Microsoft Internet Explorer, especially if they have chosen Microsoft Windows as their desktop operating system. Businesses are also enjoying the browser technology that allows them to emphasize their corporate look. Almost everything about the browser can be resized, colored, and retooled to reflect corporate style, colors, and tone. Individual users can adjust these settings, also. Some users may have difficulty viewing default font sizes, while others simply want to customize the appearance of their browsers. Experienced users can also configure both browsers to restrict or disable certain features.

Web browsers employ many of the standard user interface features found in Windows, Macintosh, UNIX and Linux operating systems. For example, the address of the current page (such as http://www.CIWcertified.com) is displayed near the toolbar, and the user can enter a new address there to access a different web page as well. All browsers make it simple to read the text, look at the pictures, and, most importantly, follow the links.

Browsers can accommodate many different types of users. For visually impaired users, speech recognition programs are available that allow the user to simply talk to the computer. The computer can then translate and type these words. Although some barriers still exist for those with disabilities, the Internet is clearly emerging with new technologies to make access easier for all users.

Legacy Browser Issues

The web browsers we will use in this book support the majority of all web-based functions. However, many companies and users still use older web browsers, called *legacy applications*. Legacy applications are programs that have existed for many years and are still used, but may not support modern technologies without being upgraded or manipulated. Individuals and companies often continue to use legacy applications, even when newer software is available, because they have invested much time and money in using these programs. Sometimes legacy applications are used because a company's legacy computer hardware cannot run newer applications.

Older browsers—especially versions before Netscape Navigator 2.0 and Microsoft Internet Explorer 3.0 which were the first consumer-oriented graphical Web browsers widely adopted by Windows users—do not support Web features considered commonplace on today's World Wide Web. For instance, frames were not supported in Netscape Navigator until version 2, and Microsoft Internet Explorer did not support frames until version 3. (Frames allow Web pages to display unchanging menus next to content in the main screen that does change.)

Some content, such as JavaScript, may also not be supported in older browsers. *Active content* consists of interactive and moving objects that create a more useful and interesting web experience, including client-side scripting languages, Java applications, and multimedia files. Netscape Navigator did not support client-side JavaScript until version 2 of its web browser, when Netscape first released the scripting language for public use. Microsoft Internet Explorer did not support client-side JavaScript until version 3 of its software. Netscape has never provided client-side support for VBScript.

Legacy issues are one reason that ISPs often send their subscribers a software CD-ROM when they sign up for service. ISPs will include a recent version of the Microsoft or Netscape web browser for the subscriber to install, in the hope that this will reduce customer complaints.

"Why doesn't my web browser show exactly what is pictured in this book?"

The CIW Foundations certification exam is written so that you do not need to know a specific version of a specific web browser or operating system. The examination questions focus on the basic tasks that can be performed with both Microsoft and Netscape web browsers.

In the next chapters, we will discuss search techniques and additional steps you can use to find more examples that are specific to your favorite web browser software. In fact, we highly recommend that you do so. This can be an important part of your Foundations work.

There are some Foundations topics in which significant differences exist between Microsoft and Netscape web browsers. Since 1996, Microsoft and Netscape have each introduced different features in their web browsers. Some of these features are supported by both companies, but may appear in different names and forms. Microsoft and Netscape regularly update and release new versions of their web browsers, also.

In many exercises and figures in this book, we have used Microsoft Internet Explorer 6. For several topics, exercises and figures, we have provided additional information related to Netscape Navigator 6. While it is easier to use the web browser we have selected for each exercise, you do not have to install or use both the Netscape and Microsoft browsers unless you want to. The Foundations exam does not ask questions about how specific brands of web browsers work.

Because of cosmetic and functional differences among different versions of web browsers, and among the various Microsoft Windows operating systems, you will encounter situations where the exercise or image in this book does not match exactly. Remember that the Internet and the World Wide Web are dynamic in nature. Web content can change without notice, and some of the web pages and websites illustrated in this book may have a different appearance or be unavailable to you.

The figures also feature the Windows 2000 operating system as configured for an English-speaking user in the United States. The Windows 2000 user interface resembles those used in Windows 95, 98, Me, and NT 4. Windows XP users will notice several cosmetic differences between their computer and the figures in this book, especially if the default Windows XP interface is installed. These differences include larger and more colorful application borders, icons, and buttons. Windows XP does offer a classic user interface option, which more closely resembles Windows 2000.

Additionally, there may be differences in language, spelling features, and overall appearance depending upon your computer's configuration and language settings.

Using Browsers to Access Web Pages

Although there are hundreds of differences in how Netscape and Microsoft web browsers support web technologies, the overall effect can be very similar. Figures 8.2 and 8.3 show the same web page displayed in Microsoft Internet Explorer and Netscape Navigator. As you can see, the images and information on the web page displayed are almost identical. The toolbar icons and arrangements vary between the browsers, but these differences have little effect on the web pages that are displayed.

FIGURE 8.2 CIWcertified.com web page viewed with Microsoft Internet Explorer

The main reason that a web page may not appear the same in different browsers is that each browser interprets HTML differently. For example, online order forms may not appear or print the same because each browser uses different fonts and layouts for forms. Web page tables, which display information in rows and columns, do not appear the same because each browser supports different table formatting commands.

FIGURE 8.3 CIWcertified.com web page viewed with Netscape Navigator

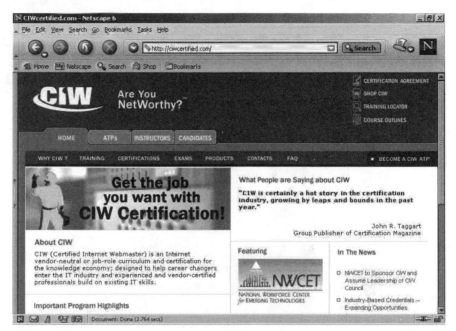

Each browser supports proprietary HTML tags and active content that are not part of the W3C HTML definition. Only the browsers that understand the proprietary code will display the web page properly. Web page authors should test their web pages in as many browsers as possible to make sure that they display properly.

In the next two sections, we'll discuss specifically how to view a specific web page in both of the major web browsers.

Viewing with Microsoft Internet Explorer

Web browsing starts with launching the client software, in this case, Microsoft Internet Explorer. All you need do is enter a web address into the Address field, which is conveniently labeled "Address" in Internet Explorer. The address field is near the toolbar buttons. Figure 8.4 shows a web page from the Sybex website.

FIGURE 8.4 The Sybex home page

You can type in the web address in one of several ways. You can specify the full URL, or *Uniform Resource Locator*, version of the address. The URL specifies the type of service or application protocol that will be used, the host and server name, and any directory or file names. For example, the full URL of the CIW certification program's default page is `http://www.CIWcertified.com/default.asp`.

Recall from Chapter 6 that web servers always have at least one default document that will be sent if a web browser does not request a specific file from the server. We can reach the same CIW default page by entering `http://www.CIWcertified.com`. The CIW web server will retrieve and send the `default.asp` web page.

Most web browsers assume that if the service name is omitted, the address entered is a web address. The web browser will then send an HTTP request to that server. So we can also enter `www.CIWcertified.com` as our web address. Recall that the web server host is usually given the host name `www`. This has become an accepted convention for web server names, although network administrators are free to name their servers anything they choose.

Finally, many network administrators configure their servers to respond to HTTP requests that omit the web server hosts name. We can also request the default page of the CIW program web site by entering `CIWcertified.com` as our web address, as long as the CIW web server has been configured to respond to this shorter address.

A standard Internet convention is the use of underlined text, as shown in the previous figure, to represent a hypertext link. If you click with the mouse on one of these hypertext links, the browser will link to and display a new web page. This new page might be on the same website or on a completely different site. For example, if you were to click on the word "Order" at the top center menu of the Sybex page, you would see the page shown in Figure 8.5.

FIGURE 8.5 The Sybex website's Order page

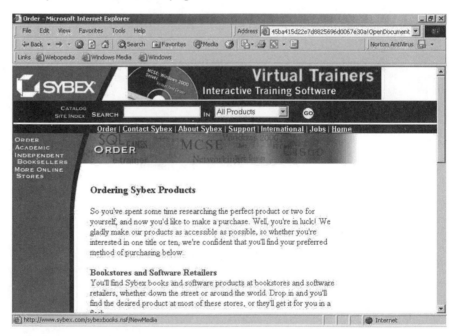

At the far left of the toolbar is the Back button, which is labeled with a left-pointing arrow. Clicking this button returns you to the previously viewed page. It is useful for quick backward navigation. Other toolbar buttons are used to accomplish a variety of specific web tasks. Some functions are easy to identify from the image displayed on the button, whereas others may require description. You will practice using these buttons in the following exercise.

EXERCISE 8.1

Viewing and Navigating Websites Using Microsoft Internet Explorer

In this exercise, you will use Internet Explorer to browse the Sybex website.

1. Start the Internet Explorer web browser.

2. Identify the vendor, version, and copyright dates of your browser by selecting the Help menu and choosing About Internet Explorer. This information is helpful in determining whether your browser is a legacy application. If your browser's copyright date is 1999 or earlier, you should consider installing a more recent version of that browser. Select the OK button.

3. In the Address field, highlight the address by clicking once in the box. Delete the address by pressing the Delete key, or by simply typing into the Address field. Enter the following address in the Address field: `http://www.sybex.com`.

4. Press Enter. The Sybex home page will appear. Locate and access the About Sybex link, as shown in Figure 8.4.

5. Select the Back button on the toolbar. The images reappear because you are visiting the previous web page, which included images.

6. Select the Forward button on the toolbar. Select the Back button again.

7. Spend a few minutes exploring the Sybex site. You can start by selecting one of the Sybex books featured on this page.

Viewing with Netscape Navigator

As noted previously, Netscape Navigator is similar to Microsoft Internet Explorer. Like IE, Netscape has an Address field, and hypertext links appear underlined. The text generally appears in one color if you have not followed the link, and in another color if you have. This color change is a helpful visual clue when navigating web pages. The cursor changes to a hand when positioned over a hypertext or graphic link.

As you can see, the toolbar and menu structures in Netscape Navigator differ only slightly from those of Internet Explorer. Although the toolbar buttons may feature different graphics, icons, and drop-down text menus, the functionality is quite similar. The toolbars for both browsers feature icon buttons for Back, Forward, Home, Stop, Refresh or Reload, and Print. These are the features you will probably use most often.

EXERCISE 8.2

Viewing and Navigating Websites Using Netscape Navigator

In this exercise, you will revisit the Sybex site using Netscape Navigator, and compare the feel of this browser to that of the Microsoft Internet Explorer browser.

1. Start the Netscape Navigator browser.

2. Identify the vendor, version, and copyright dates of your browser by selecting the Help menu and choosing About Communicator. This information is helpful in determining whether your browser is a legacy application. If your browser's copyright date is earlier than 1996, you may have legacy issues (e.g., you may be unable to view web pages that use frames). Select OK.

3. In the Netscape Navigator Location field, highlight the address by clicking once in the box. Delete the text by pressing the Delete key, or by simply typing. Enter the following address in the Location field: **http://www.sybex.com**.

4. Press Enter. The Sybex main page will appear. Locate and access the About Sybex link.

5. Select the Back button on the toolbar. The images reappear because you are visiting the previous web page, which included images.

6. Select the Forward button. Select the Back button again.

7. Spend a few minutes exploring the Sybex site, noting similarities and differences between how the site appears in the two browsers.

Customizing Your Browser

Both Microsoft Internet Explorer and Netscape Navigator allow you to customize your browser with your personal preferences or your company's. Both allow the same basic preferences, or options, although the methods to set preferences differ. In the following exercises, you will learn to configure important preference settings for your browser.

Both browsers allow you to set the size of the fonts used within the browser window. This preference is important for users who have high-resolution monitors, such as 1024×768, 1280×1024, or larger. Additionally, adjusting font size can improve readability.

EXERCISE 8.3

Configuring Font Size

In this exercise, you will access the Netscape Navigator Preferences dialog box to manipulate the font size settings.

1. Open Netscape Navigator.

2. Enter the address http://www.CIWcertified.com. Note the font sizes used on the CIW site.

3. Select the Edit menu and choose Preferences. The Preferences window will appear.

4. Click the + box next to the Appearances category to expand the selections, then select Fonts.

   Note: The majority of Netscape Navigator browser preferences are set in this Preferences window.

5. From the Size pull-down menus, make notes on what fonts and sizes are listed. Choose the font size you are most comfortable viewing on your screen.

6. In the same section of the window, you may also select which font style you want to apply. Select OK.

7. View the web page with the new font sizes.

By repeating this exercise in Internet Explorer, you can spot the differences in the way the two major browsers are configured.

EXERCISE 8.4

Configuring Font Size in Microsoft Internet Explorer

In this exercise, you will change the font size settings in Microsoft Internet Explorer.

1. Open Microsoft Internet Explorer.

2. Enter the address http://www.CIWcertified.com. Note the font sizes used on the CIW site.

3. Select the View menu and choose Text Size. A pop-up menu will appear with five font size selections. Make a note of which selection has a dot or mark next to it. Choose one of these selections.

4. From the Text Size menu, choose the font size you are most comfortable viewing on your screen.

5. View the web page with the new font size.

The Home Page

When you initially install and use a browser, the first web page that appears is the default *home page*. You can set your home page to any web page you wish. By default, Microsoft Internet explorer sets the home page of the Microsoft Network, at www.msn.com; Netscape uses its own site, home.netscape.com.

Notice that Netscape uses an unconventional address. Netscape developed one of the first large corporate websites to distribute the Netscape web browser software. The company chose the host name *home* instead of *WWW* in 1995, and has supported that host name ever since. You can also use the more conventional address www.netscape.com to reach the Netscape website.

If your ISP or another company provided or installed your web browser, they may have modified the browser's home page so that it opens the company's website. Computer manufacturers often set the home page of browsers on new computers. The home page may be the manufacturer's computer support site or that of a partnering ISP. Corporate IT departments sometimes use this feature when installing web browsers on internal computers, by setting the workstation browsers to open to the company's corporate home page or Internet site.

Special Features in Microsoft and Netscape Web Browsers

As you will notice, the Microsoft and Netscape web browsers include features that will point you to a variety of branded services. You do not have to use or register for any of these services to use the World Wide Web. However, you may find the built-in links and menu selections in these browsers convenient.

Both Microsoft and Netscape have tailored their web browsers to support these companies' offerings. Microsoft promotes its MSN ISP service and the MSNBC news network. Internet Explorer also provides support for the Windows Media Player, Microsoft e-mail applications, MSN instant messaging programs, search engines, and websites. Internet Explorer is also tightly integrated with the Microsoft Windows operating system, and the Microsoft Office productivity suite. Netscape is an operating unit of AOL Time Warner, so Netscape web browsers provide easy links to AOL Time Warner websites, AOL Instant Messenger and e-mail, as well as Netscape's search engine and web-based e-mail services.

Many corporations prefer that employees set their home page to the company's corporate website, especially if employees need to access the company's Internet frequently. Some people prefer to set the home page to a search engine. In the following exercises, you will learn how to set your home page for each browser.

EXERCISE 8.5

Setting the Home Page with Netscape Navigator

In this exercise, you will set your Netscape Navigator home page to your company's website or to a search engine of your choice.

1. Launch or restore the Netscape Navigator browser.

2. Select the Edit menu and choose Preferences.

EXERCISE 8.5 *(continued)*

3. Click the Navigator category, as shown here:

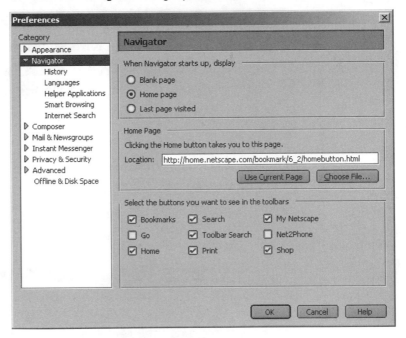

4. In the Navigator Starts With section, make sure the Home Page radio button is selected.

5. In the Home Page section, enter your company's address or a search engine address, such as http://www.yahoo.com, in the Location field.

6. Click OK.

7. To activate your new home page, click the Home button on the toolbar.

Note: You may also exit and restart Netscape Navigator to view the home page.

8. Adjust your home page to a website of your choice.

9. Minimize the Navigator window.

Now, let's take a look at how to perform the same configuration in Internet Explorer.

EXERCISE 8.6

Setting the Home Page with Microsoft Internet Explorer

In this exercise, you will set your Internet Explorer home page to your company's website or to a search engine of your choice.

1. Click the minimized Microsoft Internet Explorer icon.

2. Select the Tools menu and choose Internet Options.

3. Verify that the General tab is selected.

4. In the Home Page section, enter your company's address or a search engine address in the Address field, such as http://www.yahoo.com. Your screen should look something like this:

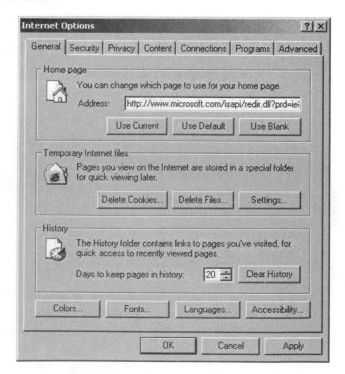

EXERCISE 8.6 *(continued)*

5. Click OK.

6. To activate your new home page, click the Home button on the toolbar.

Note: You can also exit and restart Internet Explorer to access the home page.

The History List

During each web session, your browser tracks the websites you have visited. The *history list* allows easy access to previously viewed web pages. It stores the addresses of websites you have accessed within a defined time period. The hyperlinks that you clicked to access these sites may change colors in your browser window to identify them as previously visited hyperlinks. This feature makes it easier to revisit a site if you forget exactly which hyperlinks you clicked to get there. The history list can usually be accessed by a history toolbar button, or by selecting the address bar drop-down menu.

Users may wish to modify or eliminate the history list, especially if they share a computer with several users. You can set the number of calendar days that are tracked by the history list. For example, a setting of 7 days means that the list will display all websites accessed over the last 7 calendar days. If the computer was not used during the last 7 days, no entries should appear in the history list. If you enter a zero in the time limit, the history list will be deleted when the computer is restarted. You can also clear the history list using menu commands in the browser or operating system.

In the following exercises, you will learn how to set time limits for files in the history list, as well as how to empty the history folder manually.

EXERCISE 8.7

Managing the Netscape Navigator History Folder

In this exercise, you will set a time limit for pages to be stored in the Netscape Navigator History folder, then manually empty the folder. First, you will view the contents of the History folder to check for any important pages before deleting.

EXERCISE 8.7 *(continued)*

1. Click the minimized Netscape Navigator icon.

2. Select the Tasks menu, then choose Tools ➤ History. All Web pages within the History folder will appear.

3. Double-click an item in the History folder. You will be taken to that web page.

4. Close the History folder. You will now set a time limit for History folder content, and manually empty the History folder.

5. Choose the Edit menu and select Preferences.

6. Click the Navigator History category. The screen should look something like this:

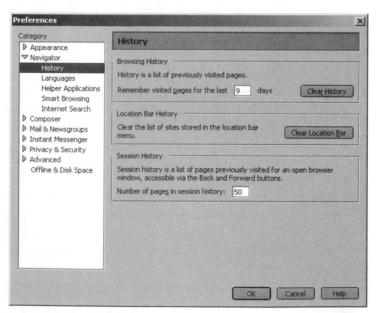

7. In the History section, change the expiration time to 1 day.

8. To clear all pages in the History folder, select the Clear History button. At the prompt, select OK to delete the contents of the History folder.

9. Click OK.

10. Minimize the Navigator window.

EXERCISE 8.8

Managing the Microsoft Internet Explorer History Folder

In this exercise, you will set a time limit for pages in the Microsoft Internet Explorer History folder, then manually empty it.

1. Click the minimized Microsoft Internet Explorer icon.

2. Select the History button on the toolbar. The History window will appear on the left side of the screen.

3. Open several folders and select a link in the History window. You will be taken to that Web page.

4. Close the History window. In the next several steps, you will set a time limit for History content, and manually empty the History folder.

5. Select the Tools menu and choose Internet Options.

6. Verify that the General tab is selected.

7. In the History section, change the expiration for the History folder to 1 day.

8. In the History section, select the Clear History button. At the prompt, select Yes to delete the contents of the History folder.

9. Click OK.

EXERCISE 8.8 *(continued)*

10. Press the History icon on the toolbar. The icon appears as a small sundial. You will see the History bar appear on the left. This window allows you to search the history list, and display it on a daily basis.

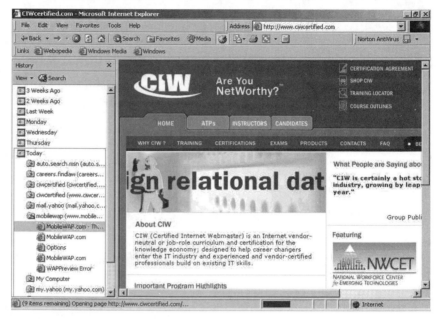

11. Minimize the Internet Explorer window.

The Browser Cache

In Chapter 6, we discussed caching servers that can store frequently accessed web content at one or more points on the Internet, which can reduce download time for Internet users. Both Microsoft and Netscape web browsers can emulate some of the caching server's functions on your computer, by using a disk or browser cache.

The *browser cache* is a folder on your hard drive that stores downloaded web files. The cache allows you to view previously accessed web pages without having to download them again. When you enter an address, your web browser checks the cache to see if the page is already stored there. If the cache contains a recent version of the page, it will display the cached version instead of downloading the page from the Web again. This feature can be especially helpful for users with dial-up connections, but browser caching can speed up any Internet connection.

Web browsers allow you to configure the cache settings so you can choose to download a page each time, regardless of whether it exists in the browser cache. By default, Netscape and Microsoft web browsers use an automatic setting that will download files that change frequently, while caching those files that rarely change. Most users never change this default setting, although web developers often alter this setting so that the web browser will always download any web file.

Depending on how much research you do on the Web, you may have an overwhelming number of files in your browser cache. It is advisable to set limits on your browser cache because cached files use hard disk space. If you do not limit the hard disk space for pages that reside in your browser cache, your hard disk space could be depleted.

If you do not set a disk limit for the files in the browser cache, then you should delete the contents of the folder every few days (or based on usage frequency). The browser cache can usually be emptied and configured from the same window that you use to clear the History folder.

Some considerations related to the web browser cache include the following:

Slow downloads   If previously visited web pages are loading slowly into your browser, your browser cache may be too small. This can force your browser to redownload web files as you request them. You can increase the size of your browser cache to display pages faster. Remember that by increasing the browser cache, you are reducing free drive space. Be careful not to increase your browser cache by a large amount.

Refresh and Reload features   To ensure that you download the most current information from a site, you should select the Refresh or Reload button on your browser toolbar. You can also use the Ctrl+R key combination.

Cached pages may appear when there is no connection   A cached web page may display even if its web server is not functioning or if you are not connected to the Internet. If you choose a hyperlink from the cached page that is not also in your cache, your web browser will not be able to display the page you requested.

Web server and file settings may interfere with browser caching   A visitor's browser cache entry must expire before an updated version of the page will display. Developers and administrators can set web servers and web files to override browser cache settings for individual web files. This is sometimes done with images that are used through a website, such as menus and buttons. By overriding the browser cache settings, these files can be sent to each user only when they do not exist in a browser cache. This technique can reduce the server's bandwidth requirements, especially if the web server has many users. You can force a web file refresh or reload by using your browser's Refresh or Reload command.

The following exercises will teach you how to configure and empty the browser caches in Navigator and Internet Explorer.

EXERCISE 8.9

Configuring the Browser Cache with Netscape Navigator

In this exercise, you will configure the browser cache with Netscape Navigator.

1. Launch Netscape Navigator.

2. Select the Edit menu and choose Preferences.

3. Expand the Advanced category and select Cache. Two caches exist: the memory cache and the disk cache. The memory cache stores web pages in RAM. The disk cache stores web pages on your hard disk.

4. To enlarge the disk cache, change the disk cache to 50,000KB (50MB). Your screen should look like this:

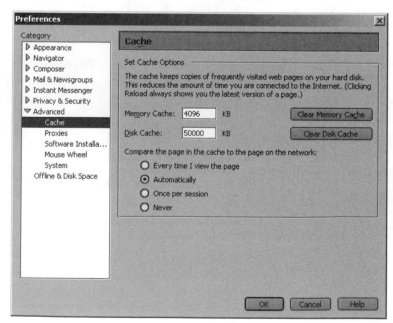

5. To clear the disk cache, select the Clear Disk Cache button. At the prompt, select OK to delete the contents of the disk cache.

6. Click OK.

Now let's try configuring the cache in Internet Explorer.

Configuring the Browser Cache with Microsoft Internet Explorer

The Internet Explorer browser cache is named Temporary Internet Files.

1. Launch Internet Explorer.

2. Select the Tools menu and choose Internet Options.

3. Verify that the General tab is selected.

4. In the Temporary Internet Files section, select the Settings button.

5. To decrease the size of the browser cache, enter **78** in the Amount Of Disk Space To Use field. Your screen should resemble this one:

EXERCISE 8.10 *(continued)*

6. Click OK.

7. To clear the Temporary Internet Files, select the Delete Files button. At the prompt, select OK to delete the contents of the browser cache.

8. Click OK.

9. Minimize the Internet Explorer window.

Bookmarks and Favorites

As you visit sites during your online research or browsing expeditions, you can save addresses for future reference to either your Bookmarks folder in Netscape Navigator or to your Favorites folders in Internet Explorer. Doing so will increase your efficiency and decrease the time you spend relocating useful sites. You can also organize addresses with similar subject matter into folders to make access more convenient.

Over time, you may collect a large number of bookmarks or favorites. Remember that Netscape bookmarks and Internet Explorer favorites are saved to the hard disk of the workstation you are using. By default, these lists are local to a specific computer, and perhaps even to a specific user account. When you use a different computer or user account, your bookmarks and favorites will be unavailable.

Netscape and Microsoft web browsers have basic features that allow you to organize your collections. Both web browsers provide limited support for collections generated by the other browser. This support is usually limited to importing a collection.

If you use regularly both Netscape and Microsoft web browsers on the same computer, you may want to consolidate your Favorites and Bookmarks into a single list. Several third-party software applications are available to manage your Bookmark and Favorites collections. We will discuss these in Chapter 10.

Yahoo! offers a service for saving bookmarks to your My Yahoo! account, which can give you access to your bookmarks using any graphical web browser on any computer. We will discuss this service in Chapter 9.

EXERCISE 8.11

Creating and Organizing Netscape Navigator Bookmarks

In this exercise, you will bookmark and organize preferred addresses into categories for easier access in Netscape Navigator.

1. Launch Netscape Navigator.

2. Enter the address **http://www.yahoo.com** in the Location field.

3. Select the Bookmarks button on the Location toolbar. A pop-up menu will appear. Click Add Bookmark.

4. To access the bookmark, select the Bookmark button again, and select the new Yahoo! entry. The Yahoo! web page appears.

5. Now you will create a folder to help organize your bookmarks by topic. Select the Bookmarks button on the Location toolbar. Click Manage Bookmarks. You will see a dialog box similar to this one.

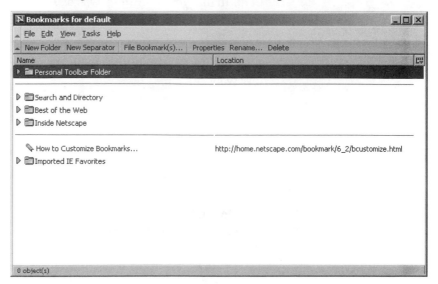

6. Select the File menu and choose New Folder.

7. Enter the folder name "Certification" and any description you want.

8. Click OK. Select the File menu and choose Close.

EXERCISE 8.11 *(continued)*

Note that you created your folder in the default location of the Bookmarks pop-up menu. It will appear as the first Bookmark folder. To create your folder in another section of the Bookmarks pop-up menu, scroll down the Edit Bookmarks window and create the folder in another location.

9. Click the Bookmarks toolbar button. Your Certification folder will appear in the pop-up menu.

10. Now you will add a bookmarked site to your Certification folder. Enter **http://www.CIWcertified.com** in the browser's Location field.

11. Select the Bookmarks button and choose File Bookmark ≻ Certification.

12. Confirm that your bookmark was saved by visiting another website, such as www.sybex.com.

13. Select the Bookmarks button and choose the Certification folder. Click the CIW bookmark you created. Navigator will take you to the CIW website.

14. Enter the address for another Internet certification site, such as www.comptia.org.

15. Add the CompTIA website to your Certifications bookmark folder. Access the site through the Bookmarks button.

Microsoft Internet Explorer uses the term favorites instead of bookmarks. This browser also has a different method of creating and organizing favorites.

EXERCISE 8.12

Creating and Organizing Internet Explorer Favorites

In this exercise, you will create Favorites and organize preferred addresses into categories for easier access in Internet Explorer.

1. Launch Internet Explorer.

2. Enter the address **http://www.yahoo.com** in the Address field.

3. Select the Favorites menu and select Add to Favorites. The Add Favorite window appears to confirm your addition.

4. Select OK.

5. To access the bookmark, select the Favorites menu again, and select the new Yahoo! entry. The Yahoo! web page appears. You can also select the Favorites button on the toolbar and choose Yahoo! from the left window of the screen.

6. Now you will create a folder to help organize your bookmarks by common topics. Select the Favorites menu and choose Organize Favorites. The Organize Favorites window will appear, as shown here.

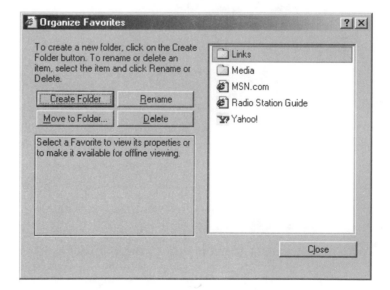

7. Select the Create Folder button.

8. Enter the folder name Certification. Click Close.

9. Select the Favorites menu. Your Certification folder will appear in the list.

EXERCISE 8.12 *(continued)*

10. Now you will add favorites to your Certification folder. Enter **http://www.CIWcertified.com** in the browser's Address field.

11. Select the Favorites menu and choose Add to Favorites. The Add Favorite window will appear.

12. Click Create In <<, then select Certification, as shown here.

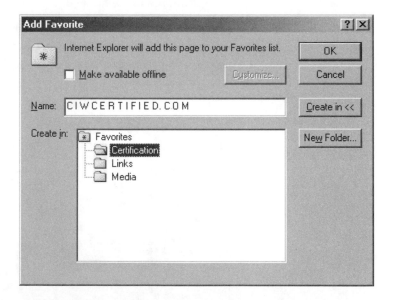

13. Click OK.

14. Confirm that the website was saved by visiting another website, such as www.sybex.com.

15. Select the Favorites menu and choose the Certification folder. Click the CIW bookmark you created. Internet Explorer will take you to the CIW website.

Images and Web Browsers

Web pages can include image files along with the text. By default, your web browser will download any images that are included in the web page. HTTP can set up multiple connections between a web client and server, so that multiple web and image files can be downloaded simultaneously. This downloading process consumes bandwidth, and slows the transfer of information between the web server and your computer.

Most graphical web browsers, including Microsoft and Netscape products, allow users to disable automatic image downloading on web pages. When images are not downloaded for a web page, only the web page text will appear in the browser window. The images are replaced by a small icon that is specified by the web browser.

You can also configure your web browser to display a text label for that image if this label is defined on the web page. (We will discuss how web authors can create these labels, called ALT tags, in Chapter 15.)

As you learned earlier in this chapter, some websites offer text-only pages. These sites usually contain a hyperlink labeled "Text Only" or a similar message, which leads to a text version of the page or site.

There are several situations in which it makes sense to disable image loading:

Slow Internet connection   If you do not have a high-speed, permanent Internet connection, you can speed up your web downloads by disabling images. Users with dial-up connections that use telephone modems, especially at speeds under 28.8Kbps, well see the most benefits. By disabling the image-loading functions in your web browser, you may also save time and telephone charges from your ISP or telephone company.

Conducting research   If you research a topic on the Internet, you may not need to view graphics or active content on your computer, because you are only looking for text on a subject.

Personal preference   Some web users prefer not to see images in their web browsers. You can tell the browser to show an image by right-clicking on an empty image, and choosing the appropriate command. In Microsoft Internet Explorer, this is the Show Picture command.

In the following exercises, you will disable image loading in Microsoft and Netscape web browsers.

EXERCISE 8.13

Controlling Image Loading with Netscape Navigator

In this exercise, you will control content in Netscape Navigator by disabling the image-loading function.

1. Launch Netscape Navigator.

2. Select the Edit menu and choose Preferences.

3. Select the Privacy and Security category, then select the Images category. On the right side of the screen, deselect the Do Not Load Any Images radio button, as shown here.

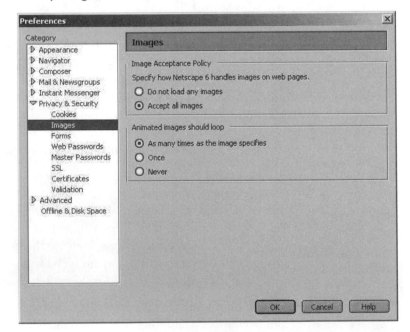

4. Click OK.

5. Enter the address **http://www.sybex.com**, or a website of your choice.

6. View the web page without images. If the images still appear, empty your browser cache and try again. Here is an example of how the Sybex page would appear without images.

EXERCISE 8.13 *(continued)*

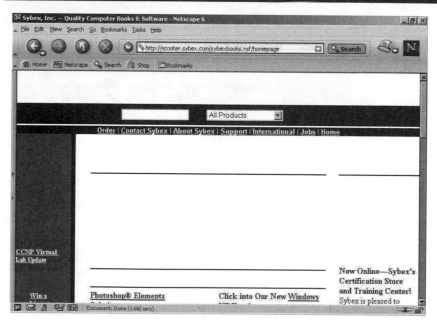

7. To restore image loading, select the Edit menu and choose Preferences.

8. Click the Privacy and Security category and then select the Images category. Click on the Accept All Images radio button. Click OK.

9. Click the Reload button on the toolbar. Is it worthwhile for you to disable images with your current Internet connection?

As you might expect, Internet Explorer uses a different set of commands to control image loading.

EXERCISE 8.14

Controlling Image Loading with Internet Explorer

In this exercise, you will control content in Internet Explorer by disabling image loading.

1. Click the minimized Microsoft Internet Explorer icon.

EXERCISE 8.14 *(continued)*

2. Select the Tools menu and choose Internet Options.

3. Click the Advanced tab. Scroll down to the Multimedia section and deselect the Show Pictures check box, as shown here.

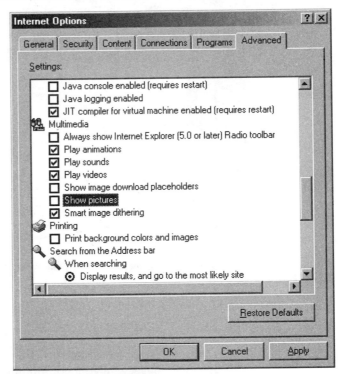

4. Click OK.

5. Enter the address **http://www.sybex.com**, or a website of your choice.

6. View the web page without images. If the images still appear, empty your browser cache and try again. Here is an example of how the Sybex page should appear without images in Internet Explorer.

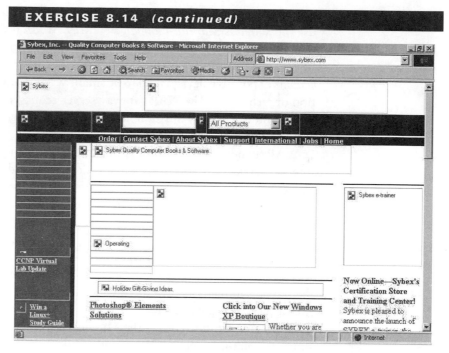

7. To restore image loading, select the Tools menu and choose Internet Options.

8. Click the Advanced tab. Scroll down to the Multimedia section and select the Show Pictures check box, then click OK.

9. Click the Refresh button. The images should appear.

Wireless Web Protocols

Another way to browse the Web is through wireless hand-held devices, such as a mobile phone or a Personal Digital Assistant (PDA). (We discussed wireless Internet connections in Chapter 2.) Many mobile devices use a protocol called *Wireless Application Protocol (WAP)*, which supports text-based web browsing and secure e-mail on wireless hand-held devices.

Instead of using HTML to present Web pages, WAP enabled web pages use the *Wireless Markup Language (WML)*. WML is a markup language that allows the text portions of web pages to be presented to wireless devices by routing the web requests through a WAP gateway server. Because the screens of portable devices tend to be small, WML presents only the text portion of web pages. The WAP gateway server requests web files from a web server and strips away any non-WML code before relaying the files to the wireless device.

WAP supports TCP/IP, so you can receive most of your web and e-mail Internet services through your wireless device. Provided that your wireless carrier supports WAP, you can access the Internet from any location where WAP service is provided. WAP is most popular in Europe and the Pacific Rim, as wireless companies in these areas were early adopters of mobile IP technology.

If developers of traditional websites want to make their sites available to wireless devices, they must implement WML in their web page code. Because the wireless industry is currently experiencing rapid growth, WAP-enabled sites are becoming more widely available.

At the time of this writing, the MobileWAP.com website offered a WAP simulator on their website. You should look for the "WAP simulator" link at `www.MobileWAP.com`. Figure 8.6 displays a WAP-enabled mobile phone. A mobile phone user would access a hyperlink by pressing the "up" and "down" buttons or by entering a URL, and then pressing an "Enter" or "Go" button on their phone.

FIGURE 8.6 Accessing web pages using WAP-enabled mobile phone

Wireless Internet service is gaining acceptance in North America as wireless carriers update their networks and device support. Some North American carriers support two earlier standards, *Handheld Device Transport Protocol (HDTP)* and the *Handheld Device Markup Language (HDML)*. HDML also requires an HDTP gateway server, and some HDTP gateways can also handle WML documents.

There are several obstacles that users must consider when accessing wireless websites. Hand-held device screens are small and difficult to read, because of the mobile telephone's small size. These screens are usually monochrome. Some manufacturers have introduced phones with color screens, but these displays usually consume battery power at a much faster rate. Even so, WAP transmits only text information. Some mobile devices, including Palms, Handsprings, and the Pocket PC, have larger screens, and they offer HTML web browsers that can download images.

Mobile phone text entry is limited to the phone's numeric keypad. Users must press a key two or more times to type many letters and punctuation marks. WAP users tend to write their messages in a form of shorthand, using abbreviations rather than spelling out entire words and sentences. A few mobile devices offer alphanumeric keypads as accessories, but these are usually miniature versions with very small keys. There are full-size folding keyboards available for some mobile devices, including Palms, Handsprings, Pocket PCs, and some Nextel telephones. But these keyboards fold down to a size that is larger than the mobile device itself.

Data transmission rates are slow compared to other Internet connections. At the time of this writing, average WAP connection speed was less than 9600Kbps. As we discussed in Chapter 3, third-generation (3G) mobile communication systems will provide faster access to WAP sites. Mobile 3G requires carriers to upgrade their networks, allowing faster downloads to wireless devices. Eventually, WAP and similar services will provide high-speed wireless multimedia data and voice access.

For many users, the fees charged by wireless carriers may be the biggest obstacle. Carriers typically charge access fees based on the kilobytes downloaded to the device. Because wireless bandwidth is usually limited, carriers ration access through their fees. As wireless carriers add bandwidth, and roll out more efficient transmission technologies, lower access fees should prevail.

Summary

In this chapter, we discussed the nature of the World Wide Web. It is a hypertext information service that runs on the Internet. Websites are linked to each other and can display a variety of text, images, active content, and multimedia files. The World Wide Web Consortium (W3C) is the organization that reviews and sets standards for web software and files.

Microsoft Internet Explorer and Netscape Navigator are two popular web browsers that you can use to access web content. Web browser software from different companies displays web pages in a similar way, although each brand has differences. Older web browsers are considered legacy applications, as they lack the features and functionality of newer browsers.

You can view a web page by entering its address in the Address field of Internet Explorer, or the Location field of Netscape Navigator. The toolbars of each browser have buttons to direct you back or forward to pages you have viewed during your web session.

Users can also set the font size for web text by using preference settings in each browser. Larger fonts can help make text more readable, but using larger fonts reduces the amount of text on the screen.

A home page for the browser can also be set using preferences. The home page is the first page loaded when the user starts the browser. Microsoft and Netscape set the default home page to their own sites. Many users and businesses reset their home page to a different site.

The history list keeps track of which sites the user has visited. You can configure the history list to monitor as many days of use as you wish, or you may clear and shut down the list as needed.

Browsers use a cache to store previously accessed web files on the computer. This technique can reduce download times, and is especially helpful for dial-up users. As with other features, users can control how big the cache grows.

Both major browsers offer ways to remember web addresses. Internet Explorer has a favorites list, while Netscape Navigator has bookmarks. Both systems allow users to maintain a list of web addresses that they can access on that computer.

Web browsers automatically download image files on web pages. Users can disable this feature, which can reduce download times for web pages.

Wireless web services can deliver websites to mobile telephones and devices. Mobile telephones usually have small, monochrome screens, so text-only web browsing is all that is possible. There are two web gateway systems used for telephones. In much of the world, the Wireless Application Protocol is popular. WAP can send the text of a website if the pages have been programmed with the Wireless Markup Language (WML). In North America, an older system called Handheld Device Markup Language (HDML) is used, along with the Handheld Device Transport Protocol (HDTP). Some mobile devices can also display HTML files and images on their screens.

Exam Essentials

Understand the World Wide Web, and explain the difference between the Web and the Internet.   The World Wide Web is an information service that allows users to view web pages, image files, active content and multimedia. The Internet is the large computer network on which the web runs.

Understand the term legacy application.   A legacy application is an old version of a software application. Legacy applications are sometimes used for months or years, especially in business organizations.

Know how to view a website with a web browser.   Enter the address of the web site in the Location field of Netscape Navigator, or the Address of Microsoft Internet Explorer. You can use the Back and Forward buttons in the toolbar to view your most recently viewed web sites.

Know what a browser's home page is.   Web browsers have a home page that they open when they start. Users can change the default page in their web browser.

Understand the history list.   Both web browsers support a history list, which tracks the web sites that were recently accessed. Both Microsoft and Netscape browsers allow you to limit the number of days that the history list maintains.

Be able to configure and empty browser caches.   A browser cache stores recently accessed web files for later use. You can change the size of the browser cache in both web browsers, but you should be careful not to make the cache too large.

Know how to save and organize frequently used Web page addresses.
In Internet Explorer, you can save web addresses as Favorites. In Netscape
Navigator, you can save them as Bookmarks. These lists appear on the
computer and browser on which they were saved.

Know how to control automatic image loading in browsers. You can
disable the automatic loading of web images in both web browsers. This
will decrease the amount of time needed to download any web page that
includes an image. In Internet Explorer by choosing the appropriate settings checkbox. In Netscape Navigator, you can disable image loading in
the Preferences.

**Know how to use the web on mobile devices, including the functions of
the Wireless Application Protocol (WAP) and Handheld Device Transport Protocol (HDTP).** Mobile devices, including mobile telephones
and handheld computers, can access the Internet if properly equipped.
Because phones have very small screens, these devices access web sites
through WAP or HDTP gateway severs. These servers can process web
pages, if the files include WML or HDML programming. Only the text of
the web pages is displayed. Some handheld computers can display HTML
and image files.

Key Terms

Before you take the exam, be certain you are familiar with the following terms:

Active content	legacy applications
anchors	links
browser cache	Uniform Resource Locator (URL)
Handheld Device Markup Language (HDML)	web browser
Handheld Device Transport Protocol (HDTP)	Wireless Application Protocol (WAP)
history list	Wireless Markup Language (WML)
home page	World Wide Web Consortium (W3C)

Review Questions

1. The World Wide Web is best described as which one of the following?

   A. The Internet

   B. A set of software programs that runs on the Internet

   C. A network similar to the Internet

   D. A set of software programs that can run on any Local Area Network

2. The World Wide Web Consortium performs which one of the following functions?

   A. Develops common standards for the World Wide Web

   B. Develops web server software

   C. Reviews and approves websites

   D. Develops web browser software

3. What are the two most popular web browsers on the market today?

   A. Opera and Microsoft Internet Explorer

   B. Netscape Navigator and Microsoft Internet Explorer

   C. Mosaic and Opera

   D. Mosaic and Netscape Navigator

4. Which one of the following is the best definition of a legacy application?

   A. Any software program that is currently used by a company

   B. A software program that can communicate with older software applications

   C. A software program that is still used, even though updated versions are available

   D. A software program that can imitate an older software program

5. In Netscape Navigator, you should enter the URL in what field?

   A. URL field

   B. Address field

   C. Location field

   D. Server field

6. Alec is looking for a website he viewed yesterday. He knows he saw a hyperlink for the site on a certain web page. He also knows that any link he used on that page will appear different in some way, to help him find it. Which choice best describes how the hyperlink will appear?

   A. The hyperlink will blink.

   B. The hyperlink will appear in a different font from the surrounding text.

   C. The hyperlink will appear in italics.

   D. The hyperlink will appear in a different color.

7. You can configure many settings in Netscape Navigator by selecting which one of the following options?

   A. The Tools Settings menu

   B. The Edit Preferences menu

   C. The View Configuration menu

   D. The Options menu

8. Caroline notices that when she starts her web browser, it always displays a certain web page. What is the most common name for this page?

   A. Start page

   B. Default page

   C. Home page

   D. Initial page

9. What is the common name of the browser feature that tracks the websites you have recently visited?

A. Favorites

B. The History list

C. Bookmarks

D. Locations

10. A browser cache performs which one of the following functions?

A. Stores frequently accessed web files on a publicly available server.

B. Saves the addresses of a user's favorite websites.

C. Saves web files for reuse when a previously downloaded page is viewed again.

D. Stores web browser settings for later use.

11. What is the name of the browser feature that allows you to save useful website addresses for quick relocation?

A. Favorites or Bookmarks

B. Bookmarks or Preferences

C. Preferences or Cool Sites

D. Cool Sites or Favorites

12. Disabling automatic image loading in a web browser results in which one of the following situations:

A. The browser loads web pages in a static state only.

B. The browser lets the user view web pages without storing them in the disk cache.

C. The browser loads web pages in text-only mode.

D. The browser allows e-mail transmissions, but provides no access to websites.

13. When you revisit a web page, it loads slowly into your browser. How can you make the revisited page display faster in your browser?

    A. Decrease your browser cache size

    B. Clear the History folder

    C. Increase the History folder size

    D. Increase the browser cache size

14. Both Netscape Navigator and Microsoft Internet Explorer allow you to customize:

    A. Speaker volume

    B. Monitor display pixels

    C. Font size

    D. Web page content

15. Wireless web protocols depend on what kind of server to help process web files for viewing?

    A. Gateway

    B. Cache

    C. Streaming media

    D. FTP

16. Web Markup Language is always used by which one of the following protocols?

    A. Handheld Device Transfer Protocol

    B. Post Office Protocol

    C. Wireless Application Protocol

    D. Hypertext Transfer Protocol

17. Which of the following services does Wireless Application Protocol (WAP) provide to wireless hand-held devices?

A. Cellular telephone network

B. Secure e-mail

C. Newsgroups

D. Digital telephone network

18. Which web browser is commonly used with America Online?

A. Netscape Navigator

B. Microsoft Internet Explorer

C. Opera

D. Mosaic

19. Nick has set his history list to save the 7 days of web addresses. What does this mean?

A. His web browser will save all the addresses he accessed during the last 7 calendar days.

B. His web browser will save all the web page content he has viewed in the last 7 days.

C. His web browser will tell him if he is viewing a page he has seen in the last 7 days.

D. His web browser will not display a web page if he has viewed it in the last seven days.

20. A web browser can always use which one of the following addresses to retrieve the Sybex website?

A. www.sybex.com

B. sybex.com

C. web.sybex.com

D. sybex

Answers to Review Questions

1. **B.** The World Wide Web is not a network, but a collection of computers and software that use the Hypertext Transfer Protocol. Web services can be run on any TCP/IP network, but the Web is generally considered to be running on the Internet.

2. **A.** The W3C is a standards-making organization. It does not develop software, or review the content of websites.

3. **B.** Netscape and Microsoft's browsers own most of the web browser market.

4. **C.** A legacy application is one that is still in use even when other, newer applications or technologies are available. Software programs can be designed to communicate or exchange data with legacy programs.

5. **C.** Netscape uses the Location field, while Internet Explorer uses the Address field. The term URL is synonymous with web address, but can denote many kinds of Internet content.

6. **D.** In Netscape and Microsoft web browsers, web links that point to previously visited sites have a different text color.

7. **B.** Netscape uses the Edit Preferences menu. The other choices are commonly used locations for program settings in other applications.

8. **C.** The page that opens automatically when a web browser is started is usually called the home page.

9. **B.** The history list is a collection of recently visited sites on a web browser. Favorites and bookmarks are web addresses that are saved by a user for future reference.

10. **C.** The browser cache reduces the time needed to display a previously viewed web page, by keeping web documents in local storage. Caching servers can store copies of content in additional network locations. The favorites and bookmark features can be used to retain the addresses of websites for later use. Preferences or options contain web browser settings.

11. **A.** Netscape calls this feature Bookmarks, while Microsoft calls it Favorites.

12. C.   When automatic image loading is disabled, the browser displays only the text portion of the web pages. The browser cache may still be used, but it will not display images. Browser image loading does not affect e-mail.

13. D.   In this situation, it is likely that the web browser has not saved the web page in its browser cache. Increasing the size of the cache will create more room to save this page's files.

14. C.   Both browsers allow users to select a function size. Speaker volume and monitor resolution are usually controlled by the operating system. Web page content can be customized in many ways.

15. A.   Wireless web systems use gateway servers to translate content for mobile devices. Cache servers store content at more convenient locations on a network. Streaming media servers transmit audio and video files. File transfer protocol servers send large files.

16. C.   WML uses WAP to translate web content for mobile devices. HDTP is used to transfer wireless web files. POP is used to retrieve e-mail. HTTP is used to transfer any kind of web file.

17. B.   WAP provides secure e-mail access on mobile devices. Telephone network services are provided by the telephone carrier.

18. B.   America Online usually uses Internet Explorer to display web content.

19. A.   The history list will retain all web addresses accessed on a browser during a period of days. The history list does not control caching of web content. It also does not indicate if content was previously viewed. The web browser will change hyperlink colors to indicate if that link has been visited previously, based on the contents of the history list.

20. A.   The machine name www is usually reserved for use by web servers. Entering only **Sybex.com** will work only if the server administrator has properly configured the DNS and web server to respond to web browser requests on that domain name. The machine name web is not usually used as a standard web server name. Entering sybex by itself will not pull up a website, as Sybex is not a valid domain name.

Chapter

9

Web Search Engines

✓ Use web browsers to access the World Wide Web and other computer resources.

✓ Customize user features in web browsers, including but not limited to: preferences, caching, and cookies.

✓ Use different types of web search engines effectively.

✓ Use the Web to obtain legal and international business information.

The Web is an enormous resource and continues to grow at an incredibly fast pace. Some observers have said that if you spent only 1 minute per web page, for 10 hours a day, it would take 4 and a half years to explore only 1 million web pages.

With so much data available on the Internet, finding exactly what you need can be difficult and frustrating. This chapter will focus on several key navigational tools that can be used to find the information you need for your personal and business practices. We will discuss what search engines and directories are, and how to use them to find information on businesses, people, products, and services. We will also discuss how search engine software operates, and how it is related to database servers. We will then discuss how you can find other Internet resources on the Web, including mailing lists and newsgroups.

Search Engines

All data on the Internet is based on computer files. The web model is a powerful form of information storage and retrieval. The Web was originally conceived as an electronic library that used hypertext to connect similar files. Like a library, there are services available to help users search for and find information. These search utilities are called *search engines*.

A search engine is a powerful software program that searches Internet databases for user-specified information. Search engines consist of large databases which are usually hosted on server farms. These databases contain information about web pages that have registered with a particular search engine.

Through *keywords*, you can find information on any subject you want to investigate. A keyword is a word that appears on a web page and is used by search engines to identify relevant URLs. Some words, such as conjunctions (and, or), articles (a, the, those), and prepositions (above, below, with), are too common to be used as keywords; search engines usually identify nouns, verbs, adjectives, and adverbs as default keywords for websites.

A search engine database typically contains information such as the title of the page, the URL, a short description of the contents, and keywords to help the search engine reference the page. When a website manager registers a web page with a search engine, their URL is added to the search engine database.

No single search engine has a universal directory of all web pages. Some website managers register their sites only with particular search engines and neglect others. Because of this selectivity and the large number of search engines, you may receive completely different results using the same keywords on different search engines.

Some search engines are highly automated and initiate a *robot* or *spider* program that automatically searches the web and indexes websites. These programs gather information about websites, Gopher sites, and newsgroups as determined by certain parameters. In some cases, only the header and URL information are indexed. In others, partial or full-page text from the website is indexed. Spiders also check the validity of the URL entered in the database to ensure accuracy.

Search engines display results in a similar manner, usually as a list of hyperlinks to the web pages with the information that most closely matches the keywords or keyword combinations you entered. Each database uses its own scoring system. Some engines, like Google, are useful for deciding whether the information is current. Others offer ways to sort results. The more searches you conduct, the better you will become at understanding how to read and quickly navigate through the results.

Directories

A *directory* differs from a search engine in that it will only find sites based on user submissions. If you do not manually submit your site to the directory, the directory will never know of or index your site, and thus never list your site in search results. Some directories, such as Yahoo!, have employees visit the website to determine the content and its relevance to the submitted topic. After the review, the web designer may receive an e-mail message asking for additional information so a site description can be created before the site is placed in the directory.

The advantage to this type of directory is that search results are more likely to contain quality content matches to any given query. However, increasing the chances for a higher placement in search results is usually not within the control of the web designer.

Many web users apply the term "search engine" to directories, as both generate lists of search results. It is helpful to know whether you are using a search engine or a directory, as this will help you understand how the results were created.

Ranking Systems

Search engines and directories often use a *ranking system* to determine how closely a site matches the topic for which you are searching. When a search is performed, a database searches for keywords or word combinations called *search strings*. The more frequently the keywords are found in a particular document, the higher the score that document receives. This concept is called *relevancy*.

Some advanced search engines use both the words you enter and their synonyms to perform a search. By combining these strategies, these search engines can provide more relevant lists of web pages.

Usually a scoring system is ranked from zero to a maximum number such as 100 or 1000. A score close to the maximum represents the highest probability of a match. Several other variations are used. If you find that one site has the highest score of all the results displayed, you should still examine the rest of the results.

The keywords for a web page can be listed in an HTML tag called the META tag. Because the actual scoring systems used by the engine databases are based on programming, clever web designers can construct a web page including popular keywords in the META tag.

The *META* Tag

The *META tag* is an HTML element you can use in a web page to embed information for search engines. This information is placed near the top of the HTML document, so the search engines can quickly access it. The more descriptive the information you list in the META tag, the more likely your website is to rank high in search results. The META tag defines meta-information about a document, such as:

- Keywords to be used by some search engines

- An expiration date for the document

- The document's author

- A description of the site's content for display in some search engines.

Most search engines scan web pages for META tag information in the following format:

```
<META NAME="Keywords"
CONTENT="keyword1,keyword2,keyword3">
```

The search engine robot program will inspect pages that use the "Keywords" value of the NAME attribute. The values specified by the CONTENT attribute are then ranked against keywords entered in the search engine by a user. Keywords in the META tag are separated by spaces or commas. Do not use the same keywords several times in the same tag. Many search engines may ignore the keyword or the entire META tag.

Another useful attribute for search engines is the "Description" value of the NAME attribute:

```
<META NAME="Description"
CONTENT="This site provides recipes.">
```

In the preceding tag, the CONTENT attribute value will appear in some search engines instead of the first few lines of your file. This description should be brief. Not all search engines recognize this tag.

One common strategy is to list the most popular search terms as keywords for a website, even when the web page does not relate to any of these keywords. There is a well-established industry of search engine specialists who continually monitor the ranking strategies used by major search engines. Search engines often change their ranking strategies to improve the quality of the engine, and some of these specialists are retained by large commercial websites to ensure that these sites are always highly ranked in search engines. Software is also available to help web designers find and insert keywords in their web pages.

Webmasters can choose to hide web documents from search engines. One popular method involves placing a text file called robots.txt in the home directory of a web server. The webmaster can include individual web document names or entire directories that they want to be excluded from search engine spider and robot programs. Many search engines will comply with robots.txt files. For more information on robots.txt files, see www.robotstxt.org/wc/robots.html.

Getting a Website Listed

If you want your website to be seen by web users, it must be registered or entered into the indexes of popular search engines and directories. Different search engines have different registration processes.

Many search engines and directories require you to complete an online form and enter the URL of your site. This will schedule a robot or spider program to visit your site and search the HTML code for keywords.

Besides the META tag, robots can also search for word occurrences, titles, heading text, and images within the web page. Unfortunately, each search engine robot gathers different information, so no guaranteed method exists to ensure a top listing.

Most search engines and directory sites offer a link, such as "Add Your Site" or "Suggest a Site," that you can access for more specific information about registering your site. You can simply visit each search engine's website and locate the registration link to add your URL.

There are also services and software available to register your site on many search engines and directories by using a single web form. This approach is very convenient, and is offered by domain name registrars and web hosting companies. Sometimes a fee is charged for mass registration services and software, although some registrars and hosts offer these search engine registration services as a feature of their regular service plans.

Search Indexes

Search engines and directories are actually programs that allow you to query indexes. These search indexes use specialized database servers that catalog millions of web page references.

You can access a search index using the site's forms, or you can manually navigate through an index's structured directory. There are three types of search indexes; the *static index*, the *keyword index*, and the *full-text index*.

Static index   This model allows users to manually search through directories to locate indexed information. Some directories are presented as a directory tree of all the indexed pages. Many websites present a *site map*, which lists the pages or sections of the site on a single page.

Keyword index   This type of index allows users to enter keywords in a search engine to query an index. The keywords are then compared to the keywords entered in the index. If the keywords match, the search engine will provide the indexed information to the users. This index type is used by web search engines and directories.

Full-text index   This index allows a user to enter any text string that might exist within a file into the search engine. This type of search requires the full contents of every page to be indexed. Many companies offer text-string indexing within their organizations and websites for document retrieval or various files. Some companies offer this service to their website visitors. Full-text indexing is not used to index the entire web or Internet because of the massive amounts of storage that would be required.

Basic Search Techniques

For basic web searches, you enter a single keyword or a short phrase within quotation marks into a search engine field. Basic searches are useful when an easy, distinguishable topic is requested. In the following section, we will go over basic web searches with Yahoo! and AltaVista. Because every search engine and directory offers different options, we will concentrate on the most common features that users will find.

Yahoo!

One of the most popular directories is Yahoo! (www.yahoo.com). It was created in 1994 by two students at Stanford University as a way to track their personal interests on the Internet. They soon customized their search utility into the hierarchical subject guide to the Internet that it has become.

Yahoo! was not intended to be a search engine, but rather an index providing several links relating to each topic. Originally, its database of links was very selective, including only carefully chosen and verified links.

Yahoo! integrated search engine features into the site in 1998, by using technologies from other vendors. Keyword searches can return results from the Yahoo! directories, and from other search engines. At the time of this writing, Google was the chief provider of search engine features for Yahoo!

Yahoo! directory categories range from the Arts and Humanities, to Business and Economy, to Culture and Society. Each of these larger categories offers subcategories. For example, under the larger heading of Business and Economy, you will find hypertext links to Companies, Investing, and Jobs.

If you select Companies, Yahoo! takes you to a more focused search-engine page that offers both an empty search-entry field and, alternately, still further-categorized and alphabetized hypertext links.

Yahoo! searches titles, categories and text to find results that contain all of your keywords. Yahoo! Searches are not case-sensitive. For example, "Dow Jones" would be read as "dow jones."

Yahoo! finds and retrieves three different types of information for each search. The searches are based on the following criteria:

- The alphabetized hypertext categories that match your keywords

- Sites that match your keywords

- Yahoo! categories that list those end sites

Yahoo! identifies its categories in bold type. End sites are displayed in plain text. To navigate down the subject hierarchy, select a category and the next-lower level of the hierarchy will display.

Yahoo! offers search engines in several different languages, usually localized to a country or geographic region. For example, the main page of Yahoo! UK and Ireland (uk.yahoo.com) uses UK English spelling and grammar, and features content, advertising, and services for those two countries. Yahoo! Deutschland (de.yahoo.com) is presented in the German language, and is designed for users in Germany, Austria, and Switzerland. You can find a list in English of the various international Yahoo! sites at `http://docs.yahoo.com/docs/family/more.html#WORLD_YAHOO_S`.

You may use either Internet Explorer or Netscape Navigator for all exercises in this chapter.

EXERCISE 9.1

Performing a Static Index Search

In this exercise, you will use Yahoo! to perform a static index search. Rather than searching by keyword, you will view the contents of predetermined subjects within the Yahoo! searchable database.

Suppose you are planning a business trip to Dallas, and you want to learn about some hotels there. (You can select a different city and country, such as Berlin, Germany, if you prefer.)

1. Enter the URL www.yahoo.com and press Enter.

2. Find the bullet labeled Regional and select the U.S. States link.

3. Select Texas.

4. Select Texas Cities, then locate and click Dallas.

5. Select Lodging.

6. Select Hotels and Motels. A listing will appear, as shown here.

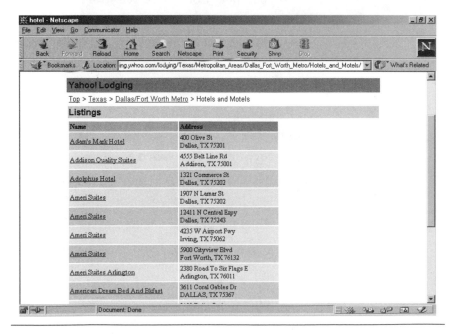

AltaVista

AltaVista (www.altavista.com) was created in 1995 by Digital Equipment Corporation, and was originally designed to index the entire Internet. AltaVista is a powerful search engine that contains one of the largest online web databases. You can search for information in multiple languages.

AltaVista allows users to choose the best search mode depending on the level of search assistance they require. Two search engines are offered: general and advanced. General offers comprehensive query results. The general engine is useful if you have a general idea of what you are seeking, but you do not have specific details. Advanced search is intended for experienced searchers who know what they want and how to get it quickly.

To ensure the most current database contents, AltaVista uses a web spider program to routinely search every web page. Pages that do not change often are checked for updates less frequently than pages that do change often.

Like many search engines, AltaVista returns your results in terms of its relevancy, with the highest likely returns posted first. The results are influenced by a combination of the following events:

- Your input words or search strings are found in the title or near the beginning of the document.

- The web document contains additional keywords or search strings.

- The web document contains input words or search strings that have been assigned a high priority by the search engine.

EXERCISE 9.2

Performing a Keyword Search

In this exercise, you will perform a keyword search for web pages with AltaVista. Compare your results with those from the previous exercise.

1. Enter the URL www.altavista.com and press Enter.

2. In the search box, enter: **Dallas hotel**. Select Search. The results that appear should be similar to those depicted here. Keep in mind that the web is always changing, so the contents and appearance of web documents may be different than you expect.

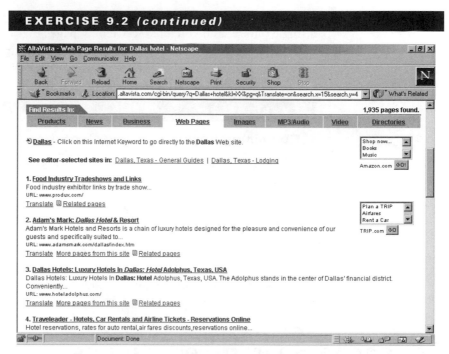

3. You will see a number of web search results. Each result is commonly called a "hit." Each result contains a description of the website. Some results may not be related to your search. The company or webmaster responsible for each site selects the keywords, so they may not represent the site properly, or the keywords may be taken out of context. Sometimes the site is related, even if the description is not. You must follow the link to find out.

4. Select one of the search result links and determine how the site is related to your search. Use the Back button on the browser to return to the list of hits and investigate another result. Did you get the same hotels as you did with Yahoo! static-index search?

Because so many search engines exist, you may get a completely different set of results when you use another search engine. For general searches, you can get good results with any of the top search engines.

To further narrow your search, most search engines allow you to use quotation marks to combine words that must appear together; this phrasing is called a search string. Using quotation marks will treat "Dallas hotel" as a single phrase, and you will receive only pages that contain both words. Quotation marks will tell most search engines to treat your keyword string as a single phrase.

EXERCISE 9.3

Combining Keywords Using Quotation Marks

In this exercise, you will narrow your search results in AltaVista by using quotation marks to combine specific words.

1. In the search box, enter "`Dallas hotel`". Be sure to include the quotation marks. Select Search.

2. You should receive more accurate web search results this way. Compare these search results with those you received when you searched without quotation marks.

Advanced Search Techniques

For basic searches, you typically enter a single keyword or a short phrase within quotation marks. Basic searches are useful when an easy, distinguishable topic is requested.

However, for more complex subjects, or to narrow the results of a standard search, advanced searches should be used. Some search engines use a separate interface for advanced searches, but many sites allow *Boolean operators* to be used in the standard search interface. A Boolean operator is a symbol or word used in Internet searches to narrow search results, or to include or exclude certain words or phrases from the results. Boolean algebra was developed by the English mathematician George Boole in the mid-19th century. Boole's theories are an important part of all computing hardware and programming languages.

In this section, you learn about the advanced features of the AltaVista website. You will use Boolean operators and various tools to refine searches, which will include searching for information on software licensing for small businesses.

Just as standard math uses addition, subtraction, division and multiplication, Boolean logic uses the AND, OR and NOT operators. When using Boolean logic for searches, you can also use NEAR operators.

Boolean operators enable users to narrow their searches by requiring important keywords or excluding keywords that may not be pertinent to a search.

For example, if you were looking for information on bats and how they fly, performing a standard search using the keyword *bats* may yield thousands of returned documents. These pages will include information on winged mammals, as well as baseball and cricket equipment.

To limit your search results, you could use a combination of a key word and Boolean operators, such as `bats AND mammal NOT baseball`. By adding the `AND mammal`, you are requiring your results to contain the words *bats* and *mammal*. By further narrowing your results with the `NOT` operator, you will exclude all pages within the results that contain the word *baseball*. This method will narrow your search results dramatically. By using additional Boolean operators to exclude other irrelevant words, such as `NOT` *cricket*, you can narrow your search even further.

In general, most operators are interchangeable among search engines; however, not all search engines recognize the same operators, or they may use commands other than Boolean operators. Table 9.1 compares some standard operators and commands with three popular search engines.

TABLE 9.1   Search Operators and Commands

Operator Action	AltaVista Advanced	Excite	Lycos Pro*
Results must include both words.	AND, &	AND	AND, &
Results must include at least one of the words.	OR, |	OR	OR, |
Results must include a particular word.	+ (plus sign does not work in advanced search)	+	+

TABLE 9.1   Search Operators and Commands *(continued)*

Operator Action	AltaVista Advanced	Excite	Lycos Pro*
Results must exclude a particular word.	AND NOT, !, − (minus sign does not work in advanced search)	AND NOT,−	NOT, !,−
Two keywords on a page are within a certain proximity to each other (near or far).	NEAR, ~		ADJ (adjacent), NEAR, FAR, BEFORE
Combine words into phrases.	" "	" "	" "
Group Boolean operator phrases.	( )	( )	( ), < >, [ ], { }
Search for root word or variances in spelling (wildcards).	* (Example: color* will return color, colors, colorize, etc.)		$ (example: color$ will return color, colors, colorize etc.)
Stop expansion of root word.			. (example: color. will return only color, not Colorado)

Boolean operators in Excite are case-sensitive; in Lycos and AltaVista they are not. Some search engines allow user-defined variances of the Boolean operators. For more information, view the Help files at each site.

In the next section, you will learn more about the advanced features and capabilities of the AltaVista, Lycos, and Ask.com search engines. You will use some of the same search criteria throughout the exercises to see how different search engines respond to the same requests.

Advanced AltaVista Search

The Advanced search features of AltaVista allow users to narrow search results from a standard search to specific criteria. You can use Boolean operators to include certain keywords, as well as sort the results using additional criteria.

EXERCISE 9.4

Using the Plus Sign (+) Parameter

In this exercise, you will use the plus sign (+) parameter to search for web pages that contain both "Paris hotel" and "pool." You will use the AltaVista standard search because the plus and minus parameters do not work in the AltaVista Advanced search.

1. Go to www.altavista.com.

2. In the search field, enter "**Paris hotel**" **+pool**.

   Note: In AltaVista, the plus sign (+) or minus sign (–) must directly precede the word it requires or excludes; do not add a space between the plus or minus sign and the associated search term.

3. Select Search. You will receive a list of pages that refer to a Paris hotel and contain the word "pool." These pages probably refer to hotels in Paris, France, or the Paris Las Vegas Resort & Casino in Las Vegas, Nevada, that have swimming pools or billiards tables.

4. Use the plus sign parameter to perform a search for some other topic.

AltaVista also supports an exclusion parameter that can omit web documents that have certain terms.

Using the Minus Sign (–) Parameter

In this exercise, you will search for word combinations using the minus sign (–) parameter in AltaVista. This method will help ensure that specific words do not appear in your search results. You will search for sites that contain Paris hotel, but do not contain references to the Paris Resort & Casino in Las Vegas, Nevada. You are now looking for hotels in Paris, France. Once again, you will use the AltaVista standard search because the plus and minus parameters do not work in the AltaVista Advanced search.

1. In the search field, enter the following search string: "**Paris hotel**"–"**Las Vegas**".

2. You will receive fewer results than the original search on "Paris hotel" because any web pages for Paris hotels that referred to Las Vegas were not included.

3. Use the minus sign parameter to perform a search for some other topic. Do you find it helpful to narrow your search using this parameter?

Let's see how using Boolean operators can affect a search.

Using the *AND/OR* Operators

In this exercise, you will use the Boolean AND/OR operators in AltaVista to influence the results of your search. You will search for web pages that contain Dallas, Texas hotels with either a pool or spa. In this scenario, a spa is an establishment with exercise and bathing facilities.

Note: To use Boolean operators, you must use the AltaVista Advanced search and type all Boolean operator parameters in the Boolean query box.

1. At the AltaVista home page, select the Advanced Search link.

2. In the Boolean Query field, enter the following search string: **Dallas hotels AND (pool OR spa)**.

EXERCISE 9.6 *(continued)*

(Note that you may also use the symbols & and | respectively.)

3. Select Any Language from the language pull-down menu, or enter a language of your choice. Your screen will resemble the one here.

Note: You can use either uppercase or lowercase letters when using Boolean operators in the AltaVista Advanced Search.

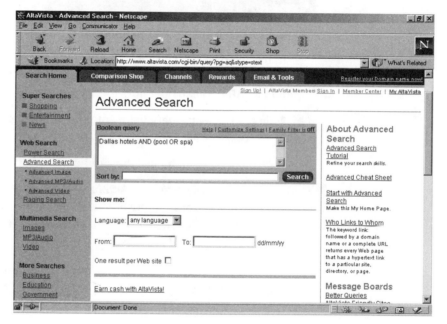

4. Select Search. You will receive fewer results than with a general search. Experiment with the AND/OR Boolean operators to narrow your results for Dallas hotels with a pool or spa.

5. Use the AND/OR operators to perform search for some other topic, such as locating automobiles by two different manufacturers. Do you find it helpful to narrow your search using these operators?

Sorting Results

When you enter a standard search, results are generally ranked by the frequency of keywords, as well as whether they are placed in the title of the linked page. However, when you enter an advanced search and only use the Boolean Query field, the results will appear in random order.

In the following exercises, you will use various search techniques in AltaVista to find information on software licensing for small businesses. Using the AltaVista Advanced Search page, you can determine the sorting results by adding keywords in the Sort By field. For the remainder of the exercises, you will sort the results.

EXERCISE 9.7

Using the *AND NOT* and *NEAR* Operators

In this exercise, you will use AltaVista to search for web pages about software licensing for small businesses. You will use the AND NOT and NEAR Boolean operators to influence the results of your search.

1. In the Boolean Query field, enter the following search string: `software NEAR licensing`.

   (Note that you may use the symbol ~ instead of NEAR.)

   This query will return all AltaVista-registered web pages that contain the words "software" and "licensing" within 10 words of each other. This search will find software licensing, but probably not other types of licensing.

2. In the Sort By field, enter `licensing`. Note that you can add several keywords to the Sort By field to modify your results.

3. Select Any Language from the language pull-down menu, or enter a language of your choice.

4. Click Search. How many results were returned? Are these results useful? Can you further narrow your search focus?

   In addition to finding software-licensing websites from around the world, your search may reveal software-licensing websites for Microsoft products. Because your small business (in this scenario) does not use Microsoft products, you can narrow your search by removing Microsoft from your search criteria. It would also help to add "small business" to your search criteria. You will use inclusive and exclusive operators together to narrow your search focus.

EXERCISE 9.7 *(continued)*

5. In the Boolean Query field, enter the following search string: `software NEAR licensing AND "small business" AND NOT Microsoft`.

6. In the Sort By field, enter licensing small business. Your screen should look something like this.

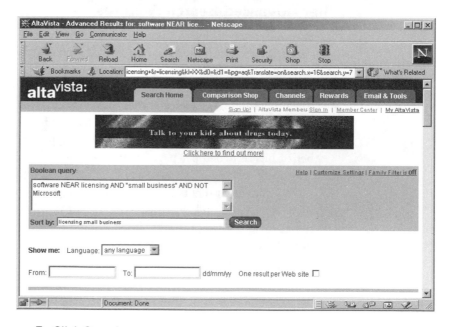

7. Click Search

8. How many results were returned? The web pages pertaining to Microsoft were not included.

9. Conduct the same search as in Steps 1 through 4, but this time capitalize Software. How many results were returned this time? Does capitalizing your keywords make a difference?

Note: Capitalization in keywords affects the results retrieved by AltaVista. If you enter "Software," you are requiring that all results be capitalized. You should always enter the words in lowercase letters; this precaution will return any variation for the keywords.

EXERCISE 9.7 *(continued)*

10. Locate websites regarding small business licensing for a particular software program, such as Adobe Photoshop. For instance, add the following string to your previous search: **AND adobe photoshop**.

Other Advanced Search Features

Several search engines and directories offer special, proprietary technology that allows various kinds of customized web searches. These sites can also display search results in several interesting formats.

Lycos offers both keyword and subject searching. Lycos uses a web spider to validate all links, to ensure that only current, existing pages are contained within the Lycos database. It also has a feature for advanced searches, called Lycos Pro, which allows you to control the types of keyword matches, number of hits returned per page, content of the result, and other useful search criteria.

Ask.com lets users type in *natural language* queries to find information. Instead of typing in keywords, a user could simply ask a question. Ask.com then provides a list of results, often pointing to other search engines as well as websites. Figure 9.1 shows the results for the natural language query, "Where is Canada?"

The Internet Archive and Alexa offer a historical search engine, which allows users to search for a website as it was displayed on a particular date. The archive is located at `web.archive.org`. Users must enter a URL that was valid at some time since January 1, 1996.

Alexa offers a search engine that displays cached versions of unavailable websites, saved on Alexa's specially designed archive server farm. If the website was archived in the Alexa server farm, the dates of various site versions will be displayed. Some features, especially database gateways, may not function because of the archive's limitations. Because websites appear and disappear on the web every day, this service can help a researcher find documents that may no longer be available on the web. Figure 9.2 shows the results for the CIW Certification Program's website.

FIGURE 9.1 Ask.com Results Page

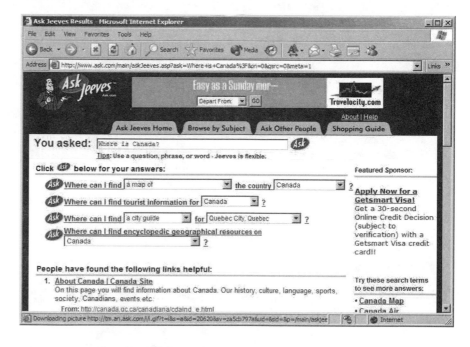

FIGURE 9.2 Internet Archive results page

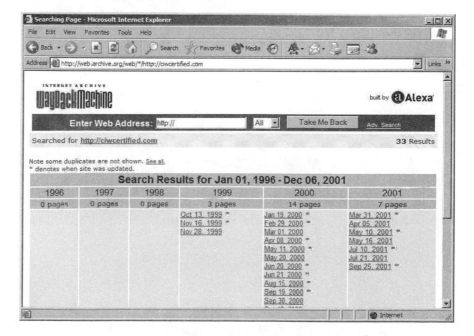

Browser Search Features

Users often set their browser's home page to their favorite search engine. There are two other ways to configure your browser for easy web searching. You can take advantage of the browser's built-in search features or install a search engine toolbar.

Netscape Navigator and Microsoft Internet Explorer each offer search features within the browser. As we discussed in Chapter 8, each manufacturer has set up their browser to use that company's search engines. Navigator defaults to the Netscape and AOL search sites, while Internet Explorer uses the MSN search engine as its default.

In Microsoft Internet Explorer, there is a Search button on the toolbar. By using this button or typing Ctrl+E, you can open a search window in the left margin of the browser window as shown in Figure 9.3.

FIGURE 9.3 Microsoft Internet Explorer search features

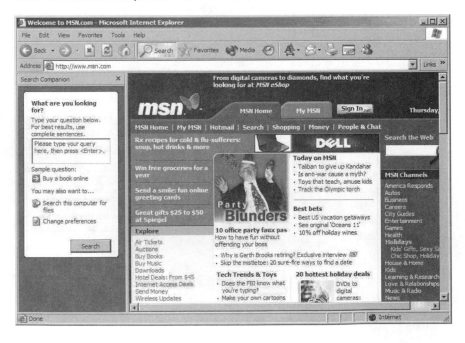

In Netscape Navigator, you can press the Search button on the toolbar to load one of several search engines in the browser window. You can also use the Sidebar feature to show a search form on the left of the browser window. Both features are shown in Figure 9.4.

FIGURE 9.4   Netscape Navigator search features

Several search engines have developed their own toolbars for use in Netscape and Microsoft browsers. A *toolbar* is a set of icons that plugs in to an application. These toolbars usually include a search field that brings up results from that search engine. Often, these toolbars include buttons that access additional site features. For example, the Google toolbar shown in Figure 9.5 also allows searches of the Google Groups site that we will discuss later in this chapter. The Yahoo! Companion toolbar shown in Figure 9.6 provides buttons that link to the Yahoo! Mail, news, and shopping services.

FIGURE 9.5 Google toolbar

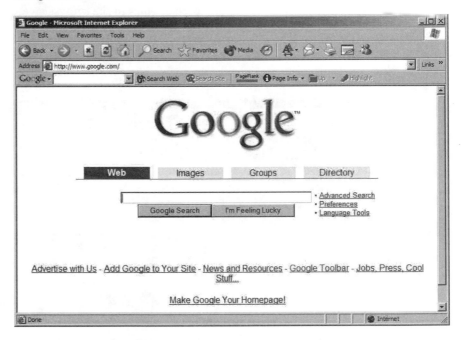

FIGURE 9.6 Yahoo! Companion toolbar

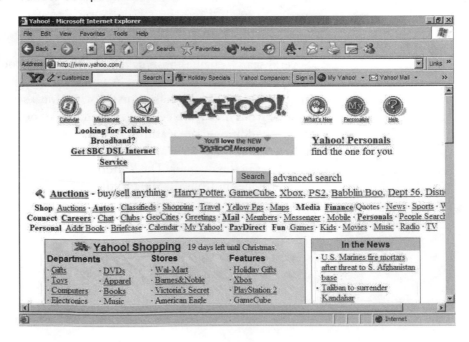

Searching for Graphics

Several search utilities can help users locate graphics and multimedia on the web. This type of search is called an *image search*. Graphic search engines are subsets of standard web search engines. However, the primary focus is the images that are contained within web pages, and not the page's text or topical content. For instance, AltaVista (`www.altavista.com`) offers the Images link from the home page.

Once you conduct a search, such as *international space station*, the search engine displays the results as a collection of *thumbnail images*. Thumbnail images are small versions or reductions of larger image files. By reducing the size of the images, the web server can easily transfer many image files to the web client.

When you select the thumbnail image, it is not a direct link to the actual image, but rather to the web page hosting the image. Once you follow the link to the web page, you may download the image. The results from an AltaVista image search for *international space station* is shown in Figure 9.7.

FIGURE 9.7   Graphic search engine results

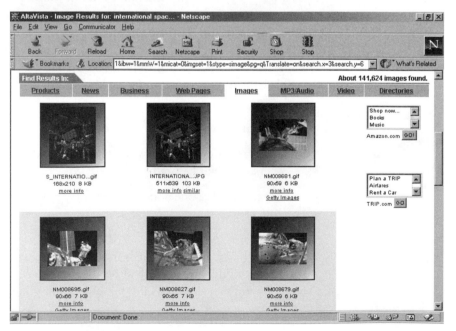

A static index search for graphic images is located at the Surf Madison Public File Libraries site (`http://surfmadison.com/library.htm`). The site offers the Clip Art, Graphics, Fonts link from the home page.

Remember that every image has a creator. You must obtain permission from the author, artist, or photographer before using the work commercially, including using it on a website. Like books and art, some images may be copyright protected. To avoid copyright infringement, you must obtain permission from and give credit to the author of any work you borrow.

Searching for Information on People

During the business day, you may need to find information about the new head of a rival corporation, the line manager of your company's Indonesia plant, the name of your legislative representative, or the address of an old school friend. You can use standard search engines to locate information about that person by using a *people search*.

If the person you are seeking has a web page or is mentioned on someone else's website, you might find him or her in this manner. If you cannot find a web page reference about the person for whom you are looking, perhaps you can find one about the company for which that person works.

If you still cannot find the person, try a website specifically made for people searches, such as WhoWhere? by Lycos (`www.whowhere.lycos.com`) or Yahoo! People Search (`people.yahoo.com`). These sites build their databases through the following sources:

- Internet activity, including people who are online

- A registration process, whereby the individual must submit his or her personal data before being listed

- Traditional phone books, proprietary phone listings, and other public directories that list people who are not necessarily connected to the Internet

You might try conducting a search for your name or a friend's name. If you do not find anyone with either of these sites, try searching for a very common name, such as Bill Gates, so that you can see the format of the results.

Searching for Mailing Lists

Earlier in this book, you learned about mailing lists. Often, a web page on a specific topic will reference a mailing list about that topic. For example, many Investor Relations sites provide information on mailing lists that discuss company business.

A number of sites are devoted to listing and hosting mailing lists. One of the better sites is Topica (`www.topica.com`) which covers more than 90,000 mailing lists. Topica was formerly known as Liszt.

You can use Topica to find and subscribe to a mailing list about a topic of your choice. When searching for mailing lists, you should choose keywords that are good general descriptions for the topic. The description of the mailing lists are typically brief, and usually do not include specific details on topics.

Topica also lets registered users create their own mailing lists. The Topica main page, which includes a list of major list categories, is shown in Figure 9.8.

FIGURE 9.8 Topica main page

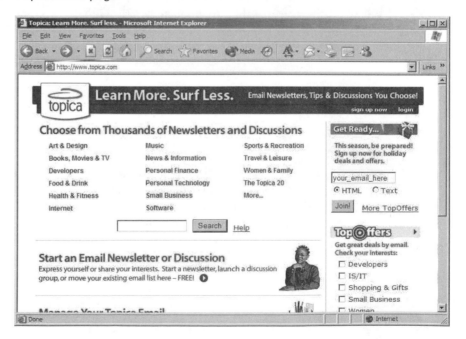

Searching for Newsgroups

Earlier in this course, you learned about newsgroups. The Google Groups website (`http://groups.google.com`) offers a way to search the Internet for newsgroups by subject, questions, keywords, or topics. Google Groups was formerly known as Deja and DejaNews before its acquisition by Google in 2000.

Web-based newsgroup searches are often easier and quicker than using a news client, because the website operator has already indexed the newsfeeds. Users can enter search strings in a web form, and receive a list of messages for viewing. With a news client, you would have to find suitable newsgroups, subscribe to them, and then download messages for searching.

Google Groups also offers a web-based method for subscribing to newsgroups. By registering with the site, you can maintain a list of newsgroups you want to read or monitor. You can read the messages in your web browser or receive summaries by e-mail.

One disadvantage is that web-based newsgroup sites, including Google Groups, do not offer a complete newsfeed. There are many local and private newsgroups that are not listed on the Google Groups site. Sometimes the site chooses not to carry newsfeeds that users may find offensive. Often, the site cannot obtain permission to carry private newsfeeds.

Other Search Tools

Before web search engines, other tools were required to access information. These search tools included Archie, Gopher, and Veronica . None of them offered a graphical user interface, but they provided ways to locate information for many years. Web search engines have rendered the majority of these services largely obsolete. However, some Gopher servers are still in use, and some contain information that cannot be found on web servers. You should be familiar with the function of these services.

Archie

One of the first internet search services available was a program called *Archie*. It conducts searches on anonymous FTP sites. To use the service, you must know the name of the file you seek. To connect to an Archie server, you can use a Telnet client, supplied with Windows, or an Archie client.

Before you conduct a search, you must know the address of an Archie server. You can use your favorite web search engine and enter **Archie server addresses**. Locating Archie servers that still provide service is becoming difficult. Many are no longer available. McGill University, where Archie was developed, has a list of Archie servers posted at `www.agrenv` `.mcgill.ca/SEARCH/ARCHIE.HTM`.

Web search engines have almost entirely replaced Archie searches. The FTP search engine offered by FAST and Lycos at `download.lycos.com/` `static/advanced_search.asp` is a popular FTP search site.

Gopher

After the Advanced Research Projects Agency (ARPA) project was completed, the information made accessible on the Internet increased in volume. Users of the Internet needed to access text-based information easily and quickly. A protocol called *Gopher* was created to allow users to navigate and search computers around the country without the addresses of the servers that stored the information.

When using Gopher, you select a menu item from a list related to the topic you are searching, and another list of choices more closely related to that topic is displayed on the screen. From this list, you pick another topic until you reach the single document, graphic, sound, or video that you want. This browsing process is sometimes called tunneling, and is similar to a static index/site map search index.

The University of Minnesota has a large Gopher site on the Internet. It contains thousands of menu items and information ranging from weather to recipes to videos of the Apollo space launches. The address for the University of Minnesota Gopher (sometimes called Gopher Home) is `gopher://` `gopher.tc.umn.edu`. To access a gopher site, enter the URL into your web browser. Both Netscape and Microsoft web browsers can be used as Gopher clients. The Gopher site will resemble an FTP site, as shown in Figure 9.9.

Although Gopher sites are now used less for research and resources than are websites, you may find yourself using a Gopher resource, often because you followed a link from elsewhere.

FIGURE 9.9   A Gopher site

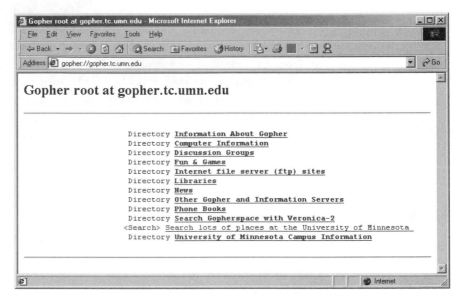

Veronica

Veronica is an index and retrieval system that can locate information on most Gopher servers. Its name is an acronym that stands for *Very Easy Rodent-Oriented Net-Wide Index to Computer Archives*. Veronica was designed to work with the Gopher protocol and make the search for information faster and easier. Veronica is used when a general search for information is performed but the Internet address of the Gopher server is not known.

Veronica servers contain basically the same information in their databases. The databases contain menu items from most of the Gopher servers on the Internet, but they are not necessarily updated at the same time. It does not make a difference which Veronica server you search, but you should search the server that is physically located closest to you.

Because there are few Veronica servers and millions of Internet users, Veronica is one of the more difficult search tools to use. Connecting with a Veronica server is sometimes difficult. Veronica is the easiest way to search Gopher, but like Gopher, it is declining in popularity.

Summary

In this chapter, we discussed how web search engines can be used to find websites. Search engines use robots or spiders to find websites, which directories rely on user submissions of URLs to catalog. Both services use robots or spiders to collect information about web pages, including keywords that may be related to the web pages contents. This information is sometimes included in the META tag of each web page.

There are three kinds of search indexes. A static index lets users manually search through ages, using a directory tree or a site map. Keyword indexes are the databases that search engines and directories help users to search. Full-text indexes can be set up for a specific website and can allow users to search on any piece of text that might be listed in that site.

We also discussed some basic search techniques. A directory such as Yahoo! offers lists of related sites. Search engines and directories always present a search field in which the user can enter keywords for location. You can refine searches by grouping keywords together in quotation marks, or using Boolean operators.

Several search engines have their own advanced features, such as Lycos' multiple searches, Internet Archive's historical searchers, and Ask.com's natural language queries. Users can also search some engines for image files, such as AltaVista.

Other searches are also available, using older Internet services. Archie is a Telnet-based application that searches FTP sites for files. Veronica is a search engine for information found on Gopher services. Archie, Gopher, and Veronica services are still available, but have been mostly replaced by the web.

Exam Essentials

Know the function of search engines and directories, and their use of keywords.   Search engines and directories allow users to find web pages based on keywords that are listed in these pages. Search engines use robot or spider programs to find and retrieve web content for indexing. Directories require users to submit URLs for indexing.

Understand how a website's ranking in search engines can be improved by using META tags and keywords. Search engines and directories rank websites based on their relevancy to the search term. The META tag can be used to include keywords on a web page, which can improve a site's ranking on a search engine.

Understand the functions of static, keyword, and full-text search indexes. Static indexes allow users to manually search through a directory tree or site map. Search engines and directories use keyword indexes, which link web pages to relevant words or phrases. Full-text search indexes are often used on individual sites, and allow users to search on any piece of text.

Be able to search Internet data using Boolean operators such as AND, OR, AND NOT, NOT, NEAR, wildcards, and plus and minus signs. Many search engines and directories offer advanced search services, which use Boolean operators to help refine standard web searches by grouping words, or excluding keywords from searches.

Be able to search for graphics, newsgroups, people, and mailing lists on the Internet. Several search engines have special features that help users search for image files, based on their contents or name. Users can read or subscribe to newsgroups at the Google Groups website. There are several services that help users locate individual people by the physical or Internet addresses. Topica.com has an index of mailing lists, and helps users subscribe to and start their own lists.

Know the purposes of Archie, Gopher, and Veronica. Archie supported file searches on FTP sites. Gopher is a text-based system that resembled hypertext. Veronica is a Gopher-based search engine. All three of these services have been replaced by web-based services.

Key Terms

Before you take the exam, be certain you are familiar with the following terms:

Archie	ranking system
Boolean operators	relevancy
directory	robot
full-text index	search engines
Gopher	site map
image search	spider
keyword index	static index
keywords	thumbnail images
META tag	toolbar
natural language	Veronica
people search	

Review Questions

1. Which one of the following services uses robots or spiders to collect information about websites?

   A. Gopher

   B. Search engine

   C. Newsgroups

   D. Archie

2. Which one of the following is the best definition of a keyword?

   A. A word that appears in the title bar of a web browser.

   B. A word that is listed in the description of a website.

   C. A word that appears in a web document and is used by search engines to identify relevant websites.

   D. A word that is listed in a website's map.

3. Which one of the following describes how a directory is different from a search engine?

   A. Search engines can search, find, and index any URL at any time.

   B. Directories can search, find, and index any URL at any time.

   C. Search engine entries must be submitted by users before the engine indexes that site.

   D. Directory entries must be submitted by users before the engine indexes that site.

4. Which of the following HTML tags is correctly formatted to store information for search engines?

   A. `<KEYWORD ="keyword1 keyword2 keyword3">`

   B. `<DESCRIPTION="keyword1,keyword2,keyword3">`

   C. `<META NAME="Keywords" CONTENT="keyword1,keyword2,keyword3">`

   D. `<CONTENT="keyword1,keyword2,keyword3">`

5. What one of the following HTML tags can provide a brief summary of the web page's information for listing in a search engine, rather than using the first few lines of the web document?

A. `<DESCRIPTION="Text">`

B. `<CONTENT="Text">`

C. `<META NAME="Description" CONTENT="Text">`

D. `<SUMMARY="Text">`

6. A static index differs from other types of searches in that it does which one of the following?

A. Requires the full content of every page to be indexed.

B. Maps the Internet, enabling users to locate directories containing indexed information.

C. Only allows users to manually search directories for indexed information.

D. Allows users to enter keywords to query an index.

7. Which type of index is usually used for a web search engine?

A. Static index

B. Site map

C. Keyword index

D. Full-text index

8. Search engines rely on which kind of internetworking server to answer user searches?

A. Certificate servers

B. Database servers

C. Directory servers

D. Transaction servers

9. Steve needs to do a web search to locate information about a supplier. Janet suggests he use Boolean operators. Which one of the following is the best explanation for Janet's suggestion?

   A. Narrow searches by allowing users to include, exclude, or combine certain keywords.

   B. Specify the parameters for manual searches.

   C. Organize the results of a search.

   D. Identify the most recent information on a particular search topic.

10. The Boolean operator OR means that the search results:

    A. May include a particular word.

    B. Must include a particular word.

    C. May include at least one of the words.

    D. Must include at least one of the words.

11. Ralph is searching for a hotel in Clearwater Beach that offers either beachfront location or a pool. Which of the following searchers would most likely return the correct results?

    A. Clearwater Beach hotels

    B. Clearwater Beach hotels AND/OR beachfront AND/OR pool

    C. Clearwater Beach hotels AND beachfront OR pool

    D. Clearwater Beach hotels AND (beachfront OR pool)

12. Which search engine was originally designed to index the entire web?

    A. Lycos

    B. Yahoo!

    C. Google

    D. AltaVista

13. Joan wants to find documents about windsurfing in Virginia. She does not want to see documents that mention North Carolina. Which one of the following search terms would present this result?

    A. `windsurfing virginia and "north carolina"`

    B. `windsurfing virginia and not "north carolina"`

    C. `windsurfing virginia without "north carolina"`

    D. `windsurfing virginia exclude "north carolina"`

14. Virginia wants to find web documents that mention the phrases "chicken sandwich" and "Turner Field." She wants to see only those documents where these two phrases are listed in the same sentence. Which one of the following queries is most likely to produce the correct results?

    A. `chicken sandwich turner field`

    B. `(chicken sandwich) and (turner field)`

    C. `(chicken sandwich) or (turner field)`

    D. `(chicken sandwich) near (turner field)`

15. Natalie wants to enter her web search queries as questions. Which one of the following search engines can support natural language queries?

    A. Yahoo

    B. AltaVista

    C. Ask.com

    D. Google

16. David is trying to access some files in his local school board's website. He knew these files were available in November 2000, but they have since been removed from the website. Which of the following search engines could help him find these files?

    A. Yahoo

    B. Ask.com

    C. Internet Archive

    D. Lycos

17. In Netscape Navigator and Microsoft Internet Explorer, where does the search bar appear on screen when activated?

A. As a toolbar, below the browser menu.

B. Below the browser window.

C. On the right side of the browser window.

D. On the left side of the browser window.

18. The Archie service is best described by which of the following statements?

A. Conducts searches on anonymous FTP sites

B. Conducts searches on newsgroups

C. Conducts searches on Gopher

D. Conducts searches on mailing lists

19. Anthony needs to find a mailing list on marathon running. Which one of the following search strategies should he use to get an answer quickly?

A. Post a message on a suitable newsgroup.

B. Search a mailing list website.

C. Open a search engine and use the keywords "marathon running."

D. Look for an entry on a directory such as Yahoo!

20. Donna is attempting to find a former roommate from college. Which service would be most helpful to her?

A. A web search engine

B. A people search service that references telephone listing

C. Veronica

D. A full-text search engine

Answers to Review Questions

1. B.   Many search engines use automated programs called robots or spiders to collect information on web documents. Gopher is a text-based information system. Newsgroups contain messages on specific topics. Archie is a telnet-based FTP search application.

2. C.   Keywords can be used in the body or header of a web page, and are intended for use by search engines.

3. D.   Directories require users to send in URLs for indexing. Search engines can proactively search and index URLs on their own schedule.

4. C.   HTML keywords are always defined in a META tag. The other tags listed are not valid HTML.

5. C.   The META tag can contain descriptions of websites. The other tags listed are not valid HTML.

6. C.   Static indexes are the less flexible of the three index types. It supports manual searching only.

7. C.   Search engines usually use keyword indexes. Static indexes and site maps are for manual searching, while full-text indexes consume too much storage space.

8. B.   Search engines rely on search indexes, which use database servers to store information. Certificate servers issue and store certificates for validating identities. Directory servers are specialized database servers that store contact information for users. Transaction servers handle financial transaction processing.

9. A.   Boolean logic is used to refine the search parameters on web search engines. Manual searches do not use Boolean logic. Search engines use their own methods for organizing search results. Boolean logic does not provide session management capabilities.

10. C.   The OR operator returns a true value if one of the two words it links is found.

11. D.   The correct choice links two conditions. For the second condition, we need to find either the keyword beachfront or pool.

12. D.   AltaVista was originally designed to index the entire web. Lycos and Google never had that goal, while Yahoo! started as a directory.

13. B. The Boolean operator AND NOT is supported on many search engines. WITHOUT is not a typical Boolean operator.

14. D. The NEAR term will locate documents that include those search terms, provided the terms are listed close together in a sentence or paragraph.

15. C. Ask.com is the only one of these search engines that supports natural language queries.

16. C. Alexa's Internet Archive allows searches on websites cached in its server farm. The other choices do not support historical searches.

17. D. This built-in feature displays web search forms, and appears on the left side of the screen by default.

18. A. Archie is a Telnet-based search application for finding files on FTP sites.

19. B. Anthony would most likely find a mailing list by using a site such as Topica. If he posts a message on a newsgroup, he will have to wait for someone to answer. His keyword search does not include anything about mailing lists, so he will likely retrieve many listings about the general subject. He may not find a suitable entry in a directory, as these are limited by the number of URLs submitted and indexed.

20. B. A people search service would be most effective for finding an individual. Web search engines will not show results unless the individual has posted content on the Web. Veronica is a Gopher search service. Full-text search engines usually cover a small number of websites.

Chapter

10

Using E-Mail and Other Clients

THE CIW EXAM OBJECTIVE GROUPS COVERED IN THIS CHAPTER:

- ✓ Use e-mail clients to send simple messages and files to other Internet users.

- ✓ Identify additional Internet services, including but not limited to: news, FTP, Gopher, Telnet.

- ✓ Transmit text and binary files using popular Internet services, including but not limited to: the Web and e-mail.

The World Wide Web is one of the most popular services on the Internet, but there are other services that you will also find useful. In this chapter, we will cover four important Internet services that every user should know how to access: e-mail, FTP, newsgroups, and Telnet.

Electronic mail is a very popular service that allows Internet users to send messages and files. In the last few years, e-mail usage has grown at an amazing rate in Europe and North America, and now rivals telephone and postal mail as a communication medium. We will discuss how to configure an e-mail client and send effective e-mail.

File Transfer Protocol is another important service that lets users share large files quickly. We will discuss how to download files with command-line and graphical FTP clients.

Newsgroups provide electronic forums for discussing topics. We will discuss how newsgroups are organized, how to read and post messages, and various rules for using these services.

Finally, we will explore how Telnet allows users to tap into Internet servers and access a variety of services. Telnet is a terminal emulation program that is often used by UNIX and Linux server administrators to configure and maintain services and networks.

Electronic Mail (E-Mail)

Electronic mail, or e-mail, has been widely embraced by the corporate communications environment. Never before has our global society been able to send and receive information so quickly. The businesses that can best handle the transfer of valuable information may become the leaders in their industries. Therefore, e-mail is a critical function to understand and master.

Internet e-mail addresses use the format of `name@domain`. Notice the @ symbol between the user name and the domain. The @ symbol represents the word "at". For example, the e-mail address for the examination department at the CIW certification program is `exam@CIWcertified.com`, and is spoken as "exam at CIWcertified dot com."

It is possible to include an IP address in an e-mail address. The IP address of the mail server would be used. The IP address that is mapped to CIWcertified.com is 63.72.51.85, so you could send an e-mail message to `exam@63.72.51.85`. Obviously, this defeats the purpose of the domain name system—providing easily remembered names, instead of requiring difficult to remember numeric addresses.

Ray Tomlinson developed the first Internet e-mail application in 1971. He worked at Bolt, Beranek & Newman, a Federal contractor on the original ARPANET project. Tomlinson is also known as the person who selected that "@" sign as the identifying character for e-mail addresses. While writing his e-mail application, he realized that each e-mail address must have a user-name and a machine name. He selected the "@" sign while searching his keyboard for a suitable character.

The part of the address before the @ identifies the user within a domain. The user name is usually mapped to an e-mail account. There is no single set of rules for creating e-mail addresses, so there are many different styles in use. Typically, the name is related to the person's name or job function, and may include dots, underscores, or numbers in addition to letters. Following are some examples:

    jsmith@company.net

    johns@company.net

    johnster@company.net

    john.smith@company.net

    john_smith@company.net

    sales@company.co.uk

webmaster@company.co.uk

webmaster2@company.co.uk

ISPs usually use your account name to create your e-mail address. Some ISPs offer an online signup form that helps you select a username.

The part of the address after the @ is the domain name of the organization or company that issues the e-mail accounts. Some businesses and organizations have carefully selected their domain name, because the domain name can quickly tell an e-mail recipient what the company is or does.

Sending E-Mail

As previously discussed, e-mail is sent using the Simple Mail Transfer Protocol (SMTP). To send e-mail, you need to configure your e-mail client with the following components:

- The outgoing mail (SMTP) server address.

- The destination e-mail addresses

- The recipient's e-mail account name

Many outgoing (SMTP) mail servers require SMTP passwords. These passwords prohibit unauthorized users from sending e-mail on the server. If the user does not enter the SMTP password, the mail will not be sent.

As we discussed in Chapter 6, there are two Internet protocols used for receiving or downloading e-mail messages to a client: Post Office Protocol (POP) or the Internet Message Access Protocol (IMAP). Most ISPs and many companies use POP. You need to configure your e-mail client with the following POP information:

Incoming mail (POP3) server address   This often includes the domain name that appears in your e-mail address. However, you should check with your ISP or server administrator.

POP3 account name   The part of the e-mail address before the @.

POP3 account password   This is provided by your ISP or server administrator.

The POP3 account is also called the POP ID (POP identity). You must log on to an incoming mail server using your POP account to download your e-mail. Logging on requires your account name and account password.

When you retrieve messages into your e-mail client using POP3, you are downloading these messages from the mail server. Most e-mail clients will delete downloaded mail messages from the server as their default behavior. You can configure your POP3 settings so that e-mail messages are not deleted at all from the server, or so that the messages are deleted after they are a few days old.

You can always delete messages you no longer wish to keep on your e-mail client. However, if you have deleted the message from the server, you will not be able to retrieve the message should you need it again.

As you continue to download e-mail to a client application, over time your e-mail inbox will have more and more messages. Most e-mail clients allow you to set up folders in the inbox, to help you organize messages you wish to keep. Some clients allow you to archive old e-mail messages, so that your inbox does not accumulate messages and waste system resources such as RAM.

If you change e-mail clients, you may be able to import your old messages to the new client. This can help you maintain your saved messages.

Address Books

E-mail programs include address books that allow you to store names and information for your frequently accessed e-mail contacts. Address books can contain e-mail addresses, names or aliases, phone numbers, street addresses, and other relevant data. You can then simply select a name from the address book list, instead of typing an e-mail address each time you want to send e-mail.

If you buy a new computer or change e-mail programs, you can save your current address book or contact list to a file, and then import the address book file to your new computer or program.

Selecting an E-Mail Client

There are many e-mail clients available for Windows users. Netscape Navigator includes an e-mail application called Communicator, which has many of the same features of Microsoft Outlook Express. America Online has its own e-mail client, which can be used to send Internet e-mail.

Internet Explorer can install an e-mail client called Outlook Express. In the next exercises, we will demonstrate how to set up and use this e-mail client to send messages.

In all likelihood, your employer will choose one e-mail program for the company and stipulate that you use it. If you choose an e-mail program for your home, you can configure as many e-mail programs as you want. For instance, you could use Netscape Messenger for your home business e-mail account and Outlook Express for your personal e-mail account. You could also configure multiple accounts on one or the other, instead of using two or more mail programs.

Your employer may have specific rules regarding the sending and receiving of personal e-mail on the company's mail servers or your computer. Please check with your IT department for more information.

EXERCISE 10.1

Configuring Microsoft Outlook Express as Your E-Mail Client

In this exercise, you will configure Microsoft Outlook Express as your e-mail client. Netscape Messenger uses a similar setup procedure.

You should not perform this exercise unless you are on your own computer and you do not have an e-mail client installed. By completing this exercise, you may be downloading and deleting unread e-mail messages from your account.

You will need the following information, which is available from your ISP or your IT department:

- POP3 server name or IP address

- SMTP server name or IP address

- Your e-mail address

- Your e-mail account name

- Your e-mail password

1. Launch Outlook Express by clicking on the icon or by selecting Start ➢ Programs ➢ Outlook Express.

2. You may be asked if you want Outlook Express to be your default e-mail program. Select No.

3. If Outlook Express has never been configured, the Internet Connection Wizard may appear. Select Cancel, then Yes to verify your cancellation of the Wizard. You will access the Wizard later in this exercise.

4. The Outlook Express Import window may appear, which allows you to import e-mail configurations from other e-mail clients on your computer. Select Do Not Import at This Time. Click Next and Finish. The Outlook Express window will open, as shown here. You may have a "Welcome" e-mail message from Microsoft. This is placed in your inbox during installation.

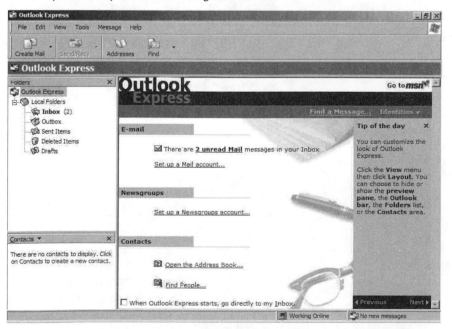

5. Select the Tools menu, choose Accounts, and select the Mail tab. To create a new mail account, click the Add button and choose Mail from the pop-up menu. The Internet Connection Wizard will launch.

6. In the Display Name window, enter your user name that will appear on your account, such as student. Select Next.

7. In the Internet E-Mail Address dialog box, select I Already Have an E-Mail Address That I'd Like To Use. Enter your e-mail account, such as user@domain.com. Select Next.

8. In the E-Mail Server Names dialog box, verify that the incoming mail server is a POP3 server. Enter your POP3 (or incoming) and SMTP (or outgoing mail) server names or IP addresses, as shown here. Select Next.

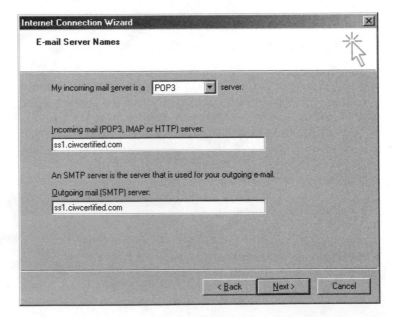

9. In the Internet Mail Logon dialog box, enter your POP3 account name and your e-mail password. Click Next.

10. In the Congratulations window, select Finish. You have configured the account and are ready to send and receive e-mail.

11. Select Close.

Next, we'll send an e-mail message using Outlook Express. Note that Netscape Messenger and other common e-mail clients have similar processes to follow for performing these tasks.

EXERCISE 10.2

Using Microsoft Outlook Express to Send E-Mail

In this exercise, you will send an e-mail message to yourself using Microsoft Outlook Express.

1. Click the Inbox on the left side of the screen. Select the New Mail button on the toolbar, or select the Message menu and choose New Message.

2. Enter your e-mail address in the To field. This step will address the message to yourself.

3. Enter a title in the Subject field. Click in the lower half of the window and type a message. Your screen should look something like this.

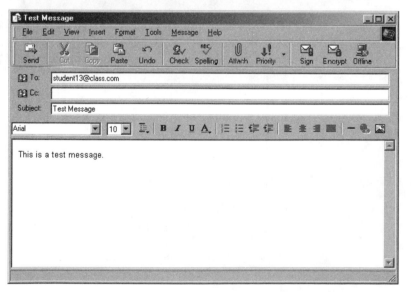

4. Select the Send button at the far left of the toolbar, or select the File menu and choose Send Message. Your message will be sent to the mail server.

Next, we'll perform retrieval of an e-mail message.

Using Microsoft Outlook Express to Retrieve E-Mail

In this exercise, you will retrieve the e-mail message you sent in the preceding exercise.

1. Select the Send/Recv button (Send and Receive) on the toolbar, or select the Tools menu and choose Send and Receive All. Note that you do not have to enter your password because it is already configured in your account.

2. The new message appears in your inbox. Double-click the message to read it in a separate window. The message will be similar to the one here.

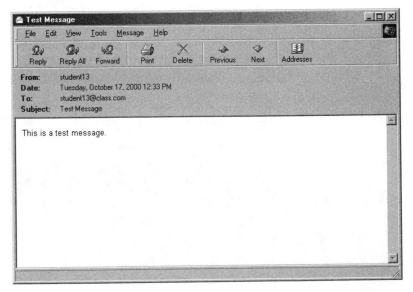

3. Close the message window by clicking the X in the upper-right corner of the window, or selecting the File menu and choosing Close.

Copying Messages

E-mail clients usually support two additional address fields, which can be used to distribute copies of a message to users other than the intended recipient.

The first of these fields is called the *Cc* field. The name comes from the term "carbon copy," which was a common way of duplicating handwritten or typed letters. By adding a user to the Cc field, you are indicating that they should read this message and understand that it is for informational purposes. The users in a Cc field are not expected to act on a message's content.

The second field is the *Bcc* field. This term is derived from the term "blind carbon copy." Recipients of an e-mail message do not see the e-mail addresses lists on a Bcc line, even though the bcc users also receive the message.

The bcc field is a convenient way to distribute a message to many users without revealing their identities. When doing this, you should list your own e-mail address in the To field. You will, of course, receive a copy of the message, but you will see that none of the bcc recipients are listed.

Web-Based E-Mail

A popular alternative to e-mail clients is web-based e-mail, where the web browser acts as the user interface for retrieving and sending e-mail messages. By using the web server as a gateway, a user can view and send e-mail on any computer that has a web connection.

Received e-mail messages are not downloaded to the web client using a mail protocol. They are sent as HTML documents that can be viewed in a graphical web browser. The web pages use form elements to present fields, icons, and buttons that are used for viewing and sending e-mail messages.

The mail messages can remain on the server until the user deletes them. Many web mail services also support POP3, so users can download messages to their regular e-mail client.

Some of the more popular web mail sites include MSN, Hotmail, Yahoo!, and AOL. Hundreds of public web mail services are available in many languages. Some of these services provide a free e-mail account with a limited amount of storage space. Others provide premium services, such as extra storage space, security, and custom domain names. Some web hosting companies and ISPs also provide web mail services for their customers' accounts.

Your company may prohibit the use of web-based e-mail on company computers. Please check with your IT department for more information.

Who Sent Me That E-Mail?

The increased popularity of web mail accounts has emphasized an important point about e-mail. It is difficult to verify who actually sent an e-mail message, unless the sender has used a certificate that was granted by a trusted authority. It is very easy to forge a return e-mail address by altering the configuration setup in the e-mail client.

Senders of unsolicited commercial mail often do this to keep replies and complaints from going to their actual e-mail account. *Unsolicited commercial e-mail (UCE)* may include advertisements, business offers, and other content that a user did not request. UCE is also called *spam*, after a popular canned luncheon meat.

You can always check the header of an e-mail message to trace its origin. When you view a message in a client, you will usually find a menu option to view the header. Outlook Express will show headers when you select the View ➢ All Headers menu command. Netscape Communicator and some web mail services also allow you to view the header as part of the e-mail message.

A sample header from a UCE message is shown in the following section. We have added line numbers to help you identify various portions of the header. These line numbers do not actually appear in an e-mail header.

```
1  Received: from wormwood.pobox.com [208.210.125.20] by
   ↳mail.pobox.com with ESMTP
   (SMTPD32-6.06) id AABDE2800FC; Tue, 11 Dec 2001
   ↳16:37:49 -0600
2  Received: from wormwood.pobox.com (localhost.pobox.com
   ↳[127.0.0.1])
   by wormwood.pobox.com (Postfix) with ESMTP id 6E2317255D
   for <bill@pobox.com>; Tue, 11 Dec 2001 17:16:55 -0500 (EST)
3  Delivered-To: bill@pobox.com
4  Received: from web21103.mail.yahoo.com
   ↳(web21103.mail.yahoo.com [216.136.227.105])
   by wormwood.pobox.com (Postfix) with SMTP id 9375372590
   for <bill@pobox.com>; Tue, 11 Dec 2001 17:16:54 -0500 (EST)
```

5 Message-ID: <20011211221653.6111.qmail@web21103.mail
↳.yahoo.com>

6 Received: from [63.194.179.202] by **web21103.mail.yahoo.com**
↳**via HTTP**; Tue, 11 Dec 2001 14:16:53 PST

7 Date: Tue, 11 Dec 2001 14:16:53 -0800 (PST)

8 From: **John Smith** <**volterradq@yahoo.com**>

9 Subject: Increase Internet Connection Speeds Up To 200%

10 To: **bill@pobox.com**

11 MIME-Version: 1.0

12 Content-Type: text/plain; charset=us-ascii

13 X-RCPT-TO: <bill@pobox.com>

14 X-UIDL: 301604328

15 Status: U

Look at line 8, which lists the e-mail address that the sender configured in his client's settings. This alone does not mean that the message was sent from yahoo.com. We can look at line 6, which identifies the server that originally sent this mail. It was a Yahoo@ web server, which we can determine by the "via HTTP" method that is listed.

This indicates that the message was sent using a web mail client. As we move up the listing, we can trace the message's path from Yahoo to the pobox.com mail server.

Because this message was UCE, we could report this message to the mail server host of the sender's account. We should forward the entire message along with the e-mail header information to the Abuse department of the sender's ISP or organization. Many companies have established the **abuse@** e-mail address as a destination for e-mail abuse complaints. The abuse e-mail department at Yahoo! Mail uses the address abuse@yahoo.com. When you forward the original UCE, you must include the e-mail header, which has information the abuse department needs to track down the sender.

How Did They Get My E-Mail Address?

UCE senders often use special programs to help them send mail. One program is an address harvester. This application scours websites for e-mail addresses and saves them in a database. One of the best defenses against this kind of spider is not to list your e-mail address on any web page. However, this tactic may not be practical, if you have posted a resume and want to be contacted by employers, for example. You may also want to post your address on the directory pages of your favorite groups and clubs so that other members can find you.

Another type of program is actually a server-side script that generates e-mail addresses based on all possible combinations of letters and numbers in the user name. A bulk mailing program then directs UCE messages to these possible usernames at known domains.

Operators of mail servers can attempt to block such mail by looking for senders who submit large quantities of undeliverable mail to a domain. If the undeliverable mail has random To addresses, the server administrator can configure the mail server to block messages sent from that domain.

However, this is not always practical. Some senders of UCE use a popular domain name such as aol.com or yahoo.com in their From field. Most server administrators would not refuse mail from these two servers, as they each represent millions of legitimate users. There are programs and options available for mail servers that can help server administrators reduce the amount of UCE that actually reaches their users.

Users can also configure their client to filter out suspicious messages. These messages can be deleted, or directed to a mailbox folder for later review. Outlook Express allows you to filter out mail by setting up a blocked senders list. Some ISPs and mail server hosts also let you configure filters or rules at the mail server. Several web mail sites offer UCE protection as part of their services, because these sites are easy targets.

Many ISPs prohibit the sending of UCE through their mail servers. This restriction is often part of the terms of service. By using server logs and e-mail headers, a skilled IT professional can identify a user who is bulk mailing UCE, and inform management to end that user's account. This is a reason why many SMTP servers require usernames and passwords—to detect unauthorized UCE mailing.

Some websites will let you opt-out of commercial e-mail that they send. This is an important aspect of user privacy that we will discuss in Chapters 12 and 13.

Netiquette

E-mail is not a new form of communication, but it is new to many users. The tendency in the busy work environment is to quickly send brief e-mail notes with little thought. Many individuals regret these hasty actions later. Treat e-mail messages as you would any other written communication.

The term *netiquette* has been coined to encourage common sense, politeness, and general rules for Internet etiquette. The following is a list of general etiquette guidelines that should be followed when using e-mail.

Remember that your e-mail message may be printed, or forwarded to other people.   This can be helpful or detrimental in a business environment. Remember that once you select Send, the message is on its way and cannot be cancelled. Proofread and check your spelling before sending your message. Use business-appropriate language in all work-related messages.

Do not type messages in all capital letters.   This practice is known as "shouting," and can indicate anger or rudeness.

Do not forward your message to many users, unless there is a genuine need to do so.   Mail recipients should immediately understand why you sent them a particular message. If you must forward a message to several users, consider using the Bcc field to conceal their addresses.

Choose an appropriate subject line for your message.   The subject line is usually visible from the inbox view. Make sure your recipient has a good idea what the message covers.

When possible, respond promptly to e-mail messages addressed to you. This practice makes a good impression, and indicates that you are monitoring your e-mail. Remember that the time and date of your reply are automatically included in your message. Some users may monitor the amount of time it takes for you to reply.

When you respond, think clearly about what you write.   Answer the message only when you have gathered all your information. If you find that you are becoming angry or emotional while writing a message, wait a few minutes after finishing the message and reread its contents. Often you will find that you have calmed down, and you will edit the message to a more pleasant tone.

Never send unsolicited commercial e-mail.   More governments and organizations are creating and enforcing penalties for sending UCE. Also, your ISP may prohibit sending UCE in its terms of service, and they can cancel your account if it detects such behavior. If you receive UCE, forward the message along with the e-mail header information to the abuse department of the sender's ISP or organization. Many companies have established the `abuse@` e-mail address as a destination for e-mail abuse complaints.

E-Mail Signatures

You may want to add a signature to your e-mail messages, or your employer may require one. An e-mail signature consists of a few lines of text that appear at the bottom of each of your messages automatically. A signature might identify your position, the department in which you work, or both. Typical signatures include the sender's name and e-mail address. Your signature can also include your business name, web address, or phone number. In addition, authors might include the title of their most recent book in their signature block, whereas software developers may cite their most recent product. The signature block is an informal reminder to your reader of your identity or the identity of your company.

EXERCISE 10.4

Creating an E-Mail Signature Text File

In this exercise, you will create a signature block for your e-mail messages. You will prepare a small text file that contains the signature block, and add it to Netscape Messenger and Microsoft Outlook Express e-mail messages in the following exercises.

1. Right-click the desktop background and select New ➤ Text Document. Rename the file `Mail Signature.txt`. Double-click the file to edit it in Notepad.

2. Enter a simple signature block such as this one:

John Doe

jdoe@company.com

Office: 1-310-555-1212

Use your own name, e-mail address, and other information. Restrict yourself to three or four lines, and try to include information that will be of interest to everyone who receives e-mail from you.

3. Save the `Mail Signature.txt` file on your desktop, and close Notepad.

This signature file can be used in the e-mail client of your choosing. In the next exercise, we'll configure Outlook Express to use the file we just created.

EXERCISE 10.5

Configuring a Signature File in Microsoft Outlook Express

In this exercise, you will configure Outlook Express to automatically load your signature file to an e-mail message.

1. Open Outlook Express. Choose the Tools menu and select Options.

2. Select the Signatures tab and select the New button. Select the check box labeled Add Signatures to All Outgoing Messages.

3. In the Edit Signature section, select the File radio button, then click the Browse button to select the `Mail Signature.txt` file you created in the previous exercise and select Open. Click OK to exit the Options window.

4. Send yourself a test message to see how your signature is added. The contents of the `Mail Signature.txt` file are appended to the end of every message you send, excluding replies and forwards.

E-Mail Privacy

In the United States, the employer has legal ownership of everything the employee creates while on the job. The same is true for the Internet workplace. Your employer has the right to read e-mail you send using company equipment and Internet connections. Your employer can also read e-mail sent to your company account from other sources; business acquaintances, friends, mailing lists, perhaps individuals you do not even know.

If you are given an e-mail address to use for company business, you should not use that address to conduct private conversations. After all, you cannot expect this correspondence to be truly private. Your employer is paying for the Internet connection, the software, the browser, and the operating system. Your IT department and perhaps your supervisor will have ready access to your mail messages. Your company may archive all sent and received e-mail messages. If you send e-mail to a co-worker about another employee, perhaps discussing a promotion or a performance appraisal, there is a chance that the other employee will be able to read that e-mail.

Some companies create *acceptable use policies* to remind their employees to use company computers and servers for business purposes only. The prudent approach is to assume your e-mail might be read, and use your business e-mail access for business purposes only, or for the occasional brief personal note. If you need to discuss company-confidential information with a co-worker, do so in person, on the phone, or with confidential memos.

If you need personal privacy in your e-mail, purchase Internet access and an e-mail account through an ISP and use it from home, on your own time. If you choose to access personal e-mail on your work computer, remember that your IT department can use network analyzer software to intercept and read the packets.

Even if your company does not mention e-mail in its nondisclosure or trade-secret policies, you should consider it to be subject to the same policies as any other form of communication. If your company stipulates that you must not reveal certain information in writing, you should not reveal it in e-mail either.

Above all, remember that e-mail is a permanent written record. Companies may monitor e-mail for no other reason than to be sure employees are not distributing software, contracts, financial information, or other confidential material to unauthorized users.

E-Mail Attachments

You can attach almost any kind of file to an e-mail message. Businesses find this a powerful tool for better communication because you can attach word-processing documents, presentations, spreadsheets, small database files, and images to your e-mail messages. Furthermore, several powerful file compression utilities enable you to compress large files into smaller ones in order to send them efficiently across the Internet.

When attaching a file, compose the message as you normally would, and be sure to mention the attachment in your message. Simply click an attachment button to send the selected file with the message. Microsoft Outlook Express and Netscape Communicator allow you to easily attach files.

Most e-mail clients display attachments in the e-mail message as separate links, such as a paper-clip icon. However, some display text attachments as additional text directly within the e-mail message.

Many ISPs and companies place limits on the size of e-mail inboxes. This restriction is a safety measure that helps prevent the e-mail server from failing if a large attachment cannot be saved to the server. If you have a large file to send, you should consider an alternate means of transmission, such as an FTP site.

You should always use a recent version of your e-mail client. Older e-mail clients detach files from your e-mail messages and put them into an attachment directory instead of leaving them attached to the message. These legacy e-mail clients do not indicate that an attachment is included, and some may not receive attachments properly. These applications may also not support MIME, which is often used to identify e-mail attachments.

There are also older technologies that converted binary files to text characters that can be included in an e-mail message. *BinHex* and *uuencode* were common means of transmitting file attachments on older e-mail systems that could handle only ASCII characters. BinHex was used on Macintosh computers, while uuencode was used on UNIX and Windows computers. Legacy e-mail clients usually displayed these text attachments as text in an e-mail message, and users had to copy and paste the text into a translation program to extract the attachments. Modern e-mail clients provide built-in support for these technologies, as SMTP does not directly support file attachments.

EXERCISE 10.6

Attaching a File to an E-Mail Message Using Microsoft Outlook Express

In this exercise, you will send yourself an e-mail message with a file attachment using Outlook Express. The procedure is similar for most e-mail clients.

1. Open Outlook Express. Prepare a test message to yourself, but do not select the Send button.

2. Select the Attach button on the toolbar or select the Insert menu and choose File Attachment.

3. In the Insert Attachment window, locate and select the `Mail Signature.txt` file on your desktop. Select Attach. Note that an Attach field appears directly below the Subject field, indicating the name of the file.

4. Send the message to yourself.

5. Retrieve the e-mail message. Notice that a paper-clip icon appears next to it. Open the message.

6. To view the attachment, double-click the file name in the Attach field. Close the attachment and the message.

EXERCISE 10.6 *(continued)*

7. You can also view the attachment in the preview pane of Outlook Express. Highlight the message and then select the paper-clip icon. A pop-up menu appears, as shown here.

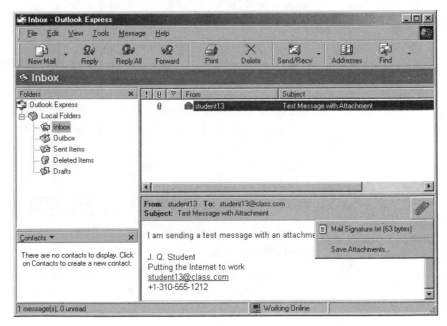

8. Select the file attachment name to view the attachment. You can save it anywhere on your hard drive using the Save Attachments option.

Other Internet Clients

The Internet presents information in a variety of ways, in addition to the Web and e-mail. File Transfer Protocol (FTP), newsgroups, and Telnet can unlock vast areas of the Internet for additional research and collaboration efforts. As you learned earlier, FTP is used to transfer files between two computers or one server and one computer, depending on the configuration. Newsgroups are part of a distributed Internet bulletin board, where information can be posted about any topic. Telnet allows users to log on and run server applications from remote computers. These tools enable business users to complete their tasks more efficiently. You will learn how to use each of these Internet resource tools in this section.

File Transfer Protocol (FTP)

As we discussed earlier, File Transfer Protocol (FTP) is a TCP/IP suite protocol that allows the transfer of files between two computers, or one server and one computer. Some sites allow guests to transfer files without requiring an account on the remote site. They are called *anonymous FTP* sites and are available to the public. Many major universities have reliable anonymous FTP servers on the Internet. Most business FTP servers require user names and passwords because the data is confidential.

For logging in to public FTP sites, a user name of "anonymous," "ftp," or "guest" is often used to gain immediate access to the FTP server. In some cases, you may be asked to enter your e-mail address as your password. Some server administrators review these passwords to determine who is using the ftp server.

The user name and password are usually sent automatically by the FTP client. Most private FTP sites require users to provide a specific user name and password that has been assigned by an FTP server administrator.

FTP users usually cannot change their FTP passwords by using a FTP client. If a password must be changed, the user must contact the FTP administrator to change it.

If you have not preconfigured an FTP client with your user name and password, you can use the following URL format to include this information:

`ftp://username:password@ftp.server.com`

If the site is an anonymous FTP site, a user name of `anonymous`, `ftp` or `guest` allows access with any password.

Many FTP servers allow only a limited number of users to log on at one time. Users are commonly denied access to popular public FTP sites because the site contains many software products or files being requested by others.

Two types of resources are available by File Transfer Protocol on the Internet: large text files and *binary files*. Large text files can be viewed within the browser, but binary files must be viewed with another application. Some binary files are executable files. They may be small software applications, images that require an association to open or compressed files that require expanding.

Navigating an FTP server is similar to navigating the directory structure of a hard drive. You start at the top by selecting a directory name that is close to the general topic in which you are interested. You then continue to select directory names that are more specific to what you are seeking, until you find the file you want. Sometimes, this navigation process may take you many levels into an FTP server's hard drive. Most FTP servers are structured similarly. Once you become familiar with FTP servers, navigating their contents becomes easy.

Downloading Files with FTP

FTP servers can contain many kinds of documents. To download these files, the FTP client program uses the `get` command. For instance, after a user logs onto an FTP server, he or she would enter the command *get filename.ext*, where `filename` and `.ext` are variables that indicate the specific name and extension of the file to be downloaded.

You can use FTP in a command-line mode. This requires you to type in each FTP command and filename that you wish to use. However, in most graphical FTP client programs, the `get` command is initiated when the user clicks on the file he or she wants to download. The client automatically uses the `get` command to download the file. The user must then identify the location to which the file should be downloaded.

FTP servers often contain popular *shareware* and *freeware* programs. Shareware programs are distributed primarily over the Internet. The program developers allow users to try the programs, and ask users to submit a registration fee if they are going to keep using the applications. Freeware programs require no registration fee.

In their original state, some files can take a long time to download and read, depending on your connection speed. To reduce download times, several compression utilities are available. These programs compress or reduce multiple files into a single archive file. The compressed archive files are then placed on the FTP servers. Thus, after you download them, you must decompress them with a decompression utility. Decompression restores the files to their original, readable states. Table 10.1 lists the file types commonly found on FTP servers. There are many file compression applications available for download.

TABLE 10.1 Popular File Types Found on FTP Servers

File Name Extension	File Type
.txt	A basic text file; can be read by any word processor or text editor.
.zip	A ZIP compressed file, and the most popular form of compressed file for the personal computer (PC). Check www.winzip.com to download the WinZip file compression program.
.exe	An executable file; typically, a self-extracting compressed file, sometimes found as an executable software program.
.asc	An ASCII text file. ASCII is a universally accepted standard text format for all computers.
.tar	A UNIX tape archive (tar) file; a form of compression used by UNIX computers.
.sea	A Macintosh Stuffit self-extracting compressed file.
.sit	A Macintosh Stuffit compressed file.

EXERCISE 10.7

Accessing an FTP Server and Downloading Files Using Microsoft Internet Explorer

In this exercise, you will view an FTP site and download a file using Microsoft Internet Explorer.

1. Open Internet Explorer.

2. Enter ftp://ftp.cdrom.com in the Address field. Your screen should resemble the one shown. Double click on the folder marked pub.

EXERCISE 10.7 *(continued)*

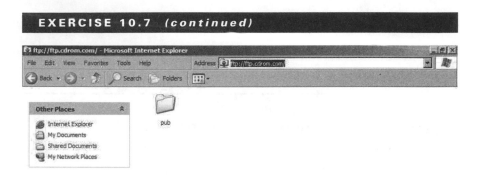

3. Select the gutenberg directory. This contains text files of classic books, called etexts, which are created and maintained by Project Gutenberg. Select one of the etext directories.

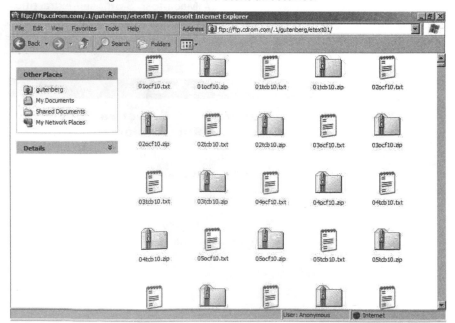

4. Find a text file, and download it by right-clicking the file and selecting Copy to Folder. The Browse for Folder window appears. Save this text file to your desktop.

5. When the save is complete, open the file with Notepad and read it.

Uploading Files with FTP

Uploading to an FTP site requires an FTP client program or a web publishing program. Many websites are published using FTP, and we will discuss this process in more detail in Chapter 14. Uploading to an FTP site also requires permission from the server administrator. If an FTP server allowed anonymous users to upload files, the server would be unmanageable. Hackers often search for unsecured FTP servers to store and share files with other users.

To upload files, an FTP client program uses the put command. For instance, after a user logs on to an FTP server, he or she would enter the command **put *filename.ext***, depending on the name and extension of the file to be uploaded. Similar to downloading FTP files, most user-friendly FTP client programs initiate the put command when the user selects an Upload button or chooses Upload from a menu, then identifies the file to upload. The client automatically uses the put command (invisible to the user) to upload the file.

There are several excellent graphical FTP clients available. You can search for these programs by using a shareware website such as Tucows (www.tucows.com) or c|net (www.download.com).

The Windows FTP Command-Line Client

On Windows machines, you can also use the Windows command prompt to access a command-line FTP client to upload files. Make sure you are familiar with the function of the open command, and the previously mentioned get and put commands.

A user must open the command prompt, then access FTP mode by entering the command ftp. To open a specific FTP server, enter the command open followed by the FTP server name, such as open ss1.ciwcertified.com. The user must enter a user name and password. For an anonymous FTP server, enter the user name **anonymous** or **ftp**. For your password, use your e-mail address or **ftp**. You can also type ftp ss1.ciwcertified.com on the command line to start the ftp client and open the site.

Once logged on, the ls (list) and dir (directory) commands display the contents of the current directory. Different directories are accessed by entering cd (change or display current directory) followed by the directory name, such as cd documentation. To change to the previous directory, enter **cd ..** or **cd /** at the prompt.

Enter the get or put command within a directory, followed by the file name, to download or upload a file. Files are downloaded into the directory in which you entered the original ftp command, which is the Windows directory by default. If you cannot find the file you downloaded, look in the Windows directory. You can also create an FTP folder on your hard drive before you begin, and then navigate to that folder using the Windows command prompt. You may then run the ftp command-line client from that folder. Figure 10.1 provides an example of such a session.

FIGURE 10.1   FTP session using the Windows command prompt

Newsgroups

Web pages are relatively formal documents, often produced at considerable expense by companies that sell products and services. Although most companies keep their pages current, they cannot modify them every day, and they naturally contain a bias toward their own product or service By contrast, online *newsgroup* articles are generally unofficial, rapidly updated, and informal. Much like traditional newspapers or the content of the evening news, online newsgroups tend to provide timely, significant, and often spirited information.

The name "newsgroup" can be misleading. Most newsgroup articles do not contain news in the traditional sense. Newsgroup articles tend to be focused on goods and services, events, people, pets, topics, concepts, ideas, and opinions.

Newsgroups are all loosely part of a huge distributed bulletin-board system that is sometimes called the *Usenet*, or User Network. Originally created in 1979 at Duke University, Usenet was intended to house news postings. There are now more than 50,000 newsgroups, covering a wide variety of subjects.

As we discussed earlier, news servers use the NNTP protocol to download news messages or articles from newsfeeds. A news server administrator can select which newsgroups to offer on a news server. The administrator also chooses how long the news messages are saved on the news server. Because there are so many newsgroups, the news server must be configured to remove old news messages on a regular basis, to make room for new messages.

Newsgroups are sometimes excellent informal sources of information. The voluntary nature of newsgroups dictates how focused each newsgroup is on its topics. Many newsgroups are unmoderated, which means that anyone may subscribe and post messages. Newsgroup users often monitor messages, and sometimes tell users when they have drifted away from the newsgroup's areas of interest. This is also called making an *off-topic post*. We will discuss other aspects of newsgroup etiquette later in this section.

Newsgroups can provide helpful information about products and services, posted by current customers. When you or your employer considers buying a product, you may want to research the subject. Visiting the producing business' web page will give you some information, but it will be biased in favor of the product. You may find necessary technical information about software updates and bug fixes, but few businesses will post negative comments about their own products or services on their website.

The Newsgroup Hierarchy

Newsgroups have a standard tree structure or *hierarchy*, wherein each branch allows the user greater access to more focused information. Of course, adjacent trees can exist also. In newsgroup name syntax, a period is used to separate each level of the newsgroup hierarchy.

For example, the `comp.sys.ibm.*` newsgroups contain discussions about IBM computers. The group would represent a cross-section of IBM computer users who have posted messages and responses about these products. The asterisk tells the user that there are at least two groups at the next level of the hierarchy.

Newsgroup names can be expanded to include more detail, such as `comp.sys.ibm.pc.hardware.networking`. This newsgroup topic discusses networking hardware for IBM's personal computer product lines.

Table 10.2 lists several newsgroup categories that are carried throughout the Internet. Hundreds more local categories are available for discussions in specific geographical areas or at specific companies or organizations.

TABLE 10.2 Newsgroup Categories

Category	Explanation
biz	Commercial topics, such as sales announcements and press releases.
comp	Topics related to computers.
news	Topics related to the newsgroup service.
rec	Topics related to recreation, including sports, games, and hobbies.
sci	Scientific topics such as medicine or linguistics.
soc	Social discussions, including cultural and religious topics.
talk	Discussions concerning controversial topics.
humanities	Topics in the humanities, such as Shakespeare or fine art.
misc	Topics not mentioned above, including business discussions.
alt	Topics that have not been assigned a category, including many controversial or adult-oriented subjects. This category has discussion areas that may be considered inappropriate for traditional business use and research.

When you want to enter a newsgroup conversation, you simply post a message or response to become a part of the ongoing discussion. You can obtain free advice on business problems from experts, and perhaps create, build and maintain a positive reputation for yourself or your company.

Newsgroup Etiquette

Newsgroups have developed their own culture and standards for behavior. This section covers points of newsgroup netiquette that have been widely discussed in newsgroups, especially `news.announce.newusers`. This is a moderated newsgroup that has many messages on how to use newsgroups effectively.

You should not insult or "flame" another user.   This is particularly important with newsgroups, as these comments will be distributed world-wide and archived. Anything you post on a newsgroup can be read years later.

Limit the amount of personal information you post on a newsgroup. You should not post your telephone number or address, for example. Some newsgroup users do not use their actual name or e-mail address.

Become familiar with a specific newsgroup before posting messages there.   This will help you determine what subjects are covered and iden-tify a proper tone for your message. When writing a newsgroup message, you should carefully choose your subject line. This is sometimes the only clue that other readers will have of your message's content. You should write clearly, and check your grammar and spelling. Most newsgroup users will know you only by what you say and how well you say it.

Never write in all capital letters, even when you want to make a point. Writing in "all caps" is considered shouting in newsgroups, just as it is in e-mail, and is a sign of an inexperienced user.

Post your message in a specific newsgroup, and then only once in that newsgroup.   Do not *crosspost* the same message to several newsgroups, especially if they are unrelated. Avoid posting off-topic messages.

Post your message locally if it is appropriate.   If your message will be of interest to users in a specific city or state, look for newsgroups that target users in those regions.

Beware of jokes and satire.   Some newsgroup messages are satire, and they are posted without any warnings. If you read a message that seems outrageous or bizarre, you should ask yourself if it may be a joke, satire, or something else. Some newsgroup users post these messages to start arguments with other users, especially in alt.* and talk.* newsgroups.

State the facts in your messages. Always include references to support your facts. It is considered rude to represent someone else's ideas as your own. Also, other users may want to read your references on their own.

Mark your spoilers. On television and movie newsgroups, you should warn users at the start of your message if you are revealing any important plot points or surprises. It is also customary to separate these *spoilers* from the top of your message by using several blank lines.

Never advertise in a newsgroup unless permitted. Some newsgroups are devoted to advertisements and sale notices. However, most news-groups do not tolerate these messages. The first unsolicited commercial advertisements, or spam, on the Internet appeared in newsgroups. News users become annoyed at seeing advertisements, especially when they are paying ISP and telephone fees to download news messages.

EXERCISE 10.8

Configuring Microsoft Outlook Express as a News Client

In this exercise, you will create a news account with the news client Microsoft Outlook Express. Then you will access a newsgroup and read messages.

To complete this exercise, your computer must have access to a news server.

If you are connected to the Internet by an ISP, check with the ISP to determine if they provide a news server, and to determine the server's domain name or IP address. (As an alternative, you can sign up for a free NNTP account with TeraNews, which operates a freely accessible news server. Go to www.teranews.com for more information.)

If you are connected to the Internet through a LAN, check with your IT department to determine if they provide a news server, and to deter-mine the server's domain name or IP address. You should also ask your IT department if your LAN filters or blocks newsgroup packets through a proxy server, firewall, or another system. You may not be able to access newsgroups with Outlook Express if filtering or block-ing is used on your LAN.

1. Open Outlook Express. Select the Tools menu and choose the Accounts option. Click the News tab. Select the Add button and select News. The Internet Connection Wizard will appear.

2. In the Display Name field, your assigned student name may appear if you have already configured Outlook Express to send and receive e-mail. If not, enter your name. Click Next.

3. In the Internet News E-Mail Address window, your e-mail address may appear with the mail server domain name if you have already configured Outlook Express for mail service. If your e-mail address does not appear, enter your e-mail address. Click Next.

4. The Internet News Server Name window will appear. In the News (NNTP) Server field, enter the name of your news server. Click Next.

5. In the Congratulations window, select Finish. Your news account has been created. Then a window similar to this one will appear:

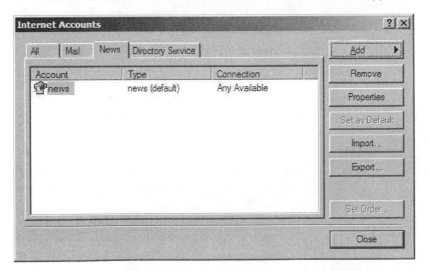

6. Select Close. Because this is the first time you accessed the server, Outlook Express will prompt you to download all the newsgroups from the news server. Click Yes to download all newsgroups.

EXERCISE 10.8 *(continued)*

If you are not immediately prompted to download all newsgroups, you will return to the main Outlook Express window. Select the news account you created from the list of accounts on the left side of the screen, then click the Newsgroups button on the toolbar.

7. All newsgroups on the news server will appear. In order to access newsgroups on the news server, you must subscribe to them by selecting one or more newsgroups, then pressing the Subscribe button. Access that newsgroup by clicking the Go To button. You may be prompted to choose Outlook Express as your default news client. Select Yes or No, depending on your preference.

8. Read some of the messages in your subscribed newsgroups, to get a sense of the group's content.

Google Groups

As we mentioned earlier in the book, Google Groups is a website that includes a newsgroup search engine. You can find Google Groups at `http://groups.google.com`.

If you want to subscribe and post to newsgroups using your web browser, you can sign up for a Google Groups account.

Google Groups is also a newsgroup archive. Most news servers delete news messages when they reach a certain age, to reduce storage requirements. Google Groups contains over 700 million newsgroup messages from as early as 1981, offering users a valuable resource for tracing the history of a topic. For example, Linus Torvalds first announced his development of Linux on a newsgroup. (In fact, many important announcements regarding Linux have been made on newsgroups.)

EXERCISE 10.9

Using Google Groups as a Web-Based News Client

In this exercise, you will use the Google Groups website to view newsgroups. Then you will access a newsgroup and read messages. This exercise is written for Internet Explorer, but you may use other graphical web browsers, including Netscape Navigator.

1. Open Internet Explorer. Enter **groups.google.com** in the Address field of the browser and press Enter.

2. In the Search field, enter the keywords **microsoft office**. Click Search.

3. You should see a results page similar to the one here. Locate a newsgroup in the microsoft.public.office.* hierarchy, and click its hyperlink.

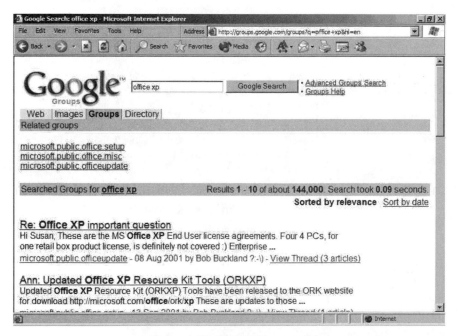

4. You should see a list of messages for this newsgroup. In the next graphic, we have selected microsoft.public.office.setup. Notice the newsgroup name in the upper left-hand corner. It is composed of four hyperlinks, each linked to a different level of the newsgroup's hierarchy, beginning with microsoft.public.office. Click on the hyperlink for office.

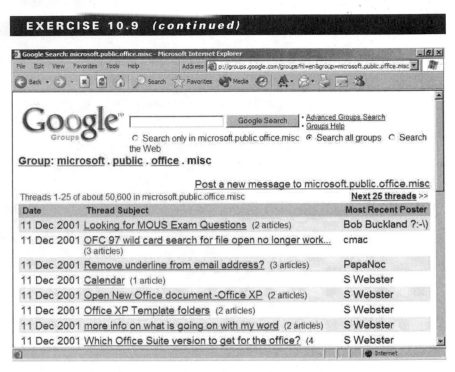

5. You should see a list of `microsoft.public.office.*` newsgroups, similar to what is shown here.

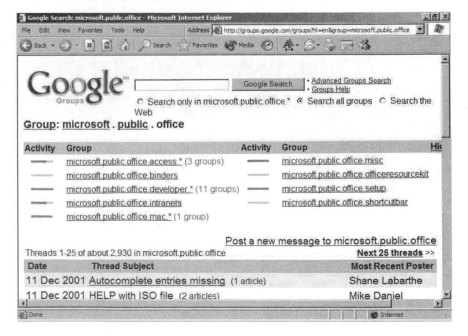

6. We can also use the search field to find a newsgroup listing, by typing in part of the newsgroups hierarchical name. Enter `microsoft.public.office` in the search field and press search. You should see a page similar the earlier one.

Telnet

Before access to the Internet was available through a graphical user interface, scientists, researchers, and educators used computers with the UNIX operating system to retrieve needed information. Occasionally, they would use a protocol called Telnet. Telnet is sometimes called a remote host connection.

A Telnet connection occurs when you establish a remote connection with a server and then use that computer to gather the information you need. You are essentially logging in to the server and accessing information as if you were sitting right at the computer.

Telnet is similar to a dial-up shell account. Each keystroke you type is sent one-by-one from the Telnet client to the Telnet host. The host interprets each keystroke, and the results are echoed back to your client screen after the host interprets it. The host, not your computer, is actually doing the work.

Because many Internet servers are run on UNIX and Linux systems, including web and FTP servers, a wide variety of information is still available through Telnet access. To use Telnet, you must have an account and a password on the host computer. You can use Telnet to access some public servers, such as public libraries and government resources, using a general logon.

Before graphical computing interfaces were widely available in the early 1990s, Telnet was the primary method for accessing the Internet. You can use Telnet to access e-mail and the web, by using command-line clients in a shell account. Because a Telnet client has few computing requirements when compared to Windows, Telnet is an easy alternative to implement. Some users still prefer this method, because they prefer to type commands rather than point and click on icons. Most users would find the command-line interfaces too challenging and difficult to use, however.

Telnet continues to be widely used by UNIX and Linux administrators. It allows them to remotely log on to a server, such as a web server, and manage it from any location that has an Internet connection.

EXERCISE 10.10

Accessing a Library Database Using Telnet

In this exercise, you will access a library database using Telnet. The Wyoming state library database services 36 libraries and supports Telnet. You will use it to locate books regarding business law or topics of your choice.

Windows, UNIX, and Linux operating systems include a command-line Telnet client in their default installations. This exercise can be run on any computer with a Telnet client and Internet access.

1. From the Start menu, select Run.

2. Enter the address telnet wyld.state.wy.us. Note that the Windows Telnet client opens automatically and accesses the Telnet site.

3. (If you are using Windows XP, you do not need to perform this step.) To communicate with the Telnet server, you may need to verify that the telnet client and the server are using the same terminal preferences. These preferences tell the client how to draw the terminal screen so that it resembles the server's screen.

   To check your client preferences, select the Terminal menu on your Telnet client and choose Preferences. Verify that the VT-100 emulation is selected.

4. Enter the username **WYLD**. No password is requested.

5. When you reach wyld.state.wy.us, select Ctrl + n (next page) to read the instructions for using this Telnet service. Each Telnet site usually has its own set of commands. The WYLD CAT site uses the arrow keys to access the menus at the top of the Telnet screen.

6. From the Telnet Find menu (highlighted by default), use the down arrow key, highlight Subject/Keyword and press the enter key. Type in a search for books about Internet Law. Do not sort the results. Your screen may look something like this.

EXERCISE 10.10 *(continued)*

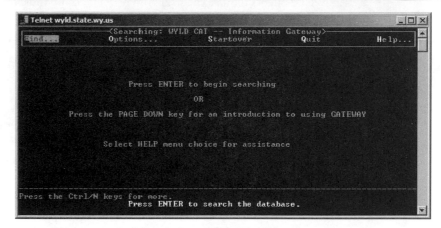

7. Experiment with Telnet and explore the site. Exit WYLD CAT by selecting the Quit menu and pressing the Enter key. You can also terminate the Telnet connection by selecting the Connect menu on the Telnet client and choosing Disconnect.

Summary

In this chapter, we discussed various client programs that help users access Internet services. Internet e-mail clients usually use the POP3 protocol to receive incoming messages from a mail server and the SMTP protocol to transmit messages. The IMAP protocol can both send and receive messages. E-mail addresses are divided into a username and a domain. The To field specifies the intended recipients of the message, and the From field lists the sender's e-mail address. The Cc field can be used to identify additional recipients who will receive informational copies of a message. The Bcc field has a similar function, but allows anonymous copying.

E-mail netiquette suggests that users write clear e-mail messages and subject lines, reply promptly to received e-mail, and avoid sending unsolicited commercial e-mail (spam). Senders can use a short e-mail signature file to include contact information at the end of an e-mail message. Employees should be aware that e-mail sent through company servers and networks can be read by corporate employees. Users can include files in their messages by sending them as e-mail attachments.

FTP clients provide access to files saved on FTP servers. Command-line FTP clients require the user to type FTP commands and file names to download and upload files. Graphical FTP clients provide a user interface that eliminates this repetitive typing. Many FTP sites allow users to connect anonymously to download files. Files are often compressed using utilities that reduce file size and combine multiple files into a single archive.

Newsgroups are discussion forums, organized into a hierarchy of topics. Users often post messages that include their opinions, questions, answers, and many other types of information. Newsgroup netiquette has some similarities to e-mail netiquette, but also asks users to consider how they discuss and post their messages. You can access newsgroups using a news client, which retrieves messages from a news server using NNTP. Browser-based news sites such as Google Groups provide a web gateway for reading and posting messages.

Telnet is a terminal emulation program that allows users to access services on Internet servers. Telnet is often used to administer UNIX and Linux Internet services. To connect using Telnet, you must know the site's domain name or IP address, a user name, and password.

Exam Essentials

Know how to send and receive e-mail messages using various e-mail client programs.   E-mail clients can use the POP3 protocol to retrieve messages from mail servers. They can also use the SMTP protocol to transmit outgoing messages to mail servers. SMTP/IMAP can both send and receive Internet e-mail, if the mail server supports this protocol. The user must know the IP address or domain name of these servers, and his or her own e-mail account name and password. The From field identified the sender's e-mail address, and the To field lists the recipients' addresses.

Know how to send copies of e-mail messages to other users.   You can use the Cc field to send a carbon copy of a message to a user who is not the intended recipient of the message. This is usually done for informational purposes only. The Bcc field sends a blind carbon copy to a user. With the Bcc field, the recipients of the copies are not revealed.

Understand and practice netiquette.   Netiquette is the practice of common sense and courtesy on the Internet. E-mail users should write carefully, choose specific users when they send messages, use appropriate subject lines, reply promptly, and never send unsolicited commercial e-mail.

Be able to create and add e-mail signatures to e-mail messages. You can create a short text file to close your e-mail messages. This text file should include your name, web address, and phone number.

Understand important issues of e-mail privacy. Employers have legal rights to employee's e-mail and Internet activities when they are using company computers and networks. Employees should consider using a personal Internet e-mail account. Company e-mail can be archived and read, so employees should consider company e-mail a permanent record of their professional activities.

Be able to attach a file to an e-mail message. E-mail clients allow users to attach many kinds of files to e-mail messages. Older technologies such as BinHex and uuencode are still used to translate files into ASCII characters for transmission as e-mail.

Know how to access and download files using File Transfer Protocol (FTP). Users can access public FTP servers by using anonymous access. FTP servers have a directory structure that resembles a hard disk drive. Binary and TXT files can be downloaded by using graphical or command-line FTP clients. These clients use various FTP commands, including `get` and `put`, to download and upload files. Large files are often reduced in size by file compression utilities before they are posted to FTP servers. File compression helps reduce bandwidth requirements and download times.

Be able to read and post messages to newsgroups. Newsgroups are collections of messages on related topics. There is a hierarchy of newsgroups, arranged by overall categories and specific topics. Newsgroups rarely contain actual news articles, as users tend to post messages of common interest.

Understand newsgroup netiquette. Newsgroup users should read messages on a specific group before posting a message. Like e-mail, it is important to write clearly and avoid unsolicited commercial messages. Writers should include references to facts that they include in their messages. You should not crosspost the same message to several different groups, or post the same message many times to the same newsgroup. Messages in television and movie newsgroups should be carefully formatted and written to warn other readers of possible spoilers. Some news messages are written simply to provoke a response from readers.

Know how to access newsgroups using a web browser. Google Groups bundles a search engine with a newsgroup archive. This website also allows users to sign up for an account that lets them subscribe and post to newsgroups.

Be able to access resources using Telnet. Telnet is a terminal emulation program that lets users tap into databases and other Internet resources. To use Telnet, you must know the Telnet server's name, a username, and a password.

Key Terms

Before you take the exam, be certain you are familiar with the following terms:

acceptable use policies	netiquette
anonymous FTP	newsgroup
Bcc	off-topic post
binary files	shareware
BinHex	spam
Cc	spoilers
cross-post	unsolicited commercial e-mail (UCE)
freeware	Usenet
hierarchy	uuencode

Review Questions

1. Which one of the following three elements is not usually required in an e-mail address?

   A. A user name

   B. An @ sign

   C. A domain name

   D. A URL

2. Jill is trying to send an e-mail message. She must configure which one of the following settings in her e-mail client to send the message?

   A. Her real name

   B. SMTP server name or address

   C. POP3 server name or address

   D. Her e-mail address

3. Which of the following best describes a POP ID?

   A. POP server name

   B. POP password

   C. POP certificate

   D. POP account name

4. Brianne wants to send Scott a copy of the e-mail she is mailing to her supervisor, Julie. She does not want Julie to realize that Scott has received a copy of the message. Which one of the following choices will work best?

   A. Brianne should include Scott along with Julie in the To field.

   B. Brianne should list Julie in the To field, and Scott in the Cc field.

   C. Brianne should list Scott in the To field, and Julie in the Cc field.

   D. Brianne should list Scott in the Bcc field, and Julie in the To field.

5. Which of the following is not considered good e-mail netiquette?

   A. Using clear, complete sentences in your message.

   B. Using a blank subject line in your message.

   C. Responding promptly to a message.

   D. Refusing to forward an unsolicited commercial e-mail to several people you do not know.

6. Jerry is creating an e-mail signature file for use on his business e-mail messages. Which one of the following suggestions should he follow?

   A. He should include his home telephone number and address in the signature file.

   B. He should add a list of his favorite newsgroups to his signature file.

   C. He should list his company, title, and office telephone number in the signature file.

   D. He should list only his office telephone number in his signature file.

7. Valerie has received an unsolicited commercial e-mail message. She wants to determine who sent the message, and report this to the sender's ISP. Which one of the following should Aimee examine?

   A. The From: field

   B. The Bcc: field.

   C. The message header

   D. The To: field.

8. Jim wants to attach 30 confidential files to a single e-mail message. Which one of the following options should he follow?

   A. Jim should use a file compression program to reduce the files into a single, smaller attachment.

   B. Jim should attach the files to the message, send it, and see if it is returned as undeliverable.

   C. Jim should send each file in its own message.

   D. Jim should post the files on the company's website so that the recipients can download them.

9. Anna is trying to access an FTP server. It allows anonymous access. How should Anna get permission to connect to the FTP server?

    A. Anna should request a secure certificate from the FTP server.

    B. Anna should e-mail the FTP server administrator and request an account and password.

    C. Anna should not enter a username or password.

    D. Anna should enter the username "anonymous," and use her e-mail address as the password.

10. Which one of the following commands does a graphical FTP client use to download a file from an FTP server?

    A. bring

    B. send

    C. get

    D. put

11. Which one of the following file compression tools is commonly associated with UNIX?

    A. TXT

    B. TAR

    C. ZIP

    D. SIT

12. Which one of the following applications cannot be used to download files to a Windows computer?

    A. Internet Explorer

    B. A graphical FTP client

    C. A command-line FTP client

    D. Telnet

13. Most public newsgroups can be described as one of the following choices:

    A. Official sources of company information and news.

    B. Informal Internet discussion groups on specific topics.

    C. E-mail lists on general topics.

    D. Databases containing a complete archive of related files and articles.

14. What protocol do web mail sites use to transmit e-mail messages to a web browser for viewing?

    A. POP3

    B. IMAP

    C. HTTP

    D. SMTP

15. Which one of the following newsgroup categories is most likely to have several newsgroups that discuss religious issues?

    A. soc

    B. news

    C. rec

    D. sci

16. What is another name for a deliberate insult on a newsgroup posting?

    A. A knock

    B. A slap

    C. A flame

    D. A slam

17. Which of these four choices should a new newsgroup user perform last?

   A. Subscribe to a newsgroup

   B. Post a reply to a message

   C. Read messages

   D. Configure their news client

18. Jeff wants to advertise a bookcase he is selling in Dallas. Which one of the following newsgroups is the best place to post an advertisement message?

   A. `rec.arts.woodworking`

   B. `misc.power-tools.sanders`

   C. `dallas.for-sale.household`

   D. `news.announce.newusers`

19. Which one of the following newsgroups is dedicated to discussions of controversial topics?

   A. `rec`

   B. `talk`

   C. `biz`

   D. `humanities`

20. Louis is typing in a Telnet session. Which of the following best describes how the computers he is using respond to each keystroke?

   A. His client displays the typed keys on the screen, and the command is sent to the host when he presses enter.

   B. The Telnet host takes direct control of the client's keyboard.

   C. His client sends every keystroke to the Telnet host, one at a time.

   D. The Telnet host detects the keystrokes and notifies the Telnet client what keys have been pressed.

Answers to Review Questions

1. D.   Only when e-mail addresses are listed as hyperlinks on a web page must they be formatted as URLs, such as `mailto://exam@ciwcertified.com`. The remaining elements are all used in normal e-mail addresses. The user name and @ sign are required, while the domain name is almost always used instead of an IP address.

2. B.   She must set an SMTP server location that will transmit the message. She should set her real name and e-mail address, but that is not required. The POP3 server address is required for receiving mail, not sending mail.

3. D.   The POP account or user name is also known as a POP ID.

4. D.   By listing Julie in the To field, the message is sent directly to her. By listing Scott in the Bcc field, he will receive a copy and Julie will not see Scott's address on the message. Julie would see Scott's address if he were listed in the To or Cc fields.

5. B.   You should always include a short, descriptive subject line in your message. The other three choices are examples of good e-mail netiquette.

6. C.   This choice is the most professional and informative, and does not reveal any personal information.

7. C.   The e-mail message header will include the originating network of the message. Valerie should forward the message along with the header to that ISP.

8. A.   Jim's best option is to use a program like WinZip to archive and compress the files. This may make the attachment small enough to mail through his company's mail server. He should not attach all the files and test to see if they will be mailed, because the files are confidential. Sending 30 messages with one attachment each might work, but it is more likely that one of the messages may not make it to its destination. Because the files are confidential, he should not post them to the website.

9. D. The username "anonymous" is a standard entry point for public FTP servers, and it usually requires an e-mail address as a password. She must enter the proper values. Anna does not need to request a secure certificate or her own password, as both are not necessary.

10. C. The `get` command is used to download a single file in FTP. There is no `bring` command. The `send` and `put` commands are both used to upload a single file to an FTP server.

11. B. Tape ARchive (TAR) is used on UNIX systems. TXT is the common extension for an uncompressed text file. The ZIP format is used on PCs. The Stuffit SIT format is geared for the Macintosh.

12. D. Telnet offers terminal emulation. It cannot perform FTP file download services. The other three applications can all download files directly to a computer from a FTP server.

13. B. Most public newsgroups are relative information discussion groups that are not used as official information sources. Newsgroups are not e-mail lists. Newsgroups do not have a central archiving function, as they are distributed lists with a limited number of recent messages in circulation. The older messages must be saved on some sort of archive server, like Google Groups.

14. C. Web mail sites use standard HTML and HTTP to display e-mail messages in a browser. Some web mail sites support POP3 downloads of mail messages to mail clients.

15. A. The `soc` hierarchy covers society, culture and religion. The `news` category is devoted to discussions about newsgroups. The `rec` category covers sports, games and recreation. The `sci` category covers scientific topics.

16. C. "Flaming" another user is the act of denigrating or insulting them based upon their newsgroup messages. You can also flame someone in an e-mail.

17. B. New users of newsgroups should find groups that interest them and read the current messages thoroughly before posting a reply or a new message.

18. C.   Jeff should select a local newsgroup that solicits advertisements. The first two newsgroups may seem appropriate, but are probably national or international in scope. The news hierarchy is devoted to discussions of the newsgroup system.

19. B.   The talk newsgroups were specifically set up for intense discussions of current topics. It is possible to discuss controversial topics on almost any newsgroup, but talk.* has been reserved for these discussions.

20. C.   The client computer monitors its own keyboard. In Telnet, each keystroke typed in a Telnet session is transmitted one at a time to the Telnet host or server. The server acknowledges each keystroke and sends any new screen instructions after each keystroke.

Chapter 11

Media and Active Content

THE CIW EXAM OBJECTIVE GROUPS COVERED IN THIS CHAPTER:

✓ Identify various technologies for enhancing the user's Web experience, including but not limited to: programming languages, multimedia technologies, and plug-ins.

As we've already discovered, the Internet and the Web are more than text-based services. Many websites, including corporate sites, include multimedia content and interactive objects. For instance, orientation sessions for new hires, audio and video messages, and training materials are often placed on the Internet or corporate intranets for employees to view.

If you want to view and use interactive audio, video, and multimedia elements on a website, it is helpful to understand what is required in order for browsers to view them. Small applications called plug-ins allow users to experience simulated three-dimensional worlds, play streaming audio and video, and interact with multimedia objects over the Internet.

We will start our discussion by examining various programming languages that are used to create multimedia applications. We have already presented Java in Chapter 7, but there are other languages such as C and C++ that are important for you to know.

This chapter will also introduce you to the source of multimedia content and the plug-in technology that allows you to view it in a web browser. It will also help you understand how to install and operate some of the most widely used plug-ins. We will discuss streaming media players including Windows Media Player, RealOne Player, and Apple QuickTime. Each media player supports a variety of formats, such as MPEG, MP3, WAV, AVI, MOV, and others.

Next, we look at Macromedia Flash and virtual reality technology, each of which provides different kinds of interactive content. We will close the chapter by discussing document viewers, small applications that allow users to see and print a file without installing the application that created it. Examples include Adobe Acrobat Reader and Microsoft PowerPoint Viewer.

Objects and Active Content

Objects enable web authors to include numerous multimedia effects, also called *active content*, on their websites. An *object* is an element on a web page that contains data and procedures for how that item will react when activated. On a web page, an object is typically a multimedia presentation. These objects can play sounds, show video clips and animation sequences, or demonstrate ideas in 3D virtual reality simulations.

In addition to making the user's web experience more enjoyable, these multimedia capabilities can greatly enhance a site's educational value. Many businesses have adopted an active approach to website design and construction, in order to effectively market their products or services. This section will discuss the different types of programming and scripting languages used to create objects and active content, and how they are related to one another.

C, Assembly, and Machine Language

Programmers must use some sort of programming language to develop and describe any application program. C is a programming language used primarily to create operating systems and applications. For instance, many UNIX operating systems have been developed using C. C can be a difficult programming language to learn, because C is much closer to assembly language than are most other high-level languages.

An *assembly language* is a programming language that is once removed from a computer's *machine language*. Machine languages consist entirely of long series of numbers. It is almost impossible for humans to read and write machine language. Assembly languages have the same structure and set of commands as machine languages, but they allow programmers to use alphanumeric names instead of numbers.

C++ and Object-Oriented Programming

Because C is so close to the underlying machine language, C programmers can write fast, efficient programming code. The low-level nature of C, however, can make the language difficult to use for developing some types of applications. An alternative model called *object-oriented programming (OOP)* has become popular among programmers.

In object-oriented programming, an application is handled as a collection of individual objects that perform separate functions, rather than as a sequence of statements that performs a specific task. OOP is a programming model based upon objects and data and how they relate to one another, rather than on logic and actions. Two examples of OOP languages are Java and a variant of C called C++. (We first encountered Java in Chapter 7.)

C++ is a superset of the C language that uses object-oriented programming. Although the names are similar, C++ uses a completely different set of programming concepts and is considered the best language for creating large applications.

The web is *event-driven*. For example, when you select something on a web page, an event occurs. Events can be almost anything: a mouse click, a mouse drag, text entered, or a page loaded (or unloaded) in the browser. JavaScript is an event-driven scripting language because it is designed to react whenever an event occurs. Traditional programming languages, such as C and C++, cause events to happen, rather than reacting to events.

We can compare full-fledged programming languages such as C and C++ to scripting languages such as JavaScript and VBScript. Scripting languages are used within existing programs to extend those programs' capabilities. JavaScript and VBScript are used to extend the interactive capabilities of web browsers, by supporting important functions like data validation. If you have ever written a macro in Microsoft Excel or used WordBasic to perform some task in a Microsoft Word document, you have already used a scripting language. VBScript is based on Microsoft application scripting languages.

Programmers cannot create objects in these scripting languages. The purpose of a scripting language is to automate routine, predefined tasks in the context of an application. There is no need for programmers to create objects, because the objects are already provided by the applications. JavaScript and VBScript are examples of *object-based programming languages*.

Java

We presented the Java programming language in Chapter 7, but it is helpful to compare Java to earlier languages such as C and C++. In fact, Java is based on C++, and is also an object-oriented programming language. However, Java is different because it concentrates on distributed objects over a network. Java is also not as complex or as difficult to learn as C or C++. These reasons, coupled with the Internet's growth, help explain why many universities and schools have included Java in their curriculums.

Java *applets* are small Java applications written in the Java language and designed to run within a web browser when accessed. While a Java application can be run directly from an operating system and within the JVM, Java applet uses the JVM, but relies on the web browser to provide its context or environment.

Applets were the first technology for bringing program objects to the web. Applets can display animated images, add functionality and interactivity, access multimedia services, and provide active content.

Java applets are treated the same way as other web-embedded objects and are displayed in the browser's content area. Your web browser must be Java-enabled to run applets. Both Netscape Navigator and Microsoft Internet Explorer support Java applets.

Unlike static objects, such as non-animated GIF and JPEG images or hyperlinks, Java applets can be dynamic and interactive. Applets can combine these properties to create complex but easy-to-use Internet applications that support the following features.

Inline video, changing text, and animation   Dynamic objects that can be embedded in web pages without the need for external helper applications or plug-ins. Applets do require the Java Virtual Machine in order to run.

Audio   Sound files played when an applet is invoked or in response to user action.

User interaction   Interaction between a user and the displayed applet. Examples of interactive applets include *user-interface controls* that allow the user to interact with an on-screen element, such as a computer game.

Real-time data feeds   Feeds that maintain an open connection between the server and an applet on a web page, or periodically poll the server to update information displayed in the browser. Examples of real-time data feeds are online clocks and up-to-the-minute stock market ticker tapes.

ActiveX Technology

ActiveX is an open set of technologies for integrating components on the Internet and within Microsoft applications and operating systems. By using

ActiveX components, web designers can offer many of the features of Java applets. ActiveX is not a programming language. Programmers can use several programming languages, including Visual Basic, Delphi, C++, and Java, to create ActiveX components.

We know web pages can include animation, audio, and video. Web content can be dynamic, providing current information on any topic, customized to the user's profile and preferences. ActiveX technology lets web designers place interactive objects on their sites, based on a common standard, and allowing the objects to work together.

ActiveX objects do not replace the static text and graphics that are a standard feature of web pages. However, ActiveX objects can play sounds, show video clips and animation sequences, or demonstrate ideas in 3D virtual reality simulations.

Microsoft Internet Explorer makes extensive use of ActiveX technology. For example, if you click on a hyperlink to a Microsoft Word document, and you have installed Word on your computer, Internet Explorer will present the Word document as an editable file, along with the Word menus.

ActiveX was first developed by Microsoft, but was then turned over to an independent organization, The Open Group, in 1998. Even though ActiveX is an open standard, Netscape does not support ActiveX and its default scripting language, VBScript, in its browsers. If you click on a hyperlink to a Word document in Netscape, the browser will usually ask to download the file to your computer. You may then use Microsoft Word to open the downloaded file.

The large base of Microsoft Office installations, along with Microsoft's seamless integration of Internet Explorer with its Windows operating system, has helped Microsoft Internet Explorer become the most popular graphical web browser on Windows computers.

Objects and Security Issues

To work with downloadable active content, such as Java applets and ActiveX objects, you should understand the security issues involved. Because Java and ActiveX content are small programs that run on your computer, they both have the potential to damage your software or create other security issues.

Most ActiveX and Java applets are designed to be downloaded and run on your system safely. However, a few developers have created hostile applets and ActiveX controls. Some of these programs simply demonstrate the possible security breaches in both technologies. A few of these programs were designed to harm systems, while others have been used to give other users control over a computer's resources. You might never inadvertently browse a page with a hostile applet or ActiveX control. But the danger is remotely possible, and you need to know how to shield your system from such problems.

To protect your system from such incursions, both Internet Explorer and Navigator provide control options to enable or disable the execution of Java programs and other active content. If you disable Java programs, you will not see applets run, nor will there be any indication that an applet would have been running, and you will not receive an error message. If you run Java programs, you will see the effects of the applet or an applet error message, if any exist. We will discuss this and other security issues in detail in the next chapter of this book.

Plug-in Technology

As browsers have evolved, features that enhance their functions have been included to support a large range of objects. Users can access the active content with plug-ins, such as Apple QuickTime and Macromedia Shockwave and Flash players, directly from the browser. A *plug-in* is a program installed as part of the browser to extend its basic functionality; it allows different file formats to be viewed as part of a standard HTML document.

Plug-ins are applications associated with a specific platform and browser such as Windows Me and Netscape Navigator. The primary goal of a plug-in is to provide efficient integration of multimedia formats with the browser and PC. This integration avoids the need for the user to download multimedia files and play them back later with a separate application. Plug-ins allow multimedia data types to execute directly from a browser.

When a browser encounters a file type that is not directly supported, it launches a plug-in application that retrieves the multimedia files from a server much as a browser retrieves standard web pages. The files are then delivered to the client system for playback.

Recall our discussion of streaming media servers in Chapter 6. Plug-ins are clients for this type of server. Instead of loading the entire file at once, plug-ins can retrieve a small portion at a time and store the data in a local disk cache or buffer. For instance, when you listen to a web audio file, you may be hearing one part of the file while the next part downloads in the background. (If you download an entire file before playing it, you are viewing non-streaming media.)

Files that have been interpreted by a plug-in appear in one of three ways, depending on the file type and additional HTML tags. (Some files will not function if additional HTML attributes are set.) The three appearance methods are:

Full-screen   In this mode, a plug-in will completely fill the browser window's inner frame. This is used for document viewers, which will discuss later in the chapter. Media players can also display videos in full-screen mode if the user so chooses.

Embedded   In this mode, the multimedia appears as part of a larger document, where the media or media player is visible as a rectangular sub-portion of a page. This method resembles an embedded GIF or JPEG image, except the media can be live and/or dynamic, and may have its own embedded functionality. Many videos, such as RealOne Player and Shockwave videos, are embedded files. Plug-ins can replay them in a portion of the browser window.

Hidden   Hidden plug-ins are not visible in the browser and run in the background. An example of a hidden plug-in might be a *Musical Instrument Digital Interface (MIDI)* player. MIDI is a standard computer interface for creating and playing electronic music. It was developed in the early 1980s to help connect musical keyboards, synthesizers, and production equipment. MIDI allows properly equipped computers to connect to musical instruments, and to recreate music in digital form for playback. Most sound hardware installed on modern personal computers includes MIDI-compatible sound synthesis hardware, and can play MIDI files.

The browser appears largely the same in spite of the plug-in. Basic browser operations, such as navigation, history, opening files and so forth, are intended to apply to all pages, regardless of which plug-ins are required to view them.

Types of Browser Plug-Ins

Technology has allowed users to download and play back high-quality audio and video from the Internet for many years. In the following pages, you will learn about several different types of multimedia and their required plug-ins. We have organized this discussion according to the functionality provided by each plug-in, including the following:

Streaming media players   These are applications that can simultaneously download and play audio and video files from streaming media servers. We will discuss three competing brands of these players, including RealOne Player, Microsoft Windows Media Player, and Apple QuickTime.

Multimedia players   These are applications that first download and then display multimedia content in web browsers. Examples include Macromedia Flash and Shockwave, and Apple QuickTime VR.

Document viewers   These are applications that can display document files with their formatting intact. Our examples include Adobe Acrobat Reader and Microsoft PowerPoint Viewer.

Streaming Media

Streaming media has become a popular Internet application, as it offers computer users the ability to hear and view many kinds of audio and video content on demand. There are several thousand radio stations that simultaneously broadcast their programs on the Internet. This makes it possible for listeners to "tune in" a radio station from their hometown or from another continent. There are also hundreds of net radio stations that only broadcast on the Internet.

Many television channels provide streaming video content on the Internet, such as news stories, sports updates, and clips from entertainment programs. Movie studios often post trailers and movie clips online as part of their marketing strategy.

Streaming content has several advantages for companies. By making content available for viewing on the Internet anytime, broadcasters can extend their audience. Streaming content has built-in protection features that make it difficult for the ordinary user to save these programs on their computer for future use. Some Internet companies have developed pay-per-view streaming media services, which can allow media companies to serve relatively small or widely scattered audiences that cannot be covered with regular broadcast, cable, and satellite services. Adult entertainment is one of the more popular pay-per-view services on the web. Sports and financial programs have also proved popular.

Can You Use Streaming Media?

Because of the wide variety of available content, we must address two aspects of streaming media. The first is the hardware requirements for using streaming media players. The second is the actual costs of using streaming media, especially on a corporate network.

When compared to the web and e-mail, streaming media requires a large amount of downloaded data.

As we mentioned in Chapter 6, streaming media quality depends upon the client computer's hardware, including the CPU, sound card, video card, and available RAM. Streaming media is not like radio or television. A radio or television is just a receiver that plays a signal as soon as it is received. Streaming media depends on the client computer to buffer the playback in RAM to reduce skips. The client computer must translate the digital file into audio and video, ideally by offloading the data to audio and video hardware to perform these tasks. Otherwise, the CPU must devote processing time to handle audio and video, which can slow down all the computer's operations.

Internet connection speed is also a critical factor. Users with dial-up connections will have acceptable results with audio streams, but video streams will be small and difficult to see. Users with faster connections can play higher quality audio streams, and may have better results with video.

Users who pay for their Internet connections by the minute or byte should consider the potential cost of viewing streaming media. They will be charged by their ISP, even when they are listening to or viewing "free" streaming content.

Each streaming media player has its own installation procedures, which you can view at the appropriate website. In addition, your computer may have one of more streaming media clients pre-installed by the manufacturer or your IT department.

Some corporate users may not be able to access streaming media, because their IT departments have installed proxy servers or firewalls that discard any incoming streaming media packets. Your administrator may have taken a less restrictive approach by blocking access to streaming media from certain external servers. Some organizations do this because they want to conserve bandwidth and reduce connection costs, as companies are often billed for the amount of Internet data downloaded by their network users.

Streaming audio has become a popular application in the workplace, because users can listen to broadcast radio stations at their computer. If your company is charged for downloaded data, you may want to consider the actual costs of listening to streaming audio on your computer. Streaming audio can be an expensive substitute for a regular radio.

Using streaming media in the workplace may violate your company's IT or employment policies. You should check with your IT department if you want to install a streaming media player on your corporate computer.

Streaming Media Players

There are three competing brands of streaming media players available from Real, Microsoft, and Apple. All three products support Windows computers, and provide limited support for Macintosh, UNIX, and Linux computers. Each brand of streaming media player offers audio and video playback features for streaming media files and other file types.

All three streaming media players share common features, including playback information and personalization. Each player displays artist and song names for most supported file formats. Each has a radio section that allows users to select their favorite net radio stations. Each allows the user to set a screen size for video playback.

Streaming media players and servers typically use UDP, which is a lossy compression technique. TCP is designed to deliver every packet of a file. This delivery method requires some network overhead in the form of confirming each received packet. Clients do not confirm when a UDP packet is received. Because listeners and viewers cannot sense every note and frame of a program, these transmission losses are usually not detectable by the user.

However, the transmission speed must be carefully chosen, based upon the Internet connection and the client's hardware. Once a UDP transmission of a streaming media file starts, the transmission speed cannot be changed. If the transmission rate is too fast, the client may not receive enough packets to ensure an acceptable playback rate. If the transmission rate is too slow, the user may receive a low quality version of the program, when their computer and connection may actually support the additional data required for higher quality playback.

Streaming media players include automatic features for determining an acceptable transmission rate. These players can also buffer or cache the streaming media data to RAM or hard disk. By saving this data temporarily, the application can continue playback even during brief interruptions in the UDP transmission.

Each player also offers audio CD playback, and can look up track names for many commercially produced compact discs. Users can run streaming media players as audio CD players, which can be useful when they cannot access an Internet connection for streaming media.

RealNetworks RealOne Player

RealNetworks pioneered the streaming media format in 1995 in their original product RealAudio. RealAudio was the first streaming media plug-in specifically designed for web browsers. In 1996, RealVideo, which uses the same streaming format as RealAudio, was developed. Real soon combined audio and video playback features into a single application called *RealPlayer*. Today, the application is called *RealOne Player*.

RealOne Player is easy to configure and use. It displays the name of the sound or video file and the playtime remaining on the track. It allows users to play, stop, pause, rewind, and fast-forward. RealOne Player sound files can be grouped into clips then played in a specified sequence, similar to a jukebox play list. The user can skip ahead or return to any part of the file. RealOne Player can also function as an external application.

RealOne Players support many different kinds of media formats that we will discuss in this chapter. Real has its own format for streaming and standard audio, which is not supported by other media players.

RealOne player is available as a free download. Users can register the program and access premium services for a nominal fee. You can learn more about RealOne Player and download the application at `www.real.com`.

Windows Media Player

The *Windows Media Player* is another popular standards-based plug-in that plays streaming audio and video. This program is based on earlier Microsoft Windows applications that could playback audio and video files from a hard drive. Windows Media Player is automatically installed during the installation of Windows Me and Windows XP. You can also install Windows Media Player as an optional part of Microsoft Internet Explorer.

Windows Media Player can display live and on-demand audio and video content. Additional features involve pay-per-view applications and increased copy protection for owners of the downloaded content.

Windows Media Player can also save and play specially formatted audio files, those which have the `.wma` file extension. Windows Media files are supported on a number of handheld audio devices. Windows Media Player also supports Microsoft's AVI video format. You can download and learn more about Windows Media Player by visiting `www.windowsmedia.com/download`. The Windows Media Player program is shown in Figure 11.1.

FIGURE 11.1 Windows Media Player running on Windows 2000

Apple QuickTime

QuickTime was first released by Apple in 1993 as a digital audio and video player for Macintosh computers. *QuickTime* is a method of storing video and audio files in digital format, and is now available for both Windows and Macintosh systems. Its plug-in lets you see and hear QuickTime content in your browser window.

The QuickTime Movie (MOV) file format was created by Apple and is supported by all QuickTime versions. Video, animation, text, and sound are combined into one file. QuickTime files are identified by a .mov, .moov, or .qt file name extension.

The QuickTime plug-in works with existing QuickTime movies and other movies that can use its fast-start feature. This feature presents the first frame of the movie almost immediately and begins playing it before the movie has been completely downloaded, much like a streaming format.

QuickTime is included with the MacOS operating system. Windows users can download QuickTime at www.apple.com/quicktime. Many samples, such as movie previews, can be viewed at the site after you download the product. Apple also offers QuickTime Pro, which supports video editing, for a nominal registration fee.

WARNING If you are using Windows NT, 2000, or XP, you may need Administrative rights to install the program. If you are using a computer at your workplace or school, check with your system administrator before installing any programs on your computer.

Installing Multiple Streaming Media Players

If you install at least two of the three software products mentioned in this section, you will find that each application, when it starts up, will attempt to associate itself with MP3 and audio CD files. Each product is also designed to associate itself with a variety of audio and video files, including some streaming file formats. This battle for file extensions can make using two or more streaming media players difficult, especially for a novice.

If you are going to use these kinds of files often, you should try playing these files in each application. Each application has different proprietary settings and features. Depending upon your computer hardware, your audio and video files may playback at different quality levels in different media players.

You should then decide which media player application you prefer to use, and use its settings or configurations menu to associate the appropriate file extensions. You can then disable the automatic file association in the other applications.

Multimedia Players

Multimedia players can present a customized environment within a normal web browser window. We will briefly discuss two multimedia products that are widely used on websites: Macromedia Shockwave and Flash, VRML Plug-ins, and Apple QuickTime VR.

Macromedia Shockwave and Flash

Macromedia Shockwave is actually a group of multimedia players designed to deliver several types of multimedia, including animation, sound, graphics, and streaming video. The Shockwave player displays interactive games, multimedia user interfaces, video, and audio. Since Shockwave was introduced in 1995, many websites have included its multimedia capabilities.

Macromedia developed another player called the Flash player. The Flash player allows browsers to view movies created with the Flash application. When you download Shockwave, you also download Flash. Flash technology is well suited for the Internet because complex animations can be downloaded quickly. Flash files are usually smaller than Java applications and applets.

EXERCISE 11.1

Downloading, Installing, and Demonstrating Macromedia Shockwave and Flash

In this exercise, you will navigate to the Macromedia website, and download and install Macromedia Shockwave and Flash. You may use either Microsoft Internet Explorer or Netscape Navigator.

If you are using Windows NT, 2000, or XP, you may need Administrative rights to install the program. If you are using a computer at your workplace or school, check with your system administrator before installing any programs.

EXERCISE 11.1 *(continued)*

1. Open your web browser.

2. Enter the URL http://sdc.shockwave.com/shockwave/download/.
   Your screen should resemble the one here, keeping in mind that
   websites are always in flux (whereas books are not).

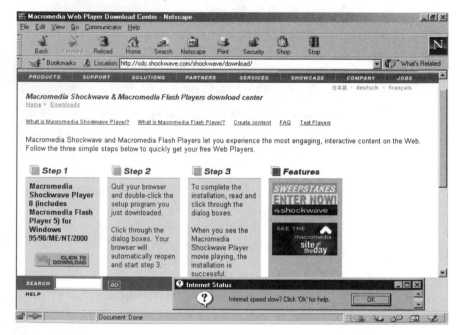

3. In the Step 1 section on your screen, select **Install now**. Save the
   file to your desktop. When the file has finished downloading, close
   your browser.

4. Double-click the Shockwave/Flash installation file you just downloaded (it should be called something like shockwaveinstaller.exe)
   to begin the setup process.

5. At the Welcome window, select Next. Select the browser in which
   you want to install Shockwave. Ensure the correct one is highlighted. Select Install.

6. Click Continue to launch your browser and download the remaining Shockwave files.

7. The registration window appears. In this exercise, you will not register the product. Select the Close (X) button in the upper-right corner of the window. The plug-in launches regardless of whether you register or not.

8. You will receive a message stating that installation is complete. Select Next.

9. Your browser plays a Shockwave demo to ensure proper installation.

10. To explore the capabilities of Shockwave and Flash, enter the URL www.macromedia.com and select the Showcase link. Explore the Showcase to see how websites are using this technology.

Virtual Reality Modeling Language (VRML) Plug-Ins

Virtual Reality Modeling Language (VRML) allows users to visit simulated 3D spaces with lifelike, fully animated objects. Virtual reality attempts to present an immersive environment, where the user can pretend they are performing certain actions, including walking or flying. Users can also interact in real time with text and images, animation, sound, music and video, as well as with embedded mini-applications.

VRML has demonstrated tremendous potential for educational, training, and commercial applications—for everything from 3D training centers to geographical information systems. However, VRML has seen limited acceptance from ordinary Internet users, in part because the hardware requirements for displaying virtual reality environments can be daunting. One common use of VRML is to display a panorama of a place, such as a stadium, or a wraparound view of an interior space, such as a car, apartment, or house.

VRML features include the following:

High-performance VRML viewing 3D spaces can be accessed at high speeds if the client computer provides support.

Animation VRML accommodates objects with lifelike behaviors.

Navigation VRML enables 3D navigation via simulated walking, flying, or pointing. Selectable camera viewpoints, sliding, optional gravity, and sound add flexibility and realism.

QuickTime VR (QTVR)

One of the most popular virtual reality viewers for web browsers is Quick-Time VR (QTVR). QTVR lets web developers expand two-dimensional photographs into a three-dimensional world. The 3D environment can be explored in 360 degrees and can include interactive elements. QTVR is automatically installed with Apple QuickTime. Figure 11.2 shows a QTVR interface featuring a corporate logo in motion.

FIGURE 11.2 QTVR interface

For more information about QTVR, including instructions for creating QTVR sequences, visit `www.apple.com/quicktime/qtvr`.

Document Viewers

A *viewer* is necessary to open certain files when the program needed to open a file type is missing from your computer. Viewers are scaled-down versions of applications, and are usually available free of charge. They do not have the full application's functionality. Often the viewer will allow you to view and print documents, but not edit them.

Because the viewer files are much smaller than program files, they are helpful when disk space is limited, or when the full program is not available. In this section, you will learn about two important viewers: Adobe Acrobat Reader and Microsoft PowerPoint Viewer.

Adobe Acrobat Reader

In 1987, Adobe created the *Portable Document Format (PDF)*, a general file format that can be created, read, and printed on any computer, regardless of the local operating system or applications. Adobe Acrobat Reader will use the printer's features to create a printed copy that is similar to the actual printed version of the document.

The Adobe Acrobat program acts as a virtual printer to capture and save document layout and formatting information to a PDF file. You can also make various settings to the PDF file. For example, you can turn off clipboard or printing support, or allow readers to highlight and make notes in portions of the document.

Although the PDF format was originally developed for corporate networks, PDF files are suitable for use on the web and Internet. The PDF format uses file compression techniques to reduce the size of the final file, which also reduces download times. Unlike the web, PDF files allow graphic designers precise control over their documents' appearance. Many corporations, government agencies and schools have adopted PDF files as a standard method for distributing content such as marketing brochures, user manuals, schedules, and forms.

Adobe offers a free viewer program called Adobe Acrobat Reader that will display and print files created in Adobe Acrobat Distiller (the program that makes PDFs). In the following exercises, you will download and install the Adobe Acrobat Reader and view a PDF document.

EXERCISE 11.2

Downloading Adobe Acrobat Reader

In this exercise, you will download and install Adobe Acrobat Reader. If you are using Windows NT, 2000, or XP, you will need Administrative rights to install the program. If you are using a computer at your workplace or school, check with your system administrator before installing any programs.

You should also check to see if you have already installed Adobe Acrobat Reader on your system. If you already have Acrobat, start the program and check the version number in the Help ➢ About Adobe Acrobat box. If the version number on the Adobe website is more recent, you may wish to download and install the newer version.

You can try this exercise in either Microsoft Internet Explorer or Netscape Navigator, as Adobe Acrobat Reader supports both browsers.

1. Open Internet Explorer.

2. Enter the URL www.adobe.com.

EXERCISE 11.2 (continued)

3. Scroll to the bottom of the Adobe home page and click the Get Acrobat Reader button, shown here.

4. Select the Get Acrobat Reader Free hyperlink.

5. The Adobe Acrobat download site will appear, shown here.

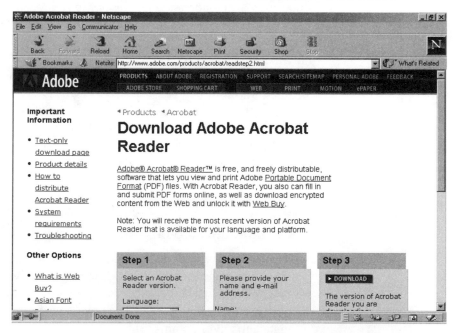

6. In the Step 1 column on your screen, select the language, platform, and nearest download location.

7. In the Step 2 column, enter your name and e-mail address. Use a valid e-mail address, such as your work or home e-mail address. If you do not wish to receive commercial e-mail from Adobe and other companies, uncheck the Notify Me About Adobe Software and Offers check box and the Allow Others to Send Me Special Offers check box.

EXERCISE 11.2 *(continued)*

8. In the Step 3 column, note the version of Acrobat you are downloading and the file size. The file is more than 5MB and may require a long time to download with slower connections. Select Download to retrieve the Adobe Acrobat Reader installation file.

9. Save the file to your desktop. When the file has finished downloading, close your browser.

10. Double-click the Adobe Acrobat Reader installation file that you just downloaded to begin the setup process. The filename will be something like ar501eng.exe.

11. At the Adobe Acrobat Reader Welcome screen, select Next. Accept the default Destination Directory and choose Next. The program will install itself, and attempt to link to the Microsoft and Netscape web browsers if they are installed on your computer. When installation is complete, a Thank You window will appear. Select OK.

Now that we have the appropriate reader, we can download and view a PDF file.

EXERCISE 11.3

Downloading and Viewing a PDF File

In this exercise, you will use Adobe Acrobat Reader to view a PDF file. You can also try this exercise in Netscape Navigator, as Adobe Acrobat Reader supports this browser.

1. Open the browser of your choice.

2. Enter the following URL: www.adobe.com/products/features/ acrobat.html.

3. Scroll down the page and click one of the PDF file hyperlinks (e.g., "PDF: 328KB/2 pages"). Adobe Acrobat Reader will open.

4. If you have not used Adobe Acrobat Reader on this computer before, you will be presented with the Adobe License Agreement. Accept the License Agreement by selecting Agree.

EXERCISE 11.3 *(continued)*

5. The file you selected will open in the Acrobat Reader window, similar to that shown here. When the PDF file has opened, use the toolbar buttons to navigate through the document.

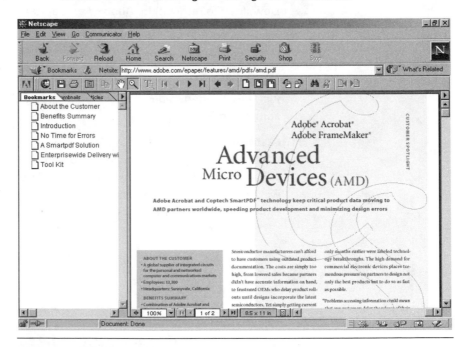

Microsoft PowerPoint Viewer

The Microsoft PowerPoint Viewer is a helpful tool for businesspeople who give slide presentations from laptop computers, or for users who have one version of PowerPoint on their computers and must give a slide presentation that was created in a newer version. PowerPoint files usually have the extension .ppt.

Installing the most recent version of the PowerPoint Viewer ensures the ability to present a slide show created with any version of PowerPoint. The PowerPoint Viewer may be downloaded and distributed freely from the Microsoft website at:

http://office.microsoft.com/downloads/2000/Ppview97.aspx

In addition to the stand-alone PowerPoint Viewer, you may also view PowerPoint slides directly within your browser. These file types are typically associated with your browser upon installation of either the browser or a new program.

Microsoft also offers viewers for other Office document formats, including Word and Excel. As we will discuss later in this chapter, users can also save Office documents in HTML versions, which can be distributed to other users on websites.

Additional Media File Formats

You will encounter other media file formats on the Internet. All of these formats were not designed for streaming. We will discuss the following file formats in this section:

- Moving Picture Experts Group (MPEG)
- MPEG-1 Audio Layer 3 (MP3)
- Audio Interchange File Format (AIFF)
- AU
- Waveform audio (WAV)

Moving Picture Experts Group (MPEG)

The *Moving Picture Experts Group (MPEG)* format is an internationally developed standard for digital audio and video compression that provides extremely high quality and resolution. The MPEG format comes in a number of specifications based on file data throughput, screen resolution, and screen size. For instance, MPEG-1 video was designed for video CDs, a format that is popular in Europe and Asia. The MPEG-3 format was created for High Definition TV (HDTV). There are MPEG plug-ins that allow browsers to view MPEG files. However, standard MPEG video files do not stream well on slower connections.

MPEG-1 Audio Layer 3 (MP3)

MP3 is a standard for compressing audio files that uses the MPEG-1 standard. An MP3 file is an MPEG file with audio data only. MP3 has gained wide popularity on the Internet because this format can compress audio files to one-twelfth their original size, while maintaining a high quality level. A normal commercial audio CD can contain up to 700MB of data. When the same tracks are saved as MP3s on a CD-ROM, it is possible to fit several audio CDs worth of files on a single disk.

MP3 files were designed to be non-streaming media, but some streaming media players can play them as if they were streamed. Many MP3 players are available as shareware and freeware on the web. Some audio CD and DVD players can also playback MP3 files.

WARNING   While software and hardware are easily available to copy and distribute CD tracks and audio files as MP3s, this use may violate international copyright laws. The MP3 format does not protect the intellectual property rights of media creators and owners. Your company, organization, or ISP may prohibit your use of their network to download or distribute MP3 files.

AIFF, AU, and WAV

Netscape Navigator and Microsoft Internet Explorer include native, or built-in, support for standard audio formats such as *Audio Interchange File Format (AIFF), AU (audio), waveform audio (WAV)*, and MIDI. AIFF was originally developed by Apple, and is still in use on Macintosh computers. The AU format was originally developed for UNIX clients. Microsoft developed the WAV audio format for audio support in early versions of the Windows operating system.

Users can play and hear these sound files embedded in HTML documents. Operating systems often provide support for playback, and streaming media players can also automatically identify and play most major audio formats used in web browsers.

Other Image File Formats

The Web made certain image formats such as JPEG and GIF popular. Many software applications provide support for these formats. Before the web was widely used, other image formats were considered standard. You may encounter files saved in two of these formats, Tagged Image File Format (TIFF) and Encapsulated PostScript (EPS).

Tagged Image File Format (TIFF) is a popular, customizable graphic format commonly used for faxing, medical imaging, and desktop publishing. TIFF supports grayscale, 8-bit and 24-bit color, and monochrome formats. Many computer fax programs can scan documents and save them in the TIFF format. TIFF files can be exchanged between applications, similar to the EPS format. TIFF files are identified by the `.tif` or `.tiff` file name extension.

Encapsulated PostScript (EPS) is a file format that you can use to import and export graphic files between operating systems and applications. EPS files are identified by an `.eps` file name extension.

EPS is based on a printing specification called PostScript. When a computer sends a document to a printer, that document must be formatted in the computer's printing language. PostScript became popular in the late 1980s because it provided a standard printing language. PostScript was usually used on laser printers, and many current models still provide PostScript compatibility.

A PostScript file only includes instructions that determine the size and orientation of a graphic file on the printed page. EPS files actually contain the *bitmap* information for the graphics file. A bitmap is a dot-by-dot representation of a graphic file.

EPS files can also display an alternative bitmap graphic that users may preview. EPS provides three preview formats for graphics: PICT for Macintosh systems, TIFF for IBM-compatible PCs, and the platform-independent EPSI.

The EPSI format is often used to transfer a graphic from a graphics-editing application such as Adobe Photoshop, into a page-layout application such as Adobe PageMaker. EPS is necessary because each application tends to use its own format. EPS acts as an intermediary that ensures no information will be lost during conversion from one format to another.

Document File Formats

There are several other document formats that are used on the Internet. Each format has its own benefits and features, which we will describe in this section. We will discuss three formats:

- Text files
- HTML
- Rich Text Format (RTF)

Text Files

Text files are the most basic computer document format for human-readable data. A text file uses alphanumeric characters, and does not include images. The simplest text is sometimes called *plaintext* or ASCII, after the character encoding system. Text files can include basic formatting marks such as carriage returns, but they do not support bold, italic, or underlining. They also do not support the use of multiple fonts.

Plaintext files can be viewed on almost any operating system. Many business applications support the import and export of plaintext files, but this process often removes formatting information. HTML files are usually saved as plaintext, although alternative encoding systems must be used for non-English languages. Unicode has emerged as a popular text format, as it provides support for hundreds of national languages.

HTML

HTML documents have become a popular file format within business applications. HTML has gained universal acceptance because of its central role in web browsing. Many e-mail clients support HTML e-mail, for example. An HTML e-mail message includes HTML formatting tags, and can reference image files.

Some business applications allow users to save and load files in HTML formats. Users can exchange HTML versions of documents between different brands of programs. They can also post these HTML documents on a web server.

A few office applications use an advanced system called XML to save and format documents. XML has several advantages over HTML, including the definition and use of proprietary tags and formatting. XML documents are saved as text, just like HTML. We will discuss XML in Chapter 15.

Rich Text Format (RTF)

First developed by Microsoft, the *Rich Text Format (RTF)* improves upon simple text files. Using RTF, you can insert images and format text within a file. Many business applications running on Windows, Linux, and Macintosh can read and write RTF files. Applications that support RTF include Microsoft Office, Corel WordPerfect, and Lotus WordPro. In Microsoft

Word, you can select File ➢ Save As, then select RTF to save something as a Rich Text document.

Although PDF files can capture formatting options that are not supported by RTF, you can only create a PDF file by using a program that can create PDF files, such as the full Adobe Acrobat application or Adobe's web-based PDF service (both of which cost the creator of the PDF money). Anyone who wants to view the PDF must install Adobe Acrobat Reader (which is, of course, free, but some recipients may be unwilling or unable to download the program). PDF files are also difficult to edit. The RTF format can deliver fairly rich, portable files that can be edited in many different applications.

Summary

In this chapter, we discussed various kinds of media and active content available on the Internet, and described how to view and use these files. Objects and active content are two terms used to describe files that can display data in an interactive manner. We discussed object-oriented programming languages, such as C++ and Java, that can be used to create active content. Java is based on C++, which is in turn based on an older language called C. C has been used to write applications and operating systems. C allows programmers to write programming code that is easily readable by people, while providing efficiency and speed that is found in assembly and machine languages.

ActiveX is a set of Microsoft technologies for creating active content. Programmers can use many different programming languages to create ActiveX objects. We closed the section with a brief discussion of security issues that relate to objects, including Java and ActiveX content that can damage a computer.

Plug-ins are small applications that work with web browsers to display different types of Internet data. Streaming media players are a popular type of plug-in. We discussed three competing brands of streaming media players from RealNetworks, Microsoft, and Apple. Microsoft Windows Media Player can also playback WMA audio and AVI video files, while QuickTime can display MOV files.

Multimedia players, such as Macromedia Shockwave and Flash and Apple QuickTime VR, are types of plug-ins that can display different kinds of user environments in web browsers. QuickTime VR builds on Virtual

Reality modeling Language (VRML), which designers can use to simulate 3D spaces.

Document viewers are a third type of plug-in. Adobe Acrobat Reader can display files in the PDF format, which simulates the layout and formatting of printed documents. Microsoft PowerPoint Viewer is another example of a document viewer that does not require users to install the application that created the file.

We closed the chapter with an overview of various file types. The MPEG format was originally developed for video, but the MP3 format has been adopted for saving and distributing audio. There are several other types of audio files, including AIFF, AU, and WAV. We discussed two image file formats, TIFF and EPS. Finally, there are various document formats that are used in the Internet, including text, HTML, and RTF.

Exam Essentials

Understand what objects and active content are and know their relationships to multimedia.   An object is an element on a web page that contains data and procedures for how that item will react when activated. Objects are sometimes called active content because they can display data in a more interactive manner than an ordinary web document.

Know the basics of C, assembly, and machine programming languages. C is a programming language used for developing operating systems and applications. C is a step above assembly language, the tool that allows programmers to use names and low-level commands to build programs. Assembly language is a step above machine language, the numerical programming language that is used to execute instructions in CPUs.

Understand object-oriented programming languages such as C++ and Java, and describe how they are related to each other.   C++ is an object-oriented version of the C programming language that is also used for application development. Java is an object-oriented programming language that has its origins in C++. Java is focused on the development of distributed objects that can communicate with each other across a network.

Understand ActiveX technology.   ActiveX is a set of Microsoft-developed technologies that let programmers develop and implement distributed objects. ActiveX is not a programming language.

Know the purpose of plug-ins.   Plug-ins are small applications that add functionality to web browsers. Plug-ins can playback media files, create different user environments, and display document files.

Be able to identify streaming media plug-ins and viewers, including RealNetworks RealOne Player, Windows Media Player, and Apple QuickTime. There are three popular plug-in applications that support streaming media on the Internet. RealNetworks RealOne is the successor to several RealNetworks audio and video players. Microsoft Windows Player supports WMA and AVI video formats. Apple QuickTime can present streaming media, as well as MOV files.

Be able to identify multimedia plug-ins and viewers, including Macromedia Shockwave and Flash players, and QuickTime VR.   Multimedia plug-ins can present different kinds of environments within a web browser. Macromedia Shockwave and Flash are used to create animated displays, games, and other environments. QuickTime VR is used to show panoramic images.

Understand the purpose of document viewers, including Adobe Acrobat Reader and Microsoft PowerPoint Viewer.   Document viewers allow users to view and print document files, without having to install the application that created the files. Adobe Acrobat Reader can view PDF files, which duplicate the layout and formatting of printed documents. Microsoft PowerPoint Viewer lets users view PowerPoint presentations.

Be able to identify various media file formats, such as MPEG, MP3, MOV, AIFF, AU, WAV, and MIDI.   The MPEG file format was designed for video playback, but the MPEG-1 Audio Layer 3 (MP3) format is often used for high quality audio files. Two media formats developed by Apple include the AIFF sound format, and the QuickTime MOV format. AU audio files were originally designed for UNIX computers. WAV files were originally developed for Windows computers.

Know various image formats including TIFF and EPS.   Tagged Image File Format (TIFF) is a graphic format commonly used for medical imaging, faxing and desktop publishing. Encapsulated PostScript (EPS) is a file format used to import and export graphic files between operating systems and applications.

Know various document formats, including text, HTML, and RTF. Text documents are the most basic file format on the Internet. HTML has become popular with the widespread adoption of the web, and is often used for formatting e-mail messages. Many applications can save files as

HTML documents, or as an earlier file format called Rich Text Format (RTF). RTF documents are easily editable in many business applications.

Understand security issues related to objects. Although ActiveX and Java objects have some built-in safeguards, there are some objects that can damage a computer, or give control over to another user.

Key Terms

Before you take the exam, be certain you are familiar with the following terms:

active content	object
ActiveX	object-based programming language
applets	object-oriented programming (OOP)
assembly language	plaintext
AU	plug-in
Audio Interchange File Format (AIFF)	Portable Document Format (PDF)
bitmap	QuickTime
C	RealOne Player
C++	RealPlayer
Encapsulated PostScript (EPS)	Rich Text Format (RTF)
event-driven	Tagged Image File Format (TIFF)
lossy	viewer
machine language	Virtual Reality Modeling Language (VRML)
Moving Picture Experts Group (MPEG)	waveform audio (WAV)
MP3	Windows Media Player
Musical Instrument Digital Interface (MIDI)	

Review Questions

1. Which one of the following choices best describes an object?

   A. An element on a web page that contains data and procedures for how that item will react when activated.

   B. An element on a web page that expedites downloading web pages.

   C. An element on a web page that condenses the amount of space a web page uses in a computer's cache.

   D. An element on a web page that interacts with all programming languages and enables them to function universally with all browsers.

2. Which programming language has been used to develop versions of the UNIX operating system?

   A. Visual Basic

   B. JavaScript

   C. C

   D. Java

3. Which one of the following is an example of an object-based programming language?

   A. Java

   B. VBScript

   C. C

   D. Machine language

4. The Java programming language is based upon what other programming language?

   A. C++

   B. JavaScript

   C. Café

   D. Oak

5. What is the best definition of a Java applet?

A. A small Java application that can run on any operating system.

B. A Java application that must be run within a web browser.

C. A Java application that has been compressed for easy downloading.

D. A Java application that is run on a server, and can connect to other servers.

6. ActiveX technology was created by what company?

A. Netscape

B. Oracle

C. Sun

D. Microsoft

7. Which one of the following statements is the best definition of a plug-in?

A. A program that is launched by a browser to extend the browser's functionality.

B. A program that must be associated with files on a computer to extend the web browser's functionality.

C. A program that is installed on computers to extend the operating system's functionality.

D. A program that acts as a separate process when accessed.

8. The fastest way to install most plug-ins is to:

A. Ask a friend to e-mail the plug-in installation file to you and install it manually.

B. E-mail the vendor and request that the plug-in installation file be mailed to you.

C. Download the plug-in installation file at the vendor's website and double-click the file to install the plug-in.

D. Search FTP sites for the plug-in installation file, download it, and install it.

9. Which one of the following file formats uses the computer's sound synthesis hardware to recreate music that was created on a digital musical instrument?

A. MIDI

B. MOV

C. PDF

D. MUS

10. Sophia's home computer hardware and software are identical to Rachel's computer. Sophia has a cable modem connection to the Internet, while Rachel uses a dial-up connection. Which one of the following situations is Rachel not likely to encounter?

A. Rachel can play full-screen streaming media on her machine, while Sophia cannot.

B. Sophia can play full-screen streaming media on her machine, while Rachel cannot.

C. Sophia can play full-screen videos that are saved on her DVD drive, while Rachel cannot.

D. Rachel can play full-screen videos that are saved on her DVD drive, while Sophia cannot.

11. Which of the following media applications was originally designed for Internet use?

A. RealPlayer

B. QuickTime

C. Adobe Acrobat

D. Windows Media Player

12. Justin has downloaded a video file with a `.mov` file extension. Which one of the following applications should he use to view the file?

A. RealOne Player

B. His favorite web browser

C. Windows Media Player

D. QuickTime

13. Which streaming media player can be installed as a part of Internet Explorer?

    A. RealOne Player

    B. Windows Media Player

    C. Macromedia Shockwave

    D. Apple QuickTime

14. Roberta notices a hyperlink to a file with the extension .pdf. When she clicks on this link, the browser downloads a file that cannot be opened. What plug-in should she install to view this file?

    A. Microsoft PowerPoint Viewer

    B. Adobe Acrobat Reader

    C. Macromedia Shockwave

    D. RealOne Player

15. Ashley has heard that she can find MP3 files from her favorite local recording artists, The Recliners. What is the official name of MP3 files?

    A. MPEG video files.

    B. MPEG-3 Audio Format.

    C. MPEG Audio Format version 3

    D. MPEG-1 Audio Layer 3

16. Which one of the following file extensions is commonly used for non-streaming Windows audio?

    A. .wav

    B. .au

    C. .aiff

    D. .mov

17. What is the Encapsulated PostScript file format?

    A. A file format used to compress video.

    B. A file format used to allow image insertion and text formatting.

    C. A file format used to compress audio files.

    D. A file format used for importing and exporting graphics between operating systems and applications.

18. Which one of the following document formats is the most basic?

    A. PDF

    B. Microsoft Word document

    C. HTML

    D. Plaintext

19. Andrea needs to send a word processing document to a colleague for some additional editing. She does not know what word processor her colleague uses. Andrea has already formatted the document, and included the images and fonts she wants to use. In which format should she send the document?

    A. Plaintext

    B. RTF

    C. Microsoft Word document

    D. PDF

20. Jerry wants to post a printable version of the company's new marketing brochure on the corporate website. What file format should he specify for this document?

    A. Plaintext

    B. RTF

    C. PowerPoint file

    D. PDF

Answers to Review Questions

1. A. An object contains programming instructions that tell it how to behave when a user selects or activates it.

2. C. C is a low-level programming language that is used to develop operating systems. Visual Basic and Java are object-oriented programming languages. JavaScript is a scripting language.

3. B. VBScript and JavaScript are object-based programming languages that are used to automate routine tasks in an application. Java is an object-oriented programming language. C is a procedural programming language. Machine language is the numerical language that is used by the CPU.

4. A. Java is derived from C++. JavaScript was in turn based on Java. Café is not the name of a computer language. Oak was the original name for the Java language.

5. B. Java applets are mini-applications that depend upon the web browser for their operating environment. Java can produce applications and applets that run on any suitable operating system. Java applications are sometimes compressed into jar files for easier downloading. Java servlets are run on a server, and can connect to other servers.

6. D. Microsoft created ActiveX technology, and provides support for it in Internet Explorer.

7. A. A plug-in is a small application that lets browsers read and display different kinds of data.

8. C. Plug-ins are usually available on vendor websites, although they are sometimes available by FTP.

9. A. The Musical Instrument Digital Interface format lets musicians record music created on digital musical instruments. MOV is an Apple video file format. PDF is Adobe's Portable Document Format used for distributing documents.

10. B. Rachel probably cannot view full-screen streaming video on her computer because her dial-up connection is too slow. Sophia should be able to use her cable modem to view full screen streaming video. Both Rachel and Sophia should be able to view full-screen video that is stored on their DVD drives, as long as their identical equipment works properly.

11. A. RealPlayer was the first streaming media application designed for Internet use. QuickTime and Windows Media Player were originally designed for viewing locally stored media. Adobe Acrobat is a document viewer.

12. D. MOV is an Apple format that is supported by QuickTime. He could try the Real or Microsoft players, but they may not support the format. His web browser cannot display the MOV file unless QuickTime is also installed.

13. B. Windows Media Player is an optional part of Internet Explorer. The other players can be used as plug-ins with Internet Explorer, but require separate installations.

14. B. Adobe Acrobat Reader can open and display Portable Document Format (PDF) files in a web browser. The PowerPoint Viewer can only open PowerPoint files, which usually have the .ppt extension. Shockwave is a multimedia viewer. RealOne player can open many types of streaming and regular media files.

15. D. The official name of MP3 files is MPEG-1 Audio Layer 3. It is one of many formats defined by the Motion Picture Experts Group.

16. A. WAV stands for Waveform audio, which was introduced on early versions of the Windows operating system. AU is a UNIX audio format, while AIFF is an Apple audio format. MOV is an Apple video format used in QuickTime.

17. D. The EPS format is used to transfer graphics files between different systems and programs.

18. D. Plaintext files use only ASCII or Unicode characters, and do not include font or formatting instructions. PDF files can display documents in their printed format. Microsoft Word documents can include many different kinds of formatting, images, and fonts. HTML documents are text documents, but they also contain HTML tags that a browser can use to display different fonts, formatting, and images.

19. B. Andrea should use Rich Text Format, because this will preserve her formatting. Plaintext removes most formatting instructions. She does not know if her colleague's word processor can load Microsoft Word documents. PDF documents are difficult to edit, and are better suited for showing the actual printed layout of the final version of this document.

20. D. The Adobe PDF format should be used, because this will show the document in its printed version. Plaintext would not include any formatting, and RTF may not include all the formatting. PowerPoint files are better suited for slide presentations.

Chapter

12

Internet Security

THE CIW EXAM OBJECTIVE GROUPS COVERED IN THIS CHAPTER:

✓ Identify security issues related to Web browsing and e-mail, including but not limited to: certificates, viruses, encryption, and patches.

✓ Identify common Internet security issues, including but not limited to: user-level and enterprise-level issues, access security, and security threats and attacks.

✓ Transmit text and binary files using popular Internet services, including but not limited to: the Web and e-mail.

As we continue to explore the fundamentals of Internet business, we now come to the critical issue of Internet security. We'll look at the overall security of computer systems and networks, which is an important part of managing any network. Crackers who try to enter and use computers without authorization also examine security, but with the purpose of defeating the hardware, software, and policies that are in place.

In this chapter, we'll cover the different types of attacks an intruder might try against you, and discuss ways to defend against those attacks. There are a variety of ways to secure an entire network, including the use of firewalls. We will discuss how using the right hardware, software, and policies can be combined to ensure that computers are used in authorized ways.

Next, we will look at how to secure an individual computer. This is especially important for home users who have direct connections to the Internet, as they have become prime targets for security violations. Finally, we'll examine how you can secure the data you transmit to the Internet, using encryption, various networking protocols, and browser features.

What Is Security?

When we deal with computers and networks, *security* concerns the safety of network assets. Anyone in charge of security must determine which people can take appropriate actions on specific items at appropriate times. Any company with a network must have a security policy that addresses appropriateness, subordination, and physical security.

We can define *network assets* as data, applications, and resources on any computing system. These assets become vulnerable whenever anyone gains access to them. Network assets can be classified into the following four resource groups. Each group lists common vulnerabilities:

Local resources   These can be workstations or individual computers on a network. Viruses and active content often damage local systems.

Network resources   These are the primary IT communications media for an entire company. IP spoofing, system snooping, and other unauthorized acquisitions of information can help a cracker gain access or control of your network.

Server resources   This includes your web, e-mail, and FTP servers. Unauthorized entry allows crackers to gain access to server resources, where they can then access and control other resources.

Information resources   The most vital IT asset of any company is how it organizes and disseminates information, especially databases. If crackers gain unauthorized access to company databases, they can find a company's trade secrets, customer data, and other vital information.

Crackers try to take control of these network assets using a systematic process of analysis to identify entry points. A *cracker* is a computer user who is trying to gain unauthorized use of another computer or network. (A *hacker*, on the other hand, is a very knowledgeable computer user.) A cracker can conduct many different attacks using many different techniques.

We are using the term *cracker* throughout this chapter. Hacker is the term that is used in the mainstream press, but in the computer press, a hacker can simply be a very proficient programmer or user; they may not be doing anything wrong. A cracker is doing something illegal.

The Cracker Process

Although the primary motivation for connecting systems is to share information and resources, this connectivity also makes systems and data vulnerable to unwanted activity by crackers.

Not all crackers have criminal intent. Most are users who enjoy the challenge of entering a system. Once they get inside, they may do little more than brag about their exploits to friends. While this behavior may seem innocent, in many cases this qualifies as unauthorized entry of a computer system and is illegal. It is the minority of crackers who intend to cause damage to the systems they enter. In either case, the unauthorized use of computer systems and networks may violate local, national, and international laws.

The primary weapon of a cracker is a thorough understanding of the methods required to successfully discover, penetrate, and control a system.

Stage 1: Discovery   The cracker gathers as much information as possible about the target system by mapping your system. A large amount of information about your system is freely and legally available to crackers. In fact, crackers can obtain most of the information they need simply by conducting what would be otherwise legitimate queries of the network. For instance, a WhoIs search can determine the name, server, IP address, and domain range. Alternatively, a user can ping a particular machine or web server to discover its IP address.

Stage 2: Penetration   Once the cracker has determined the scope of your systems, they will choose a specific target for penetration. Usually, this target will be the one with the weakest security or one for which the cracker has the most tools. System defaults and bugs are major concerns.

Stage 3: Control   Once a cracker successfully penetrates your system, they will immediately attempt to control it. Typical goals in this stage include destroying evidence of activity, obtaining root and administrative access, opening new security holes, creating new accounts, and moving to other systems. If the cracker is successful at implementing even a few of these steps, detecting or terminating the penetration will be difficult.

Types of Attacks

Crackers use a variety of different attacks to help discover, penetrate, and control network assets. You can usually categorize those methods into one of the following types:

- Denial of service (DoS)
- Spoofing or masquerade
- Man-in-the-middle (hijacking)

- Insider

- Brute-force

- Trapdoor

- Replay

- Trojan horse

- Social-engineering

- Software-based attacks (Viruses and Worms)

In this section, we will briefly discuss the first eight attacks. We will then discuss denial-of-service attacks, as they are a most common form of attack on the Internet. We will follow this with discussions of viruses and worms, two forms of software-based attack that are often used against personal computers.

Denial-of-Service Attacks

Denial-of-service (DoS) attacks are the most common type of attack. They occur when the host or system cannot perform properly because another program or node on a network is using all its resources. Additionally, a denial-of-service attack can crash the entire system. Crackers often conduct denial-of-service attacks via spoofing attacks (see next section); if a cracker is imitating another network or device, they do not want to find that the legitimate network is sending packets. Therefore, the cracker will generate a rapid flood of information, such as a large number of ping packets, to overburden or crash the network device. This type of tactic, called a *ping flood*, is one reason why some server administrators configure their servers, routers, and firewalls not to respond to external pings.

Mail bombing, also called mail flooding, is another denial-of-service attack that occurs when a user receives a massive amount of e-mail. For instance, if you were to receive thousands of 1MB files in your e-mail, this load could cause your mail server to fail in some cases. Mail bombing is sometimes used by crackers to retaliate against senders of UCE.

A *SYN flood* is a denial-of-service attack that initiates but does not complete the establishment of a connection-oriented session, called a *TCP handshake*. SYN is an abbreviated code for "synchronize," and is used in TCP to establish the connection-oriented session. A SYN flood is similar to extending your hand to initiate a handshake with someone, then pulling your hand away as they extend a hand to you. If the frustrated person then continues to try to shake your hand, their attention has been diverted. In a SYN flood, the attacked computer allocates more and more resources as it attempts to finish the handshake. A server may eventually fail due to a SYN flood. One possible defense against a SYN flood is to restrict the amount of SYN packets your router will recognize within a given time; the router would ignore any additional SYN packets.

Server administrators can reprogram their routers to ignore packet floods sent from a single host. Crackers sometimes write and distribute programs that can create a *distributed denial-of-service attack*. In a distributed denial-of-service (DDoS) attack, the cracker leverages the distributed networks that form the Internet to create a much stronger level of attack. Hundreds of computers run a program that issues ping or SYN floods against a single host. These programs are often sent out as viruses or worms, which we'll discuss in a later section.

Spoofing or Masquerade Attacks

Spoofing attacks occur when a host, a program, or an application assumes the identity of a legitimate network device or host. Victims of a spoofing attack are convinced they are communicating with a trusted host, and will probably engage in compromising transactions. Usually, a cracker who engages in such an attack will manipulate legitimate data.

For example, in IP spoofing, a cracker alters the IP packet header so that it appears to have originated from a trusted network. This activity allows crackers to gain access to engage in *system snooping*, or the actions of a cracker who enters a computer network and begins mapping the system's contents. For example, they might start examining directories, files, and permissions to determine if they can access, copy, or delete data. Also, the cracker may examine system configuration settings to find additional weaknesses they might exploit.

Man-in-the-Middle (Hijacking) Attacks

Man-in-the-middle attacks occur when a cracker captures packets being sent from one host to another. This type of attack is used in many other attacks, such as spoofing. This type of attack is sometimes called *hijacking*, because the packets are being redirected away from their original destination.

To conduct a man-in-the-middle attack, the cracker must be literally between the two communicating hosts to intercept the packets. Once the cracker has the packets, they then send them to a destination other than the one the sender had intended.

Insider Attacks

Insider attacks are common, mostly because employees or personnel can easily misuse their legitimate access to a network or computer. Recent estimates indicate that insiders are responsible for over 60 percent of all attacks on corporate networks.

The same methods that are used in external perimeter attacks to gain unauthorized access can also be used internally, sometimes with greater ease because security measures expect mostly external violations. Two insider-attack techniques are eavesdropping on messages between applications and compromising existing control mechanisms.

Brute-Force Attacks

Brute-force attacks, also called *front-door attacks*, occur when a cracker attempts to gain access as a legitimate user. Because a cracker has complete information to fraudulently identify herself as a legitimate user, they can simply walk in through the system's front door.

In a brute-force attack, a cracker uses a "dictionary program" containing obvious passwords and names. Crackers sometimes resort to using very powerful computers to analyze and defeat a network's password scheme. If you notice multiple logon failures, you may be witnessing a brute-force attack. For example, the cracker may already know the user's account name, and they may be attempting to obtain the corresponding password by the sheer force of trying multitudes of possible alternatives.

Trapdoor Attacks

Trapdoor attacks occur when crackers establish certain commands that open potential unauthorized access. For example, although logon accounts may be secured with good passwords, an account used for running diagnostics, which usually has a high degree of privilege, may leave the application vulnerable to intrusion. Even though the intruder cannot log on to that account, they can view and possibly execute system programs and utilities. This is dangerous, because there are a wide variety of these programs, and their functions can be highly destructive when used incorrectly. The format utility in DOS and Windows can be used to destroy all data on a hard drive, for example.

Replay Attacks

A *replay attack* occurs after a cracker has captured and altered a key part of a message, such as the header of a network data packet. Crackers can intercept packets using a network analyzer program, as we discussed in Chapter 5. The intruder will often edit a packet header with false information that can aid their attack. By resending or replaying this altered message, they can often obtain valuable information or gain access to a system.

Trojan Horse Attacks

A *Trojan horse attack* is a variation of the trapdoor attack that involves hiding an unauthorized command within a commonly used function to cause a breach. A Trojan horse is a file or application that purports to operate in a legitimate way, but has an alternative, secret operation.

For example, imagine that an executable application is attached to an e-mail message, which explains that the program is a multimedia Christmas greeting. An unsuspecting user runs the greeting card program, and thus loads the Trojan program into memory. The Trojan may appear to be executing as the innocent original program. However, the Trojan then executes unauthorized functions in the background, such as sending files, passwords or other information to a cracker.

Social-Engineering Attacks

A *social-engineering attack* occurs when someone attempts to obtain information about a network through simple psychological tricks. A cracker, for example, might engage in social engineering by convincing people to disregard their better judgment, and give the cracker some information that could be used to enter a computer system.

For example, a group of high school students who wanted to gain access to the school district's computers created a "social studies" project that involved a survey. The students gave the survey form to the school's principal, secretaries, and teachers. The survey asked for seemingly innocent information, such as the names of their spouses, children, and pets, as well as birthdays and anniversaries. With this information, the students were able to break in to the computer system because many of the school's administrators and teachers had used their spouses' or children's names as passwords. While this is a common technique for breaking into systems, one should remember that any unauthorized access may violate company or network policy, and may also be illegal.

Software-Based Attacks

Viruses and worms are a different form of attack, based on uploading and executing particular software on a client or server. The cracker who creates a virus or worm either tricks a user into running the software, or exploits a known security hole in the computer itself.

A *virus* is a malicious program designed to damage computers. Specifically, a virus is a self-replicating program that assumes control of system operations, often with harmful results. You can spread viruses to other files or computers unknowingly through floppy disks and e-mail attachments. For example, a virus might have written itself onto every floppy disk that you used. If you pass an infected disk to a colleague, that colleague's system can also be infected.

As you can imagine, the Internet has become a primary distribution method for viruses. As Internet e-mail became a worldwide standard, crackers tried to infect computers with e-mail virus attachments in the form of executable e-mail messages. If a recipient ran the attachment, the virus automatically infected the computer.

It is important to note that viruses usually affect programs running at the Application layer (Layer 7). Viruses can harm the application software and operating system on a computer. The level of damage may be so great that the user may lose their data files, and the software may need to be reinstalled. On a network, viruses do not affect OSI/RM Layer 1 and Layer 2 devices. For instance, cables, NICs, bridges, repeaters, and hubs are immune to viruses. A virus cannot directly harm networking hardware.

A *worm* is similar to a virus, in that it tries to replicate itself across a network. What makes a worm different is that it will also try to shut down an infected computer. A worm keeps accessing an infected computer's drives and memory in an attempt to consume system resources. When enough resources are compromised, the computer fails. Worms are often targeted against Internet servers.

Virus Types

There are several types of viruses, each with its own methods of distribution and attack. Later in this chapter, we will discuss how you can use antivirus programs to find and remove infected files from your computer.

Macros These viruses are small programs written in macro code for word processing or spreadsheet applications such as Microsoft Word or Excel. When the infected file is opened, the macro is executed. Macros tend to be the weakest form of virus, because their abilities are constrained by the application program's own macro programming language.

Executables These are viruses that attach themselves to executable programs (or are executable themselves) that are activated when the user launches the program. If you receive an executable program from an unknown source, you are advised not to run the program until it has been scanned for viruses.

Boot sector These viruses copy themselves to the boot sector of hard drives or floppy disks, allowing themselves to be loaded into memory each time a system is started. The *boot sector* is a dedicated portion of a disk that contains the first parts of an operating system's startup files. Once in memory, a boot sector virus tries to replicate itself to other drives.

Stealth A stealth virus attempts to avoid detection by redirecting hard-drive read requests away from the virus-scanning software or by manipulating directory structure information. This action causes the virus-scanning program to miss the stealth virus in its scanning process, leaving the virus on the system.

Polymorphic Perhaps the most difficult virus to detect, a polymorphic virus has programming code enabling it to change its action and programming code each time it is run. Because a polymorphic virus can appear as a different process each time, this virus can avoid being detected by older virus-scanning software. Modern virus scanners use a variety of techniques to identify polymorphic viruses.

Defending Your Network

There are various methods we can use to defend a computer network from the attacks that we have described. We must first identify the areas and assets that can be attacked, and then use several different methods to secure these vulnerabilities.

Auditing

The best way to determine a network's ability to withstand discovery, penetration, and control is to conduct a thorough *auditing* process.

Auditing is the process of examining your systems and procedures to determine their efficiency, such as your network's ability to withstand cracker activity. For example, you can audit the settings of routers and servers, to determine if they can successfully handle a flood attack. You might also review your software for known security issues. Auditing should be an ongoing activity, and effective security involves both manual and automated analysis.

Following is a description of three key auditing steps you should take when determining the level of security needed for a network.

Step 1: Status Quo Analysis   Determines the current level of security at the site. It includes asking administrators questions such as "In your opinion, how effective is the existing security? How would you improve security?" It also includes determining the physical security of the servers. For instance, is the server located in a locked room, or is it behind the receptionist's desk? You should also attempt to learn the types of services your network is operating, and determine whether those services are necessary. This knowledge will help you decrease the chance of a cracker entering your system through a vulnerable service.

Step 2: Risk Analysis   Determines which network systems are vulnerable to an attack. For instance, if your web server uses CGI scripts, then your network is at some risk because of the nature of CGI itself. If your FTP server requires password protection and your employees use these passwords to access other, more sensitive areas, then your FTP server presents a greater risk than is necessary because standard FTP passwords are sent across the network as clear text (non-encrypted). Furthermore, if you have not changed your servers' default directories, you are also exposing yourself to some risk.

Step 3: Threat Analysis   Determines probable attacks. Attacks come from both inside and outside a system, and it is necessary to determine how such attacks can occur. A cracker can penetrate a firewall, but even a temporary worker can easily obtain key information or conduct an attack on your system. For example, an employee can bring a disk to work and unwittingly spread a virus, or deliberately steal certain files.

In summary, the primary difference between a risk analysis and a threat analysis is that the risk analysis examines internal system resources, whereas the threat analysis attempts to determine an attacker's attitudes or inclinations.

Authentication

Authentication is the ability to determine a user's true identity, and is a crucial part of defending any computer system. To communicate effectively, users in enterprise networks must ensure that they are actually communicating with the person they want to address. However, IP spoofing, falsified e-mail, social engineering, and other techniques all intervene to defeat the authentication process.

Networks can employ three methods to prove a user's identity and achieve authentication.

What you know   The most common form of authentication; it involves the use of passwords. When you log on to a computer network, you will often be asked for a password. This information is something that you alone should know. Because a password is a simple text string, it is relatively easy to defeat this level of authentication.

What you have   This method requires that you use a physical item, such as a key, for authentication. An example is a building entry card. Anyone who moves the card over a scanner will be granted access to the building. In this case, the authentication is based on possessing the card.

Who you are   Biometrics is the science of connecting authentication schemes to unique physical attributes. Examples of this method include the use of fingerprints, visual and photographic identification, and physical signatures. More sophisticated methods include retinal scans, facial maps, voice analysis, and digital signatures. Each method attempts to validate an individual's claim concerning their identity.

The term *strong authentication* describes extensive steps, including the use of encryption, to ensure authentication. It is a combination of what you know, what you have, and who you are. Strong authentication combines several levels of protection that can help turn away crackers.

Firewalls

A *firewall* is the collection of hardware, software, and corporate policies that protects a LAN from the Internet. On one side of a firewall is your company's production network, which you supervise, control, and protect. The other side contains a public network, such as the Internet, over which you have no control.

In computer networking, a network firewall acts as a barrier against potential malicious activity, while still allowing a door for people to communicate between a secured network and the open, unsecured network. The most common location for a firewall is between a corporate LAN and the Internet.

A firewall is intended to do the following:

- Restrict unauthorized users

- Retain control of private information

- Prevent unauthorized export of proprietary data and information

A firewall controls access to your private network. It can also create secure intranet domains. Furthermore, it is the primary means of enforcing your security policy, which can help a system administrator determining threats and use countermeasures.

A firewall can further enhance privacy by hiding your internal systems and information from the public. For example, firewalls can conceal open ports on computers, that might otherwise be exploited. Firewalls can be inconvenient for business users who are protected by them. For example, users may be unable to access an external e-mail provider or to upload files to external servers. Some standardized Internet plug-ins, such as RealOne Player, do not function well through firewalls. If your employer's firewall interferes with your use of the Internet, and your company's policies allow the use of streaming media players, you might work with your IT department's firewall administrators to achieve a more transparent form of protection.

Firewall Functions

Before you implement your firewall, you should know which services your company requires, and which services will be available to both internal and external users. The availability of services on both sides of the firewall largely determines which firewall functions you will use.

In the following sections, we will discuss three functions of a firewall:

- Packet filtering
- Proxy server
- Virtual Private Networks (VPNs)

You can use these functions in a variety of combinations. Sometimes they will be used on individual machines, but most often they will be combined. Together, these functions form your firewall's building blocks.

Packet Filtering

A *packet filter* is a device that inspects the headers of each packet. Recall that the headers contain important information, such as port numbers, that indicate the type of data carried. Although it does not provide error-proof protection, it is almost always the first line of defense. Packet filtering is an inexpensive defense, mainly because most routers can perform this task. Engineers usually filter packets at the external router, which can then discard certain types of network activity entirely, based on the packet's contents. This method is very useful for front-line defense.

Packet filtering works at the Data Link, Network, and Transport layers of the OSI reference model. Implementation requires instructing the router to filter the IP packets based on the following fields in the packet:

- Source IP address
- Destination IP address
- TCP/UDP source port
- TCP/UDP destination port

We mentioned in Chapter 11 that some companies restrict the use of streaming media players on their networks. This is often done through packet-level filtering. The router can be configured to filter out ports that are used for streaming media, thus restricting any streaming media access from within the network.

Proxy Servers

You have already learned about the proxy server concept in Chapter 5. However, proxies are very important to firewall applications because a proxy replaces the network IP address with another, contingent address. This process effectively hides the actual IP address from the rest of the Internet, thereby protecting the entire network from discovery. A proxy has several uses, especially in relation to the beginning stages of the cracker process.

For enterprise-level firewalls, proxies come in two basic forms: the circuit-level gateway and the application-level gateway.

Circuit-Level Gateways

A *circuit-level gateway* acts as a proxy between the Internet and your internal systems. It is a firewall component that monitors and transmits information at the transport layer of the OSI model. It hides information about the network. A packet passing through this type of gateway appears to have originated from the firewall.

A circuit-level gateway firewall receives an outbound network packet and transfers it on behalf of the internal system. Inbound traffic works in a similar way. As shown in Figure 12.1, the circuit-level gateway shields the internal system.

FIGURE 12.1   Circuit-level gateway

The transmission process begins when the internal system sends a series of packets destined for the Internet. These packets then go to the firewall, which checks them against its predetermined set of rules. If the packets do not violate any rules, the firewall sends the same packets on behalf of the internal system. The packets that appear on the Internet originate at the router's external port, which is also the device that receives any replies. This process effectively shields all internal information, such as IP addresses, from the Internet.

The circuit-level gateway has the same weakness as a packet filter; it does not examine the bytes of the information sent, meaning that it cannot examine the nature of the packets it allows.

Both circuit and application gateways create a complete break between your internal and external systems. This break gives your firewall system an opportunity to examine all transmissions before passing them into or out of your internal networks.

Application-Level Gateways

Application-level gateways perform a similar function to circuit-level gateways, but they filter packets on a program-by-program basis. For example, an application-level gateway can serve as an SMTP firewall. In that case, external inbound e-mail messages would be received from the Internet at the firewall's external port. The firewall could then verify the source of the e-mail messages and scan all attachments for viruses before transmitting the mail into the internal network.

Although this process is rather involved, it is often necessary. Neither source verification nor virus-scanning capabilities are built into SMTP specifications. An application-level gateway provides an easy method to implement this type of security.

Most firewall systems today are combinations of packet filtering, circuit-level gateways, and application-level gateways. They examine packets by piece, and they use predetermined rules. Only packets that engage in acceptable activities as defined by your networks' security policy are allowed into and out of the network.

If your network uses a proxy server, all users must be properly configured. For example, to browse the Web, users must enter the correct address of that proxy server into their browsers. Otherwise, the proxy server will ignore any requests.

Furthermore, you must configure every application to work with your proxy server, including web browsers, Telnet applications, and FTP programs. Otherwise, not all applications will be able to access outside networks. Browsers from both Netscape and Microsoft provide proxy server configuration, and you can obtain third-party programs that will allow almost any application to work properly with a proxy server. By default, Internet Explorer automatically detects your proxy server.

Virtual Private Networks (VPNs)

The use of a *Virtual Private Network (VPN)* is a technique that allows secure communication, usually for a company extranet. A VPN can extend the corporate LAN to the Internet, providing secure worldwide connectivity. In a VPN, the Internet is often the corporate network backbone, thereby eliminating the dichotomy of inside network and outside network, as well as the need to maintain many networks. VPNs are appropriate for any organization requiring secure external access to internal resources. For example, a VPN is appropriate for companies whose facilities are spread over long distances but need to communicate as if they were located together. Another reason VPNs are important is that they allow companies to embed non-Internet protocols within TCP/IP.

All VPNs are *tunneling protocols*; their information packets or payloads are encapsulated or tunneled into the network packets. Encryption occurs at the source, and decryption occurs at the destination.

Tunneling can be used to interconnect TCP/IP networks to other network protocols. For example, imagine that you administer the network of a company that has two offices, one in Dallas and the other in Tokyo. Each office has a LAN that runs IPX/SPX. Using the Internet, you can use a VPN to create a connection between offices and tunnel or encapsulate IPX/SPX packets within TCP/IP. You can encapsulate other protocols as well.

Security fundamentals such as authentication, message integrity, and encryption, are very important to VPN implementation. Without such authentication procedures, a cracker can impersonate anyone and then gain access to the network. Message integrity is required because the packets can be altered as they travel through the public network. Without encryption, the information may become truly public.

VPN is also used to provide remote access to authorized users, by tunneling packets through a firewall. This provides a secure method for letting external users access an extranet, for example.

There are three popular standards for implementing VPNs:

Point-to-Point Tunneling Protocol (PPTP)   *Point-to-Point Tunneling Protocol (PPTP)* is a popular VPN tunneling protocol that encapsulates protocols and transmits them over the Internet using encryption. It is designed to establish a private channel between a client and a server over a public network such as the Internet. The protocol encapsulates data and information/control packets using the Internet Generic Routing Encapsulation protocol version 2 (GREv2).

Layer-2 Tunneling Protocol (L2TP)   *Layer-2 Tunneling Protocol (L2TP)* is an IETF standard tunneling protocol. It is primarily used to support VPNs over the Internet for non-IP protocols. For instance, Apple networks can create VPNs over the network, as can Novell networks, using L2TP. It is a combination of PPTP and Cisco's Layer 2 Forwarding (L2F) protocol.

IP Security (IPSec)   *IP Security (IPSec)* is another Internet Engineering Task Force standard that provides packet-level encryption, authentication, and integrity for VPNs. It functions at Layer 3 of the OSI/RM and can secure all packets transmitted over the network. IPsec is expected to become the VPN standard because it was designed for IP and is IPv6-compatible.

Firewall Topology

Most enterprise security professionals consider the firewall to be the choke point through which all traffic must pass. Enterprise networks use four different models to implement that choke point, depending on their needs and available resources. Each model is designed to create a matrix of filters and points that can process and secure information. The four common firewall implementations are:

- Packet filtering
- Single-homed bastion host
- Dual-homed bastion host
- Screened subnet with DMZ

The Packet-Filtering Firewall

The *packet-filtering firewall* option is the most simple of the four models, and consequently the most common. Roughly 60 to 70 percent of organizations that use firewalls employ packet filtering.

Figure 12.2 shows a diagram of a packet-filtering router. It is inexpensive, but it still provides a significant degree of protection. A packet filter inspects only Internet addresses and port numbers after analyzing network header fields. This strategy can contain, or filter, much unwanted traffic.

FIGURE 12.2 Packet-filtering configuration

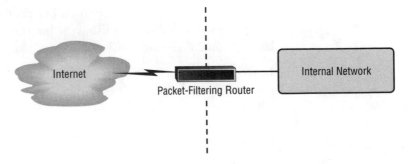

A potential drawback to packet filtering is that the degree of safety it offers depends greatly on the expertise of the people who implement the filters. Another drawback is that the security of your entire network depends primarily on a single device; if a cracker defeats the packet filter, your network will no longer have a firewall in place. Another drawback is that a packet filter cannot implement effective logging and alarms.

Single-Homed Bastion

The second prevalent type of firewall is a screened host that uses a *single-homed bastion*. The phrase "single-homed" means the bastion is composed of one computer that acts as both a firewall component and the network interface.

In a simple packet-filtering configuration, the packet filter acts as both the firewall and the network interface. Any information coming from an external network first goes to the bastion. After the bastion processes this information, it forwards the packets to your company's network.

The screened-host firewall is so named because it can screen all packets that come to and from the internal hosts at the application level. In this firewall implementation, the router is configured to forward all incoming traffic to the bastion host. It allows traffic only from the bastion host; all other traffic is discarded. The bastion host serves as both a circuit gateway and an application gateway, controlling access to and from the internal systems and any externally accessible servers, such as a web or FTP server. A single-homed bastion host is shown in Figure 12.3.

FIGURE 12.3 Single-homed bastion configuration

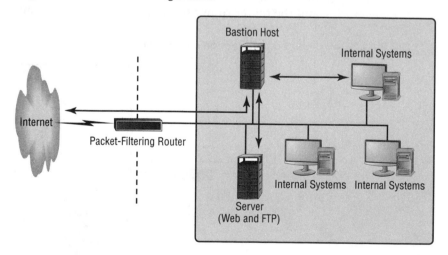

This implementation is superior to the packet-filtering firewall for several reasons. First, it adds a bastion host as well as circuit and application gateways. In addition, the bastion itself constitutes a second security device that is significantly more difficult to subvert than a router. Now, the cracker must subvert not only the router, but also a separate computer that is not designed to accept logon requests. With a screened-host firewall, the cracker's task becomes doubly difficult.

The disadvantages of this method, at least compared with packet filtering, are increased cost and reduced performance. Because the bastion host processes information, the network often takes more time to respond to user requests. Finally, the screened-host firewall can make user access to the Internet more difficult because it can be configured to disallow file downloading. This may be helpful for a network administrator, especially if they must enforce a company policy that prohibits downloading.

Dual-Homed Bastion

A *dual-homed bastion* host is a different kind of screened-host firewall that adds a significant level of security to the previous method by using a computer with two or more NICs with their IP forwarding features disabled. Software-imposed firewall rules help forward valid packets between subnets.

As shown in Figure 12.4, this firewall implementation is more secure because it creates a complete physical break between your network and any external network, such as the Internet. As with the single-homed bastion, all external traffic is forwarded directly to the bastion host for processing. In this implementation, however, a cracker must subvert the bastion host and the router to bypass the protection mechanisms.

FIGURE 12.4 Dual-homed bastion configuration

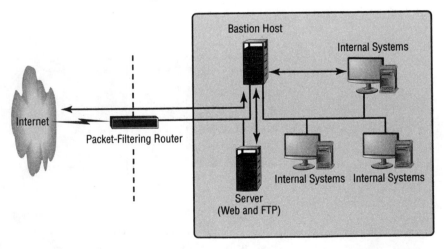

A single-homed implementation still may allow a cracker to modify the router so that packets cannot be sent to the bastion host. This action would bypass the bastion and allow the cracker directly into the network. Such a bypass usually does not happen, however, because a network using a single-homed bastion is typically configured to send packets only to the bastion host and not directly to the Internet. For a cracker to bypass a network that is properly configured for a single-homed bastion firewall, they must reconfigure the entire network to bypass the firewall.

A dual-homed bastion eliminates this possibility, however. Furthermore, even if crackers can defeat one of the computers, they will still need to penetrate the other, greatly slowing their progress.

Screened-Subnet Firewall with DMZ

The fourth commonly used implementation of a firewall is the screened subnet. This configuration is also known as a *demilitarized zone (DMZ)*, because it creates a fairly secure space, or subnetwork, between the Internet and your network. It is the most secure of the four general implementations because it uses a bastion host to support both circuit-level and application-level gateways while defining the DMZ.

In this configuration, all publicly accessible devices, including modem pools and other such resources, are placed inside this zone. The DMZ then functions as a small isolated network positioned between the Internet and the internal network. The DMZ can be used to host publicly accessible inter-networking servers, including web and FTP servers. Figure 12.5 shows an example of this type of firewall.

FIGURE 12.5   Screened-subnet firewall

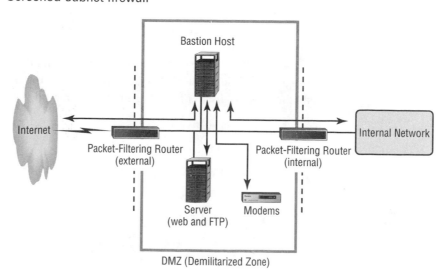

This configuration uses external and internal routers. Each is configured so that its traffic flows only to or from the bastion host. This arrangement prevents any traffic from directly traversing the subnetwork, or DMZ. The external router uses standard filtering to restrict external access to the bastion host and rejects any traffic that does not come from the bastion host.

In this configuration, a cracker wanting to access your network must subvert three separate devices without being detected. The internal network is effectively invisible to the Internet, because all packets leaving and entering go directly to the DMZ and not to your network. This arrangement makes it impossible for a cracker to gain information about your internal systems. Only the DMZ is advertised in routing tables and other Internet information. Thirdly, because this routing information is contained within the network, internal users cannot access the Internet without going through the bastion host.

Packets sent directly from the internal network cannot receive a reply from the Internet because there will be no routing tables to return the packet to the internal network from the Internet. This configuration prevents internal users from bypassing your security measures.

Defending Your Computer

While defending a network is an important step, each computer user should know how they can defend and secure their own computer. After all, it can only take one computer inside a network to compromise the entire network's security.

We will discuss various security steps you can take when using the Internet, ranging from securing your system to securing the data you transmit. The methods we'll discuss for securing your personal system include:

- Antivirus software

- Personal firewalls

- Internet Explorer security levels

Virus-Protection Software

The best defense an end-user has against a virus is to regularly run an industry-recognized, currently updated antivirus program on your client computer. *Antivirus software* identifies and removes viruses from your computer. Updates are important because even the best program will not protect you if its antivirus files are a year old.

Virus-scanning software uses *signature files* to recognize patterns that indicate viruses. Because new viruses appear often, manufacturers update these signature files frequently. Administrators should regularly update these files on their individual systems. Some virus software will download the latest file automatically. A virus-scanning program is only as effective as the signature file it uses.

Antivirus software is not included as a part of your computer's operating system, although some computer manufacturers do preinstall antivirus programs on their products. Antivirus programs for the Windows operating systems are sold by the companies listed in Table 12.1.

TABLE 12.1 Popular Antivirus Programs

Product	Company	URL
McAfee VirusScan	Network Associates	www.mcafee.com
Norton AntiVirus	Symantec	www.symantec.com
Panda AntiVirus	Panda Software	www.pandasoftware.com
Sophos Anti-Virus	Sophos	www.sophos.com
PC-cillin	Trend Micro	www.antivirus.com

Virus-scanning software is available for workstations and servers, and should be installed on both machine types to provide optimal protection. Because viruses do not affect OSI/RM Layer 1 and Layer 2 devices, virus-protection software is not required for devices such as cables, NICs, bridges, and hubs.

Antivirus software should be installed and run on all company servers. Antivirus software exists for specific Internet server applications, such as mail servers. Because viruses are often spread as e-mail attachments, server-based antivirus protection can be an effective way to prevent viruses from entering or leaving a computer network.

Using antivirus software is not effective unless you also follow some basic rules for safe computing. No antivirus program can provide complete protection, especially if the user does not follow the following recommended practices.

Install an antivirus program. Make sure you have a current antivirus program installed on your computer. Corporate IT departments often specify a standard antivirus application for office use.

Update your antivirus program regularly. Use your antivirus program's update features to download and install new signature files on a regular basis. In some programs, you can schedule automatic updates.

Scan your hard drives regularly. Your antivirus program can scan your hard drive for viruses on a regular basis. These automatic scans can also disinfect any files that contain viruses.

Scan floppy disks. Install antivirus programs that automatically scan floppy disks every time they are used.

Scan every executable attachment. If you receive an executable program from someone you do not know, do not execute it. Many antivirus programs can scan incoming mail messages, and disable or delete infected attachments.

Beware of unknown mail senders. If you receive an e-mail message and attachment from a user you do not know, do not run the attachment.

Keep your IT department informed. If you suspect a virus or detect unusual activity on your office or university system, inform the IT department immediately. Often, they can help you disinfect the system while they help prevent other users from being infected.

Personal Firewalls

If you use a direct Internet connection for your home computer, you should consider installing a *personal firewall* to protect your computer from crackers. A personal firewall is a smaller, inexpensive version of a full-scale corporate firewall that does not provide support for running or protecting internetworking servers. Like a corporate firewall, a personal firewall can use software and hardware to hide and protect one or more computers. Personal firewalls tend to be weaker than full-scale corporate firewalls, but they can provide a good level of protection by concealing your computer from other users.

Using a direct connection, such as a cable modem or DSL, means that your computer will keep its assigned IP address for as long as your computer is running. A direct connection can provide you with speedy Internet access, but it also provides crackers with speedy access to your computer.

There are users who often use scripts and application programs to scan many computers for open ports. These scripts and programs are widely available on the Internet, along with directions for their use. A popular name for those who use these tools is *script kiddies*, because there is little skill involved in downloading and running scan scripts.

Software-Based Personal Firewalls

A software-based personal firewall is a program that is installed on a user's computer. The software can perform packet-filtering to identify possible attacks. Firewall software can also make the computer's Internet ports appear closed to other users.

Several personal firewall programs for the Windows operating systems are sold by the companies listed in Table 12.2. Some of these programs also offer antivirus protection, privacy monitoring, and other features.

TABLE 12.2 Popular Personal Firewall Programs

Product	Company	URL
Black Ice Defender	Internet Security Systems	www.iss.net
McAfee Personal Firewall	Network Associates	www.mcafee.com
Norton Internet Security	Symantec	www.symantec.com
ZoneAlarm	ZoneLabs	www.zonelabs.com

The Microsoft Windows XP operating system includes a modest personal firewall feature. While this firewall is not as powerful as those listed above, it does provide some protection without installing an additional program.

You should not run personal firewall software on any desktop computer that is connected to a corporate network. Software-based personal firewalls can block various protocols that are used for network management. Your network servers need to see your computer on the network, and the firewall may make necessary Internet ports appear closed. A corporate laptop user may benefit from personal firewall software, especially if they connect to the Internet from home and other locations outside the office, where there is no hardware firewall protection.

Hardware-Based Personal Firewalls

Home users may also consider installing a hardware-based personal firewall, to use on its own or in combination with a software-based firewall. These hardware firewalls can be relatively inexpensive, and are sold under a variety of names, including *broadband routers*.

Hardware-based personal firewalls form a first line of defense, by obtaining an IP address from the ISP. The hardware firewall then uses Network Address Translation (NAT) to assign addresses to any internal computers that are connected to it using DHCP. NAT can foil basic cracker attacks, simply by concealing the actual IP address of any computers behind the firewall.

As the name broadband router implies, most hardware-based personal firewalls can connect several computers to a single Internet connection. Some hardware-based personal firewalls can also provide packet filtering. This feature can help the performance of software-based firewalls, because each computer's CPU will not have to scan the port numbers of the offending inbound packets. The hardware firewall will have already screened out these packets. More expensive devices designed for small businesses can also provide VPN services.

Configuring Browser Security

Web browsers also have their own security features. Netscape Navigator offers a security button on the toolbar to immediately determine whether a site is secure. Microsoft Internet Explorer offers safety levels to stop potentially dangerous material from downloading to your computer. These settings will often determine whether you can download active content, such as Java applets or ActiveX objects.

For each safety level, a certain action or request is handled, depending on the content of the web page. For example, if the *High* setting is selected as the security level, and a web page with active content is encountered, the active content will not display and the notification message shown in Figure 12.6 will appear. The High safety level setting does not give you the option to view the active content.

FIGURE 12.6 Microsoft Internet Explorer High security notification

If the *Medium* safety level setting is selected, you may receive a digital certificate message similar to that shown in Figure 12.7. You are given the option to download and install the content or decline the request.

FIGURE 12.7 Microsoft Internet Explorer Medium security warning

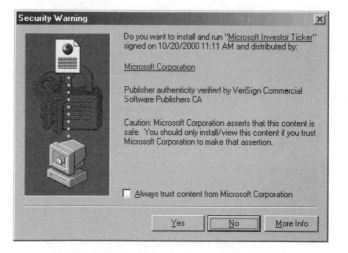

If *Low* is selected for the safety level, you will not be warned or receive any confirmation messages, and you will not be protected from most active content. You will still be prompted when downloading unsigned and unsafe ActiveX controls. The content that prompted the warning in the preceding figure is deemed safe, so with a low safety level setting, you would not be prompted with a warning.

If you are not denied access or prompted, then active web content will download and operate through your browser automatically. In the following exercise, you will learn how to set these security levels.

Setting Safety Levels on Microsoft Internet Explorer

In this exercise, you will change the security level for active content downloading with Internet Explorer. Because we are downloading ActiveX content, you must use Internet Explorer. Netscape Navigator does not support ActiveX.

1. Launch Internet Explorer.

2. Select the Tools menu and choose Internet Options. Click the Security tab.

3. Verify that the Internet zone is selected. Click the Custom Level button to set your security settings.

4. By default, your security settings are set to Medium, which warns you before running potentially damaging content.

5. In the Reset Custom Settings section, select High and click the Reset button. Select Yes to confirm that you want to change the security zone. The High setting prohibits you from downloading content that could damage your computer; this includes all ActiveX controls and plug-ins, as shown here:

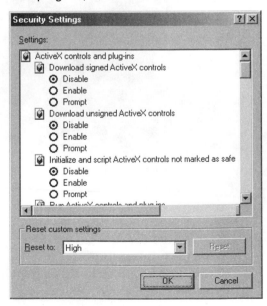

6. Click OK twice to return to your browser.

7. Browse the Web and notice the number of times you are warned about security. You will be unable to download most active content. For instance, visit `http://moneycentral.msn.com/investor/home.asp`. Locate and click the CNBC Ticker hypertext link. It may be on the lower-half of this web page, and will look like this.

You will be unable to download the ActiveX object.

8. When you are finished, reset your browser security level to Medium.

Safety levels are important for all web users. With the extremely rapid growth of the Internet, and the number of files and active programs transferred over it, security awareness will become increasingly important. You may find it annoying to be warned for every cookie or active content item you encounter, but the warnings will serve as a constant reminder of the importance of web security.

Defending Your Transmitted Data

Even if your network and computer are secure, your data may still be vulnerable. As we discussed in Chapter 11, text documents are the most basic form of communication on the Internet. While plaintext is used by default to transmit web and e-mail data, you can choose to secure the data you transmit by using different services and features:

- Encryption
- Secure Socket Layer (SSL)
- Identifying secure web forms
- Monitoring cookies
- Digital certificates

Encryption

Encryption is the encoding of data so that its contents are concealed while in transit. Encryption is the primary means to ensure privacy across the enterprise. This technique is often used to assist authentication efforts, as well. Encryption applications reduce the possibility of information theft, and dramatically reduce the risk by scrambling information using mathematical algorithms. Encrypted text cannot be understood by anyone without the correct encryption *key*, so even if your information is copied, there should be no risk to you. A key is a string of numbers used by software that scrambles your message from plain text, readable by anyone, into encrypted text.

Currently, you can choose from three encryption models: symmetric-key, asymmetric-key, and one-way. Symmetric-key encryption is the most familiar form of encryption, but for enterprise-wide communication, asymmetric-key and one-way encryption are also used.

Encryption always implies the use of algorithms. At the networking level, algorithms often create keys, or text strings, that scramble and descramble information. As you will see, generating and delivering these keys are critical issues.

Symmetric-Key Encryption

In *symmetric-key encryption*, a single key is used to encrypt and decrypt messages. Even though single-key encryption is a simple process, all parties must know and trust one another completely, and have confidential copies of the key. The first transmission of the key is crucial. If it is intercepted, the interceptor knows the key, and confidential material is no longer protected. Figure 12.8 illustrates single-key encryption.

FIGURE 12.8 Symmetric-key encryption

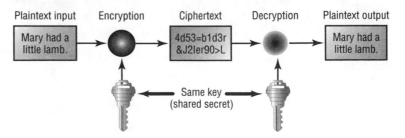

An example of a symmetric key is a simple password you use to log on to your Internet account at your ISP.

Although you can create a symmetric key with many different algorithms, the most common commercial algorithms are those provided by RSA, Inc. The specific algorithms include RC2 and RC4. Each of these methods can use keys between 40 and 128 bits. Contact www.rsasecurity.com for more information about the RC series of algorithms.

The benefits of symmetric encryption are its speed and strength. These features allow you to encrypt a large amount of information in less than a second. The drawbacks of a symmetric key are that all recipients and viewers must have the same key, and all users must have a secure way to retrieve the key.

However, to pass information across a public medium such as the Internet, users need a way to transfer this password key among themselves. In some cases, the users can meet and transfer the key physically. The problem is that network users cannot always meet with one another in person.

In addition to this concern, crackers can compromise symmetric keys that use passwords by using a *dictionary program*. A dictionary program is specifically written to break into a password-protected system. It has a relatively large list of common password names it repeatedly uses to gain access.

Another method of finding passwords is *password sniffing*. This is a method of intercepting the transmission of a password during the authentication process using a sniffer program designed to intercept passwords.

If the cracker has access to the office or building where the computer is stored, they may look for clues to the password. Although it is unwise, some users write their password somewhere near the computer, so they will not forget it.

Asymmetric-Key Encryption

Asymmetric-key encryption uses a key pair in the encryption process rather than the single key used in symmetric-key encryption. A key pair is a mathematically matched key set in which one key encrypts and the other key decrypts. Key A encrypts that which Key B decrypts; and Key B encrypts that which Key A decrypts.

An important aspect to this concept is that one of these keys is made public, whereas the other is kept private, as shown in Figure 12.9. The key that you publish is called a public key, and the key kept secret is the private key. Initially, you can distribute either key. However, once one key of the pair has been distributed, it must always remain public, and vice versa. Consistency is critical. Because one key is public, asymmetric encryption is also called public-key encryption.

FIGURE 12.9 Encrypting information into ciphertext, using public-key encryption

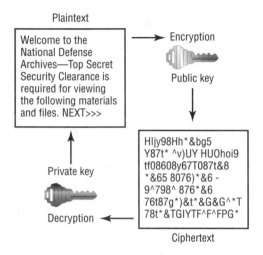

An example of asymmetric-key encryption is as follows: To send a secret message to Maria, you encrypt the message with Maria's public key, then send the encrypted text. When Maria receives the encrypted text, she will decrypt it with her private key. Anyone who intercepts the message cannot decrypt it without Maria's private key.

Although private and public keys are mathematically related to one another, determining the value of the private key from the public key is extremely difficult and time consuming.

One of the drawbacks of asymmetric-key encryption is that it is quite slow, owing to the intensive mathematical calculations the program requires. Even a rudimentary level of asymmetric encryption can require a great deal of time.

For communication over the Internet, the asymmetric-key system makes key management easier because the public key can be distributed while the private key stays secure with the user.

One-Way Encryption (Hash Encryption)

One-way encryption typically uses a hash table that contains a hash function. A hash is a table of hexadecimal numbers that are used used for encryption. One-way encryption is used for information that will not be decrypted or read. In this case, decryption is theoretically and mathematically impossible.

Permanent encryption may seem illogical and useless, but it is actually widely used. This is because one-way encryption allows someone to verify but not copy information. For example, an automated teller machine does not actually decrypt the personal identification number (PIN) entered by a customer. The magnetic stripe has the customer's code encrypted one-way. This one-way encryption is the hash code. The automated teller machine calculates the hash on the PIN that the customer enters, which yields a result. This result is then compared with the hash code on the card. By using this method, the PIN is secure, even from the automated teller machine and those who maintain it.

Pretty Good Privacy (PGP)

When individuals want to communicate securely over long distances, they generally use combinations of the encryption schemes described previously. For example, a program such as Pretty Good Privacy (PGP) (www.pgp.com) uses symmetric-key encryption to scramble the original message you want to send. Then, it uses asymmetric-key encryption to encrypt only the symmetric key you just used. Finally, PGP uses a hash code (one-way encryption) to "sign" the message and ensure that no one can tamper with it.

This combination employs the strengths of each encryption method. Asymmetric encryption is quite slow, but PGP and methods such as SSL use it only to encrypt the symmetric key, not the actual message. Because symmetric-key encryption is so fast, it encrypts the message itself. Hash encryption then signs the message efficiently. You will learn more about the details of SSL shortly.

E-mail applications such as Netscape Messenger, Microsoft Outlook Express, and Qualcomm Eudora Pro use the same combination. The main difference among the three is the algorithms they use to create the ciphertext.

Country-Specific Encryption Standards

You can create a key with many different algorithms. The most common commercial algorithms are those provided by RSA. Typical commercial encryption uses 40-bit or 128-bit keys. The more bits included in the key, the more difficult the message is to descramble without the correct key.

Different countries have different encryption policies; a global policy has yet to be agreed upon. For instance, the United States did not allow the export (not publication) of 128-bit encryption until 1999. Because 128-bit encryption can be extremely difficult and time consuming to descramble, the U.S. government felt it could be a potential security hazard if the encryption was used with malicious intent. Many countries, such as France, are stricter than the United States.

Some national governments want to establish their own key-escrow systems, and require any user or company using strong encryption (128-bit encryption or higher) to provide a copy of the decryption key to the government. The decryption key would be used only by authorities with a court order. You can read about this highly controversial issue at the Electronic Frontier Foundations website (`www.eff.org`).

Secure Sockets Layer (SSL)

The *Secure Sockets Layer (SSL)* protocol allows applications to privately exchange data over public networks, thereby preventing eavesdropping, tampering, and message forgery. SSL is a particularly elegant solution because it allows the transparent exchange of symmetric and asymmetric keys, allowing two parties to communicate without ever having to establish a prior relationship. SSL is not necessarily a Network-level protocol because it encrypts long-term sessions. However, because it is vital to secure transactions on the Web, it is a protocol you need to understand.

SSL enables two hosts to communicate over the network by authenticating with a *digital certificate*. A digital certificate is a specific form of an asymmetric key. Certificates provide authentication and assign responsibility. SSL also ensures message reliability using encryption and message digest. SSL is a thin layer above the transport protocol (usually TCP/IP). Specifically, it provides an extra layer of protection between the transport and session layers of the OSI. All browsers support SSL, so the applications using it need no special code for the SSL.

SSL 2.0 was originated by Netscape and became a standard in 1995. All major browsers, such as Netscape Navigator, Microsoft Internet Explorer, NCSA Mosaic, and Lotus Personal Web Browser, support SSL 3.0 (the current standard, which was defined in 1996). When you visit a website and are redirected to a secure site that uses Hypertext Transfer Protocol Secure (HTTPS), or you see `https://` in the address field, you are using SSL.

Secure Web Forms

Most business web pages encourage you to subscribe to, register for, or purchase something the business offers. These business web pages are usually directly or indirectly soliciting personal information. This type of information is often necessary for a business to be able to offer its products or services. If you enter information in a web form and submit it, how do you know that your personal data will be securely transmitted?

Many new web users may be unfamiliar with basic Internet security measures. Businesses should inform customers of potential risks associated with submitting information over the Internet, and should offer the customer the option to cancel submission.

If you are entering a secure site, your browser will display a locked icon on the bottom border of the window. The icon will resemble Figure 12.10. When you complete and submit a form on a secure website, SSL encryption is used to scramble the data between your computer and the web server. Therefore, even if your data is intercepted, it will be unreadable.

FIGURE 12.10   Locked security icon

 When a secure site loads into your browser, look closely at the URL. A secure site is identified by a URL beginning with https:// instead of http:// meaning it is using the *Hypertext Transfer Protocol Secure (HTTPS)* protocol to access a secure web server. The session is then managed by a security protocol. For instance, https://login.yahoo.com is a secure site, but http://www.yahoo.com is not.

Cookies

Cookies are small text files placed on a website visitor's computer so website managers can gain marketing information about their visitors, and can customize their website to a visitor's preferences. Cookies are also called persistent client-side information, because they are settings that can be made and saved to your web browser by a web server.

Cookies are not harmful to a computer. It is difficult for a cookie to contain an executable virus or worm program, as a cookie is simply a formatted string of text.

If users configure their browsers to allow cookie downloads from a website, then each time a user revisits that site, the user's computer will send the cookie to the web server at the moment they revisit the site. The cookie can inform the web server of the visitor's preferences, such as local news and favorite stocks, and which sections of the site the visitor has previously navigated. Cookies are connected to a database entry on the server site. These types of cookies enable the issuing cookie authority to customize distribution of its web content to the visitor's operating system and browser.

The cookie is stored in a specific directory on your computer. Cookies are considered to be so secure that both Internet Explorer and Netscape Navigator allow them by default. However, both browsers allow you to control cookie functions. Depending on security settings, the browser warns users before accepting a cookie, and then allows them to view, restrict or disable cookies completely.

Some of the personal firewall software we have discussed can also manage which cookies are saved on your computer. Microsoft Internet Explorer introduced a privacy management system in version 6 of their software. This system can use the privacy settings published by websites to manage cookies.

Digital Certificates

For SSL to work, a certificate server must generate and authenticate certificates. A digital certificate is an electronic identification card that is used in conjunction with public key encryption. *Digital certificates* verify the sender's identity. A trusted third party, called the certificate authority (CA), is responsible for verifying the legitimacy of the digital certificate.

Digital certificates contain the following data about the certificate owner:

- Name, company, and address
- Public key
- Certificate serial number
- Dates the certificate is valid
- Identification of the certifying company
- Digital signature of the certifying company

Digital certificates contain digital signatures to ensure a message has not been altered during transmission from the sender. The typical implementation of a digital signature is as follows.

1. Kent first reduces his message using a hash algorithm, then encrypts his message with his private key. He has created an encrypted file that contains a distinct signature. This digital signature is an encrypted digest of the text that is sent with the text message.

2. Lisa receives the message and decrypts the digital signature with Kent's public key. This decryption allows Lisa to verify the digital signature by recomputing the signature's hash value and comparing it with the received signature's hash value. If the values match, the message has not been altered, and is authenticated.

The digital signature does not ensure authentication. Authentication requires a digital certificate verified by a CA.

Summary

In this chapter, we discussed many aspects of Internet security, which concerns ensuring the safety of computers connected to the Internet. We defined four kinds of network assets that must be secured: local resources, network resources, server resources, and information resources. We then discussed how crackers attempt to gain access to computers by using discovery, penetration, and control techniques, including various kinds of attacks.

We paid particular attention to the most common type of attacks, denial-of-service (DoS), viruses, and worms. A DoS attack uses one or more hosts to flood another host with packets, preventing legitimate users from accessing that host. A virus is program code that is downloaded to another computer in an attempt to make its user lose control. A worm is similar to a virus, but it tries to use a system's resources to the point of failure.

We then discussed various methods of defending your network, starting with an audit. Auditing helps identify potentially vulnerable network assets through status quo, risk, and threat analyses. Authentication helps verify who has access to network assets by verifying what they know, who they are, or what they have.

Firewalls play an important part of network security by combining software, hardware, and policies to control LAN access to the Internet. A firewall can include a packet filter to remove incoming packets that are accessing protected services. Proxy servers use circuit-level and application-level gateways. Virtual private networking provides a secure means for authorized users to tunnel through a firewall. We presented four different firewall models: packet filter, single-homed and dual-homed bastions, and screened-subnet. The last three kinds use a dedicated proxy server computer called a bastion as a choke-point for traffic.

We then discussed how users can defend their own computers. Antivirus software can help identify and remove infected files before they are executed. Users can create their own personal firewalls with hardware and software. Internet Explorer lets users set security levels to block content.

Users should also protect the data they send to the Internet, as by default, much Internet data is sent as plaintext. Plaintext is easily readable by crackers who intercept a transmission. Encryption can scramble data so it cannot be easily read. Various means are available for encrypting e-mail and web data. Secure Socket Layer (SSL) is an encryption method that can be combined with Hypertext Transfer Protocol Secure (HTTPS) to encrypt web forms and sessions. Websites can use cookies to save information to a user's computer, but the user can manage these cookies using browsers and software. Digital certificates can also be used to verify identities on the Internet.

Exam Essentials

Understand security.   Security concerns the safeguarding of network assets, including local, network, server, and information resources.

Know what a cracker is and explain the process crackers use to enter systems without authorization.   A cracker is someone who tries to gain unauthorized access to a computer or network. Such access may violate company policies, as well as local, regional, and national laws. Crackers use a three-step process of discovery, penetration, and control.

Be able to identify various types of cracker attacks.   Crackers use a variety of attacks to gain entry to a system or network, including spoofing or masquerade, man-in-the-middle (hijacking), insider, brute-force, trapdoor, replay, Trojan horse, and social-engineering techniques.

Understand a denial-of-service (DoS) attack. In a DoS attack, repeated messages or packet floods are used to keep a server busy, thus denying service to legitimate users. A distributed denial-of-service attack (DDoS) uses multiple computers to send packet floods.

Understand computer viruses and worms. A virus is a program that, when downloaded and executed on a host, can damage or interfere with that computer. Viruses can appear in macro, executable, boot sector, stealth, or polymorphic form. A worm is like a virus, but it tries to consume resources until it shuts down the computer.

Understand the audit process. The audit process uses status quo, risk and threat analysis to identify vulnerable network assets.

Know authentication principles. Authentication is the ability to determine a user's identity, based on what they know, what they have, or who they are.

Understand a packet filter and what it does. A packet filter examines each of the headers for information such as port numbers, and discards packets that do not conform to policies. Most routers can perform packet-filtering, so this is usually a first-line method of network defense.

Understand proxy servers and how they operate. A proxy server replaces an IP address with a contingent address. Circuit-level gateways are used to create this effect. An application-level gateway filters packets based upon the applications that use or create them, by examining the packet's port number and content.

Know what a Virtual Private Network (VPN) does. A VPN allows secure communication between hosts by using a tunneling protocol. VPNs can allow external users to safely penetrate firewalls and access internal systems.

Be able to list and discuss the four major types of firewalls. A firewall uses software, hardware, and network policies to protect a LAN from the Internet. Packet filters are one type of firewall. Single-homed bastions use a single computer to screen all Internet communications. A dual-homed bastion uses a computer with two NICs to protect the internal network. A screened-subnet firewall uses a bastion and a proxy server to protect network computers. This model also creates a demilitarized zone (DMZ) that can host internetworking servers.

Know how to protect your computer from virus attacks. You can use an antivirus program to scan and delete viruses on your computer. You should also follow safe computing practices, including file and disk scanning and not opening e-mail attachments from unknown senders.

Understand and explain personal firewalls. A personal firewall is a combination of hardware, software, and policies designed to protect home systems, especially those that use direct connections to the Internet.

Know the three major types of encryption. Encryption is the encoding of data to conceal its contents by using one or more keys that a recipient requires to decode the data. Symmetric-key encryption uses a single key. Asymmetric encryption uses a pair of mathematically-matched keys. One-way encryption cannot be used to decrypt information, but can be used to verify encrypted information.

Understand Secure Sockets Layer, and how it can be used to protect web data. The Secure Sockets Layer protocol is used to encrypt data that is transmitted from web forms to a web server. SSL can also be used to transmit secure data from a server to a browser.

Know what cookies are and understand their purpose. Cookies are small formatted text files that are saved to a web client by a web server. Cookies can be used to save the state of a session, to save a user's preferences, or to help a website tailor its marketing toward a particular user.

Understand the purpose of a digital certificate. A digital certificate is used to verify identity on the Internet. Digital certificates can be used with SSL to prove that the identity of a web server is as it claims to be.

Key Terms

Before you take the exam, be certain you are familiar with the following terms:

antivirus software	auditing
application-level gateways	boot sector
asymmetric-key encryption	brute-force attacks

circuit-level gateway

cookies

cracker

demilitarized zone (DMZ)

denial-of-service (DoS) attacks

dictionary program

digital certificate

distributed denial-of-service (DDoS) attack

dual-homed bastion

encryption

firewall

front-door attacks

hijacking

Hypertext Transfer Protocol Secure (HTTPS)

insider attacks

IP Security (IPSec)

key

Layer-2 Tunneling Protocol (L2TP)

man-in-the-middle attacks

Network Address Translation (NAT)

network assets

one-way encryption

packet filter

packet-filtering firewall

password sniffing

personal firewall

ping flood

Point-to-Point Tunneling Protocol (PPTP)

replay attack

script kiddies

Secure Sockets Layer (SSL)

security

signature files

single-homed bastion

smart card

social-engineering attack

spoofing attacks

strong authentication

symmetric-key encryption

SYN flood

system snooping

TCP handshake

trapdoor attacks

Trojan horse attack

tunneling protocols

virus

worm

Review Questions

1. Which one of the following choices is not a network asset?

   A. Local resources

   B. Network resources

   C. Server resources

   D. Message resources

2. What kind of virus executes differently each time it is run?

   A. Web

   B. Executable

   C. Polymorphic

   D. Macro

3. A SYN flood is best described as which one of the following attacks?

   A. Social-engineering

   B. Denial-of-service

   C. Masquerade

   D. Accidental

4. Which device does not pass an outgoing packet from one network to another, to help shield the network address of the originating computer?

   A. Circuit-level gateway

   B. Application-level gateway

   C. Proxy server

   D. Certificate server

5. Amanda uses a cable modem to connect the Internet to her home computer. What is the most appropriate type of security system that she can install to protect her computer from common Internet attacks?

   A. Web browser

   B. Subnet-screened firewall

   C. Personal firewall

   D. VPN

6. Which one of the following choices is the first step in an auditing scheme?

   A. Risk analysis

   B. Status quo analysis

   C. Threat analysis

   D. Critical analysis

7. Which of the following is an example of the "What you have" method of authentication?

   A. Password

   B. Fingerprint

   C. Voice

   D. Smart card

8. Which one of the following terms means that only one key is used to encrypt and decrypt a message?

   A. Symmetric-key encryption

   B. Asymmetric-key encryption

   C. Hash encryption

   D. One-way encryption

9. Which of the following protocol types encapsulates a data packet into another packet?

   A. Cocoon protocol

   B. Tunneling protocol

   C. Fragmentation protocol

   D. Extension protocol

10. Which item from the following list does not require antivirus software?

    A. Operating system

    B. E-mail program

    C. Network Interface Card

    D. Word processor program

11. Which one of the following firewalls creates a demilitarized zone between an internal network and a WAN?

    A. Packet filter

    B. Single-homed bastion

    C. Dual-homed bastion

    D. Screened-subnet

12. Grant is attempting to crack a network system. He is targeting the network assets that are too weak to withstand some of his cracking tools. What stage of the cracker process is described here?

    A. Control

    B. Penetration

    C. Discovery

    D. Definition

13. Julie uses a diagnostic account on the server to check network performance each day. She executes several programs to perform these checks. One day, she notices that the diagnostic account was used to

delete several accounting files from the system. She also notices that one of her diagnostic programs was replaced the previous evening. What kind of attack has occurred?

A. Replay

B. Worm

C. Trapdoor

D. Hijacking

14. Which one of the following statements best describes a cookie?

A. Small text files placed on a website visitor's computer.

B. Applications that a user installs on their computer to enhance website viewing.

C. Small files that are used to confirm an e-mail message.

D. Small text files that enhance the download of streaming media files.

15. Which protocol is used to protect data sent by secure web forms?

A. Hypertext Transfer Protocol

B. Secure Sockets Layer

C. Secure MIME

D. Hypertext Markup Language

16. Which one of the following choices best describes authentication?

A. Verifying the identity of the person who developed a website

B. Verifying the identity of a user who is logging on to a computer system

C. Identifying a third person or organization to verify the identity of party sending information

D. Identifying a third person or organization to verify the identity of party receiving information

17. Franklin believes his computer system has a virus. Which one of the following actions should he perform first?

    A. E-mail all his colleagues to warn them about the virus.

    B. Copy any documents he has open to another computer so he can continue working on them.

    C. Run an antivirus program to disinfect his computer.

    D. He should let the virus execute on his computer.

18. Which of the following poses a security risk when sending information over the Internet?

    A. Cookies stored on your hard drive

    B. Digital certificates

    C. Plaintext password transmission

    D. Websites that use HTTPS

19. Which one of the following technologies is used to restrict unauthorized users and prevent unauthorized export of private or proprietary data on a LAN?

    A. Firewall

    B. Browser security alert

    C. Digital certificate

    D. Encryption

20. Hypertext Transfer Protocol Secure (HTTPS) allows users to do which one of the following?

    A. Create digital certificates

    B. Make a secure connection to a web server

    C. Send secure e-mail messages across a LAN

    D. Prevent unauthorized access to a LAN

Answers to Review Questions

1. **D.** Individual messages are not a network asset. Local resources are workstations. Network resources include transmission media. Server resources include internetworking servers.

2. **C.** A polymorphic virus changes its execution pattern or signature to avoid detection.

3. **B.** A SYN flood is an example of a DoS attack, in which the attacker is attempting to limit authorized access to a computer by sending multiple messages to that computer. In social-engineering, an authorized user is tricked into revealing sensitive information that may allow network access. In a masquerade attack, the attacker spoofs or changes legitimate data to enter a network. SYN floods are usually not accidental; they are deliberately staged to disable a network or server.

4. **A.** A certificate server issues digital certificates. Proxy servers help shield internal networks by using circuit-level and application-level gateways to block packets to an external network.

5. **C.** A personal firewall can provide effective protection against cracker attacks, without the expense of an enterprise firewall. A web browser does not protect a computer from attacks. A VPN encrypts data, and does not provide firewall protection against attacks.

6. **B.** Status quo analysis is the first step, in which the auditor determines the current level of security at the site. Risk analysis is the second step, and threat analysis is the third step. There is no step that is called critical analysis.

7. **D.** A smart card is a physical item that a user must present during authentication. A password is something that a user knows. Voice and fingerprint identification are examples of the "who you are" method of authentication.

8. **A.** Symmetric-key encryption uses a single key for encryption and decryption. Asymmetric-key encryption uses a key pair. Hash or one-way encryption is sometimes called one-way encryption; it uses a single key but does not allow decryption.

9. **B.** A tunneling protocol allows different networking protocols to be encapsulated and sent within another protocol. Tunneling protocols are used in Virtual Private Networks (VPNs).

10. C. A NIC operates at Layer 2 of the OSI/RM; it places and receives data from a transmission medium. Layer 2 does not require virus protection, because we are dealing with the actual transmission of datagrams and packets. Antivirus programs must work at levels that allow them access to the actual data that is being transmitted. E-mail and word-processing programs work at Layer 7, the Application level. Operating systems work at several layers.

11. D. The screened-subnet creates a secure subnet between an external and an internal router. Packet filters merely review content and discard any violating packets. Single-homed and dual-homed bastions sit on the LAN behind a packet-filtering router.

12. B. Grant is attempting to penetrate this system. He has already discovered the network, and needs to penetrate one or more network assets to gain control.

13. C. This describes a trapdoor attack, in which one of the diagnostic programs was replaced by an intruder to delete the files. A replay attack uses captured data that has been altered to enter a system. A worm consumes system resources until the computer can no longer function. In a hijacking, packets are intercepted between hosts.

14. A. Cookies are small text files that a web server places on a web client's computer to store information.

15. B. SSL is used to manage symmetric and asymmetric-key encryption on web sessions. HTTP is used to download web documents from a web server. Secure MIME is used to encrypt e-mail messages. HTML is the language used for formatting web documents.

16. B. Authentication is the ability to determine a system user's true identity. This can be done by checking what they know, what they have, or who they are.

17. C. Franklin should use an antivirus program to remove the virus from his computer. He should not e-mail anyone until the virus is removed, because some viruses are transmitted by e-mail messages. He should not copy his open documents to another computer, because this may also transmit the virus.

18. C. When passwords are transmitted as plaintext, anyone with a network analyzer program can intercept and read them.

19. A.   A firewall controls user access to networks with a combination of software, hardware, and policies. A browser security alert is a dialog box that appears to remind the user they may be transmitting data on an unsecure connection. A digital certificate is used to confirm identity. Encryption encodes a message so that it is difficult to read if intercepted.

20. B.   HTTPS provides secure connections to web servers. They do not protect LANs or issue digital certificates.

Chapter 13

E-Commerce Fundamentals

THE CIW EXAM OBJECTIVE GROUPS COVERED IN THIS CHAPTER:

- ✓ Define e-commerce, including technologies and concepts.
- ✓ Identify project management issues associated with developing a corporate website.

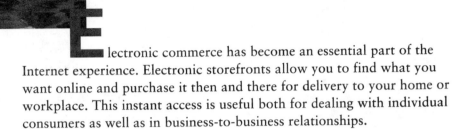

Electronic commerce has become an essential part of the Internet experience. Electronic storefronts allow you to find what you want online and purchase it then and there for delivery to your home or workplace. This instant access is useful both for dealing with individual consumers as well as in business-to-business relationships.

The Certified Internet Webmaster (CIW) program tests individuals on the most important aspects of electronic commerce including project management. In order to be able to manage a project of any size, you must be able to implement solid skills and procedures and stay on top of all aspects of the venture. It is important to understand the ramifications that result anytime one portion of a project exceeds the resources originally allotted to it—whether that be in terms of time, cost, or any other perceptible resource.

In this chapter, you will learn these e-commerce basics.

Electronic Commerce (E-Commerce)

Electronic commerce, or *e-commerce*, is becoming a competitive necessity for business owners. As the Internet becomes more accessible to the global population, it brings electronic commerce to new levels. Electronic commerce on the Internet is commonly referred to as *Internet commerce*, *web commerce*, or *e-commerce*.

In this chapter, you will establish the fundamental background for understanding the web commerce model and discuss the advantages of deploying a web commerce infrastructure. You will also discuss the various aspects of ensuring that a traditional business can be e-commerce–enabled.

Evolving a business into a web storefront can be deceptively simple. However, if the goals and expectations of the business are not well defined, the transition may produce poor results. The Web provides everything needed to transform a business into an e-commerce–enabled organization.

Definition of Electronic Commerce

Commerce can be defined as the exchange of goods and services for fees on a large scale. With few exceptions, the fees so far consist of currency (checks, bank drafts, credit card transactions, or other equity that is understood by all parties to have monetary value). Traditionally, data management for transactions was limited to manual or computer-based bookkeeping, and security was largely absent in the traditional transaction model.

Electronic commerce was previously defined as commerce conducted via any electronic medium. Issues such as data management and security were well understood. The Internet, however, has forced us to reconsider the definition to a certain degree. Electronic commerce can be conducted on the Internet, but special care must be taken with data management and security.

These main elements of electronic commerce can be described as follows:

Communication   These services support the transfer of information between the buyer and the seller. Unlike traditional transactions, the communication aspects extend beyond sharing the same spoken language (or using a translator) to sharing the same digital language.

Data management   These services define the exchange format of the information. In the classic sense, data management also includes the databases involved, the catalog, customers, orders, etc. Under CIW definitions, data management can also include a common digital language to successfully complete electronic transactions.

Security   These mechanisms authenticate the source of information and guarantee the integrity and privacy of the information. Security mechanisms are of paramount importance because, unlike traditional transactions, electronic transactions do not require the buyer and seller to be physically close.

Therefore, electronic commerce must be defined on a broader scope: it is the integration of communications, data management, and security capabilities that allows organizations to exchange information related to the sale of goods and services.

Electronic vs. Traditional Commerce

Electronic commerce differs from traditional commerce in the way information is exchanged and processed. Traditionally, information was exchanged via direct person-to-person contact, or through the use of telephones or the postal system. In electronic commerce, information is carried through an electronic medium such as a computer system operating over an electronic network.

In traditional commerce, participating individuals act on information accompanying a typical business transaction. In electronic commerce, manual presence is limited and almost the entire process is automated.

Electronic commerce uses various business support services, including e-mail, online directories, ordering and logistical support systems, settlement support systems, inventory control systems, and management information and statistical reporting systems. These services, provided by the merchant, are called *merchant systems*.

In traditional commerce systems, the participating entities are physically close. *Nonrepudiation (the ability to prove that a transaction took place)* and authentication can be verified by asking for a receipt and a standard identification item such as a driver's license or a passport. The electronic commerce infrastructure does not lend itself to this model: Nonrepudiation and authentication must be provided digitally. Digital signatures and encryption frameworks have been developed to address security issues.

E-Commerce Types

There are two models of e-commerce: the business-to-business model and the business-to-consumer model.

The Business-to-Business Model   In the business-to-business model, commerce is conducted between two businesses. For example, consider a Fortune 500 company that wants to allow its employees to purchase sundry items such as staplers, tape, and so forth online. It can set up a memorandum of understanding with an office supplier and allow employees to access the supplier's Internet site to make purchases. This type of model is characterized by *high-volume, lower-price* margins (i.e., 100 consumers buying a stack of adhesive notes at $1.25 each).

The Business-to-Consumer Model   In the business-to-consumer model, commerce is conducted between a business entity and a consumer (e.g., a home user on a PC). For example, consider the practice of buying books or CDs on the Internet. The consumer accesses the business' Internet site and purchases products. The business-to-consumer model is characterized by *low-volume*, *higher-price* margins (i.e., one consumer buying a CD or book costing more than $20). Although the price margins are higher than in the business-to-business model, they are often lower than going to a retail outlet to purchase the same product.

EDI and SET

There are two important technologies that set the standards for e-commerce—EDI and SET. The following sections discuss these technologies and the importance of each.

Electronic Data Interchange (EDI)

If electronic commerce is to succeed, a standard method of transferring information between computers and companies is necessary. *Electronic Data Interchange (EDI)* is such a standard. EDI establishes the format for electronic documents exchanged between participating computers.

EDI is defined as the interorganization exchange of documents in standardized electronic form directly between participating computers. EDI can be thought of as an electronic replacement of many paper-based transactions; it is primarily used for purchase orders and invoices.

EDI is designed to standardize electronic commerce among business organizations. To that extent, its goals are as follows:

- To enable easy and inexpensive communication of structured information throughout the lifetime of an electronic transaction.

- To reduce the amount of data capture and transcriptions; this reduction will improve processes due to fewer errors, less time spent handling errors, and fewer delays due to incorrect and/or unformatted data.

- To ensure faster handling of transactions and get an equivalent increase in cash flow.

The overall penetration of EDI so far has been limited. E-commerce might act as a catalyst to start EDI, because agreeing on a standardized document exchange is key to expanding e-commerce. In the past few years, EDI has found a niche in certain specific industry groups, including automotive, retail, chemical, electronics, electrical, petroleum, metals, paper, and office products. The widespread use of EDI has been hampered due to lack of a standardized document exchange format. Each industry used its own flavor of EDI.

The advent of the Internet and the resulting e-commerce push has done more to standardize EDI than any previous initiative. Today, EDI messages are encoded in a standard data format governed by ANSI X12 and UN/EDIFACT specifications.

Besides lack of standardization, cost has also been a mitigating factor in establishing EDI as a prominent vehicle for data interchange. In the past, EDI was deemed costly to implement. That perception seems to be changing now as EDI matures and becomes a standard. As e-commerce grows and becomes more far-reaching, EDI will be increasingly important in binding the different elements of electronic commerce together.

Companies or industries that possess one or more of the following characteristics are strong candidates for conversion to EDI:

- Handle a large volume of repetitive standard transactions

- Operate on a very tight margin

- Face strong competition, requiring significant productivity improvements

- Operate in a time-sensitive environment

- Have received requests from partner companies to convert to EDI

Secure Electronic Transaction (SET)

EDI is not the only standard used for electronic transactions. There are several other protocols that work either in place of or in conjunction with EDI to make electronic transactions possible; one of which is the *Secure Electronic Transaction (SET)*, which could represent a substantial advance in security and capabilities for e-commerce. Although SET is not widely used currently because it has recently emerged from the test phase, it offers significant capabilities. SET will probably become the predominant protocol for both business-to-consumer and business-to-business e-commerce.

SET is a standard protocol currently used on the Internet to secure online credit card payments. In a given transaction, all three parties involved must use the SET protocol: the user, the merchant, and the bank.

SET was first proposed by MasterCard. Visa originally had a competing protocol but later tests showed the MasterCard proposal to be superior. With a few minor modifications, the proposal has now been endorsed by both MasterCard and Visa.

Tests were conducted by MasterCard, IBM, and NationsBank to run several live transactions using the protocol for verification purposes. Simultaneously, the protocol has been deployed in Japan, Switzerland, and Denmark, where it is widely used on a commercial basis.

Principal Features of SET

The first primary feature of the SET protocol is enhanced identification. The only identification required by the protocol is on the part of the server. SET requires that all participants have certificates for definite identification.

Currently, a significant opportunity for fraud exists, not just by consumers but by merchants as well. Requiring all transactions to be signed and identified by each participant at each step of the process greatly reduces the potential for fraud. In fact, by requiring cryptographic identification, the authentication will actually surpass that of non-electronic transactions. The high potential for fraud forces merchants conducting e-commerce with credit cards to assume the risk.

Additionally, the use of SET may help merchants avoid the higher percentages charged by the acquirer for e-commerce transactions. For example, in a conventional, "card present" credit card transaction, the merchant is typically subject to a charge between 1 percent and 3 percent. The fee for "card not present" transactions (the classification currently used for Internet credit card transactions) is often in the 6 percent to 12 percent range. MasterCard and Visa have indicated that transactions from companies using SET will be classified as "card present" transactions due to the strong authentication. This fee reclassification will represent a significant cost savings to merchants.

The second differentiating characteristic of the SET protocol is that the merchant never sees the credit card number. All credit card information from the consumer is sent encrypted to the merchant's bank only. The merchant never gets an opportunity to abuse, either deliberately or inadvertently, the credit card or transaction information.

The third advantage of SET is that it requires that all sensitive information among all parties must be encrypted and signed. This encryption is used to achieve four goals: data confidentiality, data integrity, authentication, and nonrepudiation.

Finally, because the SET protocol was designed specifically for use in financial transactions, it also supports such activities as credits, returning of goods, reversing authorizations when a product is not available, and charge-backs. These credit card situations currently cause difficulties with most *payment gateways*. Including them in the protocol alleviates this problem.

Advantages of E-Commerce

E-commerce has the potential to markedly increase the speed, accuracy and efficiency of business and personal transactions. Establishing a web store-front can be as simple as leasing a T1 line with Internet access. Compare this to the costs associated with leasing and upkeep of a prime real-estate parcel.

The benefits of e-commerce include the following:

- Instant and ubiquitous availability. The storefront is open continu-ously and is accessible to a global audience.

- A streamlined buyer-to-seller relationship with simplified communi-cation channels and direct interaction.

- Reduced paperwork for a greater concentration on customer needs.

- Reduced errors, time, and overhead costs in information processing without requirements for re-entering data.

- Reduced time to complete business transactions (specifically, reduced time from delivery to payment).

- Easier entry into new markets, especially geographically remote markets. For instance, a web storefront selling Persian rugs can be accessed with the same URL from the Middle East and from North America.

- New business opportunities as entrepreneurs develop innovative ways to use the Internet for commerce.

- Improved market analysis. The large base of Internet users can be targeted for the distribution of surveys to analyze the marketability of a new product or service idea.

- Wider access to assistance and advice from experts and peers.

- Improved product analysis, as businesses are able to collect, collate, and publish product information over the Internet.

- Streamlined and automated purchasing processes. Companies allow customers to generate and send purchase orders online, minimizing the costs associated with handling sales orders.

Issues in E-Commerce

So far, you have studied the ways in which e-commerce is beneficial to both the consumer and the producer. However, e-commerce also presents some issues that require careful consideration before implementing a site.

E-commerce may lead to a greater degree of vulnerability. With the introduction of Internet transactions—which include names, addresses, and credit card numbers of buyers—the potential for fraud increases.

Other issues to consider include the following:

Intellectual property Protecting intellectual property becomes a problem when it is so easy to copy material from other sites.

Security Mechanisms to pay online merchants for goods and services add a degree of risk because financial information must be sent over the public network. The confidential transmission of data, authentication of the parties involved, and the integrity of order data and payment instructions are all components of the new electronic business model.

Taxation Suppose a web user living in Illinois purchases some goods from a web store hosted in California. Is sales tax charged? If so, is it Illinois or California sales tax?

Customs The Internet spans national boundaries. Is it lawful to buy a product that is outlawed in your country from a website hosted in another country where that product is legal? Given that some governments restrict the export of cryptography technology, will some countries' products be more secure than others' when cryptography is used?

Regulations Government bodies and regulators may enforce restrictions that invade privacy or hinder security.

Fraud The U.S. Electronic Funds Transfer Act stipulates that a maximum of $50 can be charged to the cardholder in cases of fraud. In e-commerce, what legal actions protect cardholders in cases of unauthorized or fraudulent transactions?

Trust If a web storefront is easy to establish, it is equally easy to dismantle. In traditional transactions, the buyer and seller see each other before completing the transaction. How does a newly opened web storefront assure its customers that it will still be there the next time they visit or if the product malfunctions?

Ubiquitous availability If availability is an advantage, it is also a risk. What happens to lost business opportunities through the disruption of service?

The following sections discuss some of these and other issues relevant to e-commerce.

Multi-Language Support

You should consider multi-language support on your e-commerce site. Website visitors from other countries may avoid your site if it is not localized in their language, and they will probably never become customers. You must determine whether translating your site into other languages is cost effective. Usually only large organizations, such as governments and international conglomerates, can afford to translate. The costs of translating a site will vary. If your site is a candidate, you can hire a translator, or use software or translation tools located on the Internet. If you use software or Internet sites for translation, be aware that the vocabularies are limited and often translate language out of context.

Another multi-language option is *Unicode*, which is a text and script character that can interchange, process, and display text of most of the world's languages. Unicode is a format for text files that can be translated by a user's interface, such as a browser. Provided that web pages are created using Unicode and a browser supports Unicode, the website can be translated into almost any language in the world. The Unicode Standard is currently in its third version and might one day replace ASCII, which is the most common text file format used on the Internet.

Visitor Tracking

Monitoring visitors to your website can help you make important decisions about your site. Counters are available to clock visitor access, and code can be written to provide information about a visitor's actions during a visit to the site.

Using this collection process, a business (such as an online book publisher) can collect visitor information. All or any part of it can be relayed to the correct party. Statistics showing the number of hits can go to management, whereas statistics related to customer inquiries can go directly to the sales department.

Visitor tracking can be customized by a programmer or webmaster to track virtually any aspect of a website. If certain pages are never accessed by visitors, those pages may need to be modified, moved, or removed. If no one is visiting your site, your company may need a new promotion to attract visitors.

For example, visitor tracking can reveal the time periods during which visitors access your site:

```
For the 24 hours covered on 31-Jan-01:
 5 a.m.    —    6 a.m.    =     23 visitors
 6 a.m.    —    7 a.m.    =     35 visitors
 7 a.m.    —    8 a.m.    =     42 visitors
 8 a.m.    —    9 a.m.    =     69 visitors
 9 a.m.    —   10 a.m.    =    105 visitors
10 a.m.    —   11 a.m.    =    323 visitors
```

If you are interested in the early-morning web-browsing population, you may want to add a news section to your site. Most web server applications are equipped with visitor-tracking software.

International Currencies

It is important to consider international currencies. Customers from other countries may not be able to pay you with your local currency. You must be prepared to accept multiple currencies or lose part of your potential customer base. Most high-end e-commerce applications, such as IBM Net.Commerce, provide multiple currency support. If you have a small website with moderate business, you can use a currency converter on the Web for calculations, then visit your local bank for actual cash conversions.

International Shipping and Supply

If you are shipping products, you must consider international issues. Because an e-commerce site opens your business to the world, you must be able to efficiently ship your products worldwide.

First, consider shipping costs. It may become costly to ship your products from one location to all your customers. Many companies distribute their products from several hubs on different continents. Although the initial costs are more expensive, this approach may reduce costs over time. If you use a distributed shipping method, you must also consider the ramifications of resupplying your distribution centers with your products.

Secondly, you must ensure that delivery services, such as DHL or FedEx, can deliver to your customer destinations. If a customer from a remote area orders your product, how will you deliver it?

Payment Processing

Payment processing is fundamental to the success of an e-commerce site. The merchant must verify and transfer funds from the consumer's credit card, checking account, ATM card, or smart card to the bank. Approval must be quick so the merchant can expedite shipment of the order and still be sure of getting paid.

Most merchant software for e-commerce provides payment-processing software.

Generally speaking, the three models for payment in electronic commerce are:

- The cash model
- The check model
- The credit model

A fourth payment method, the smart card, is slowly gaining industry acceptance. Smart cards are far more common in Europe and Asia than in the United States. Smart cards will be discussed in this section.

The Cash Model

The cash model, or e-cash, is the easiest to understand, albeit the hardest to implement in the web infrastructure. E-cash can be visualized as the minting of electronic money or tokens. In electronic cash schemes, buyers and sellers trade electronic value tokens, which are issued or backed by some third party, usually an established bank.

The consumer buys the digital equivalent of money from an established bank and deposits it in his or her digital wallet, which is stored on the PC. When the consumer makes a purchase from a website that accepts e-cash, the ordering software will automatically deduct the requisite amount from the consumer's digital wallet. The advantage is that during a transaction, the transfer of funds is immediate and no back-end processing is required.

One of the vendors at the forefront of e-cash is DigiCash (www.digicash.com).

The Check Model

Using this model, a consumer presents a digital version of a check to a web business. The digitized check is encrypted using the appropriate technologies. The web business verifies the check through its financial institution, which in turn consults the consumer's financial institution to ensure the availability of funds. The biggest disadvantage of this model, at least for the storefront, is that the funds are not transferred immediately.

Like the cash model, the check model operates on the assumption of a digital checkbook stored on the consumer's PC. When the consumer makes a purchase from a website that accepts electronic checks, the ordering software will automatically deduct the requisite amount from the consumer's digital checkbook. One of the leading vendors in this area is CheckFree (www.checkfree.com).

The Credit Model

The credit model fits well into the web infrastructure. Part of the reason is that existing credit card processing already uses much of the network infrastructure that is needed for e-commerce. For instance, when presented with a credit card, a merchant in a traditional transaction scans the card through a reader and in turn authorizes the transaction through a financial institution. This authorization may be performed over the existing phone network using modems.

In a web storefront, when a consumer enters the credit card number on a web order form, the Internet can deliver that information to an authorization server immediately. From there on, the transaction proceeds similarly in both the traditional and electronic commerce scenarios: Assuming that authorization succeeded, the consumer's credit account is charged for the purchase amount and the storefront is paid by the credit company.

The Smart Card

Imagine a card that replaces the magnetic strip with an integrated circuit for storing and/or processing data! Payment processing using *smart cards* is gaining global acceptance. Smart cards may eventually replace credit cards and ATM cards. Instead of using a magnetic strip on the back like ATM and credit cards, a smart card has a small integrated circuit inserted into it. This chip can contain several different technologies. Regardless of the specific type of technology inside it, a smart card is much more capable than an ATM or credit card.

Smart cards are about the same size as normal credit cards, although usually a bit thicker due to the integrated circuit. The electronic module, which can contain a CPU and/or memory, can allow you to receive, store, and transmit data over a network. Some smart cards can hold almost 100 times more information than a standard magnetic strip. In fact, certain types of smart cards, such as optical memory cards, can hold up to 4MB of information.

The chief benefit of a smart card is that it enhances the ability to verify a person's identity, a process that is known as *authentication*. Smart cards can store and update passwords and other security information for use on computer networks. For example, they can process encryption schemes to ensure secure communication, perform instantaneous currency conversion, and protect cellular communications from fraud. Smart cards can also process vast amounts of information that you can organize, store, and delete at will.

The main disadvantage of smart cards is their cost. Whereas it costs less than 10 cents (U.S.) to create and distribute a standard ATM card, a microprocessor card costs about $10. However, government programs and initiatives by companies such as Microsoft, IBM, and MasterCard promise to make smart cards more common. Also, Visa has announced the creation of GlobalPlatform, a forum established to standardize smart card technology globally.

Security

Security constitutes a major concern for a consumer conducting an electronic transaction: Will a credit card number be stolen? Will someone exploit the consumer's home address? Although these are valid questions, web transactions are at least as secure as traditional transactions in which consumers routinely hand their credit cards to waiters in restaurants or supply account numbers to vendors over the phone. What prevents a waiter or a phone vendor from noting the credit card number for future fraudulent charges?

Consumers should be made to feel secure about transmitting personal information over the Internet. This reassurance can come with using certificates that authenticate both parties in a transaction and encrypt the transaction. VeriSign (`www.verisign.com`) is a leading vendor in certificates. With a VeriSign certificate to authenticate the parties, and a technology embedded in web servers and browsers, called *Secure Sockets Layer (SSL)* to encrypt the traffic, web transactions can be made very secure.

PKI (Public Key Infrastructure) is a method of verifying and authenticating those involved in a transaction across the Internet. This can be accomplished via digital certificates or other means, but is crucial to successful electronic commerce.

In addition to these measures, teaching consumers about security issues is important. An educated consumer is better able to discern what measures are being taken and how to detect these measures to ensure the security and privacy of their own personal information.

E-Commerce Solutions

There are two main ways to establish a web storefront:

- In-house solution

- Instant storefront solution

In-House Solution

With this approach, a web business owner must buy, develop, and implement an e-commerce software package, a service platform, redundant Internet connections, secure payment-processing network connections, and 24-hour maintenance. Generally, only a large business with an IT staff that understands e-commerce can afford this solution.

The advantages of the in-house solution include:

- Complete control of the hardware and software infrastructure

- Easier integration into existing back-end enterprise systems

The in-house solution also allows complete control of *online cataloging*—the process of creating a catalog of data; the catalog then becomes a searchable index that is available online. An online catalog may contain all the products a company offers, such as CDs. Users can search the catalog to locate an artist of their choice. Also, if inventory of a certain CD is running low, an automatic reorder can occur. Furthermore, when a search returns a specific CD, similar music and additional merchandise can be advertised on the results page.

The disadvantages of the in-house solution are primarily monetary in nature. It can cost upwards of $250,000 (U.S.) to implement and maintain a complex, in-house web storefront system. However, recent technologies and software products are making web storefronts far more cost-effective than they have been in the past.

Instant Storefront Solution

The alternative to an in-house solution is to use a software package from a vendor. Typically, these packages require very little technical knowledge to use. The better ones allow for customization of the storefront and also automate the technology so business staff can concentrate on sales.

The two types of instant storefront packages are online and offline. With an online package, the entire e-commerce software program is on the service provider's infrastructure; the storefront accesses the software with an Internet browser. The advantage of an online storefront is that it can be managed remotely. The business is freed from constant upgrades and other logistical issues associated with maintaining an Internet infrastructure. The disadvantage is that the software package is controlled by the service provider, and maintenance can be time-consuming, depending on the speed of the Internet connection.

An offline solution typically involves installing software on the business's computing infrastructure. The owner builds and maintains the storefront inside the application. When changes are ready to be published, the owner connects to the Internet and transmits the website. Advantages of an offline package include control (the business owns the software) and speed (changes to the store can be made quickly). The disadvantages include lack of software portability and installation/upgrade problems.

Small-business owners often do not have the time or energy to worry about technology. The quickest and easiest way for a small business to establish a web presence is with an online, ready-to-use package.

Copyrights, Licensing, and Trademarks

Intellectual property—that property which cannot be handled in a traditional physical way—offers some challenges when implemented in the digital world. While it may seem like a good idea to you to share thoughts on an exam you've just taken with the rest of the world, for example, the vendor behind that exam will think otherwise. The vendor has spent a great deal of time and money in creating the exam and the content of it—the intellectual property, in this case—is something that they want to protect and guard tightly.

The Internet has added new challenges to copyright, trademark, and licensing law enforcement. Because the Internet spans countries and each government has its own set of rules, new enforcement techniques must be applied. This section will discuss copyrights, trademarks, and licensing.

Copyrights

Copyright laws protect original works of authorship that are fixed in a tangible medium of expression. The basic elements are:

- Expression
- Originality

An Internet user who makes an unauthorized copy of someone else's work is probably violating the copyright owner's rights. Works of authorship include literary works (including computer programs); musical works; pantomimes and choreographic works; pictorial, graphic, and sculptural works; motion pictures and other audiovisual works; sound recordings; and architectural works.

Contrary to popular belief, an "international copyright" does not exist. To protect your copyright of your original material, you must contact the government agency that handles copyrights in the country where you reside. For instance, in the United States, you would contact the Library of Congress Copyright Office. You can request the forms (depending on your specific work) by phone, or download forms online from www.loc.gov/copyright. In Brazil, you would contact the Ministry of Culture Copyright Coordination unit at www.minc.gov.br.

A copyright is a protection afforded to a fixed piece of work when it is created. This exists the moment you create the item—whether or not you submit it to the copyright office itself. The trick, however, is proving that you did create the work and exactly *when* you did create it. That is the primary reason for submitting the work to the copyright office—to have the proof as to the time of submission and thus to establish ownership.

If you or your company copyrights your website material, you should place the copyright symbol (©) and year at the bottom of each page that contains the copyrighted material. Copyright symbols are not required, but are highly recommended, because they are often the first line of defense against copyright infringement.

The Information Infrastructure Task Force (IITF)

To codify copyright law as it applies to digital information, the Information Infrastructure Task Force (IITF) was formed in 1993. The IITF in turn established a working group on intellectual property rights to examine the intellectual property implications.

In 1994, the group published "Green Paper," a preliminary draft report on intellectual property rights. The working group recognized the need to review current copyright laws in light of the fact that copying and disseminating information are extremely easy in the digital age. At this time, copyright law is murky in respect to the Internet. It may be several years until legislation is passed, and it may be impossible to enforce.

World Intellectual Property Organization (WIPO)

The World Intellectual Property Organization (WIPO) is a specialized United Nations agency formed to protect intellectual property worldwide. *Intellectual property* consists of industrial property (trademarks, inventions) and copyrighted works. WIPO attempts to enforce copyright laws by cooperation between countries. More than 170 countries are currently members of WIPO.

If you register a copyright for a book in the United States and someone reproduces and sells it in Germany without your permission, you would be able to prosecute that person in both the United States and Germany because both countries have signed copyright agreement documentation. You can visit the WIPO site at `www.wipo.org`, which lists the copyright administration office for each member country.

Precedent Copyright Law and Internet Cases

Two precedent-setting cases have been decided by the courts in conjunction with copyright laws and the Internet.

Sega Enterprises Ltd. vs. MAPHIA   In *Sega Enterprises Ltd. vs. MAPHIA*, the courts decided in favor of Sega Enterprises, which brought suit against MAPHIA, an electronic bulletin board system (BBS). Sega Enterprises claimed that MAPHIA copied a game to its BBS and made it available for user downloads. The court found that MAPHIA sometimes charged users a direct fee for downloading privileges, or bartered for the privilege of downloading the Sega game. Because Sega's game was protected by copyright, MAPHIA violated that copyright by obtaining unauthorized copies of Sega's games and placing them on storage media of the BBS to be downloaded by unknown users.

Playboy Enterprises vs. Frena   In *Playboy vs. Frena*, Playboy brought a lawsuit against the defendant George Frena, an independent BBS operator. Playboy claimed that Frena distributed unauthorized copies of Playboy's copyright-protected photographs from his BBS. Frena's BBS was available by fee to anyone. Frena admitted that he did not obtain authorization from Playboy to copy or distribute the photographs. The courts found evidence of direct copyright infringement, and stated that the fact that Frena may not have known of the copyright infringement was irrelevant.

Another heavily publicized court case is still pending. The following case may impact the way music is distributed on the Internet for generations, and may have eventual implications for movies as well.

Recording Industry Association of America (RIAA) vs. Napster   This copyright-infringement case was filed by the RIAA to contest the distribution of copyrighted music files over the Internet using a popular program called Napster. This program allows users who have installed the Napster software on their computers to share MP3 music files with other users who have the Napster software. There is no cost for copying files from one user's computer to another. The RIAA wants artists and record companies to receive royalty payments from users who swap these copyrighted files. Napster is currently in the process of developing a subscription service that will allow users to share copyrighted MP3 files while observing a permission agreement. This arrangement will allow artists and record companies to receive payment for their copyrighted music.

Licensing

If you want to *license* someone else's copyright-protected material, you must contact the copyright owner and ask for permission. This task might involve contacting the legal department of a large organization, or a copyright specialist at a small to mid-size organization, or simply contacting one individual by phone or e-mail.

If you are granted permission to use the copyrighted work, the copyright holder determines the terms of use. For instance, there may be no cost but you might rather have to credit the owner for the work. In most cases, you must license the work from the owner under the terms of an agreement between both parties. The agreement usually determines how the work may be used (limited or unlimited reproduction) and how payment will be arranged (royalties or one lump payment).

Trademarks

A *trademark* is any word, slogan, symbol, name, package design or device (or any combination thereof) that marks and distinguishes a product from other products in trade. For instance, AltaVista and Rolls Royce are both trademarks. Trademarks are protected worldwide by participating WIPO countries.

To register a trademark, you must contact the government agency in your country that handles trademarks. For instance, in the United States, you would contact the U.S. Patent and Trademark Office. You can request the forms by phone, or download forms online from `http://www.uspto.gov`. In Canada, you would contact The Canadian Intellectual Property Office at `cipo.gc.ca`.

Project Management

Project management is a skill that touches all industries. Whether you are creating an e-commerce site or designing a new hospital wing, the same basic rules apply. This section will focus on the fundamentals of project management, including essential terms and concepts.

What Is Project Management?

To understand project management, you must first understand the concept of a project. A project is a temporary effort to create a unique product, such as an e-commerce website. It has defined beginning and ending dates, objectives, and a budget. The unique product can include software, hardware, services, processed materials, structures, and even intangible products such as skills and knowledge.

Projects include many elements that must be managed, usually by a project manager. The main elements are:

- Project schedule

- Costs

- Performance risks

Project management is the set of techniques, practices and principles that assists managers in controlling these main elements. You begin the project management process by creating realistic objectives and establishing the scope of the work to be completed.

Scope and Scope Creep

Scope refers to the size of a project. Project scope varies greatly depending on the complexity and number of tasks required to complete a project. For example, building an e-commerce website is a project of greater scope than designing a company newsletter. A project manager must consider the project's scope when planning a project of any size.

A common problem associated with project management is the tendency for the project's scope to increase over time. Any changes in the schedule, cost, or performance required to complete the project affect its scope. Issues often arise during the project that were not initially considered. You may be able to contain the project scope but only at the price of introducing sub-projects that also must be managed.

Changes in project scope tend to occur in small rather than large degrees, and therefore might seem negligible. However, small increases in scope will begin to add up. These gradual changes are called *scope creep or project creep*. If scope creep is not controlled, it can be detrimental to the success of your project.

Design/Development Project Cycle

A design/development project is one in which the team designs and develops the product itself, rather than beginning at the production or testing stage.

All projects have various stages, which constitute the project cycle. A design/development project cycle includes the following five stages:

1. Business process/functionality design

2. Technology/architecture design

3. Implementation/development

4. Pilot/parallel

5. Cutover/live

Business Process/Functionality Design

This first stage of the project management cycle determines the overall goals of the project. Business process/functionality design often involves executive managers from both the customer and supplier companies. They must determine a process that will fulfill the expectations of all people, called stakeholders, who have a business or personal interest in its end result. They also select the project team members.

This stage includes two important documents that should be completed as a result: the *business requirements* and *scope matrix documents*.

Business requirements document   A report that identifies the customer's needs. It can include the goals of the project, its features and functions, the budget, deadlines, and any company information that might assist the project.

Scope matrix document   A table or spreadsheet that lays out the project scope in rows and columns. It organizes the project's structure. Hierarchical models can also be used, depending on the environment.

Technology/Architecture Design

The second stage of the project management cycle is used to plan the project's design. The technology/architecture design stage begins with further refinement of the scope, which must incorporate realistic results, resources, and deadlines. The project team must determine the specific resources needed and estimate the time it will take to create the initial product. They must also include a workable budget and an efficient schedule.

All members of the team, such as programmers and contractors, are involved to determine how to meet the project objectives. The plan must be approved by the appropriate stakeholders at this stage.

This process includes an important document that should be completed as a result: the *technical architecture document*, a project management report that contains the design and formal specifications of a product. The fine-tuned budget should always include a section for the design and formal specifications, as it is a likely source for scope creep.

Implementation/Development

The third stage of the project management cycle involves developing the product according to the project plan. Implementation/development includes securing all required resources, keeping efforts properly focused, resolving conflicts, and maintaining communication with stakeholders.

Implementation/development also involves monitoring the project for deviation. If scope creep occurs, quick steps must be taken to reassess the situation. For example, the project might have to be rescheduled, the resources modified (such as temporary *co-location*, or placement of third-party equipment in a company), or the scope firmly limited. All changes must be accepted at the technology/architecture stage before implementation.

Pilot/Parallel

The fourth stage of the project management cycle involves inspecting and testing the product. During pilot/parallel, the supplier must comply with the project plan. If the product does not comply, it must be re-evaluated at the technology/architecture stage. It might require minor modifications or a complete redesign.

The fourth stage is closely tied to the third stage. In complex products, elements can be tested at different time periods. Therefore, development and testing of various project elements can occur in parallel.

If your company is launching an e-commerce website, for example, the pilot stage includes pre-launch testing to make sure the site is functional. This process should include:

Testing hot links   Make sure all the links on your site, including hot links, function properly. Hot links are connections that are interrelated: When one page changes, it updates other pages. For instance, if a database changes (such as the pricing of all store items), it should automatically update the pages that display pricing from that database.

Testing different browsers   Make sure the web pages in your site render correctly in as many browsers as possible. Older browsers may not support some of your website's functionality.

Testing for e-commerce site failure and corruption   Make sure the e-commerce aspects of your site, such as online transactions, function properly. Test all possible scenarios until you are sure the site will function properly when it goes live.

Testing heavy traffic   Make sure the web servers can handle many simultaneous users.

Testing various connection speeds   Make sure all users, regardless of the connection speed they use, can download pages and content in a reasonable amount of time.

Cutover/Live

Once a product passes the fourth stage, it is ready for the next step: live release. The project team is disbanded and the resource operations are halted. The project should also be analyzed for results, accomplishments, and learning experiences. The customer and all stakeholders should review the product, and a final report should be created.

From a project management viewpoint, the end product is the final step. However, many companies will require customer service and support to continue throughout the life of the product.

Further Study of Project Management

Many resources exist to further your knowledge of project management. Two key resources are the Project Management Institute (PMI) and the International Organization for Standardization (ISO) 9000 series.

Project Management Institute (PMI)

The Project Management Institute (PMI) is a non-profit membership organization that publishes standards and offers education regarding the project management profession.

The PMI *Guide to the Project Management Body of Knowledge (PMBOK)* identifies nine topic areas that define project management, including human resources, communications, integration, and procurement. Each topic area provides a set of principles and techniques to help you manage projects.

The PMI *Scalable Project Management Methodology Guide* introduces each project management topic discussed in the PMBOK.

To learn more about the Project Management Institute and obtain copies of the PMBOK guides, visit the institute online at www.pmi.org.

International Organization for Standardization (ISO) 9000 Series

The International Organization for Standardization (ISO) is a worldwide grouping of national standards bodies from more than 120 countries. It develops technical specifications for intellectual, scientific, technological, and economic activities worldwide.

The ISO offers a certification program for management system standards titled 9001. ISO 9001 details the steps recommended to produce high-quality products using a quality-management system. ISO 9001 certification is one document in the *ISO 9000* series, which standardizes quality-management systems.

To learn more about ISO 9001 certification and the ISO 9000 series for project management, visit the ISO online at www.iso.ch.

Summary

In this chapter, we defined electronic commerce and learned the advantages and disadvantages associated with it. To ensure that e-commerce is a success, you must understand standards such as Electronic Data Interchange (EDI), Secure Electronic Transaction (SET), and smart cards.

You also learned about many issues that must be carefully considered before implementing an e-commerce site. E-commerce may lead to a greater degree of vulnerability. With the introduction of Internet transactions—which are complete with names, addresses, and credit card numbers of buyers—the potential for fraud increases.

Protection can be added to property via a number of different methods. Written property can be protected via copyrights, while patents apply to processes and trademarks to phrases and expressions.

Finally, we studied the fundamentals of project management. A project is a temporary effort to create a unique product, such as an e-commerce website. It has defined beginning and ending dates, objectives, and a budget. The unique product can include software, hardware, services, processed materials, structures, and even intangible products such as skills and knowledge.

Exam Essentials

Be able to define electronic commerce and compare it to traditional commerce.   Traditionally, information was exchanged via direct person-to-person contact, or through the use of telephones or the postal system. In electronic commerce, information is carried through an electronic medium, such as a computer system operating over an electronic network.

Know the principal features of Electronic Data Interchange (EDI) and Secure Electronic Transaction (SET).   EDI is defined as the inter-organization exchange of documents in standardized electronic form directly between participating computers. EDI can be thought of as an electronic replacement for many paper-based transactions; it is primarily used for purchase orders and invoices.

The first primary feature of the SET protocol is enhanced identification. The second differentiating characteristic of the SET protocol is that the merchant never sees the credit card number. The third requirement of SET is that all sensitive information among all parties must be encrypted and signed.

Understand the advantages and key issues of e-commerce.   The benefits of e-commerce include: instant and ubiquitous availability, a streamlined buyer-to-seller relationship, reduced paperwork, reduced errors, reduced time to complete business transactions, easier entry into new markets, new business opportunities, improved market analysis, wider access to assistance and advice from experts and peers, improved product analysis, and streamlined and automated purchasing processes.

Key issues to consider include: intellectual property, security, taxation, customs, regulations, fraud, trust, and ubiquitous availability.

Be able to define the payment models for e-commerce.   The three models for payment in electronic commerce are: cash model, check model, and credit model. Under the cash model, buyers and sellers trade electronic value tokens, which are issued or backed by some third party, usually an established bank. Under the check model, consumers present digital versions of checks to web businesses. The web business verifies the check through its financial institution, which in turn consults the consumer's financial institution to ensure the availability of funds. The credit model fits well into the web infrastructure because existing credit card processing already uses much of the network infrastructure needed for e-commerce. When a consumer enters a credit card number on a web order form, the Internet can deliver that information to an authorization server immediately. The transaction then proceeds similarly in both the traditional and electronic commerce scenarios.

Know the international issues involved with e-commerce.   Issues involved with international e-commerce include currency exchange, shipping, and translation. Currency exchange rates can vary greatly from day to day. Shipping can be difficult to regions that do not have a major infrastructure in place. Translation can be difficult from the standpoint of explaining and understanding a product across boundaries.

Know the functions and advantages of smart cards.   Rather than having a magnetic strip on the back, smart cards have small integrated circuits inserted into them. Regardless of the specific type of technology inside it, a smart card is much more capable than an ATM or credit card. Smart cards may eventually replace credit cards.

Understand copyrights, licensing, and trademarks.   Copyright laws protect original works of authorship that are fixed in a tangible medium of expression. Licensing is obtaining permission to someone else's copyright-protected material from the copyright owner. A trademark is any word, slogan, symbol, name, package design, or device (or any combination thereof) that marks and distinguishes a product from other products in trade.

Be able to describe the fundamentals of project management, including the major stages of a design/development project cycle.   Project management is the set of techniques, practices, and principles that assists managers in controlling the main elements of a project. A project is a temporary effort to create a unique product, such as an e-commerce website. It has defined beginning and ending dates, objectives, and a budget.

Projects include many elements that must be managed, usually by a project manager. The main elements are: project schedule, costs, and performance risks.

Key Terms

Before you take the exam, be certain you are familiar with the following terms:

authentication	payment gateway
co-location	project management
business requirements document	scope creep
copyright	scope matrix document
data management	Secure Electronic Transaction (SET)
Electronic Data Interchange (EDI)	Secure Sockets Layer (SSL)
electronic commerce	security
intellectual property	smart cards
ISO 9001	technical architecture document
license	trademark
merchant system	ubiquitous availability
nonrepudiation	Unicode
online cataloging	

Review Questions

1. E-commerce differs from traditional commerce in that e-commerce:

   A. Is conducted through an electronic medium.

   B. Is more secure.

   C. Is more personal in nature.

   D. Is limited geographically.

2. What is the primary feature of the Secure Electronic Transaction (SET) protocol?

   A. Sensitive information is confirmed via telephone.

   B. Credit card information is stored in the merchant's database.

   C. All participants of the transaction must be authenticated.

   D. Market analysis is performed concurrent with the transaction.

3. Which of the following is a key advantage of e-commerce?

   A. Verification that ordered merchandise is actually available

   B. Easier connection with merchants' customer service departments

   C. More personalized service

   D. Reduced time and overhead costs in information processing

4. Which of the following payment models is the most difficult to implement in the web infrastructure?

   A. Cash

   B. Check

   C. Credit card

   D. Smart card

5. What is the chief benefit of a smart card?

   A. Easier return of merchandise

   B. More timely transactions

   C. Enhanced authentication

   D. Improved magnetic strip

6. What is a primary concern regarding international e-commerce?

   A. Ability to convert currency

   B. Ability to deliver products in a timely manner

   C. Ability to trust international merchants

   D. Ability to communicate verbally if the need arises

7. An agreement to use someone else's copyrighted material is called:

   A. A fair-use agreement

   B. A copyright agreement

   C. A trademark agreement

   D. A license agreement

8. What three main elements of a project must be managed by a project manager?

   A. Project functionality, costs, and performance risks

   B. Project costs, design elements, and functionality

   C. Project schedule, costs, and design elements

   D. Project schedule, costs, and performance risks

9. Which of the following are the components of successful e-commerce?

   A. Language, project management, security

   B. Communication, data management, security

   C. Security, project management, volume

   D. Volume, data management, risk

10. Electronic commerce uses various business support services, including e-mail, online directories, ordering, and logistical support systems, for example. What are these merchant-provided services known as?

    A. Merchant systems

    B. Merchant controls

    C. Repudiation

    D. Nonrepudiation

11. Which e-commerce model is characterized by high-volume, low-price margins?

    A. Trade model

    B. Consumer-to-business model

    C. Business-to-business model

    D. Business-to-consumer model

12. Which company first proposed SET?

    A. Visa

    B. Microsoft

    C. VeriSign

    D. MasterCard

13. What is the name for a system that interfaces between the merchant and the merchant's bank to perform credit card authorizations?

    A. Fee doorway

    B. Payment gateway

    C. Payment entryway

    D. Compensation doorway

14. Which of the following is a text and script character standard that can interchange, process, and display text of all principal written languages?

    A. ASCII

    B. SET

    C. EDI

    D. Unicode

15. Which electronic commerce payment models utilize cards that replaces the magnetic strip with an integrated circuit for storing and/or processing data?

    A. Smart card

    B. Check

    C. Cash

    D. Credit

16. Which of the following defines authentication?

    A. The integration of communications, data management, and security capabilities to allow organizations to exchange information related to the sale of goods and services

    B. The interorganization exchange of documents in standardized electronic form directly between participating computers

    C. The ability to verify a person's identity

    D. A standard protocol used on the Internet to secure online credit card payments.

17. Which of the following organizations published a preliminary draft report on intellectual property rights known as "Green Paper"?

    A. IITF

    B. WIPO

    C. RIAA

    D. MAPHIA

18. What is the process of creating a catalog of data (that then becomes a searchable index available online) known as?

   A. Inventory analysis

   B. Store-fronting

   C. Online cataloging

   D. Indexing

19. Which of the following terms refers to the size of a project?

   A. Extent

   B. Degree

   C. Depth

   D. Scope

20. What is the term for the tendency for a project's scope to increase over time?

   A. Lag

   B. Creep

   C. Crawl

   D. Bulk

Answers to Review Questions

1. A. Traditionally, information was exchanged via direct person-to-person contact, or through the use of telephones or the postal system. In electronic commerce, information is carried through an electronic medium such as a computer system operating over an electronic network.

2. C . The first primary feature of the SET protocol is enhanced identification.

3. D. The benefits of e-commerce include: instant and ubiquitous availability, a streamlined buyer-to-seller relationship, reduced paperwork, reduced errors, reduced time to complete business transactions, easier entry into new markets, new business opportunities, improved market analysis, wider access to assistance and advice from experts and peers, improved product analysis, and streamlined and automated purchasing processes.

4. A. The cash model, or e-cash, is the easiest to understand, albeit the hardest to implement in the web infrastructure.

5. C. The chief benefit of a smart card is that it enhances authentication. Smart cards can store and update passwords and other security information for use on computer networks. For example, they can process encryption schemes to ensure secure communication, perform instantaneous currency conversion, and protect cellular communications from fraud. Smart cards can also process vast amounts of information that you can organize, store, and delete at will.

6. B. First, consider shipping costs, which would be the primary concern in this instance. Second, you must ensure that delivery services, such as DHL or FedEx, can deliver to your customer destinations.

7. D. A license agreement is permission to use someone else's copyright-protected material granted by the copyright owner.

8. D. The main elements of a project are: project schedule, costs, and performance risks.

9. B. The three main elements of electronic commerce are communication, data management, and security.

10. A.   These services, provided by the merchant, are called merchant systems.

11. C.   The business-to-business model is characterized by high-volume, low-price margins. The business-to-consumer model is characterized by low-volume, higher-price margins, and the other two choices do not exist.

12. D.   MasterCard first proposed the Secure Electronic Transaction (SET) protocol.

13. B.   A payment gateway is the system that interfaces between the merchant and the merchant's bank to perform credit card authorizations. All other terms are nonexistent.

14. D.   Unicode is a text and script character standard that can interchange, process, and display text of all principal written languages. SET is a standard protocol used to secure online credit card payments. EDI establishes the format for electronic documents exchanged between participating computers. ASCII is the most common text file format used on the Internet.

15. A.   A smart card replaces the magnetic strip with an integrated circuit for storing and/or processing data.

16. C.   Authentication is the ability to verify a person's identity.

17. A.   In 1994, the IITF (Information Infrastructure Task Force) published "Green Paper," a preliminary draft report on intellectual property rights.

18. C.   Online cataloging is the process of creating a catalog of data; the catalog then becomes a searchable index that is available online.

19. D.   Scope refers to the size of a project.

20. B.   Project creep, or scope creep, is the tendency for the project's scope to increase over time.

Chapter

14

Basic HTML

THE CIW EXAM OBJECTIVE GROUPS COVERED IN THIS CHAPTER:

- ✓ Format HTML files to maintain compatibility with older Web browsers.

- ✓ Add images and graphical formatting to HTML files by manual coding in a text editor.

HTML (Hypertext Markup Language) is the standard authoring language used to develop web pages. Web page authoring, to continue the thought, is the process of creating web pages. There are many ways to create a web page, depending on your preferences. Since the World Wide Web's popularity has increased the Internet's prevalence in society, the skill of web page creation has become vital to many careers. This chapter will teach you how to create web pages using text editors and graphical user interface (GUI) editors. Each tool creates similar pages, but the processes are completely different.

This chapter introduces you to the basics of HTML and creates a foundation of knowledge that is built upon further in the next chapter, "Advanced HTML."

What Is HTML?

Tim Berners-Lee of MIT invented Hypertext Markup Language (HTML) with colleagues from CERN, the European Particle Physics Laboratory, as a means of distributing nonlinear text, called *hypertext*, to multiple points across the Internet. One document links to another through pointers called hyperlinks. *Hyperlinks* are embedded instructions within one text file that call another file whenever the link is accessed, usually by a click of a mouse. The global set of linked documents across the existing Internet framework grew into what is now known as the World Wide Web.

Hypermedia is an extension of hypertext. It includes images, video, audio, animation, and other multimedia data types, which can be incorporated into HTML documents. The Web can accurately be described as a hypermedia system.

Hypertext was first conceived by Ted Nelson in 1965. The first widely commercialized hypertext product was HyperCard, conceived by Bill Atkinson and introduced by Apple Computer in 1987. It incorporated many hypertext and hypermedia concepts, but was a proprietary system that worked only on Macintosh computers.

In contrast, HTML is a cross-platform language that works on Windows, Macintosh, and UNIX platforms. In addition, HTML and the Web are client/server systems; HyperCard works only on standalone Macintosh computers.

A markup language is very different from a programming language. Program files and data files exist separately in traditional applications. In a markup language, the instructions and the data reside in the same file. In addition, HTML does not provide data structures or internal logic, as do procedural programming languages such as C or Pascal.

HTML has evolved from other markup languages. IBM created the Generalized Markup Language (GML) in the late 1960s as a way to move formatted documents across different computer platforms. GML evolved into the Standard Generalized Markup Language (SGML) in 1986 and was ratified by the International Organization for Standardization (ISO). SGML is a powerful markup language; however, it is also very complex and difficult to learn.

HTML is an application of SGML. Although it has fewer language elements than SGML, HTML is easier to use and has become the standard method of encoding information for web documents. As with GML, HTML facilitates data exchange through a common document format across different types of computer systems and networks on the Web.

Whereas SGML is used specifically to define context (as opposed to appearance), HTML has evolved into both a contextual and a formatting language. For example, by applying a heading style to text using HTML, you are marking that text contextually as an important topic that begins a new section, *and* you are also applying the visual format element of boldface and a larger font size. HTML files are plain text files that have been "marked up" with special language elements called tags, which are embedded in the text.

Tags are pieces of text, enclosed in angle brackets (or "wickets"), that provide instructions to programs designed to interpret HTML. Suppose, for example, that you want to change the color of some text in your file. You can apply this formatting by embedding opening and closing tags around the text that you want colored. If you want an image to appear in your document, you can use a tag to specify the source and placement of the image.

HTML interpreters are programs that process the HTML pages and render them to the user as text pages formatted in accordance with the embedded instructions. Examples of HTML interpreters are Netscape Navigator and Microsoft Internet Explorer, which, as you've learned, are also called web browsers.

HTML interpreters are not limited to browsers. Many programs that have come on the market since 1996 include HTML reading, exporting, and creation capabilities as built-in features. Netscape Communicator, for example, now allows you to send and receive HTML messages, post fully formatted HTML messages to discussions and newsgroups, and create HTML pages automatically using a graphical user interface (GUI) editor.

Although HTML was specifically designed for use on the World Wide Web, many businesses are finding uses for HTML documents that have little or nothing to do with the Web. HTML files are very small and extremely portable, making this format an ideal choice when exchanging documents across any type of network.

HTML Standards

The World Wide Web Consortium (W3C) is the standards organization that controls the evolution of HTML. When the W3C fully endorses a technology, it publishes a "recommendation" to the Internet community. When the W3C evaluates a proposed recommendation, the specifics of the technology are in a state of constant flux. Be sure the code you use conforms to the latest recommendation from the W3C.

Generally, you should not write code to specifications indicated in working drafts; these versions are undergoing discussion and consideration, and are generally not yet supported by the major vendors. Recommendations from the W3C become the standards to which vendors pledge full support. To see current W3C recommendations, you can access the W3C website at www.w3.org/.

The W3C establishes standards for additional technologies, including Extensible Markup Language (XML), the Document Object Model (DOM), and Cascading Style Sheets (CSS).

HTML 3.2 Standard and HTML 4.01

HTML 3.2 is an older but still fully functional HTML standard. Many web pages and HTML editors (such as Microsoft FrontPage and NetObjects Fusion) still use the 3.2 standard. This standard is quite universal because many people surf the Web using older web browsers that cannot process all the elements required by the newer HTML 4.01 Recommendation.

The HTML 4.01 Recommendation was released December 24, 1999, and contains the latest specifications. You can access it at www.w3.org/TR/html4/. The 4.01 specification includes minor modifications to the 4.0 specification. Throughout this chapter, the specification will be referred to as both HTML 4.0 and 4.01.

HTML 4.01 enables you to use *Cascading Style Sheets (CSS)*—a technology that uses embedded information to define the fonts, colors, and phrase elements used on a particular HTML page—and supports multiple languages.

For example, languages such as Hebrew are read from right to left. HTML 4.01 allows you to create web pages that read in this way. HTML 4.01 also allows you to create ambitious tables and forms, as well as to incorporate scripting languages. You will learn more about scripting solutions, such as DHTML (Dynamic HTML), later in the chapter.

The W3C regulates the development of standards regarding Cascading Style Sheets (CSS).

As you develop web pages in HTML 4.01, you should understand that it has three distinct variants, or "flavors."

HTML 4.01 Flavors

The HTML 4.01 flavors ensure that you can use the latest specification yet remain backward-compatible with older web browsers. The following is a short description of each flavor:

HTML 4.01 Transitional   This flavor enables developers to insert formatting using either CSS or traditional layout instructions (e.g., fonts, colors, and phrase elements). This version will render features such as CSS in browsers that do not support HTML 4.01.

HTML 4.01 Strict   This flavor requires the exclusive use of CSS when defining layout instructions.

HTML 4.01 Frameset   This flavor is required for pages that use HTML frames. Frames separate the web page into two or more sections.

You specify the flavor of HTML by using a Document Type Declaration (DTD) tag. You will learn more about the DTD tag later in this chapter.

The majority of this book is written to the HTML 4.01 Transitional flavor. However, you will use the HTML 4.01 Strict and Frameset specifications in various sections.

Extensible Hypertext Markup Language (XHTML)

The *Extensible Hypertext Markup Language (XHTML)* is the latest formulation of HTML. XHTML combines HTML with the *Extensible Markup Language (XML)*. Whereas HTML describes a document's visual layout, XML allows you to describe the function and context of the actual information contained in a document. You will learn more about XML and XHTML later in this book. The relationship is shown in Figure 14.1.

FIGURE 14.1   Relationship of HTML, XML, and XHTML

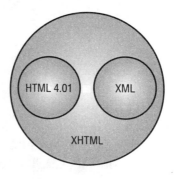

The HTML 4.01 Recommendation is one of the foundations for XHTML. Because the HTML 4.01 specification defines the meanings of the HTML tags used in XHTML, you need to master HTML.

XHTML is based specifically on the HTML 4.01 Recommendation, which repairs the "bugs" of HTML 4.0.

Because XHTML uses HTML for page formatting, it uses the same flavors: transitional, strict, and frameset. Following is a short description of each flavor.

XHTML Transitional   This flavor enables developers to insert formatting using either CSS or traditional layout instructions (e.g., fonts, colors, and phrase elements). This version will render in browsers that do not support HTML 4.01 features such as CSS.

XHTML Strict   This flavor requires the exclusive use of CSS when defining layout instructions.

XHTML Frameset   This flavor is required for pages that use HTML frames. Frames separate the web page into two or more sections.

Although XHTML will be discussed in later sections, the *Web Page Authoring Fundamentals* portion of the exam focuses on HTML. For more information about how XHTML, HTML, and XML work together, visit `www.w3.org/MarkUp/`.

Web Browsers and Standards

You should already be familiar with the function of web browsers. Web browsers are applications designed specifically to render hypermedia documents from the Internet. Browsers deliver HTML pages, sound files, images, videos, and other media across the Internet or enterprise intranet to the end user. An *intranet* is an internal network, using Internet technology, encased behind an enterprise's firewall. Web browsers are also called *user agents*, which is the W3C term for any application that renders HTML for display to users, such as a web browser or help engine.

Although the W3C attempts to create standards that will render the same results across different browsers, each browser manufacturer supports additional code that others may or may not support. Using this non-standard, proprietary code will likely cause the page to be rendered differently across browsers.

Usually, good page coding involves ensuring that the content is rendered appropriately regardless of which browser is in use. If you are writing code for an HTML page for your company's intranet, and all employees use the same browser, you can feel comfortable using proprietary language extensions and technology. In this case, you can be relatively sure that your HTML will render consistently every time.

However, a different generation of the same browser may differ in the way it interprets HTML. The term *generation* refers to a web browser's version number. Netscape Navigator 4.0 and Microsoft Internet Explorer 5 are fourth- and fifth-generation browsers, respectively. Internet Explorer 5.5 uses an HTML-rendering engine that has been significantly revised from version 4.0. You should always consider how each vendor and each version implements HTML standards differently.

The HTML code used in this chapter will function in all browsers, but was written to Netscape Navigator.

If you are preparing a site for public use, it is advisable to write your HTML code using the most widely supported standards.

HTML Coding

You can create an HTML document in any text editor, including the Windows platform editor, Notepad. You can also use sophisticated programs to write your text and corresponding HTML code; however, you must save your file as plain text. Any formatting instructions embedded in a file by a word-processing program, for example, will prevent the file from functioning as an HTML document.

In this section, you will learn how to use the most common HTML tags to create simple HTML documents. These documents, when written for the Web, are commonly referred to as *pages*. The default or starting page at a website is the *home page* for that site.

If you are creating your page for use on the Web, you will eventually need to upload the file to a web server, which is a server specifically designed to handle Hypertext Transfer Protocol (HTTP) requests. As we learned earlier, *HTTP* is the protocol used to transport HTML documents over the Internet. Uploading to a web server is beyond the scope of this book; check with your web server administrator if you have questions regarding this procedure.

Markup Tags

HTML markup tags are HTML element names enclosed in angle brackets. Tags are the essential building blocks of HTML files. Tags embed the HTML element information into the document so that an HTML interpreter will treat text according to the associated HTML element function. For example, using the boldface tags around text would cause the browser to display text contained by such tags in boldface. Text surrounded by tags becomes an *element*; text between an opening heading tag and a closing heading tag, for example, would be considered a heading element.

The combination of HTML tags and text is loosely referred to as *code*. While HTML is not a programming language, the tags do instruct the browser to perform certain actions, and so the use of the term "code" is appropriate in this context.

Container Tags and Empty Tags

There are two types of tags: container and empty. *Container tags* come in pairs; *empty tags* stand alone.

Container tags use opening and closing tags. For example, when you want italic text, you will contain the text between opening and closing <I> tags.

The following demonstrates the proper use of a container tag:

```
<TITLE>My Home Page</TITLE>
```

The <TITLE> tag contains text between an opening <TITLE> and a closing </TITLE> tag. Note that the closing tag is denoted by the presence of the slash (/) character.

An empty tag stands alone. If you want to include an image in your page, for example, you use a single tag to indicate where the image is to be inserted. An image tag has no closing tag; therefore, it is an empty tag. A list item (an item in a numbered or bulleted list) is also indicated by an empty tag, as shown below:

```
<LI>This is an item in a list
<LI>This is another item
```

The majority of tags are container tags, but many empty tags exist as well. Many tags carry additional information called attributes within the tag character itself. We will discuss attributes in more detail shortly.

Are Tags Case Sensitive?

Tags, or elements, are not case sensitive. As you become proficient in HTML, however, you will learn that tags are difficult to distinguish from text. Good coding practice is to use all capital letters for tag names. This technique is recommended, but it is not required.

According to the W3C HTML 4.01 specification: "Element names are written in uppercase letters (e.g., BODY). Attribute names are written in lowercase letters (e.g., lang, onsubmit). Recall that in HTML, element and attribute names are case-insensitive; the convention is meant to encourage readability."

In this chapter, both elements and attributes are written in uppercase letters to enhance readability, especially in paragraphs of text. When a discussion of an attribute takes place within a paragraph, it is easier to identify the attribute if it is not buried within the text.

What Constitutes a Tag?

A tag can consist of the following three items inside the angle brackets, or wickets.

An element   An *element* provides the main instruction of the tag. Elements include <TITLE>, <FONT>, <TABLE>, and many others.

An attribute   An *attribute* specifies a quality or describes a certain aspect of the element. For example, <DIV (which marks up divisions in a document) has several attributes, including ALIGN.

A value   A *value* gives value to the element and its attribute. For example, <DIV ALIGN="center"> has a value that instructs the text to be centered.

It is important that you understand this terminology as you continue through this chapter.

Some HTML tags use only an element and do not support attributes and values. Others, such as the <DIV> tag, support attributes *and* values.

Quotation marks are not always necessary when creating attribute values. However, good coding practice dictates that you enclose all values in quotes. Using quotation marks will never get you into trouble; omitting them may cause unexpected results.

Make sure to close any quotation marks that you open. If you do not close them, the page content up to the next occurrence of the quotation mark character may disappear.

Document Structure Tags

At a minimum, an HTML 4.01 document must contain the following tags, in the sequence shown. Italic type indicates document text that will vary from page to page.

```
<!DOCTYPE HTML PUBLIC "-//W3C//DTD HTML 4.01 Transitional
↳//EN""http://www.w3.org/TR/html4/loose.dtd">
<HTML>
<HEAD>
<TITLE>Descriptive Page Title</TITLE>
</HEAD>
<BODY>
Page text and media
</BODY>
</HTML>
```

The Document Type Declaration (DTD) statement begins your HTML code by specifying the HTML version number and type used in the document. You should note that the DTD statement is technically not an HTML statement, but an SGML statement.

The opening <HTML> and closing </HTML> tags enclose the entire page. <HTML> is an optional tag because the DTD contains the HTML version information. However, it is useful if you specify the LANG attribute in a web page. The LANG attribute identifies the base language of the document, which includes the text content and the attribute values (not the elements). For instance, a web document written in English would use <HTML LANG="en"> and a document written in French would use <HTML LANG="fr">. This attribute is helpful for search engines and speech synthesizers.

Within any page are two document sections: the HEAD and the BODY. Each of these sections has corresponding <HEAD> and <BODY> container tags that enclose any text or other tags pertaining to those sections.

In the exercises in this chapter, the only element you will be adding to the document HEAD is the mandatory TITLE element. Every page should have a title, enclosed within <TITLE> tags in the HEAD section. The title is very important. Text between <TITLE> tags will appear in the title box of the browser window, in the history list, and on the page when printed. Title text also becomes the bookmark name if the page is bookmarked or added to a browser Favorites folder.

All text to be displayed on the page through the browser or HTML interpreter needs to appear between the <BODY> and </BODY> tags.

Table 14.1 provides a quick reference to the HTML structure tags.

TABLE 14.1 HTML Structure Tags

Element	Usage
HTML	Identifies the document type as HTML.
HEAD	Encloses the HEAD section of the document. The title will appear in the HEAD section.
TITLE	Encloses the text that will appear in the browser title bar when the page is loaded. The TITLE container is itself contained within the <HEAD> tags.
BODY	Encloses the BODY of the document. Text typed in the BODY section will appear in the browser window when that page is loaded.

The DTD tag is not an HTML structure statement. This tag is placed before any HTML information. You will learn more about the DTD in the following section.

The Document Type Declaration (DTD)

The *Document Type Declaration (DTD)*, denoted by the <!DOCTYPE> tag, describes the nature of your HTML code. As mentioned earlier, this declaration is technically not HTML; it is actually SGML. The DTD states the version of HTML used by the page, as well as the document's primary language. It also includes an optional web address that contains the proper DTD structure for the HTML version used. For instance, the HTML 4.01 Transitional DTD contains the website address www.w3.org/TR/html4/loose.dtd. If you visit the site, you will find an example of the correct format of the HTML 4.01 Transitional DTD.

You should use the DTD for two reasons. First, it is always worthwhile to consider the future and how your code might be used. For example, a vendor might require you to use the DTD to take advantage of a particular browser's advanced features. Second, you might want to use an HTML validator, which checks your HTML code for errors. These programs require the DTD.

The W3C has a popular HTML validation tool at http://validator.w3.org/.

If you want to validate your HTML, the validating program you use will require you to specify the HTML version it is supposed to check. Some examples of DTD tags follow.

HTML 4.01   The following DTDs are used for files written in the specified flavors of HTML 4.01. The web addresses are optional.

Transitional

```
<!DOCTYPE HTML PUBLIC "-//W3C//DTD
⮑HTML 4.01 Transitional//EN"
"http://www.w3.org/TR/html4/loose.dtd">
```

Strict

```
<!DOCTYPE HTML PUBLIC "-//W3C//DTD
⮑HTML 4.01//EN"
"http://www.w3.org/TR/html4/strict.dtd">
```

Frameset

```
<!DOCTYPE HTML PUBLIC "-//W3C//DTD
↳HTML 4.01 Frameset//EN"
"http://www.w3.org/TR/html4/frameset.dtd">
```

HTML 3.2   The following DTD is used for HTML 3.2 files.

```
<!DOCTYPE HTML PUBLIC "-//W3C//DTD HTML 3.2 Final//EN">
```

HTML 2.0   The following DTD is used for HTML 2.0 files.

```
<!DOCTYPE HTML PUBLIC "-//W3C//DTD HTML 2.0//EN">
```

XHTML   The following DTDs are used for the specified flavors of XHTML. XHTML approximates the HTML 4.01 DTDs. If you are using the XHTML Transitional flavor and you are not including XML in your document, there will be little difference between an HTML 4.01 and XHTML document. The Web address is optional.

Transitional

```
<!DOCTYPE HTML PUBLIC "-//W3C//DTD
↳XHTML 1.0 Transitional//EN"
"http://www.w3.org/TR/xhtml1/DTD/
↳xhtml1-transitional.dtd">
```

Strict

```
<!DOCTYPE HTML PUBLIC "-//W3C//DTD
↳XHTML 1.0 Strict//EN"
"http://www.w3.org/TR/xhtml1/DTD/
↳xhtml1-strict.dtd">
```

Frameset

```
<!DOCTYPE HTML PUBLIC "-//W3C//DTD
↳XHTML 1.0 Frameset//EN"
"http://www.w3.org/TR/xhtml1/DTD/
↳xhtml1-frameset.dtd">
```

By using the DTD tag, you will improve your page's ability to work with browsers. The DTD can help you create a more efficient interface.

DTD Placement

Because the DTD is not an HTML statement, you place it before any HTML information. Thus, it resides above the <HTML> tag.

EXERCISE 14.1

Creating a Simple HTML Page

In this exercise, you will create an HTML page titled "My Page" that contains a single line of text.

1. Create a new file using Notepad (or other text editor).

2. Enter the following code:

```
<!DOCTYPE HTML PUBLIC "-//W3C//DTD HTML 4.01 Transitional//EN"
"http://www.w3.org/TR/html4/loose.dtd">
<HTML>
<HEAD>
<TITLE>My Page</TITLE>
</HEAD>
<BODY>
Welcome to my page!
</BODY>
</HTML>
```

3. Save the file as mypage.htm.

4. Launch your browser and load mypage.htm. You should see a single line of text in your browser.

Examine the title bar of the browser window. Notice that the text you entered between the <TITLE> tags appears there.

You just created your first HTML page.

In some books about HTML, you may read that some of these structure tags are optional. Although this statement is true, it is not good coding practice to omit structure tags, and it is not recommended. Most HTML interpreters will infer the presence of certain tags if they are missing. However, many people will judge you and your knowledge level by the clarity and structure of your code. Include the structure tags shown here, and you will be respected among other web page developers.

The *<META>* Tag

The <META> tag is quite useful with search engines because many spider programs look for it. A *spider* is a program that automatically searches web pages and indexes them for searches. The <META> tag is an empty tag that describes the contents of your page. You place it between the <HEAD> tags in your HTML document.

To make your pages more accessible to search engines, you can use the <META> tag to specify keywords. This strategy will increase your hit rate. You can also use it to provide a short summary of the page's contents, and to identify the author of the page. Many GUI HTML editors will insert information about the authoring tool used to create the page. You can also use the <META> tag to automatically refresh a page.

To provide keywords for search engines, you can use the <META> tag as follows:

```
<META NAME="Keywords" CONTENT="TCP/IP, networking, Java,
↳CIW, certification">
```

If you want to use the META element to provide a detailed description of your page, use syntax similar to the following:

```
<META NAME="Description" CONTENT="You can enter a useful
↳description of the page here. You can type sentences, as
↳you would in an e-mail or letter, though you should keep
↳it concise.">
```

To name the author of the web page, use META with the NAME attribute:

```
<META NAME="Author" CONTENT="Rosa Estelle Rodriguez">
```

You can even use the <META> tag to make your page refresh automatically after a specified number of seconds:

```
<META HTTP-EQUIV="Refresh" Content="5;
    URL=http://www.ciwcertified.com">
```

An extended discussion of the <META> tag is beyond the scope of this book. However, the <META> tag is a very effective back-end tool for ensuring that your pages perform well across networks. The <META> tag was discussed in this section because it is placed within the document structure tags.

Paragraph Formatting and Block-Level Elements

HTML elements that affect an entire paragraph or multiple paragraphs are referred to as *block-level elements*. HTML elements that can affect something as small as a character or a word are referred to as *text-level elements*.

Block-level elements are automatically preceded and followed by paragraph breaks. Text-level elements are not followed by breaks unless the breaks are manually included.

Paragraph Breaks and Line Breaks

The most basic block-level element is the paragraph element. The line break element is technically a text-level element, but it is included here in the context of formatting paragraphs. The <P> tag defines the start of a new paragraph. HTML 4.01 states that the <P> tag can be either a container or empty tag, but a container tag is strongly recommended. The <BR> tag specifies that a line break should be inserted wherever the tag occurs;
 is always an empty tag.

The following exercise demonstrates the difference between the <P> tag and the <BR> tag, and the necessity of using both.

EXERCISE 14.2

Inserting Paragraph Breaks and Line Breaks

In this exercise, you will use the <P> and <BR> tags to add paragraph breaks and line breaks to a web page.

1. In the text editor, open the file mypage.htm, which you created in the previous exercise.

2. Move the cursor to the end of the single sentence in this file (Welcome to my page!), and press Enter twice.

3. Add a second sentence that reads:
   This should be the start of a second paragraph.

4. Save the file.

5. In your browser, load mypage.htm. Notice that although you added two returns, no spacing information was passed to the browser.

6. In the text file, move to the beginning of the text you just added. Insert a <P> tag in the blank line before the second paragraph, and a closing </P> tag after the second paragraph. Save the file.

7. Reload the file in the browser. You should now see these two sentences appear as separate paragraphs in the browser.

8. In the text file, position the cursor to the left of the word "start." Insert a <BR> tag here.

9. Save the file.

10. In the browser, reload your file. You should now see a line break just before the word "start" in the middle of the second paragraph.

11. To demonstrate that more than one space character is treated as a single space, in the text editor file, add five spaces between the words "should" and "be" in the text file. Move to the end of "be" and press Enter.

12. Save the file.

13. Reload the file. Notice that neither the spaces nor the return you added had any effect on the way the file displayed in the browser. This important concept will affect the way you write code.

The preceding exercise demonstrates that the appearance of text in the editor will not necessarily match the appearance of text in the browser. Do not become frustrated when the text in your browser does not appear as you intended. Determine what you need to do to achieve the desired appearance, and add the appropriate code into your file.

Heading Levels

Even the most basic HTML documents will usually include at least one heading, and more likely, several. Denoting text as heading elements emphasizes the start of different sections on your page, and draws attention to that text. Heading tags have built-in styles associated with them. For example, text formatted as a heading-level-1 element is rendered, by default, in a large, bold, serif font.

A *serif* font is a font in which the individual characters have little flourishes at the outermost points of the character. Times Roman is an example of a serif font. By contrast, *sans serif* means "without a serif." Arial and Helvetica are examples of sans serif fonts.

HTML uses six heading styles. Headings are container tags that open and close around the affected text. <H1> and </H1> cause text to be rendered in the heading-level-1 style, <H4> and </H4> cause text to be rendered in the heading-level-4 style, and so forth. The largest heading is level 1. Heading-level-4 text is rendered the same size as normal text. Heading levels-5 and -6 are smaller than normal text and should be used sparingly, if at all.

Because headings are block-level elements, they are automatically preceded and followed by paragraph breaks, regardless of the relative position of the element to other text in the HTML source code.

EXERCISE 14.3

Using HTML Headings

In this exercise, you will create a page upon which you will build in later exercises. This page is the home page for the fictitious enterprise Sun & Sand Tours.

1. Create a new file using Notepad (or other text editor).

2. Enter the following text in the file:
   ```
   <!DOCTYPE HTML PUBLIC "-/ /W3C/ /DTD
   ⮑HTML 4.01 Transitional/ /EN"
   "http://www.w3.org/TR/html4/loose.dtd"
   <HTML>
   <HEAD>
   <TITLE>Sun & Sand Tours</TITLE>
   </HEAD>
   <BODY>
   Sun & Sand Tours

   Welcome to Sun & Sand Tours.
   Take off your shoes,
   take off your socks,
   and imagine your toes in the sand...

   What You'll Find Here:

   Travel Tips
   Tour Package Information
   Information Request Form

   For more information, send mail to tours@sunsand.com
   </BODY>
   </HTML>
   ```

3. Save the file as home.htm. The .htm file name extension will allow you to render this file in a browser.

4. Load the file home.htm in your browser and notice how the lines all run together.

5. Add heading, paragraph, and line-break tags as shown here:

```
<!DOCTYPE HTML PUBLIC "-//W3C//DTD HTML 4.01
↪Transitional//EN"
"http://www.w3.org/TR/html4/loose.dtd">
<HTML>
<HEAD>
<TITLE>Sun & Sand Tours</TITLE>
</HEAD>
<BODY>
<H1>Sun & Sand Tours</H1>
Welcome to Sun & Sand Tours. Take off your shoes, take
↪off your socks, and imagine your toes in the sand...
<H3>What You'll Find Here:</H3>
Travel Tips<BR>
Tour Package Information<BR>
Information Request Form<P>
For more information, send mail to tours@sunsand.com
</BODY>
</HTML>
```

6. Save the file.

7. Reload the file. Your page should display in a clearly designed format.

Primitive Formatting with the *<PRE>* Tag

Sometimes you may want to use text that has already been formatted using a fixed-width font, such as Courier or Lucida Sans Typewriter. (A *fixed-width font* is a font in which every character, including the space character, has equal width. In *proportional-width fonts*, letters such as *i* and *j* have less width than letters *m* or *b*.) With the preformatted text tag, all line breaks and spacing will be displayed in a browser exactly as they appear in the original text. This tag is useful for adding spaces and line breaks freely where desired. The <PRE> tag is a container tag, requiring its closing </PRE> tag. This tag is especially useful for displaying plain text files in their original format.

The <PRE> tag is commonly used to display tabular data.

As you will learn in a later section, HTML tables are more attractive and functional for presenting tabular data. But if you do not have much time, the <PRE> tag is quick and simple to use.

Indenting and Centering Text

There are several options for indenting a paragraph of text. First, you can use the HTML 4.01 <DIV> container tag. The syntax is as follows:

```
<DIV ALIGN="center"> This text is centered </DIV>
```

This code shows the standard way to create centered text using HTML 4.01. In this example, the DIV element indicates the text you want to center. The ALIGN attribute tells the browser that the text should be aligned. You can use the <DIV> tag for many functions. Most often, you will use it to align content. You can, for example, center text, tables and images. You can also use <DIV> to justify items to the right or left on a page. For example, consider the following code:

```
<DIV ALIGN="right"> This text is on the right </DIV>
```

In this example, the text would render on the right side of the page.

Consult Appendix C for a quick HTML 4.01 reference.

The <BLOCKQUOTE> tag centers and indents text. <BLOCKQUOTE> is a container tag.

The <CENTER> tag also centers text. Like <BLOCKQUOTE>, it is a container tag. Many developers and WYSIWYG HTML editors use <CENTER>. However, the HTML 4.01 Recommendation deprecates this tag in favor of <DIV>. The word "center" should now be used only as an attribute value. For instance, HTML 4.01 uses "center" as an ALIGN attribute in the <P> container tag as follows:

```
<P ALIGN="center"> Your text here. </P>
```

EXERCISE 14.4

Indenting and Centering Text

In this exercise, you will indent and center text in the file you created in the previous exercise.

1. In the text editor, open the file home.htm.

2. Modify your code as indicated in bold:

```
<!DOCTYPE HTML PUBLIC "-//W3C//DTD HTML 4.01
↳Transitional//EN"
"http://www.w3.org/TR/html4/loose.dtd">
<HTML>
<HEAD>
<TITLE>Sun & Sand Tours</TITLE>
</HEAD>
<BODY>
<H1>Sun & Sand Tours</H1>
<BLOCKQUOTE>
Welcome to Sun & Sand Tours. Take off your shoes, take
↳off your socks, and imagine your toes in the sand...
</BLOCKQUOTE>
<H3>What You'll Find Here:</H3>
Travel Tips<BR>
Tour Package Information<BR>
Information Request Form<P>
<DIV ALIGN=CENTER>
For more information, send mail to tours@sunsand.com
</DIV>
</BODY>
</HTML>
```

3. Load the file home.htm in your browser. You should see the first paragraph indented and the last paragraph centered.

Additional Block-Level Elements

You can incorporate additional block-level elements into your HTML pages. These include forms, divisions, horizontal ruling lines, and lists. By this point, you should understand how to use the most common block-level tags: <P>, <H1> through <H6>, <BLOCKQUOTE>, and <DIV>. Other elements are discussed later in this section and in the sections that follow. The key point to remember is that all block-level elements are automatically preceded and followed by paragraph breaks.

 Paragraph tags are not actually added to the HTML document when using block-level elements (except when you use the <P> tag manually). The block-level elements are interpreted by the client browser, which inserts the additional spacing.

Text-Level Elements

Text-level elements can affect a section of text as small as a single character or as large as an entire page. In the discussion that follows, you will learn how to use several text-formatting elements to emphasize text and embellish your pages.

Bold, Italic, and Underline

Simple text-level elements include the following: B and STRONG for boldface, I and EM for italic, and U for underline. The STRONG and EM elements are standard; it is recommended that you use them instead of B and I. As a general rule, you should avoid the use of underline because it is used predominantly to designate hyperlinks in web page text.

Text-formatting tags are simple to use. Open the tag before the text to be affected, and close the tag where you want that effect to end.

Font Style Elements vs. Phrase Elements

The B and STRONG elements both create boldface text. However, each element accomplishes this effect differently. The difference is that B specifically means apply the bold font style, whereas STRONG indicates that the text is to be given a strong appearance. In short, B represents a specific font instruction; STRONG represents the weighting of the phrase relative to surrounding text. The B element is called a font style element; STRONG is called a phrase element. The same is true of I and EM, respectively, which both create italic (or emphasized) text.

HTML was originally created to describe the *function*, not *appearance*, of text. The reasoning behind this was that HTML was and is viewed as a language that can describe more than text. HTML can also be used by speech-output systems. There is no such thing as "bold" speech, but the term "strong" can be used both to denote bold text when printed, and strongly spoken text when output through an audio device.

For printed output, you can use phrase and font elements interchangeably. However, if you are coding for the future (as you should be), you should consider how the HTML might be used in a different context, then apply the most appropriate tag.

Table 14.2 lists text-level elements, their usage, and their appearances.

TABLE 14.2 Text-Level HTML Elements

Element	Usage	Appearance
B	Font style element	**bold text**
BIG	Font style element	larger text
CITE	Phrase element (for program sample output)	*italic text*
CODE	Phrase element (for program code examples)	`fixed-space font`
DFN	Phrase element (for word definitions)	normal text (or *italic* text in Internet Explorer 4.0)
EM	Phrase element (for emphasis)	*italic text*
I	Font style element	*italic text*
KBD	Phrase element (for user text to be typed)	`fixed-space font`
SAMP	Phrase element (for program sample output)	`fixed-space font`
SMALL	Font style element	smaller text
STRONG	Phrase element	**bold text**

TABLE 14.2   Text-Level HTML Elements *(continued)*

Element	Usage	Appearance
SUB	Font style element (for subscript)	smaller text lowered below the baseline, as in H_2O
SUP	Font style element (for superscript)	smaller text raised above the baseline, as in $E=MC^2$
STRIKE	Font style element	~~strikethrough text~~
TT	Font style element	`fixed-space font`
U	Font style element	<u>underline</u>
VAR	Phrase element (for variable text in program code)	*italic text*

In the following exercise, you will apply a few of these elements to existing text.

EXERCISE 14.5

Using Text-Level Formatting Tags

In this exercise, you will add text-level formatting tags to the file you worked with in the previous exercise.

1. In the text editor, open home.htm.

2. Modify the code indicated in bold to incorporate changes:

```
<!DOCTYPE HTML PUBLIC "-//W3C//DTD HTML 4.01
Transitional//EN"
"http://www.w3.org/TR/html4/loose.dtd">
<HTML>
<HEAD>
<TITLE>Sun & Sand Tours</TITLE>
</HEAD>
<BODY>
<H1>Sun & Sand Tours</H1>
```

```
<BLOCKQUOTE>
<BIG><EM>Welcome to Sun & Sand Tours.
⤷Take off your <STRONG>shoes</STRONG>, take off
⤷your <STRONG>socks</STRONG>, and imagine your toes in
⤷the sand...</EM></BIG>
</BLOCKQUOTE>
<H3>What You'll Find Here:</H3>
Travel Tips<BR>
Tour Package Information<BR>
Information Request Form<P>
<DIV ALIGN=CENTER>
<EM><STRONG>For more information, send mail to
⤷tours@sunsand.com</STRONG></EM>
</DIV>
</BODY>
</HTML>
```

3. Save the file.

4. Load the file home.htm in your browser.

Now that you know how to use the text formatting tags, you will work with lists.

Lists

A common HTML function is to create bulleted and numbered lists. Lists are compound, block-level elements. Inside list definition tags are individual list item tags. A paragraph break precedes and follows the entire list. Individual list items are separated by single line breaks.

There are two types of HTML lists (see Table 14.3):

- An *ordered list* is a numbered list that uses the <OL> element and requires a closing tag.

- An *unordered list* is a bulleted list that uses the <UL> element and also requires a closing tag.

Both lists use identical syntax. Each list item is specified using the list item (<LI>) element, and the closing tag is optional.

TABLE 14.3 Ordered and Unordered List Syntax

Ordered List	Unordered List
<H2>Ordered List</H2>	<H2>Unordered List</H2>
<OL>	<UL>
<LI>This is the first numbered item.	<LI>This is the first bulleted item.
<LI>This is the second item.	<LI>This is the second item.
<LI>This is the last item.	<LI>This is the last item.
</OL>	</UL>

EXERCISE 14.6

Creating Lists

In this exercise, you will change the three single lines in the file home.htm into a bulleted list. Using what you have learned so far, you will also create a second file that will contain a numbered list.

1. In the text editor, open the file home.htm.

2. Modify this portion of code as indicated in bold. Where strike-through has been applied, delete the indicated tags.
<H3>What You'll Find Here:</H3>
<UL>
<LI>Travel Tips**
**
<LI>Tour Package Information**
**
<LI>Information Request Form**<P>**
</UL>

EXERCISE 14.6 *(continued)*

3. Save your file.

4. Load the file home.htm in the browser. Each bulleted item will eventually link to a separate page.

5. In the text editor, open the file home.htm.

6. Change the bulleted list to a numbered list by making the following changes:
   ```
   <UL><OL>
   <LI>Travel Tips
   <LI>Tour Package Information
   <LI>Information Request Form
   </UL></OL>
   ```

7. Modify the code indicated in bold to be able to distinguish between the earlier file:
   ```
   <!DOCTYPE HTML PUBLIC "-//W3C//DTD HTML 4.01
   ↳Transitional//EN"
   "http://www.w3.org/TR/html4/loose.dtd">
   <HTML>
   <HEAD>
   <TITLE>TIPS</TITLE>
   </HEAD>
   <BODY>
   <H1>TIPS</H1>
   ```

8. Save the file as tips.htm.

9. Load tips.htm in your browser. Your page should display with numbers instead of bullet points. If it does not, review your code.

You have already learned many of the basic tags that HTML provides for formatting text and paragraphs. In the sections that follow, you will learn how to incorporate graphics, create links, work with tables, and create HTML forms.

Adding Hidden Comments

You can bury comments within your HTML source code that will not appear on the page. The syntax for including a comment within your document is as follows:

```
<!-- comment text here -->
```

Hidden comments are useful for adding messages to yourself or other developers who might be updating your code.

Good Coding Practice

Now that you have learned the basics of working with HTML tags, you should consider not simply which tags to use, but how to best use them in conjunction with your text.

If you are coding an HTML page and you are the only one who will ever look at the code, you may think the appearance of your code does not matter. This statement is basically true. But suppose you must share your work with others. Some coding techniques provide enhanced readability, and make finding and changing code a simple operation. Other coding techniques produce a busy, confusing format that makes it difficult to decipher and edit the code.

When applying two or more tags to the same text, you must consider the sequence of the tags as a matter of good coding practice. For example, either of the following two lines would be considered good coding:

```
<B><I> ... text here ... </I></B>
<I><B> ... text here ... </B></I>
```

In both lines, the first tag opened is the last tag closed and the last tag opened is the first tag closed. The following line demonstrates the incorrect way to code the same text:

```
<I><B> ... text here ... </I></B>
```

In this example, the first tag opened is also the first closed. This usage is improper and occasionally will produce unexpected results. Sometimes the sequence in which tags are opened and closed is irrelevant in terms of effect. But for the few times that the sequence *will* matter, it is best to always use good coding practice and avoid the last method shown here.

HTML Horizontal Rules and Graphical Elements

Many times the information on a page needs to be divided to make it more readable, or to be chunked into smaller elements more likely to catch a user's attention. A simple method of doing this is to add horizontal lines—known as rules—and graphical elements into the page.

In the next few sections, we will look at how to add horizontal rules to web pages, work with horizontal rule attributes, and incorporate image files as standalone graphics. We will also look at how to use the web-safe color palette, change the page background color, and use a tiled image across the page background.

Adding Horizontal Ruling Lines

There are several simple graphical elements that you can add to a web page to provide structure and visual interest. One such element that is easy to add in HTML is the horizontal *rule*, which is simply a line or series of lines. The term is related to "ruler," a tool of measurement that can be used to draw straight lines. To add a horizontal rule to your page, insert the <HR> tag at the position where you want the line to appear. <HR> is an empty tag, requiring no closing tag.

Horizontal rules do not appear as distinctly on a white background as they do on a colored or textured background. You will learn how to change the page background later in this section.

Consider the following code:

```
<H1>Horizontal Rules</H1>
<HR>
Horizontal rules are lines that can be used to make
↳visual divisions in your document.
```

By default, these lines include a 3D shading effect, which can be disabled. In addition, the lines can be set to various sizes, widths, and alignments. But the line is added by a single tag: <HR>. So how is this other information passed to the browser?

Horizontal Rule Attributes

In the previous section, you learned about the three components of a tag. You also learned about the <DIV> element's associated attributes and values. The HR element has a width attribute that controls how far across the screen the line extends. The WIDTH attribute controls the length of the line. The value of the attribute, by default, is 100 percent. If you want the line to extend across only 50 percent of the window, you would write the tag as follows:

```
<HR WIDTH="50%">
```

Note that the attribute name (in this case, WIDTH) precedes an equal sign (=). Following the equal sign is the desired value for this attribute, in this case 50 percent.

You are already familiar with the ALIGN attribute from your work with the DIV element. You can use ALIGN with the HR element as well. For example, to create a line starting at the left margin that extends halfway across the page, you could use either of the following two tags:

```
<HR WIDTH="50%" ALIGN="left">
<HR ALIGN="left" WIDTH="50%">
```

The element name must be the first text in the tag. The order in which the attributes appear is not dictated. You cannot, however, reverse the attribute name and value; the attribute name must always precede the equal sign and value.

Table 14.4 lists the attributes and accepted values for the HR element.

TABLE 14.4 Horizontal Rule Attributes

Attribute Name	Accepted Values
ALIGN	Alignment can be Left, Right, or Center. If no alignment is specified, center is the default value used for this attribute.
NOSHADE	Not all attributes take values. The NOSHADE attribute stands alone; its presence in the tag indicates the inclusion of the attribute. When the NOSHADE attribute is included, the 3D shading effect is not present; the browser will present a solid, instead of etched, line.

TABLE 14.4 Horizontal Rule Attributes *(continued)*

Attribute Name	Accepted Values
SIZE	The SIZE attribute can be specified in terms of pixels, which are very small units of the screen. Pixels are not an absolute measurement, but are relative to the display resolution.
WIDTH	WIDTH can be specified in terms of percentage of the window width or number of pixels.

EXERCISE 14.7

Assigning Attribute Values in *<HR>* Tags

In this exercise, you will learn how to assign and change the values of attributes in the <HR> tag.

1. Create a new file using Notepad (or other text editor).

2. Enter the source code shown here:

```
<!DOCTYPE HTML PUBLIC "-//W3C//DTD HTML 4.01
↳Transitional//EN"
"http://www.w3.org/TR/html4/loose.dtd">
<HTML>
<HEAD>
<TITLE>Lines</TITLE>
</HEAD>
<BODY>
<DIV ALIGN="center"><H1>Lines and Attributes</H1></DIV>
<HR WIDTH="4%">
<HR WIDTH="12%">
<HR WIDTH="20%">
<HR WIDTH="12%">
<HR WIDTH="4%">
</BODY>
</HTML>
```

3. Save the file as lines.htm.

4. Load the file lines.htm in your browser.

5. Modify the code for the horizontal rules as indicated in bold:

```
<HR WIDTH="4%" NOSHADE>
<HR WIDTH="12%" ALIGN="left" SIZE="5">
<HR WIDTH="20%" SIZE=10 NOSHADE>
<HR WIDTH="12%" ALIGN="right" SIZE="5">
<HR WIDTH="4%" NOSHADE>
```

6. Save the file.

7. Reload the file in the browser.

In some instances, many web authors choose to use graphic images and bars in place of horizontal lines. This takes longer for the pages to load and is not always practical. You need to know how to use horizontal lines to be able to serve an audience that may not have a fast connection, as well as to pass the Foundations exam. Remember that HTML can define function as well as appearance, as was illustrated here. You may have a reason to choose the HR element in the future because HR may designate some contextual meaning.

Incorporating Images into Web Pages

You may have heard the saying that a picture is worth a thousand words. Most web developers must believe this, because the Web is inundated with graphic images. Images can be big or small; they can function as links; they can be used to launch script actions; and they can be used as image maps. Although scripting is not discussed in this chapter, you will be introduced to clickable image maps in a later section. In this section, you will focus on using images purely as graphic enhancements.

The <IMG> tag displays a graphic image on your page. The key attribute that will always be present in this tag is SRC. Use SRC to specify the name and, if necessary, the location of your image file. The <IMG> tag is an empty tag, so it requires no closing tag.

Standard image tag syntax is as follows:

```
<IMG SRC="imagefile.gif">
```

Image File Formats

Two widely supported web image formats are Graphics Interchange Format (GIF) and Joint Photographic Experts Group (JPEG). Microsoft Internet Explorer also supports the display of Windows Bitmap (BMP) images when used in an HTML document; Netscape Navigator does not currently support that format.

GIF   Typically, GIF files support fewer colors than JPEG files, and are best suited for line art, custom drawings, and text used as a graphic. Two GIF versions exist: GIF 87a and GIF 89a. GIF 89a is more popular because it supports the following techniques:

Transparency   The ability to make any part of the image invisible so the page background shows through. The image thus appears to blend into the background.

Interlacing   The ability for an image to "fade in" as it renders.

Animation   A series of images appearing in sequence to create the effect of motion.

You will learn more about animation, transparency, and interlacing later in the chapter.

JPEG   The JPEG format supports many more colors than GIF, and is typically used for photographs and complex images. This format also supports compression, meaning that you can reduce the image's file size. However, the more you compress the image, the more you will likely reduce its quality. Image compression of this type is called *lossy* compression.

PNG   Portable Network Graphics (PNG) is an emerging format, proposed as a future standard. This proposed format has not yet been widely implemented. However, you should check whether your current graphics software can produce or export an image into this format. PNG is designed to compress image information, allowing shorter download times and quicker image rendering in the browser.

When chosen carefully, images can greatly enhance your pages. Too many images, however, can slow the loading of pages, waste costly online time, and even displease users by making the page look too cluttered. Be creative but sparing in your use of images.

In the exercises that follow, you will incorporate several images into Web pages.

EXERCISE 14.8

Incorporating Images in a Web Page

In this exercise, you will learn how to place and align an image relative to text.

1. Open the file home.htm.

2. Modify the top portion of the code as indicated in bold, and save the file:

```
<BODY>
<IMG SRC=sun&sand.jpg>
<H1>Sun & Sand Tours</H1>
```

3. Load home.htm in your browser. You should see an icon representing that no image is available at the top of the screen.

4. Copy the file sun&sand.jpg from the CD to the same folder in which the home.htm file has been created.

5. Load home.htm in your browser. You should see an image appear at the top of the page.

6. Return to the text file, and center the image by adding the <DIV ALIGN=CENTER> tag. Save the file.

7. Reload the file. Your image should be centered.

You have successfully placed an image on a web page. You then centered the image by using the <DIV ALIGN=CENTER> tag.

If you upload your web pages to a web server and the images do not appear, check the <IMG SRC=" "> value of each image. If you created all of your images in a separate directory, make sure you uploaded that directory as well.

The preceding exercise demonstrated that simple design elements can enhance a website. If you will be creating web pages for a living, you may want to invest in an image-editing program. If you have some artistic ability, you will want to learn to use the more complicated graphics applications.

If you spend time browsing pictures on the Internet, you might be tempted to use graphics created by others in your Web pages. Be aware that any content—text, sound files, or images—is the sole property of the original owner. You may be subject to penalties under copyright laws if you use some-one else's creation without express, written permission. This is true of text as well, which is protected by copyright laws.

Aligning Images Relative to Text

Once you start working with images, you will see that placing an image on your page is only the first step. You will need to know how to position images relative to the text on the page. The syntax for the ALIGN attribute is as follows:

```
<IMG SRC="imagefile.gif" ALIGN="alignment choice">
```

Table 14.5 lists the values that you can use in conjunction with the ALIGN attribute in the <IMG> tag.

TABLE 14.5 Alignment Options for Images

ALIGN Attribute Value	Description
Bottom	The default alignment. The image is positioned so that the bottom of the image aligns with the baseline of adjoining text.
Middle	A vertical, not horizontal, alignment option. This value aligns the middle of the image to the baseline of adjoining text.

TABLE 14.5 Alignment Options for Images *(continued)*

ALIGN Attribute Value	Description
Top	Aligns the top of the image with the top of adjoining text.
Left	Floats the image to the left of the text paragraph into which the <IMG> tag is inserted. The top of the image will align with the left and top of the adjoining text.
Right	Floats the image to the right of the text paragraph into which the <IMG> tag is inserted. The top of the image will align with the right and top of the adjoining text.

Using the *ALT* Attribute with Images

Every image should follow good coding practice by containing the ALT attribute with a corresponding value. ALT designates alternate text to appear while the graphic is loading or in place of the graphic for those using non-graphical browsers, such as Lynx. This text will also display if the image fails to load or if the user has configured the browser not to display images.

The syntax for using the ALT attribute is as follows:

```
<IMG SRC="image.gif" ALT="alternate text">
```

Resizing Images

Sometimes, you will want to use a graphic in a size other than the natural size of the image. If you need to resize an image, you must maintain its relative measurements. For example, if you have an image that is 200 pixels wide by 300 pixels tall, you would not want to change the size to be 100 pixels wide by 300 pixels tall; this would distort the information and make it appear taller and narrower than it was originally. If you were trying to shrink the graphic to one-half of its size, you would instead change the width to 100 and the height to 150. By shrinking both dimensions by an equal percentage (in this case, by 50 percent), you maintain the original ratio of the image.

The syntax for specifying image height and width information is as follows:

```
<IMG SRC="imagename.gif" HEIGHT="HeightInPixels"
   WIDTH="WidthInPixels">
```

If you are not certain of the original dimensions of your image, you can ensure that the size will be changed proportionately by specifying *either* the height or the width; the other measurement will then be calculated for you based on the original image size.

It is considered good practice to specify the width of your image even if you are not changing the image from its original dimensions. This practice allows the browser to load surrounding text faster, because the browser then knows how much space to allot for your image before it loads.

EXERCISE 14.9

Labeling an Image with the *ALT* Attribute

In this exercise, you will create a page with an image that you will later use as an image map.

1. Load the file home.htm in your text editor.

2. Modify the top portion of the code as indicated in bold:
```
<DIV ALIGN=CENTER>
<IMG SRC=sun&sand.jpg><IMG SRC=sun&sand.gif>
<DIV>
<H1>Sun & Sand Tours</H1>
```

3. Save the file.

4. Reload the file in your browser. You should see an icon representing that no image is available at the top of the screen.

5. Modify the top portion of the code as indicated in bold:
```
<DIV ALIGN=CENTER>
<IMG SRC=sun&sand.gif ALT="Image of fun">
<DIV>
<H1>Sun & Sand Tours</H1>
```

6. Save the file.

7. Reload the file in your browser. You should see the phrase "Image of fun" beside the icon, representing that no image is available at the top of the screen.

You should develop the habit of including ALT text in your images. You should always include this attribute and the appropriate value when using images (other than graphic line and bullet character images).

Special Characters

Sooner or later you will need to include a non-keyboard character in your page. You can include non-keyboard characters if you know either the ANSI character value or the special HTML code for the character. In the Resources directory of your supplemental disc, the file named `charcodes.htm` contains a list of codes for special characters. Table 14.6 defines some of the most commonly used characters. As you can see, each special character code begins with the ampersand character (&) and ends with the semicolon character (;).

TABLE 14.6 HTML Special Character Codes

Character	Description	HTML Code
©	Copyright symbol	© or ©
®	Registered trademark symbol	® or ®
é	Lowercase e with an acute accent	é
<	Less-than symbol	<
>	Greater-than symbol	>

Sometimes you will see   in HTML code. This code denotes a non-breaking space character. Although more than one regular space is ignored in HTML, non-breaking space characters are never ignored. You can use these characters to insert more than one space in a row.

Specifying Colors in HTML

So far, all the files you created have used the same color scheme: black text on a white background. The Web would be very boring if no one ever strayed from this combination. Instead, you can specify alternate page and text color combinations.

You can easily specify colors for text and the page background in HTML documents. To do this, you need to supply a value representing a color. This value can take the form of a recognized color name (such as "yellow" or "blue"), or the value can be a hexadecimal code representing a color. The term *hexadecimal* refers to a base-16 number system that allows large numbers to be displayed by fewer characters than if the number were displayed in the regular base-10 system. In the hexadecimal system, the number 10 is represented as the letter A; 15 is represented as the letter F; and 16 is represented as 10.

Colors are often specified in terms of their RGB values. RGB stands for Red Green Blue. If you are mixing paint, you will know that mixing red, green, and blue together creates a rather muddy color. But on a monitor, you are mixing light, and the mixture of red, green, and blue light produces white, which is the presence of all colors. Black is the absence of all colors. In other words, the higher the numeric value representing a color, the lighter that color will be. The lower the value, the darker the color.

RGB colors are specified in values ranging from 0 to 255. The RGB value of 255 is FF is in hexadecimal code. Therefore, #FFFFFF represents the highest possible value for all three colors, producing white. The value #000000 represents the absence of all colors, or black. The number character (#) is not required by current generation browsers, but you should include this symbol for full backward compatibility.

The Web-Safe Color Palette

Colors are formulated on a computer screen through a combination of red, green, and blue; thus, colors are often referred to as the RGB values.

Whenever you use a color in a web page (whether for a background, font, or image), you are enabling a combination of the RGB values. This limited color palette is necessary because computer screens are generally cathode ray tubes (CRTs), which have certain design limitations.

You will want your pages to render consistently no matter which browser or operating system is used to view them. In other words, if you define a blue background color, you will want it to appear the same in a Macintosh system using a version of Netscape Navigator as it would in a Windows system using a version of Microsoft Internet Explorer. You want your image colors to appear consistently. If your HTML code asks for a color that the browser or operating system cannot support, the computer will compensate through *dithering*, or the ability for a computer to approximate a color by combining the RGB values. The results of dithering are unpredictable and often unsightly.

When Netscape Corporation marketed the first browser that supported *inline images* (images rendered in a web page), it created a standard of 216 colors that would render consistently, known as the web-safe color palette. Microsoft Internet Explorer, NCSA Mosaic, and other browsers conform to this list of colors.

Sometimes the web-safe color palette is called the "Netscape safe palette" or the "browser-safe palette."

As mentioned earlier, the file on the accompanying CD named 216.html contains a list of the 216 colors in the web-safe palette. To further ensure cross-browser capability, you can specify colors in hexadecimal format, rather than by name.

Page Colors and Backgrounds

You can add color information to the <BODY> tag to control the colors of the background of the page, as well as the colors of the text and links on the page. In addition, you can tile an image across the page for a background.

To specify a color for a page background, add the BGCOLOR attribute to the BODY element using the following syntax:

```
<BODY BGCOLOR="color">
```

To designate the color of text on a page, use the TEXT attribute of the BODY element. In the next section, you will learn how to create hyperlinks. If you are using links, you can control the color of links from the <BODY> tag as well. Table 14.7 outlines the <BODY> tag color attributes.

TABLE 14.7 <BODY> Tag Color Attributes

Attribute Name	Sample Values	Description
BGCOLOR	#FF0000 red	The value of this attribute determines the background color of the page.
TEXT	#00FF00 green	The value of this attribute determines the color of non-link text on the page.
ALINK	#0000FF blue	The value of this attribute determines the color of the link when the mouse is pressed but not released over the link.
LINK	#FFFFFF white	The value of this attribute determines the color of unvisited links.
VLINK	#000000 black	The value of this attribute determines the color of visited links.
BACKGROUND	myback.gif tiledimage.jpg	The value of this attribute determines the image that will be tiled behind the contents as a background for the page.

If the BACKGROUND and BGCOLOR attributes are both used, the BACKGROUND attribute will take precedence and the BGCOLOR attribute will be ignored.

EXERCISE 14.10

Changing Page Colors and Backgrounds

In this exercise, you will learn how to specify and change document colors for the page background and any text on the page. You will also learn how to use an image as a page background.

1. Open the file home.htm in your editor.

2. Modify the <BODY> tag as indicated in bold:
   <BODY **BGCOLOR="#FFFF00"**>

3. Save the file. Reload it within the browser and you should see a background of bright yellow.

4. Open the file home.htm in the editor again.

5. Modify the <BODY> tag as indicated in bold:
   <BODY BGCOLOR="**navy**" TEXT="**cyan**">

6. Reload the file in your browser. You should see light turquoise-blue text on a dark blue background.

7. Delete the BGCOLOR attribute and value, and include the BACKGROUND attribute instead, as indicated in bold:
   <BODY **BACKGROUND="sun&sand.jpg"**>
   <DIV ALIGN=CENTER>
   <IMG SRC=sun&sand.gif ALT="Image of fun">
   <DIV>
   <H1>Sun & Sand Tours</H1>

8. Reload the file in the browser.

As you can see, using images and colors instantly changes a plain-looking page to an attractive, vibrant presentation. The most important element to consider when creating a web page, however, is not how attractive the page looks, but how readable it is. Although you may prefer an unusual combination of colors, keep your target audience in mind and consider whether your choices will make the page more readable or less.

Partial color blindness is much more widespread than commonly realized. If your target audience is the entire world, read about color blindness to determine which combinations are most easily read by the largest number of people. You can find several sites relating to color blindness by visiting www.yahoo.com and searching for the keywords "color blindness."

Specifying Font Information

The <FONT> tag is a container tag that allows you to change the size, color, and typeface of the enclosed text. The next exercise will demonstrate the use of the <FONT> tag. The <FONT> tag supports three attributes: SIZE, COLOR, and FACE. The HTML 4.01 standard has deprecated this tag in favor of using Cascading Style Sheets (CSS). This means that future versions of HTML—and Web browsers—may not support <FONT>. However, this tag is still quite popular.

When using the <FONT> tag, the SIZE attribute takes values 1 through 7, with 7 being largest, 3 being the normal size of default text, and 1 being two sizes smaller than normal. In addition, you can set the value of the <FONT> tag's size attribute to +1, -2, and so forth to make changes relative to the font's default size.

When you specify a value for the COLOR attribute, use the same values that you learned for specifying a page background color.

The FACE attribute specifies the typeface (i.e., font name) to be used. Remember to always close your <FONT> tag with </FONT> at the end of the text to be affected.

If you specify a font that is not available on all systems, some users will not see the font face you chose; the font will display as a default font face instead. Be aware of this when planning your pages.

EXERCISE 14.11

Changing Font Face, Size, and Color with the <FONT> Tag

In this exercise, you will learn how to change the font style of text using the <FONT> tag.

1. Create a new file with your text editor.

```
<!DOCTYPE HTML PUBLIC "-//W3C//DTD HTML 4.01
↳Transitional//EN"
"http://www.w3.org/TR/html4/loose.dtd">
<HTML>
<HEAD>
<TITLE>Tour Package Information from Sun & Sand
↳Tours</TITLE>
</HEAD>
<BODY>
<H1>Tour Packages</H1>
<FONT SIZE="7">
Sun & Sand Tour Packages
</FONT>
<PRE>
Destination     Duration  Cost
Tahiti          5 Nights  $899
Virgin Islands  9 Nights  $1499
Seychelles      8 Nights  $2499
</PRE>
<SMALL>
All tours are subject to change without notice.<P>
Return to our home page
</SMALL>
</BODY>
</HTML>
```

2. Save the file as tours.htm.

3. Load the file in your browser.

4. Modify the opening <FONT> tag as indicated in bold:

<FONT SIZE=4 COLOR="purple" FACE=Arial>

5. Reload the file in the browser.

When you tagged text to appear as a heading-level-1 element, you saw that the text became larger and bold as well. The same is not true when you increase size using the <FONT> tag. In the next step, you will add boldface to your specified font.

6. Modify your code as indicated in bold:
   `<B>`Sun & Sand Tour Packages`</B>`
   `</FONT>`

7. Reload the file in the browser. The text you changed should now appear in bold as well.

As you learned in the preceding exercise, you can specify certain font information through the use of the `<FONT>` tag. However, some information, including boldface and other font attributes you learned earlier, cannot be specified using the `<FONT>` tag.

With practice, you can embellish your HTML pages quickly and easily by using simple graphical elements and by adding attributes to the basic elements of the page. In the next section, you will learn to join your pages into a website using hyperlinks.

HTML Hyperlinks

What makes the World Wide Web a "web" are the links that connect web pages to other files across the Internet. The ability to create hyperlinks is in fact more fundamental than the ability to include multimedia objects in your HTML documents. Even users with non-graphical browsers, such as Lynx, can select links in web pages to navigate and explore the Web. The critical element is the ability to move from page to page by clicking on linked text or images.

A text hyperlink is a section of text that is specially tagged as a link. An image or icon may also be enclosed in anchor tags and used as a link to another file. In both cases, clicking the link will take the user to the destination of the link.

You can link to external files as well as to points within the current file. On a long page, you can jump between sections of the page with links. Such a link is called an internal link. You create internal and external links with the anchor tag.

Anchor Tag

Links are created with the anchor tag, <A>. Anchor tags are container tags surrounding the text or image (or both) to be used as the link. The HREF attribute is used to specify the link's hypertext reference, or the target of the link. You can specify a fully qualified URL or a relative URL reference for any file, page, or site.

The syntax for using the anchor tag to create a link is as follows:

```
<A HREF="URL"> linked text or image (or both) </A>
```

Table 14.8 lists examples of values for the URL when referencing external links.

TABLE 14.8   URL Options for External Links

Type of Reference	Examples
Fully qualified URL	http://www.someserver.com/somepage.html ftp://ftp.someserver.com/pub/somefile.ext
Partial URL	http://www.someserver.com/somepage.html /pub6/images/mybullet.gif

EXERCISE 14.12

Creating Local Text Hyperlinks

In this exercise, you will link together some of the files you already created.

1. Open the file home.htm.

2. You will link the first bullet list item to the corresponding travel tips page you created in an earlier section. Modify the code as indicated in bold to create a hyperlink using the anchor tag:

```
<UL>
<LI><A HREF="tips.htm">Travel Tips</A>
<LI>Tour Package Information
<LI>Information Request Form
</UL>
```

3. Save the file.

4. Load the file home.htm. "Travel Tips" should appear in blue and underlined. This indicates that the text is now a link.

5. Test the link by clicking it. You should see the Travel Tips page load into the browser.

6. Click the Back button on the browser to return to the home page.

7. On your own, link the second bullet text to the tours.htm page.

8. Reload the file.

9. Click the new link. You should see the Tour Packages page.

As you have seen, creating links can be a simple operation. In the previous exercise, you linked to other files located in the same directory as the file containing the link. In the next exercise, you will enter a fully qualified URL to link to a page on the U.S. State Department website.

EXERCISE 14.13

Linking to an External Site

In this exercise, you will use the anchor tag to link a piece of text to a file on an external website.

1. Open the file home.htm.

2. The U.S. State Department maintains a page of travel advisories for U.S. citizens traveling to foreign destinations. This page is located at http://travel.state.gov/travel_warnings.html. Add a fourth bullet to the list as indicated in bold:

```
<LI>Information Request Form
<LI>Check out any
<A HREF=http://travel.state.gov/travel_warnings.html>
State Department Travel Advisories
</A>
before you leave.
</UL>
```

EXERCISE 14.13 *(continued)*

3. Save the file.

4. Load the file in your browser. The text should now appear underlined.

5. Verify that you are connected to the Internet, then click the link. You should see the U.S. State Department's Travel Warnings page.

6. Click the browser's Back button to return to the home page.

Using Images as Links

You are not limited to using text to link to another file. You can surround image tags with opening and closing anchor tags to use a graphic image as a link. The following exercise will demonstrate how to use an image as a link.

EXERCISE 14.14

Using an Image as a Link

In this exercise, you will add a small image of an Exit sign to the bottom of the `tips.htm` and `tours.htm` pages. This graphic will function as a return link to the home page for Sun & Sand Tours.

1. Copy the file `exit.jpg` from the CD to the directory where your `.htm` files exist.

2. Open the file `tips.htm` in your editor.

3. Place the cursor just before the closing `</BODY>` tag and add the following image tag near the bottom of the page:
   ```
   <IMG SRC=exit.jpg HEIGHT=50 WIDTH=75>
   </BODY>
   </HTML>
   ```

4. Save the file.

5. Load the file `tips.htm` in your browser. You should now see a small image of an Exit sign at the bottom left of the page.

6. Within the editor, add an anchor tag around the image tag to use the image as the link as indicated in bold:

   <A HREF=home.htm><IMG SRC=exit.jpg HEIGHT=50
   ↳WIDTH=75>**</A>**

7. Save the file.

8. Reload the file in your browser. You should see a box around the image. This box indicates that the image is a link.

9. Click the exit sign image. The home page for Sun & Sand Tours should appear.

10. Click the Travel Tips link to return to the Tips page.

11. Most web page authors do not like the box to appear around an image used as a link. You can choose to make the box invisible by using the BORDER attribute of the <IMG> tag. Within the editor, modify the <IMG> tag as indicated in bold:

    <A HREF=home.htm><IMG SRC=exit.jpb HEIGHT=50 WIDTH=75
    ↳**BORDER="0">**</A>

    Note that you can specify either BORDER="0" or BORDER="none". Both of these are acceptable values for the BORDER attribute. The other acceptable value is a positive integer, which can be used to specify the width of the border that appears when the image is used as a link.

12. Save the file.

13. Reload the file in the browser. The border around the image should now be gone; however, the image should still function as a link.

14. Click the image to return to the Sun & Sand Tours home page.

15. Click the Travel Tips link to return to the Tips page.

16. You will add text to the link so that the same pair of anchor tags links both text and the image. Within the editor, modify your code as indicated in bold:

    <A HREF=home.htm><IMG SRC=exit.jpg HEIGHT=50 WIDTH=75
    ↳BORDER="0"> **Return to the Home Page**</A>

17. Save the file.

18. Reload the file. You should now see linked text appearing next to the image. By doing this, users who have turned off image display or are not using a graphical browser can still return to your home page.

So far, you have created external links using full and partial URLs. In the next section, you will learn how to create a link within a page to a different area of the same page.

Creating Internal Links

On a long web page, you may want to include links that target other areas within the same page so that users can easily find the section of the page that interests them.

Internal links require internal bookmarks, called anchors. Creating an internal link requires two steps. You must first use the anchor tag, <A>, with the NAME attribute to define an area as a target. Then, in another portion of the page, you create a link that points to that target area using the anchor tag with the hypertext reference, HREF, attribute. The syntax for creating an internal link is as follows:

```
<A NAME="TargetArea1">
target anchor text or image (or both)
</A>
... other page content here ...
<A HREF="#TargetArea1"> text/images linking to
↳TargetArea1 </A>
```

The NAME attribute of the anchor tag defines an internal bookmark or anchor in the page. Note that for the HREF value, the # symbol is used. This symbol, called a hash, tells the browser to look for an anchor by this name within the current document. Without this hash, the browser will look for an external file by that name.

Accessing an External File's Internal Link

Suppose you want to link to a specific point in another page without first accessing the top of that page. To link to an internal anchor in another file, use the following syntax:

```
<A HREF="URL/filename.ext#AnchorName">link text/image</A>
```

You can start with a full or partial URL, but you must specify the file name, followed by the hash symbol, followed by the name of the internal anchor to which you want to direct the link.

Summary

In this chapter, you learned the origins of HTML and the purpose for its creation. You learned that the W3C is the standards organization governing the evolution of HTML. You also learned that HTML editors may provide a simple interface to help you create HTML pages, but without the core knowledge to write HTML code manually, you are limited in your web page development.

You also learned how to use container and empty HTML tags. You learned the basic structure tags that must be present in any HTML document. You learned how to format both text and paragraphs, and you learned how to use the <PRE> tag. You also created a bulleted list in one file and a numbered list in another. Finally, you were introduced to the concept of good coding practice and the importance of correct application and sequence of your code.

You were introduced to graphic elements such as horizontal rules, images, and colors. You learned how to position graphics relative to text, and how to resize images for display. In addition, you were introduced to the <FONT> tag, which specifies font face, size, and color information.

You learned how to link text and images to other files and sites. You learned that you can use full or partial URLs in your links, and you learned how to link to an internal anchor point within the current document or even within another document.

Exam Essentials

Know the origins of HTML. Tim Berners-Lee of MIT invented Hypertext Markup Language (HTML) with colleagues from CERN, the European Particle Physics Laboratory, as a means of distributing nonlinear text, called hypertext, to multiple points across the Internet.

Understand the standards organization that controls the various versions of HTML. The World Wide Web Consortium (W3C) is the standards organization that controls the evolution of HTML. When the W3C fully endorses a technology, it publishes a "recommendation" to the Internet community.

Know the HTML 4.01 flavors. There are three HTML 4.01 flavors that ensure use of the latest specification, yet remain backward-compatible with older Web browsers: HTML 4.01 Transitional, HTML 4.01 Strict, and HTML 4.01 Frameset.

Be able to explain how HTML is related to XHTML. The Extensible Hypertext Markup Language (XHTML) is the latest formulation of HTML. XHTML combines HTML with the Extensible Markup Language (XML).

Be able to identify HTML document structure tags. Document structure tags are the bare minimum needed tags for an HTML page. The required tags are: HTML, HEAD, TITLE, and BODY.

Understand the <META> tag and the Document Type Declaration (DTD). The <META> tag is an empty tag that describes the contents of your page. You place it between the <HEAD> tags in your HTML document. The <META> tag is quite useful with search engines because many spider programs look for it. The Document Type Declaration (DTD) statement begins your HTML code by specifying the HTML version number and type used in the document.

Be able to name two image file formats supported across the Web. Two widely supported web image formats are Graphics Interchange Format (GIF) and Joint Photographic Experts Group (JPEG).

Know the alignment options available for aligning images relative to text. There are five alignment options available: Bottom, Middle, Top, Left, and Right.

Understand hexadecimal color values. Colors are specified in values ranging from #000000 to #FFFFFF. Although the number character (#) is not required by current generation browsers, you should include this symbol for full backward-compatibility.

Know the two types of URLs you can reference outside a web page when creating hyperlinks (i.e., located on either an external site or another page on the same site). You can specify a fully qualified URL or a relative URL reference for any file, page, or site.

Understand the syntax used to link to an internal anchor in another file without first accessing the top of that page. To link to an internal anchor in another file, use the following syntax:

`<A HREF="URL/filename.ext#AnchorName">link text/image</A>`

You can start with a full or partial URL, but you must specify the file name, followed by the hash symbol, followed by the name of the internal anchor to which you want to direct the link.

Key Terms

Before you take the exam, be certain you are familiar with the following terms:

animation	Document Type Declaration (DTD)
attribute	element
block-level element	empty tag
Cascading Style Sheet (CSS)	fixed-width font
container tag	frameset
dithering	hexadecimal

horizontal rule

HTTP (Hypertext Transfer Protocol)

hyperlink

hypertext

interlacing

intranet

lossy

proportional-width font

rule

spider

strict

tag

text-level element

transitional

transparency

user agent

value

XHTML (Extensible Hypertext Markup Language)

XML (Extensible Markup Language)

Review Questions

1. What are the pointers that connect text images and image maps to multiple locations across the Internet known as?

   A. Websites

   B. Hyperlinks

   C. Hyperconnectors

   D. Web links

2. Which of the following requires the exclusive use of Cascading Style Sheets when defining layout instructions?

   A. HTML 4.01 Transitional

   B. HTML 4.01 Strict

   C. HTML 4.01 Extensible

   D. HTML 4.01 Frameset

3. What is the primary function of HTML?

   A. To display graphics on a web page

   B. To broadcast audio across a web page

   C. To enhance the use of animation on a web page

   D. To position content on a web page

4. What embeds the HTML element information into the document to instruct an interpreter how to render text?

   A. Markup tags

   B. Hyperlinks

   C. Body tags

   D. Attributes

5. Which of the following must be used in pairs?

   A. Attribute values

   B. Empty tags

   C. Elements

   D. Container tags

6. Which of the following tags would usually enclose the main portion of an HTML document?

   A. <TITLE> tag

   B. <BODY> tag

   C. <HEAD> tag

   D. <HTML> tag

7. Into which of the following tags could you add a brief summary of your web page's contents?

   A. <HEAD>

   B. <DTD>

   C. <META>

   D. <HTML>

8. Which attribute eliminates the default "shadow" of a horizontal rule?

   A. NOSHADE

   B. NOSHADOW

   C. SHADING

   D. SHADOWING

9. Transparency, interlacing, and animation are the three techniques supported by:

   A. GIF 91a

   B. GIF 89a

   C. GIF 87a

   D. GIF 84a

10. You have uploaded a website to the Web, but when you view the web page in your browser, the images do not appear. What should you check on your web pages?

    A. Interlacing properties

    B. `<IMG SRC="">` value

    C. Image alignment value

    D. Transparency properties

11. Which of the following attributes controls the color of a link when a mouse is pressed but not released over the link?

    A. ALINK

    B. VLINK

    C. LINK

    D. TEXT

12. What is a computer's ability to approximate a color by combining RGB values called?

    A. Dithering

    B. Blending

    C. Transparency

    D. Rendering

13. Which of the following attributes determines the image that will be tiled behind the contents of a page?

    A. BGCOLOR

    B. TEXT

    C. BACKGROUND

    D. VLINK

14. When is it necessary to use a fully qualified URL?

    A. When using an image as a link

    B. When linking to another location on the same site

    C. When linking to an external site

    D. When accessing a file's internal link

15. Which tag is used to create hyperlinks that connect web pages to other files on the Internet or to text within the same page?

    A. <HREF> tag

    B. <HEAD> tag

    C. <LINK> tag

    D. <A> tag

16. To use an image as the link to another file, you would:

    A. Add an image tag.

    B. Add an anchor tag around an image tag.

    C. Add an image tag around an anchor tag.

    D. Place the IMAGE attribute inside an anchor tag.

17. Which anchor tag attribute defines an internal bookmark within a page?

    A. NAME

    B. INTERNAL

    C. BOOKMARK

    D. HREF followed by the hash symbol

18. Which anchor tag attribute creates a hyperlink to a defined internal bookmark?

    A. `NAME = "TargetArea"`

    B. `EXTERNAL = "#TargetArea"`

    C. `BOOKMARK = "TargetArea"`

    D. `HREF = "#TargetArea"`

19. Which of the following individuals first conceived hypertext?

    A. Al Gore

    B. Bill Gates

    C. Dennis Ritchie

    D. Ted Nelson

20. Which of the following values is not accepted with the `ALIGN` attribute for horizontal rules?

    A. `Middle`

    B. `Right`

    C. `Center`

    D. `Left`

Answers to Review Questions

1. B.   Hyperlinks are used to provide methods of connecting text images and image maps to multiple locations across the Internet.

2. B.   HTML 4.01 Strict adheres to a set standard and requires the exclusive use of Cascading Style Sheets (CSS).

3. D.   HTML can be used for a number of things, but the primary function of the language is to format content on a web page.

4. A.   Markup tags are used to embed HTML element information into a document. The browser reads the tags and interprets the instructions on rendering held within.

5. D.   Container tags must always be used in pairs in HTML.

6. B.   The main portion, or body, of the document is held within the <BODY> and </BODY> tags.

7. C.   Summaries of a web page's content can be added within <META> tags.

8. A.   The NOSHADE attribute is used to eliminate the shadow that, by default, accompanies a horizontal rule.

9. B.   GIF 89a added animation to graphic possibilities and supports transparency and interlacing.

10. B.   Images on a page are identified by the <IMG SRC=" "> values. If the images do not appear, you should verify that they are properly referenced within those tags.

11. A.   The ALINK attribute is used to control the color of a link when a mouse is pressed.

12. A.   Dithering is the computer's ability to approximate a color by combining RGB values.

13. C.   The BACKGROUND attribute specifies the background image that will be tiled behind the contents of a page.

14. C.   Relative URLs can be used to reference internal sites, but when linking to an external site, you must always use a fully qualified URL.

15. D.   The <A> tag is used to create hyperlinks that connect web pages to other files.

16. B.   Adding an anchor tag around an image tag will allow the image to serve as a link to another file.

17. A.   The NAME anchor tag attribute is used to define internal bookmarks.

18. D.   The HREF = "#TargetArea" anchor tag attribute creates a hyperlink to a defined internal bookmark.

19. D.   Ted Nelson first conceived of hypertext in 1965.

20. A.   The three accepted values for the Align attribute are Right, Center (the default), and Left.

Chapter

15

Advanced HTML

THE CIW EXAM OBJECTIVE GROUPS COVERED IN THIS CHAPTER:

- ✓ Add images and graphical formatting to HTML files by manual coding in a text editor.
- ✓ Create a basic HTML form that accepts user input.
- ✓ Test and analyze website performance.
- ✓ Identify the purpose and function of Extensible Markup Language (XML).

As you learned in the preceding chapter, HTML (Hypertext Markup Language) is the standard authoring language used to develop web pages. This chapter builds upon the basics of the HTML language by showing you how to enhance web pages by adding tables, creating forms, and employing image techniques. Further, we'll discuss how to utilize frames and HTML extensions to increase the types of content you offer on your website.

HTML Tables

You will often find that you need to align text and images, horizontally or vertically (or both) on a page. When you want to create the appearance of tabular or structured text, you can use the table tags provided in HTML to make useful and attractive grids. Tables were first introduced in HTML 2.0, and have been expanded upon for HTML 4.01.

Figure 15.1 describes the individual elements that compose an HTML table. Each of these elements will be explored in this section.

FIGURE 15.1 HTML table elements

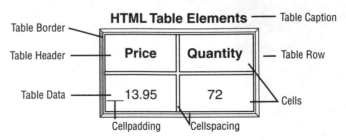

The code for the table in the preceding figure could be written as follows:

```
<TABLE BORDER="3" CELLPADDING="4" CELLSPACING="2">
<CAPTION>HTML Table Elements</CAPTION>
<TR>
<TH>Price</TH><TH>Quantity</TH>
</TR>
<TR>
<TD>13.95</TD><TD ALIGN="center">72</TD>
</TR>
</TABLE>
```

The CELLPADDING attribute in the preceding code is used to identify space between cell text and cell border. The tags that correspond to each element in Figure 15.1 are described in Table 15.1.

TABLE 15.1 Table Tags

Element	Tag	Usage
Table	<TABLE>...</TABLE>	Required to create a table; it contains all the other table elements.
Table Caption	<CAPTION>...</CAPTION>	Optional; can be used to add an attached caption to the table.
Table Row	<TR>...</TR>	Required; contains all data for the current table row.
Table Header	<TH>...</TH>	Optional; typically designates the top row or left column. By default, text in a header cell will appear bold and centered.
Table Data	<TD>...</TD>	Mandatory unless <TH> is being used. Table data tags enclose table cell contents.

Tables can be very complex or very simple, as is the one you will create in the following exercise. Straightforward tables are easy to create, once you understand where each element should be placed. As your tables become more complex, you will understand why GUI HTML editors are so popular.

EXERCISE 15.1

Creating a Simple Table

In this exercise, you will view a simple table, add a border, and change the table's overall width.

1. Load the file `table.htm` from the CD into your browser. You should see a small table resembling the one shown here:

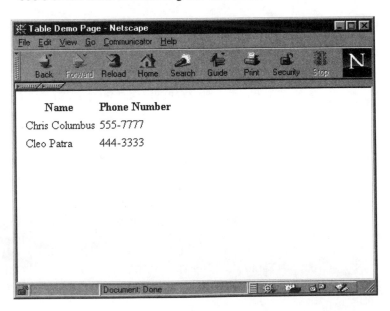

EXERCISE 15.1 *(continued)*

2. Open table.htm in your editor. Your screen should resemble this one.

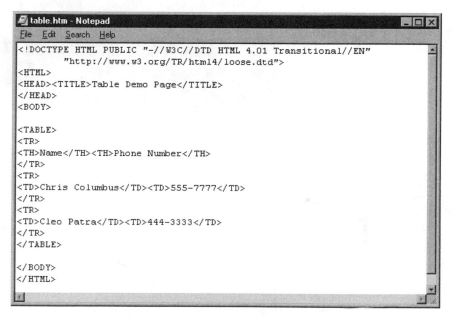

```
table.htm - Notepad                                        _ □ ×
File  Edit  Search  Help
<!DOCTYPE HTML PUBLIC "-//W3C//DTD HTML 4.01 Transitional//EN"
        "http://www.w3.org/TR/html4/loose.dtd">
<HTML>
<HEAD><TITLE>Table Demo Page</TITLE>
</HEAD>
<BODY>

<TABLE>
<TR>
<TH>Name</TH><TH>Phone Number</TH>
</TR>
<TR>
<TD>Chris Columbus</TD><TD>555-7777</TD>
</TR>
<TR>
<TD>Cleo Patra</TD><TD>444-3333</TD>
</TR>
</TABLE>

</BODY>
</HTML>
```

3. Add the BORDER attribute to the <TABLE> tag as indicated in bold:

   <TABLE **BORDER="1"**>

   <TR>

   <TH>Name</TH><TH>Phone Number</TH>

   </TR>

   <TR>

   <TD>Chris Columbus</TD><TD>555-7777</TD>

   </TR>

   <TR>

   <TD>Cleo Patra</TD><TD>444-3333</TD>

   </TR>

   </TABLE>

4. Save the file.

5. Reload the file in the browser. You should now see a border outlining the cells of your table, like this one.

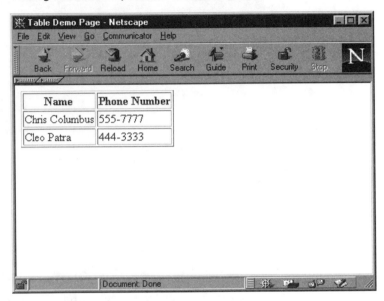

6. Note that by default, a table will only fill as much space as it needs, based on the text in the cells. If you want more white space between your text and the cell borders, you have some options. One way to add space is to widen the whole table. Modify the <TABLE> tag as indicated in bold:
   <TABLE BORDER="1" **WIDTH="80%"**>

7. Save the file.

8. Reload the file. Your table should now resemble this one:

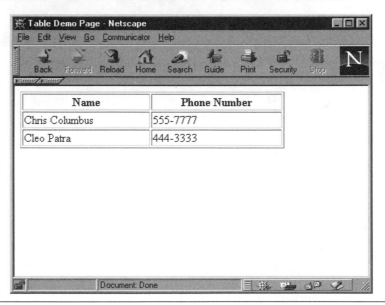

Table and Data Alignment Options

Frequently you will want to align cell content in a manner that differs from the default alignment. By default, table header cells are aligned to the center of the cell. By default, table data cells are aligned to the left. Consider the example in Figure 15.2.

As you can see, by default, cell contents are aligned vertically to the middle of the cell. You can change this for an individual cell or for an entire row. The attribute you use to specify horizontal alignment is ALIGN; for vertical alignment, use VALIGN.

FIGURE 15.2 Vertical alignment of cell content

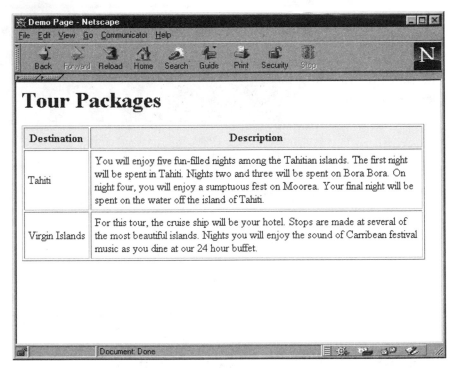

Either of the following code samples in Figure 15.3 could be used to produce the vertical alignment.

FIGURE 15.3 Two ways to change vertical alignment

```
<TR VALIGN="top">
<TD>
Tahiti
</TD>
```

```
<TR>
<TD VALIGN="top">
Tahiti
</TD>
```

The example on the left in Figure 15.3 sets the alignment of the entire row to `"top"`, meaning all cell content in that row will start at the top of the cell. The example on the right specifies a vertical alignment only for the cell containing Tahiti. The cell to the right of Tahiti is already aligned to the top because it is completely full.

You can align the contents of any table cell to the left, right, or center. In addition, you can align the table itself relative to the surrounding page text by adding the ALIGN attribute to the <TABLE> tag. Tables can float to the left or right of page text. You also have the option to align the table to the center of the page.

Table 15.2 outlines the various alignment attributes and the table elements with which these attributes can be used.

TABLE 15.2 Alignment Attributes Used with Table Elements

Element	Attribute	Values	Description
<TR><TH> <TD>	VALIGN	top, middle, bottom	Vertically aligns the contents of the cell or row to the top, center, or bottom of the cell. The default alignment is middle.
<TABLE> <TR><TH> <TD>	ALIGN	left, center, right	Horizontally aligns the contents of the table, cell(s) or row to the left, right, or center. For tables and table data cells, the default alignment is left. For table header cells, the default alignment is center.
<CAPTION>	ALIGN	top, bottom	A caption can be added above your table. The caption is by default aligned to the top center above your table. You can specify bottom to have the caption appear below the table.

You can change the height or width of the table and individual cells by specifying pixel or percentage values. For example, HEIGHT="50%" will set the height to 50% of the browser window. Likewise, WIDTH="80%" will set the width of a column to 80% of the browser window.

HEIGHT=50 will set the height to 50 pixels, whereas WIDTH=80 will, correspondingly, set the width to 80 pixels.

Column and Row Spanning

Sometimes you will want to apply a heading across several cells. In other cases, you may need one cell to span more than one row. The following code demonstrates a cell that horizontally spans three columns, as well as a cell that vertically spans four rows. This effect is accomplished by using the ROWSPAN and COLSPAN attributes. The tags used to create the table above have been minimized so that you can focus on the overall structure in the following code: Most of the attributes and text have been removed to facilitate your focus on key tags. Note especially the code in bold and its effects.

```
<TABLE CELLSPACING=10 WIDTH="100%">
<TR><TH COLSPAN=3>Conservation...</TH></TR>
<TR><TD ROWSPAN=4><IMG SRC="paloalto.gif"></TD>
<TH>Date</TH><TH>Activities</TH></TR>
<TR><TD>November 17</TD><TD>Discussion of ...</TD></TR>
<TR><TD>November 23</TD><TD>Naturelands hike...</TD></TR>
<TR><TD>December 12</TD><TD>The movie ...</TD></TR>
</TABLE>
```

When you change the width or height of any one cell, that action will have a ripple effect across related cells. If you decrease the width of one cell, you are increasing the width of other cells. If you increase the height of one cell, you are increasing the height of other cells in the same row.

HTML Forms

HTML forms, also known as web forms, are standard in all flavors of HTML 4.01. Before you create a web form, however, you should first learn about the processes involved when a user sends a form to a web server.

HTTP allows you to send almost any type of data across the Internet to a web server. One critical type of data is input from visitors to the site. Websites use forms to obtain input from users. You can place many different fields into one form for user input—for example, a user name, address, or credit card number could all be put into one form. The information entered into a form is then submitted to a server where it is stored and/or processed.

To be truly functional, a form requires the use of a Common Gateway Interface (CGI) program to process the script. CGI is the *de facto* standard, but other technologies exist to process forms, such as Active Server Pages (ASP) and Java Server Pages (JSP). CGI programs use a server-side script. This is in contrast to a client-side script, which is executed on the client.

A *server-side script* is code that resides on a server to help process a form. Server-side CGI scripts are commonly written in Perl. A *client-side script* is code embedded into the HTML and downloaded by a user. It resides on the client and helps to process a form. Common client-side scripting languages include JavaScript and VBScript.

A CGI script residing on a server performs two important functions: it receives data from a web browser, and then it processes and formats the data. Without some sort of CGI script running on the server, the server cannot receive the form data. Most CGI scripts do more than just receive data; they also remove extraneous information and format the data. Many scripts, servers, and utilities are available on UNIX, Macintosh, and Windows platforms to simplify this process. Such scripting utilities are available commercially, or as freeware or shareware.

Uploading or e-mailing form data is referred to as *submitting* a form. A Reset button often is available on web pages to clear entered data and reset the form to the default values.

Now that you understand the basic processes of a web form, you will learn about the elements that compose a web form.

The *<FORM>* Tag

The <FORM> tag begins and ends an HTML form. <FORM> is a container tag, which means you must supply both opening and closing tags. In some browsers, if you fail to supply the closing </FORM> tag, the form will not render. Internet Explorer displays form fields even if no <FORM> tag is present. However, you would be unable to submit any form information because without the <FORM> tag, you cannot instruct the browser where to send data. In Navigator, form fields not enclosed in <FORM> tags will not appear at all.

Following is sample syntax for a <FORM> tag:

```
<FORM
METHOD="post" ACTION="http://www.anyserver.com/cgi-bin/scriptfile">
<INPUT ...>
<SELECT> ... </SELECT>
</FORM>
```

For now, ignore the INPUT and SELECT elements. The FORM element has two attributes associated with it: METHOD and ACTION.

METHOD Attribute   The METHOD attribute specifies which method the browser will use to send form data to a web server. The METHOD attribute takes two values: get and post. Table 15.3 describes each of these methods.

TABLE 15.3   Form Submission Methods

Method	Description
get	Form data is appended to the URL for use in a query string.
post	Form data is posted to the URL specified by the ACTION attribute. Post is the most common method for sending form data. It can send more characters, although sometimes post requires more processing by the CGI script.

ACTION Attribute   The ACTION attribute specifies the name and location of the CGI script used to process the form. The contents of the form will be processed by the script and acted upon according to the instructions in the script.

Most ISPs offer the use of certain scripts to their customers. Check with your provider for available CGI scripts and any other information you need to use forms on your own site. If you host your own server, you will have to write and manage your own scripts.

You can use the <INPUT>, <SELECT>, and <TEXTAREA> tags to create form fields by placing them within the FORM element. The <INPUT> tag is empty; you use it to create text boxes, check boxes, radio buttons, and the Submit and Reset buttons. The <SELECT> tag is a container tag used to create select lists and multiple-select lists. The <TEXTAREA> container tag creates text area spaces.

The INPUT element uses a TYPE attribute. Add a value to TYPE to designate whether you want a text box, a radio button, a Submit or Reset button, a password field, or a check box. For example, to create a radio button with the INPUT element, use the following syntax:

```
<INPUT TYPE="radio" NAME="AddToList">
```

You can change the value of TYPE to create other buttons or fields. You can also add additional attributes to customize the element's behavior. You will learn more about the NAME and VALUE attributes shortly.

Web Form Fields

Table 15.4 describes each type of form field discussed in this section.

TABLE 15.4 Web Form Fields

Form Field	Description
Text box	A text field into which a user can enter characters
Radio button	Round option buttons in a group of two or more mutually exclusive options
Check box	Square boxes in a group of two or more non-exclusive options
Select list	A drop-down list of two or more options from which a single selection can be made
Multiple-select list	An exposed list of two or more options, optionally scrollable, from which the user can make multiple selections
Text area	A scrolling text field into which the user can enter multiple lines of text
Password field	A text box that visually masks characters entered with asterisks
Submit button	A button that, when clicked, causes the form's action statement to process; labeled "Submit" or "Submit Query" by default, but can display any label
Reset button	A button that, when clicked, clears all form data and sets all form fields back to the default values for those fields; labeled "Reset" by default, but can display any label

The value names for each type of form field will be discussed shortly.

All form field elements share one attribute: NAME. The NAME attribute identifies information you receive from a user and associates it with a value you specify. The NAME attribute helps you organize user input. For example, you could use a series of check boxes to learn about a user's preferences for gardening, sailing, and biking; you could name the group of boxes "Interests." Thus when you receive information from the forms, you can use the names to determine the user's choices. If the user checks the "sailing" check box, you will receive the following information: Interests=sailing. To understand how the NAME attribute works, you need to learn more about how CGI handles forms.

Remember that a CGI script residing on a server receives data from a web browser, and then processes the data into human-readable format (or any other format you require). Figure 15.4 shows a simple form.

FIGURE 15.4 A simple HTML form

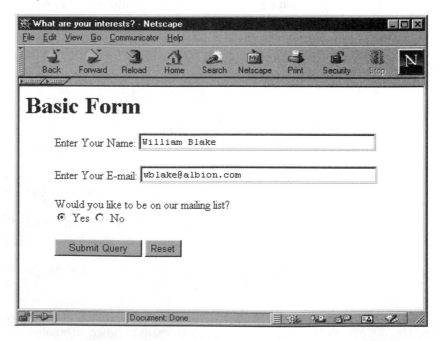

A basic form allows users to supply their name and e-mail address, then indicate whether they want to be placed on the company's mailing list. When the user clicks the Submit Query button, the browser sends the contents of this form to the web server as a raw text string.

The basic element of a raw text string is a name=value pair. The NAME attribute of the FORM element organizes information input from the user into name=value pairs. For example, the form in the preceding figure organizes user input according to the following code. Pay special attention to the code shown in bold:

```
Enter Your Name: <INPUT TYPE="text" NAME="Name" SIZE="40">
Enter Your E-mail: <INPUT TYPE="text" NAME="Email" SIZE="40">
Would you like to be on our mailing list? <BR>
<INPUT TYPE="radio" NAME="AddToList" VALUE="yes"> Yes
<INPUT TYPE="radio" NAME="AddToList" VALUE="no"> No
```

When the browser sends this data, it will use the NAME values "Name", "Email", and "AddToList" as the basis for creating the raw text string. You can use any words to specify NAME values. In this example, the server receives a raw text string that resembles the following:

```
Name=William+Blake&Email=wblake@albion.com&AddToList=yes
```

This raw text string consists of name=value pairs, delimited by ampersands (&). Name=value pairs replace spaces with plus signs (+). If a form field is left empty, only the first part of the name=value pair will be returned. For example, if this user left the mailing list option blank, the corresponding name=value pair would return "Email=" without any information after the equal symbol.

Once the server receives this information, a CGI script can parse and format the raw text string into a human-readable format similar to the following:

Name:	William Blake
E-mail:	wblake@albion.com
Mailing List:	Yes

The form you will create in this section will use Name and Email, as well as other form field names that depend upon their function.

For more information about how CGI works, see the NCSA discussion of HTML forms and CGI at www.ncsa.uiuc.edu/SDG/Software/Mosaic/Docs/fill-out-forms/overview.html.

Now that you understand some of the basic conventions used in forms, you can begin studying and coding individual form fields.

Text boxes A *text box* is used to collect a single line of data from the user, such as name, e-mail, or address information. The text box is the most common form field.

The syntax for creating a text box is as follows:

```
<INPUT TYPE="text" NAME="FieldName">
```

If you want the text box to appear with some default text inside, use the additional attribute of VALUE as shown:

```
<INPUT TYPE="text" NAME="FieldName" VALUE="Default Text">
```

Additionally, you can use a SIZE attribute to specify the width of the text box in characters. The SIZE attribute has no effect on the amount of text the user can enter; it restricts only the visual appearance of the field. Contrast this with the MAXLENGTH attribute. The value of MAXLENGTH restricts user entries to the specified number of characters; it has no effect on the display width of the field.

Submit and Reset buttons When you specify the INPUT TYPE value as "reset" or "submit", you create a button that performs a specific action. Clicking the Submit button sends the data from the form fields to be processed by the ACTION specified in the <FORM> tag. Clicking the Reset button clears all form fields and resets fields to their default settings.

EXERCISE 15.2

Creating a Simple Web Form

In this exercise, you will create a basic form using the <FORM> and <INPUT> tags. The ACTION attribute in the <FORM> tag points to a public test engine you can use to check form output. You would never use this URL in an actual production setting. Use it only to verify that your form is functioning as expected.

1. Create a file named myform.txt using Notepad.

2. Enter the source code indicated in bold:

```
<!DOCTYPE HTML PUBLIC "-//W3C//DTD
⮡HTML 4.01 Transitional//EN"

"http://www.w3.org/TR/html4/loose.dtd">
```

```
<HTML>

<HEAD>

<TITLE>Basic Form</TITLE>

</HEAD>

<BODY>

<H1>Basic Form</H1>

<FORM

METHOD=POST

ACTION="http://ss1.ciwcertified.com/cgi-bin/process.pl">

Enter Your Name: <INPUT TYPE="text" NAME="Name"
↳SIZE="40"><P>

Enter Your E-mail: <INPUT TYPE="text"
↳NAME="Email" SIZE="40"><P>

<INPUT TYPE="SUBMIT">
↳<INPUT TYPE="RESET">

</FORM>

</BODY>

</HTML>
```

3. Save the file as myform.htm.

4. Open the file myform.htm in your browser.

5. Enter a name and e-mail address into the text boxes, and then click the Submit button. You should see in the status bar that a server connection is being made. After a few seconds (or minutes if your connection is slow), you should see the results of your input echoed back to you on a separate page.

6. Click the Back button in the browser to return to your form page.

7. Click the Reset button to clear all form data.

Radio buttons   *Radio buttons*, which are never used as stand-alone items, are round option buttons in a group of two or more mutually exclusive options. To ensure exclusivity, a group of radio buttons must share the same NAME, although they will pass individual values. The following example code shows two buttons representing mutually exclusive answers to the same question.

```
Have you seen this movie? <BR>
<INPUT TYPE="radio" NAME="SawMovie" VALUE="yes"> Yes
<INPUT TYPE="radio" NAME="SawMovie" VALUE="no"> No
```

You will probably want to mark one of the options to be selected by default. To preselect an option, add the attribute CHECKED inside the <INPUT> tag.

Check boxes   *Check boxes* are used for non-exclusive choices. You have two options when naming check boxes, and your decision will be based on how you plan to use the data gathered. Consider the following scenario. You want a list of the user's favorite hobbies. You plan to store the user's selections in a database. Are you going to store the user's response (which might include multiple hobbies) in a single field? Or will each hobby separately correspond to a separate database field? Your choice will affect how you name the fields.

The syntax for creating a check box is as follows:

```
<INPUT TYPE="checkbox" NAME="name" VALUE="value">
```

Notice that the keyword used to specify a check box as the TYPE attribute value is "checkbox" written as all one word with no space.

As with the radio buttons, you can preselect check boxes by adding the attribute CHECKED into the tag.

The following could be a check box section on a form:

```
Tours of interest (check all that apply):<BR>
<INPUT TYPE="checkbox" NAME="Tahiti"> Tahiti<BR>
<INPUT TYPE="checkbox" NAME="V-Isles"> Virgin Islands<BR>
<INPUT TYPE="checkbox" NAME="Seych"> Seychelles<BR>
```

In this check box example, the tags can also be written as follows:

```
<INPUT TYPE="checkbox" NAME="Tours" VALUE="Tahiti">
<INPUT TYPE="checkbox" NAME="Tours" VALUE="V-Isles">
<INPUT TYPE="checkbox" NAME="Tours" VALUE ="Seych">
```

With this syntax, each choice is treated as part of a single field named `"Tours"`. Either method is acceptable; one will be more appropriate depending on how you plan to use the data.

Select lists   *Select lists* are drop-down lists of predetermined options. Technically, they are not input types because they limit the input a user can send to the web server. Depending on the settings, these lists can allow single or multiple selections. Select list tags are similar to the bulleted and numbered list tags you learned about in an earlier section, in that a container tag contains multiple empty tags that indicate individual list items.

Single-option select list   The syntax for creating a drop-down, single-option select list is as follows:

```
<SELECT NAME="name">
<OPTION>Option 1
<OPTION>Option 2
...
<OPTION>Option n
</SELECT>
```

The value that is passed when the form is submitted is the text to the right of the `<OPTION>` tag. However, if you want to pass a value different from the text that appears in the list, you can add `VALUE="value"` into any or all of the `<OPTION>` tags.

Multiple-option select list   Within the `<SELECT>` tag, you can include the `MULTIPLE` attribute. The presence of this attribute automatically changes the list to allow users to select multiple options. Because multiple selections are possible, these lists are usually presented with several, if not all, options already exposed.

The SIZE attribute controls how many items will appear in a scrolling list box. If no size is specified, the number of items that will appear by default will vary between browsers. Navigator 4.0 and later, for example, will display all the items by default. Internet Explorer 4.0 and later, at the time the exam was written, will display only the first four options unless a size is specified.

Scrolling text area box   To gather more than a line of text from a user, you will use the TEXTAREA form element. TEXTAREA provides a scrolling text box into which a user can enter a few sentences, an address, letters to the editor, or other text.

<TEXTAREA> is a container tag. The only content this tag can contain is text. Text between <TEXTAREA> tags will appear as default text within the box.

The TEXTAREA element has several key attributes, which you will want to understand and use. Table 15.5 outlines these attributes and accepted values.

TABLE 15.5   TEXTAREA Element Attributes

Attribute	Value	Description
COLS	Integer value	Specifies the width in characters of the scrolling text box.
ROWS	Integer value	Specifies the number of rows of text to display in the box.
WRAP	"none" or "virtual"	If "none" is specified, text the user enters continues on one line; the user must scroll horizontally to read what they have entered. If "virtual" is specified, text entered into the box will wrap as it approaches the box border. As indicated by the value name, such a wrap is in appearance only. The text string submitted to the script will take the form of one long line of text.

The WRAP attribute is deprecated in HTML 4.01. Text wrapping is now the responsibility of the user agent (i.e., browser). Recall that this attribute is still permissible in HTML 4.01 Transitional.

HTML Image Techniques

One of the primary ingredients of any successful web page is well-placed graphics. You have already learned about the image formats used on the Web. In this section, you will learn more about image techniques used to create web pages. These include the following:

- Image maps
- Image transparency
- Interlacing
- Animation

Image Maps

An *image map* is a set of coordinates that creates a "hot spot" area on a particular image. Each of these "hot spots" acts as a hyperlink. You can create multiple image maps on an image. Image maps call either a client-side or a server-side set of coordinates to determine how to process the user's mouse action. Client-side image maps use code embedded within the HTML itself. You can create an image map for any image format supported by a web browser.

The most difficult aspect of working with image maps is determining the coordinates of the map areas you want to use as links. Once that task is completed, you simply specify which URLs correspond to which regions. Many graphic-creation applications show you the coordinates of any position in a graphic as you move the cursor across the image. If you do not know the coordinates for different regions of your image but know the image's pixel height and width, you can perform mathematical calculations to determine which coordinates define which regions.

Examine the graphic shown in Figure 15.5.

FIGURE 15.5 Image to be used as map

Suppose you want to send the user to a map of Capitol Hill if they click on the Capitol Dome. The Dome could roughly be represented by a rectangle surrounding it, as shown in Figure 15.6.

In the preceding figure, the rectangle is defined by four coordinates. The four coordinates represent the upper-left and bottom-right corners of the image. The coordinates that define this particular area are 57, 79, 160, and 225. The number 57 represents the number in pixels from the left of the image to the left edge of a rectangle that could encompass the Capitol Dome.

This number is the upper-left x coordinate for a rectangle. The number 79 represents the number in pixels from the top of the image to the top of the same rectangle; this is the upper-left y coordinate. The two numbers together, 57 and 79, would designate the upper-left corner of a rectangle. The numbers 160 and 225 respectively represent the bottom-right x and y coordinates of a rectangle encompassing the Capitol Dome.

FIGURE 15.6 Image map coordinates

The defined area will not be visible on a web page as it is here in the book. This figure only provides a representation of the area defined by the coordinates mentioned. Once an area is defined by means of an image map, you can then attach a URL to that area so that when a user clicks that portion of the image, the file designated by the URL is loaded.

> Applications that simplify the image map creation process are available at www.sausage.com/, www.1automata.com/hotspots/mapper.html, and www.tucows.com.

Defining a Client-Side Image Map

Once you obtain your image and coordinates, you can include them in your HTML. You can create client-side or server-side image maps. Server-side image maps require a CGI script. Client-side image maps are much more common. The advantage of using a client-side map is that you can place all the code relating to the image map directly into your HTML file. The syntax for defining a client-side map for an image is as follows:

```
<MAP NAME="MapName">
<AREA SHAPE="shape" COORDS="coordinates" HREF="URL">
<AREA SHAPE="shape" COORDS="coordinates" HREF="URL">
<AREA SHAPE="shape" COORDS="coordinates" HREF="URL">
</MAP>
<IMG SRC="imagemap.gif" USEMAP="#MapName">
```

Note the relationship between the USEMAP attribute value and the *MapName* value. USEMAP indicates that the image is to be used with a map. The hash symbol (#) indicates that the *MapName* represents a map within the same HTML file.

<MAP> is a container tag. It encloses <AREA> tags, which are empty tags that define the regions of the image map. Acceptable values for the SHAPE attribute are "rect" for a rectangle, "circle" for a circular area, or "polygon" for any other shape. The number and meaning of coordinates you specify will vary based on the shape specified. The *URL* value refers to the page that will load when the user clicks that area of the map. You can use as many or as few areas as you want when defining regions within an image.

You can define your map before or after the related image tag; either sequence is acceptable.

Defining a rectangle   Any two points can define a rectangle. Each point is represented by a horizontal (x) coordinate and a vertical (y) coordinate. Rectangles are defined by four coordinates representing the upper-left and bottom-right corners of the rectangle, as shown in Figure 15.7.

FIGURE 15.7 Four coordinates define rectangle

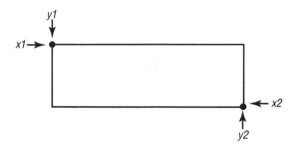

You can define a rectangular area using the following syntax:

`<AREA SHAPE="rect" COORDS="x1,y1,x2,y2" HREF="URL">`

The *x1* indicates the leftmost point of the area to be defined. The *y1* indicates the topmost point of the area to be defined. The *x2* indicates the farthest point to the right in the area to be defined, and *y2* indicates the lowest point. These four coordinates will necessarily define a rectangle. Figure 15.8 shows a rectangular image functioning as an image map.

FIGURE 15.8 Original rectangular image

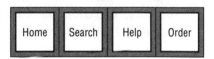

This image file is 312 pixels wide and 75 pixels high. Each square is 78 pixels wide. Using basic math, you should be able to determine the top-left and bottom-right *x* and *y* coordinates for this graphic. The code for map for this graphic could resemble the following:

```
<IMG SRC="buttons.gif" USEMAP="#ButtonMap">
<MAP NAME="ButtonMap">
<AREA COORDS="0,0,78,75" HREF="home.htm">
<AREA COORDS="78,0,156,75" HREF="search.htm">
<AREA COORDS="156,0,234,75" HREF="help.htm">
<AREA COORDS="234,0,312,75" HREF="order.htm">
</MAP>
```

Defining a circle area Circles are defined by two coordinates and a radius. The pair of coordinates specifies the circle's center, and the third number specifies the desired half-width or radius of the circle.

The syntax for defining a circle area is as follows:

`<AREA SHAPE="circle" COORDS="x1,y1,radius" HREF="URL">`

Figure 15.9 shows how the coordinates and radius are determined.

FIGURE 15.9 Two coordinates and radius define a circle

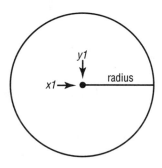

Defining a polygon Whenever you need to define an area that is neither a circle nor a rectangle, you can use SHAPE="polygon" and specify coordinates for each point that defines the polygon.

Examine Figure 15.10. Note that the coordinates define the polygon in sequence. You could not, for example, switch the *x4* and *y4* coordinates with the *x2* and *y2* coordinates without altering the shape of the image.

FIGURE 15.10 Polygon defined by four or more pairs of coordinates

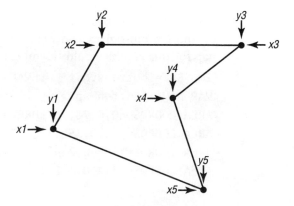

You can use up to 100 pairs of coordinates to define a polygon. The syntax for defining a polygon area is as follows:

`<AREA SHAPE="polygon" COORDS="x1,y1,x2,y2,...xn,yn"`
`HREF="URL">`

Image Transparency

An image that supports transparency will contain elements that automatically blend in with the background color of your HTML page. The background of the web page simply shows through the transparent part of the image. Most developers use *image transparency* to remove the background of an image so that it blends in with the rest of the page. However, you can make any element of an image transparent.

The only web-ready formats that support transparency are GIF 89a and PNG. The GIF 89a format is the most popular.

Technically, only the 89a version of the GIF format supports transparency. However, some graphics-editing programs allow you to save a GIF 89a as an 87a and choose to retain the transparency information.

In Figure 15.11, you see a non-transparent GIF 89a image rendered in a browser. Notice that you can see the image's background, and that it obscures the page's background.

FIGURE 15.11 Standard GIF image

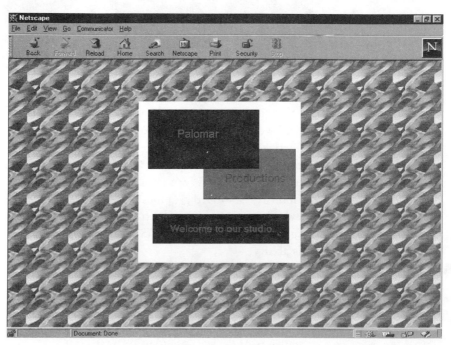

Although an image may certainly retain its visible background, some designs look better when the images blend in with the page background. Figure 15.12 shows the same image with a transparent background, allowing the page background to show through.

FIGURE 15.12 Same image with transparent background

You can no longer see the white background that belongs to the image. Even if you change the web page's background or background color, it will still appear through the image's background. Most developers refer to this type of GIF as a "transparent GIF," but remember that you can achieve this effect with the PNG format as well.

Industry-standard graphics applications such as Adobe Photoshop (www.adobe.com) can convert images and create transparencies. Less powerful applications, such as JASC Paint Shop Pro (www.jasc.com), also have this ability.

Interlacing

Interlacing is the technique that allows an image to progressively display itself in a browser as it downloads. It will appear in stages over the period of downloading time. This action makes your pages more accessible to users with slower Internet connections.

Standard image formats are read from top to bottom. The top of a non-interlaced image will appear after the browser has read 50 percent of the image. The bottom half will render some time later. A non-interlaced image can remain invisible to a user who is downloading an image across a slow connection.

An interlaced image, on the other hand, appears to "fade in" as it renders in the browser because it is interpreted differently. An interlaced image repeatedly scans the entire image from left to right. The first pass will render roughly 13 percent of the entire image. The second pass delivers 25 percent, and then continues in 25-percent increments until the image renders completely. During this process, the image will at first appear fuzzy, but will continuously sharpen.

The only web-ready formats that support interlacing are GIF and PNG. Both GIF formats, 87a and 89a, support interlacing.

Interlacing will sometimes make your image file size increase. Consider the size, especially if you expect users to download images over a network.

Animated GIFs

One reason the GIF image format remains so popular is because it enables you to combine several GIF images to create an animation sequence. Currently, GIF 89a is the only format that supports animation.

Programs such as GIF Construction Set allow you to incorporate several images into one file, as well as several mini-programs that control how those images will render in a browser. Most animation programs allow you to set the interval of appearance between images, and to create many other effects. You can obtain a copy of GIF Construction Set at Tucows (www.tucows.com) or at the Mind Workshop home page (www.mindworkshop.com/alchemy/gifcon.html).

You can obtain other image animation shareware programs at Tucows, or at Download.com (www.download.com).

HTML Frames

In this section, you will work with existing sets of frames and create a new set of frames, called a frameset. A frameset is defined in an HTML file called a *frameset document*, which we will discuss later in this section.

Frames were introduced as an extension of the HTML 3.2 standard, and were first supported by the Netscape Navigator 2.0 browser. The frames technology was submitted to the W3C for consideration as an HTML standard, and is currently part of HTML 4.01.

Frames offer new possibilities for web designers and authors, allowing elements that site users should always see, such as navigation links, copyright notices and title graphics, to be placed in a static, individual frame. As users navigate the site, the static frame's content will remain, even though the contents of the adjoining frames may change.

Frames are most useful when you want to combine static and dynamic information. Figure 15.13 shows a web page with a table of contents in the left frame. This frame contains links that, when clicked, display the target URLs' contents in the adjoining frame. The frameset document contains two separate files loaded into two frames.

FIGURE 15.13 Two frames in one web page

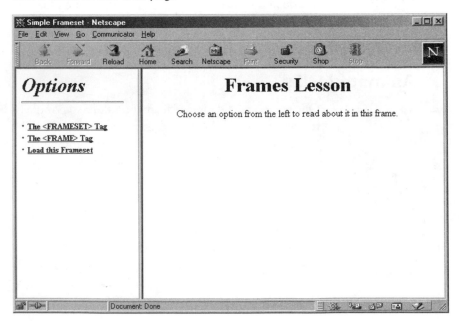

You can add frames to a web page form so that queries can be submitted and answered on the same page: One frame displays the query form, and the other frame presents the query results.

<FRAMESET> Tag

The <FRAMESET> tag, or element, is a container tag that allows you to define regions in your browser window and assign separate files to each. It requires a mandatory attribute of either COLS or ROWS that designates the number and size of columns or rows in a browser window.

The frameset in the preceding figure has two frames; one column occupies 35 percent of the available screen width, and the other column occupies the remaining 65 percent. The source code for this frameset is as follows:

```
<FRAMESET COLS="35%,65%">
```

You can specify the COLS and ROWS attribute in two ways: by percentages or pixels. In addition, you can use a wildcard character to accommodate various user screen widths and resolutions. For example, consider the following tag:

```
<FRAMESET ROWS="160,*">
```

This tag specifies that the first 160 pixels are used for the top-row frame, and the remaining space is used for the bottom-row frame.

<FRAME> Tag

The <FRAME> tag defines the content in each frame and is placed within the <FRAMESET> tag. The SRC attribute (abbreviation for "source") specifies the file that will appear in the frame.

In the following example, the frame source for the top frame is the file f1-toc.htm, and the frame source for the lower frame is f1-second.htm. The frameset defines two rows and opens the frames with the files specified in the <FRAME> tags.

```
<FRAMESET ROWS="160,*">
<FRAME SRC="f1-toc.htm">
<FRAME SRC="f1-second.htm">
</FRAMESET>
```

The frame source can be a local document or a URL pointing to a website.

Frameset Document

The <FRAMESET> and <FRAME> elements will create frames only if they are placed correctly into an HTML file called the frameset document. In the frameset document, the <FRAMESET> element takes the place of the <BODY> element.

The frameset document defines the <FRAMESET>, <FRAME>, and <NOFRAMES> elements. You will learn about the <NOFRAMES> element in the next section.

The following example demonstrates proper code structure for the frameset document. This HTML source code created the frames shown in Figure 15.13.

```
<!DOCTYPE HTML PUBLIC "-//W3C//DTD HTML 4.01 Frameset//EN"
http://www.w3.org/TR/html4/frameset.dtd>
<HTML>
<HEAD>
<TITLE>Simple Frameset</TITLE>
</HEAD>
<FRAMESET COLS="35%,65%">
<FRAME SRC="fl-toc.htm">
<FRAME SRC="fl-second.htm">
</FRAMESET>
</HTML>
```

Remember these two key points:

- The opening <FRAMESET> tag follows the closing </HEAD> tag.

- The <FRAMESET> tag must contain either the ROWS attribute or the COLS attribute. You cannot specify both ROWS and COLS in the same <FRAMESET> tag.

EXERCISE 15.3

Creating Frames with Rows and Columns

In this exercise, you will create a frameset document that defines two horizontal panes using the ROWS attribute.

1. In your text editor, open the frameplay.htm file from the CD.

2. Modify the following source code as indicated in bold:

EXERCISE 15.3 *(continued)*

```
<!DOCTYPE HTML PUBLIC "-//W3C//DTD
↳HTML 4.01 Frameset//EN"
http://www.w3.org/TR/html4/frameset.dtd>
<HTML>
<HEAD>
<TITLE>Frame Lesson</TITLE>
</HEAD>
<FRAMESET ROWS="50%,50%">
<FRAME SRC="a.htm">
<FRAME SRC="b.htm">
</FRAMESET>
</HTML>
```

3. Save the file.

4. Open the frameplay.htm file in your browser.

5. Your screen should display in two horizontal frames.

6. In the text editor, continue working on the frameplay.htm file.

7. Modify the following source code as indicated in bold:

```
<!DOCTYPE HTML PUBLIC "-//W3C//DTD
↳HTML 4.01 Frameset//EN"
http://www.w3.org/TR/html4/frameset.dtd>
<HTML>
<HEAD>
<TITLE>Frame Lesson</TITLE>
</HEAD>
<FRAMESET COLS="25%,75%">
<FRAME SRC="a.htm">
<FRAME SRC="b.htm">
</FRAMESET>
</HTML>
```

8. Save the file.

9. Open the `frameplay.htm` file.

   Note that if you are working with frames in Netscape Navigator, you must reopen the file containing the frameset (instead of refreshing it) to see the changes you made.

10. Your screen should display in two horizontal frames.

The *<NOFRAMES>* Tag

Some Internet users have early-generation browsers that cannot render frames. To provide content (other than a blank screen) for these users, you can add a <NOFRAMES> tag section to your frameset document. The <NOFRAMES> tag is a container tag used to display text or images in browsers that do not support frames. Browsers that can display frames will ignore the information between the opening and closing <NOFRAMES> tag.

The following example extends the HTML source code from the previous example to accommodate users who cannot view frames. You can format the content as desired, or include a link to a non-frames version of your website.

```
<!DOCTYPE HTML PUBLIC "-//W3C//DTD HTML 4.01 Frameset//EN"
http://www.w3.org/TR/html4/frameset.dtd>
<HTML>
<HEAD>
<TITLE>Simple Frameset</TITLE>
</HEAD>
<FRAMESET COLS="35%,65%">
<FRAME SRC="fl-toc.htm">
<FRAME SRC="fl-second.htm">
<NOFRAMES>
If you had a frames-capable browser, you would see frames here.
</NOFRAMES>
</FRAMESET>
</HTML>
```

Targeting Frames with Hyperlinks

In the previous examples, you could not click a link in one frame and change the content of another frame. To do this, you must target the individual frames for links. If you add the NAME attribute to each <FRAME> tag, you can click a link in one frame and open a different frame for the file targeted by the link.

The syntax for the <FRAME> tag is as follows:

<FRAME SRC="*URL*" NAME="*framename*">

The anchor tag <A> specifies the text that will serve as the hyperlink. Clicking the hyperlink causes the corresponding page to appear in the other frame. The syntax for the anchor tag is as follows:

<A HREF="*URL*" TARGET="*framename*">Link Text</A>

To target a link from the table-of-contents or TOC frame (left) and cause the content to appear in the main (right) frame, create the following link:

<A HREF="*URL*" TARGET="main">

Similarly, to open a new set of options into the TOC frame from the main frame, you would create the following link:

<A HREF="*URL*" TARGET="toc">

If you do not specify a target, the linked content will open into the same frame as the link itself.

If you specify a target name that does not match the name of any existing frame, the browser will launch itself again and open the file into this new browser window. You should avoid this situation unless you want this specific effect.

Specifying a BASE Target

It can be time-consuming to enter targets manually into every link on the page. By specifying a *BASE target*, you can automatically set a default target for all links.

A special empty tag called the <BASE> tag enables you to specify both the URL for a document and a default TARGET frame for all the links in that file.

For example, if you want all the links in the TOC frame to target the main frame, you could include the following source code in the <HEAD> tag section:

```
<BASE HREF="URL" TARGET="main">
```

The optional HREF attribute can be used to indicate the full URL in case the page on which this tag resides is read out of context. For example, if users download this page to their systems, how will they know where it came from? If you have indicated a BASE URL, users will be able to find your site again.

As mentioned earlier, the TARGET attribute specifies a default target for all hyperlinks on the page. However, you can still link to targets other than the BASE. If the TARGET attribute is specified in the anchor tag <A HREF>, then that target will be used. Only when no target is present will the BASE target be used (if the BASE target is present).

Borderless Frames

The FRAMEBORDER attribute can be added to the <FRAME> tag of the frameset document. It designates borders around each frame. A value of 0 leaves no visible borders; a value of 1 causes borders to display.

The MARGINWIDTH and MARGINHEIGHT attributes can also be added to the <FRAME> tag. The values assigned to these attributes designate the space, in pixels, between the frame's contents and the left and right margins, or top and bottom margins, respectively. A value greater than 0 is required. The default space depends on the browser that is viewing the page.

You can learn about additional <FRAME> element attributes, and other elements and attributes of HTML frames, by visiting the W3C website (www.w3.org) and accessing the HTML 4.01 specification.

Graphical User Interface HTML Editors

You can create web pages using a graphical user interface (GUI) HTML editor, also called a *WYSIWYG* (pronounced WIZZY-wig, for "what you see is what you get") editor. These editors allow web authors to create web pages without typing the requisite HTML code. Many

WYSIWYG editors exist, such as Macromedia Dreamweaver, Microsoft Front Page and FrontPage Express, Allaire HomeSite, and Netscape Composer.

In this section, you will use the Netscape Composer program as your GUI HTML editor for several reasons. First, Composer is used for web page creation, not website management. This feature greatly simplifies the program because it focuses on the creation of one page at a time, which is similar to the way you approached HTML coding in the previous sections. Once the pages are created, you can then link them together using hyperlinks. The program offers no comprehensive site management tools (and site management is beyond the scope of this exam). Secondly, Composer is already built into Netscape Communicator, so you do not need to download another program.

To learn about site management concepts and tools, it is recommended that you pursue the CIW Site Designer series.

Types of GUI HTML Editors

As previously mentioned, there are two types of GUI HTML editors: page editors and site management editors. Both are WYSIWYG programs.

GUI page editors help you create a web page using your mouse and a toolbar. Functionality is usually limited to creating individual web pages. Software programs that provide only page editor functionality include:

- Netscape Composer

- Microsoft FrontPage Express

GUI website editors provide both web page creation and site management functionality. Once you create the web pages, you can then manage the entire website as a whole. Site management includes task automation and workflow integration with other programs (such as Microsoft Office and web applications) in a production environment. Software programs that provide these functions include:

- Macromedia Dreamweaver

- Microsoft FrontPage

- Allaire HomeSite

Macromedia Dreamweaver is a site management tool. It displays a centralized view of a website, which includes the pages as well as the directories in which the files are located.

GUI Editor Functionality

GUI HTML editors allow you to create web pages. In most cases, you enter and exit text similar to the way you would in a word-processing application. Images, tables, links, bookmarks, and so forth, can be created just as easily because the application writes the HTML code automatically.

The following is a list of features offered by most GUI editors:

Templates and wizards   Allow you to create custom web pages to your specifications.

Text style options   Allow you to insert text in different font styles, alter text size and color, and apply formats such as centering, boldface and italics.

Icon bars   Offer the same functions found in sometimes lengthy text-based toolbars, using easily identifiable graphic icons.

Inline images feature   Allows you to easily insert graphic images into a web page.

Hypertext links feature   Allows you to create hypertext links to pages and files inside your website, and to pages and files on the World Wide Web. Once the link has been created, the editor displays the target page.

Import HTML pages feature   Allows you to open pages from the World Wide Web and, when permissible, save them to a website or local file system. If desired, the editor can import all images on a page into a website or file system.

Table creation feature   Allows you to add tables to arrange data or organize a page layout.

Publish documents on the Internet feature   Allows you to click a button to post pages to a web server. This feature automatically copies files from a local hard drive to a directory on an ISP's server.

Creating Web Pages in a GUI Editor

The following exercise will familiarize you with the toolbar, menus, and functions of Netscape Composer. Most of these features are similar regardless of the type of GUI HTML editor you use. However, the interface will differ from one application to another.

EXERCISE 15.4

Creating a Web Page Using a GUI Editor

In this exercise, you will create a web page using the Netscape Composer editor. The web page, similar to a résumé, will promote your skills to potential employers.

1. Open Netscape Communicator by double-clicking the Netscape Communicator icon on your desktop. The Navigator browser will open by default.

2. Select the Communicator menu and choose Composer. Netscape Composer will open.

3. Select Heading 1 from the paragraph style drop-down menu.

4. Type your first, middle, and last name. Highlight your name and center it by selecting the Format menu, then choosing Align ➤ Center. You can also click the Alignment button (on the right side of lower toolbar), then select the Center button from the drop-down menu that appears.

5. Deselect your name by clicking anywhere else on the web page.

6. Move the cursor to the line below your name (similar to a word processor, place the cursor at the end of your name and push the Enter key). The paragraph style should return to normal. If not, select Normal from the paragraph style drop-down menu.

7. Enter the text: **Internet Certified and Ready to Succeed**! Highlight the text and make it boldface by selecting the **Bold** button on the toolbar. Then center the text.

8. Create a new folder on your desktop and name it Promo.

9. Select the Save button. Name your file default.htm and save it in the Promo folder. A Page Title dialog box will appear.

10. Enter a title for your web page. For example, enter your name, followed by –**Internet Certified**. This title will appear in the window title and the Bookmarks or Favorites folders of web browsers. Select OK.

11. To view the web page in a browser, click the Preview button on the toolbar. The Navigator browser will open and display your web page. You can now read the entire title in the browser's title bar. When finished, exit the Navigator window.

HTML Text Editors vs. GUI Editors

The following sections describe some of the advantages and disadvantages of HTML text editors and GUI editors. The type of editor you choose depends on your personal preferences.

In most cases, you will use both types of HTML editors. You can create the majority of your website quickly with a GUI HTML editor, and then use a text editor (most GUI editors include one) to enter scripts for advanced functionality.

HTML Text Editors

- If you are considering learning a scripting language such as JavaScript or VBScript, you must learn how to write code from scratch. If you want to add forms to your web pages, it is also helpful to be proficient in HTML.

- If you know HTML code, you can maximize the benefit of GUI HTML editors by manually adding code outside the editor.

- You can learn the fundamentals of HTML, and can update pages to the latest version of HTML.

- A disadvantage of using an HTML text editor is that typing code can be extremely time-consuming and complicated.

GUI HTML Editors

- GUI editors place HTML code into files for you, which enables you to create HTML pages quickly by simply clicking your mouse.

- Most GUI editors allow you to modify your HTML code manually.

- A disadvantage of manually entering HTML code in a GUI editor is that some editors will alter or ignore the code you enter. For instance, you can manually add a paragraph tag <P>, but the GUI editor may not recognize it. This situation can be frustrating if you want to format a web page your own way.

- A disadvantage of using GUI HTML editors is that most GUI editors have not kept pace with the evolution of HTML, and thus do not provide options for using some of the recently developed tags.

HTML Extensions

When the World Wide Web first became popular, HTML was the only language developers could use to create web pages. HTML delivered a page of text and/or graphics, but offered limited interactivity with the web page itself. Now, most computer users are accustomed to interactive web interfaces. They click buttons to execute command sequences, conduct online business, and watch an array of visual effects that enhance the web browsing experience. This rise in user abilities and expectations has resulted in the continual improvement and extension of HTML, which includes Cascading Style Sheets (CSS), JavaScript, Dynamic HTML (DHTML), and the Extensible Hypertext Markup Language (XHTML). This section will explain the design issues and key technologies of these HTML extensions so that you can pursue the technologies that interest you most when you return to your home or office.

Cascading Style Sheets (CSS)

Cascading Style Sheets (CSS) is a specification for creating lists of formatting instructions, called style sheets, which you can use to customize your web pages. The strict flavor of HTML 4.01 demands that you use only CSS to impose layout and formatting for your pages. You can use style sheets to override some or all of the default properties presented by HTML elements. The new properties you define will remain in force throughout the document. You can use style sheets within a document, or you can create external style sheets to which your documents can refer.

Using a linked style sheet, you can declare styles in a separate text file, then link any or all of your web pages to that file. All linked pages will follow the instructions contained in that text file. If you then want to change those instructions (for example, the style of <H1> headings), you need not change every page manually. You need only change a line in the style sheet file, then all your <H1> headings will change their appearance to conform to the style sheet. This technology can save a great deal of development and maintenance time, as well as make a more consistent, accessible interface.

Currently, two standards exist for style sheets: Cascading Style Sheets 1 (CSS1) and Cascading Style Sheets 2 (CSS2). CSS1 governs the basic structure of HTML style sheets. CSS2 adds more capabilities to the CSS1 specification, including the ability to support media types (such as specific printers) and work with HTML tables.

HTML 4.01 adopts CSS1 and CSS2 as the preferred ways to format an HTML page. Because CSS1 contains the instructions you will use most often, this section will focus on the standards presented therein.

CSS1 Terminology

Before you deploy CSS, you should learn its terminology. The most important terms to understand are selector, property, value, declaration, and rule. Figure 15.14 illustrates the anatomy of these style sheet elements as they are found in linked, imported and embedded style sheets. Inline styles are declared differently.

FIGURE 15.14 Anatomy of CSS rule

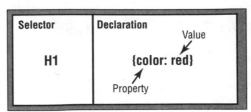

Most developers use Cascading Style Sheets to override some or all of the properties found in existing HTML tags. As shown in the preceding figure, you could decide to change the color of all <H1> tags in a document. To make such a change, you must identify the element you want to change, then refer to it in a style sheet. In a style sheet, any HTML element you want to include is called a *selector*.

Once you have chosen a selector, you can customize it by selecting a property and setting a value. By selecting a *property*, you will change the way the selector renders in the browser. For example, you could alter the selector's color, size, background, font family, font size, and so forth. These changes will apply to all subsequent instances of the HTML element you define as a selector.

A property must then have a value. If, for example, you change a selector's size property, you must set a value to determine that size. For example, you could decide to change the font size of your H1 headings to 24 points, and so forth.

In the following example, you will see a CSS1 declaration, which consists of a property and a value contained within curly brackets:

```
BODY {color: teal}
```

The name for a selector, property, and value all grouped together is a *rule*. The following rule will change the color of the body background to teal, then set the font color to white:

```
BODY {color: teal; font: white}
```

To define multiple declarations for one selector within a rule, as in the previous example, you must separate each declaration with a semicolon. You can also place a semicolon between a value and the end bracket.

Notice from these examples that the property and the value must be placed within curly brackets. This practice is standard for all style sheet rules, except when declaring inline styles. You will learn more about different ways to define styles later in this section.

CSS1 and CSS2 declarations are not case-specific. You should, however, use letter case consistently when declaring styles.

Inheritance

The concept of inheritance is essential to Cascading Style Sheets. In fact, the word "cascading" refers to inheritance. The style you define will flow, or cascade, throughout the document, unless another style specifically overrides it. Many styles can be used together to create a completely formatted document. For example, a *style sheet rule* will override the BGCOLOR element, as well as the default body font color, which is black. However, certain properties (such as text size) remain in force. All these characteristics, whether they are defined in a style sheet or exist by default, are inherited throughout the rest of the document.

CSS1 and HTML

Now that you understand CSS1 terminology and syntax, you need to know how to implement it with an HTML page. You can apply CSS1 styles in four ways. You can:

- Declare an inline style
- Create an embedded style sheet
- Link to an external style sheet
- Use an imported style sheet

Declaring an Inline Style

Declaring an inline style means that you modify the HTML inside the body of the HTML document. You can apply an inline style using either the <SPAN> tag by itself or the <STYLE> tag within a standard HTML element.

If you use the <SPAN> tag, you need not refer to a specific HTML tag. For example, in the following code, the text "CIW Associate" will appear in black font with a red background (provided that you have not declared any other styles):

```
<SPAN STYLE="background: red">CIW Associate</SPAN>
```

Because <SPAN> is a container tag, it will alter all text contained between it and the closing </SPAN> tag.

If you use the <STYLE> tag to define an inline style, you must first use standard HTML code, as shown in Figure 15.15. The style definition given in this figure will remain in force until the browser encounters the </H1> tag. Because this style defines a color, a font family and a size, it overrides the color and font-family information normally associated with the <H1> tag. However, this style would inherit any other properties of <H1>.

FIGURE 15.15   Inline style using <STYLE> tag

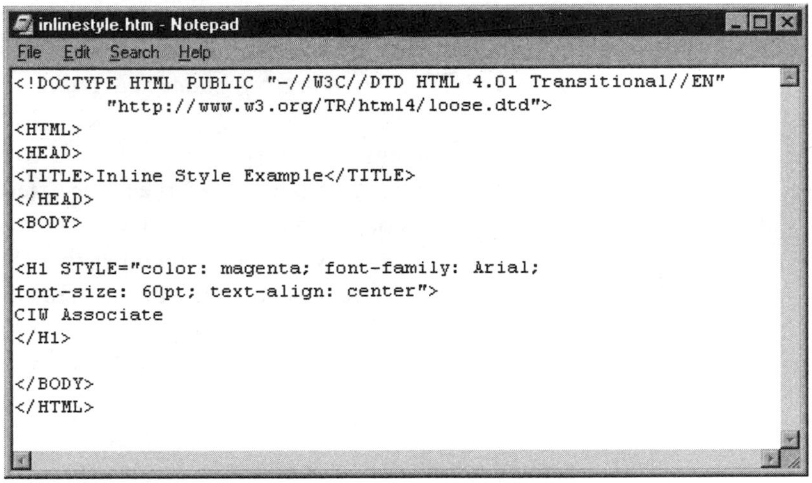

```
inlinestyle.htm - Notepad
File  Edit  Search  Help
<!DOCTYPE HTML PUBLIC "-//W3C//DTD HTML 4.01 Transitional//EN"
        "http://www.w3.org/TR/html4/loose.dtd">
<HTML>
<HEAD>
<TITLE>Inline Style Example</TITLE>
</HEAD>
<BODY>

<H1 STYLE="color: magenta; font-family: Arial;
font-size: 60pt; text-align: center">
CIW Associate
</H1>

</BODY>
</HTML>
```

The <STYLE> tag in CSS is meant to replace the deprecated <FONT> tag in HTML.

Creating an Embedded Style Sheet

You can use the <STYLE> tag within the <HEAD> tag to create an embedded style sheet, as follows:

```
<HTML>
<HEAD>
<TITLE>Certified Internet webmaster
</TITLE>
<STYLE>
<!--
H1 {color: magenta; font-family: arial; font-size: 20pt}
-->
</STYLE>
</HEAD>
```

Once you define an embedded style, it will remain in force until you override it with an inline style.

Linking to an External Style Sheet

A linked style sheet is a popular way to ensure that all pages have the same look and feel. This form of style sheet adopts a two-part strategy. First, you create a text file separate from your HTML document. To this file you add rules.

You can add as many rules as you want, and you can name the style sheet whatever you like. You can use any file name extension you want, although most developers prefer to use the standard .css extension. You should try to give the file a descriptive name. Remember that this is not an HTML document; it is a simple text document with the .css extension.

The second step is to place the <LINK> tag within the <HEAD> tag of your HTML document. Excellent examples on how this can be done are available at: www.htmlhelp.com/reference/css/style-html.html#external.

Without a declared style sheet, the page should appear as it has throughout past sections. According to the HTML code, the horizontal rule created by the <HR> tag should occupy the entire width of the screen. The text between the <H1> tags should appear in its default bold Times New Roman size. No background color should be specified for this text.

The styles you define and link alter the appearance significantly.

Using Imported Style Sheets

This type of style sheet also requires an external file. However, the imported style sheet is different in that it contains the following code at the beginning of the file: @import url(filename.css). You must refer to the imported style sheet in your HTML document using the following syntax:

```
<!DOCTYPE HTML PUBLIC "-//W3C//DTD HTML 4.01//EN"
"http://www.w3.org/TR/html4/strict.dtd">
<HTML>
<HEAD>
<TITLE>Certified Internet webmaster</TITLE>
<STYLE type="text/css">
@import url(import.css);
</STYLE>
</HEAD>
```

You can, of course, name the style sheet whatever you like.

Style Sheets and Browser Compatibility

Style sheets have the potential to create consistency across a page or an entire site. However, a vast gulf often exists between potential and practice.

As an HTML developer, understand that style sheets can lead to compatibility problems because the Microsoft and Netscape browsers interpret style sheet commands differently. You may also encounter difficulty predicting how earlier versions of the same browser will interpret the same style sheet. Therefore, you should test your code in as many browsers and browser versions as possible.

JavaScript

JavaScript is an object-based scripting language that allows developers to add interactivity to their web pages. JavaScript code must reside inside HTML documents in order to run. JavaScript adds the following functions to a web page or site:

- Pop-up windows, such as alert, dialog, and prompt boxes
- Automatic date and time changes
- Image and text that change upon a mouse rollover
- Cookie creation and identification

Unlike traditional programming languages, such as C and Pascal, a scripting language is used within a program to extend its capabilities. If you have ever written a macro in Microsoft Excel or used WordBasic to perform some task in a Microsoft Word document, you have already used a scripting language.

JavaScript syntax closely resembles that of C and Pascal. The code is placed within your web document so that when your browser retrieves a page that incorporates JavaScript, it runs the programs and performs the appropriate operations.

The term "object-oriented" is common in programming languages. An *object-oriented* program handles data as a collection of individual objects that perform different functions, rather than as a sequence of statements that completes a specific task.

JavaScript is an object-based language that has a collection of built-in objects. You can also create your own objects depending on your programming needs.

The following advantages of JavaScript make it a natural choice for easily and quickly extending HTML pages on the Web:

Quick development   Because JavaScript does not require time-consuming compilation, scripts can be developed in a relatively short period of time. Most of the interface features, such as forms, frames, and other GUI elements, are handled by the browser and HTML code, further shortening the development time. JavaScript programmers do not have to create or handle these elements of their applications.

Easy to learn   Though JavaScript shares many characteristics with the Java programming language, the JavaScript syntax and rules are simpler. If you know any other programming languages, it will be much easier for you to learn JavaScript.

Platform independence   Like HTML, JavaScript is not specific to any operating system. The same JavaScript program can be used on any browser on any system, provided that the browser supports JavaScript.

Embedding JavaScript into HTML

JavaScript must reside within an HTML document. It is embedded into an HTML document using the <SCRIPT> tag. Note that JavaScript placement is not restricted to the <BODY> element. The following example demonstrates the basic structure of an HTML file with JavaScript.

```
<HTML><HEAD>
<TITLE>JavaScript</TITLE>
<SCRIPT>
JavaScript code goes here.
</SCRIPT>
</HEAD>
<BODY>
<SCRIPT>
JavaScript can go here too.
</SCRIPT>
</BODY>
</HTML>
```

In JavaScript, the web author can communicate with the user through the `alert()` and `prompt()` functions. These functions are both properties of the `window` document. The web author can also use the `document.write()` function to output text to the client window in sequence with an HTML file. The `alert()` function displays an alert dialog box. The `prompt()` function requests user input in a text area within a dialog box. The `prompt()` function initiates a conversation or true dialog. The result returned by the `prompt()` can be used as an argument to another method, such as the `document.write()`.

The following exercise will demonstrate these functions. Note that the text entered into the prompt dialog box is output to the web page.

EXERCISE 15.5

Incorporating Simple JavaScript in a Web Page

In this exercise, you will incorporate a simple JavaScript function into a web page.

1. Open the file named `javascript.htm` from the CD in your text editor.

2. Add the JavaScript code indicated in bold:

```
<!DOCTYPE HTML PUBLIC "-//W3C//DTD HTML 4.01 Transitional//EN"
"http://www.w3.org/TR/html4/loose.dtd">
<HTML>
<HEAD>
<TITLE>A Simple JavaScript</TITLE>
</HEAD>
<BODY>
<H1>A Simple JavaScript</H1>
<HR>
<SCRIPT> language="JavaScript">
alert("Welcome to my Web Site!");
document.write("Hello, ")
var answer=prompt("What is your name?, ")
document.write("<BR>Welcome to JavaScript!")
</SCRIPT>
</BODY></HTML>
```

3. Save the file.

4. Open `javascript.htm` in the browser.

5. Select the OK button. A dialog box will appear asking for your name. Enter your name in the text field, and then click OK. Your name will appear in the greeting.

Copyright Protection with JavaScript

JavaScript can also be used for copyright protection. A simple script can stop your website from being included within another site's frame. The following example displays JavaScript code that ensures your web page is at the top of the browser window, and not part of a frame.

```
<HTML>
<HEAD>
<TITLE>No Frames Allowed</TITLE>
<SCRIPT LANGUAGE="JavaScript">
<!--
if (self != top) top.location.href = location.href;
//-->
</SCRIPT>
</HEAD>
<BODY>
web page content .
</BODY>
</HTML>
```

JavaScript detects whether your web page is at the top of the browser window. If your web page is loaded into a frame, JavaScript will replace whatever is in the window with `location.href`, which is a location object that has an HREF property (hypertext reference). This property holds the URL for the current web page.

JavaScript has been included in this section only to show you its capabilities. To learn more about JavaScript, enroll in the CIW JavaScript Fundamentals course.

Dynamic HTML (DHTML)

Dynamic HTML (DHTML) is an HTML enhancement that allows animation, interaction, and dynamic updating in web pages. With DHTML, you can create a web page that reacts to user actions without contacting the server or downloading complex, bandwidth-consuming applications.

Because it eases the burden on the server, DHTML is an effective front-end and back-end solution.

You can use DHTML to control the way in which an image will perform. For example, you can make an image become animated only when a mouse passes over it. Or the page can automatically scroll text headlines, similar to a Java applet or ActiveX control. Additional DHTML uses include the following:

- Automatic adjustment of font sizes and colors. You can use a DHTML *event handler* to animate text when a user passes a mouse over certain parts of the page.

- Absolute positioning. You can create text that moves to certain positions in reaction to user input.

- New document content without having to refresh the browser window.

- Granular control over animation, audio, and video. Rather than coding a page to constantly present a video clip, you can code it to begin a sequence at a certain time, or after a certain event.

DHTML is slowly becoming accepted. As an emerging technology, DHTML is imperfectly applied at present but will probably become a standard in the future.

To use DHTML, you must master three technologies: HTML 4.01, Cascading Style Sheets (CSS1 and CSS2), and the Document Object Model (DOM). You have already learned about HTML and Cascading Style Sheets. In the next section, you will learn about the DOM.

Document Object Model (DOM)

A *Document Object Model (DOM)* describes the elements, or objects, within a document rendered by a web browser. It is meant to be a vendor-neutral, cross-platform standard. With the DOM, you can open a new browser instance and control its functions. For example, you can determine the size of the new browser instance, which toolbars will be open, and so forth. You can also create pop-up dialog boxes, change the font and colors used in the current document, and alter the address bar or almost any other component of the browser.

Currently, the DOM is not as universal as one would expect. Each of the major browsers uses its own DOM. Lack of a clear standard may be the main cause for the relatively slow industry acceptance of some technologies, such as DHTML. On the other hand, acceptance of JavaScript is almost universal. Both Netscape and Microsoft have promised to support the W3C DOM specification. You can learn more about the W3C DOM by visiting www.w3.org/DOM/.

Accessing a Browser's DOM

To use the DOM for any browser, you need to use a scripting language, such as JavaScript or VBScript. JavaScript is more difficult to learn, but more universal. At present, VBScript works only with Microsoft Internet Explorer.

Do not confuse the DOM with the Component Object Model (COM). The DOM describes documents within a browser. The COM is a Microsoft specification for creating applications. The Distributed Component Object Model (DCOM) describes the ability to create applications that work well over network connections.

Undefined Object Error

You may receive an "Undefined Object Error" if you visit a web page and your browser does not support a specific DOM. In other cases, you may simply view an unformatted document in plain text. Not all versions of a browser support the same DOM. Therefore, not all objects can be defined.

If a particular DOM is not supported, another browser will usually render the web page successfully. This relationship is common with Microsoft Internet Explorer and Netscape Navigator.

HTML 4.01, the DOM, and Browser Compatibility

Most HTML 4.01 elements and attributes are backward compatible. However, some of the more ambitious improvements, including frames and the ability to respond to users, do not work well (or at all) with earlier browser versions. Additionally, the 4.0 and later browser versions interpret many HTML 4.01 commands quite differently, which means that your pages will render differently from browser to browser. Some DHTML solutions will work well in one browser but disable another. JavaScript appears slightly differently, depending on the browser.

Extensible HTML (XHTML)

In January 2000, HTML and Extensible Markup Language (XML) were combined into a specification called *Extensible HTML (XHTML)*. XHTML relies on the HTML 4.01 and the XML 1.0 specifications. Because of this reliance, the XHTML specification is relatively condensed. You can read the XHTML specification at www.w3.org/TR/xhtml1.

The W3C specification defines XHTML as "a reformulation of HTML 4 as an XML 1.0 application, and three DTDs corresponding to the ones defined by HTML 4."

Whereas HTML describes a document's visual layout, XML allows you to describe the function and context of the actual information contained in a document. XML is a tool that will help describe and organize the data that passes through networks. In web-based computing, you must understand when to use a particular tool. XML enables developers to create persistent documents that can be searched quickly and efficiently.

To understand XHTML, you must first understand HTML and XML. The remainder of this section will focus on XML. You can view the XML 1.0 specification at www.w3.org/XML.

The details of XHTML and its implementation of XML are advanced topics that extend beyond the scope of this exam.

Extensible Markup Language (XML)

XML is a language that allows you (within certain limits) to create your own custom markup language. Technically, you do not use XML to describe the meaning of information in your document. You use it to create your own language that in turn describes the meaning of information in your document. In this sense, XML is a *meta-language*—a language used to create languages. Any tags you define yourself are said to *extend* XML.

The chief benefit of XML is that it enables you to focus on the meaning and context of the information in a document. Banks, e-commerce sites, search engines, and large networks that serve complex documents require just such a solution.

XML is, in many ways, a reduced version of Standard Generalized Markup Language (SGML), because it allows you to declare your own tags without the complexity of SGML. *SGML* is a meta-language used to create other languages, including HTML and XML. The W3C now governs the development of XML.

An XML document has two characteristics:

- It must be well-formed.

- It must be valid.

Tree Structure of a Well-Formed XML Document

In XML, you must create what is called a "well-formed" document. For a document to be well-formed, it must contain a DTD and a root element, and have properly declared tags. You will learn about the XML DTD shortly. A root element is a container tag that surrounds all other elements, similar to the <HTML> tag. In XML, all properly declared tags must nest in the correct order.

The primary characteristic of a well-formed document is that it forms a tree-like structure that stems from the root. Figure 15.16 demonstrates one way in which you could represent this tree structure visually.

FIGURE 15.16 Tree structure of elements in an XML document

The following is an example of a document patterned after the hierarchy illustrated in the preceding figure:

```
<?xml version="1.0"?>
<CATALOG>
<BOOK>
<TITLE>A Certain Justice</TITLE>
<AUTHOR>P.D. James</AUTHOR>
```

```
<YEAR-PUBLISHED>1998</YEAR-PUBLISHED>
<ISBN>0375401091</ISBN>
</BOOK>
<BOOK>
<TITLE>Ashworth Hall</TITLE>
<AUTHOR>Anne Perry</AUTHOR>
<YEAR-PUBLISHED>1997</YEAR-PUBLISHED>
<ISBN>0449908445</ISBN>
</BOOK>
<BOOK>
<TITLE>L.A. Confidential</TITLE>
<AUTHOR>James Ellroy</AUTHOR>
<YEAR-PUBLISHED>1997</YEAR-PUBLISHED>
<ISBN>0446674249</ISBN>
</BOOK>
<BOOK>
<TITLE>Shadow Woman</TITLE>
<AUTHOR>Thomas Perry</AUTHOR>
<YEAR-PUBLISHED>1997</YEAR-PUBLISHED>
<ISBN>0679453024</ISBN>
</BOOK>
</CATALOG>
```

This XML document is well-formed, but it is not yet valid. To create a valid XML document, you must declare a DTD.

XML and Valid Documents: The DTD

Unlike HTML documents, an XML document must include a DTD, usually of the document author's creation. The DTD defines the validity of all subsequent tags. If an XML document does not have a DTD, it will not render.

The XML DTD is necessary because you must define the meanings and structure of all XML tags. Remember that XML allows you to create a language that describes your text. XML is not a specified language, like HTML. Therefore, you must think ahead and define every element. In many ways, the DTD is the most important part of an XML document because it provides the rules, or the grammar, for the descriptive tags. Specifically, it defines the syntax, structure, and vocabulary of the XML document.

Generally, you place the DTD in a separate text file, but you can include it within the XML document if you prefer.

XML and Style Sheets

Because XML does not provide formatting instructions like HTML does, you must use a style sheet to format an XML document. You can use either CSS or *Extensible Stylesheet Language (XSL)*. One of the benefits of XSL is document transformation; With XSL, you can translate (i.e., transform) an XML page into an HTML page so that a browser can render it. You can also use XSL and CSS together. For more information about XSL, consult the W3C site at `www.w3.org/Style/XSL/`.

Summary

In this chapter, you learned that you can enhance the functionality and provide useful information to users by utilizing, creating, and manipulating tables, creating forms, using imaging techniques, and employing frames on a website. Using the basic structure tags such as <TR>, <TH>, and <TD>, you can generate a table, its rows, and individual cells. Not only can you create a table, but you can also align cell content, span cell content across rows and columns, add background colors to both tables and cells, and mix text and graphics in cells.

HTML forms are also known as web forms. They are standard in all flavors of HTML 4.01 and allow you to send almost any type of data across the Internet to a web server. Fields are used to collect user input (such as a user name, address, or credit card number) on the form. Once entered, the data is then submitted to a server where it is stored and/or processed. *Common Gateway Interface (CGI)* is the *de facto* standard language for programs that process the interface script, but other technologies exist to process forms as well.

This chapter also discussed how an image map functions and how to create a client-side image map. As we noted earlier, an image map is just a set of coordinates that creates a "hot spot" area (hyperlink) on a particular image and multiple image maps can exist on a single image. Client-side image maps use code embedded within the HTML itself.

We also discussed how frames allow you to create attractive websites that allow more creative control over the user's experience. Frames also make navigation easier by allowing certain links and information to remain visible. The <FRAMESET> tag, or element, is a container tag that allows you to define regions in your browser window and assign separate files to each. It requires a mandatory attribute of either COLS or ROWS that designates the number and size of columns or rows in a browser window.

Finally, you were introduced to the concept of GUI HTML editors and how Cascading Style Sheets (CSS) can be extremely helpful in large websites with tens or hundreds of web pages, because each page does not have to be formatted separately.

Exam Essentials

Know the measurements used to modify an HTML table.   An HTML table can be modified by specifying measurements in either pixels, or by a percentage of the window. Pixels are convenient to use because they represent static numbers, but a percentage of the window is often easier to choose and manipulate in regard to other elements on the page.

Know the <TABLE>, <INPUT>, <PRE>, etc. tags and their uses.   The <TABLE> tag creates tables. The <INPUT> tag is used to create text boxes, check boxes, radio buttons, and submit and reset buttons. The <PRE> tag is used to create a simple table by preserving spacing and breaks.

Know the components of table appearance and their uses.   The contents of a table can be aligned within the cells. The table itself is aligned within the window of the browser and the table is aligned with other text. You can format all by using the ALIGN attribute.

Know the uses of ROWSPAN and COLSPAN.   The ROWSPAN attribute is used to span a single cell across multiple rows. The COLSPAN attribute is used to span a single cell across multiple columns.

Understand the difference between a select list and a multiple-select list in a web form.   A select list is a drop-down list of multiple options from which a single selection can be made. A multiple-select list is identical to a select list, except that the user can make multiple selections and it is optionally scrollable.

Understand an image "hot spot."   An image map is a set of coordinates that creates a "hot spot" area on a particular image. You can create multiple image maps on an image. Each of these "hot spots" acts as a hyperlink. Image maps call either a client-side or a server-side set of coordinates to determine how to process the user's mouse action. Client-side image maps use code embedded within the HTML itself. You can create an image map for any image format supported by a web browser.

Know how to create an animated GIF.   An animated GIF is made by combining a sequence of several GIF images into one file. Most animation tools allow you to set the interval of appearance between images, and to create many other effects to be employed by the animated GIF.

Know how frames can be useful in a website.   Elements that users should always see, such as navigation links, copyright notices, and title graphics, can be placed in a static, individual frame. As users navigate the site, the static frame's content can remain fixed, even though the contents of the adjoining frames may change.

Know how your frames-enabled website can accommodate browsers that do not support frames.   You can add the <NOFRAMES> tag to the frameset document to add alternative text that appears in the browser in place of the frameset. If a user's browser cannot handle frames, then the alternate text appears within their browser.

Understand Cascading Style Sheets.   Cascading style sheets are used to apply formatting to an entire website, instead of formatting each page manually. For instance, if your site consists of hundreds of pages, CSS can be used to create a consistent format to all of the pages rather than needing to have an administrator to apply a style to each one individually.

Be able to name the four ways in which you can apply a style sheet when implementing CSS1 with HTML.   You can apply CSS1 by declaring an inline style, creating an embedded style sheet, linking to an external style sheet, or using an imported style sheet.

Know what Dynamic HTML is and does.   Dynamic HTML is a programming language based on HTML that creates animation, interaction, and dynamic updating on web pages without contacting the server for each request.

Understand XML.   Extensible Markup Language (XML) is a programming language that gives context and meaning to the information in a document. XML is a language that allows you (within certain limits) to create your own custom markup language. Any tags you define yourself are said to extend XML.

Key Terms

Before you take the exam, be certain you are familiar with the following terms:

ALIGN	image transparency
animation	interlacing
BASE target	JavaScript
Cascading Style Sheets (CSS)	meta-language
CELLPADDING	object-oriented
check box	property
client-side script	radio button
Common Gateway Interface (CGI)	rule
Document Object Model (DOM)	select lists
Dynamic HTML (DHTML)	server-side script
event handler	Standard Generalized Markup Language (SGML)
Extensible HTML (XHTML)	style sheet rule
Extensible Markup Language (XML)	style sheet selector
Extensible Stylesheet Language (XSL)	table
frame	text box
frameset document	VALIGN
image map	WYSIWYG

Review Questions

1. Into which tag would you add the BORDER attribute to add a border to a table?

   A. <TABLE>

   B. <TR>

   C. <TH>

   D. <TD>

2. The CELLPADDING attribute refers to:

   A. The space between rows

   B. The space between cell text and cell border

   C. The space between columns

   D. The space between the table and surrounding text

3. You are creating a form, and want to incorporate a text field in which users can add comments about your web page. Which of the following form fields would you use?

   A. Text box

   B. Select list

   C. Scrolling text area

   D. Multiple-select list

4. Which of the following attributes must you include in the <FORM> tag to specify the location and name of the script that will process form data?

   A. TRIAL

   B. CHECK

   C. TEST

   D. ACTION

5. A polygon-shaped area is defined by how many coordinate pairs?

  A. Between four and one hundred

  B. Two

  C. One plus a radius

  D. Four

6. What does an image transparency do?

  A. Enables an animated object to take on the colors of the web page background.

  B. Enables a static image to be transformed into an image map.

  C. Enables any part of an image to blend with the web page background.

  D. Enables portions of an image to disappear behind another image.

7. The action of an image progressively displaying on a web page is called what?

  A. Interlacing

  B. Scrolling

  C. Progression

  D. Image transparency

8. Which of the following Graphics Interchange Formats supports simple animation?

  A. GIF 91a

  B. GIF 89a

  C. GIF 87a

  D. GIF 84a

9. Which of the following tags creates a frameset with two columns, each occupying half of the browser window?

    A. <FRAMESET COLS="50,50">

    B. <FRAME COLS="50,50">

    C. <FRAMESET COLS="50%,50%">

    D. <FRAME COLS="50%,50%>

10. What is the purpose of the <FRAME> tag?

    A. It identifies the content of each frame in the frameset.

    B. It defines the number of columns or rows in a frameset.

    C. It defines the percentage or pixel value of each frame.

    D. It identifies the relationship of hyperlinks between frames.

11. You create a frameset in which one frame targets another frame. When visitors click any navigation link in one frame, the corresponding web page will appear in the other frame. Which tag allows you to accomplish this task most easily?

    A. <NAME>

    B. <TARGET>

    C. <BASE>

    D. <HREF>

12. Which attribute and value makes frame borders invisible?

    A. MARGINWIDTH="0"

    B. FRAMEBORDER="0"

    C. MARGINHEIGHT="1"

    D. FRAMEBORDER="1"

13. You want a program that creates web pages and offers advanced management tools for integrating your website with other applications. What type of program should you choose?

A. Page editor

B. GUI editor

C. Site management editor

D. Text editor

14. Which of the following is a reason for choosing an HTML GUI editor to create a web page?

A. GUI editors often modify HTML code that is entered manually.

B. Typing HTML code is time consuming.

C. You will always be using the most up-to-date version of HTML.

D. Typing code teaches you HTML fundamentals.

15. Which of the following is the best reason for learning HTML code?

A. HTML text editors are simple to use and require no training.

B. You do not need to learn HTML code to create a website with advanced functionality.

C. HTML text editors place the code into files for you.

D. If you want to enhance the functionality of your web pages with scripting languages, you must learn HTML code.

16. Which of the following is a reason to use JavaScript on your website?

A. It creates interactive dialog boxes.

B. It gives context and meaning to the information in a document.

C. It creates applications, such as Microsoft Word.

D. It can be compiled.

17. What type of error usually indicates that your browser does not support a specific DOM?

    A. HTTP 404–File Not Found

    B. Undefined property

    C. Undefined object

    D. DOM error

18. Which Cascading Style Sheet implementation allows a web designer to create a separate CSS text file and use the `<LINK>` tag within each HTML document to point to that text file?

    A. Inline style

    B. External style sheet

    C. Embedded style sheet

    D. Imported style sheet

19. Which technique enables web pages and computer languages to react to user input?

    A. An event handler

    B. The `<SPAM>` tag

    C. An inline image

    D. A Document Object Model

20. Extensible Markup Language (XML) does which of the following?

    A. Enables the movement of otherwise static objects.

    B. Allows HTML to work with all other markup languages.

    C. Allows you to create your own markup language.

    D. Allows you to create HTML code without regard to proper formatting structure.

Answers to Review Questions

1. A. The <TABLE> tag is used to add a border to a table.

2. B. The CELLPADDING attribute is used to identify space between cell text and cell border.

3. C. The scrolling text area can be used to create a text field in which users can add comments about your web page.

4. D. The ACTION attribute must be included in the <FORM> tag to specify the location and name of the script that will process form data.

5. A. Between four and one hundred coordinate pairs are used to define a polygon-shaped area.

6. C. An image transparency enables any part of an image to blend with the web page background.

7. A. The action of an image progressively displaying on a web page is called interlacing.

8. B. The GIF 89a format supports simple animation.

9. C. The <FRAMESET COLS="50%,50%"> tag creates a frameset with two columns, each occupying half of the browser window.

10. A. The <FRAME> tag identifies the content of each frame in the frameset.

11. C. The <BASE> tag allows visitors to click any navigation link in one frame, and have the corresponding web page appear in the other frame. While <TARGET> would work, it is not correct because of the "most easily" clause in the question.

12. B. FRAMEBORDER="0" makes frame borders invisible.

13. C. A site management editor creates web pages and offers advanced management tools for integrating your website with other applications.

14. B. A compelling reason for using an HTML GUI editor to create a web page is that typing HTML code is time consuming.

15. D.   You must learn HTML code if you want to enhance the functionality of your web pages with scripting languages.

16. A.   JavaScript can be used to create interactive dialog boxes.

17. C.   An undefined object error usually indicates that your browser does not support a specific DOM.

18. B.   External style sheets allow a web designer to create a separate CSS text file and use the <LINK> tag within each HTML document to point to that text file.

19. A.   An event handler enables web pages and computer languages to react to user input.

20. C.   XML allows you to create your own markup language.

Appendix A

Compiled vs. Interpreted Languages

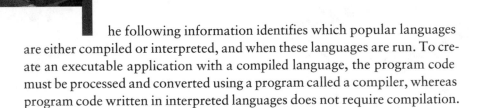

The following information identifies which popular languages are either compiled or interpreted, and when these languages are run. To create an executable application with a compiled language, the program code must be processed and converted using a program called a compiler, whereas program code written in interpreted languages does not require compilation.

Compiled Languages

These three languages share the same requirement: the program code must be compiled before execution. This compiling creates a standalone, executable program that cannot be viewed at the source code level by anyone other than the author(s). When writing programs in Visual Basic, for example, you must choose to compile the program into an EXE (executable) before it can be run on another machine that does not have Visual Basic on it. Please note that there are many compiled languages in use besides the three listed here.

C   C can be used to create applications, drivers, and operating systems. As with Java applications, C applications are run when the user opens the program, and then they run when the user inputs some data into the program. The individual parts of the program execute depending on what the program is intended to do.

C++   C++ programs are generally standalone programs. As with C programs, they run when the user opens the program, and then they run when the user inputs some data into the program. The individual parts of the program execute depending on what the program is intended to do.

Visual Basic   Visual Basic programs are generally standalone applications that depend on user input (or some type of event) to determine when particular parts of the program execute. Again, it depends on what the program is intended to do as to when individual parts of the program execute.

Interpreted Languages

Interpreted languages are sometimes called scripting languages. Just as an actor in a play recites a script line-by-line, programs written in interpreted languages must be run line-by-line when executed.

In contrast, some languages create a set of instructions that need not be compiled. The proper command or directive within the HTML page will tell the browser to execute the code that follows. The code continues to be in ASCII format and can be viewed by others who choose to look at the source code.

JavaScript   JavaScript program code is either included in an HTML source file or referenced by an HTML file as an include file. A script engine handles JavaScript interpretation. Script engines are built into browsers. The script engine checks the script for syntax, checks, and stores any variables that may be present, and executes any in-line script or script that is not part of a function. Scripts that include named functions can have those functions execute based on events that occur in the browser, such as a page loading, a user clicking on a button, or a user submitting a form. So again, when it executes depends on what the script is intended to do.

VBScript   VBScript program code is included in an HTML source file. A script engine handles VBScript interpretation. Script engines are built into browsers. The script engine checks the script for syntax, checks and stores any variables that may be present, and then executes any in-line script or script that is not part of a function. Scripts that include named functions can have those functions execute based on events that occur in the browser, such as a page loading, a user clicking on a button, or a user submitting a form. So again, it all depends on what the script is intended to do when it executes.

JScript   JScript is the Microsoft implementation of JavaScript. Like JavaScript program code, JScript code can either be included in an HTML source file or referenced by an HTML file as an include file. A script engine handles JScript interpretation. Script engines are built into browsers. The script engine checks the script for syntax, checks and stores any variables that may be present, and then executes any in-line script or script that is not part of a function. Scripts that include named functions can have those functions execute based on events that occur in the browser, such as a page loading, a user clicking on a button, or a user submitting a form. So again, it all depends on what the script is intended to do when it executes.

Extensible Markup Language (XML)   XML is different in that it is a language used to describe other languages. It is a meta-language that can be used to encode data in a machine-readable format. XML code is executed inline by an XML parser, which often uses a reference called a document type definition (DTD) that helps define how data is presented. DTDs are often specific to particular industries and applications, and can be customized by developers to include new forms of data.

Virtual Reality Markup Language (VRML)   VRML is used to create and define simulated 3D environments in a 2D computing environment. The VRML file is actually parsed by a browser or browser plug-in. How the code is transformed into its final presentation depends on the browser or plug-in. The browser plug-in displays the shapes and sounds in a scene graph. The presentation is known as a virtual world. The user (either a human or a mechanical entity) navigates the virtual world with the browser.

Active Server Pages (ASP)   ASP code is embedded inside HTML pages and is marked by special delimiters. A client requests an ASP page by sending an HTTP GET Request to a server. The page is then sent to the ASP scripting engine to be parsed. The ASP scripting engine is an integral part of the web server. Microsoft includes this engine in IIS. ASP engines for other servers are available from third-party publishers such as Chili!Soft. The Scripting Host, located in an executable program called `asp.dll`, can do two things. If it is the first ASP page to be sent to this client from the server, it means a new session, and possibly a new application, has begun. The Scripting Host checks the `global.asp` file and performs any scripted functionality before it gets to the requested page. Once that is done, the

Scripting Host executes all the embedded server-side scripting code in the page. Once this is done, the scripting engine passes back one of these three things: an error page, an object moved status code, or an HTML page.

Personal Home Page (PHP)   PHP code is embedded inside HTML pages. PHP is very similar to ASP in execution. The obvious difference is that a PHP interpreter executes the PHP script prior to returning the results to the client. Other than that (especially with the advent of PHP 4.0, which supports sessions and application-level variables), ASP and PHP are very similar.

Perl and Java

The Perl and Java languages do not exactly fit the definition of either a compiled language or an interpreted language.

Java   Java applications represent an interesting form of computer program. Java applications can be developed so that they are written once yet executable on a variety of different computing platforms. Java is not a compiled language, although it has its roots in C++. Java programs are prepared for distribution by a conversion into bytecode. When the program is executed, the Java Virtual Machine interprets this bytecode into machine language appropriate for the operating system and processor. This state represents an intermediate step between interpreted and compiled languages.

Java applications typically depend on user input. In other words, they run when the user opens the program, and then they run when the user inputs some data into the program. Individual parts of the program execute depending on what the program is intended to do.

Java applets are mini-applications that are downloaded to a browser, generally over the Internet or an intranet. The applets may be programs that execute and perform a function after they are downloaded, or, like applications, they may require user input in order to provide their functionality. However, the applet requires an operating environment provided by the browser in order to execute. Again, it depends on what the applet is intended to do when it executes.

Java servlets are similar to CGI programs. They execute on a server when information is received from a client. A servlet can request and receive data from another server or database. This process of servlet chaining allows a web application to securely display third-party data to a web user.

Perl Perl originated as a scripting language for report development. In Perl, the individual elements of a script are compiled into a tree of opcodes, which differ from machine code in that they are executed by a virtual machine, whereas machine code is executed directly by hardware. Opcodes are optimized objects intended to perform specific tasks. When a Perl program is executed, it is compiled into opcodes, and these opcodes are then executed by a virtual machine. Consequently, Perl provides the advantages of a scripting language and the execution speed of a compiled program. Perl can be considered both compiled and interpreted.

Just as with a Java program, a Perl program can execute upon opening by a user, or it can await input from a user on which it acts. Most Perl programs perform automated tasks, so they run when either another program or a script calls them. If the Perl program is CGI-oriented, it runs on a server when it receives data from a client.

Appendix

B

Internet Technology

As we have discussed throughout this book, the Internet provides a method for sharing and delivering files and information through standard sets of protocols. Protocols define how networks talk to one another, and how the communicated data is structured as files. The files can be opened and displayed by a variety of user applications. In some cases, files can be compressed to reduce their size and transmission time. Finally, we can use Internet search engines to locate documents and files containing relevant data.

Protocol Syntax

A list of Internet protocols is shown in Table B.1. The URL Syntax column lists the syntax that can be entered into a browser address field to open the proper client for each protocol. The URLs that include an asterisk (*) can also be directly accessed using specific client programs, such as e-mail, news, and FTP clients.

TABLE B.1 URL Protocol Syntax

Protocol	Server Type	URL Syntax
SMTP/POP/IMAP	Mail	`mailto:address` `mailto://address` *
NNTP	News	`news:address` `news://address` *

TABLE B.1 URL Protocol Syntax *(continued)*

Protocol	Server Type	URL Syntax
Gopher	Gopher	`gopher://address`
FTP	FTP	`ftp://address*`
HTTP	Web	`http://address`
Microsoft Internet Explorer	Files on local drive (not a server type)	`c:\directory\filename`
Netscape Navigator	Files on local drive (not a server type)	`file://c:/directory/filename`

Shareware and Freeware

Plenty of software is available on the Web. Shareware is inexpensive. Download and install it, and if you like the application, send the vendor a payment. Freeware is absolutely free. These programs may be less robust than retail or shareware applications, but there is no charge for using freeware. Major software companies, such as Microsoft and Netscape, often give away free copies to help you get started, but more complete versions are available for a fee. Plug-ins, or software that extends a browser's capabilities, and helper applications that your browser opens to play or view multimedia files are often free, also.

File Compression

When you download files from the Internet, such as compressed files attached to e-mail messages, you should save them to your desktop or a special folder so that you will always be able to find them.

When compressed files are extracted, you will have two files: the compressed file and a folder with the extracted files. Eventually, you will want to delete the compressed file. Also, remember to compress files you use infrequently to conserve space.

Table B.2 shows compression file types used by compression programs to send data over the Internet.

TABLE B.2 Compression Standards

File Name Extension	Type of Compression
.zip	A Windows file generated from shareware, such as WinZip or PKZIP; a popular compression type used for PCs.
.exe	A Windows executable file. Typically, a self-extracting compressed file, sometimes a software program. Automatically expands when double-clicked; a compression utility is not necessary to decompress it.
.sit	An Apple StuffIt file; a popular compression type used for Macintosh.
.sea	An Apple self-extracting file, usually a SIT file that automatically expands when double-clicked; a compression utility is not necessary to decompress it.
.tar	A UNIX tape archive (tar) file; a form of compression used by UNIX computers.

Internet Indexes and Search Engines

Table B.3 lists Internet indexes and search engines you can use to find information on the Web.

TABLE B.3   Indexes and Search Engines

Name	URL
AltaVista	www.altavista.com
Excite	www.excite.com
Lycos	www.lycos.com
HotBot	hotbot.lycos.com
Google	www.google.com
Google Groups	groups.google.com
MetaCrawler	www.metacrawler.com
WebCrawler	www.webcrawler.com
Yahoo!	www.yahoo.com

Appendix C

HTML Elements and Attributes

he following table describes the elements and attributes included in the HTML 4.01 recommendation. HTML is the non-proprietary language used for creating web pages and was originally based upon SGML. HTML standards are maintained by W3C, and if you are new to HTML, consider the "Getting Started with HTML" tutorial they offer at www.w3.org/MarkUp/Guide/.

Element	Attributes	Tags	Closing Tag? (R) Required (F) Forbidden (O) Optional	Description
A	ACCESSKEY, CHARSET, CLASS, COORDS, DIR, HREF, HREFLANG, ID, LANG, NAME, ONBLUR, ONCLICK, ONDBLCLICK, ONFOCUS, ONKEYDOWN, ONKEYPRESS, ONKEYUP, ONMOUSEDOWN, ONMOUSEMOVE, ONMOUSEOUT, ONMOUSEOVER, ONMOUSEUP, REL, REV, SHAPE, STYLE, TABINDEX, TARGET, TITLE, TYPE	`<A></A>`	(R)	Denotes anchor; facilitates hypertext linkage.
ABBR	CLASS, DIR, ID, LANG, ONCLICK, ONDBLCLICK, ONKEYDOWN, ONKEYPRESS, ONKEYUP, ONMOUSEDOWN, ONMOUSEMOVE, ONMOUSEOUT, ONMOUSEOVER, ONMOUSEUP, STYLE, TITLE	`<ABBR>` `</ABBR>`	(R)	Denotes an abbreviation.

Element	Attributes	Tags	Closing Tag? (R) Required (F) Forbidden (O) Optional	Description
ACRONYM	CLASS, DIR, ID, LANG, ONCLICK, ONDBLCLICK, ONKEYDOWN, ONKEYPRESS, ONKEYUP, ONMOUSEDOWN, ONMOUSEMOVE, ONMOUSEOUT, ONMOUSEOVER, ONMOUSEUP, STYLE, TITLE	\<ACRONYM\> \</ACRONYM\>	(R)	Indicates an acronym, such as POTS, WAN, and so forth.
APPLET	ARCHIVE, CLASS, CODE, CODEBASE, HEIGHT, HSPACE, ID, NAME, OBJECT, STYLE, TITLE, VSPACE, WIDTH	\<APPLET\> \</APPLET\>	(R)	Embeds Java applets. May contain the PARAM attribute. *Note:* The W3C has deprecated this element in favor of OBJECT.
AREA	ACCESSKEY, ALT, CLASS, COORDS, DIR, HREF, ID, LANG, NOHREF, ONBLUR, ONCLICK, ONDBLCLICK, ONFOCUS, ONKEYDOWN, ONKEYPRESS, ONKEYUP, ONMOUSEDOWN, ONMOUSEMOVE, ONMOUSEOUT, ONMOUSEOVER, ONMOUSEUP, SHAPE, STYLE, TABINDEX, TARGET, TITLE	\<AREA\>	(F)	Identifies the area of an image map.
B	CLASS, DIR, ID, LANG STYLE, TITLE, ONCLICK, ONDBLCLICK, ONKEYDOWN, ONKEYPRESS, ONKEYUP, ONMOUSEDOWN, ONMOUSEMOVE, ONMOUSEOUT, ONMOUSEOVER, ONMOUSEUP	\<B\>\</B\>	(R)	Creates bold text.

Element	Attributes	Tags	Closing Tag? (R) Required (F) Forbidden (O) Optional	Description
BASE	HREF, TARGET	<BASE>	(F)	Indicates document base URL.
BASEFONT	COLOR, FACE, ID, LANG, SIZE	<BASEFONT> </BASEFONT>	(R)	Sets base font size.
BDO	CLASS, DIR, ID, LANG, STYLE, TITLE	<BDO></BDO>	(R)	Overrides the bi-directional algorithm in browsers.
BIG	CLASS, DIR, ID, LANG, STYLE, TITLE, ONCLICK, ONDBLCLICK, ONKEYDOWN, ONKEYPRESS, ONKEYUP, ONMOUSEDOWN, ONMOUSEMOVE, ONMOUSEOUT, ONMOUSEOVER, ONMOUSEUP	<BIG></BIG>	(R)	Creates large text.
BLOCK QUOTE	CITE, CLASS, ID, LANG, DIR, ONCLICK, ONDBLCLICK, ONKEYDOWN, ONKEYPRESS, ONKEYUP, ONMOUSEDOWN, ONMOUSEMOVE, ONMOUSEOUT, ONMOUSEOVER, ONMOUSEUP, STYLE, TITLE	<BLOCKQUOTE> </BLOCKQUOTE>	(R)	Indents text; useful for long quotations.
BODY	CLASS, ID, DIR, LANG, ONCLICK, ONDBLCLICK, ONKEYDOWN, ONKEYPRESS, ONKEYUP, ONLOAD, ONMOUSEDOWN, ONMOUSEMOVE, ONMOUSEOUT, ONMOUSEOVER, ONMOUSEUP, ONUNLOAD, STYLE, TITLE	<BODY> </BODY>	(O)	Encloses the body of the HTML document.
BR	CLASS, CLEAR, ID, STYLE, TITLE	 	(F)	Creates a forced line break without white space.

Element	Attributes	Tags	Closing Tag? (R) Required (F) Forbidden (O) Optional	Description
BUTTON	ACCESSKEY, CLASS, DISABLED, ID, NAME, ONBLUR, ONCLICK, ONDBLCLICK, ONFOCUS, ONKEYDOWN, ONKEYPRESS, ONKEYUP, ONMOUSEDOWN, ONMOUSEMOVE, ONMOUSEOUT, ONMOUSEOVER, ONMOUSEUP, STYLE, TABINDEX, TITLE, TYPE, VALUE	<BUTTON> </BUTTON>	(R)	Inserts push button.
CAPTION	ALIGN, CLASS, DIR, ID, LANG, ONCLICK, ONDBLCLICK, ONKEYDOWN, ONKEYPRESS, ONKEYUP, ONMOUSEDOWN, ONMOUSEMOVE, ONMOUSEOUT, ONMOUSEOVER, ONMOUSEUP, STYLE, TITLE	<CAPTION> </CAPTION>	(R)	Creates a table caption.
CENTER	CLASS, ID, LANG, ONCLICK, ONDBLCLICK, ONKEYDOWN, ONKEYPRESS, ONKEYUP, ONMOUSEDOWN, ONMOUSEMOVE, ONMOUSEOUT, ONMOUSEOVER, ONMOUSEUP, STYLE, TITLE	<CENTER> </CENTER>	(R)	Centers text or other elements on a horizontal line. *Note:* The W3C has deprecated this element in favor of the text-align CSS property.
CITE	CLASS, DIR, ID, LANG, ONCLICK, ONDBLCLICK, ONKEYDOWN, ONKEYPRESS, ONKEYUP, ONMOUSEDOWN, ONMOUSEMOVE, ONMOUSEOUT, ONMOUSEOVER, ONMOUSEUP, STYLE, TITLE	<CITE> </CITE>	(R)	Employs citation style used for quoting other works or titles.

Element	Attributes	Tags	Closing Tag? (R) Required (F) Forbidden (O) Optional	Description
CODE	CLASS, DIR, ID, LANG, ONCLICK, ONDBLCLICK, ONKEYDOWN, ONKEYPRESS, ONKEYUP, ONMOUSEDOWN, ONMOUSEMOVE, ONMOUSEOUT, ONMOUSEOVER, ONMOUSEUP, STYLE, TITLE	\<CODE\> \</CODE\>	(R)	Indicates citation of computer code text strings.
COL	ALIGN, CHAR, CHAROFF, CLASS, DIR, ID, LANG, ONCLICK, ONDBLCLICK, ONKEYDOWN, ONKEYPRESS, ONKEYUP, ONMOUSEDOWN, ONMOUSEMOVE, ONMOUSEOUT, ONMOUSEOVER, ONMOUSEUP, SPAN, STYLE, TITLE, VALIGN, WIDTH	\<COL\>	(F)	Divides table into vertical groups or columns.
COLGROUP	ALIGN, CHAR, CHAROFF, CLASS, DIR, ID, LANG, ONCLICK, ONDBLCLICK, ONKEYDOWN, ONKEYPRESS, ONKEYUP, ONMOUSEDOWN, ONMOUSEMOVE, ONMOUSEOUT, ONMOUSEOVER, ONMOUSEUP, SPAN, STYLE, TITLE, VALIGN, WIDTH	\<COLGROUP\> \</COLGROUP\>	(O)	Divides a table into vertical groups.
DD	CLASS, DIR, ID, LANG, ONCLICK, ONDBLCLICK, ONKEYDOWN, ONKEYPRESS, ONKEYUP, ONMOUSEDOWN, ONMOUSEMOVE, ONMOUSEOUT, ONMOUSEOVER, ONMOUSEUP, STYLE, TITLE	\<DD\>\</DD\>	(O)	Designates a definition. Used with DL.

Element	Attributes	Tags	Closing Tag? (R) Required (F) Forbidden (O) Optional	Description
DEL	CITE, CLASS, DATETIME, DIR, ID, LANG, ONCLICK, ONDBLCLICK, ONKEYDOWN, ONKEYPRESS, ONKEYUP, ONMOUSEDOWN, ONMOUSEMOVE, ONMOUSEOUT, ONMOUSEOVER, ONMOUSEUP, STYLE, TITLE	\<DEL>\</DEL>	(R)	Indicates text deleted from the previous version.
DFN	CLASS, DIR, ID, LANG, ONCLICK, ONDBLCLICK, ONKEYDOWN, ONKEYPRESS, ONKEYUP, ONMOUSEDOWN, ONMOUSEMOVE, ONMOUSEOUT, ONMOUSEOVER, ONMOUSEUP, STYLE, TITLE	\<DFN>\</DFN>	(R)	Indicates the defining instance of the enclosed term.
DIR	CLASS, COMPACT, DIR, ID, LANG, ONCLICK, ONDBLCLICK, ONKEYDOWN, ONKEYPRESS, ONKEYUP, ONMOUSEDOWN, ONMOUSEMOVE, ONMOUSEOUT, ONMOUSEOVER, ONMOUSEUP, STYLE, TITLE	\<DIR>\</DIR>	(R)	Used for directory lists. *Note:* The W3C has deprecated this element; use \<UL> in place of \<DIR> and \<MENU>.
DIV	ALIGN, CLASS, DIR, ID, LANG, ONCLICK, ONDBLCLICK, ONKEYDOWN, ONKEYPRESS, ONKEYUP, ONMOUSEDOWN, ONMOUSEMOVE, ONMOUSEOUT, ONMOUSEOVER, ONMOUSEUP, STYLE, TITLE	\<DIV>\</DIV>	(R)	Creates a division for formatting and manipulation purposes.

Element	Attributes	Tags	Closing Tag? (R) Required (F) Forbidden (O) Optional	Description
DL	CLASS, COMPACT, DIR, ID, LANG, ONCLICK, ONDBLCLICK, ONKEYDOWN, ONKEYPRESS, ONKEYUP, ONMOUSEDOWN, ONMOUSEMOVE, ONMOUSEOUT, ONMOUSEOVER, ONMOUSEUP, STYLE, TITLE	\<DL>\</DL>	(R)	Creates a definition list.
DT	CLASS, DIR, ID, LANG, ONCLICK, ONDBLCLICK, ONKEYDOWN, ONKEYPRESS, ONKEYUP, ONMOUSEDOWN, ONMOUSEMOVE, ONMOUSEOUT, ONMOUSEOVER, ONMOUSEUP, STYLE, TITLE	\<DT>\</DT>	(O)	Designates a DL term.
EM	CLASS, DIR, ID, LANG, ONCLICK, ONDBLCLICK, ONKEYDOWN, ONKEYPRESS, ONKEYUP, ONMOUSEDOWN, ONMOUSEMOVE, ONMOUSEOUT, ONMOUSEOVER, ONMOUSEUP, STYLE, TITLE	\<EM>\</EM>	(R)	Creates emphasis; usually rendered as italic style.
FIELDSET	CLASS, DIR, ID, LANG, ONCLICK, ONDBLCLICK, ONKEYDOWN, ONKEYPRESS, ONKEYUP, ONMOUSEDOWN, ONMOUSEMOVE, ONMOUSEOUT, ONMOUSEOVER, ONMOUSEUP, STYLE, TITLE	\<FIELDSET>\</FIELDSET>	(R)	Forms control group.
FONT	CLASS, COLOR, DIR, FACE, ID, LANG, SIZE, STYLE, TITLE	\<FONT>\</FONT>	(R)	Determines the font in a specific instance.

Element	Attributes	Tags	Closing Tag? (R) Required (F) Forbidden (O) Optional	Description
FORM	ACCEPT-CHARSET, ACTION, CLASS, DIR, ENCTYPE, ID, LANG, METHOD, ONCLICK, ONDBLCLICK, ONKEYDOWN, ONKEYPRESS, ONKEYUP, ONMOUSEDOWN, ONMOUSEMOVE, ONMOUSEOUT, ONMOUSEOVER, ONMOUSEUP, ONRESET, ONSUBMIT, STYLE, TARGET, TITLE	`<FORM>` `</FORM>`	(R)	Creates an interactive HTML form.
FRAME	CLASS, FRAMEBORDER, ID, LONGDESC, MARGINHEIGHT, MARGINWIDTH, NAME, NORESIZE, SCROLLING, SRC, STYLE, TITLE	`<FRAME>`	(F)	Defines the contents of a frame within a frameset.
FRAMESET	CLASS, COLS, ID, ONLOAD, ONUNLOAD, ROWS, STYLE, TITLE	`<FRAMESET>` `</FRAMESET>`	(R)	Specifies the structure, position and layout of the frames in the browser window.
H1	ALIGN, CLASS, DIR, ID, LANG, ONCLICK, ONDBLCLICK, ONKEYDOWN, ONKEYPRESS, ONKEYUP, ONMOUSEDOWN, ONMOUSEMOVE, ONMOUSEOUT, ONMOUSEOVER, ONMOUSEUP, STYLE, TITLE	`<H1></H1>`	(R)	Styles as level-one heading.
H2	ALIGN, CLASS, DIR, ID, LANG, ONCLICK, ONDBLCLICK, ONKEYDOWN, ONKEYPRESS, ONKEYUP, ONMOUSEDOWN, ONMOUSEMOVE, ONMOUSEOUT, ONMOUSEOVER, ONMOUSEUP, STYLE, TITLE	`<H2></H2>`	(R)	Styles as level-two heading.

Element	Attributes	Tags	Closing Tag? (R) Required (F) Forbidden (O) Optional	Description
H3	ALIGN, CLASS, DIR, ID, LANG, ONCLICK, ONDBLCLICK, ONKEYDOWN, ONKEYPRESS, ONKEYUP, ONMOUSEDOWN, ONMOUSEMOVE, ONMOUSEOUT, ONMOUSEOVER, ONMOUSEUP, STYLE, TITLE	\<H3>\</H3>	(R)	Styles as level-three heading.
H4	ALIGN, CLASS, DIR, ID, LANG, ONCLICK, ONDBLCLICK, ONKEYDOWN, ONKEYPRESS, ONKEYUP, ONMOUSEDOWN, ONMOUSEMOVE, ONMOUSEOUT, ONMOUSEOVER, ONMOUSEUP, STYLE, TITLE	\<H4>\</H4>	(R)	Styles as level-four heading.
H5	ALIGN, CLASS, DIR, ID, LANG, ONCLICK, ONDBLCLICK, ONKEYDOWN, ONKEYPRESS, ONKEYUP, ONMOUSEDOWN, ONMOUSEMOVE, ONMOUSEOUT, ONMOUSEOVER, ONMOUSEUP, STYLE, TITLE	\<H5>\</H5>	(R)	Styles as level-five heading.
H6	ALIGN, CLASS, DIR, ID, LANG, ONCLICK, ONDBLCLICK, ONKEYDOWN, ONKEYPRESS, ONKEYUP, ONMOUSEDOWN, ONMOUSEMOVE, ONMOUSEOUT, ONMOUSEOVER, ONMOUSEUP, STYLE, TITLE	\<H6>\</H6>	(R)	Styles as level-six heading.
HEAD	DIR, LANG, PROFILE	\<HEAD> \</HEAD>	(O)	Encloses the document header.

Element	Attributes	Tags	Closing Tag? (R) Required (F) Forbidden (O) Optional	Description
HR	ALIGN, CLASS, ID, NOSHADE, ONCLICK, ONDBLCLICK, ONKEYDOWN, ONKEYPRESS, ONKEYUP, ONMOUSEDOWN, ONMOUSEMOVE, ONMOUSEOUT, ONMOUSEOVER, ONMOUSEUP, SIZE, STYLE, TITLE, WIDTH	\<HR\>	(F)	Adds horizontal rule.
HTML	DIR, LANG, VERSION	\<HTML\> \</HTML\>	(O)	Identifies document as HTML.
I	CLASS, DIR, ID, LANG, ONCLICK, ONDBLCLICK, ONKEYDOWN, ONKEYPRESS, ONKEYUP, ONMOUSEDOWN, ONMOUSEMOVE, ONMOUSEOUT, ONMOUSEOVER, ONMOUSEUP, STYLE, TITLE	\<I\>\</I\>	(R)	Defines italic text.
IFRAME	ALIGN, CLASS, FRAMEBORDER, HEIGHT, ID, LONGDESC, MARGINHEIGHT, MARGINWIDTH, NAME, SCROLLING, SRC, STYLE, TITLE, WIDTH	\<IFRAME\> \</IFRAME\>	(R)	Defines a floating frame.
IMG	ALT, BORDER, CLASS, DIR, HEIGHT, ID, ISMAP, LANG, LONGDESC, ONCLICK, ONDBLCLICK, ONKEYDOWN, ONKEYPRESS, ONKEYUP, ONMOUSEDOWN, ONMOUSEMOVE, ONMOUSEOUT, ONMOUSEOVER, ONMOUSEUP, SRC, STYLE, TITLE, USEMAP, VSPACE, WIDTH	\<IMG\>	(F)	Inserts an image.

Element	Attributes	Tags	Closing Tag? (R) Required (F) Forbidden (O) Optional	Description
INPUT TYPE= "button"	ACCESSKEY, CLASS, DIR, DISABLED, ID, LANG, NAME, ONBLUR, ONCHANGE, ONCLICK, ONDBLCLICK, ONFOCUS, ONKEYDOWN, ONKEYPRESS, ONKEYUP, ONMOUSEDOWN, ONMOUSEMOVE, ONMOUSEOUT, ONMOUSEOVER, ONMOUSEUP, ONSELECT, READONLY, SIZE, STYLE, TABINDEX, TITLE, TYPE, VALUE	\<INPUT>	(F)	Defines a button.
INPUT TYPE= "checkbox"	ACCESSKEY, CHECKED, CLASS, DISABLED, ID, NAME, ONBLUR, ONCHANGE, ONCLICK, ONDBLCLICK, ONFOCUS, ONKEYDOWN, ONKEYPRESS, ONKEYUP, ONMOUSEDOWN, ONMOUSEMOVE, ONMOUSEOUT, ONMOUSEOVER, ONMOUSEUP, READONLY, STYLE, TABINDEX, TITLE, TYPE, VALUE	\<INPUT>	(F)	Defines a check box.
INPUT TYPE= "file"	ACCEPT, ACCESSKEY, CLASS, DISABLED, ID, NAME, ONBLUR, ONCHANGE, ONCLICK, ONDBLCLICK, ONFOCUS, ONKEYDOWN, ONKEYPRESS, ONKEYUP, ONMOUSEDOWN, ONMOUSEMOVE, ONMOUSEOUT, ONMOUSEOVER, ONMOUSEUP, ONSELECT, READONLY, SIZE, STYLE, TABINDEX, TITLE, TYPE, VALUE	\<INPUT>	(F)	Defines a field into which a file name can be entered for uploading a file. *Note:* A form that includes a file input must specify the following in the \<FORM> tag: METHOD="post" ENCTYPE="multipart /form-data".

Element	Attributes	Tags	Closing Tag? (R) Required (F) Forbidden (O) Optional	Description
INPUT TYPE= "hidden"	ACCESSKEY, CLASS, DIR, DISABLED, ID, LANG, MAXLENGTH, NAME, ONBLUR, ONCLICK, ONDBLCLICK, ONFOCUS, ONKEYDOWN, ONKEYPRESS, ONKEYUP, ONMOUSEDOWN, ONMOUSEMOVE, ONMOUSEOUT, ONMOUSEOVER, ONMOUSEUP, ONSELECT, READONLY, SIZE, STYLE, TABINDEX, TITLE, TYPE, VALUE	\<INPUT\>	(F)	Defines a hidden file field that can carry information unseen by the user.
INPUT TYPE= "image"	ALT, ACCESSKEY, CLASS, DISABLED, ID, NAME, ONBLUR, ONCLICK, ONDBLCLICK, ONFOCUS, ONKEYDOWN, ONKEYPRESS, ONKEYUP, ONMOUSEDOWN, ONMOUSEMOVE, ONMOUSEOUT, ONMOUSEOVER, ONMOUSEUP, SRC, STYLE, TABINDEX, TITLE, TYPE, USEMAP, VALUE	\<INPUT\>	(F)	Defines an image that functions as a Submit button.
INPUT TYPE= "password"	ACCESSKEY, CLASS, DISABLED, DIR, ID, LANG, MAXLENGTH, NAME, ONBLUR, ONCLICK, ONDBLCLICK, ONFOCUS, ONKEYDOWN, ONKEYPRESS, ONKEYUP, ONMOUSEDOWN, ONMOUSEMOVE, ONMOUSEOUT, ONMOUSEOVER, ONMOUSEUP, ONSELECT, READONLY, SIZE, STYLE, TABINDEX, TITLE, TYPE, VALUE	\<INPUT\>	(F)	Defines a text field in which entered text is masked by asterisks.

Element	Attributes	Tags	Closing Tag? (R) Required (F) Forbidden (O) Optional	Description
INPUT TYPE= "radio"	ACCESSKEY, CHECKED, CLASS, DISABLED, ID, NAME, ONBLUR, ONCHANGE, ONCLICK, ONDBLCLICK, ONFOCUS, ONMOUSEDOWN, ONMOUSEMOVE, ONMOUSEOUT, ONMOUSEOVER, ONMOUSEUP, ONKEYDOWN, ONKEYPRESS, ONKEYUP, READONLY, STYLE, TABINDEX, TITLE, TYPE, VALUE	\<INPUT\>	(F)	Defines a radio button group for selecting mutually exclusive options.
INPUT TYPE= "reset"	ACCESSKEY, CLASS, DISABLED, ID, NAME, ONBLUR, ONCHANGE, ONCLICK, ONDBLCLICK, ONFOCUS, ONKEYDOWN, ONKEYPRESS, ONKEYUP, ONMOUSEDOWN, ONMOUSEMOVE, ONMOUSEOUT, ONMOUSEOVER, ONMOUSEUP, STYLE, TABINDEX, TYPE, TITLE, VALUE	\<INPUT\>	(F)	Defines a Reset button.
INPUT TYPE= "submit"	ACCESSKEY, CLASS, DISABLED, ID, NAME, ONBLUR, ONCHANGE, ONCLICK, ONDBLCLICK, ONFOCUS, ONKEYDOWN, ONKEYPRESS, ONKEYUP, ONMOUSEDOWN, ONMOUSEMOVE, ONMOUSEOUT, ONMOUSEOVER, ONMOUSEUP, STYLE, TABINDEX, TITLE, TYPE, VALUE	\<INPUT\>	(F)	Defines a Submit button.

Element	Attributes	Tags	Closing Tag? (R) Required (F) Forbidden (O) Optional	Description
INPUT TYPE= "text"	ACCESSKEY, CLASS, DIR, DISABLED, ID, LANG, MAXLENGTH, NAME, ONBLUR, ONCLICK, ONDBLCLICK, ONFOCUS, ONKEYDOWN, ONKEYPRESS, ONKEYUP, ONMOUSEDOWN, ONMOUSEMOVE, ONMOUSEOUT, ONMOUSEOVER, ONMOUSEUP, ONSELECT, READONLY, SIZE, STYLE, TABINDEX, TITLE, TYPE, VALUE	\<INPUT>	(F)	Defines a text field.
INS	CITE, CLASS, DATETIME, DIR, ID, LANG, STYLE, TITLE, ONCLICK, ONDBLCLICK, ONKEYDOWN, ONKEYPRESS, ONKEYUP, ONMOUSEDOWN, ONMOUSEMOVE, ONMOUSEOUT, ONMOUSEOVER, NMOUSEUP	\<INS>\</INS>	(R)	Indicates text added since the previous version.
ISINDEX	CLASS, DIR, ID, LANG, PROMPT, STYLE, TITLE	\<ISINDEX>	(F)	Specifies that the URL given with the HREF attribute is searchable. *Note:* The W3C has deprecated this element in favor of INPUT.
KBD	CLASS, DIR, ID, LANG, ONCLICK, ONDBLCLICK, ONKEYDOWN, ONKEYPRESS, ONKEYUP, ONMOUSEDOWN, ONMOUSEMOVE, ONMOUSEOUT, ONMOUSEOVER, ONMOUSEUP, STYLE, TITLE	\<KBD>\</KBD>	(R)	Designates text that is typed by a user, typically rendered in a monospaced font. Commonly used in instruction manuals.

Element	Attributes	Tags	Closing Tag? (R) Required (F) Forbidden (O) Optional	Description
LABEL	ACCESSKEY, CLASS, DIR, FOR, ID, LANG, ONBLUR, ONCLICK, ONDBLCLICK, ONFOCUS, ONKEYDOWN, ONKEYPRESS, ONKEYUP, ONMOUSEDOWN, ONMOUSEMOVE, ONMOUSEOUT, ONMOUSEOVER, ONMOUSEUP, STYLE, TITLE	\<LABEL\> \</LABEL\>	(R)	Attaches caption information to controls. Designed to enable both aural and visual presentation.
LEGEND	ACCESSKEY, ALIGN, CLASS, DIR, ID, LANG, ONCLICK, ONDBLCLICK, ONKEYDOWN, ONKEYPRESS, ONKEYUP, ONMOUSEDOWN, ONMOUSEMOVE, ONMOUSEOUT, ONMOUSEOVER, ONMOUSEUP, STYLE, TITLE	\<LEGEND\> \</LEGEND\>	(R)	Assigns a caption to a FIELDSET.
LI	CLASS, DIR, ID, LANG, ONCLICK, ONDBLCLICK, ONMOUSEDOWN, ONMOUSEUP, ONMOUSEOVER, ONMOUSEMOVE, ONMOUSEOUT, ONKEYPRESS, ONKEYDOWN, ONKEYUP, STYLE, TITLE, TYPE, VALUE	\<LI\>\</LI\>	(O)	Designates a list item within a UL or OL element.
LINK	CHARSET, CLASS, DIR, HREF, HREFLANG, ID, LANG, MEDIA, ONCLICK, ONDBLCLICK, ONKEYDOWN, ONKEYPRESS, ONKEYUP, ONMOUSEDOWN, ONMOUSEMOVE, ONMOUSEOUT, ONMOUSEOVER, ONMOUSEUP, REL, REV, STYLE, TARGET, TITLE, TYPE	\<LINK\>	(F)	Creates a media-independent link.

Element	Attributes	Tags	Closing Tag? (R) Required (F) Forbidden (O) Optional	Description
MAP	CLASS, LANG, MAP, ONCLICK, ONDBLCLICK, ONKEYDOWN, ONKEYPRESS, ONKEYUP, ONMOUSEDOWN, ONMOUSEMOVE, ONMOUSEOUT, ONMOUSEOVER, ONMOUSEUP, STYLE	\<MAP>\</MAP>	(R)	Defines a client-side image map.
MENU	CLASS, COMPACT, DIR, ID, LANG, ONCLICK, ONDBLCLICK, ONKEYDOWN, ONKEYPRESS, ONKEYUP, ONMOUSEDOWN, ONMOUSEMOVE, ONMOUSEOUT, ONMOUSEOVER, ONMOUSEUP, STYLE, TITLE	\<MENU> \</MENU>	(R)	Creates a menu list. *Note:* The W3C has deprecated this element; use \<UL> in place of \<DIR> and \<MENU>.
META	CONTENT, HTTP–EQUIV, LANG, NAME, SCHEME	\<META>	(F)	Lists information about the page, author, and HTML language version; designates keywords for use with search engines.
NOFRAMES		\<NOFRAMES> \</NOFRAMES>	(R)	Encloses content displayed when a browser cannot render frames.
NOSCRIPT		\<NOSCRIPT> \</NOSCRIPT>	(R)	Encloses content displayed when a browser cannot render script.

Element	Attributes	Tags	Closing Tag? (R) Required (F) Forbidden (O) Optional	Description
OBJECT	ALIGN, ARCHIVE, BORDER, CLASS, CLASSID, CODEBASE, CODETYPE, DATA, DECLARE, DIR, HEIGHT, HSPACE, ID, LANG, NAME, ONCLICK, ONDBLCLICK, ONKEYDOWN, ONKEYPRESS, ONKEYUP, ONMOUSEDOWN, ONMOUSEMOVE, ONMOUSEOUT, ONMOUSEOVER, ONMOUSEUP, STANDBY, STYLE, TABINDEX, TITLE, TYPE, USEMAP, VSPACE, WIDTH	\<OBJECT\> \</OBJECT\>	(R)	Used for inserting content supported by the browser and external applications. *Note:* This element should be used instead of APPLET.
OL	COMPACT, CLASS, DIR, ID, LANG, ONCLICK, ONDBLCLICK, ONKEYDOWN, ONKEYPRESS, ONKEYUP, ONMOUSEDOWN, ONMOUSEMOVE, ONMOUSEOUT, ONMOUSEOVER, ONMOUSEUP, START, STYLE, TITLE, TYPE	\<OL\>\</OL\>	(R)	Designates an ordered (numbered) list; contains LI elements.
OPTGROUP	CLASS, DIR, DISABLED, ID, LABEL, LANG, MULTIPLE, ONCLICK, ONDBLCLICK, ONKEYDOWN, ONKEYPRESS, ONKEYUP, ONMOUSEDOWN, ONMOUSEMOVE, ONMOUSEOUT, ONMOUSEOVER, ONMOUSEUP, STYLE, TITLE	\<OPTGROUP\> \</OPTGROUP\>	(R)	Creates a group of related form elements.
OPTION	CLASS, DIR, DISABLED, ID, LABEL, LANG, ONCLICK, ONDBLCLICK, ONKEYDOWN, ONKEYPRESS, ONKEYUP, ONMOUSEDOWN, ONMOUSEMOVE, ONMOUSEOUT, ONMOUSEOVER, ONMOUSEUP, SELECTED, STYLE, TITLE, VALUE	\<OPTION\> \</OPTION\>	(O)	Creates an option choice in a select list.

Element	Attributes	Tags	Closing Tag? (R) Required (F) Forbidden (O) Optional	Description
P	ALIGN, CLASS, DIR, ID, LANG, ONCLICK, ONDBLCLICK, ONKEYDOWN, ONKEYPRESS, ONKEYUP, ONMOUSEDOWN, ONMOUSEMOVE, ONMOUSEOUT, ONMOUSEOVER, ONMOUSEUP, STYLE, TITLE	`<P></P>`	(O)	Creates a line break with space.
PARAM	ID, NAME, TYPE, VALUE, VALUETYPE	`<PARAM>`	(F)	Defines parameter for an APPLET element.
PRE	ID, CLASS, DIR, LANG, ONCLICK, ONDBLCLICK, ONKEYDOWN, ONKEYPRESS, ONKEYUP, ONMOUSEDOWN, ONMOUSEMOVE, ONMOUSEOUT, ONMOUSEOVER, ONMOUSEUP, STYLE, TITLE, WIDTH	`<PRE></PRE>`	(R)	Used to render pre-formatted text.
Q	CITE, CLASS, DIR, ID, LANG, ONCLICK, ONDBLCLICK, ONKEYDOWN, ONKEYPRESS, ONKEYUP, ONMOUSEDOWN, ONMOUSEMOVE, ONMOUSEOUT, ONMOUSEOVER, ONMOUSEUP, STYLE, TITLE	`<Q></Q>`	(R)	Used for short inline quotations.
S	CLASS, DIR, ID, LANG, ONCLICK, ONDBLCLICK, ONKEYDOWN, ONKEYPRESS, ONKEYUP, ONMOUSEDOWN, ONMOUSEOUT, ONMOUSEMOVE, ONMOUSEOVER, ONMOUSEUP, STYLE, TITLE	`<S></S>`	(R)	Denotes strike-through text. *Note:* The W3C has deprecated this element.

Element	Attributes	Tags	Closing Tag? (R) Required (F) Forbidden (O) Optional	Description
SAMP	CLASS, DIR, ID, LANG, ONCLICK, ONDBLCLICK, ONKEYDOWN, ONKEYPRESS, ONKEYUP, ONMOUSEDOWN, ONMOUSEOUT, ONMOUSEMOVE, ONMOUSEOVER, ONMOUSEUP, STYLE, TITLE	<SAMP> </SAMP>	(R)	Used for rendering examples and program code output.
SCRIPT	CHARSET, DEFER, LANGUAGE, SRC, TYPE	<SCRIPT> </SCRIPT>	(R)	Creates containers for blocks of script, such as VBScript and JavaScript.
SELECT	CLASS, DIR, DISABLED, ID, MULTIPLE, NAME, ONBLUR, ONCHANGE, ONCLICK, ONDBLCLICK, ONFOCUS, ONKEYDOWN, ONKEYPRESS, ONKEYUP, ONMOUSEDOWN, ONMOUSEMOVE, ONMOUSEOUT, ONMOUSEOVER, ONMOUSEUP, SIZE, STYLE, TABINDEX, TITLE	<SELECT> </SELECT>	(R)	Creates a drop-down list form field that contains OPTION elements.
SMALL	CLASS, DIR, ID, LANG, ONCLICK, ONDBLCLICK, ONKEYDOWN, ONKEYPRESS, ONKEYUP, ONMOUSEDOWN, ONMOUSEMOVE, ONMOUSEOUT, ONMOUSEOVER, ONMOUSEUP, STYLE, TITLE	<SMALL> </SMALL>	(R)	Used for creating small text.
SPAN	CLASS, DIR, ID, LANG, ONCLICK, ONDBLCLICK, ONKEYDOWN, ONKEYPRESS, ONKEYUP, ONMOUSEDOWN, ONMOUSEMOVE, ONMOUSEOUT, ONMOUSEOVER, ONMOUSEUP, STYLE, TITLE	<SPAN> </SPAN>	(R)	Defines inline style; adds structure to documents.

Element	Attributes	Tags	Closing Tag? (R) Required (F) Forbidden (O) Optional	Description
STRIKE	CLASS, DIR, ID, LANG, ONCLICK, ONDBLCLICK, ONKEYDOWN, ONKEYPRESS, ONKEYUP, ONMOUSEDOWN, ONMOUSEMOVE, ONMOUSEOUT, ONMOUSEOVER, ONMOUSEUP, STYLE, TITLE	`<STRIKE>` `</STRIKE>`	(R)	Creates strike-through text (draws a line through the text).
STRONG	CLASS, DIR, ID, LANG, ONCLICK, ONDBLCLICK, ONKEYDOWN, ONKEYPRESS, ONKEYUP, ONMOUSEDOWN, ONMOUSEMOVE, ONMOUSEOUT, ONMOUSEOVER, ONMOUSEUP, STYLE, TITLE	`<STRONG>` `</STRONG>`	(R)	Strong emphasis (similar to bold).
STYLE	DIR, LANG, MEDIA, TYPE	`<STYLE>` `</STYLE>`	(R)	Defines a style sheet for an HTML document; placed in the HEAD section.
SUB	CLASS, DIR, ID, LANG, ONCLICK, ONDBLCLICK, ONKEYDOWN, ONKEYPRESS, ONKEYUP, ONMOUSEDOWN, ONMOUSEMOVE, ONMOUSEOUT, ONMOUSEOVER, ONMOUSEUP, STYLE, TITLE	`<SUB></SUB>`	(R)	Renders text as subscript.
SUP	CLASS, DIR, ID, LANG, ONCLICK, ONDBLCLICK, ONKEYDOWN, ONKEYPRESS, ONKEYUP, ONMOUSEDOWN, ONMOUSEMOVE, ONMOUSEOUT, ONMOUSEOVER, ONMOUSEUP, STYLE, TITLE	`<SUP></SUP>`	(R)	Renders text as superscript.

Element	Attributes	Tags	Closing Tag? (R) Required (F) Forbidden (O) Optional	Description
TABLE	ALIGN, BORDER, CELLPADDING, CELLSPACING, CLASS, DIR, FRAME, ID, LANG, ONCLICK, ONDBLCLICK, ONKEYDOWN, ONKEYPRESS, ONKEYUP, ONMOUSEDOWN, ONMOUSEMOVE, ONMOUSEOUT, ONMOUSEOVER, ONMOUSEUP, RULES, STYLE, SUMMARY, TITLE, WIDTH	\<TABLE\> \</TABLE\>	(R)	Creates an HTML table.
TBODY	ALIGN, CHAR, CHAROFF, CLASS, DIR, ID, LANG, ONCLICK, ONDBLCLICK, ONKEYDOWN, ONKEYPRESS, ONKEYUP, ONMOUSEDOWN, ONMOUSEMOVE, ONMOUSEOUT, ONMOUSEOVER, ONMOUSEUP, STYLE, TITLE, VALIGN	\<TBODY\> \</TBODY\>	(O)	Denotes the main section of the table.
TD	ABBR, ALIGN, AXIS, CHAR, CHAROFF, CLASS, COLSPAN, DIR, HEADERS, HEIGHT, ID, LANG, NOWRAP, ONCLICK, ONDBLCLICK, ONKEYDOWN, ONKEYPRESS, ONKEYUP, ONMOUSEDOWN, ONMOUSEMOVE, ONMOUSEOUT, ONMOUSEOVER, ONMOUSEUP, ROWSPAN, SCOPE, STYLE, TITLE, VALIGN, WIDTH	\<TD\>\</TD\>	(O)	Inserts table cell information.

Element	Attributes	Tags	Closing Tag? (R) Required (F) Forbidden (O) Optional	Description
TEXTAREA	ACCESSKEY, CLASS COLS, DIR, DISABLED, ID, LANG, NAME, ONBLUR, ONCHANGE, ONCLICK, ONDBLCLICK, ONFOCUS, ONKEYDOWN, ONKEYPRESS, ONKEYUP, ONMOUSEDOWN, ONMOUSEMOVE, ONMOUSEOUT, ONMOUSEOVER, ONMOUSEUP, ONSELECT, READONLY, ROWS, STYLE, TABINDEX, TITLE	\<TEXTAREA\> \</TEXTAREA\>	(R)	Creates a multi-lined scrolling text field.
TFOOT	ALIGN, CHAR, CHAROFF, CLASS, DIR, ID, LANG, ONCLICK, ONDBLCLICK, ONKEYDOWN, ONKEYPRESS, ONKEYUP, ONMOUSEDOWN, ONMOUSEOVER, ONMOUSEMOVE, ONMOUSEOUT, ONMOUSEUP, STYLE, TITLE, VALIGN	\<TFOOT\> \</TFOOT\>	(O)	Denotes the footer section of a table.
TH	ABBR, ALIGN, AXIS, HEADERS, CHAR, CHAROFF, CLASS, COLSPAN, DIR, HEIGHT, ID, LANG, NOWRAP, ONCLICK, ONDBLCLICK, ONKEYDOWN, ONKEYPRESS, ONKEYUP, ONMOUSEDOWN, ONMOUSEMOVE, ONMOUSEOVER, ONMOUSEUP, ONMOUSEMOVE, ROWSPAN, SCOPE, STYLE, TITLE, VALIGN, WIDTH	\<TH\>\</TH\>	(O)	Creates a table header cell.

Element	Attributes	Tags	Closing Tag? (R) Required (F) Forbidden (O) Optional	Description
THEAD	ALIGN, CHAR, CHAROFF, CLASS, DIR, ID, LANG, ONCLICK, ONDBLCLICK, ONKEYDOWN, ONKEYPRESS, ONKEYUP, ONMOUSEDOWN, ONMOUSEMOVE, ONMOUSEOUT, ONMOUSEOVER, ONMOUSEUP, STYLE, TITLE, VALIGN	\<THEAD\> \</THEAD\>	(O)	Denotes the header section of the table.
TITLE	DIR, LANG	\<TITLE\> \</TITLE\>	(R)	Specifies the document title. TITLE belongs in the HEAD element. *Note:* LANG and DIR can be used in this element.
TR	ALIGN, CHAR, CHAROFF, CLASS, DIR, ID, LANG, ONCLICK, ONDBLCLICK, ONKEYDOWN, ONKEYPRESS, ONKEYUP, ONMOUSEDOWN, ONMOUSEMOVE, ONMOUSEOUT, ONMOUSEOVER, ONMOUSEUP, STYLE, TITLE, VALIGN	\<TR\>\</TR\>	(O)	Defines a table row.
TT	CLASS, DIR, ID, LANG, ONCLICK, ONDBLCLICK, ONKEYDOWN, ONKEYPRESS, ONKEYUP, ONMOUSEDOWN, ONMOUSEMOVE, ONMOUSEOUT, ONMOUSEOVER, ONMOUSEUP, STYLE, TITLE	\<TT\>\</TT\>	(R)	Employs typewriter style using a monospaced font.

Element	Attributes	Tags	**Closing Tag?** **(R) Required** **(F) Forbidden** **(O) Optional**	Description
U	CLASS, ID, DIR, LANG, ONCLICK, ONDBLCLICK, ONKEYDOWN, ONKEYPRESS, ONKEYUP, ONMOUSEDOWN, ONMOUSEMOVE, ONMOUSEOUT, ONMOUSEOVER, ONMOUSEUP, STYLE, TITLE	`<U></U>`	(R)	Employs underlined text style.
UL	COMPACT, CLASS, DIR, ID, LANG, ONCLICK, ONDBLCLICK, ONKEYDOWN, ONKEYPRESS, ONKEYUP, ONMOUSEDOWN, ONMOUSEMOVE, ONMOUSEOUT, ONMOUSEOVER, ONMOUSEUP, STYLE, TITLE, TYPE	`<UL></UL>`	(R)	Creates unordered (bulleted) lists; contains LI elements.
VAR	CLASS, DIR, ID, LANG, ONCLICK, ONDBLCLICK, ONKEYDOWN, ONKEYPRESS, ONKEYUP, ONMOUSEDOWN, ONMOUSEMOVE, ONMOUSEOVER, ONMOUSEOUT, ONMOUSEUP, STYLE, TITLE	`<VAR></VAR>`	(R)	Used to denote a variable or program argument.

Glossary

A

acceptable use policies   Rules or regulations regarding authorized network and computer use and activities, including e-mail content.

access control list (ACL)   A list that defines the permissions for a resource by specifying which users and groups have access to the resource.

active content   Interactive and moving objects that create a more useful and interesting web experience, including client-side scripting languages, Java applications, and multimedia files.

Active Server Pages (ASP)   A set of technologies developed by Microsoft for developing and hosting networked database applications.

ActiveX   An open set of technologies for integrating components on the Internet and within Microsoft applications.

ActiveX Data Objects (ADO)   The Microsoft model for creating applications that can work together across a network even though they were created using different computer languages. Uses the Microsoft Object Linking and Embedding Database (OLE DB) model to access the database or other information. Part of the Component Object Model (COM).

adapter   A device that provides connectivity between at least two systems.

Address Resolution Protocol (ARP)   A Network layer protocol used to convert a numeric IP address into a physical address, such as a MAC address. Used for direct or indirect routing.

Advanced Research Projects Agency (ARPA)   A U.S. Department of Defense agency that originated the first global computer network. Now referred to as DARPA.

Advanced Research Projects Agency Network (ARPANET)   See *ARPANET*.

adware   Software that is distributed free of charge, but includes advertisement banners to defray development and distribution expenses.

analog   A measurement format in which data is represented by continuously variable, measurable, physical quantities, such as time, frequency, or voltage.

anchor   A component of a hyperlink. Properly formatted hyperlinks are a source anchor which leads to a destination anchor, which may be any Internet resource such as a web document, FTP site, newsgroup, and so forth.

anonymous FTP   A method for legitimately accessing an FTP server without an assigned username or password.

antivirus software   Applications that scan, detect, repair, and remove virus infections on a computer.

applets   Small programs, written in Java, which are downloaded as needed and executed within a web page or browser.

application   An executable program typically used to perform functions on data including retrieval, transmission, display, editing, and formatting.

Application layer 1) Layer 7 in the OSI/RM, responsible for presenting data to the user. 2) The top layer of the Internet architecture, corresponding to the Application and Presentation layers of the OSI/RM.

application program interface (API) A method that allows a programmer to make requests of an operating system or application.

application-level gateway A firewall component that filters packets on a program-by-program basis and provides strong authentication.

Archie A search vehicle for locating publicly available files on anonymous FTP servers.

arp A utility that displays ARP information, including the physical address of computers with which you have recently communicated.

ARPANET A computer network, funded by the Advanced Research Projects Agency (ARPA), which served as the basis for early networking research and was the backbone during the development of the Internet.

assembly language A programming language that is once removed from a computer's machine language. Can be used to develop fast, efficient programs.

asymmetric-key encryption An encryption method using a pair of keys, one of which is made public and the other kept private.

asynchronous Characterized by the absence of a clock in the transmission media. The access device is not synchronized with the network device. Data is transmitted as individual characters. Each character is synchronized by information contained in the start (header) and stop (trailer) bits.

asynchronous transfer mode A fast packet–switching technology that uses fixed-sized cells (instead of frame relay's variable-length packets) and PVCs to support data as well as real-time video and voice. Both LANs and WANs can use ATM, but ATM is most commonly used as an Internet backbone.

attenuation The weakening of a transmission signal as it travels farther from its source.

AU Audio format used by UNIX servers, which make up the majority of web servers. Most web browsers can read AU.

Audio Interchange File Format (AIFF) High-quality audio format developed by Apple Computer.

Audio Video Interleave (AVI) The standard file format for the Microsoft Video for Windows.

auditing The ongoing process of examining systems and procedures to determine their efficiency, including the ability to withstand cracker activity. Involves both manual and automated analysis.

authentication The ability to verify a person's identity.

B

backbone   Network part that carries the majority of network traffic; usually a high-speed transmission path spanning long distances, to which smaller networks typically connect.

bandwidth   The amount of information, sometimes called traffic, that can be carried on a network at one time. Measured in bits per second.

baseband   A transmission method that uses the entire media bandwidth for a single channel.

bastion   A computer that houses various firewall components and services.

Bcc   Short for *blind carbon copy*. When an e-mail address is listed in the Bcc field, that address will receive a copy of the message but will not be listed in the e-mail header.

binary file   A file containing data or instructions written in terms of zeros and ones (computer language).

bind   The act of attaching a networking protocol to a network adapter such as NIC.

BinHex   A method for encoding file attachments for transmission to or from Mac OS computers.

bitmap   A graphics file format that assigns information to individual pixels.

block-level element   Any HTML element that will affect at least an entire paragraph.

BNC connector   A device commonly used to connect coaxial cable to NICs, hubs and other network devices. The connector is crimped to the cable using a bayonet mount that connects the two wires (signal and ground) in the coaxial cable to the connector. The connector is then inserted into another connector and turned, which causes the bayonet mechanism to pinch two pins into the BNC's locking groove. Also called British Naval Connector, or Bayonet Neill-Concelman connector.

Boolean operator   A symbol or word used in Internet searches to narrow search results, or to include or exclude certain words or phrases from the results.

boot sector   A dedicated portion of a disk that contains the first parts of an operating system's startup files.

BOOTstrap Protocol (BOOTP)   An Application-layer protocol that provides an alternative method to RARP for diskless workstations and X terminals to determine their IP addresses. Used along with TFTP.

bottleneck   Any element (a hard drive, I/O card, or network interface card) that slows network connectivity rates.

bridge   A hardware device that filters frames to determine whether a specific frame belongs on a local segment or another LAN segment, by using hardware addresses to determine which segment will receive the frame.

broadband   A transmission method that uses frequency division multiplexing (FDM) to transmit multiple signals over a single transmission path.

broadcast address   An IP address used to send messages to all network hosts and used only as destination addresses. Usually includes the number 255.

brouter   A hardware device that combines the functions of a bridge and router, by connecting networks, forwarding outbound packets, and providing other services.

browser   An application that displays a document for viewing and printing. Typically used to refer to web browsing applications.

browser cache   An area kept by a web client on a hard drive to store downloaded web documents and images for later viewing.

brute-force attacks   A method of network invasion that repeatedly tries different possible passwords from a "dictionary program" that contains obvious passwords and names in order to gain unauthorized access to network assets. Also called a *front door attack*.

buffer   A cache of memory used by a computer to store frequently used data. Buffers allow faster access times.

bus topology   A type of network that requires that all computers, or nodes, tap into the same electrical cable or bus. Network data must be transmitted to each computer along the cable. Only the destination computer reads the sent message; the rest of the computers ignore the data.

business logic   See *process logic*.

business requirements document   A project-management report that identifies the requirements of the customer.

C

C   A programming language used primarily to create operating systems and applications, including many versions of UNIX. One step removed from assembly language, and two steps removed from machine language.

C++   An object-oriented programming language based on C.

cable modem   A hardware device that connects a computer to a WAN, such as the Internet, using cable television lines. A cable modem works by demodulating transmissions from the cable network, modulating the computer's transmissions to the WAN, and using one or more channels on the cable television line for these transmissions.

cache   An area of RAM or disk storage used to store frequently accessed information for speedy retrieval.

caching server   An internetworking server that caches frequently accessed network data, such as web documents or streaming media.

callback   Authentication technique that calls a remote computer back after an initial login to authenticate the remote computer.

Carrier Sense Multiple Access/Collision Detection (CSMA/CD)   The LAN access method used by Ethernet. Checks for network access availability with a signal. After detecting a collision, each computer waits a random delay time and then attempts to retransmit their message.

Cascading Style Sheets (CSS)   A technology that uses embedded information to define the fonts, colors, and phrase elements used on a particular HTML page.

catalog server   An internetworking server that provides a single point of access for users by indexing databases, files, and information across a large network and allows keyword, Boolean, and other searches.

Cc   Short for *carbon copy*. When an e-mail address is listed in the Cc field, that address will receive a copy of the message and will be listed in the e-mail header.

certificate server   An internetworking server that issues or validates keys.

Channel Definition Format (CDF)   A Microsoft proprietary file format used to deliver pushed content to Microsoft Internet Explorer 4.0 or later.

Channel Service Unit/Data (or Digital) Service Unit (CSU/DSU)   A hardware device that terminates physical connections and is required when using dedicated circuits, such as T1 lines. Converts digital network signals to a format that is suitable for line transmission.

circuit-level gateway   A firewall component that monitors and transmits information at the Transport layer of the OSI model. It hides information about the network; a packet passing through this type of gateway appears to have originated from the firewall.

Class A address   An IP address that uses the first byte for the network portion and the last three bytes for the host portion. Class A addresses range from 1.0.0.0 to 127.255.255.255.

Class B address   An IP address that uses the first two bytes for the network portion and the last two bytes for the host portion. Class B addresses range from 128.0.0.0 to 191.255.255.255.

Class C address   An IP address that uses the first three bytes for the network portion and the last byte for the host portion. Class C addresses range from 192.0.0.0 to 223.255.255.255.

Class D address   An IP address that supports multicasting and is targeted to a group that is identified by a network address only. No host portion exists in the address. The first byte can range from 224 to 239.

Class E address   An IP address that is reserved for future use. The first byte can range from 240 to 247.

client   A system or application that requests a service from another computer (the server).

client/server model   A distributed computing system in which computing tasks are divided between the server and the client.

client-side script   Code embedded into the HTML and downloaded by a user; it resides on the client and helps process a form. Common client-side scripting languages include JavaScript and VBScript.

coaxial cable   High-capacity two-wire (signal and ground) cable; the inner wire is the primary conductor and the metal sheath serves as a ground. Also called *coax*.

collision   An event that occurs when signals from two computers meet simultaneously on the same network segment.

co-location   The placement of third-party equipment, such as servers and other networking hardware, in a company. The hosting company provides infrastructure support, such as electrical power and bandwidth.

command-line interface   A common method for accessing computers and operating systems that requires users to type and enter commands on a keyboard or console.

Common Gateway Interface (CGI)   A program that processes data submitted by the user.

Common Object Request Broker Architecture (CORBA)   An architecture designed to allow programs written in different languages to work together, regardless of which operating system they use.

compile   A process used to convert programming code into machine code for an executable object or application.

compiled languages   High-level programming languages that require a special program called a compiler to process statements written in a specific language; the compiler converts the language into code understood by a computer processor. Examples include FORTRAN, Pascal, C, and Java.

Conseil Européen pour la Recherche Nucléaire (CERN)   The European Council for Nuclear Research—the birthplace of the World Wide Web.

copyright   A legally recognized protection that bestows ownership and other protections on the registered holder of a creative work such as a book, computer program, musical composition, artwork, or other creative output.

cookie   A small text file created by a web server that resides on a client's computer and preserves the state of a client-server session. May be used to store data, settings, and other information.

CORBA   See *Common Object Request Broker Architecture*.

core   In fiber optic cables, the two strands that send and receive data.

cracker   A computer user who attempts to gain unauthorized access to another computer or network asset for nefarious purposes.

cross-post   The act of posting the same message to several mailing lists or newsgroups.

D

daemon   A UNIX program that is usually initiated at startup and runs in the background until required.

database   A file or series of files used to organize information by storing data in a consistent format so that users can search the files for specific information.

database management system (DBMS)   Software that manages a flat file database.

datagram   A packet at the Network layer of the OSI/RM.

data validation   The process of checking or confirming data entered into fields by a user.

default gateway   The IP address of the router on your local network.

demand priority   The LAN access method used by 100VG-AnyLAN networks. Hubs specify how and when nodes get network access by prioritizing transmissions.

demilitarized zone (DMZ)   A protected area between an external and internal router where public servers may be hosted outside the firewall.

demultiplexing   The process of decoding a network packet into usable data, by removing and checking headers and CRCs.

denial-of-service (DoS) attack   An attack meant to deny authorized users access to a network, usually by flooding one or more network assets with packets or messages that consume server resources.

dictionary program   A program specifically written to break into a password-protected system. It has a relatively large list of common password names it repeatedly uses to gain access.

digital   A data representation format that uses a series of two integers, 1 and 0, to store the data.

digital certificate   A digital ID issued by a certificate authority to authenticate and validate Internet data transfers. A digital certificate is a specific form of an asymmetric key.

Digital Subscriber Line (DSL)   A high-speed direct Internet connection that uses all-digital networks.

direct routing   The process performed when directing packets between two computers on the same physical network.

directory   A type of web search engine that requires manual submission of URLs by webmasters.

directory server   An internetworking server that stores contact information for individuals in a database.

disk cache   A storage space on a computer hard disk used to temporarily store downloaded data.

distributed denial-of-service attack (DDoS)   A form of DoS attack that uses multiple computers to conduct a coordinated assault on a network asset.

dithering   The ability for a computer to approximate a color by combining the RGB values.

Document Object Model (DOM)   A model that specifies how objects are manipulated through script.

Document Type Declaration (DTD)   A declaration of document or code type embedded within and HTML, XML, or SGML document; identifies the version and nature of code used. Denoted by the <!DOCTYPE> tag.

Domain Name System (DNS) A system that maps uniquely hierarchical names to specific Internet addresses.

dongle A hardware cable that connects two devices to each other.

dotted quad Common term for describing an IPv4 address, such as 127.0.0.1.

dual-homed bastion A firewall that funnels traffic through a computer with two or more NICs with their IP forwarding features disabled. Software-imposed firewall rules help forward valid packets between subnets.

dynamic Constantly changing.

Dynamic Host Configuration Protocol (DHCP) An Application-layer protocol designed to assign Internet addresses, DNS servers, and gateway addresses to nodes on a TCP/IP network during initialization. Commonly used to configure workstations and computers on an ISP, IAP, or LAN.

Dynamic HTML (DHTML) A combination of HTML, script, styles, and the Document Object Model (DOM) that provides web page interactivity.

dynamic link library (DLL) A program element used in Microsoft operating systems, that can be shared and executed by several applications at once on a single computer.

dynamic router Routers that can receive and exchange routing information tables.

E

E1 A European digital carrier standard for synchronous data transmission at a speed of 2.048Mbps.

E3 A European digital carrier standard for synchronous data transmission at a speed of 34.368Mbps.

e-commerce (electronic commerce) The integration of communications, data management, and security capabilities to allow organizations to exchange information related to the sale of goods and services.

Electronic Data Interchange (EDI) The organization and exchange of documents and data in standardized electronic formats by a vendor and purchaser, directly between participating computers of both parties.

e-mail (electronic mail) A system for transferring messages from one computer to another over a network. Messages may include data in text-only format or text with attachments.

encapsulated PostScript (EPS) File format used for importing and exporting graphics.

encryption The encoding, or scrambling, of information to a scrambled (unreadable) form by using specific algorithms, usually a string of characters known as a *key*.

enterprise networks Networks that provide connectivity among all nodes in an organization, regardless of their geographical location, and run the organization's mission-critical applications. Enterprise networks can include elements of peer-to-peer and server-based networks. An enterprise network may consist of several different networking protocols.

Ethernet   A set of hardware technologies and networking protocols for LANs, including MAC and CSMA/CD. Also defined as IEEE 802.3. First developed at Xerox PARC in 1972.

event-driven   Reacting to signals that are triggered when a particular user action occurs or when the browser has completed a specific task.

event handler   A technique that allows a program to react to user input.

extensible   Able to be customized and expanded.

Extensible HTML   See *XHTML*.

Extensible Markup Language   See *XML*.

Extensible Stylesheet Language (XSL)   See *XSL*.

extranet   A network that connects enterprise intranets to the global Internet. Designed to provide access to selected external users to expedite the exchange of products, services and key business information.

F

fast packet switching   A transmission method for mesh-type switching networks, where the network does not perform packet sequencing and acknowledgments. See also frame relay and asynchronous transfer mode.

fault tolerance   The ability of a system to respond gracefully to an unexpected hardware or software failure.

Fiber Distributed Data Interface (FDDI)   A high-speed LAN standard that uses two counter-rotating rings to provide redundancy and allow the network to function if one ring fails. See also *municipal area network*.

fiber optic cable   A type of transmission media that uses light to transmit signals. It consists of a core wrapped in glass or plastic cladding. Each core and cladding element is wrapped with a plastic reinforced with Kevlar fibers.

field   A space allocated for the storage of a particular item of information. Usually the smallest unit of information in a database.

File Transfer Protocol (FTP)   An Application-layer protocol used to transfer files between computers, that allows file transfer without corruption or alteration.

firewall   The collection of hardware, software, and corporate policies that protects a LAN from the Internet.

fixed-width font   A font in which every character, including the space character has equal width. In proportional-width fonts, letters such as *i* and *j* have less width than *m* or *b*.

flat file database   A database in which all information is kept in a single file. Also called non-relational databases.

frame 1) A scrollable region in which pages can be displayed; a single element of a frameset. Each frame has its own URL. 2) A packet at the Data Link layer, used to traverse an Ethernet network.

frame relay A streamlined version of X.25, that uses variable-length packets and allows high-speed connections using shared network facilities and Permanent Virtual Circuits (PVCs).

frameset document A web page that defines a set of frames in which other web pages are displayed.

freeware Software that is distributed free of charge.

frequency division multiplexing (FDM) The transmission of multiple signals over a single transmission path, where each signal is within a unique frequency range or carrier. Used in broadband transmissions.

front door attack See *brute force attack.*

full-text search A type of search that compares the keyword to every word included on the indexed documents.

fully qualified domain name (FQDN) The complete domain name of an Internet computer, such as www.CIWcertified.com.

functions Standalone, reusable segments of program code that are not part of an object.

G

gateway A device that converts signals from one protocol stack to another. Also called a protocol converter.

GNU A variety of non-proprietary UNIX-compatible software and operating systems. GNU software formed the basis for Linux. The acronym stands for "Gnu's Not UNIX."

Gopher 1) An Application-layer protocol that allows clients to retrieve text menus of information from servers. 2) An older menu-based program in UNIX-based systems that is used to find resources.

graphical user interface (GUI) A front-end or shell used as a substitute for a command-line interface in operating systems such as Windows, Mac OS, and many varieties of UNIX and Linux. Provides visual navigation with menus and screen icons, and performs automated functions at the click of a button.

H

hacker A computer user who knows an application, operating system, or hardware very well.

Handheld Device Markup Language (HDML) A method for describing which portions of a web document should be downloaded to a handheld web client.

Handheld Device Transport Protocol (HDTP) A protocol for transmitting suitable web documents to a handheld client.

hexadecimal A base-16 system that allows large numbers to be displayed by fewer characters than if the number were displayed in the regular base-10 system. In hexadecimal, the number 10 is represented as the letter A, 15 is represented as F, and 16 is represented as 10.

hierarchy A system that ranks and classifies concepts, objects, people, or other elements into an order that implies dominance of higher-order elements over lower-order elements.

hijacking The process of diverting a stream of packets transmitted from a client computer and intended for one specific destination to another destination, without the authorization of consent of the sender.

history list A list of previous viewed URLs maintained in a web browser.

home page 1) The web document that a web client opens when it is first executed. 2) The initial page of a website.

hop One link between two network devices. The number of hops between two devices is considered a *hop count*.

host A computer that other computers can use to gain information; in network architecture, a host is a client or workstation.

hosts file A file that links IP addresses to alphanumeric names, such as nicknames and domain names. Before the DNS was developed, hosts files on each Internet computer contained a complete mapping of all registered Internet node names to their IP addresses.

hub A hardware device that connects computers in a star-configured network so they can exchange information. Most hubs are active hubs; they have a powered supply and can act as repeaters. Also called a *concentrator*.

hybrid topology A topology that combines elements of the *bus*, *star*, and *ring* topologies.

hyperlinks Embedded instructions within a text file that link it to a separate file. Also called *links*.

hypertext Electronic text that, unlike static text in a book, contains links to other text or to various media, including sound, video, animation, and images.

Hypertext Markup Language (HTML) The standard authoring language used to develop web pages.

Hypertext Transfer Protocol (HTTP) An Application-layer protocol for transporting HTML documents across the Internet. HTTP requires a client program on one end (a browser) and a server on the other, both running TCP/IP.

Hypertext Transfer Protocol Secure (HTTPS) An application-layer protocol used to access a secure web server.

I

image map A set of coordinates on an image that creates a "hot spot." When the hot spot is clicked, it acts as a *hyperlink*.

image search A type of web search that finds appropriate image files in web documents, based on the keyword and the HTML surrounding the image files.

index A list of unique identifiers or *keys* that identify each record. In a relational database table, unique keys are used to help maintain the integrity of the data table. Also used by a database management system to provide faster searches of the data table.

indirect routing The process used to send the IP packet to a router for delivery when two computers are not on the same physical network.

inetd The internet daemon, a UNIX application that responds to received requests and starts an appropriate Internet service.

Information Technology (IT) department An in-house computer and network systems department entrusted with the setup, operation, and maintenance of all computer systems within an organization.

inline images Images rendered in a web page.

in process An executable program that uses a threading model to eliminate the need to launch a separate process each time it is accessed.

insider attacks An attack against a network asset mounted by an internal user of a computer network.

Institute of Electrical and Electronics Engineers (IEEE) An organization of scientists and engineers, accredited by the American National Standards Institute (ANSI), that creates standards for computers and communications.

Integrated Services Digital Network (ISDN) An international standard that defines the transmission of data, voice, and video over digital lines at 64Kbps. An ISDN line consists of a 64-Kbps channel, which can be combined for faster speeds.

intellectual property The output of a creative process, such as a technology, creative work, document, or composition, which is claimed by an owner.

interactive The characteristic of some hardware and software, such as computers, games and multimedia systems, that allows them to respond differently based on a user's actions.

Internet The global wide area network that uses TCP/IP and other protocols to interconnect other WANs, LANs, and computers.

Internet Access Provider (IAP) An organization that maintains a gateway to the Internet and rents access to customers on a per-use or subscription basis. Sometimes referred to as an *Internet Service Provider*.

Internet architecture A four-part model that provides a reference to the internal workings of the Internet and TCP/IP networks. See also *Application layer*, *Transport layer*, *Internet layer*, and *Network Access layer*.

Internet Control Message Protocol (ICMP) The troubleshooting Network layer protocol of TCP/IP that allows Internet hosts and gateways to report errors through ICMP messages that are sent to network users.

Internet Corporation for Assigned Names and Numbers (ICANN) The international organization responsible for domain name registration. In 1998, ICANN inherited responsibilities originally performed by InterNIC. Performs Internet address space allocation, protocol parameter assignment, and root server management. Can be found on the Web at www.icann.org.

Internet Engineering Task Force (IETF) The main standards organization for Internet technologies. IETF is an organization of network designers, operators, vendors, and researchers concerned with the evolution of the Internet architecture and the smooth operation of the Internet.

Internet Group Management Protocol (IGMP) A Network layer protocol used for multicasting, in which one source sends a message to a group of subscribers who belong to a multicast group.

Internet layer OSI/RM layer responsible for addressing and routing packets, using a protocol such as IP: Layer 4 of the OSI/RM. Also known as the Network layer of the OSI/RM.

Internet Message Access Protocol (IMAP) Provides the same services as POP, but is more powerful. Allows sharing of mailboxes and multiple mail server access. The latest version is IMAP4.

Internet Network Information Center (InterNIC) Until 1998, the cooperative organization formed by an agreement between the United States Department of Commerce and Network Solutions that registered domain names for the `.com`, `.net` and `.org` top-level domains.

Internet Protocol (IP) The data transmission standard for the Internet. Every computer connected to the Internet has its own IP address, which allows a packet or unit of data to be delivered to a specific computer.

Internet Research Task Force (IRTF) A research organization for Internet technologies.

Internet Server Application Programming Interface (ISAPI) A web server extension that allows the server to execute other programs and scripts without the expensive processing associated with CGI. Supported on Microsoft operating systems, and some third-party gateways.

Internet Service Provider (ISP) An organization that maintains a gateway to the Internet and rents access to customers on a per-use or subscription basis. Sometimes referred to as an *Internet Access Provider*.

Internet standard A protocol designated as an official standard by the *IETF*. Also called full standard.

interoperability The ability of one computer system to communicate with another; often refers to different operating systems working together.

interpreted languages Programming languages that require specific software, called interpreters, to run,; interpreters run languages line-per-line at run time.

intranet An internal network, using Internet technology, that is not accessible to Internet users at large.

IP address A numeric address that identifies a computer or device on a TCP/IP network. IPv4 addresses are 32 bits in length, and arranged in a dotted quad such as 127.0.0.1. IPv6 addresses are 128 bits in length and uses eight sections of hexadecimal numbers each delimited by a colon.

ipconfig A program that displays TCP/IP network settings on the Windows NT, 2000 or XP operating system.

IPSec IP Security (IPSec) is an authentication and encryption protocol that provides security over the Internet; it functions at Layer 3 of the OSI/RM and can secure all packets transmitted over the network.

ISO 9001 An International Organization for Standardization specification that defines the documentation of a corporate quality management system.

J

Java   An object-oriented programming language developed by Sun Microsystems that is fully cross-platform functional.

JavaScript   An interpreted, object-based scripting language developed by Netscape Communications that adds interactivity to web pages.

Java servlet   A dedicated Java program that resides on a server. Java servlets extend a server's functionality.

Java Virtual Machine (JVM)   A small, efficient operating system that resides on top of other operating systems. It creates an environment that supports Java programs.

K

kernel   The essential part of an operating system; provides basic services; always resides in memory.

key   A string of numbers used by software that scrambles your message from plaintext, readable by anyone, into encrypted text. Some software encrypts and decrypts with the same key, whereas other software relies on a pair of keys.

keyword   A word that appears on a web page and is used by search engines to identify relevant URLs. Some words, such as "the" or "and," are too common to be used as keywords.

keyword index   A type of search engine that categorizes documents based on a ranking

system that assigned a numeric score based on each document's relationship to a keyword.

L

latency   The delay caused when data is sent between two computers. Each computer wastes time waiting to communicate, when that time could be used for actual computations.

Layer-2 Tunneling Protocol (L2TP)   An IETF standard tunneling protocol primarily used to support VPNs over the Internet for non-IP protocols.

legacy applications   Applications that have existed for years and may not support modern technologies without manipulation or upgrades.

license   A credential issued by an entity that gives one permission to perform a set of defined acts.

Lightweight Directory Access Protocol (LDAP)   A protocol based on X.500 for transmitting data from a directory server to a client.

links   See *hyperlinks*.

Linux   A popular version of the UNIX operating system, designed for personal computers under the supervision of Linus Torvalds. Linux is an open-source network operating system licensed under the GNU framework. Many Linux distributions include a graphical user interface. Pronounced LIH-nucks.

LiveScript   The Netscape-developed scripting language that was the predecessor to JavaScript.

load balancing   The process of distributing processing and communications activity evenly across a computer network so that no single device is overwhelmed.

local area network (LAN)   A group of computers connected within a confined geographic area so that their users can share files and services.

Logical Link Control (LLC)   Along with Media Access Control, one of two sublayers of the IEEE 802.2 standard. Provides connection-oriented and connectionless services at the Data Link layer, which manages network transmissions. Used in IPX/SPX and NetBIOS.

loopback   A set of IP addresses used to test and diagnose network connections. The common loopback address is 127.0.0.1.

lossy compression   A type of file compression that allows the loss or omission of data.

M

MAC address   See *Media Access Control address*.

Mac OS   The brand name for a series of network operating systems developed by Apple Computer for Macintosh personal computers.

machine language   The numerical language that computers use to execute programs. All computer languages must be translated to machine language at some point.

mail server   An internetworking server that stores and/or transmits mail messages.

mainframe   This centralized approach employed central servers, or mainframes, and remote diskless or dumb terminals that could only request information. Diskless terminals could not store or read data locally, but data storage was relatively expensive and providing local storage was cost prohibitive. Also called centralized computing.

man-in-the-middle attacks   An attack in which a cracker captures packets being sent from one host to another, and redirects the packets. Also called *hijacking*.

media   Any material that allows data to flow through it or be stored on it, including hard and floppy disks, wire, cable and fiber optics.

Media Access Control   Along with Logical Link Control, one of two sublayers of the IEEE 802.2 standard. Provides access to LAN media by placing the data on the network, and provides a physical address, hardware address, or Ethernet address.

Media Access Control (MAC) address   A unique hardware address that is assigned and burned by the NIC manufacturer, and can be used to identify a specific computer on a network.

merchant systems   A series of computer applications that are used to support e-commerce, including e-mail, online directories, ordering and logistical support systems, settlement support systems, inventory control systems, and management information and statistical reporting systems.

mesh topology   Connects devices with multiple paths so that redundancies exist, ensuring that a connection can always be made, even if one is lost. All devices are cross-connected so the best path can be chosen at any given moment in the event of a connection failure.

META tag   An HTML tag located in the document header that can be used to link descriptions, keywords, author information, and other data to a web document.

meta-language   A language used for defining other languages, such as XML.

MIME type   Identifies the contents of a file in the MIME encoding system using a type/subtype format; examples are image/jpg and text/plain.

mirroring   A process that causes two sets of disk writes to occur for each original disk write that takes place. Uses a mirror set that is established between two or more physical hard drives or partitions.

mission-critical applications   Applications that are absolutely essential for the day-to-day operation of a business environment.

modem   A device that enables a computer to communicate with other computers over telephone lines by translating digital data into audio/analog signals (on the sending computer) and then back into digital form (on the receiving computer). The term is derived from the device's function as a modulator/demodulator.

Moving Picture Experts Group (MPEG)   A high-quality video compression format.

MP3   A common file extension for audio files that use the MPEG Layer 3 standard. The files can be recorded at high bit rates to maintain sound quality while providing file compression.

multimode fiber optic cable   Uses a large number of frequencies or modes for transmission. The cable's core is larger than that of single-mode. Usually specified for LANs and WANs.

Multipurpose Internet Mail Extensions (MIME)   Protocol that identifies a file type, encodes the file using the file type, and decodes it at the receiving end to display properly. Used for e-mail attachments and by HTTP servers; file types are classified as MIME types.

Multistation Access Unit (MAU)   The network device that is the central connection point for token ring networks.

municipal area network (MAN)   A network used to communicate over a city or geographic area.

Musical Instrument Digital Interface (MIDI)   A standard computer interface for creating and playing electronic music. It allows computers to recreate music in digital form for playback.

N

National Science Foundation (NSF)   An independent agency of the U.S. government that promotes the advancement of science and engineering.

natural language   A type of search that allows users to input their queries as written questions.

netiquette A set of cultural standards for proper Internet usage, including the formatting and writing of e-mail and newsgroup messages.

netstat A utility that displays the contents of various network-related data structures, such as the state of sockets.

network A group of two or more computer systems linked together.

Network Address Translation (NAT) A process that assigns addresses to any internal computers that are connected to a device, such as a firewall or router, by using DHCP. Using NAT conceals the actual IP address of any computers behind the firewall.

Network Access Layer A layer of the Internet architecture that corresponds to the Physical and Data Link layers of the OSI/RM. Includes the operating system's device driver, corresponding network interface card (NIC), and physical connections.

network adapter card See *network interface card*.

network analyzer A software program that can intercept and decode network transmissions, including packets.

network assets Network devices that include local resources, network resources, server resources, and information resources.

network interface card (NIC) A hardware device installed in a computer that serves as the interface between a computer and a network. When using a cable modem, an additional cable connects a computer's NIC to the modem. Also called a network adapter card.

Network layer Layer 4 of the OSI/RM, responsible for addressing and routing packets, using a protocol such as IP. Also known as the Internet layer of the Internet architecture.

Network News Transfer Protocol (NNTP) An Application-layer Internet protocol that allows the exchange of newsgroup articles.

network operating system (NOS) An operating system that manages network resources.

newsfeed A source that transmits newsgroup information and messages to NNTP servers.

newsgroups An Internet discussion group that allows users to read and post messages using NNTP.

node Processing locations on a network, such as a computer, printer, or other device.

nonrelational database A database format in which all related information is contained within a single table. Also called a flat file database.

nonrepudiation The capacity to ensure that an individual party to a communication, agreement or other contract cannot refute or deny the authenticity of their signature on a document or the sending of a message that they originated.

nonroutable Describes protocols that will not function through a router such as NetBEUI and DLC.

Novell NetWare A network operating system developed by Novell to provide file and print services for LANs, servers and personal computers. Versions 1 through 4 used IPX/SPX as the default protocol. Later versions used TCP/IP.

O

object   An element on a web page that contains data and procedures for how that item will react when activated.

object-based programming   Programming concept that allows the use of predefined objects, but not the definition of new objects. Used in web scripting languages such as JavaScript and VBScript.

object database management system (ODBMS)   An application or computer program that manages object-oriented databases.

object-oriented programming (OOP)   Programming concept based on objects and data, and how they relate to one another, instead of logic and actions; C++ and Java are OOP languages.

off-topic post   A mailing list or newsgroup message that does not readily conform to the group's defined subjects and topics.

one-way encryption   An encryption method that is used for information that is not meant to be decrypted. The encrypted message can be checked against a hash table of hexadecimal numbers to confirm its validity. Also called hash encryption.

online cataloging   The process of creating a catalog of data; the catalog then becomes a searchable index that is available online.

Online Transaction Processing (OLTP) The process of updating master files or databases immediately when a transaction takes place, including sending a transaction confirmation.

Open Shortest Path First (OSPF)   A prtocol for authenticated exchanges of updates to routing information tables. Also supports multiple routes to a given destination, load balancing, and network areas.

open source   The act of providing free source code to the development community-at-large to develop a better product; Apache Web server, Netscape Communicator, and Linux are all open source creations.

Open Systems Interconnection Reference Model (OSI/RM)   A Seven-Layer Networking Model Used to Break down the Many Tasks Involved in Moving Data from One Host to Another. See also *Application*, *Presentation*, *Session*, *Transport*, *Network*, *Data Link*, and *Physical layers*.

out-of-process   An executable program (EXE) that launches a separate process each time it is loaded or referenced.

P

packet   Data processed by protocols so it can be sent across a network.

packet filtering   A function of routers and firewalls that screens packets based on their contents, and discards offending packets.

password sniffing   A method of intercepting the transmission of a password during the authentication process. A *sniffer* is a program used to intercept passwords.

patch cord   A cable used to cross-connect networked computers that are wired to the patch panel.

patch panel A centralized location of sockets representing various network devices so that these devices can be cross-connected as desired, such as connecting a workstation to a hub/switch.

payment gateway The system (usually software) that interfaces between the merchant and the merchant's bank to perform credit card authorizations.

peer-to-peer network A network formed by two or more computers that are linked to each other without centralized controls. Each computer can have as much control as the other over the network.

people search A type of web-based search that locates web documents, e-mail addresses, and contact information based on a person's name.

permanent virtual circuits (PVC) Logical, dedicated, end-to-end connections used for data transfer in frame relay connections.

permissions 1) Instructions given by an operating system or server (or a combination thereof) that restrict or allow access to system resources, such as files, user databases, and system processes. 2) An owner's granting of the rights to another for the use of copyrighted or licensed intellectual property.

personal firewall A combination of hardware, software, and policies designed to protect a personal computer from attacks launched through an Internet connection.

ping A utility that tests Internet connectivity by using ICMP to send packets to a host. From the term Packet Internet Groper.

ping flood The act of flooding a server with repeated pings, perhaps as part of a *DoS attack*.

plaintext Unencrypted text that can be easily viewed by the sender, receiver, or an intermediary.

plenum Space between building floors; usually contains air and heating ducts, as well as communication and electrical wires.

plug-in A program installed as part of the browser to extend its basic functionality. Allows different file formats to be viewed as part of a standard HTML document.

Point-to-Point Protocol (PPP) An improved version of SLIP that allows a computer to connect to the Internet over a phone line. If an ISP offers you a choice of a SLIP or a PPP connection, choose PPP.

Point-to-Point Tunneling Protocol (PPTP) Encapsulates protocols and transmits them over the Internet, using encryption, which allows Virtual Private Networks to be established over the Internet.

port number Addresses contained in the headers of TCP and UDP packets that identify the appropriate communication process.

Portable Document Format (PDF) A file format developed by Adobe that can be transferred across platforms and retain its formatting; designated by the file name extension `.pdf`.

Portable Network Graphics (PNG) A bitmapped graphic format that provides additional features including layers, file compression, large color palettes and animation.

Post Office Protocol (POP)   A protocol that resides on an incoming mail server. Sorts mail into the correct user mailbox for the user to download. The latest version is POP3.

print queue   A process that stores print requests until they are passed to a printing device.

process   An executing program or task.

process logic   Methods used to access a physical database, modeled after the actual business practices that the database supports. Also called business logic or business rules.

project management   The process of administering and supervising the implementation of a specific project.

protocol   Communication rules that define and describe how computers and networks can communicate with each other.

proxy server   An intermediary server that stands between a network host and other hosts outside the network. Provides enhanced security, manages TCP/IP addresses, and speeds access to the Internet by providing caching server functions for frequently used documents.

pull technology   A technology involving a client that requests information from a computer or program; constitutes the majority of data transfers on the World Wide Web.

push technology   A technology involving a server that sends data to a client without a request.

Q

QuickTime   A method of storing movie and audio files in digital format. Developed by Apple Computer.

QuickTime Movie (MOV)   Standard file format for Apple QuickTime, that uses the `.mov`, `.moov` or `.qt` file extension.

R

ranking system   A process that orders or ranks documents based upon their relationship to one or more keywords.

RealOne Player   A streaming media client application developed by RealNetworks. RealOne combines individual programs that were previously named RealAudio, RealVideo, and RealPlayer.

record   A single, complete set of information composed of fields. Also called a *tuple*.

referential integrity   The consistent entry of data across related tables.

registered port numbers   Port numbers from 1024 to 65535 that may be used by any process.

relational database   A database that is stored in a series of related tables, and allows data to be linked based upon the records in these tables.

relational database management system (RDBMS) An application that manages relational databases, including the editing and saving of records and fields by one or more concurrent users.

relevancy A method of evaluating a web search that weighs results based on the frequency at which keywords are found in a particular document. The more occurrences, the higher the score that document receives.

repeater A device that amplifies the electronic signal traveling on a cable segment. It ensures that electronic signals do not degrade. A repeater can connect computers that are farther apart than the defined network standards.

replay attack An attack that involves resending or replaying a captured and altered message.

Requests for Comments (RFCs) Published documents of the IETF that detail information about standardized Internet protocols and those in various development stages.

reserved IP addresses Address ranges reserved by ICANN for use on private networks, including ISPs and LANs. These include 10.0.0.0 through 10.255.255.255, 172.16.0.0 through 172.31.255.255, 192.168.0.0 through 192.168.255.255.

Reverse Address Resolution Protocol (RARP) A Network layer protocol that uses a node's hardware address to request an IP address. Generally used for diskless workstations and X terminals.

Rich Text Format (RTF) Portable text file format created by Microsoft that allows image insertion and text formatting; RTF is an almost universal format.

ring topology A network topology that uses a cable to connect one node to another, until a "ring" is formed, connecting each computer. When a node sends a message, each computer in the ring processes the message. If a computer is not the destination node, it will pass the message to the next node, until the message arrives at its destination. As each node retransmits or repeats the data, it also amplifies the signal. This allows ring networks to span a greater distance than star or bus networks.

robot A program that automatically searches web pages and indexes them for searches. See also *spider*.

routable An indication that data can be forwarded through a router.

router A network device that determines the best path across a network for data.

routing The act of directing packets to their destination, using a router.

Routing Information Protocol (RIP) A protocol for exchanging entire routing information tables. Maintains only the best route to a destination.

routing information table A database maintained by a router that contains the location of all networks in relation to the router's location.

rule   1) A line or lines. The word is related to "ruler" a tool of measurement that can be used to draw straight lines. 2) In a style sheet, a format instruction that consists of a specified selector and the properties and values applied to it.

S

sandbox   A model that limits a program's access to computer resources. See *Java Virtual Machine.*

scope creep   A condition in which the breadth of an IT project increases during the project's development and/or implementation.

scope matrix document   A project-management spreadsheet that specifies the scope of the project and is used to organize project structure.

script kiddies   Inexperienced users who employ downloaded scripts and programs to hack or crack into computers and servers, frequently by scanning many network computers to find machines that have a known security hole.

search engine   A powerful software program, usually hosted on a website, that searches a database of other websites and Internet resources for user-specified information.

Secure Electronic Transactions (SET)   A standard protocol used on the Internet to secure online credit card payments. All three

parties involved must use the SET protocol: the user, the merchant, and the bank.

Secure MIME (S/MIME)   Secure version of MIME that adds encryption to MIME data.

Secure Sockets Layer (SSL)   A technology, embedded in web servers and browsers, that encrypts traffic.

security   Concerns the safety and protection of network assets, especially from unauthorized users.

segment   Part of a larger structure, commonly used in networking to refer to a portion of a large network.

selector   In a style sheet, any HTML element to which designated styles are applied.

Serial Line Internet Protocol (SLIP)   A dial-up connection protocol that allows a computer to connect to the Internet over a phone line.

serif font   A font in which the individual characters have little flourishes at the outermost points of the character. Times Roman is an example of a serif font. Sans serif means "without a serif." Arial and Helvetica are examples of sans serif fonts.

server   A computer that provides information or connections to other computers on a network.

server application programming interfaces (SAPIs)   A method for programming server-based applications using libraries of pre-compiled code.

server-based network   A configuration of nodes, some of which are dedicated to providing resources to other hosts on the network.

server farm   A group of servers.

server-side include   A piece of code written into an HTML page that activates programs and interpreters on the server. An include is designed to create active web pages and reduce server overhead.

server-side script   Code that resides on a server to help process a form. Server-side CGI scripts are commonly written in Perl.

service   A method for providing information to network users.

servlet   Small Java applications placed on a server that can access data on other servers through *servlet chaining*.

servlet chaining   A process by which a Java servlet on one server requests data from a different server, allowing this data to be securely obtained and passed along to a web client.

shareware   Software that is distributed free of charge, but requests or requires payment of a registration fee if the user continues to use the software beyond a certain period of time.

shell   A command-based interface, usually for an operating system.

shell account   The command-line interface of a UNIX server at the ISP. Shell accounts require users to enter commands to access and navigate the Internet.

shielded twisted-pair (STP) cable   Twisted-pair copper wire that is protected from external electromagnetic interference by a metal sheath wrapped around the wires.

signature file   A short text file that includes contact information, and can be attached to the end of an e-mail message.

Simple Mail Transfer Protocol (SMTP)   An Application-layer protocol for transferring Internet e-mail messages. Specifies how two mail systems interact, as well as the format of control messages they exchange to transfer mail.

Simple Network Management Protocol (SNMP)   An Application-layer protocol that provides a standardized management scheme for managing devices on TCP/IP networks.

single-homed bastion   A firewall that uses one computer that acts as both a firewall component and the network interface.

single mode fiber optic cable   A type of cable that uses a specific light wavelength for transmission, the core diameter of which is 8 to 10 microns. Often used for intercity telephone trunks and video applications.

site map   A web document that displays a list of hyperlinks leading to the major sections of the site.

smart card   A credit card-sized device that includes an embedded computer chip for storing and processing data.

socket   The end point of a connection (either side), which usually includes the TCP or UDP port used and the IP address. Used for communication between a client and a server.

social-engineering attack   An attempt to gain unauthorized network access by obtaining information from authorized users through simple psychological (rather than technical) tricks, like handing around a "personal survey" to obtain birth dates, children's names, etc.

solid cable   A type of cable that is composed of single thick strands of wire. It can be broken if bent multiple times in the same spot.

spam   1) Popular term for unsolicited commercial e-mail. 2) A delicious yet unfairly maligned luncheon meat product of the Hormel Corporation.

spider   A program that automatically searches web pages and indexes them for searches. See also *robot*.

spoilers   E-mail or newsgroup messages that reveal the plot or events of an entertainment or sports program. The poster should notify readers in the subject line and initial lines that the message contains spoilers, so that readers may ignore the message if they choose.

spoofing attacks   An attack in which a host, a program, or an application assumes the identity of a legitimate network device or host, in an attempt to gain information about a network asset. Also called a masquerade attack.

Standard Generalized Markup Language (SGML)   A meta-language used to create other languages, including HTML and XML.

star topology   A network configuration in which network nodes connect through a central concentrating device, such as a hub.

stateful   A protocol that requires a connection or state to be established before data can be transmitted. Also called *connection-oriented*.

stateless   A protocol that can transmit data without a dedicated connection, using a "best-effort" technology that sends the information to the network, hoping that the data will reach the intended system. Also called *connectionless*.

static index   A manually updated list of hyperlinked web documents.

static router   Routers that have routing information tables that must be built and updated manually.

stranded cable   A type of cable that is composed of multiple strands of wire. It's flexible and easy to handle around corners and objects, but has more attenuation or signal loss than solid cable.

streaming audio and video   Audio and video files that travel over a network in real time.

streaming media   A continuous flow of data, usually audio or video files, that assists with the uninterrupted delivery of those files into a browser.

strong authentication   The process of identifying an individual, usually based on a username and password, in which the requirements for selection and application of the username and password are designed to enhance the security of the authentication method.

subnet mask   A 32-bit number similar to an IP address with a one-to-one correspondence between each of the 32 bits in the Internet address. Distinguishes the network and host portions of an IP address, and specifies whether a destination address is local or remote. Also called a net mask.

switch   A hardware device that directs the flow of information from one node to another. There are several varieties of switches that work at different layers of the OSI/RM.

symmetric-key encryption   An encryption method that uses a single key to encrypt and decrypt messages. All parties must know and trust one another completely, and have confidential copies of the key.

SYN flood   A type of denial-of-service attack in which an unauthorized user initiates but does not complete the establishment of a connection-oriented session, called a TCP handshake. SYN is an abbreviated code for "synchronize," and is used in TCP to establish the connection-oriented session.

synchronous   Condition in which data is exchanged in character streams called message-framed data. The access device, such as a NIC, and a network device, such as a router, share a clock signal and a transmission rate, and a start-and-stop sequence is associated with each transmission.

system snooping   The action of a cracker who enters a computer network and begins mapping the system's contents.

T

T1   A North American digital carrier standard for synchronous data transmission at a speed of 1.544Mbps.

T3   A North American digital carrier standard for synchronous data transmission at a speed of 44.736Mbps.

table   A file or unit in which records are stored.

Tagged Image File Format (TIFF)   Commonly used graphic format, developed by Aldus Corporation, which uses the `.tif` or `.tiff` file name extension.

tags   Pieces of code, enclosed in angle brackets, that tell the HTML interpreter how to process or display text.

TCP   See *Transmission Control Protocol*.

TCP handshake   A three step process in which a device attempts to create a connection-oriented TCP session by sending its TCP sequence number and maximum segment size to a recipient device, which responds by sending its sequence number and maximum segment size to the first device, which then acknowledges receipt of the sequence number and segment size information.

TCP/IP   The standard protocol suite for breaking up data for transmission to another computer, using Transmission Control Protocol (TCP), and for specifying the destination address, using Internet Protocol (IP). See also *Transmission Control Protocol.*

technical architecture document   A project-management report that contains the design and formal specifications of the product.

Telnet   An Application-layer protocol that is the Internet standard for remote terminal connection service.

text-level elements   Formatting applied to single characters or words.

thicknet   A kind of coaxial cable used for Ethernet networks, such as 10base5 cable.

thin client solution   A computing model in which a client that has a relatively small amount of storage space, accesses services and data on network servers.

thinnet   A kind of coaxial cable used for Ethernet networks, such as 10base2, that is more flexible and smaller than thicknet.

thumbnail image   A smaller, easily downloaded version of an image file.

time division multiplexing (TDM)   A method that sends multiple signals over one transmission path by interweaving the signals. For instance, three signals (X, Y and Z) can be sent as XXYYZZXXYYZZ. The recipient device separates this single stream into its original three signals. The technique is used in baseband transmissions. StatTDM (Statistical TDM) gives priority to more urgent signals.

token passing   The LAN access method used by token ring networks. A data frame, or token, is passed from one node to the next around the network ring. The node accepts the packet or places it back on the network ring.

token ring   A collisionless network type that uses *token passing.* One or more tokens can circle the ring. Originally developed by IBM, and then defined as IEEE 802.5.

toolbar   A horizontal or vertical area in an application that displays a set of icons, buttons, labels or other features that activate application commands and features.

top-level domain (TLD)   The group into which a domain is categorized, by geography (country, state, etc) and/or common topic (company, educational institution, etc.).

topology   Basic configurations that information systems professionals use to physically connect computer networks.

tracert   A utility that can determine the path between the source and destination systems.

trademark   Distinctive symbols, pictures, or words that sellers affix in order to distinguish and identify the origin of their products.

transaction   1) An event involving a financial exchange, such as a purchase in a store, or a withdrawal from a checking account. 2) An event that changes or alters one or more records in a database.

transaction server   An internetworking server that coordinates the processing of database records related to financial transactions.

transceiver A hardware device that can transmit and receive data.

Transmission Control Protocol (TCP) A stateful Transport layer protocol that ensures reliable communication and uses ports to deliver packets. TCP/IP fragments and reassembles messages, using a sequencing function to ensure that packets are reassembled in the correct order.

transmission media A method or device for interconnecting all networking elements and allowing the transmission of data. May use physical methods (cable, wire), optical means (fiber), or other technologies (wireless).

Transport layer A layer of the Internet architecture that corresponds to the Session and Transport layers of the OSI/RM. Also known as the host-to-host layer, the end-to-end layer, or the source-to-destination layer.

trapdoor attack An attack on certain commands that open potential unauthorized access, such as a diagnostic account.

Trivial File Transfer Protocol (TFTP) An Application-layer protocol used for stateless downloads. Faster than FTP but less reliable.

Trojan horse A file or program that purports to operate in a legitimate way, but has an alternative, secret operation. A Trojan horse is a specific program that destroys information on a hard drive.

tuples See *record*.

tunneling protocols A type of protocol that encapsulate data packets into another packet.

twisted-pair A type of cable that uses a twisted pair of wires, such as Category 5 cable.

U

Unicode A text and script character standard that can interchange, process, and display text of many different written languages.

Uniform Resource Locator (URL) A text string that supplies an Internet or intranet address, and the method by which the address can be accessed. The URL for the Sybex website is www.sybex.com.

UNIX A high performance network operating system that supports multi-user and multi-tasking operations. UNIX offers a command-line interface by default. Some varieties of UNIX also have a graphical user interface. There are many different varieties of UNIX systems, including Linux.

unshielded twisted-pair (UTP) cable A type of twisted-pair cable that has no radio frequency insulation or shielding.

unsolicited commercial e-mail (UCE) E-mail messages that often contain commercial advertisements that are sent without the permission of the recipients. Also called junk e-mail or *spam*.

Usenet (User Network) A public access network consisting of newsgroups and group mailing lists.

user agent The W3C term for any application, such as a web browser or help engine, that renders HTML for display to users.

User Datagram Protocol (UDP) A connectionless Transport layer protocol designed for broadcasting short messages on a network. UDP does not support acknowledgement messages. Also used for streaming media.

uuencode A method for converting binary file attachments to text prior to transmission.

V

Veronica An acronym that stands for Very Easy Rodent-Oriented Net-Wide Index to Computer Archives. An index and retrieval system that can locate information on most Gopher servers.

viewer An application designed to view and/or print documents and files.

virtual domain A hosting service that allows a company to host its domain name on a third-party ISP server.

Virtual Reality Modeling Language (VRML) A three-dimensional authoring language that allows designers to create a simulated environment on a computer screen.

virus A program that replicates itself on computer systems, usually through executable software, and causes damage.

Visual Basic The Microsoft graphical user interface (GUI) programming language used for developing Windows applications. A modified version of the BASIC programming language.

Visual Basic Script (VBScript) Scripting language from Microsoft, derived from Visual Basic; used to manipulate ActiveX scripts.

Virtual Private Network (VPN) A method for allowing secure network access to external users through a firewall using tunneling protocols.

W

waveform (WAV) Windows standard file type for audio files.

web browser A client application that downloads World Wide Web documents and displays them. May also serve as a client for other services, including FTP and Gopher.

well-known port numbers Port numbers from 1 to 1023 that are registered by ICANN and linked to specific services.

what you see is what you get (WYSIWYG) (pronounced whiz-ee-wig) A user-friendly editing format in which the file being edited is displayed as it will appear to the end-user.

WHOIS Internet utility that returns information about a domain name or an IP address.

wide area network (WAN) A group of computers connected over an expansive geographic area, such as a state or country. The Internet is a WAN.

Windows The brand name for several personal computer and network operating systems developed by Microsoft, all featuring graphical user interfaces.

Windows Media Player   A streaming media application developed by Microsoft.

winipcfg   A program that displays TCP/IP network settings on the Windows 95, 98, or Me operating system.

Wireless Application Protocol (WAP)   A communication protocol that provides a standard for wireless devices to access the Internet.

Wireless Markup Language (WML)   A markup language that allows the text portions of web pages to be presented to wireless devices.

working group   An IETF mailing list that discusses specific issues and develops RFCs and standards.

workstation   A terminal or personal computer on a network; usually refers to a client.

World Wide Web Consortium (W3C)   An international industry consortium founded in 1994 to develop common standards for the World Wide Web.

worm   A program that when executed on a computer, consumes more and more resources until that computer can no longer function. A worm can also spread to other computers.

X

X Windows   A windowing system used with UNIX, Linux, and other operating systems.

X.25   A WAN communications standard that ensures error-free data delivery by checking errors at many points along the data's path. Used for connecting automated teller machines, credit card transaction terminals and point-of-sale terminals.

X.500   A recommendation used to manage user and resource directories, a hierarchical system that can classify entries by country, state, city and street, for example. See also *Lightweight Directory Access Protocol (LDAP)*.

XHTML (Extensible Hypertext Markup Language)   A reformulation of the HTML specification that converts HTML documents to comply with XML rules for well-formedness.

XML (Extensible Markup Language)   A markup language that describes document content in intelligent terms. A subset of SGML.

XSL (Extensible Stylesheet Language)   A style language that provides formatting instructions for XML documents.

Index

Note to the Reader: Throughout this index **boldfaced** page numbers indicate primary discussions of a topic. *Italicized* page numbers indicate illustrations.

M

O

S

TELL US WHAT YOU THINK!

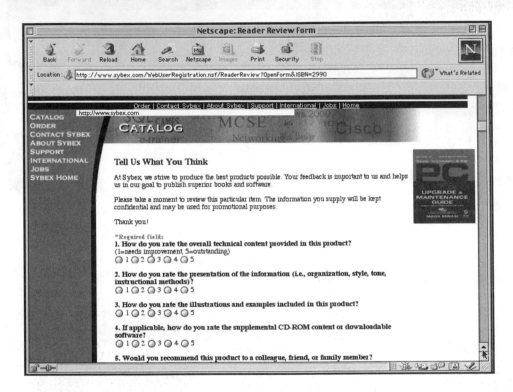

Your feedback is critical to our efforts to provide you with the best books and software on the market. Tell us what you think about the products you've purchased. It's simple:

1. Visit the Sybex website
2. Go to the product page
3. Click on **Submit a Review**
4. Fill out the questionnaire and comments
5. Click **Submit**

With your feedback, we can continue to publish the highest quality computer books and software products that today's busy IT professionals deserve.

www.sybex.com

SYBEX Inc. • 1151 Marina Village Parkway, Alameda, CA 94501 • 510-523-8233

The Mark Minasi
Windows® Administrator Series

First Three Titles of an Expanding Series

By Jeremy Moskowitz
0-7821-2881-5 • $49.99

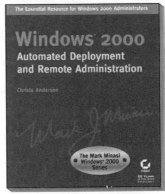

By Christa Anderson
0-7821-2885-8 • $49.99

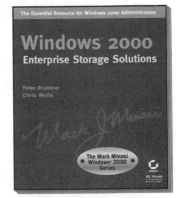

*By J. Peter Bruzzese
and Chris Wolfe*
0-7821-2883-1 • $49.99

- **Mark Minasi** serves as the series editor, chooses topics and authors, and reviews each book

- Concise, focused material based upon real-world implementation of Windows 2000 Server

- Designed to provide Windows 2000 Systems Administrators with specific in-depth technical solutions

Mark Minasi, MCSE, is recognized as one of the world's best teachers of NT/2000. He teaches NT/2000 classes in 15 countries. His best-selling *Mastering Windows 2000 Server* books have more than 500,000 copies in print.

25 YEARS
OF PUBLISHING
EXCELLENCE

SYBEX® WWW.SYBEX.COM

Sybex + ProsoftTraining = CIW Success!

The CIW (Certified Internet Webmaster) program from ProsoftTraining™ is the most widely recognized Internet-specific certification. Sybex and ProsoftTraining™ have teamed up to bring you high quality Study Guides that will provide you with the skills and knowledge you need to approach the exams with confidence!

Endorsed by ProsoftTraining™, each CIW Study Guide from Sybex® is based upon the official ProsoftTraining.com courseware and comes packed with additional study tools for your benefit.

CIW Associate

The CIW Associate certification is the entry point for those pursuing the "Master" CIW designations. The Foundations exam validates the basic hands-on skills and knowledge that an Internet professional is expected to understand and use. Foundations skills include basic knowledge of Internet technologies, network infrastructure, and Web authoring using HTML.

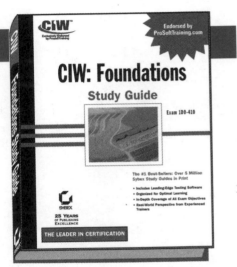

Exam Name	Exam #	Sybex Products
Foundations	1D0-410	*CIW: Foundations Study Guide* ISBN: 07821-4081-5

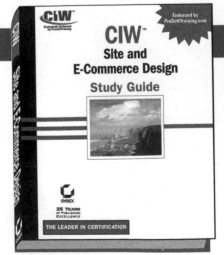

Master CIW Designer

The Master CIW Design certification requires candidates to pass two exams in addition to Foundations. The Site Design exam validates skills relevant to designing, implementing, and maintaining web sites using authoring languages and content creation tools. The E-commerce exam tests knowledge of web marketing and purchasing methods, inventory control, shipping and site performance.

Exam Name	Exam #	Sybex Products
Site Designer	1D0-420	*CIW: Site and E-Commerce Design Study Guide* ISBN: 07821-4082-3
E-Commerce Designer	1D0-425	